Strategic management and organisational dynamics

PEARSON
Education

We work with leading authors to develop the strongest educational materials in business and management, bringing cutting-edge thinking and best learning practice to a global market.

Under a range of well-known imprints, including Financial Times Prentice Hall, we craft high quality print and electronic publications which help readers to understand and apply their content, whether studying or at work.

To find out more about the complete range of our publishing, please visit us on the World Wide Web at: www.pearsoned.co.uk

Strategic management and organisational dynamics

The challenge of complexity to ways of thinking about organisations

Fifth Edition

Ralph D. Stacey

FT Prentice Hall
FINANCIAL TIMES

An imprint of **Pearson Education**
Harlow, England • London • New York • Boston • San Francisco • Toronto • Sydney • Singapore • Hong Kong
Tokyo • Seoul • Taipei • New Delhi • Cape Town • Madrid • Mexico City • Amsterdam • Munich • Paris • Milan

Pearson Education Limited
Edinburgh Gate
Harlow
Essex CM20 2JE
England

and Associated Companies throughout the world

Visit us on the World Wide Web at:
www.pearsoned.co.uk

First published under the Pitman Publishing imprint 1993
Second edition published 1996
Third edition published 2000
Fourth edition published 2003
Fifth edition published 2007

ISBN 978-0-273-70811-7

British Library Cataloguing-in-Publication Data
A catalogue record for this book is available from the British Library

Library of Congress Cataloging-in-Publication Data
A catalogue record for this book is available from the Library of Congress

10 9 8 7 6 5 4 3 2
11 10 09 08 07

Typeset in 10/12.5pt Sabon by 35
Printed and bound in China (GCC/02)

The publisher's policy is to use paper manufactured from sustainable forests.

To the memory of my mother Auriel

Contents

Supporting resources

Visit **www.pearsoned.co.uk/stacey** to find valuable online resources

For instructors
- Teaching notes

For more information please contact your local Pearson Education sales representative or visit **www.pearsoned.co.uk/stacey**

List of boxes

List of tables

Preface

This is a textbook of *ways of thinking* about organisations and their management, particularly strategic management. While most strategic management textbooks are concerned with presenting the key elements and prescriptions of strategic management to be found in the dominant discourse on the matter, this book is concerned with the implicit, taken-for-granted assumptions made in the ways of thinking expressed in that dominant discourse. The intention, then, is not to summarise what key strategic thinkers have written about generic strategies that managers should follow to secure competitive advantage and so produce superior organisational performance. Nor is the intention to convey received wisdom on how to design and implement conditions and processes conducive to effective organisational learning and knowledge management. The intention is, rather, to explore the ways of thinking reflected in the prescriptions for successful strategic content and process so as to highlight taken-for-granted assumptions. In order to do this, it is necessary to locate current thinking about strategy in the history of Western thought. The book raises and explores questions rather than presenting further explicit prescriptions

For example, why do we think that an organisation is a system, and what are the consequences of doing so? What view of human psychology is implicit in prescribing measures that managers should take to select the direction of an organisation's movement into the future?

This book, then, seeks to challenge thinking rather than describe the current state of thinking about strategy and organisational dynamics. The challenge to current ways of thinking is presented in the contrasts that this book draws between systemic and responsive processes ways of thinking about strategy and organisational dynamics. While the systemic perspective is concerned with improvement and movement to a future destination, process thinking is concerned with complex responsive processes of human relating in which strategies emerge. From this perspective, strategy is defined as the emergence of organisational and individual identities so that the concern is with how organisations come to be what they are and how those identities will continue to evolve. From a responsive processes perspective, the questions of performance and improvement have to do with participation in processes of communicative interaction, power relating and the creation of knowledge and meaning. The challenge to ways of thinking presented in this book also comes in the form of insights from the complexity sciences. The book will explore the differences for organisational thinking between a way of interpreting these insights in systemic terms and a way of interpreting them in process terms. The purpose of this book is to assist people to make sense of their own experience of life in organisations, to explore their own thinking, because how they think powerfully affects what they pay attention to and so what they do. If we never challenge dominant modes of thinking we end up trapped in modes of acting that may no longer be serving us all that well.

This central emphasis on ways of thinking has consequences for how this book is structured and presented. It does not focus just on what has come to be accepted as the academic discipline of strategic management but takes account of other organisational disciplines such as matters that would normally come under organisational behaviour. These distinctions between academic disciplines are rather artificial when it comes to making sense of what managers actually do. Also the book reaches into the disciplines of psychology, sociology and philosophy in seeking to understand the ways of thinking reflected in the dominant discourse. There are no traditional case studies and few examples of how people have managed successfully. Case studies tend to be carefully structured accounts of someone else's organisational experience, usually written with some point in mind, which the reader is supposed to see. Examples of successful management practices are often introduced to subtly 'prove' that a particular prescription works. These devices are not consistent with the purpose of assisting readers to make sense of their own experience. Since this is a book about ways of thinking, the examples it provides are examples of ways of thinking. Part 3 of the book, concerned with a complex responsive processes perspective on organisations, provides four reflective management narratives, that is, personal accounts of the experience of life in organisations. Readers are invited to think about the sense they make of this experience. The main point, however, remains for readers to use the material in this book to make sense of their own experience.

The structure of this fifth edition is the same as the last edition in that Part 1 deals with the dominant discourse on strategic management and related organisational disciplines, Part 2 introduces the complexity sciences and Part 3 presents the theory of complex responsive processes as a way of thinking about organisations and their strategy. However, Part 1 has been significantly reduced in coverage and less space has been allocated to the complexity sciences. Part Three has been significantly expanded, bringing in more recent developments of the theory of complex responsive processes to do with values, ideology and the link between local interaction, the micro, and population-wide patterns, the macro. These developments reflect a growing literature on the complex responsive processes perspective mainly coming from graduates of a research degree programme run at the Complexity and Management Centre at the Business School of the University of Hertfordshire. The reflective management narratives I referred to earlier have been written by members of this programme and so provide a useful way of indicating how thinking in these terms affects what people do in organisations. I have introduced each chapter and management narrative with what seem to me to be the key points for reflection which the chapter points to. At the end of each chapter and management narrative I have given a few questions as an aid to further reflection.

I am grateful to users of previous editions who have made helpful comments and to my colleagues and other participants in the MA/Doctor of Management programme on organisational change at the University of Hertfordshire for the contribution they continue to make to how I find myself thinking.

Ralph Stacey
University of Hertfordshire
March 2006

Acknowledgements

We are grateful to the following for permission to reproduce copyright material:

Taylor & Francis Group Plc for extracts from *The Paradox of Control in Organizations* by Philip J Streatfield published by Routledge 2001.

Chapter 1

Thinking about strategy and organisational change

1.1 Introduction

I want to introduce this book with what seem to be a number of perfectly obvious statements. Human beings live in communities and whatever they do is a joint performance conducted by them in communities of practice. This joint activity is accomplished through communicative interaction between conscious and self-conscious persons. In other words, joint activity is carried out in ongoing conversation between people in which they negotiate what they are doing and how they are making sense of what they are doing. In this activity, they become who they are – together they construct their identities. The form of such conversation is thus of central importance, because in establishing what it is acceptable for people to talk about in a community, and how it is acceptable to talk, the conversational form, or discourse, establishes people's relative power positions and therefore who they are and what they do together. Every such community of practice is characterised by a dominant discourse, the most acceptable way to converse, which reflects power positions supported by ideologies. Most communities of practice are also characterised by some resistance to, or criticism of, the dominant discourse. A community of practice can change in the tension between the dominant discourse and the critique of it.

This book is addressed to the community of practice constituted by people who manage organisations, those who consult to them, those who research and write about organisational activity and those who study all of this as part of gaining entry to, and developing the knowledge and skill required to participate in, the community of practice. Such participation requires the ability to engage in the community's dominant discourse. This dominant discourse is reflected in how managers usually talk together about the nature of their managerial activity. It is also reflected in the kind of organisational research that attracts funding from research bodies, the kind of papers that prestigious research journals will publish, and the kind of courses taught at business schools and in organisational training and development activities.

It is usual for textbooks to survey and summarise the dominant discourse and, in the case of the community of organisational practitioners, to present prescriptions for successful management together with some kind of evidence backing the prescriptions, usually in the form of case studies. Most strategy books focus attention, either explicitly or implicitly, on what managers are supposed to do to improve the performance of an organisation. The immediate concern is then with the scope of an organisation's activities, its future direction and how it secures competitive advantage. Many, probably most, textbooks on strategy simply present the major strand in the dominant discourse, together with its prescriptions, with little questioning, as if the underlying way of thinking was self-evident. Most of these textbooks, largely reflecting the origins of the major strand in the dominant discourse in economics, present a view of strategic management that is rational, formal and orderly. Some textbooks, however, do bring out the multifaceted nature of the dominant discourse and the sometimes conflicting strands of thinking reflected in that discourse. They clarify how early, rather simplistic, accounts of strategic management, largely drawn from economics, have been subjected to strenuous critique which presents much messier processes of strategic management involving politics, culture, acts of interpretation and expressions of emotion. To understand these messier aspects, this second category of textbook draws on ideas from psychology, sociology and philosophy.

This book is similar in some respects to this latter category in that it too points to the less rational, less orderly aspects of strategic management, also drawing on ideas from psychology, sociology and philosophy. This is signalled by the term 'organisational dynamics' in the title of the book. 'Dynamics' refers to patterns of movement over time, for example, whether the pattern of movement is regular or irregular. 'Organisational dynamics', therefore, refers to the patterns of movement over time in the interactions between the people who are the organisation, the community of practice. Such patterns could be described, for example, as regular patterns of dependence and conformity, or as irregular patterns of aggression and noncompliance. In the literature on organisations, organisational dynamics is often regarded as a discipline of its own, called organisational behaviour, for example, which is quite distinct from the discipline of strategic management, which is itself often distinguished from operational management. In coupling strategic management and organisational dynamics, the title signals that this book will not make what I regard as artificial splits between aspects of organisational activity that seem to me to be inseparable. It is people who practice management, whether strategic or otherwise, and it is therefore essential to understand the behaviour of people, the dynamics of their interactions, if one is to understand the practice of strategising.

However, while similar in some respects to the second category of strategic management textbooks mentioned above, this book also differs significantly from them and this is signalled in the subtitle of the book. The subtitle refers to a 'challenge to ways of thinking about organisations' where that challenge is presented from a particular viewpoint, namely, 'complexity'. The term 'complexity' here refers to important insights coming from the natural complexity sciences to do with the intrinsic uncertainty and unpredictability of a great many natural phenomena, to the importance of diversity in the evolution of novel forms, and to the self-organising, emergent nature of that evolution. The insight is that novel global, population-wide forms emerge unpredictably in self-organising, that is local, interaction, in the absence of any blueprint, programme or plan for the global, population-wide form.

Since the major strand in the dominant discourse is based on assumptions to do with predictability and planning the development of the whole organisation, the insights from complexity clearly present a challenge. These insights, however, also challenge the critique of the rational, planning strand in the dominant discourse because most of the critiques retain some notion of at least influencing the whole from some external position.

The purpose of this book, therefore, is to explore *ways of thinking* about organisations and their management. It seeks to identify the usually taken-for-granted, fundamental assumptions upon which particular ways of thinking are based. It further seeks to clarify how these assumptions lead to particular lines of argument that focus attention on organisational matters in particular ways. Taken-for-granted assumptions carry with them certain entailments that have an enormous impact on the kind of actions people in organisations take. The purpose of this book is *not* to simply summarise various strands of the dominant discourse and the criticisms that may be made of them or to indicate how the ensuing prescriptions have led to success or failure by presenting examples and case studies. Instead, the book provides brief summaries of the various strands in the dominant discourse only in the interests of bringing out what the implicit, taken-for-granted assumptions are. This book will also be locating various discourses about organisations in the wider traditions of Western thought, paying attention to how they have developed historically.

Part 1 of the book, then, is an exploration of the dominant discourse. This dominant discourse is understood to include all perspectives on organisations that make the following assumptions. The first assumption is that organisations are, or are to be thought of 'as if' they were, systems. The second assumption is that these systems are external to the individuals forming them. Individuals are thought of as existing at one level whereas organisational systems are thought of as existing at a higher level. The third assumption is that it is the individual who is primary – the autonomous individual. The dominant discourse is built on the foundations of cognitivist, constructivist, humanistic and psychoanalytic psychology where, for all of them, the individual is the primary unit of concern. Fourth, associated with this focus on the individual, is the notion of the organisation and the social as systems being constructed by the actions of individuals, with those constructions then acting back on individuals as a cause of their behaviour. The fifth assumption is that since they are external to and constructors of the organisational system, individuals can plan, design, or at the very least influence the movement of the system.

Part 2 of the book looks at insights from the complexity sciences and describes how these are usually taken up within the dominant discourse and so do not lead to any serious challenge to that discourse.

Part 3 interprets the insights from the complexity sciences in a different way, moving away altogether from the notion of organisation as a system and from the focus on the individual. Instead it draws on certain strands of thinking in sociology that stress human interdependence and regard individuals as thoroughly social selves that arise in human interaction. That interaction can be described as complex responsive processes of human relating. These responsive processes of interaction take the form of conversation, patterns of power relations and ideologically based choices. Furthermore, these continually iterated responsive processes occur as the living present, the present we live in, and are essentially local in nature. It is in such responsive local interaction that population-wide patterns emerge. Organisations are such population-wide patterns constituting collective identities. For example, the university where I work is the continual iteration of patterns of behaviour described as lectures, seminars, examinations, committee meetings and so on. Part 3 of the book responds to the challenge of complexity by reconceptualising an organisation as ongoing patterning in the interactions between people and denies that it constitutes a system or even that it is useful to think of an organisation 'as if' it were a system. No one can step outside the ongoing responsive processes of interaction and so no one can influence the emerging patterns from any external position. The only influence any of us can have is in our participating in the ongoing responsive process of relating to each other. This is not to take an ideological position in which relating is somehow good, because oppression, ethnic cleansing, racial abuse, murder and war are also iterated, ongoing, responsive processes of people relating to each other. The dominant discourse separates macro (global or population-wide) and micro (local) levels of existence or study, reflected in distinctions between the parts and the whole of a system and the separation of the individual and the group (organisation or society). The alternative presented in Part 3 takes the view that the macro is continually emerging in the micro as individuals simultaneously form, and are formed by, the social. This leads to a very different focus of attention with regard to organisational life and therefore has very different implications for action.

This book, then, differs from most textbooks in that it quite explicitly advocates a particular way of thinking about organisations, and according to some reviewers this means that it is not a textbook at all. Whatever it is, this book is concerned with *ways of thinking about how organisations change over time*. It explores explanations of how organisations have become what they are, and how they will become whatever they will be in five, ten or however many years' time.

There are many different theories that seek to explain how organisations change, or fail to change, but none of them is universally accepted. Even those that dominate academic and management discourses provide only partial explanations of life in organisations. The purpose of this book is to examine what is similar in these competing theories, and how they differ. To put it another way, the purpose of this book is to explore different ways of making sense of one's experience of life in organisations. It is from my own experience that I describe, compare and comment on the various theories I will be presenting in the chapters that follow. My own experience inevitably colours how I describe those theories and what I have to say about them. In writing this book, therefore, I am revealing how I currently make sense of my experience of life in organisations and I am inviting you to consider whether this resonates in any way with your own experience.

The chapters that follow will briefly summarise various organisational theories, including their descriptions of, and prescriptions for, managing change. The aim will be to point to the assumptions made, and reasoning processes used, in these theories, matters that are often not made explicit by those presenting them. A distinction will be drawn between systemic and responsive processes ways of thinking about organisations and their strategies.

Two basic questions

What I am setting out to do in this book, then, is to review and compare different ways of explaining what strategy is, how it arises and how organisations change.

It is very tempting to jump straight into defining what a strategy is and how it should be formulated and implemented, or to describe and explain immediately how organisations change and how this change should be managed. I want to avoid this temptation because, as I hope to show, the result of such haste is the obscuring of what lies behind the definitions and prescriptions. There is no universally true explanation of how organisations evolve, only a number of increasingly contested accounts. If one is to avoid blindly following one of these accounts, mistakenly taking it to be the truth, then I think that it is necessary to stand back and ask two fundamental questions:

1. What are the phenomena that are being talked about when the terms 'strategy' and 'organisational change' are used?
2. How do human beings make sense of phenomena, including those that this book is concerned with, and in what traditions of thought is such sense making located?

The second question is important because there are different explanations of how humans make sense of anything. The particular explanation one adopts directly affects the particular account one gives of any phenomena, including those to which the concepts of strategy and organisational change apply. The following section takes up the question to do with the phenomena of interest and the one after that considers different explanations of *how* we know anything.

1.2 The phenomena of interest

Before attempting any definition of what a strategy is, or what is meant by organisational change, consider the general phenomena that strategy and organisational change are both concerned with in our experience. If I reflect upon my own experience of life in organisations I am first of all aware that people in any organisation that I have ever worked for interact with people in other organisations in what I would think of as a population of organisations.

Populations of organisations

Over any time period, say one, five, ten years, in any geographic region, say Europe, thousands upon thousands of new organisations are set up, and within the same time frame many thousands are dissolved, mostly small ones but sometimes very large ones. In other words, in each period, there are large numbers of small organisational dissolutions and small numbers of large ones. Some organisations go on for a very long time: the Roman Catholic Church is more than 1,500 years old and a few commercial organisations have survived for more than a century. On average, however, the lifespan of commercial organisations in Western countries is about 40 years. In any time period, some organisations merge into others, while yet others split into separate organisations. Many acquire others and some sell parts of their organisation to others. Organisations supply each other with goods and services. Some exert regulatory power over others.

Over the years, surviving organisations change their structures and the composition of their activities and as they do so they threaten, or create opportunities for, others. Whole new industries appear as new technologies are developed, creating niches of new activities for both new and old organisations, while other industries disappear. Many organisations reduce their workforces in downsizing, delayering activities. Many relocate their activities from one country to another. Some focus on one locality while others operate globally. From time to time, there are major changes in how organisations are governed. There are private and public, commercial and charitable, governmental and industrial organisations all interacting with each other in many different ways.

Dynamic phenomena

What is striking, I think, is just how much change is going on but also, at the same time, how some organisations change very little. In other words, the phenomena of interest, namely populations of organisations, are highly dynamic ones. *Dynamics* means movement, and concern with the dynamics is concern with the patterns phenomena display as they evolve over time. Dynamic phenomena are ones that display patterns of change over time and a study of dynamics is concerned with what generates these patterns and what properties of stability and instability, regularity and irregularity, predictability and unpredictability they display. One of the key features distinguishing one theory of strategy and organisational change from another is how they deal with the matter of dynamics. I will be pointing to this in the reviews of a number of theories in the chapters that follow.

It is striking how unstable the dynamics of populations of organisations are, on the one hand, but how stable they are, on the other. Or, to put it another way, what is striking is just how unpredictable are the moves made by organisations and yet how predictable they are. What I mean by this is that it is virtually certain that mergers and takeovers will take place and it is often clear in which industries this will happen. At the same time, however, it is often very surprising that one particular organisation should buy, or merge with, another. Members of an organisation, including its most senior managers, often experience such unpredictability and instability as anxiety provoking and stressful. Another striking point is how some organisations are merging with others, while yet others are splitting themselves into two or more parts. In other words, some are integrating while others are dividing.

Paradoxical phenomena

Populations of organisations change over time in ways that display both stability and instability at the same time, both predictability and unpredictability at the same time, both creation and destruction at the same time. What is one to make of it when the phenomena one is trying to understand, changes in populations of organisations, display such contradictory tendencies? Is this an apparent contradiction which arises for me simply because I do not understand the phenomena fully? Or is it a paradox, the genuine, simultaneous coexistence of two contradictory movements? How one answers these questions has important implications for the kind of theory of organisational change one develops. Some theories see only contradictions to be solved by further work, while others see paradox that can never be resolved.

This position on paradox will be one of the features I will use to distinguish one theory of organisational change from another. I will return to this point later in this chapter and take it up again in subsequent chapters as I review a number of theories of organisational change.

Degrees of detail

Now, however, I think it is important to notice how I have been talking about organisations as 'whole' organisations interacting 'within' a whole population as if they were individual entities, which is a very common way of talking about organisations. In other words, the descriptions are at the macro level, that is, the level of the large, or the whole, rather than the small, or the entities that make up the whole, that is, the micro level. This too will be an important feature in the comparison between different theories of organisational change in the chapters that follow. Some theories focus on the macro level, some on the micro level and yet others on both, looking for how the micro and the macro might be linked.

More fundamentally, however, is the matter of how one thinks about these 'levels'. In some theories, the micro and the macro are thought of as distinct levels of reality, each of which has its own distinctive properties as wholes. So, one level is the individual human being understood from some psychological perspective. The next level is the group having its own properties. The level above that may be the organisation consisting of groups of individuals to be understood in terms of organisational principles and above that are the levels of industry, economy and society. In these theories, then, organisational phenomena are wholes classified at different ontological levels. In other theories, however, the micro and the macro are not thought of as separate levels with distinctive properties. Instead, they are thought of as simply different degrees of examination. In these theories, individuals, groups and organisations are not wholes at different ontological levels but are simply aspects of the same processes of human interaction.

Moving now to the micro degree of examination, each organisation is itself a population of interacting groupings of individual people. In my experience, this interaction between members of an organisational population is characterised by political activity as people push for, or try to stop, particular activities. They may become angry with each other or feel betrayed. If you think of your experience of being promoted, having others promoted above you, or having the threat of downsizing hanging over you, you can see how emotions of some kind are inseparable from interactions between people within and between organisations. Another feature I will be pointing to, as I review a number of theories in the chapters that follow, is just how much account those theories take of the political activity and emotion involved in organisational evolution.

The phenomena of interest in this book have to do with life in organisations and this is not some interaction between abstract entities, but interactions between people that directly affect the meaning of their lives and their health. To gain some understanding of these interactions one has to participate in them and one's understanding will arise in one's own experience. From a macro perspective, it may well be possible to take the position of the objective observer who stands outside the phenomena of interest and offers explanations of their behaviour. However, explanation and understanding from the micro perspective relies much more on one's own personal experience. Here the explanation is offered from the position of a participant in organisational life. This is another distinguishing feature of the theories I will review, namely the extent to which the theory is offered from the position of the objective observer as opposed to the enquiring participant.

Interaction

Another important point to note about the phenomena that strategy and organisational change are concerned with is that they are all about interactions. For example, one kind of interaction takes place when one company buys another and another kind of interaction takes place when one company supplies another. From the perspective of an individual organisation, one kind of interaction takes place when a director resigns and another kind takes place when a director is handsomely rewarded. Furthermore, one interaction will inevitably touch off many more. When one pharmaceutical company merges with another, it changes the competitive balance for all of the others, making it highly likely that many of them will look for merger partners. This is because they are interconnected. Another very important feature distinguishing one theory of strategy and organisational change from another is the manner in which interaction and interconnection are understood.

Most theories think of interaction as constituting a network or a system. Individual minds might be thought of as a system consisting of, say, interacting concepts. A group may be thought of as a system consisting of, say, interacting individuals, while an organisation might then be thought of as a system consisting of interacting groups. An industry would then be thought of as a supra-system consisting of interacting organisations. When thought of in this way, interaction is always interaction between systems, producing yet another system, all of them nesting hierarchically in each other at different levels. Different theories of strategy and organisational change are built on different theories of the nature of a system. One of the main focuses of this book will be on different theories of systems and how these underpin different theories of organisational evolution. However, although most theories of strategy and organisational change are couched in systemic terms, there is an alternative. This is to think of interaction as responsive processes of direct communicating and relating between human bodies. Such a perspective yields responsive processes theories of strategy and organisational change. This distinction between systemic and process theories provides the principal way of distinguishing between different theories of strategy and organisational change. Parts 1 and 2 will review systemic theories and Part 3 will explore responsive processes theories.

In summary, then, the phenomena that this book is concerned with are continuously evolving populations of organisations where each organisation is itself an evolving population of groupings of individual people, each of whom is also evolving. In other words, we are concerned with dynamic patterns of interaction and interconnection. We can think about these patterns of interaction in terms of *systems* or in terms of *responsive processes*. We can take a macro or micro perspective and we can think of these as different ontological *levels* or simply as different *degrees of detail being examined*. We can notice the contradictions and we can adopt a *dualistic* way of thinking that resolves them or we can adopt a way of thinking that sees the contradictions as essential *paradoxes* that cannot be resolved. Finally, we can try to think from the position of the *objective observer* or from that of the *participative enquirer*. Which of all of these choices is made determines the kind of theory of strategy and organisational change one comes up with.

Having obtained some idea of the nature of the phenomena that strategy and organisational change are concerned with, consider now the second question posed at the end of Section 1.1, namely how to make sense of the phenomena.

1.3 Making sense of the phenomena

The question of how we make sense of ourselves in our world is, of course, a very old one. One answer to that question is *realism*. From this perspective, it is the nature of reality itself that determines the patterns we perceive and the meaning we make of our experience. The notion here is that there is a reality external to humans that exists before they try to interpret or explain it; that is, reality is pre-given. This means that the categories into which people classify specific instances are already there in the phenomenon they are trying to explain. A rose falls into the category 'roses' because there is a real difference between roses and other categories of flowers. An organisation falls into the category 'coal industry' because there is a real difference between organisations in this industry and those in the gas industry. If the categories exist in reality then any other classification people might make would not produce an adequate explanation, a fact that they would discover when they tried to act in accordance with that explanation. Most natural scientists would probably adopt this position in relation to the natural phenomena that they try to explain. If one adopts this position then it is quite natural to suppose that a human being can stand outside the phenomena to be explained, taking the role of the objective observer who builds increasingly accurate explanations, or models, through experimentation. Mostly, realists do not see any inherent limitation on human ability to comprehend reality in its entirety. For them, it is only a matter of time before research progressively uncovers more and more of reality.

The opposite position to realism is *relativism* or *scepticism*, nowadays known as postmodernism. Here the categories into which people classify their experiences are held to exist only in their minds, not out there in reality. Any explanations they come up with are, therefore, simply projections of their own minds. Those who hold this position maintain that there is no pre-given reality outside of humans. There is no reality, only the stories we tell each other and, according to those who take this position to the extreme, one story is as good as another.

Another position avoids the extremes of both realism and scepticism and this is *idealism*. Here, too, it is held that it is the way we think that determines the patterning of our experience. However, idealists do not believe that this means that our entire sense-making activity is purely relative. Chapters 2 and 10 will explore idealist ways of making sense in more detail. Chapter 2 will describe Kant's transcendental idealism, in which it is argued that humans inherit mental categories and understand their world in terms of them. Understanding is then not relative at all but determined by pre-given categories in individual minds. Chapter 10 will briefly review Hegel's absolute or Romantic idealism according to which human understanding is a social process that avoids relativism.

There are also more recent views that might be understood as idealist. *Constructivists* (*see* Chapter 4) hold that, because of biological evolution, humans are capable of perceiving the world in one way but not others (Maturana and Varela, 1987). For example, the human visual apparatus receives light waves on three channels; it is trichromate. Some other animals have dichromate (two channels) or quatrochromate (four channels) vision. Each type of creature, therefore, sees the world of colour in a different way, in effect, through biological evolution, selecting aspects of reality for attention. It is impossible for one type of creature to see the world of colour that another type sees. Similarly, constructivists would point to limitations on human capacity to perceive reality imposed by the evolved nature of the human brain. By its very nature, the human brain selects aspects of reality to pay attention to. This position has something in common with realism in that it supposes a reality that exists outside of the human organism and is not simply the result of the mind's projection. Unlike realism, however, this is not an unproblematically pre-given reality but, rather, an individually constructed, enacted or selected reality.

Another position taken on the nature of the human capacity to explain experience is that of *social constructionism* (Gergen, 1985), which is a form of idealism. Some social constructionists adopt the sceptical position, holding that there is no reality out there, but others tend towards an idealist position in which social reality is socially constructed in language. Here, reality is not a pre-given world determining our explanation but, rather, our explanation is being socially constructed in our encounters with each other in the world. This form of social constructionism is similar to constructivism but with a very important difference. While constructivists focus upon the selective nature of the individual human being, social constructionists point to social interaction, particularly in conversation, as the selecting process. The constructionist position is this: every explanation people put forward of any phenomenon is a socially constructed account, not a straightforward description of reality. If this view is held then it is impossible to adopt the role of the independent, objective observer when trying to explain any phenomenon. Instead, one can only come up with an explanation through participation in what one is trying to explain.

Social constructionists hold that it is impossible to take the position of objective observer and that those who claim to do so are simply ignoring the impact of their own participation or lack of it. This leads to the closely related notion of *reflexivity* (Steier, 1991). Reflexive entities are entities that bend back upon themselves. Humans are reflexive in the sense that any explanations they produce are the products of who they are, as determined by their histories. For example, I am trying, on these pages, to explain the different ways in which humans explain their experience. If I hold the reflexive position then I cannot claim any objectively given truth for my way of doing this. Instead, I have to recognise that the approach I am adopting is the product of who I am and how I think. This, in turn, is the distillation of my personal history of relating to other people over many years. If I accept the argument about reflexivity, I can never claim to stand outside my own experience, outside the web of relationships that I am a part of, and take the role of objective observer. Instead, I have to take the role of enquiring participant (Reason, 1988). Furthermore, reflexivity is not simply an individual activity dependent on that individual person's history alone. This is because we are always members of a community that has a history and traditions of thought. Reflexivity, therefore, involves being aware of the impact on how one thinks of both one's personal history and the history and traditions of thought of one's community. It is for this reason that Chapters 2 and 10, particularly, give brief accounts of the central traditions in Western thought.

The individual and the group

The move to a Romantic idealist, reflexive, social constructionist position is very significant in terms of what is being assumed about the relationship between the individual and the group. Realist, transcendental idealist and constructivist positions are all presented in terms of the capacities and limitations of the autonomous human individual. The individual is taken to be prior and primary to the group and groups can then only be seen as consisting of individuals. On the other hand, some social constructionists see the group as prior and primary. Individuals are then the products of the group in some way. Other perspectives, mostly derived from Romantic idealism, are paradoxical in that neither the individual nor the group is primary. One forms and is formed by the other at the same time. This question of how to think about the individual and the group is central to the reviews of ways of thinking about strategy and organisational change explored in this book.

So, there are a number of different, contradictory ways of explaining how human beings come to know anything. Furthermore, there is no widespread agreement as to which of these explanations is 'true' or even most useful. The realist position probably commands most support amongst natural scientists and those social scientists, probably the majority, who seek the same status for their field as is accorded to the natural sciences. Social constructionists point to a significant difference between natural and social phenomena. Humans interpret natural phenomena, those phenomena do not interpret themselves. However, when it comes to human phenomena, we are dealing with ourselves, phenomena that are already interpreting themselves. Many constructionists hold, therefore, that while the traditional scientific approach might be applicable in the natural sciences it is not in the human sciences.

At this point, you might be wondering why I have apparently moved so far away from the central concern of this book, namely strategy and organisational dynamics. The reason is this: any view you take of the nature of strategy and change in organisations immediately implies a view on the nature of human knowing. If you think that an organisation's strategy is the choice made by its chief executive, following a rational process of formulation, then you are assuming a realist, transcendental idealist or perhaps constructivist position. You are implicitly assuming that the individual is primary and that this individual takes the position of the objective observer of the organisation. Since this tends to be the dominant approach to explaining what strategy is, it is quite easy to take it for the truth. However, what I have been trying to show in the above paragraphs is that this would be a completely unwarranted assumption. Just how human beings know anything, and whether the individual or the group is primary, are hotly contested issues with no clear truth. Simply going along with today's dominant views on strategy, without questioning the foundations upon which they are built, amounts to shutting one's eyes to other possibilities which might make more sense of one's experience. For example, if one shifts perspective and considers that an organisation's strategy might emerge from conversational processes in which many participate, then one would be moving towards a social constructionist position and assuming that the group is primary or to some kind of absolute idealism where neither the individual nor the group is primary. Perhaps this might assist in making more sense of the experience of life in organisations.

Different theories of strategy and organisational change imply different ways of explaining how human beings know or do anything. If one wants to understand just what the differences are between one explanation of strategy and organisational change and another, then one needs, I believe, to understand what assumptions are implicitly being made about how humans know anything. The key aspect distinguishing explanations of human knowing is the way they treat the relationship between the individual and the group. In the rest of this book, I will be reviewing how various ways of understanding strategy and organisational change differ. I will be pointing to how some of the most important differences relate to the implicit assumptions made about human knowing and the relationship between the individual and the group.

I now want to move on to another extremely important aspect of how we make sense of the world and this has to do with the nature of causality.

The nature of causality

One way of thinking about the relationship between cause and effect in Western culture is linear and unidirectional. There is some variable Y whose behaviour is to be explained. It is regarded as dependent and other 'independent' variables, X_1, $X_2, \ldots$, are sought that are causing it. Linear relationships mean that *if* there is more of a cause *then* there will be proportionally more of the effect. This is the efficient, 'if . . . then' theory of causality.

For example, in organisations, a frequent explanation for success is that it is caused by a particular culture, a particular management style, or a particular control system. The more that culture, style or control system is applied the more successful the organisation will be. Opposition parties always say that the government of the day has caused recession and inflation. More of the government's policies will, they say, lead to more recession and more inflation. All of this is what is meant by straight-forward unidirectional, linear connections between cause and effect.

Many scientists, both social and natural, are increasingly realising that this view of the relationship between cause and effect is far too simplistic and leads to an inadequate understanding of behaviour. They hold that greater insight comes from thinking in terms of mutual or circular causality. The demand for a product does not depend simply on customer behaviour; it also depends upon what the producing firm does in terms of price and quality. In other words, the firm affects the customer who then affects the firm. Management style may cause success but success affects the style managers adopt. The government's policies may cause recession and inflation, but recession and inflation may also cause the policies they adopt.

When organisms and organisations are thought of as systems then complex forms of causality become evident to do with interconnection and interdependence, where everything affects everything else. In addition to the circular causality and inter-dependence of systems, there is also *nonlinearity*. This means that one variable can have a more than proportional effect upon another. Nonlinear systems then involve very complex connections between cause and effect. It may become unclear what cause and effect mean. The links between them may become distant in time and space and those links may even disappear for all practical purposes. If in these circumstances one proceeds as if simple linear links exist even if one does not know what they are, then one is likely to undertake actions that yield unintended and surprising results.

How one thinks about causality, then, will have an important impact on how one thinks about strategy and organisational change. This is a matter to which subsequent chapters will pay a great deal of attention.

Closely linked to the matter of causality is that of paradox. I have already said that how different theories deal with paradox is an important feature distinguishing them, so it is important to be clear about what paradox means.

The nature of paradox

There are a number of different ways in which we deal with the contradictions we encounter in our thinking. The first is to regard them as a *dichotomy*, which is a polarised opposition requiring an 'either . . . or' choice. For example, managers faced with the need to improve quality, requiring an increase in costs, may also be faced with the need to cut costs. If they think in terms of a dichotomy then they choose one or the other of these opposing alternatives. Or they could think of the choice facing them as a *dilemma*, which is a choice between two equally unattractive alternatives. Improving quality is unattractive because it increases costs, and cutting costs means destroying jobs, which is unattractive for humanitarian reasons. Dilemmas also present 'either . . . or' choices. Thirdly, a contradiction may be thought of in terms of a *dualism or a duality*. For example, managers may be faced with the need to customise their products to meet localised customer requirements but they may also be faced with the need to standardise their products to meet global competition. If those managers think about this in dualistic terms then they might come up with the resolution or elimination of the contradiction through '*both* thinking globally *and* acting locally'. The mode of thinking in dualistic terms has a 'both . . . and' structure. Instead of choosing between one or the other, one keeps both but locates them in different spaces or times. So in the above example, one pole of the contradiction is located in thinking and the other in acting. The 'either . . . or' thinking of dichotomies and dilemmas and the 'both . . . and' thinking of dualisms/dualities all satisfy a precept of Aristotelian logic, which requires the elimination of contradictions because they are a sign of faulty thinking.

Finally, one might think of a contradiction as a *paradox*. There are a number of different definitions of a paradox. First, it may mean an apparent contradiction, a state in which two apparently conflicting elements appear to be operating at the same time. Paradox in this sense can be removed or resolved by choosing one element above the other all the time or by reframing the problem to remove the apparent contradiction. There is little difference between paradox in this sense and dualism/dualities and this is the meaning of paradox that is usually taken up in the literature on systemic views of organisations.

However, paradox may mean a state in which two diametrically opposing forces/ideas are simultaneously present, neither of which can ever be resolved or eliminated. There is, therefore, no possibility of a choice between the opposing poles or of locating them in different spheres. Instead, what is required is a different kind of logic, such as the dialectical logic of Hegel (*see* Chapter 10). As it is used in this book, the word paradox means the presence together, at the same time, of self-contradictory, essentially conflicting ideas, none of which can be eliminated or resolved.

There are many examples of paradoxes in organisations. Each individual in an organisation has a paradoxical desire for freedom and the excitement that goes with chance and uncertainty, while at the same time fearing the unknown and wanting order and discipline. Businesses have to produce at the lowest cost, but they have to increase costs to provide quality. Organisations have to control what their employees do, but they have to give them freedom if they want to retain them and if they want them to deal with rapidly changing circumstances.

Many theories of organisation emphasise either/or choices. They prescribe either stability and success, or instability and failure. They usually do not recognise paradox as fundamental and, when they do, they prescribe some kind of harmonious, equilibrium balance between the choices. In this way the paradox is in effect eliminated; its existence is a nuisance that is not fundamental to success.

The way one perceives paradox says much about the way one understands organisational dynamics. The idea that, for success, paradoxes must be resolved, and that the tension they cause must be released, is part of the paradigm that equates success with the dynamics of stability, regularity and predictability. The notion that paradoxes can never be resolved, only lived with, leads to a view of organisational dynamics couched in terms of continuing tension-generating behaviour patterns that are both regular and irregular, both stable and unstable and both predictable and unpredictable, all at the same time, but which lead to creative novelty.

1.4 Key features in comparing theories of organisational evolution

In the previous sections of this chapter, I have been describing what I think the phenomena are that I am trying to explain when I talk about strategy and organisational change. Those phenomena are populations of organisations of various kinds and populations of people and groupings of people that make up each of those organisations. These populations of organisations and people are continuously interacting with each other in ever-changing but also repetitive ways. I have also been talking about how human beings come to know the phenomena of their worlds, including those of populations of organisations and people dynamically interacting with each other. In the course of describing the phenomena and how one might come to know them, I have listed a number of factors that I want to use to distinguish between various theories of strategy and organisational dynamics. These factors are:

- How the dynamics are understood.
- How paradox is handled in thought.
- What ontological states and what degree of descriptive detail are focused upon – macro or micro.
- What part emotion is seen to play.
- How the interactive/relational nature of the phenomena are conceptualised.
- How causality is understood.

- Whether the theory assumes a pre-given or a constructed reality.
- Whether it takes the methodological stance of the objective observer or the reflexive, participative enquirer.
- What theory of human knowing and behaving it assumes, particularly how it deals with the relationship between individuals and groups.

I now want to pull these factors together into four questions that I will put to each of the theories to be considered in the chapters that follow. The questions are:

1. How does the theory understand the nature of human interacting and relating? I will be considering whether the theory takes a systemic or a responsive processes perspective, and how each of these deals with dynamics and the nature of causality.

2. What theory of human psychology, that is ways of knowing and behaving, does each theory of strategy and organisational change assume? I will be focusing particularly on how each psychological theory deals with the relationship between individual and group and the questions of emotion and power.

3. What methodology underlies each theory of strategy and organisational change? I will be asking whether the theory takes the position of objective observer of a pre-given reality or whether it takes the position of the reflexive, participative enquirer seeking to understand a constructed reality.

4. How does each theory of strategy and organisational change deal with the paradoxical nature of the population of organisations and groupings of people? I will be asking whether the theory sees opposing ideas as dichotomies, dilemmas, dualisms/dualities or paradoxes.

In the chapters that follow I am going to classify different explanations according to the answers they give to the above four questions. What I am trying to do is to tease out strands of thinking in order to expose assumptions and reasoning processes for comparison.

1.5 Outline of the book

As already indicated, this book consists of three parts. Each part starts with a short introduction setting out the purpose of that part. Each part is divided into a number of chapters. It is usual nowadays to indicate at the start of chapters in a textbook what the learning outcomes are supposed to be for those reading the chapter. This practice reflects a particular theory of communication and learning that will be described in Chapter 3. According to this theory, meaning arises in an individual mind and is transmitted to another mind. If the idea is described with clarity and the transmission is successful then the writer of a chapter can convey it to the reader who ought to be able to learn it. For reasons that I hope will become clear in Part Three, I do not find this a convincing theory of communication and instead ascribe to a view in which meaning arises in interaction between people, so that the meaning of what I write is located not in my words alone but in your response to them. It follows that I cannot know what the learning outcomes will be for you if you read a chapter.

So instead of setting out learning outcomes, at the start of each chapter, I list the points about a particular way of thinking that I am trying to draw attention to and invite readers to draw on their own organisational experience to reflect upon these points. I try to indicate why I think the material in a particular chapter is important. Each chapter ends with a list of questions about the material in the chapter. These have not been designed as a kind of examination in which readers can check whether they have learned the material. Instead the questions are intended as an aid to further reflection on the ways of thinking that have been discussed in the chapter.

It is also usual for a textbook to have a number of case studies that describe successful or unsuccessful managerial action. Readers are then supposed to analyse the case studies and draw conclusions about successful management practice. Since this book is about ways of thinking, some of which are incompatible with the case study method, I have not included any case studies or even examples that might convey the idea of 'right' management practices. Instead the book provides four Reflective Management Narratives, one after each of Chapters 11, 12, 13 and 14. These are pieces written by graduates from, or current participants in, a doctoral programme that I direct at the University of Hertfordshire. This is a part-time programme for organisational practitioners whose research is their work. The methodology they pursue is one that can be summarised as 'taking experience seriously'. What this involves is narrating some current organisational activity that the writer is involved in and reflecting upon, and making sense of, that activity in the light of traditions of thought. Each of the four narratives therefore provides the reader with an opportunity to reflect upon, and perhaps discuss with others, just how a particular practitioner makes use of the ideas presented in Part 3 to make sense of what they are doing in organisations. In discussing these experiences readers may develop further their own thinking.

Turning now to the content of the book, Part 1 reviews theories of strategy and organisational change that are based on some form of systems thinking combined with some individual-based psychological theory.

Chapter 2 explores the origins and development of systems thinking and the notion of the autonomous rational individual in the thought of the German philosopher Kant. These notions are the main pillars upon which are built the theories of organisational strategy covered in Part One.

Chapter 3 is concerned with strategic choice theory, which prescribes formal, analytical procedures for formulating long-term strategies to produce successful performance and the design of administrative systems for their implementation. The chapter will explore how this theory is fundamentally based upon cybernetic systems theory and primarily cognitivist psychology.

Chapter 4 turns to alterative theories of how organisations evolve and change through processes of organisational learning. The theoretical foundations of these theories are to be found in an alternative theory of systems known as systems dynamics combined with cognitivist psychology, as in strategic choice theory, and also humanistic psychology.

Chapter 5 reviews a combination of yet another theory of systems, general or open systems theory and psychoanalytic perspectives on human action. This psychodynamic systems theory focuses attention on unconscious group processes and the way people defend themselves against anxiety, drawing attention to how these all create obstacles to rational task performance and learning.

Chapter 6 explores the development of second-order systems thinking, reviewing the move these system thinkers have been making to more social perspectives.

Chapter 7 reviews the way in which those engaged in the dominant discourse have addressed the question of strategy process, that is, the matter of *how* strategising activities are conducted.

Part 2 of the book moves from the systems theories developed in the late 1940s and early 1950s to those developed more recently in what have come to be known as the complexity sciences.

Chapter 8 describes the theories of chaos, dissipative structures and the agent-based models of complex adaptive systems.

Chapter 9 reviews a number of applications of chaos and complexity theory to organisations. I argue that most of these applications continue to be made within the systemic and cognitivist psychological perspective of the dominant discourse with the consequence of collapsing the potentially radical insights of chaos and complexity theory into that dominant discourse. The result is the re-presentation of existing theories in new language.

Part 3 moves from systemic to responsive processes thinking. The latter perspective is a way of understanding organisations as ongoing temporal processes of interaction between persons in which what they are creating is simply further patterns of interaction rather than any system.

Chapter 10 reviews the origins of responsive processes thinking in the thought of the German philosopher Hegel, and its further development in the work of the American pragmatist philosophers Mead and Dewey, and the processes sociologist Elias.

Chapters 11 to 15 review the theory of complex responsive processes as a perspective from which to understand strategy and organisational change. They develop an alternative psychological perspective in which relationship is key to understanding human action, including organisations. This theory focuses on the self-organising and constructive nature of conversation, power relations and ideology in organisations. The first four of these chapters are followed by a Reflective Management Narrative in which leaders, managers and consultants write about some aspect of their experience of life in organisations.

Chapter 16 examines how the theory of complex responsive processes might answer the four key questions posed earlier in this chapter.

Part 1

Systemic ways of thinking about strategy and organisational dynamics

The purpose of Part 1 is to explore the ways of thinking reflected in the dominant discourse about organisations and their management as well as the most prominent critiques of this discourse to be found in organisational and management literature. What the chapters that follow will be trying to do is tease out the taken-for-granted assumptions being made in the dominant discourse and the critiques of it.

Common to both the dominant discourse and most of its major critiques is the taken-for-grated assumption that organisations are systems. It is now usual, amongst both organisational practitioners and organisational researchers and writers, to talk about organisations as entities that actually exist outside of human interaction. Human individuals with minds inside them are located at one level of existence and organisations as things called systems which actually exist are located at another level of existence. Human individuals are thought to create organisations as systems in their interaction with each other and these systems are then thought to act back on individuals as a cause of their behaviour. The dominant discourse, therefore, reifies organisations, sometimes regarding them as mechanistic things and sometimes claiming that they are living things, organisms, with purposes and intentions of their own. We have come, then, not only to reify organisations but to anthropomorphise them. It is widely assumed that individuals, as leaders and managers, can take the position of objective observer of such organisational systems and design them to achieve purposes ascribed to them or at least intervene in them and influence the direction they take. The dominant discourse thus reflects an implicit and powerful ideology to do with managerial control. Chapters 3, 4 and 5 will explore just how these taken-for-granted assumptions are expressed in the dominant theories of strategic choice, organisational learning and psychodynamic systems.

The prevailing assumption that organisations are actually existing things, whether mechanistic or organic, has not gone unchallenged. Chapter 6 will explore a particularly coherent critique presented within the tradition of second-order systems thinking by soft and critical systems thinkers. Writers in these traditions hold that organisations are not actual systems to be found in the real world. Instead, they argue that organisations are to be thought of 'as if' they are systems; indeed some of these writers hold that human thinking is innately systemic. This critique therefore represents an important movement in thought from a realist to an idealist approach in which organisations as systems are mental constructs. However, this does not amount to a movement away from the idea of system. An organisation is to be thought of 'as if' it is a system in order to structure organisational problems in the interest of finding more effective solutions. It continues to be taken for granted that organisational phenomena are at a different level to human individuals who can design, intervene, influence and solve systemic problems. However, here too there is a challenge to the dominant discourse and its ideology of managerial control. This flows from the recognition that individuals cannot simply be objective observers external to an organisational system because they are also participants in it. This leads to an emphasis on participation, social interaction, politics, culture and ethics in what amounts to an ideology of improvement, emancipation, democracy and respect for the plurality of points of view. However, the fundamental assumptions to do with systems and the primacy of the individual remain intact in the critique mounted by second-order systems thinking.

Other critiques of the dominant discourse have also been presented and these will be considered in Chapter 7. One outstanding critique has been presented to the taken-for-granted assumption in the dominant discourse that managers are rational decision makers. This critique has pointed to the considerable limitations placed on the possibility of rational decision making by the economic costs of gathering and analysing data, the information processing capacity of the human brain, the influence of cognitive frames of reference on what people pay attention to, the interpretations people make of their situations, and the impact of emotion, fantasising and unconscious processes (see Chapter 5). Linked to this major critique are the descriptive studies of what managers actually do, which reveal how idealised an image the dominant discourse presents of managers as rational planners. This critique points to how messy actual decision making is and how at least some major aspects of strategy emerge, which is understood as occurring by chance as opposed to intention. Then there are the relatively few studies of whether the prescriptions of the dominant discourse do actually achieve what they are supposed to. Taken together, these studies are inconclusive at best and tend to point to how ineffective the prescriptions of the dominat discourse prove to be.

However, these critiques again make the same fundamental assumptions as the dominant discourse to do with the systemic nature of organisations and the primacy of the individual, the latter being reflected even when social interaction is taken into account.

Another critique is also important and this relates to the nature of organisational process. In a reaction to the focus on that content of strategies which will lead to successful performance, some writers have called for a focus on how strategy is formed, that is, on strategy process rather than strategy content. However, the process field continued to think about organisations as a whole, at the macro level, and took a macro view of the strategy process. Over the last few years there has been a reaction to this, taking the form of a call for focusing attention on the micro level of what people actually do on an ordinary, daily basis when they strategise. This leads to a concern with conversations, ways of sense making, politics, emotion and identity.

However, once again this critique continues to be based on systemic thinking about organisations and individual-focused cognitivist, constructivist and humanistic psychologies.

Given the taken-for-granted nature and fundamental importance of the idea of system and the concept of the individual in the dominant discourse, as well as the critiques of it, Chapter 2 will explore the origins and implications of these notions.

Chapters 3 and 4 then go on to briefly summarise the main elements of the dominant discourse on organisation and strategy with a view to identifying the fundamental underlying assumptions. In talking about the dominant discourse, I am not talking about a monolithic, uncontested way of thinking but a number of often conflicting strands held together by the common underlying assumptions of the autonomous individual and the organisation as a system. There are various ways of classifying these strands. One common classification is to distinguish between those approaches to strategy that focus on content and those that focus on process (Chakravarthy and Doz, 1992). However, this distinction has been criticised because all theories focusing on content make at least some implicit assumptions about process and vice versa. I will be looking specifically at the assumptions made about process in Chapters 7 and 10. An often quoted classification of strategic schools of thought is that provided by Mintzberg *et al.* (1998) who make the following distinctions:

Prescriptive schools

- The *design school*, in which strategy is a deliberate process of conscious thought where responsibility rests with top management. The strategy seeks to match the internal capabilities of a firm with the opportunities proved by its external environment (Andrews, 1987; Chandler, 1962; Selznick, 1957).
- The *planning school*, where specialist strategic planners adopt formal, step-by-step techniques to do much the same as the design school (Ansoff, 1965).
- The *positioning school*, which is built on the design and planning schools but focuses on strategy content (Porter, 1980, 1985).

Descriptive schools

- The *entrepreneurial school*, in which strategy is seen as a visionary process carried out by leaders (Peters and Waterman, 1982).
- The *cognitive school* (Bogner and Thomas, 1993; Regner and Huff, 1993), which focuses on the mental and interpretive processes of strategisers.
- The *learning school*, where strategies emerge as people learn over time (Lindblom, 1959; Nelson and Winter, 1982; Quinn, 1980) as distinct from deliberate strategy (Mintzberg and Walters, 1982).
- The *power school*, which sees strategy as a political process (Pettigrew, 1977).
- The *cultural school*, which is concerned with the influence of culture on strategic stability (Peters and Waterman, 1982).
- The *environmental school*, which sees the environment as the active cause of strategy while the organisation is passive (Hannan and Freeman, 1989).

Synthesis

- The *configuration school*, which integrates the views of all the other schools in terms of configurations or in terms of transformations (Miller and Freeson, 1980; Mintzberg, 1983).

Another writer, Whittington (2001), distinguishes amongst:

- The *classical approach*, which relies on the rational planning models.
- The *evolutionary approach*, which draws on the metaphor of biological evolution where change depends on chance and competition.

Table A.1 Classification of schools of strategy thinking

School	Strategic choice	Organisational learning
Mintzberg *et al.*	*Prescriptive schools:* design planning positioning	*Descriptive schools:* entrepreneurial cognitive learning power cultural
Whittington	classical	processualists systemic

- The *processualists*, who emphasise the imperfect processes of forming strategies which, in practice, emerge from pragmatic processes of learning and compromise.
- The *systemic approach*, which regards strategy as linked to the cultures and power structures of the system in which it takes place.

In reviewing the dominant discourse in this part, I intend to adopt a simpler classification, distinguishing between those approaches that regard strategy as a more or less unproblematic choice and those that regard strategy as arising in some form of purposive organisational learning. The relationships between these classifications are roughly as set out in Table A.1. The school Mintzberg *et al.* (1998) call the environmental school coincides more or less with what Whittington calls the evolutionary approach. I have not included these under the heading of either strategic choice or organisational learning because evolutionary approaches claim that what happens to an organisation happens mainly as a consequence of chance and competition. In making this claim they mount what is, perhaps, the major critique within the dominant discourse of the intentional, purposive basis of all the other theories. Not surprisingly, given its emphasis on chance and passivity, evolutionary approaches feature very rarely in the discussions of organisational practitioners while the vocabulary of all the other schools is common parlance amongst them. I will refer in subsequent chapters to the evolutionary approaches in drawing attention to the critiques of the dominant discourse.

I will be arguing that all of the theories categorised in Table A.1 under the headings of both strategic choice and organisational learning, as well as the evolutionary critiques thereof, share two fundamental, taken-for-granted assumptions. First, they all think of organisations in terms of systems. Second, they are all based, implicitly or explicitly, on one or more of the individual-centred theories of human psychology, namely, cognitivism, constructivism, humanistic psychology or psychoanalysis. Chapter 3 will be concerned with the theory of strategic choice while Chapter 4 will explore the way of thinking reflected in theories of organisational learning. Chapter 5 will look at ways of thinking about obstacles to learning from a psychoanalytic perspective, while Chapter 6 will consider more recent developments in systems thinking, namely, second-order systems and autopoiesis. Chapter 7 will then review the manner in which strategy process is dealt with in the dominant discourse.

The purpose of Part 1 of the book, then, is to explore the ways of thinking underlying theories found in the dominant discourse. These chapters provide the basis for comparison with the perspective to be described in Part 3, which turns to ways of thinking that depart from both of the dominant discourse's underlying assumptions mentioned above. This way of thinking takes organisations to be ongoing processes of human interaction rather than systems, and views human psychology not in terms of the autonomous individual and consequent individual-centred psychologies, but in terms of people being fundamentally interdependent.

Chapter 2

The origins of systems thinking

This chapter invites you to draw on your own experience to reflect on and consider the implications of:

- How the idea of a system arose and what it consists of.

- The 'as if', hypothetical nature of original systems thinking and how this was lost in the later development of systems thinking.

- The notions of causality reflected in the idea of a system.

- The notion of the autonomous rational individual and the theory of causality that this implies.

- The dualistic 'both . . . and' structure of systems thinking.

- The caution against applying the notion of system to human action.

- The possibility of explaining novelty in terms of systems.

- How systems sciences, including theories of organisation, developed on the basis of systems thinking.

As subsequent chapters will show, the concept of system and the notion of the rational autonomous individual are both fundamental to the dominant discourse on organisations and their management. For the purpose of reflecting upon and becoming critically aware of the way of thinking reflected in this discourse it is therefore of great importance to think about the origins of the concept of system and the notion of the autonomous rational individual and what their explanatory limitations might be. Taking a reflexive stance does not simply mean taking into account one's personal history and how this impacts on how one is arguing, it also means taking into account the history of the social traditions of thought in which one is embedded and how this impacts on what one is arguing. Awareness of the history of the concept of systems and autonomous individuals then becomes a key element in taking a critical position. Already in Kant's thought we can see how organisations have come to be thought of as systems external to individuals and how these rational individuals have come to be thought of as the designers of organisational systems, or at least interveners in them who can influence the direction of their movement. Part 3 of this book presents a fundamental challenge to both of these notions.

2.1 Introduction

Some time ago, I joined a task force of senior executives in a large international corporation. This task force had been appointed by the chief executive who was concerned about the strategic direction of the corporation. He felt that the corporation had become increasingly unable to cope with the rapid changes confronting it. It seemed to carry on operating as it always had done in a world that was now completely different. The chief executive believed that the organisation needed to change substantially from an inflexible bureaucracy into a nimble entrepreneurial organisation capable of developing new forms of competitive advantage. He also believed that this change would only take place if the people throughout the *whole* organisation changed the way they behaved and he was convinced that such behavioural change would only happen if the values driving behaviour were transformed. This was the task he set for the task force I joined, namely, identifying the new set of values required to transform the organisation and recommending the actions required to instil these new values into the organisation. This task force had been meeting for some time and when I joined them their frustration was evident. Despite sharing the chief executive's beliefs and despite their undoubtedly intelligent efforts, they had been unable to identify the required values, let alone how such values might be instilled in the *whole* corporation. Furthermore, they had no satisfactory way of explaining why they had not been able to carry out their task.

What struck me when I joined them was how they had not been questioning the way of thinking that led them to believe that they could change their whole corporation in the manner proposed. They were not exploring the assumptions they were making when they held this view. Instead, they were simply taking it for granted that it was possible to do what they had been asked to do. It seemed to me that they were implicitly thinking of their organisation as a whole, as a system, operating according to particular values. They thought that if they could identify these values and then change them, they could change the direction, the strategy, of the organisation. They seemed to be thinking about themselves as autonomous individuals who could objectively observe the organisational system and determine the values according to which it should operate and then ensure that it did in fact operate according to these values.

For me, the big question was whether it was possible to do what they were proposing to do and it was clear that they were not even asking themselves this question. Unless they could begin to reflect upon their way of thinking and its taken-for-granted assumptions, they would probably continue with their frustrating attempts to formulate and change values. To take the reflexive stance I am suggesting, it seems to me to be essential to understand how particular ways of thinking originated. Ways of thinking evolve – they have a history and understanding this history enables us to understand the nature of the assumptions we are making now as we approach important practical issues. It is for this very practical reason that this chapter introduces the subjects of strategy and change by turning to philosophy and the history of Western thought.

In order to understand the taken-for-granted assumptions made in theories of strategic management, therefore, it is helpful in a very practical way to understand something of the history of those theories within the wider history of Western thought. The chapters in this part of the book will be drawing attention to the manner in which all of the major theories of strategic management today depend upon systems thinking and take for granted the assumptions upon which that thinking is built. This chapter will explore the origins of systems thinking in Western philosophy and to do this it is necessary to go back some four hundred years and consider how people in the West thought about themselves and the world they lived in, and how they thought about the way in which they came to know anything about themselves in the world they lived in.

In the Middle Ages, people in the West thought that the world was created by God and they thought about themselves as creatures in nature and therefore also made by God, in fact in the image of God. The purpose of nature was to express the glory of God in following His eternal, timeless laws. These laws applied to human beings too but with one major difference: unlike other creatures, humans were believed to have souls enabling them to choose whether to obey the laws of God or not. Obedience led to rewards in the afterlife and disobedience led to eternal punishment. Knowledge of God's creation was through divine revelation so that humans knew what they knew because God had revealed it to them in the Scriptures. Knowing was a process of interpreting the eternal truth to be found in the Holy Scriptures. Individuals thought of themselves in terms of their place in the community rather than as separate individuals. There was no notion of an existential gap between individuals because who one was flowed from one's membership of a community and this was fixed by birth.

People thought in this way for hundreds of years, and then about four hundred years ago changes in social and political structures began a long process of weakening the Church and absolute monarchies, and this process was intertwined with changes in the way people thought. This gradual process of change in the way people thought has come to be known as the Scientific Revolution, leading to the Age of Reason.

2.2 The Scientific Revolution

The Scientific Revolution was a movement of thought in which people came to hold that the eternal, timeless laws of nature could be understood not through revelation but through human reason. For example, Copernicus and others worked in the early sixteenth century, observing and measuring the movement of the planets and putting forward theories on the laws governing their movement. Galileo took this work up in the early seventeenth century, as did Newton and Leibniz later on in the seventeenth century. Also during this period, the philosophers Bacon and Descartes powerfully articulated the way in which people were coming to experience themselves as individuals with minds inside them. As Descartes put it, human minds are 'thinking things' and all we can be sure of is our own individual capacity to doubt. Everything is to be subjected to doubt and it is in this rational process of doubting that humans can come to know themselves and their world. By the end of the seventeenth century, then, the scientific method had been established, as had a highly individualistic way of thinking about ourselves.

Central to the scientific method is the individual scientist who objectively observes nature, formulates hypotheses about the laws governing it and then tests these laws against quantified data, so progressively moving towards a fuller and more accurate understanding of the laws. These laws were understood to take the form of universal, timeless, deterministic, linear 'if–then' causal links. For example, *if* twice as much force is applied to an object in a vacuum *then* it will move twice as far. The consequence of this Scientific Revolution, extending over more than a century, was that people in the West had come to experience themselves as autonomous individuals with a non-corporeal mind inside them, taking the form of internal worlds consisting of representations of the external world. This view of how people experienced themselves was concisely formulated in the philosophy of Leibniz. He saw individuals as windowless monads who internally represented external worlds, perceived both consciously and unconsciously, and related to each other across an existential gulf.

However, this way of thinking posed fundamental questions. First, the question arose as to how reasoning individuals were able to formulate hypotheses, involving the categorisation of phenomena in nature and the identification of relationships between them. For the realists, the answer lay in the nature of reality. There was no problem about knowing because our bodies simply perceived reality as it was through the senses. For others, however, there was a problem about knowing that needed explanation. Descartes and Leibniz dealt with the problem by arguing that the mind contained innate ideas through which it recognised clear, distinct truths about the real external world. In other words, there is nothing problematic about knowing: external reality exists and we directly know it because we are born with minds having the capacity for knowing reality. However, Locke took a more sceptical position and argued that the mind had no innate ideas of reality but was initially a blank tablet waiting for experience to write upon it in the form of sensory impressions that represent external, material objects. The question then became how we could know that our mental representations correspond to reality.

Writing around the middle of the eighteenth century, Hume took a radically sceptical position and said that the mind imposes an order of its own on the sensations coming from the external real world but that this order is simply an association of ideas, a habit of human imagination through which it assumes causal connections. There is nothing innate about knowing and the causal connections we postulate are simply the accidents of repeated connections in the mind. Ideas result from connections in experience, not from an independent reality, and intelligibility reflects habits of mind, not the nature of reality. Hume claimed that there was no necessary order to our ideas other than the ways they were combined in our minds according to habit and the laws of association.

With this radically sceptical argument, Hume threw into doubt the Enlightenment idea that reason could unaided discover the order of the real world. As a result, the philosophy of Descartes, Leibniz and Locke no longer seemed to provide a firm foundation for science. Scepticism, with its conclusion about the relativity and unreliability of knowledge, threatened the very basis of science. This debate between the dogmatic rationalists, or realist scientists, and the radical sceptics about the nature of human knowledge is much the same as the more recent debate between modernist science and postmodernism. In both cases, science posits the existence of a unitary reality that can be reliably observed as truth, while radical scepticism/postmodernism points to the constructed, relative and plural nature of accounts of the world in which there is no truth, only many different 'stories' with, at the extreme, none necessarily better than any other.

Another fundamental question posed by the Scientific Revolution had to do with human freedom and choice. Since humans were part of nature they had to be subject to its deterministic laws; but if they were, then it followed that they could not be free.

These two questions, one to do with the nature of human knowing and the other to do with the possibility of human choice, were taken up by the philosopher Kant. Systems thinking can be said to have originated in Kant's answers to these questions.

2.3 Kant: natural systems and autonomous individuals

Kant was impressed by the advances in human knowledge brought about by the scientific method but he also recognised that it was not sufficient to simply dogmatically postulate that we know reality directly. He accepted that we know what we know through sensations coming from the real world and that the mind imposes some kind of order on these sense data so that we cannot know reality in a direct manner. He therefore postulated a dualism. On the one hand there was reality, which he called noumenal, and on the other hand there was the appearance of reality to us in the form of sensations, which he called phenomenal. He argued that we could never know reality in itself, the noumenal, but only the appearance of reality as sensation, the phenomenal. This bears some similarity to the position of the radical sceptics but Kant departed from them when he held that our inability to know reality itself does not mean that all our knowledge is purely relative, simply the result of habits of association. Instead, the mind consists of innate categories which impose order on the phenomenal.

In this way he agreed with the radical sceptics in holding that we could not know reality directly but also agreed with the scientific realists in holding that there were innate ideas that imposed order on experience so that knowledge and truth were not simply relative. Examples of the innate categories of mind are time, space, causal links and what Kant called 'regulative ideas'. *Regulative ideas* are to be distinguished from *constitutive ideas*. A constitutive idea, or hypothesis, is a statement of what actually happens in reality. For example if we say that an organisation actually is a system operating to fulfil some real purpose, then we are putting forward a constitutive idea. We are saying that the organisation really exists and it is really fulfilling some real purpose. However, if we put forward an hypothesis in which we are thinking about an organisation 'as if' it were a system operating 'as if' it had a purpose, then we are thinking in terms of regulative ideas. Obviously Kant would not talk about constitutive ideas because he held that we could never know reality in itself. The activity of the scientist then becomes clear in Kant's scheme of things. The scientist has a mind consisting of categories of time, space, causal links and the capacity for forming 'as if' hypotheses, which enable him or her to formulate hypotheses about the appearances of reality and then test them.

Scientists, such as Newton and Leibniz, had understood nature in mechanistic terms and Kant was able to explain why this understanding was neither purely relative nor directly revealing of the reality of nature. He resolved the contradiction between realist and relative knowledge by taking aspects from each argument and holding them together in the 'both . . . and' way of a dualism. Knowledge of appearances was real and reliable while knowledge of reality itself was indeed impossible. In a sense *both* the scientific realists *and* the radical sceptics had a point and the *contradictions between them could be eliminated* by locating their conflicting explanations in different realms. This is typical of Kant's dualistic thinking in which paradoxes are eliminated so satisfying the rule of Aristotelian logic according to which paradox, the simultaneous existence of two contradictory ideas, is a sign of faulty thinking. I want to stress this key aspect of Kantian thinking because it has become very widespread in the West. The ideas of figure and ground, of different lenses through which to understand the world, and different levels of existence such as the individual at one level and the organisation at another, are examples of this.

Kant, then, developed transcendental idealism as an alternative to realism, on the one hand, and to scepticism, on the other. His thinking can be labelled as idealism because he held that we know reality through the capacities of the mind and it is transcendental because the categories through which we know are already given outside our direct experience. In this way, Kant provided a sophisticated justification for the scientific method.

Self-organising systems

However, Kant went further than providing a philosophical justification of the mechanistic understanding of nature provided by scientists. He held that while it was useful to understand inanimate nature in this way, it was not adequate for an understanding of living organisms. He suggested that organisms could be more usefully understood as *self-organising systems*, which are very different from mechanisms.

A mechanism consists of parts that form a functional unity. The parts derive their function as parts from the functioning of the whole. For example, a clock consists of a number of parts, such as cogs, dials and hands, and these are assembled into a clock, which has the function of recording the passing of time. The parts are only parts of the clock insofar as they are required for the functioning of the whole, the clock. Therefore, a finished notion of *the whole is required before the parts* can have any function and the *parts must be designed* and assembled to play their particular role, without which there cannot be the whole clock. Before the clock functions, the parts must be designed and before they can be designed, the notion of the clock must be formulated.

However, the parts of a living organism are not first designed and then assembled into the unity of the organism. Rather, they arise as the result of interactions within the developing organism. For example, a plant has roots, stems, leaves and flowers that interact with each other to form the plant. The parts emerge, as parts, not by prior design but as a result of internal interactions within the plant itself in a self-generating, self-organising dynamic in a particular environmental context. The parts do not come before the whole but emerge in the interaction of spontaneously generated differences that give rise to the parts within the unity of the whole (Goodwin, 1994; Webster and Goodwin, 1996). The parts, however, have to be necessary for the production of the whole, otherwise they have no relevance as parts. The parts have to serve the whole; it is just that the whole is not designed first but comes into being with the parts. Organisms develop from a simple initial form, such as a fertilised egg, into a mature adult form, all as part of an inner coherence expressed in the dynamic unity of the parts. An organism thus expresses a nature with no purpose other than the unfolding of its own mature form. The organism's development unfolds what was already enfolded in it from the beginning.

Kant described this unfolding as 'purposive' because although an organism is not goal oriented in the sense of moving towards an external result, it is thought of as moving to a mature form of itself. The development to the mature form, and the mature form itself, will have some unique features due to the particular context in which it develops but the organism can only ever unfold the general form already enfolded in it. In talking about development being purposive, Kant introduced his notion of organism developing according to a 'regulative idea'. Since he held that we could not know reality, it followed that we could not say that an organism actually was following a particular idea. In other words, we cannot make the claim of a constitutive idea in relation to the organism. Instead, as observing scientists, we can claim that it is helpful to understand an organism 'as if' it were moving according to a particular purpose, namely, the regulative idea of realising a mature form of itself, that is, its true nature or true self.

For Kant, the parts of an organism exist because of, and in order to sustain, the whole as an emergent property (Kauffman, 1995). Organisms are self-producing and therefore self-organising wholes, where the whole is maintained by the parts and the whole orders the parts in such a way that it is maintained. In suggesting that we think in terms of systems, Kant was introducing a causality that was teleological and formative rather than the simple, linear, efficient (if–then) causality assumed in the mechanistic way of understanding nature. In systems terms, *causality is formative* in that it is in the self-organising interaction of the parts that those parts and the whole emerge. It is 'as if' the system, the whole, has a purpose, namely, to move towards a final state that is already given at its origin as a mature form of itself. In other words, nature is unfolding already enfolded forms and causality might be referred to as formative (Stacey *et al.*, 2000) in which the dominant form of causality is the formative process of development from an embryonic to a mature form. It follows that emergence has a particular meaning in Kant's thought. In Kant's systemic thinking, self-organisation means interaction between parts and what emerges in this interaction is the developmental pattern of the whole. Since the system is unfolding what is already enfolded in it this emergent developmental pattern is not unknown or unpredictable. The system does not move towards that which is unknown. What is unknown, however, is reality itself so the system hypothesis cannot be a claim that reality itself moves towards the known.

Note how this understanding of nature as system is quite consistent with the scientific method in that it is the human objective observer who identifies and isolates causality in natural systems and then tests hypotheses ('as if' or regulative ideas) about the purposive movement of those systems. It is not that organisms actually are systems or that they actually are unfolding a particular pattern in movement to a mature form. It is the scientist who finds it useful to think 'as if' they are. It is not that the laws are actually in nature but that the scientist is giving the laws to nature.

A very important point follows from this way of thinking about organisms, namely that it is *a way of thinking that cannot explain novelty*, that is, how any new form could come into existence. In thinking of an organism as unfolding an already enfolded form, Kant's systems thinking can explain the developmental cycle from birth to death but cannot explain how any new form emerges, that is, how evolution takes place. This is obviously a serious problem if what one wants to understand is creativity, innovation or novelty. The key point is that in Kant's systems thinking, causality is formative rather than transformative.

Also, Kant argued that the systemic explanation of how nature functioned could never be applied to humans because humans are autonomous and have a soul. Humans have some freedom to choose and so the deterministic laws of nature cannot be applied to rational human action.

The autonomous individual

For Kant, the human body could be thought of as a system because it is an organism. As such, it is subject to the laws of nature and when human action is driven by the passions of the body then it too is subject to the laws of nature and so not free. However, when acting rationally, humans could not be thought of as parts of a system because then they would exist because of, and in order to maintain, the whole. A part of a system is only a part because it is interacting with other parts to realise themselves in the purposive movement of the emergent whole and the emergence of that whole is the unfolding of what is already enfolded, so excluding any fundamental spontaneity or novelty. If a part is not doing this then it is irrelevant to the system and so not a part acting to produce the whole. However, a part in this sense cannot be free, that is, it cannot follow its own autonomously chosen goals because then it would be acting for itself and not as a part. Furthermore, as parts of a whole that is unfolding an already enfolded final state, neither whole nor parts can display spontaneity or novelty. There can be nothing creative or transformative about such a system. This way of thinking, therefore, cannot explain how the new arises.

It follows that rational human action has to be understood in a different way. Kant held that human individuals are autonomous and so can choose the goals of their actions and they can choose the actions required to realise them using reason. The predominant form of causality here is teleological, namely, that of autonomously chosen ends made possible because of the human capacity for reason. The principal concern then becomes how autonomously chosen goals and actions mesh together in a coherent way that makes it possible for humans to live together. This is a question of ethics and Kant understood ethical choice in terms of universals, namely, those choices that could be followed by all people. We may call this *rationalist causality* (Stacey *et al.*, 2000).

So, Kant developed a systems theory with a theory of formative causality to explain how organisms in nature developed, arguing that this could not be applied to human action, and another kind of explanation for human action, involving rationalist causality. It is particularly important to note these points because when later forms of systems thinking were developed in the middle of the twentieth century, they were directly applied to human action, and individuals came to be thought of as parts in a system called a group, organisation or society. It immediately follows that any such explanation cannot encompass individual human freedom. Nor can a systemic explanation encompass the origins of spontaneity or novelty. To explain these phenomena within systems thinking, we have to rely on the autonomous individual standing outside the system. In other words, change of a transformative kind cannot be explained in systemic terms, that is, in terms of

Box 2.1	Key concepts in Kantian thinking

- Organisms in nature can be thought about 'as if' they are systems.
- Systems are wholes consisting of parts interacting with each other in a self-generating, self-organising way and it is in this interaction that both parts and whole emerge without prior design.
- However, systems are 'purposive' in that they move according to a developmental pattern from an embryonic to a mature form of themselves.
- Causality may then be described as formative in that it is the process of interaction between the parts that is forming the developmental path, unfolding that which was already enfolded from the beginning.
- Humans are autonomous rational individuals who are able to choose their own goals and the actions required to realise them.
- Causality may then be described as rationalist.
- Kantian thinking is fundamentally dualistic in that one kind of causality applies to an organism and another to a human individual.

interactions between parts of the system, with one important exception that I will come to in Chapter 8. Any transformative change can then only be explained in terms of the mental functioning of the individual.

There are two other points to be borne in mind about Kant's systems thinking. It is essentially dualistic, that is, it takes a 'both . . . and' form that eliminates paradox (Griffin, 2002) by locating contradictions in different spaces or time periods. So, with regard to knowing there is *both* the known relating to phenomena *and* the unknown relating to noumena. With regard to the paradox of determinism and freedom there is *both* the determinism of mechanism and organism in nature *and* the freedom of rational human action. Emergence is located in nature and intention in human individuals. Linked to this there is the essentially spatial metaphor underlying all systems thinking. *A system is a whole separated by a boundary from other systems, or wholes.* In other words, there is an 'inside' and an 'outside'. For example, one thinks of what is happening inside an organisation or outside in the environment. Or one thinks of the mind inside a person and reality outside it. The key concepts in Kantian thinking are summarised in Box 2.1.

2.4 Systems thinking in the twentieth century

Kant's thinking provoked many controversies and has continued to have a major impact on the evolution of Western thought up to the present time. This impact is evident in the major development of systems thinking in the twentieth century. Scholars in many different areas were working from the 1920s to the 1940s to develop systemic ways of thinking about physiology, biology, psychology, sociology, engineering and communication. This work culminated in the publication of a number of very important papers around 1950. These papers covered systems of control, the development of computer language, theories of communication (Shannon and Weaver, 1949) and the development of a new science of mind in reaction to behaviourism, namely, cognitivism (Gardner, 1985; McCulloch and Pitts, 1943). These ways of thinking amounted to a new paradigm, namely, a shift from mechanistic, reductionist science in which the whole phenomenon of interest was understood to be the sum of its parts, requiring attention to be focused on the nature of the part rather than the interactions between them. In the new paradigm of systems thinking, the whole phenomenon was thought of as a system and the parts as subsystems within it. A system in turn was thought to be part of a larger supra-system, its environment. The parts were now not simply additive in that they affected each other. The whole came to be understood as more than the sum of the parts. The focus of attention shifted from understanding the parts, or entities, of which the whole was composed, to the interaction of subsystems to form a system and of systems to form a supra-system. An essential aspect of this way of thinking is the *different levels of existence* it ascribes to phenomena. For example, individual minds are thought of as subsystems forming groups, which are thought of as systems forming an organisation, which is thought of as a supra-system. Here each level is a different kind of phenomenon to be understood in a different way.

The new systems theories developed along three pathways over much the same period of time:

- *General systems* theory (Boulding, 1956; von Bertalanffy, 1968) developed by biologists and economists. The central concept here is that of homeostasis, which means that systems have a strong, self-regulating tendency to move towards a state of order and stability, or adapted equilibrium. They can only do this if they have permeable boundaries that are open to interactions with other systems. This strand in systems thinking will be explored in Chapter 5.

- *Cybernetic systems* (Ashby, 1945, 1952, 1956; Beer, 1979, 1981; Wiener, 1948) developed by engineers. Cybernetic systems are self-regulating, goal-directed systems adapting to their environment, a simple example being the central heating system in a building. Here, the resident of a room sets a target temperature and a regulator at the boundary of the heating system detects a gap between that target and the actual temperature. This gap triggers the heating system to switch on or off, so maintaining the chosen target through a process of negative feedback operation. The impact of this strand of thinking on strategic management will be explored in Chapter 3.

- *Systems dynamics* (Forrester, 1958, 1961, 1969; Goodwin, 1951; Philips, 1950; Tustin, 1953) developed largely by engineers who turned their attention to economics and industrial management problems. In systems dynamics, mathematical models are constructed of how the system changes states over time. One important difference from the other two systems theories is the recognition that the system may not move to equilibrium. The system is then no longer self-regulating but it is self-influencing: it may be self-sustaining or self-destructive. The impact of this strand of systems thinking will be explored in Chapter 4.

These three strands of systems thinking began to attract a great deal of attention in many disciplines from around 1950, as did the new cognitivist psychology, and of course, computers. Engineers, bringing with them their notion of control, took the lead in developing the theories of cybernetic systems and systems dynamics, while biologists, concerned with biological control mechanisms, developed general systems theory. This systems movement, particularly in the form of cybernetics, has come to form the foundation of today's dominant management discourse, so importing the engineer's notion of control into understanding human activity. The development of systems thinking amounted to the rediscovery of formative causality. The move from mechanistic thinking about parts and wholes to systems thinking, therefore, amounted to a move from a theory of causality couched entirely in efficient terms (if–then) to one of both efficient causal links and formative causal process as found in Kant's philosophy.

It is important to note that in applying systems thinking to human action, all of the strands of systems thinking indicated above did exactly what Kant had argued against. They postulated that human action could be understood in terms of systems. Some of the systems thinkers at this time did explore the difficulties created by the fact that the observer of a system was also a participant in it in what is called second-order systems thinking. This perspective will be considered in Chapter 6.

2.5 Thinking about organisations and their management

So far in this chapter, I have been describing the movement from revelation as a way of knowing to the Scientific Revolution with its rational way of knowing. I have talked about some of the reactions to the scientific method and to some key aspects of its development, namely, the move from mechanistic and reductionist ways of thinking to holistic and systemic ways of thinking. These developments have, of course, been reflected in thinking about organisations and their management during the course of the twentieth century.

Scientific management

The mechanistic and reductionist approach of the early Scientific Revolution is quite evident in what has come to be known as scientific management. Frederick Taylor (1911) in the United States and Henri Fayol (1916) in Europe were the founding figures of scientific management and both were engineers. Taylor's central concern was with the efficient performance of the physical activities required to achieve an organisation's purpose. His method was that of meticulously observing the processes required to produce anything, splitting them into the smallest possible parts, identifying the skills required and measuring how long each part took to perform and what quantities were produced. His prescription was to provide standardised descriptions of every activity, specify the skills required, define the boundaries around each activity and fit the person to the job requirement. Individual performance was to be measured against the defined standards and rewarded through financial incentive schemes. He maintained that management was an objective science that could be defined by laws, rules and principles: if a task was clearly defined, and if those performing it were properly motivated, then that task would be efficiently performed. Fayol's approach to management was much the same. He split an organisation into a number of distinct activities (for example, technical, commercial, accounting and management) and he defined management as the activity of forecasting, planning, organising, co-ordinating and controlling through setting rules that others were to follow.

Management science equated the manager with the scientist and the organisation with the phenomenon that the scientist is concerned with. The particular approach that the manager is then supposed to take towards the organisation is that of the scientist, the objective observer, who regards the phenomenon as a mechanism. The whole mechanism is thought to be the sum of its parts and the behaviour of each part is thought to be governed by timeless laws. *An organisation is, thus, thought to be governed by efficient (if–then) causality and the manager's main concern is with these causal rules.* There is a quite explicit assumption that there is some set of rules that are *optimal*, that is, that produce the most efficient global outcome of the actions of the parts, or members, of the organisation.

There is, however, an important difference between the scientist concerned with nature and the analogous manager concerned with an organisation, which is not acknowledged in scientific management. The scientist discovers the laws of nature while the manager, in the theory of management science, chooses the rules driving the behaviour of the organisation's members. In this way, something like Kant's autonomous individual and the accompanying rationalist causality is imported into theories of scientific management, but with some important differences. First, it is only the manager to whom rationalist causality applies. It is he or she who exercises the freedom of autonomous choice in the act of choosing the goals and designing the rules that the members of the organisation are to follow in order to achieve the goals. Those members are not understood as human beings with autonomous choices of their own but as rule-following parts making up the whole organisation. Closely linked to this point about freedom is that of acting into the unknown. Kant argued that individuals make choices in the form of hypotheses about an unknowable reality and they discover the efficacy of these choices in acting. In its use in scientific management, rationalist causality is stripped of the quality of the unknown, and also of the ethical limits within which action should take place, to provide a reduced rationalist causality. In fact scientific management does what Kant argued against. It applies the scientific method in its most mechanistic form to human action. Secondly, Kant's coupling of autonomous human action with universal ethical principles is absent in the rationalist causality of management science, which regards human action as a reflex-like response to stimuli in accordance with the behaviourist psychology of its time.

The ethical aspect appears to some extent in the reaction of the Human Relations school to scientific management. By the 1930s, the view that Taylor and Fayol took of human behaviour was being actively contested by, for example, Elton Mayo (1945), a social psychologist. He conducted experiments to identify what it was that motivated workers and what effect motivational factors had on their work. He pointed to how they always formed themselves into groups that soon developed customs, duties, routines and rituals and argued that managers would only succeed if these groups accepted their authority and leadership. He concluded that it was a major role of the manager to organise teamwork and so sustain co-operation. Mayo did not abandon a scientific approach but, rather, sought to apply the scientific method to the study of motivation in groups.

From the 1940s to the 1960s, behavioural scientists (for example, Likert, 1961) continued this work and concluded that effective groups were those in which the values and goals of the group coincided with those of the individual members and where those individuals were loyal to the group and its leader. Efficiency was seen to depend upon individuals abiding by group values and goals, having high levels of trust and confidence in each other in a supportive and harmonious atmosphere. In extending freedom to all members of an organisation and paying attention to motivational factors, the Human Relations school took up a fuller notion of rationalist causality.

Taking scientific management and Human Relations together, we have a theory in which stability is preserved by rules, including motivational rules, which govern the behaviour of members of an organisation. Change is brought about by managers when they choose to change the rules, which they should do in a way that respects and motivates others so that the designed set of rules will produce optimal outcomes. Organisations are thought to function like machines achieving given purposes deliberately chosen by their managers. Within the terms of this framework, change of a fundamental, radical kind cannot be explained. Such change is simply the result of rational choices made by managers, and just how such choices emerge is not part of what this theory seeks to explain. The result is a powerful way of thinking and managing when the goals and the tasks are clear, there is not much uncertainty and people are reasonably docile, but inadequate in other conditions. Truly novel change and coping with conditions of great uncertainty were simply not part of what scientific management and Human Relations theories set out to explain or accomplish.

The principles discussed above were developed a long time ago, and they have been subjected to heavy criticism over the years, but they still quite clearly form the basis of much management thinking.

The shift to systems thinking

The wider paradigm shift from mechanistic to systemic thinking described in the previous section is also evident in theories of organisations and their management. For example, general systems theory was combined with psychoanalysis to develop a systemic understanding of organisation (*see* Chapter 5) which emphasises clarity of roles and task definition and equates management with a controlling role at the boundary (Miller and Rice, 1967). The influence of the cybernetic strand of systems thinking is even more in evidence (*see* Chapter 3). All planning and budgeting systems in organisations are cybernetic in that quantified targets are set for performance at some point in the future, the time path towards the target is forecast and then actual outcomes are measured and compared with forecasts, with the variance fed back to determine what adjustments are required to bring performance back to target. All quality management systems take the same form as do all incentive schemes, performance appraisal and reward systems, management and culture change programmes, total quality management and business process re-engineering projects. The thinking and talking of both managers and organisational researchers, therefore, tends to be dominated by cybernetic notions. The third strand of systems thinking, namely systems dynamics, originally had little impact on management thinking but more recently it has attracted much interest as a central concept in the notion of the learning organisation (*see* Chapter 4). Here, instead of thinking of a system moving towards an equilibrium state, it is thought of as following a small number of typical patterns or archetypes. Effective management requires the recognition of these archetypes and the identification of leverage points at which action can be taken to change them and so enable management to stay in control of an organisation, in effect controlling its dynamics.

The shift from reductionist management science to holistic, systemic perspectives on organisations does not, however, entail any substantial challenge to the scientific method. The manager continues to be equated with the natural scientist, the objective observer, and just as the scientist is concerned with a natural phenomenon, so the manager is concerned with an organisation. Now, however, the organisation is understood not as parts adding to a whole, but as a system in which the interactions between its parts are of primary importance in producing a whole that is more than the sum of its parts. The manager understands the organisation to be a self-regulating or a self-influencing system and it is the formative process of self-regulation or self-influence (formative cause) that is organising the pattern of behaviour that can be observed. In the case of general systems and cybernetics, that pattern is movement towards a chosen goal, an optimally efficient state, and the pattern of behaviour is held close to this goal/state when the system is operating effectively. In the case of systems dynamics, the form towards which the system moves is a typical pattern or archetype enfolded in the system, which the manager can alter by operating at leverage points. In all of these systems theories, therefore, the final form of the system's behaviour, that towards which it tends, is a state already enfolded, as it were, in the rules governing the way the parts interact. The manager is the objective observer standing outside the system and through reason designs it, changes it, and sets objectives for it.

In the decades after 1950, the first wave of modern systems thinking about organisation, described above, paid as little attention as management science did to ethics, ordinary human freedom and the unknown nature of the final state towards which human action tends. As soon as one thinks of a human organisation as a system that can be identified or designed one immediately encounters the problem that the identifier or the designer is also part of the system. This problem was recognised by the systems thinkers of the mid-twentieth century and later led to the development of second-order systems thinking (*see* Chapter 6). Also, some more recent developments of systems thinking (soft systems and critical systems) in the 1980s and 1990s actively took up the issues of participation and ethics, but they did so in a way that did nothing to alter the underlying theory of causality (*see* Chapter 6). The systems movement continues to build on a theory of rationalist causality applied to the understanding and design of organisations as systems that are governed by formative causality (*see* Chapters 8 and 9).

Back to the values task force

I started this chapter by referring to the task force appointed by the chief executive of a major international company. I suggest that the way he and the members of the task force were thinking about change in their organisation clearly reflects the history of systems thinking outlined in this chapter. They were taking it for granted that they, as autonomous individuals, could objectively observe their organisation, understood as a system, and change the values that drive its operation. In other words, they were assuming that they could enfold into the organisational system the purposes that it would then unfold. In doing this, they had lost sight of Kant's notion of a regulative idea. Instead of thinking that they could understand the system 'as if' it were unfolding a purpose they were hypothesising, they were thinking that their organisation was a system that really could/would unfold the purpose they determined for it. More than that, however, they were doing what Kant strongly advised against. They were applying the notion of system to the human actions that are the organisation and thereby thinking of the organisation's members, including themselves, as parts of the system. In this way of thinking, ordinary human freedom to make a choice is lost sight of. However, all individuals in an organisation have some choice regarding the part they play in together forming the values that guide their behaviour. Attempts to determine these values for them are then bound to fail, if indeed individuals have at least some degree of choice. Furthermore, the systemic way of thinking cannot explain in its own terms the very matter that these managers were concerned with, namely the transformation of their organisation. This is simply because systems thinking cannot explain, in its own terms, novelty or creativity. What may seem, in this chapter, to be a rather abstract philosophical discussion is in fact a highly practical matter.

2.6 How systems thinking deals with the four questions

Systems thinking essentially seeks to understand phenomena as a whole formed by the interaction of parts. Whole systems are separated from others by boundaries and they interact with each other to form a supra-whole. There are thus different levels at which phenomena either exist or need to be thought about. These notions of wholes, boundaries and levels are central distinguishing features of systems thinking. How does this kind of thinking deal with the four questions posed at the end of Chapter 1?

The first question has to do with how interaction is understood. In systems thinking, interaction between parts produces the whole and the parts are relevant as parts only because they produce and sustain the whole. The form of causality is the formative process of interaction between parts. Process here means the process of producing a whole and participation means participating in the production of a whole.

The second question has to do with the nature of human beings. In systems thinking, the answer to this question is a dualism. On the one hand, humans are thought of as rational, autonomous individuals who objectively observe systems and ascribe purposive behaviour to them. Causality here is rationalist and rational humans are free to choose. On the other hand, humans are also thought of as parts or members of the system being observed and so subject to formative causality. As such they cannot be free to choose but are subject to the purpose and formative process of the system. This problem has not gone unnoticed by systems thinkers but in Chapter 6 I will argue that the problem has not been resolved.

Taken together, the systems thinkers' answers to these two questions imply a particular way of thinking about human experience, that is, the patterning of interaction between people. The implication is that the cause of experience, the cause of the patterning of interaction between people, lies in some system, created by people, that lies above or below that experience. So, in the task force I referred to, the particular patterning of the interactions between people in the organisation was assumed to be caused by a system of values existing somehow outside the direct experience of the people interacting.

Turning to the third question to do with the method used to understand human action, it is clear that the method of the systems thinking so far discussed is that of objective observation. Generally, when applied to organisations, this is done in a realist way. People then think that systems actually exist in reality and organisations really are systems that have their own purposes. Organisations and systems are thereby reified, that is, understood to have an existence as things. Kant's idealist position on systems is thereby lost. However, in later critical systems thinking (*see* Chapter 6) Kant's 'as if' position has been recovered. Critical systems thinkers argue against the notion that systems actually exist and regard them as mental structures. Second-order systems thinking also moves away from simple objective observation and seeks to understand humans as participants in systems.

The fourth question has to do with paradox. Systems thinking originated as a dualistic way of thinking that eliminated paradox, for example by postulating one causality for nature and another for human action. Since Kant, systems thinkers have retained, often implicitly, a dual theory of causality, formative and rationalist, and applied them both to human action. They eliminate the paradox, not by different spatial locations, but in different temporal sequencing. First, managers are thought of as autonomous individuals subject to rationalist causality when they are determining the organisational system's purpose and then as subject to formative causality in their role as members of the system. In this way they preserve the 'both . . . and' structure of Kantian thinking.

2.7 Summary

This chapter has described some key aspects in the development of Western thought over the last four centuries. Its particular concern has been with the origins of systems thinking in Kantian philosophy and his articulation of the autonomous individual, as well as later developments in systems thinking and its application to human action around the middle of the twentieth century. The purpose has been to highlight the key aspects of systems thinking and the particular problems it poses when applied to human action. The main problem has to do with how, in system terms, we are to understand human participation, freedom and transformation. Chapters 3 to 5 will explore systemic theories of organisational strategy and change. Chapter 6 will describe later developments in systems thinking taking the form of second-order systems, including critical systems thinking.

Further reading

The origins and philosophical nature of systems thinking are reviewed in more depth in Stacey *et al.* (2000) and in Griffin (2002).

Questions to aid further reflection

1. What are the key elements of a system and what are the consequences of thinking about organisations in this way?

2. What are the distinctions between efficient, formative and rationalist causality?

3. How does the development of management thinking reflect changes in ways of thinking in the natural sciences?

4. In what way does systems thinking about organisations reflect a dualist, 'both . . . and' way of thinking and what are the consequences?

5. How would you explain learning, creativity, spontaneity and choice in the way systems thinking has been applied to understanding organisations?

6. Where in your own experience do you see organisational manifestations of the thinking described in this chapter?

Chapter 3

Thinking in terms of strategic choice

Cybernetic systems, cognitivist and humanistic psychology

This chapter invites you to draw on your own experience to reflect on and consider the implications of:

- The origins and nature of thinking that organisations are cybernetic systems.

- The origins and nature of thinking about the human individual in terms of cognitive and humanistic psychology.

- The origins and nature of thinking about human communication in terms of a sender–receiver model.

- The role of the objective autonomous individual observer who can control.

- The dual theory of causality implied by strategic choice theory.

- The requirement for predictability on which the theory of strategic choice depends.

- What it means to be practical in terms of strategic choice theory.

- The manner in which control, leadership and group behaviour are thought about in the theory of strategic choice.

- The technically rational process that is assumed in the theory of strategic choice.

- How the theory focuses attention and what this entails for what managers do.

It is important to understand the theories of cybernetic systems and cognitivist/humanistic psychology because they provide the key assumptions that tend to be taken for granted in the theory of strategic choice. Without this understanding it is not possible to reflect rigorously on the entailments of thinking in terms of strategic choice and so evaluate the prescriptions of the theory.

3.1 Introduction

The major part of most textbooks on strategic management is devoted to the prescriptions and analytical techniques of formulating and implementing strategic plans of one kind or another. In other words, they express the theory of strategic choice. What these textbooks devote very little attention to is the way of thinking that strategic choice theory reflects. The underlying assumptions of the theory are taken for granted rather than explored and so the entailments of making those assumptions are not examined. While this chapter gives a brief description of the key elements of the theory of strategic choice, its main purpose is not to provide a comprehensive review but to explore the way of thinking reflected in that theory. This theory has strong critics and there has been a shift in thinking over the past two decades to notions of the learning organisation (*see* Chapter 4), but strategic choice is probably still the dominant theory of strategy and organisational change. You can hear it in the way that most management practitioners talk about strategy and change in their organisations, and you can read it in a great many of the books and articles written about strategy and organisational design and development.

According to the theory of strategic choice, the strategy of an organisation is the general direction in which it changes over time. The general direction encompasses the range of activities it will undertake, the broad markets it will serve, how its resource base and competences will change and how it will secure competitive advantage. The purpose of the strategy is to secure sustainable competitive advantage that will optimise the organisation's performance. This strategy is chosen by the most powerful individual in the organisation or by a small group of managers at the top of the management hierarchy, that is, the dominant coalition. The prescribed way of making the choice is first to formulate a strategy by following an analytical procedure to prepare a plan, that is, a set of goals, the intended actions required to achieve the goals, and forecasts of the consequences of those actions over a long period of time. Having chosen the general direction, or strategy, the managers at the top of the hierarchy are then required to design an organisational structure to implement it. The structure they design should be a largely self-regulating system in which people are assigned roles and objectives that will realise the chosen strategy. Implementation is the procedure of designing systems to ensure that the plans are carried out in the intended manner and periodically adjusted to keep the organisation on track to achieve its goals. A brief description of the formulation and implementation procedures is provided later in this chapter.

From this brief description it can be seen that strategic choice theory makes particular assumptions about how people interact with each other. They are thought to interact within a particular kind of system, which has been designed by the dominant coalition of managers in the organisation. This is a cybernetic system, the nature of which will be described in the next section of this chapter. The ability to predict is crucial to the ability to control an organisation understood as a cybernetic system.

Strategic choice theory assumes that it is possible for powerful individuals to stand outside their organisations and model them in the interest of controlling them. The theory assumes that organisations change successfully when top executives form the right intention for the overall future shape of the whole organisation and specify in enough detail how this is to be achieved. It prescribes the prior design of change and then the installation of that change. The theory of strategic choice therefore places the individual, and the rational choices made by the individual, at the very centre of its explanation of how organisations become what they become. The cause of an organisation's 'shape' and performance is the strategy rationally chosen by its most powerful members. It therefore immediately implies a particular theory of human psychology, that is, a theory of how humans know and act. The theory implied is that of cognitivism, which will be described later in the chapter. Furthermore, the need to motivate people to achieve objectives also implies a psychological theory of motivation and this is usually based on humanistic psychology. This will also be described later in this chapter.

The foundations of strategic choice theory therefore reflect a particular way of thinking about what organisations are and how they become what they become. This way of thinking derives essentially from Kant (*see* Chapter 2) and combines cybernetic systems theory with the cognitivist and humanistic psychological theories that the rest of this chapter will explore.

3.2 Cybernetic systems

Cybernetics is an application of the engineer's idea of control to human activity. During the Second World War, the superiority of the German air force led British scientists to consider how they might improve the accuracy of anti-aircraft defences. One of these scientists, Norbert Wiener, saw a way of treating the evasive action of enemy aircraft as a time series that could be manipulated mathematically using negative feedback to improve the gunner's predictions of the enemy plane's future position (Wiener, 1948, p. 6).

Negative feedback and equilibrium

Negative feedback simply means that the outcome of a previous action is compared with some desired outcome and the difference between the two is fed back as information that guides the next action in such a way that the difference is reduced until it disappears. The effect is to sustain a system in a state of stable equilibrium. When anything disturbs a cybernetic system from its state of stable equilibrium it will return to that equilibrium in a self-regulating manner if it is governed by negative feedback control. A commonly quoted example of a cybernetic system is the domestic central heating system.

A domestic heating system consists of an appliance and a regulator. The regulator contains a device that senses room temperature connected to a device that turns the heating appliance on and off. A desired temperature, that is, an external reference point, is set in the regulator by an observer outside the system. When the room temperature falls below this desired level, the control sensor detects the discrepancy between actual and desired states. The regulator responds to a negative discrepancy with a positive action – it turns the heat on. When the temperature rises above the desired level the opposite happens. By responding to the deviation of actual from desired levels in an opposite or negative way, a cybernetic system dampens any movement away from desired levels. The system keeps the room temperature close to a stable level over time utilising negative feedback.

Negative feedback and human action

Wiener and his colleagues held that negative feedback loops were important in most human actions – a loop in which the gap between desired and actual performance of an act just past is fed back as a determinant of the next action. If you are trying to hit an object by throwing a ball at it and you miss because you aimed too far to the right, you then use the information from this miss to alter the point at which you aim the next shot, so offsetting the previous error. In this sense the feedback is negative – it prompts you to move in the opposite direction. You keep doing this until you hit the object. Wiener and his colleagues thought that this negative feedback was essential to all forms of controlled behaviour and that breaking the feedback link led to pathological behaviour.

Another example is provided by the operation of markets. In classical economic theory, markets are assumed to tend to a state of equilibrium. If there is an increase in demand, then prices rise to encourage a reduction in demand and an increase in supply to match the demand. If demand then stays constant, so will price and supply. Any chance movement of the price away from its equilibrium level will set in train changes in demand and supply that will rapidly pull the price back to its equilibrium level. In other words, a cybernetic system does not have an internal capacity to change. Instead, any significant change is simply a self-regulating adaptation to some external, environmental change. *Dynamic equilibrium* is a movement over time in which a system continuously adapts to alterations in a continually changing environment.

However, the self-regulating operation of cybernetic systems is not as simple as it sounds. Cyberneticists realised that when negative feedback becomes too fast, or too sensitive, the result could be uncontrolled cycles of over- and under-achievement of the desired state. So, for example, you may be taking a shower and find the water too hot. This leads you to raise the flow of cold water. If you do not take sufficient account of the lag between your action and the subsequent drop in temperature you may increase the cold water flow again. This may make the water too cold so you raise the flow of hot water, which then makes it too hot again. Unless you get the time lag between your action and its consequence right, the system will not stabilise. So, if a negative feedback control system is operating too rapidly, behaviour will fluctuate in an unstable manner instead of settling down to a desired level.

Those studying such systems therefore sought to establish the conditions for stability and instability in negative feedback control systems. As a result of this kind of work, governments came to accept that their attempts to remove cycles in the level of activity in the economy were usually counterproductive. Just as the economy was recovering from a slump, impatient governments tended to cut taxes and increase expenditure, so fuelling an excessive boom accompanied by rapid inflation. Just as that boom was collapsing on its own, fearful governments increased taxes and cut expenditure, so pushing the economy into a deeper slump than it would otherwise have experienced. To secure stability through negative feedback you must be able to predict not only the outcome of an action but also the time lag between an action and its outcome. The design of a control system that works at the right speed and the right level of sensitivity relies upon such predictions. Given the ability to predict, it is then possible to specify in a precise mathematical way exactly what conditions will produce stable equilibrium for any negative feedback system.

The key point about all forms of equilibrating systems is that they are regular, orderly and predictable without any internal capacity to change. Such regular, orderly, predictable movement depends upon clear-cut links between cause and effect of the 'if–then' kind. Most theories of management and organisation have been developed within an equilibrium framework reflecting an underlying assumption that organisations should be designed as cybernetic systems.

Consider now how cybernetics has been applied to the control of organisations (Ashby 1945, 1952, 1956; Beer [1959] 1967, 1966).

Goal-seeking adaptation to the environment

According to cybernetic theory, two main forces drive an organisation over time. The first force is the drive to achieve some purpose: from this perspective organisations are goal-seeking systems and the goal drives their actions. The second force arises because organisations are connected through feedback links to their environments: they are subsystems of an even larger environmental supra-system. Reaching the goal requires being adapted to those environments. Thus, in the cybernetics tradition, organisations are driven by attraction to a predetermined desired state that is in equilibrium with the environment. The state a given organisation comes to occupy is determined by the nature of its environment.

For example, on this view, a company operating in, say, the electronics industry may be driven by the goal of achieving a 20 per cent return on its capital. In order to achieve this it must deliver what its customers want. If customers have stable requirements for standardised low-cost silicon chips to be used as components in their own products, then the company has to adapt to this environment by employing mass production methods to produce standardised products at lower costs than its rivals. It will have to support these production methods with particular forms of organisational structure, control systems and cultures: functional structures, bureaucratic control systems and conservative, strongly shared cultures. The company will look much the same as its rivals in the same market because the overall shape of each is determined by the same environment.

If, however, the electronics market is a turbulent one with rapidly changing technology and many niche markets where customers look for customised chips, then there will be very different kinds of organisation, according to cybernetics theory. A company will have to adapt by emphasising R&D and continually developing new products to differentiate itself from its rivals. It will support these production methods with particular forms of structure, control systems and culture: decentralised structures of separate profit centres, greater emphasis on informal controls, and change-loving cultures.

But how do organisations come to be adapted to their environments and achieve their goals?

Regulators

According to cybernetics, organisations deploy regulators that utilise negative feedback in order to reach their goals and the desired states of adaptation to their environments. The central problem is how to keep an organisation at, or near to, some desired state and the answer to the problem lies in the design of the regulator, that is, the design of the control system. Cybernetics is the science of control, and management is the profession of control. There are two types of regulator: the error-controlled regulator and the anticipatory regulator.

If the regulator is placed so that it senses the disturbance before that disturbance hits the organisation, then it can take anticipatory action and offset the undesirable impact of the disturbance on the outcome before it occurs. An immediately recognisable example of this kind of regulator is of course a planning system. Such a regulator takes the form of sensing devices such as market research questionnaires or analyses of market statistics. On the basis of these, realistically achievable desired states are established. These desired states, or goals, are based on forecasts of sales volumes, prices and costs at some future point. Action plans to realise the selected goals in the predicted environment are also prepared; that is, patterns in future actions are identified. As the organisation moves through time it continually senses the environment, picks up disturbances before they occur and prepares planned actions to deal with them before they hit the organisation. This is ideal control without making mistakes: preventing deviations from plan occurring in the first place.

If it is not possible to establish such an anticipatory regulator, or if such a regulator cannot work perfectly, then a regulator must be placed so that it can sense the outcome once that outcome has occurred. This is the classic error-controlled regulator. An immediately recognisable example of this type of regulator is the monitoring, reviewing and corrective action system of an organisation. It is what an organisation's board of directors does each month when it meets to review what has happened to the organisation over the past month, monitors how the performance measures are moving and decides what to do to correct deviations from plan that have already occurred. Note, however, that even error-controlled regulators depend on some form of predictability. When you take a corrective action you have to be able to predict not only its outcome and the time delay between corrective action and its consequences but also the time lag between an event and its detection. To function effectively, cybernetic systems depend upon predictability at a rather detailed level.

An essential requirement for the most effective application of this whole approach to control, therefore, is the availability of quantitative forecasts of future changes in the organisation and its environment, as well as forecasts of the consequences of proposed actions to deal with these changes and the time lags involved. For self-regulating control to work adequately the forecasts need to be at a rather detailed level of description and can only function, therefore, over a time span where this is possible. The tools available for such quantitative forecasts are those derived from statistical theory. Statistical forecasting methods are based on the assumption that the disturbances hitting the organisation from its environment take the form of groupings of large numbers of closely similar events that can be described by a probability distribution. It is implicitly assumed that uniquely uncertain events will be relatively unimportant.

Cybernetics sees the main cause of the difficulty in designing regulators not in terms of the uniqueness of events, but in terms of their variety, or complexity. Variety is the number of discernibly different states the environment can present to the organisation and the number of discernibly different responses the organisation can make to the environment. It is the function of the regulator to reduce variety so retaining stability within a system, despite high variety outside it. In other words, the huge variety of disturbances presented by the environment must be neutralised by a huge number of responses such that the outcome can match the one desirable state selected in advance that will fit the environment. In order to be able to do this, the regulator must be designed to have as much variety as the environment; the number of potential responses must match the number of potential disturbances so that they can cancel each other out and produce a single desired outcome. This is Ashby's law of requisite variety: the complexity and speed of the firm's response must match the complexity and speed of change of the environment.

Cybernetics and causality

The law of requisite variety makes it unnecessary, according to the cybernetics tradition, to understand the internal feedback structures of the organisation and the environment. Cyberneticists recognised that feedback means circular causality – event A causes event B which then causes event A. They argued that one can determine the direction this circular causality takes for any pair of events simply by observing which precedes which in a large number of cases. But when dealing with large numbers of interconnected pairs it all becomes too difficult. These internal structures are so complex that one cannot hope to understand them – they constitute a 'black box'. Note how an unquestioned assumption is being made here. Those arguing this position are assuming that there is always a specific cause for each specific outcome, the problem being that it is all too complex for us to understand.

The cyberneticists, however, argued that causal connections exist but one does not need to understand them because one can observe a particular type of disturbance impacting on a system and also can observe the outcome of that disturbance; that is, how the system responds. If the regulator has requisite variety, that is, a large enough variety of responses to counteract the variety of disturbances, then it will normally respond to a particular type of disturbance in the same way. From large numbers of observations of such regularities statistical connections can be established between particular types of disturbance and particular organisational responses.

The importance of this notion of causal connection is that it allows the use of statistical techniques for control in a negative feedback way, despite system complexity so great that one cannot hope to understand it, at least according to the cyberneticists. What matters to them are pragmatic factors such as what is observed and what is done. It is not necessary to devote much energy to understanding and explaining, they claim, because observing and doing is what matters in a complex world. These writers were not concerned with the dynamic patterns of behaviour that organisations generated or with the complexities of the internal workings of the organisation.

Cybernetics, then, is an approach that seeks to control an organisation by using feedback without understanding the feedback structure of the organisation itself. It sees effective regulators as those that cause the system to be largely self-regulating, automatically handling the disturbances with which the environment bombards it. It sees effective regulators as those that maintain continual equilibrium with the environment. The result is stable behaviour, predictable in terms of probabilities of specific events and times.

The key points on organisational dynamics made by the cybernetics tradition are summarised in Box 3.1. Whenever managers use planning, monitoring, reviewing and corrective action forms of control, they are making the same assumptions about the world as those made by cyberneticists. Whenever management consultants install such systems they too make the same assumptions. Whenever managers engage in trial-and-error actions in the belief that this will take them to an envisioned end-point in a turbulent environment, that is, whenever they implement the advice

---

Box 3.1   Cybernetics: main points on organisational dynamics

- Organisations are *goal-seeking*, *self-regulating* systems adapting to pre-given environments through negative feedback.

- Cybernetics thus takes a realist position on human knowing.

- The system is *recursive*. This means that it feeds back on itself to repeat its behaviour.

- It follows that causality is circular. However, although the causality is circular it is *linear*. Cybernetics does not take account of the effects of nonlinearity. Causal structures cannot be understood because they are too complex. However, regularities in the relationships between external disturbances and the system's response can be statistically identified. Circular causality is thus recognised but then sidestepped by saying that it is too complicated to understand.

- Predictability of specific events and their timings is possible in a probabilistic sense. Disturbances coming from the environment are not primarily unique.

- Effective control requires forecasts and a control system that contains as much variety as the environment. Change must be probabilistic so that large numbers of random changes and random responses cancel out, otherwise unique small changes might amplify and swamp the system.

- No account is taken of positive, or amplifying, feedback. There is thus no possibility of small changes amplifying into major alterations.

- Behavioural patterns themselves, especially of the system as a whole, are not thought to be interesting enough to warrant special comment.

- The self-regulation process requires the system's actual behavioural outcomes to be compared with some representation of, or expectation about, its environment. There is an external point of reference according to which it is controlled. The system internally *represents* its environment and then responds to that representation.

- There is a clear boundary between system and environment, between inner and outer. Although the system is adapting to its environment, it is itself a closed system. It operates/changes with *reference to a fixed point at the boundary* with its environment.

- Its state is determined by flux in the environment expressed through the fixed point of reference. Instability comes from the environment.

- It is a homeostatic, or *equilibrium-seeking*, system.

- *History is not important* in that the current state of the system is not dependent upon the sequence of previous states, only on the 'error' registered at the regulator. The system does not evolve of its own accord. Any change must be designed outside the system and then installed.

- Effective organisations are self-regulating, an automatic mechanical feature flowing from the way the control system is structured.

- Success is a state of stability, consistency and harmony.

of writers such as Peters and Waterman (1982), then they are assuming that the law of requisite variety is valid. The problem is that managers and consultants are normally not fully aware of what they are assuming. It is extremely important to be aware of these assumptions because if life in organisations diverges significantly from them, cybernetic systems will not work. For example, if unique tiny changes can escalate through amplifying feedback, a cybernetic system will no longer be able to self-regulate.

Consider now how this systems theory is reflected in the prescriptions strategic choice theory provides for the formulation and implementation of strategic plans.

3.3 Formulating and implementing long-term strategic plans

Section 3.2 has described the assumptions about interaction that underly strategic choice theory. This theory of strategic management is concerned with anticipatory and error-controlled regulators. Anticipatory regulation consists of the formulation of long-term strategic plans and the implementation of these plans is based on the operation of error-controlled regulation consisting of various administrative and monitoring systems. The literature on strategic choice provides many prescriptions for formulating and implementing strategic plans (for example, Andrews, [1971] 1987; Ansoff, 1965, 1990; Barney, 1991; Porter, 1980, 1985). This literature is primarily concerned with formal, analytical procedures to do with planning and monitoring.

The words 'plan' and 'planning' are often used loosely by managers. For example, managers may say that they have a long-term plan simply because they have set out some long-term financial targets or because they have identified one or two specific actions that they intend to undertake, for example, make an acquisition. However, these words have more precise meanings in the theory of strategic choice. A strategic plan is a formally articulated choice of a particular future composition of activities and a particular market position for the whole organisation such that it will achieve an optimal level of performance in a future context. Strategic planning involves choosing aims and objectives for the whole organisation well in advance of acting. Strategic planning also involves managers sharing a common intention to pursue a sequence of actions to achieve that chosen future state. Before managers can intentionally choose an intended state and an intended sequence of future actions, however, they have to identify the future environment in which they are to achieve their aims – their intentions must be anchored to a specific future reality. In other words, managers cannot possibly plan unless they can also make reasonably reliable forecasts of the future time period they are planning for. The future must not only be knowable, it must be sufficiently well known in advance of required performance. The time span and the level of detail must be that which produces the required performance. A long-term plan requires long-term predictability otherwise there is only a sequence of short-term plans.

Many managers will immediately realise that in a rapidly changing world they are rather unlikely to encounter the degree of predictability required to formulate long-term plans satisfying the definition just given. Some of them, and some writers on strategy too, then dismiss the whole approach as impracticable. Others argue that while it may not be possible to plan the future in the way just described it is still possible for them to choose a broad direction for their organisation. What is being suggested is that in practice a watered-down form of long-term planning is what is required. However, this still requires enough predictability to set a direction. The theory of strategic choice, however, goes further than simply setting some general direction and provides tools and techniques for doing more than this.

In addition to formulating plans, managers must set milestones along the path to the intended future state, couched in terms of results, if what they are doing is to qualify as controlling and developing an organisation's long-term future in the planning mode. This will enable the outcomes of actions to be checked and deviations from plan to be corrected. Action is both implementation of the planned sequence of actions and corrections to keep results on course. Only then is control being exercised in a planned manner. The ability to control by plan depends upon the possibility of establishing intention relating to the organisation as a *whole* and making predictions at the appropriate level of detail over the relevant time span.

Prediction is a process of analysing the past and the present and then using that analysis as the basis for forecasting the future. Once managers know something about the nature of their future environment they can then deduce what alternative action options might deliver their performance objectives. The rational criteria of acceptability, feasibility and suitability, to be discussed below, must then be applied to evaluate each option and select that option which best satisfies the criteria. This then becomes an organisation's strategy.

Since most organisations of any size consist of a collection of different activities organised into units, a distinction is drawn between corporate plans and business unit plans (Hofer and Schendel, 1978; Porter, 1987). The corporate plan is concerned with what activities or businesses the organisation should be involved in and how the corporate level should manage that set of businesses. In other words, corporate strategy is about a portfolio of businesses and what should be done with them. Business unit plans set out how a business unit is going to build a market position that is superior to that of its rivals, so enabling it to achieve the performance objectives set by the corporate level. In other words, business unit strategy is about the means of securing and sustaining competitive advantage. Since business units are generally organised on a functional basis – finance, sales, production, and research departments, for example – the business unit strategy will have to be translated into functional or operational strategies. The result is a hierarchy of long-term objectives and plans, the corporate creating the framework for the business unit, and the business unit creating the framework for the functional. Furthermore, this collection of long-term plans provides the framework for formulating shorter-term plans and budgets against which an organisation can be controlled in the short term.

The theory of strategic choice prescribes analytical criteria for evaluating strategic options. The evaluation criteria are intended to enable managers to conclude whether or not a particular sequence of actions will lead to a particular future state that will produce some target measure of performance. The criteria are there to enable managers to form judgements about the outcomes of their proposed actions before they take those actions. The purpose is to prevent surprises and ensure that an organisation behaves over long time periods in a manner intended by its leaders.

Evaluating long-term strategic plans

There are three very widely proposed criteria for evaluating long-term strategic plans and these are acceptability or desirability, feasibility, and suitability or fit. These are reviewed in the following sections.

Acceptability

There are at least three senses, it is argued, in which strategies have to be acceptable if they are to produce success. First, performance in financial terms must be acceptable to owners and creditors. Second, the consequences of the strategies for the most powerful groupings within an organisation must be acceptable in terms of their expectations and the impact on their power positions and cultural beliefs. Third, the consequences of the strategies for powerful groups external to an organisation must be acceptable to those groupings. Consider what each of these senses entails.

- *Acceptable financial performance.* Determining whether the long-term plans are likely to turn out to be financially acceptable requires forecasting the financial consequences of each strategic option: cash flows, capital expenditures and other costs, sales volumes, price levels, profit levels, assets and liabilities including borrowing and other funding requirements. The forecasts are used to calculate prospective rates of return on sales and capital in order to compare them with those required by owners and fund providers. This is not as simple as it sounds because there are many different rates of return on sales and capital and the one used depends upon the purpose of use and also on accounting conventions. There are also many difficulties of measurement, for example, the problems of measuring depreciation, skill, knowledge and other costs and benefits that are not traded on markets. The analysis may therefore involve subjective judgements and disagreements that cannot be resolved by rational argument. Scenarios and simulations may be used to identify variables that performance is particularly sensitive to in order to manage risk.

- *Acceptable consequences for internal power groups.* If carried out, strategic plans may well change the way people work, whom they work with, what relative power they have, and how they are judged by others. Long-term plans could produce consequences that people believe to be morally repugnant or against their customs and beliefs in some other way. If this is the case, those plans are unlikely to succeed because people will do their best to prevent the plans' being implemented. The prescription is, therefore, to submit long-term plans to the test of acceptability in terms of the expectations, relative power positions and cultural beliefs of key individuals and groups within the organisation. In order to determine whether a plan is likely to be acceptable in cultural terms it is necessary to analyse people's shared beliefs. Analysis of the culture is thought to reveal whether options being considered fall within that culture or whether they require major cultural change. One would not necessarily reject options that require major cultural change, but then plans to bring this about would have to be formulated. It is also necessary to analyse the power structure of an organisation to determine whether plans are likely to be acceptable.

- *Acceptable consequences for external power groups.* Power groups outside an organisation also determine the acceptability of that organisation's strategies. For example, a community pressure group may find the noise level of a proposed factory expansion unacceptable. Even if the factory itself turns out to be a financially acceptable investment, the total consequences for the image of the corporation could render the strategy unsuccessful. Another example is provided by the electricity and gas industries in the UK. To succeed, strategies of companies in these sectors have to be acceptable to the industry regulators and consumer pressure groups. A further example is where the strategies of one organisation could have damaging consequences for the distributors of that organisation's products or for the suppliers to that organisation. Such damage could provoke those distributors and suppliers to retaliate in highly detrimental ways. The reactions of competitors to strategies are also of major importance. Some strategies pursued by one company could provoke greater than normal competitive responses from competitors. Those competitors may regard the strategies of the first company as unfair competition and this could lead to price wars, hostile mergers or lobbying of the national political institutions, all of which could cause a strategy to fail.

Feasibility

Analysis may show that strategies are likely to be acceptable in terms of financial performance, and to major power groupings both within and outside an organisation, but yet fail because they are not feasible. To be feasible there must be no insurmountable obstacle to implementing a strategy. Such obstacles could be presented by:

- *Financial resources*. One of the immediately obvious resources that must be available if a strategy is to be carried out is the money to finance the strategy over its whole life. If a company gets halfway through a strategy, which is on target to yield acceptable performance, but nevertheless runs out of the funds to continue, then clearly the strategy will fail. The prescription is therefore to carry out a flow-of-funds analysis of the strategy options, before embarking on any of them, to ascertain the probability of running into cash flow problems. A flow-of-funds analysis identifies the timing and size of the capital expenditures and other costs required for each project that makes up the strategy, and the timing and size of the revenues that those projects will generate. A flow-of-funds analysis makes it possible to calculate the break-even point, where a project, a set of projects constituting a strategy or a corporation as a whole makes neither a loss nor a profit.

- *Human resources*. In addition to financial resources, the availability of the right numbers of skilled people will also be a major determinant of the feasibility of strategic options. This makes it necessary for managers to audit the human resources inside their organisation, those available outside and the availability of training resources to improve the skills of people.

Suitability or fit

Having established that their strategies are acceptable and feasible, the next hurdle managers must cross to select an appropriate strategic plan is that of demonstrating that a strategy has a *strategic logic*. Strategic logic means that a proposed sequence of actions is consistently related to the objectives of the organisation on the one hand and matches the organisation's capability (including its structure, control systems and culture) in relation to its environment on the other. The idea is that all the pieces of the strategic puzzle should fit together in a predetermined manner – the pieces should be *congruent*. When this happens we can say that the strategies fit, that they are suitable. The prescription is to use analytical techniques to determine the strategic logic of a sequence of actions (Hofer and Schendel, 1978). The analytical techniques available to do this are:

- *SWOT analysis*. This is a list of an organisation's strengths and weaknesses indicated by an analysis of its resources and capabilities, plus a list of the opportunities and threats that an analysis of its environment identifies. Strategic logic obviously requires that the future pattern of actions to be taken should match strengths with opportunities, ward off threats and seek to overcome weaknesses.

- *Industry structure and value chain analysis*. Michael Porter (1980, 1985) has put the classical economic theories of market form into a framework for analysing the nature of competitive advantage in a market and the power of a company in that market, as well as the value chain of the company. These analytical techniques identify key aspects determining the relative market power of an organisation and its ability to sustain excess profits. Strategic logic entails taking actions that are consistent with and that match the nature of the organisation's market power. Industry structure is held to determine what the predominant form of competitive advantage, and thus the level of profit, is. Some market structures mean that sustainable competitive advantage can be secured only through cost-leadership strategies. Other structures mean that competitive advantage flows from differentiation. Strategic logic means matching actions to those required to secure competitive advantage. Value chain analysis identifies the points in the chain of activity from raw material to consumer that are crucial to competitive advantage.

- *Product life cycle.* To be suitable in market terms a strategy must take account of the stages in the product life cycle. Most products are thought to follow typical developmental stages: *embryonic* in which the product is developed; *growth* in which rapid market growth materialises, attracting other competitors; *shake-out* in which some of the competitors cannot compete and therefore leave; *mature* in which growth in the demand for the product slows and a small number of competitors come to dominate the market; *saturation* in which demand for the product stabilises and competitors have difficulty filling their capacity; and *decline* in which demand begins to switch to substitute products. These stages in the evolution of a product indicate different general types of strategies – different generic strategies. Which of these generic strategies is suitable is said to be dependent upon the stage of evolution of the product's market and the competitive strength of the company producing it. So, for example, a company with a strong capability should invest heavily in the embryonic stage and establish a position before others arrive.

- *Experience curves*. The idea of the experience curve is based on the observation that the higher the volume of a particular product that a company produces, the more efficient it becomes at producing it. The cost per unit therefore declines as volume increases, at first rapidly and then more slowly as the learning opportunities for that particular product are exhausted. As a company moves down the learning curve it is in a position to reduce the price it charges customers for the product because its costs are falling. These price and cost curves can be linked to the idea of a product life cycle and the different strategies that strong and weak competitors should pursue. In the early stages of product evolution, a strong competitor will achieve higher volumes than a weak one and so move further down the learning curve. This will enable the strong competitor to reduce prices faster, stimulating demand and so increasing volumes even more to move even faster down the learning curve. Soon, the weaker competitor, or the latecomer, will have no chance of catching up.

- *Product portfolio*. The earliest and simplest form of product portfolio analysis is the growth share matrix of the Boston Consulting Group (BCG) (Henderson, 1970). To analyse their organisation in this way, managers review their whole business, dividing it up into all its different products, or market segments, or business units. They then calculate the relative market share they hold for each product, or market segment or business unit. The relative market share provides a measure of the firm's competitive capability with regard to that product, segment or business unit, because a high market share indicates that the firm is well down the experience curve compared with rivals. Next, managers must calculate the rate of growth of the product demand or market segment. The rate of growth is held to be a good measure of the attractiveness of the market – the stage in its evolution that it has reached. Different combinations of market share and growth rates indicate which particular generic strategies should be followed. The suitable options will be those that have some balance between the different possibilities in terms of cash generation.

Implementing long-term strategic plans

Once long-term plans have been formulated and evaluated and the optimal ones selected, they need to be implemented. Implementation is primarily the design and installation of cybernetic systems as follows.

- *Designing organisational structures*. The structure of an organisation is the formal way of identifying who is to take responsibility for what; who is to exercise authority over whom; and who is to be answerable to whom. The structure is a hierarchy of managers and is the source of authority, as well as the legitimacy of decisions and actions. The appropriate structure follows from the strategy that an organisation is pursuing and structure displays typical patterns of development or life cycles (Chandler, 1962). Embryonic organisations have very simple structures in which people report rather informally to someone that they accept as their leader. Growth strategy makes it necessary to change the structure to one based on more formal specialisation of functions and identification of authority and responsibility. This leads to the problem of integrating specialised functions so that the structure has to be made even more formal with clearer definition of lines of authority and communication. Strategies of diversification into new products and markets make it necessary to set up marketing and manufacturing organisations in different geographic areas. Further diversification leads to setting up largely independent subsidiaries in divisionalised or holding company structures.

- *Designing systems of information and control*. The information and control systems of an organisation are basically procedures, rules and regulations governing what information about the performance of an organisation should flow to whom and when. It also covers who is required to respond to that information and how they are authorised to respond, in particular what authority they have to deploy the resources of the organisation. To implement strategies, information and control systems are required to enable the flows of information that implementation requires and provide appropriate control mechanisms to enable managers to monitor the outcomes of the strategy implementation and do something if those outcomes are not in accordance with the strategy. Management control is defined as the process of ensuring that all resources – physical, human and technological – are allocated so as to realise the strategy. Control ensures proper behaviour in an organisation and the need for it arises because individuals within the organisation are thought not to be always willing to act in the best interests of the organisation. The process of control involves setting standards or targets for performance, or expected outcomes of a sequence of actions, then comparing actual performance or outcomes against standards, targets or expectations, and finally taking corrective action to remove any deviations from standard, target or expectation. The principal form taken by the control system in most organisations is that of the annual plan or budget. The budget converts strategy into a set of short-term action plans and sets out the financial consequences of those action plans for the year ahead. Control is then a process of regularly comparing what happens with what the budget said would happen. Budgets allocate the resources of an organisation with which different business units and functions are charged to carry out the strategy. Budgets establish the legitimate authority for using the resources of the organisation.

- *Installing and operating human resource systems*. Effective strategy implementation should occur when the people required to take action to this end are motivated to do so. One of the most powerful motivators is the organisation's reward system (Galbraith and Kazanian, 1986). Appropriate rewards stimulate people to make the effort to take actions directly relevant to an organisation's strategy. The way in which people's jobs are graded and the pay scales attached to these grades will affect how people feel about their jobs and the effort they will make. Differentials need to be perceived to be fair if they are not to affect performance adversely. Bonuses, profit-related pay, piecework and productivity schemes are all ways of tying monetary rewards to the actions that strategy implementation requires. Non-monetary rewards are also of great importance in motivating people. These rewards include promotion, career development, job enrichment, job rotation, training and development. They all help individuals to be more useful to an organisation while developing greater self-fulfilment. Simpler forms of reward are also of great importance, for example, praise, recognition and thanks. Training and development is an important implementation tool, not only because it motivates people, but also because it provides the skills required for strategy implementation (Hussey, 1991). The objectives of training and development programmes should be aligned with those of an organisation's strategy and those objectives should consist of measurable changes in corporate performance.

- *Culture change programmes*. Just as the reporting structure of an organisation should fit the particular strategy the organisation wishes to pursue, so too should its culture, the attitudes and beliefs that people within an organisation share. Just as structures need to fit a particular strategy and just as they tend to follow a life cycle from the simple to the functional to the divisional, so too do cultures according to strategic choice theory. Implementation may well therefore require that an organisation change its culture and the conventional wisdom prescribes that such change should be planned. The reasons why people might resist a change in culture need to be identified and plans formulated to overcome the resistance. Participation, communication and training are all seen as ways of overcoming resistance. The process of overcoming resistance involves a stage called unfreezing when the existing culture is questioned, and is followed by a period of reformulation where people consider what new beliefs they need to develop and share with each other. Finally there is the re-freezing stage where the new culture is fixed in place.

- *Developing appropriate political behaviour*. It is inevitable that people in an organisation will sometimes come into conflict and, when they do, they engage in political behaviour (Pfeffer, 1981). Interdependence, heterogeneous goals and scarce resources taken together produce conflict. If the conflict is important and power is distributed widely enough, then people will use political behaviour, that is, persuasion and negotiation, to resolve their conflict. If power is highly centralised then most will simply do as they are told – they will not have enough power to engage in political behaviour. The kinds of political strategies people employ to come out best from conflict are the selective use of objective criteria, the use of outside experts to support their case, forming alliances and coalitions, sponsoring those with similar ideas, empire building, intentionally doing nothing, suppressing information, making decisions first and using analysis afterwards to justify them, and many more. The above view of politics as a manipulative process of dubious ethical validity leads to the belief that steps should be taken to reduce the incidence of political behaviour. Such steps are those that reduce the level of conflict and the most powerful of these is to preach and convert people to a common ideology.

This section has very briefly summarised the general prescriptions, tools and techniques that have been put forward to formulate and implement the long-term plans embodying the strategic choices made by an organisation's dominant coalition. Condensing what is a huge body of literature in this way inevitably produces something of a caricature. There has been considerable research into the effectiveness of generic strategies and debates about many issues, some of which will be briefly reviewed in Section 3.6. There has also been some research into whether formal planning systems of the kind outlined above produce what they are intended to produce. The evidence is very far from conclusive. However, the summary presented in this section, although somewhat simplistic, does indicate the underlying way of thinking represented by strategic choice theory, which makes it very evident how heavily conditioned this way of thinking is by the notion of cybernetic systems.

The rational decision-making process put forward by the theory of strategic choice also implies a particular psychological theory, that of cognitivism, and a particular theory of human communication, namely, the sender–receiver model. In recognising that people need to be motivated in order to implement strategies, strategic choice theory also implies humanistic psychology. The next section explores the implicit assumptions about human psychology and communication.

3.4 Cognitivist and humanistic psychology

The review of cybernetic theory in Section 3.2 has already brought out how cybernetics is a theory about human behaviour. It assumes that human beings are cybernetic entities and that they learn through an essentially negative feedback process. In fact, the development of cybernetic systems theory was closely associated with the development of cognitive science. Furthermore, both cybernetics and cognitivism were closely associated with the development of computers and technologies of communication.

Cognitive psychology and the sender–receiver model of communication

In 1943, McCulloch and Pitts (1943) published an important paper in which they claimed that brain functioning and mental activity could be understood as logical operations. They held that the brain was a system of neurons that functioned according to logical processing principles. The brain was thought to be a deductive machine and this notion was applied to develop machines that could operate in the same way, namely computers. In essence, the claim was that human minds were cybernetic systems. So, a theory about the operation of the brain was fundamental to the development of computers and those computers then came to be taken as an analogy for brain functioning. Computers were developed to mimic what brains were thought to do and, this having been done, the brain was then thought to be like a computer, an essentially circular argument.

The next significant development in cognitive science occurred in 1956 at two meetings in Cambridge, Massachusetts, when Simon, Chomsky, Minsky and McCarthy set major guidelines for the development of cognitive science (Gardner, 1985). Their central idea was that human intelligence resembles computation so much that cognition, that is, human knowing, could be understood as a process of computing representations of reality, those representations being made in the form of symbols. Just as computers process digital symbols so the human brain processes symbols taking the form of electrochemical activity in the brain. This is the central idea, just as it is with cybernetic systems. Humans are assumed to act on the basis of representations of their environment that are processed in their brains. Learning is a process of developing more and more accurate representations of external, pre-given reality utilising negative feedback processes. In a life experience of development and learning, human minds build up models, maps or schemas representing reality and then act on the basis of these models. Cognitivism focuses on the individual mind and claims that this mind is an information-processing device that is the basis of rational thinking. Human thinking is claimed to be an essentially calculating process that is highly rational when functioning properly. In focusing on rational choices made by powerful individuals, the theory of strategic choice is making just these assumptions about human psychology.

What should be noted here is the importance of internal representations of the external environment and the error-activated nature of the learning process that cybernetics specifies. These are central assumptions in a cognitivist approach to psychology and they have enormous implications for how human agency, groups and organisations are understood.

About the same time as the developments described above, Shannon and Weaver (1949) published an important paper on the science of human communication. What they proposed was a model of communication derived from telephony in which one individual formulates an idea in the mind, translates it into language and then sends it to another individual who receives the words and translates them back into the idea. If the translation processes are accurate and there is no 'noise' in the transmission then the communication will be effective. If there is any failure of communication, then the receiving individual sends a message or signal to the sender indicating a gap, which the sender must then try to remove. This sender–receiver model is clearly a cybernetic theory of communication and it has come to be the one underlying the dominant discourse on organisations. Strategic choice theory, then, is built upon the assumptions of cognitivist psychology and the accompanying sender–receiver model of communication.

Human beings are regarded, in strategic choice theory, as living cybernetic systems that can understand, design, control and change other cybernetic systems, including their own minds. The implication is that an individual human can stand alone as a system. Implicit in a cybernetic approach to human affairs, then, is the assumption that humans are monads, that is, autonomous individuals who can exist outside relationships with others. The individual is prior and primary to the group. Again, there is the assumption, dominant in Western thinking, of the primacy of the masterful, rational, autonomous individual. Box 3.2 summarises the main assumptions of cognitivism.

Box 3.2   Cognitivism: main points on human knowing and communicating

- The brain processes symbols (electrochemical pulses) in a sequential manner to form representations or internal templates that are more or less accurate pictures of the world. This means that the brain is assumed to act as a passive mirror of reality.

- The world so pictured by the brain can be specified prior to any cognitive activity. This means that the world being perceived would have particular properties, such as light waves, and it would be these already existing real properties that would be directly registered by the brain. The world into which humans act is found, not created.

- The templates formed are the basis upon which a human being knows and acts. Repeated exposure to the same light wave would strengthen connections along a specific neuronal pathway, so making a perception a more and more accurate representation of reality. This would form the template, stored in a particular part of the brain, against which other light wave perceptions could be compared and categorised, forming the basis of the body's response. Representing and storing are, thus, essentially cybernetic processes. There is a fixed point of reference, external reality, and negative feedback of the gap between the internal picture and this external reality forms a self-regulating process that closes this gap. Knowing, knowledge creation and learning are essentially adaptive feedback processes, as is communication between people.

- The biological individual is at the centre of the whole process of knowing and acting.

- Since all normal individuals have much the same biologically determined brain structures and all their brains are processing symbolic representations of the same pre-given reality, there is no fundamental problem in individuals sharing the same perceptions. They share perceptions by communicating in what is essentially an engineering process of transmission.

Humanistic psychology

Humanistic psychology was developed mainly in the United States as a reaction to what was felt to be the pessimism and conservatism of psychoanalysis. Humanistic psychology takes a basically optimistic view of human nature and its perfectibility. One of its roots was in inspirational religious revivalism and it saw the main problem of human existence as the alienation of an individual from his or her true self. From this perspective people can be motivated by providing experiences for them in which they can experience more of their true selves. You see the influence of these ideas in the theories of motivation of Maslow and Hertzberg, mentioned below. The prescriptions for establishing visions and missions that inspire people also arise from this kind of thinking about human nature.

So far, this chapter has reviewed the stages of formulation, evaluation and implementation of long-term strategic plans, which is the centrepiece of the theory of strategic choice. However, those writing in this tradition also recognise that the factors of human motivation and leadership affect how an organisation's strategy is implemented. For example, Peters and Waterman (1982) questioned the rational techniques of decision making and control reviewed in this chapter, pointing to their limitations in conditions of turbulence. Instead, they emphasised human motivation, values, beliefs and the importance of leadership. They stressed the importance of working harmoniously together, and strongly sharing the same culture, values, beliefs and vision of the future. Their prescriptions were to choose a vision of the whole organisation's future, convert people to believing in it, promote internal harmony by encouraging the strong sharing of a few cultural values, and empower people.

However, although critical of rational techniques, Peters and Waterman did not depart in any way from cognitivist assumptions about human nature, or in any essential way from the assumption that an organisation is a cybernetic system. This is evident when they talk about charismatic leaders who choose a vision of the future and certain core values that they then inspire others with, converting them into believing the vision and the values. If anything, the autonomous individual becomes even more heroic in their view of organisational change. The system is still cybernetic because it is controlled by referring to the vision and the values and damping out any deviations from them.

A number of similar theories of motivation have been put forward in the management literature on how to secure consensus, co-operation and commitment. For example, Hertzberg (1966) pointed out that people are motivated to work in co-operation with others by both extrinsic motivators such as monetary rewards and intrinsic motivators such as recognition for achievement, achievement itself, responsibility, growth and advancement. Intrinsic motivation is the more powerful of the motivators and is increased when jobs are enriched, that is when jobs are brought up to the skill levels of those performing them.

Maslow (1954) distinguished between: basic physiological needs, such as food and shelter; intermediate social needs, such as safety and esteem; and higher self-actualisation needs, such as self-fulfilment. Maslow held that when the conditions are created in which people can satisfy their self-actualisation needs, those people are then powerfully motivated to strive for the good of their organisation.

Schein (1988) and Etzioni (1961) distinguished three categories of relationship between the individual and the organisation. The relationship may be coercive, in which case the individual will do only the bare minimum required to escape punishment. The relationship may be a utilitarian one where the individual does only enough to earn the required level of reward. Third, the relationship may take a normative form where individuals value what they are doing for its own sake, because they believe in it and identify with it. In other words, the individual's ideology coincides with an organisation's ideology. This provides the strongest motivator of all for the individual to work for the good of an organisation.

Pascale and Athos (1981) stressed organisational culture as a result of their study of Japanese management. They recognised that people yearn for meaning in their lives and transcendence over mundane things. Cultures that provide this meaning create powerfully motivated employees and managers.

What all these studies suggest is that an organisation succeeds when its people, as individuals, are emotionally engaged in some way, when they believe in what their group and their organisation are doing, and when the contribution they make to this organisational activity brings psychological satisfaction of some kind, something more than simple basic rewards. Others have argued that people believe and are emotionally engaged when their organisation has a mission or set of values and when their own personal values match those of the organisation. Organisational missions develop because people search for meaning and purpose and this search includes their work lives (Campbell and Tawady, 1990). To win commitment and loyalty and to secure consensus around performing tasks it becomes necessary to promote a sense of mission. The development of a sense of mission is seen as a central leadership task and a vitally important way of gaining commitment to, loyalty for and consensus around, the nature and purpose of the existing business. An organisation with a sense of mission captures the emotional support of its people, even if only temporarily. A sense of mission is more than a definition of the business, that is, the area in which an organisation is to operate. A sense of mission is also to be distinguished from the ideas behind the word 'vision' or 'strategic intent'. The word 'vision' is usually taken to mean a picture of a future state for an organisation, a mental image of a possible and desirable future that is realistic, credible and attractive. The term mission differs in that it refers not to the future but to the present. A mission is a way of behaving.

The underlying assumption is that organisations succeed when individuals are motivated to perform, as individuals. The humanistic psychology on which the above writers draw accords the same primacy to the individual as cognitivism does. The difference is that the former places much more emphasis on emotional factors, predominantly of a positive inspirational kind. Note how leaders are supposed to choose appropriate motivators.

Box 3.3 summarises the key assumptions upon which are built humanistic views of knowing and communicating.

3.5 Leadership and the role of groups

From a strategic choice theory perspective, the primary focus is on the leader as one who translates the directives of those higher up in the hierarchy into the goals and tasks of the group. Leaders monitor the performance of the task in terms of goal

Box 3.3	Humanistic psychology: main points on human knowing and communicating

- The biological individual is at the centre of human experience and emotion and spirituality are fundamental to this experience.
- Each individual has a true self and is most motivated to act when such action realises the true self.
- Emotions, values and beliefs are fundamental and people work most effectively when they are in harmony with each other. Rational choice is a limited aspect of human experience.
- People yearn for meaning and transcendence of the mundane.
- Organisations will be successful when people are emotionally engaged and inspired by visions and a sense of mission and it is the role of leaders to choose these.

achievement and ensure that a cohesive team is built and motivated to perform the task. Leaders supply any skills or efforts that are missing in the team and, most important of all, they articulate purpose and culture, so reducing the uncertainty that team members face.

When leadership is defined in these terms, the concern is with the qualities leaders must possess and the styles they must employ in order to fulfil these functions effectively and efficiently. Those who have put forward explanations of this kind on the nature of leadership have differed from each other over whether the effective leader is one who focuses on the task, or one who focuses on relationships with and between people. A related area of concern is whether the effective leader is one who is autocratic, or one who delegates, consults and invites full participation. The question is which style of leadership motivates people more and thus gets the task done better. Consider three prominent theories: those of Fiedler (1967), Hersey and Blanchard (1988) and Vroom and Yetton (1973). According to these theories, leadership styles are to be chosen by the individual manager and, to be successful, a style that matches certain pre-given situations must be chosen. The leader should arrive at the group with particular skills developed beforehand. The required personality, skills and styles (or, as they are sometimes called, competences) are supposed to be identified in advance to suit a foreseeable situation. Here, leadership is about motivating people and the concern is with the appropriate role of the leader in securing efficient performance of known tasks.

The relevance of the group

A group is understood to be any number of people who interact with each other, are psychologically aware of each other and perceive themselves to be a group. Formal groups in an organisation may be permanent, for example the sales department; or they may be temporary, as is the case when special task forces or multi-disciplinary teams are appointed to deal with a particular task. Whether they are temporary or permanent, formal groups have clear goals and tasks; it is the purpose of formal groups to find solutions to structured problems. They usually have appointed leaders – leaders and managers have power given to them. However, they may also be autonomous, self-managing or democratic work groups that elect their own leader and design their own approach to a given structured task.

Within, alongside and across the formal groups, there is a strong tendency for informal groups to develop. These may be horizontal cliques amongst colleagues on the same hierarchical level, vertical cliques that include people from different hierarchical levels, or random cliques. Informal groups develop primarily because of proximity (Festinger *et al.*, 1950): through the contacts people make with each other given their physical location in relation to each other, the nature of their work and the time pressures they are under. The immediate concern about these informal groups is whether they will support or counter the operation of formal groups. The concern is with motivating people to cohere into functional teams that will focus on clearly defined tasks, not dissipate energies in destructive informal groups. The concern is primarily with the authority, responsibility and performance of individual managers in carrying out their pre-assigned tasks. From this perspective, the interest in groups relates to the circumstances in which groups may be more effective than individuals.

The underlying assumption about the relationship between individuals and groups in the notions reviewed in this section is that of the objective observer standing outside the system of groups and teams. The explicit or implicit prescription is that leaders and managers should take this position too, identify the nature of the situation and select leadership styles and motivational factors that are appropriate in the sense that they fit the situation. In essence, this amounts to installing appropriate feedback loops in the organisation so that it operates like a cybernetic system.

As far as the relationship between individuals and groups is concerned, again it is clear how the primacy of the individual is assumed. Groups are made up of individuals and these groups then affect those individuals, meeting some of their needs but deskilling them in other ways. In order to prevent adverse effects of groups on individuals, leaders need to pay attention to factors to do with the environment of the group, its composition in terms of members and their sensitivity to group dynamics. Formal groups are to be preferred over informal ones. It is recognised that informal groups are inevitable but the mainstream view seems to be that they threaten control. This attitude towards groups reflects cognitivist and humanistic assumptions.

3.6 Key debates

Previous sections of this chapter have provided a very brief description of key aspects of strategic choice theory in order to bring out its underpinning way of thinking. This section explores some of the key debates that have arisen in the development of the theory. These debates, which have not questioned the underlying way of thinking with its taken-for-granted assumptions about organisations and human interaction, have had to do with:

- whether strategy determines organisational structure or whether it is structure that determines strategy;
- whether market position or the resource base of an organisation determines its competitive advantage;

- what the limitations of strategic choice are, particularly when it comes to uncertainty and the impact of cognitive frames in interpreting situations, leading to questioning the very possibility of strategic choice;
- process versus content leading to an emphasis on learning rather than simple choice.

A brief indication of some of these debates is provided in this section.

Market position and the resource-based view of strategy

Previous sections have described strategic choice as the choice of the overall direction and shape of a whole organisation and its parts for some long time period into the future. The central purpose of the choice is to secure sustainable competitive advantage for the whole organisation and this choice was thought to be the single most important cause of successful performance. Furthermore, it was held that the choice of market position was the single most important cause of competitive advantage. This view was based on neo-classical economic theory, particularly theories to do with industry structure. The idea was that managers needed to analyse and understand the structure of their industry or market and select strategies that were appropriate to that structure.

Others, however, also drawing on neo-classical economics, argued that market position alone was not the cause of competitive advantage and took a resource-based view of strategy. Here a firm is viewed as a blend of resources that enable certain capabilities, options and accomplishments (Wernerfelt, 1984), which determines competitive advantage far more than market position. One firm outperforms another if it has superior ability to develop, use and protect core competences and resources, which are the foundations for creating the future (Hamel and Prahalad, 1990, 1994). Internal capabilities are what enable a firm to exploit external opportunities, and competitiveness is a function of the exploitation and leveraging of these internal resources. Strategies are designed to capitalise on core competences and distinctive assets form the basis of creating a sustainable competitive advantage. Complementary interdependence makes a firm's capabilities difficult to imitate. Resource and competence are built up historically, evolving in a continuous way with cumulative effects. Capabilities are building blocks that can be combined in mutually reinforcing ways into unique capacities and the different unique combinations lead to different unique futures. To prevent imitation, attention is focused on intellectual capital, firm-specific practices, relationships with customers and other intangible ways of working together. Strategic intent relates to choices about competences to secure a desired future and success comes from focusing attention on a few primary success factors.

Hamel and Prahalad (1989) also stress the role of organisations in creating their own environments instead of simply adapting to them. They have studied a number of global companies in North America, Europe and Japan and they suggest that what distinguishes the noticeably successful (Honda, Komatsu and Canon, for example) from the noticeably less so (General Motors, Caterpillar and Xerox, for example) are the different mental models of strategy guiding their respective actions. This research questions one of the basic tenets of strategic choice, namely the notion that successful organisations are those that fit, or adapt to, their environments.

Hamel and Prahalad found that the less successful companies follow strategic choice prescriptions and so seek to maintain strategic fit. This leads them to trim their ambitions to those that can be met with available resources. Such companies are concerned mainly with product market units rather than core competences. They preserve consistency through requiring conformity in behaviour, and they focus on achieving financial objectives. These companies attempt to achieve their financial objectives by using generic strategies, selected according to criteria of strategic fit, in order to secure sustainable competitive advantage. Hamel and Prahalad report that this approach leads to repetition and imitation.

On the other hand, Hamel and Prahalad found that successful companies focus on leveraging resources, that is, using what they have in new and innovative ways to reach seemingly unattainable goals. The main concern of these companies is to use their resources in challenging and stretching ways to build up a number of core competences. Consistency is maintained by all sharing a central strategic intent and the route to this successful state is accelerated organisational learning, recognising that no competitive advantages are inherently sustainable. Here, managers are not simply matching their resources to the requirements of the environment, leaving to others those requirements their resources are incapable of delivering. Instead, managers creatively use the resources they have, they create requirements of the environment that they can then meet, they push to achieve stretching goals and so they continually renew and transform their organisation. They question the idea of adapting to the environment, proposing instead creative interaction and stressing the importance of local learning, so suggesting a shift from classical strategic choice theory towards the perspective of strategy as a learning process, which will be taken up in Chapter 4.

While these authors question some assumptions of strategic choice theory, they preserve others. In particular, they continue to see organisational success as flowing from clear, prior, organisation-wide intention. They stress what they call strategic intent, a challenging, shared vision of a future leadership position for the company. This strategic intent is stable over time. It is clear as to outcome but flexible as to the means of achieving the outcome. It is an obsession with winning, and winning on a global scale cannot be secured either through long-term plans or through some undirected process of intrapreneurship or autonomous small task forces. Instead, success is secured by discovering how to achieve a broad, stretching, challenging intention to build core competences. However, in stressing intention, harmony and consistency, the resource-based view falls within strategic choice theory.

Uncertainty and the limitations to strategic choice

It has already been pointed out that cybernetic control depends on the possibility of making reasonably reliable forecasts of action outcomes and time lags involved at the required level of detail and over the required time span. When this is not possible, cybernetic control may still be effective if small and essentially random actions by the organisation can be relied upon to cancel out small and essentially random changes in the environment – the law of requisite variety. In other words, cybernetic systems require a fairly high degree of certainty about environmental change, either in the sense that a specific cause can be related to a specific effect or in the probabilistic sense of small changes cancelling out. This is the same as saying that cybernetic systems function effectively when they operate in rather repetitive environments.

Many writers on strategic management have, of course, been well aware of the uncertainty, ambiguity and conflicting goals that managers have to deal with and have developed different ways of understanding the nature of strategic choice. One influential example is the notion of logical incrementalism, which will be discussed in Chapter 7. Logical incrementalism represents a move from the more mechanistic view of classical strategic choice theory towards an understanding of strategy as a continual process of small incremental changes within an overall, chosen logic.

The view that competitive advantage could be sustained for long time periods was criticised by some who pointed to the rapid change in competitive conditions. They held that hypercompetition made it impossible to sustain competitive advantage for any length of time. Those taking this view argue that hypercompetition requires a new view of strategy (D'Aveni, 1995). From this perspective, one firm outperforms another if it is adept at rapidly and repeatedly disrupting the current situation to create a novel basis for competing. Hypercompetition requires a discontinuously redefined competitive advantage and radical changes in market relationships. Success is built not on existing strengths as in the resource-based view, but on repeated disruptions. This enables a firm to continuously establish new but temporary competitive advantages. Tactical actions keep competitors off-balance. Competitive advantage is temporary and firms destroy their own and others' competitive advantage. Organisation units and actions are loosely coupled and competition requires aggressive action unconstrained by loyalty and compassion. Successful strategies rely on surveillance, interpretation, initiative, opportunism and improvisation.

The writers in the organisational evolution tradition (Hannan and Freeman, 1989) went even further and questioned the ability of managers to choose the state of their organisation in any way. They took a neo-Darwinian view and held that organisations changed through random events that were then selected for survival by competitive selection.

Process versus content

Another debate arose between those who argued that strategy research focused too much on the content of generic strategies required to produce successful performance. Arising from the discussion of the limits to rationality, some argued for looking at how managers actually made strategy. They called for a focus on how strategies were constructed, the process, rather than what they consisted of, the content. The whole question of process will be taken up in Chapter 7. This emphasis on process was taken up by some as a move from simple choice to a view of strategy as a learning process. For example, Mintzberg (1994) made a direct call for a move from strategic choice and long-term planning to an understanding of strategic management as a process of learning. This perspective will be explored in Chapter 4.

3.7 How strategic choice theory deals with the four key questions

The purpose of this section is to reflect upon the underlying assumptions and reasoning processes of strategic choice theory, including the debates it has led to, in order to identify what it focuses attention on and the extent to which it helps to make sense of one's experience of life in organisations.

In Chapter 1, I suggested that the phenomena of interest when one talks about strategy are populations of organisations of various kinds that interact with each other. Each organisation is itself a population of groupings of individuals that interact with each other. These populations are continually changing in that new organisations and groups within them come into being, while already existing ones disappear altogether, merge with others, split apart, develop new activities, alter structurally, grow or decline. As they relate to each other in their groups, people experience enthusiasm and boredom, excitement and anxiety, anger and fear, jealousy and envy, fulfilment and disappointment, pleasure and frustration.

Making sense of the phenomena

Strategic choice theory makes sense of these phenomena from a realist position. In other words, the theory assumes a pre-given reality. Section 3.2 on the formulation and evaluation of a strategy shows how each step in the formulation process makes this assumption. For example, a suitable strategy is one that fits, or is adapted to a particular market. In order to determine whether or not this is so, the market must be analysed in terms of customer requirements, competitor positions, entry barriers and so on. These factors are treated as realities that already exist, not stories about a reality that is being socially constructed by those who are participating in that market.

In addition, to establish the suitability of a strategy, managers must forecast, envision or imagine the state of these market factors some years into the future. That future is talked about as a pre-given reality too. You can hear this when people talk about getting to the future first, or use the analogy of Columbus setting sail for America, or President Kennedy announcing the dream of putting a man on the moon. These are all metaphors of a future reality that already exists, waiting to be discovered rather than created. Another example of this realist position is the discussion of leadership. Different leadership styles are related to different situations and the recommendation is that individuals should choose a leadership style that fits the situation. Again, the situations and the styles already exist before any individual comes to take them up. They are not created in the act of leading but are discovered and adopted in advance. Emotion tends to be understood from a humanistic point of view as a source of motivating followers and workers but the strategic choice itself focuses firmly on Kant's autonomous, rational individual.

Furthermore, strategic choice theory makes a particular assumption about the nature of causality. It assumes that linear causal links can be identified and that, therefore, predictions can be made. For example, it states that success is caused by choosing a strategy that is feasible, acceptable and suitable. Another example is provided by the understanding of groups. It is postulated that groups of people will function effectively as teams if certain environmental factors and certain kinds of members are chosen to form the group. Such linear causality is not the only possible view. Chapter 8 will review notions of nonlinear causal connections and look at theories indicating that it could be impossible to identify causal links at all in certain circumstances.

The point I am making, then, is that strategic choice theory takes a particular position in relation to the way that humans know anything and the debates it has led to largely continue to do the same. As with any other position, this immediately moves the reasoning process down one avenue and excludes others. The result is to deal with the four questions posed in Chapter 1 in a particular way. Consider how strategic choice theory deals with these four questions.

The nature of interaction

In strategic choice theory, interaction is understood in systemic terms, where the entities comprising the system are organisations that interact with each other in industry groupings, or markets. An organisation is also thought of as a system that consists of people grouped into divisions, subsidiary companies, departments, project teams and so on, all of which interact with each other to form the organisational system. The immediate consequence is a tendency to reify, that is, to think of an organisation and a system as a thing.

The concept of a system in strategic choice theory is a very specific one. It is a cybernetic system, that is, a goal-driven, self-regulating system. The self-regulation takes the form of a negative feedback process through which an organisation adapts to its environment, that is, its markets. Negative feedback is a process of referring back to a fixed point of reference established outside the organisation. The market demand to which the organisation must adapt provides the fixed point of reference. The negative feedback works through the system taking account of the difference between its offering and that market demand, so as to remove the difference. The organisation is itself also a cybernetic system consisting of groups of people. The fixed point of reference for these groups is the goals and targets set for them by their manager. Negative feedback operates by taking account of the difference between performance and targets, so as to remove the difference. Uncertainty, ambiguity and conflict are supposed to be dealt with largely by more elaborate negative feedback loops. Thinking about motivation, political activity and culture change is all in terms of negative feedback loops. Note how strategic choice theory takes no account of the effect of positive or amplifying feedback loops in human affairs.

The result is a theory that focuses primarily on the macro level with very little attention to micro interactions or micro diversity. In other words, differences amongst the system entities are averaged out. Interactions between the entities are assumed to be average, or at least normally distributed around the average. This allows the cyberneticist to disregard the dynamics of interaction between the entities of which the system is composed and concentrate on the system as a whole. What is then focused on is the regularities in the system's responses to changes in its environment. The system responds to differences between externally imposed goals and its actual behaviour. Or, it responds to differences between an expectation, or prediction, of some state it should achieve and what it actually does. In organisational terms, the focus of attention is on how the whole organisation responds to the actions of other whole organisations that constitute its environment. Little attention is paid to the differences in the people that belong to the organisation or the nature of their interactions with each other.

A single, whole organisation is the primary unit of analysis. Intention, or choice, is related to this whole. By focusing attention on a single organisation, 'the organisation', strategic choice theory tends to ignore the fact that other organisations are making choices too. What happens to one depends not only on what it chooses but on what all the others are choosing too. You can see the importance attached to a single organisation making choices for the whole in the emphasis placed on: strategic intent, choosing a vision, choosing financial targets, choosing a culture, choosing strategic management styles, and so on. The possibility of making such choices successfully depends heavily on the ability to predict at rather fine levels of detail and over rather long time spans. That in turn depends upon the possibility of identifying causal links between action and outcome at a rather fine level of detail over rather long time spans.

For example, to achieve financial targets, investments must be chosen to deliver those targets. The discounted cash flow method prescribed for choosing between alternative investments requires the forecasting of detailed cash flows over periods as long as 25 years. Whether an investment is a success or not depends on the fine detail of what it costs and what revenues it generates over many years, once it is in operation. Forecasts at a coarse level of detail, or for short time periods, will then not capture the factors upon which success depends. The choice cannot then be made as prescribed, which is to make the choice in a rational way that takes account of the actual factors that lead to success. Success will not be the result of rational choice but will depend on the chance capturing of the most important factors in the coarse forecasts.

Strategic choice theory takes a particular view of organisational dynamics. Since it is a cybernetic theory, the dynamics are those of a move to stable equilibrium. Success is equated with stability, consistency and harmony. Instabilities arise largely in the organisation's environment.

Strategic choice theory is usually formulated in a way that focuses on the interaction between components and so ignores the richness of human relationships. In viewing people as parts of a system it fails to take account of ordinary human spontaneity, which will always be affecting what happens. Cybernetic systems are incapable of any kind of novelty, innovation, creativity or transformation. They can only unfold what their designers, the observing humans outside them, put into them. The cause of the system's movement is the formative process of negative feedback. From this perspective, organisations are thought of as wholes formed by interacting parts. These parts exist in order to sustain the purpose of the whole and so cannot be free. The cybernetic system unfolds the purpose already enfolded in it, namely the target set from outside of it. Cybernetics cannot explain novelty or transformation.

Nature of human beings

This chapter has indicated how strategic choice theory is built on a particular view of human nature. It is assumed that individuals are essentially cybernetic entities. They make representations of a pre-given reality taking the form of regularities built up from previous experience and mentally stored in the form of sets of rules, or schemas, cognitive maps or mental models. Through experience they make more and more accurate representations, more and more reliable cognitive maps. This process is essentially one of negative feedback in which discrepancies between the cognitive map and external reality are fed back into the map to change it, closing the gap between it and reality. Strategic choice theory pays very little attention to emotion and the impact that this might have on how an organisation functions. To the extent that this theory does pay attention to emotion it does so from a humanistic psychology perspective in which individuals are motivated by opportunities to actualise their true selves. Little attention is paid to the notion that unconscious processes might influence how people perceive and know anything.

So, when it comes to the micro level, strategic choice theory alternates between two views of human nature, the cognitivist and the humanistic. The former tends to be predominant when the theory focuses on control systems and the latter when it focuses on motivation, leadership and culture. The way both are used, however, has an element in common. It is implicitly assumed that the individual members of an organisation are all the same and that interactions between them are all the same. It is assumed that everyone responds in the same way to the same motivational factor, for example. Another example is the implicit assumption, when talking about leadership styles, that everyone will respond in the same way to a given leadership style. Differences between individuals, and deviant and eccentric behaviour, have no role to play in how an organisation evolves. Indeed, they are seen as dangerous disruptions to be removed by more controls or additional motivators. The emphasis is on everyone sharing the same values to produce uniformity and conformity. The very way members of an organisation are referred to as the staff, or the management, indicates how differences within the categories are obliterated while differences between them are highlighted.

There is an important consequence of this ignoring of individual differences and deviant behaviour that will be taken up in Part Three. Systems in which the entities and their interactions are all the same cannot spontaneously generate anything new. For strategic choice theory this means that the only possible explanation of creativity is located in the individual's intention to do something creative. How individuals do this is not explained in strategic choice theory. It is simply assumed.

Individuals feature in strategic choice theory primarily in terms of how they affect the organisation as a whole. Individuals make the choices and do the controlling. Individuals appoint people to roles and they put them into teams. They set targets for those teams and motivate, reward or punish people according to performance. An individual forms a vision and individuals articulate missions for others. Power is possessed by individuals who exert it over other individuals. In this way the individual is consistently held to be prior and primary to the group. While the organisation as a system is understood to be driven by formative causality, a different theory of causality applies to the humans who design it. This is the rationalist causality of the autonomous individual choosing goals and actions.

The point I am making here is that strategic choice theory implicitly makes a number of important assumptions about human beings that should not be mistaken for the 'truth'. They are all assumptions that can quite properly be contested and, when they are, the whole of strategic choice theory is questioned too (*see* Part 3).

Methodology and strategic choice

Both cybernetics and cognitivism take a realist position on human knowing. In other words, they assume that there is a reality to be dealt with that exists before people perceive it. They take the traditional scientific perspective of looking for laws, or regularities, to explain behaviour. They seek to apply the principles of logic. In doing this they take the position of the objective observer who stands outside the system of interest and makes hypotheses about it. They build models of the system to guide behaviour. The emphasis is on the ability to control. Little importance is attached to the notion that people may construct reality in their social interaction with each other. There is no notion of reflexivity and the position of understanding through participating. Individuals stand outside the system they are talking about and construct models of it as the basis for prescription and action. This has methodological implications for research and it has even more important consequences for how managers understand their role.

When a manager takes this position, that manager immediately assumes that it is his or her task to design and install some system, set of actions, motivators and so on. For example, the top executive is supposed to analyse the values of an organisation. This requires the executive to step outside the value system of which he or she is a part and look at it from the outside, as it were. The next step is to design and install a new value system. Another example is provided by the discussion of leadership styles. Again, the manager is required to step outside the situation and determine whether it is one in which a particular leadership style is required. If this differs from the one the manager currently practises, then the appropriate one must be installed.

Paradox

The theory of strategic choice pays no attention to the possibility of paradox, that is, the simultaneous presence of contradictory ideas. The primary example of this is the way in which people are implicitly regarded as parts of an organisational cybernetic system, and so not free, on the one hand, and yet also as autonomous individuals who can design it and so are free, on the other hand. This is not sensed as paradoxical at all. In fact any paradox has been eliminated in a temporal sequencing in which the human is first thought of as a part and then thought of as autonomous.

Contradictions are to be solved, tensions and conflicts smoothed away and dilemmas resolved. In terms of what might be major paradoxes of organisational life, strategic choice consistently occupies one pole of the contradiction. Individuals and groups are not paradoxical since groups simply consist of autonomous individuals. Predictability is emphasised and the possible implications of simultaneously present unpredictability are not seriously explored. Control is emphasised and freedom to act is made consistent with it through motivational factors. Order is required for success and disorder or any form of deviance or eccentricity is to be curbed and removed. Success is equated with rational choice and chance with the potential for failure.

Again, the point I am making is that strategic choice theory implicitly makes assumptions about opposing forces in organisational life that cannot simply be taken for granted. It is quite possible to take a different view and so construct a different theory.

Making sense of experience

The question now is how this theory assists one to make sense of one's experience of life in organisations. My experience is that, despite the rational analysis, the forecasts, the visions, strategic intents, team building and so on, organisational outcomes are very frequently surprising and unexpected. I find it very difficult to make sense of this experience by taking a strategic choice perspective, as indeed do many others as described in Section 3.6 above. The theory leads one to believe that it is possible to make choices that lead to organisational success if one follows the prescribed procedures. So when managers follow the prescriptions and the surprising, the unexpected and the downright unpleasant occur, they are left with little option but to conclude that they, or more likely that other people, have been incompetent in some way. A variation on this is to blame the surprise on ignorance of enough facts. Alternatively, the blame might be placed on people who do not implement the strategic choice as required. When one makes sense of experience from the strategic choice perspective the most widespread response to the unexpected takes the form of some kind of blame.

The response is then to put more effort into gathering and analysing information to overcome ignorance. Or more intensive efforts are made to acquire the necessary competences to manage strategically and so avoid accusations and feelings of incompetence. Or new motivating and controlling systems are installed to prevent poor implementation and bad behaviour. When the surprise is a large one, these responses are usually accompanied by the removal from the organisation of individuals who are conspicuously associated with the surprise. However, none of these responses puts a stop to the whole sequence of events happening again. Instead, in my view, these responses raise levels of fear and place people under increasing stress. Is this inevitable or is there a problem with trying to make sense of experience from the strategic choice standpoint?

If you take the psychoanalytic perspective to be reviewed in Chapter 5, you might reach a different conclusion. It could be that many of the prescriptions of strategic choice theory are little more than defences against the anxiety of not being able to forecast and stay in control. If this is so, then they are not very good defences because, as I have just suggested, they may actually increase levels of anxiety. If you take the perspective that I will suggest in Part 3, you might conclude that it is the nature of organising itself that generates the unexpected and the surprising. Then it may be that no one is to blame but, rather, uncertainty needs to be accepted as an inescapable fact of life that need not provoke despair or paralyse action.

3.8 Summary

This chapter has reviewed the theory of cybernetic systems and the closely associated cognitivist theory of human behaviour upon which the theory of strategic choice is built. These theories are the foundations upon which the strategic choice theory of organisational change is built. Cybernetic systems depend upon the possibility of prediction over a long enough time period at a fine enough level of detail, if they are to achieve the control that is their central concern. Cognitivist psychology assumes that individuals are autonomous and that they learn in an essentially negative feedback manner. It heavily emphasises the logical capacities of the human being and it is these that enable choices to be made. These are central themes that run through strategic choice theory.

This chapter has also reviewed the rational, analytical sequence of steps prescribed by strategic choice theory for the formulation and evaluation of long-term strategic plans. The steps involve analysing and forecasting market development, as well as the financial, other resource or competence and power implications of alternative action options. The result should be a blueprint to guide the development of the organisation for some reasonably long period into the future. It is the template against which the actions of individual managers are to be measured. The assumption is that if the plan has been put together skilfully enough it will go a long way to ensuring the organisation's success. However, the formulated plan only provides the blueprint against which action is to be evaluated. Success requires effective implementation.

Implementation is in effect the construction of cybernetic systems. Detailed targets and objectives are derived from the strategic plan and hierarchical structures and detailed sets of procedures for measuring and comparing outcomes with expectations are designed to monitor movement towards the detailed objectives. Even 'softer' elements such as belief systems, power and management style are prescribed in much the same way.

The chapter then reviewed behavioural factors in organisations from a strategic choice perspective, primarily to do with the motivation of people working in the organisation and the nature of leadership. These were understood in terms of what amounts to negative feedback loops, displaying the way in which organisations are treated as if they are, or should be, cybernetic systems. In all of these areas the individual is treated as primary, displaying the underlying assumption of cognitivism and humanistic psychology. Another common assumption is that managers can and should take the position of independent observer and choose appropriate feedback loops in relation to motivation, leadership, politics and culture. Throughout, the assumption is that human beings behave like cybernetic systems themselves, the underlying tenet of cognitivism.

The conclusion I reach is that this theory provides a partial and limited explanation of how organisational life unfolds. It provides powerful explanations of, and prescriptions for, the predictable, repetitive aspects of organisational life over short time frames into the future. These are indeed very prominent and important aspects of organisational life. However, if you believe, as I do, that life in organisations is the interplay of the predictable and the unpredictable, the stable and the unstable, the orderly and the disorderly, then it provides a very partial explanation. On its own, it leaves one feeling puzzled by constant surprise and worried about the inability to stay in control that it prescribes. Creativity and innovation remain largely mysterious if strategic choice theory is the only way to understand organisations. The creativity and destructiveness of relationships between people is absent. It prescribes predominantly top-down processes, even when empowerment and self-managing teams are suggested. They are always the result of decisions made by those at the top of the hierarchy but, as those at the top know only too well, people rarely do exactly as they are told. These conclusions are not at all new – similar points have been made in the debate around strategic choice theory for a long time now. What is surprising, perhaps, is that despite the debate around it and the dubious evidence base for it, strategic choice theory continues to dominate most strategic management textbooks and features frequently in the ways in which practising managers talk about their organisation and its strategies.

Further reading

Richardson (1991) provides an excellent account of cybernetics and the use of feedback thinking about human systems. Baddeley (1990) provides a very good exposition of the cognitivist position and Varela *et al.* (1995) provide a cogent critique of cognitivism. To obtain further information on analytical techniques and models for evaluating strategies turn to Hofer and Schendel (1978) as well as Rowe *et al.* (1989) and Johnson *et al.* (2005). Also see Ansoff (1990) for a very different perspective from the one presented in this book. Hussey (1991) provides further material on management control and Goold and Campbell (1987) provide a thorough analysis of strategic management styles. Campbell and Tawady (1990) should be referred to for a greater understanding of the mission concept. For further detail on particular decision-making modes turn to Quinn (1978), Mintzberg *et al.* (1976) and Cohen *et al.* (1972). Good summaries of counter views are to be found in Hurst (1982). Hurst (1986), Argyris (1990), Schein (1988), Morgan (1997) and Mintzberg (1994) are well worth reading. For the resource-based view see Hamel and Prahalad (1989).

Questions to aid further reflection

1. What are the essential features of a cybernetic system and what assumptions does such a theory make about the world it is trying to explain?

2. If you think in the way suggested by the theory of strategic choice how would you explain what an organisation is?

3. What role does the notion of the objective observer play in cybernetic systems and cognitivist psychology?

4. What theory of communication is central to cognitivist psychology?

5. What taken-for-granted assumptions does the theory of strategic choice make about human individuals and the social world they live in?

6. What theories of causality are implied by the theory of strategic choice?

7. What does it mean to be practical if you subscribe to this theory?

Chapter 4

Thinking in terms of organisational learning and knowledge creation

Systems dynamics, cognitivist, humanistic and constructivist psychology

This chapter invites you to draw on your own experience to reflect on and consider the implications of:

- The importance and consequences of nonlinearity.

- The importance and consequences of positive feedback.

- What it means to think in terms of mental models.

- The consequences of the move from cognitivist to constructivist psychology.

- How control is presented as operation at leverage points.

- The dual causality to be found in organisational learning theories.

- The role of teams and of the social generally in learning processes.

- The role of leaders in learning and knowledge creation.

- The move to notions of organisations as living systems and the connection made to the mystical.

The ideas presented in this chapter are important because they constitute the assumptions on which theories of organisational learning are built. The recent popularity of notions of organisational learning and knowledge management reflects some realisation of the limitations of strategic choice theory. If one is to avoid naïve applications of learning and knowledge management prescriptions it is necessary to understand the way of thinking they reflect and understand the limitations of this way of thinking.

4.1 Introduction

Chapter 3 reviewed strategic choice theory, showing how its theoretical foundations are to be found in the theory of cybernetic systems and a primarily cognitivist view of human nature. According to this theory, organisations become what they become because of the strategic choices of their leaders. That chapter also described how a number of writers have taken issue with the strategic choice perspective and suggested instead that an organisation's strategic development could be better understood as arising in processes of learning. According to this theory, organisations become what they become because of the quality of their learning processes and strategy and strategic direction are caused by such learning. It is the role of the leaders to design learning processes and inspire effective learning.

This chapter, therefore, explores the theoretical foundations of learning organisation theory and knowledge management which have attracted increasing attention since the early 1990s. This approach has much in common with strategic choice theory but there are significant differences. Most important, perhaps, is how it points to the limits of predictability and more complex processes involved in strategising in organisations. The main theoretical difference is that learning organisation theorists employ a somewhat different theory of interaction. They still see interaction in systemic terms but the systems theory is systems dynamics rather than cybernetics. The same cognitivist view of human action is usually retained, however, although some writers move to a constructivist perspective and humanistic psychology becomes more important than it was in the theory of strategic choice. Strategic choice theory held that organisations change when their managers make choices about a wide range of issues. According to the theory of the learning organisation, change flows from a process of organisational learning. It is when people in an organisation learn effectively together and so create knowledge that it changes. However, the concern with control remains.

One of the most influential expositions of the concept of the learning organisation is that given by Senge (1990). Senge believes that an organisation excels when it is able to tap the commitment and capacity of its members to learn. He sees this capacity as intrinsic to human nature and he locates it in the individual, although he does see such learning as occurring when individuals experience profound teamwork. He identifies five disciplines required for an organisation that can truly learn:

- systems thinking;
- personal mastery;
- mental models;
- shared vision;
- team learning.

Each of these will be considered in the sections that follow.

4.2 Systems dynamics: nonlinearity and positive feedback

Senge understands organisations from the perspective of systems dynamics and holds that a learning organisation requires its people to think in systems terms. People should not think about their work purely in terms of their own roles. Instead, they should develop an understanding of the negative and positive feedback structure of the system of which they are a part. This should enable them to obtain some insight into the unexpected consequences of what they are doing. The purpose of thinking in systemic terms is to identify leverage points, that is, those points in the web of negative and positive feedback loops where change can have the largest beneficial effects. As in strategic choice theory, the purpose is to stay in control as much as is possible in a very complex system.

Systems dynamics has its intellectual roots in the same tradition as cybernetics. It is also built on the engineer's notion of control. However, from this common root and around the same time, it developed in a somewhat different way from cybernetics. While cyberneticists focused on the structure of negative feedback loops, those who developed systems dynamics sought to model the system as a whole in mathematical terms. The most important figures in this development were economists seeking to model economic cycles for whole economies or some aspect of them such as inventory cycles. Some of the most important figures here were Goodwin (1951), Philips (1950) and Tustin (1953). Systems dynamics thinking was also extended to industrial management problems (Forrester, 1958; Simon, 1952).

In their modelling work, systems dynamicists used *nonlinear* equations that incorporated *positive* feedback effects and generated rather complex dynamics. These models also display some cyclical behaviour that is due to the structure of the system itself, not just changes in the environment. However, just as with cybernetics, the system cannot spontaneously change, a matter I will return to in Chapter 8.

This section will give a brief review of some of the key concepts in systems dynamics, starting with the nature of nonlinearity.

Nonlinearity

Nonlinearity occurs when some condition or some action has a varying effect on an outcome, depending on the level of the condition or the intensity of the action. For example, the availability of inventories of goods in an inventory affects shipment rates of those goods, but the effect varies. When the inventory is close to a desired level, there will be virtually no impact of inventory levels on shipment rates. The firm ships according to its order inflow rate. However, when inventory is very low, inventory availability has a powerful constraining effect on shipments.

Instead of a system that operates only according to negative feedback, as in cybernetics, there is now a system that operates according to both positive and negative feedback. Systems dynamics therefore introduces the possibility that a system may display non-equilibrium behaviour as it flips between positive and negative feedback. The result is much more complex patterns of movement over time, that is, much more complex dynamics. Behaviour can now be cyclical and those cycles might be very irregular if the system is perturbed by environmental fluctuations. Systems dynamics was very important in understanding the nature of economic cycles, such as cycles in inventory and other forms of investment. Systems dynamics also points to the limits of predictability by introducing nonlinear circular causality, which makes it difficult to say what causes what, or what precedes what.

Perhaps the most important development of systems dynamics models for application to organisational and social policy issues has been by Jay Forrester (1958, 1961). His background was that of a servomechanisms engineer, digital computer pioneer and manager of a large R&D effort. He developed an approach to understanding human systems that is based on concepts of positive and negative feedback, nonlinearity and the use of computers to simulate the behaviour patterns of such complex systems. Feedback is the basic characteristic of his view of the world and he firmly links human decision making to the feedback concept.

Production and distribution chains

Forrester has illustrated his approach by modelling the behaviour of production and distribution chains. A factory supplies a product, say beer, to a number of distributors who then ship it to an even larger number of retailers. Orders for the product flow back upstream from retailers to distributors and from them to the factory. The factory, the distributors and the retailers form a system and the links between them are flows of orders in one direction and flows of product in the other. Each part of the system tries to do the best it can to maintain inventories at minimum levels without running out of product to sell. Each attempts to ship product as fast as possible. They all do these things because that is the way to maximise their individual profits. But because of its very structure – the feedback and lags in information flows – this system shows a marked tendency to amplify minor ordering disturbances at the retail level. An initial 10 per cent increase in orders at the retail level can eventually cause production at the factory to peak 40 per cent above the initial level before collapsing.

Peter Senge (1990) reports how he has used this example as a game with thousands of groups of managers in many countries. Even when people know about the likely consequences of this system, he has always found that the consequences of a small increase at the retail level are, first of all, growing demand that cannot be met. Inventories are depleted and backlogs grow. Then beer arrives in great quantities while incoming orders suddenly decline as backlogs are reduced. Eventually almost all players end up with large inventories they cannot unload.

Senge concludes that it is only by being aware of how the system as a whole functions, rather than simply concentrating on their own part of it, that managers can ensure that the extreme instabilities of the cycles are avoided. It seems, however, that these cycles can never be removed altogether.

Principles of systems dynamics

By running computer simulations of a great many different human systems, researchers in the systems dynamics tradition have identified a number of principles about complex human systems. These are set out below.

1. Complex systems often produce unexpected and counterintuitive results. In the beer game, retailers increase orders above their real need expecting this to lead to

bigger deliveries, but because all retailers are doing this, and because of lags in information flows, the unexpected result is lower deliveries.

2. In systems with nonlinear relationships, or with positive and negative feedback, the links between cause and effect are distant in time and space. In the beer game, the causes of increased demand appear at the retail end, distant in space from the factory and distant in time because of the lags in order flows. Such distance between cause and effect makes it very difficult to say what is causing what. Those playing the beer game always think that the fluctuations in deliveries are being caused by fluctuations in retail demand when in fact they are due to the manner in which the system operates. The problem is made worse by many coincident symptoms that look like causes but are merely relational. This means that it is extremely difficult to make specific predictions of what will happen in a specific place over a specific time period. Instead, quantitative simulations on computers can be used to identify general qualitative patterns of behaviour that will be similar to those one is likely to experience, although never the same. Simulation here is being used not to capture the future specific outcome within a range of likely outcomes, but to establish broad qualitative features in patterns of behaviour.

3. Systems are highly sensitive to some changes but remarkably insensitive to many others. These systems contain some influential pressure, or leverage, points. Managers can exert influence at these points and so can have a major impact on the behaviour of the system. The problem is that they are difficult to identify. In the beer game, the leverage points lie in the ordering practices of retailers and distributors. Unfortunately these pressure points, from which favourable chain reactions can be initiated, are extremely difficult to find. More usually, it seems, systems are insensitive to changes and indeed counteract and compensate for externally applied correctives. So when retailers find that deliveries from the distributors are curtailed, they respond by ordering even more and so make the situation worse. Because of the natural tendency to counteract and compensate, that is, to move to stability, it is necessary to change the system itself rather than simply apply externally generated remedies.

The above points lead to the conclusion that attempts to plan the long-term future are likely to prompt counter-forces and lead to unexpected and unintended changes.

Archetypes of feedback processes

The strong possibility that systems will counteract correctives and produce unintended consequences makes it necessary for managers to analyse and understand the feedback connections in the system, to understand the system as a whole. Through their simulations, systems dynamicists have built up a set of templates, or archetype feedback processes, that are very commonly found in organisations of all kinds. The purpose of these archetypes is not to make specific predictions of what will happen, but to recondition perceptions so that people are able to perceive the structures at play, to see the dynamic patterns of behaviour and to see the potential leverage in those structures. The templates are meant to be used in a flexible way to help understand patterns in events. For example, Senge describes an archetype called limits to growth, which occurs when a reinforcing positive feedback process is installed to produce a desired result (a positive growth loop) but it inadvertently creates secondary effects (a negative limiting loop) that put a stop to the growth. The 'limits to growth' structure is found wherever growth bumps up against limits. The most immediate response to this structure is that of pushing harder on the factors that cause growth. In fact this is counterproductive because it causes the system to bump even more firmly against the limits. The solution is to work on the negative loop, on relaxing the limits.

For example, a company may grow through introducing new products flowing from its R&D efforts. As it grows it increases the size of the R&D department, which becomes harder to manage. Senior engineers then become managers and the flow of new product ideas slows. Pressing for more new product ideas will simply lead to a bigger R&D department and that will exacerbate the management problems, so reducing the flow of new ideas. Instead, there is a need to rethink the whole process of developing new products and running R&D activities. The leverage point is the way in which the actual R&D effort is organised, and to see how this should be done one needs to understand the whole system of which R&D is a part.

Box 4.1 summarises the key points that the theory of systems dynamics makes on patterns of organisational change over time.

4.3 Personal mastery and mental models: cognitivist psychology

The second discipline required in a learning organisation is personal mastery. Senge does not mean by this some form of domination but, rather, a high level of proficiency such as that possessed by a master craft worker. Those who have personal mastery consistently obtain the results that they want and it requires commitment to lifelong learning. It is a process of continually deepening one's personal vision, focusing energy, developing patience and seeing reality objectively. He links it with spiritual foundations. The strongly humanistic flavour of his view of human nature is evident and takes the same line of inspirational motivation as that described in Chapter 3 in relation to strategic choice theory.

The third discipline required for the learning organisation is an understanding of the notion of mental models. These are deeply ingrained assumptions, or generalisations, often taking the form of pictures or images in individual minds. Individuals are mostly not aware of their mental models: they are hidden, or unconscious, mental constructions. Senge emphasises how mental models restrict perceptions and points to Royal Dutch Shell, claiming that it developed the skill of surfacing and challenging the mental models of managers. Mental models are internal pictures of the external world and he claims that individuals can learn to surface them and subject them to rigorous scrutiny. Institutional learning is a process in which management teams work together to change their shared mental models of their company and its markets. This is cognitivist psychology as in strategic choice theory.

According to cognitive science, humans are compelled by their limited brain capacity for processing new information to simplify everything they observe. They are unable to know reality itself; all they can do is construct simplifications, that is, mental models of reality. The influence of Kant (*see* Chapter 2) is very clear in this

Box 4.1	Systems dynamics: main points on organisational dynamics

- Organisations are goal-seeking feedback systems, but amplifying feedback loops and nonlinearity mean that they are not self-regulating in the cybernetic sense. Instead, they are self-influencing and this may take a self-sustaining or a self-destructive form. They may be adapting to pre-given environments through negative feedback or diverging from them through positive feedback.

- Systems dynamics takes a realist position on human knowing.

- The system is recursive. This means that it feeds back on itself to repeat its behaviour.

- It follows that causality is circular. However, in systems dynamics causality is nonlinear. Causal links are distant and often difficult to identify.

- Predictability of specific events and their timings is very difficult and this makes it important to recognise qualitative patterns.

- Control becomes difficult but if the structure of the system is understood, leverage points can be identified. These are points where efforts to change behaviour have the most effect. These points are difficult to find. Changes there might simply provoke compensating and offsetting behaviour.

- Instability is an essential part of what goes on and one cannot simply ignore it or write it off as something to be banished by negative feedback controls. There is too much evidence that this focus on negative feedback alone leads to unintended positive loops and unintended consequences.

- Behavioural patterns of the system as a whole are of great importance. Behavioural patterns can emerge without being intended; in fact they often emerge contrary to intention. The result is unexpected and counterintuitive outcomes. The systematic feedback structure of the organisation itself determines the pattern of behaviour over time.

- Because the analysis is conducted in feedback terms there is still the notion of an external point of reference. The system still operates on the basis of representations of its environment.

- There is a clear boundary between system and environment, between inner and outer. Although the system is adapting to its environment, it is itself a closed system. It operates/changes with reference to a fixed point at the boundary with its environment, either amplifying or damping in relation to that fixed point.

- Its state is determined by its own structure as well as flux in the environment expressed through the fixed point of reference. Instability comes from within the system as well as the environment.

- The system is no longer homeostatic, or equilibrium seeking, but far more likely to be in non-equilibrium. However, left to its own devices, the system has a tendency to stabilise and so deteriorate in the face of change.

- History is important in that the current state of the system does depend upon the sequence of previous states. However, the system does not evolve of its own accord. Any change must be designed outside the system and then installed.

- The goal is still to achieve as much stability, consistency and harmony as is compatible with changing to adapt to the environment.

kind of thinking. When people look at a particular situation, they see it through the lens provided by the mental models built up through past experience and education. Humans approach each situation every day with a mindset, a recipe they have acquired from the past, that they use to understand the present in order to design actions to cope with it. When they take actions that fail to have the desired result, the reason often lies in the way the problem is perceived in the first place. The remedy is to amend the mental model, the perspective, the mindset, the paradigm with which the task is being approached.

Managers will not simply observe a given environment and a given organisational capability – the facts. They, like all other humans, will sometimes inevitably invent, to some extent, what they observe. The whole process of simplifying and selecting means that the environment is in a real sense the invention and the creation of the managers observing it. It will then only be possible for managers to make sense of what they are doing after they have done it (Weick, [1969] 1979). In highly complex and uncertain situations, then, explanations of strategic management need to take account of the possibility that environments may be invented or created in managers' minds and that they can often only make sense of what they are doing with hindsight. This is a move from cognitivism to contructivism.

Constructivist psychology

Maturana and Varela (1987) argue for a constructivist view of human psychology. They hold that people do not simply respond to stimuli presented by the environment but select aspects of their environment according to their own identities. In other words, they enact, or bring forth, the environment that is relevant to them. This is a view of cognition, that is, of recognising and responding, that is active rather than simply passively registering what is already there. The world of an individual is an active construction by that individual of his or her own world, not a passive representation of a pre-given world. Each in a sense creates his or her own world.

This notion of selecting, or calling forth, a world is illustrated by the perception of colour (Varela *et al.*, 1995). Primates have evolved a trichromate system for perceiving colour. That is, they possess one channel, or receptor, which responds to medium-wave light, another which responds to an excess of long-wave over short-wave light and a third to an excess of medium- over long-wave light. The colours perceived depend upon which receptors are dominant and which are dormant. Not all species, however, have trichromate systems. Squirrels and rabbits, for example, have dichromate systems, that is, two receptors, while pigeons and ducks have tetra-chromate systems, that is, four receptors. These other creatures, therefore, cannot see the world of colour that humans see and similarly humans are at a loss to know what the world of colour looks like to a duck or a rabbit. Which is reality? The question is meaningless because specific evolutionary histories have produced one of a number of possible visual systems for each species. Evolutionary history has operated to select, to call forth or enact, one of a number of possible worlds for a particular species.

Maturana and Varela present evidence for their view that the human brain does not simply register stimuli but creates patterns associated with them. The brain does not process information or act as a passive mirror of reality to form more or less accurate representations of the world. Instead, it is perturbed, or triggered, by external stimuli into actively constructing global patterns of electrochemical activity. Furthermore, these patterns are not stored in specific parts of the brain because each time a stimulus is presented to the body, the brain constructs a pattern anew that involves whole ensembles of neurons in many different parts of the brain. This leads

Maturana and Varela to conclude that the nervous system does not simply represent a world; rather, it creates, calls forth or enacts a world. The world people act into is the world they have created by acting into it. In other words, Maturana and Varela adopt a constructivist perspective rather than the cognitivist one usually underlying the theory of strategic choice and many views of the learning organisation.

This change in the underlying theory of psychology is important because it presents a serious challenge to the cognitivist underpinnings of the theories of strategic choice and the learning organisation. It presents a view of mental process as one of perpetual construction, thereby moving away from the notion that brains faithfully represent an external reality and also any idea of the brain as storing and retrieving representations in any simple way. The Maturana and Varela perspective brings bodily action to the forefront and develops the notion of enactment, that is, of humans acting into what they have constructed.

However, the individual is still held to be primary and the theory is still a systems theory. They present a theory of autopoietic systems (*see* Chapter 6) where the individual, understood as a system, is the fundamental unit of analysis and the conservation of individual identity as the fundamental principle. Here, individuals are bounded, self-determining entities. The constructivist position is not inconsistent with the notion of mental models since it can be taken to be an alternative way of understanding how mental models are constructed. The individual mind is then functioning purely in terms of an identity, on one side of a boundary, constructing variations in itself, triggered by changes in other identities contained within their boundaries.

Enactment and sense making in organisations

One influential writer on organisations who adopts a constructivist approach is Weick (1995). He emphasises enactment and also the role of storytelling in communities of practice as processes of sense making, which have the following features:

1. Active agents place stimuli in some kind of framework so that they can comprehend, explain, attribute, extrapolate and predict. Weick often uses the metaphor of a map and talks about individual mental models.

2. Individuals form conscious and unconscious anticipations and assumptions as predictions of what they expect to encounter, and sense making is triggered when there is a discrepancy between such expectations and what they encounter. The need for explanation is triggered by surprise and takes the form of retrospective accounts to explain those surprises. Meaning is ascribed retrospectively as an output of a sense-making process and does not arise concurrently with the detection of difference.

3. Sense making is the process people employ to cope with interruptions of ongoing activity.

4. It is a process of reciprocal interaction of information seeking and meaning ascription, that is, it includes environmental scanning, interpretation and associated responses.

5. A distinction may be drawn between generic (collective) and intersubjective (individual-relating) forms of sense making.

Weick regards sense making as both an individual and a social activity and argues that it attends to both how a 'text' is constructed and how it is interpreted, to both creation/invention and discovery. He argues that sense making is grounded in identity construction, where identities are constructed in the process of interaction between people. He emphasises its retrospective nature, where meaning is the kind of attention directed to experience. Sense making is a process of relating in which people co-create, or enact, their environment. This leads him to place particular emphasis on talk, discourse, conversation, storytelling and narrative. In this process, people notice, extract and embellish cues, which he regards as the simple, familiar structures from which people develop a larger sense of what may be occurring. For him, the metaphor of a 'seed' captures the open-ended quality of sense making because a seed is a form-producing process. He quotes Shotter (1983), who describes how an acorn limits the tree that grows from it to an oak tree but does not specify it exactly. Rather, it grows unpredictably. Notice here how this assumes a theory of formative causality (*see* Chapter 2).

Weick ascribes particular importance to novel moments in the process of sense making. He locates the origins of novelty in dissonance, surprise, gaps, differences, disruptions, unexpected failures and uncertainty. For him it is events of this kind that trigger sense making, which could produce novel explanations. He describes the process as one that involves emotion and is necessarily confusing. What he does not question is the split between individual and social and the dual causality that goes with it.

Box 4.2 lists the key points about knowing that are made by cognitivist psychology.

So far, I have been describing two theories of mental models, namely, the cognitivist theory in which mental models are internal representations of external reality and constructivist theory in which mental models are active constructions that create the world that people act into. Whatever the perspective, however, learning has to do with changing mental models. A very influential theory of learning as change in mental models derives from the work of Bateson (1972) and later that of Argyris and Schön (1978). They distinguish between single- and double-loop learning.

Single- and double-loop learning

A person would function very slowly if for every action that person had consciously to retrieve and examine large numbers of previously acquired mental models and then choose an appropriate one. Experts therefore act on previously acquired models

Box 4.2	**Constructivist psychology: main points on human knowing**

- The biological individual is at the centre of human knowing.
- Individual brains do not represent a given world but rather actively select the world into which they act. They therefore create or enact their worlds.
- Sense making is triggered by discrepancies between what people expect and what they encounter.

which have become unconscious. One process of learning, therefore, involves the repetition of an action in order to make the design of later similar actions an automatic process. The expert seems to use some form of recognisable pattern in a new situation automatically to trigger the use of past models developed in relation to analogous previous situations. Experts do not examine the whole body of their expertise when they confront a new situation. Instead, they detect recognisable similarity in the qualitative patterns of what they observe and automatically produce models which they modify to meet the new circumstances. This is single-loop learning. Each time people act they learn from the consequences of the action to improve the next action, without having consciously to retrieve and examine the unconscious models being used to design the action.

But expert behaviour based on single-loop learning and unconscious mental models brings not only benefits; it also carries with it significant dangers. The fact that the mental models being used to design actions are unconscious means that they are not being questioned. The more expert one is, the more rapidly one acts on the basis of unconscious models. This means that one more easily takes for granted the assumptions and simplifications upon which the mental models are inevitably built. This is efficient in stable circumstances but when those circumstances change rapidly it becomes dangerous. The possibility of skilled incompetence (Argyris, 1990) then arises. The more expert people are, that is, the more skilled they are in designing certain actions, the greater the risk that they will not question what they are doing. It follows that they are more likely to become skilled incompetents. This gives rise to the need for double-loop learning. Here people learn not only in the sense of adjusting actions in the light of their consequences, but in the sense also of questioning and adjusting the unconscious mental models being used to design those actions in the first place.

There may well be a difference between espoused models and models in use (Argyris and Schön, 1978). Experts are quite likely to say one thing and do another. The more expert people become in working together as a group the more prone they are to do this. Ask managers what they do and most will say that they organise and plan. Observe what managers actually do and you may see that they dash from one task to another in a manner that is not very organised or planned.

When it is recognised that there are frequent differences between what expert managers say they are doing and what they are actually doing, differences of which they themselves are not usually aware, it can be seen how easy it is for managers to play games and build organisational defences against facing up to what is really happening (Argyris, 1990). For example, most managers espouse a rational model of action and believe that they should uncover the facts and consider a sensible range of options before they take action. Most espouse free and open discussions because that is a rational position to take. But at the same time there is a widespread norm in organisations requiring subordinates to withhold the truth from their superiors, especially if they believe that the superior will find the truth unwelcome and accuse them of being negative. Games of deception and cover-up are therefore played. All know they are being played but none openly discusses what is happening, despite espousal of rational behaviour. Managers sometimes say one thing, but do the direct opposite, and rarely find this strange. Add to this the existence of skilled incompetence and you can see how very difficult it will be to change these games and break down these defences. Attempts to explain how strategic management is actually carried out and attempts to prescribe how to do it better will be misleading and perhaps dangerous unless they explicitly recognise the existence of skilled incompetence, the difference between espoused models and models in use, and the behavioural dynamics these lead to.

Double-loop learning begins when people question their own unique mental models and when together they start questioning the mental models they share with each other. As soon as they do this they arouse fears to do with failing to produce anything that functions in place of what they are destroying, as well as the fear of embarrassing themselves and others with questioning and discussion that may appear incompetent, or threatening or even crazy. As soon as such fears are aroused, people automatically defend themselves by activating defence routines of one kind or another. The raising of such defensive routines in an organisational setting is what is meant by covert politics. It is a form of game playing that all are aware is going on but which all agree, tacitly, not to discuss (Argyris, 1990).

Defence routines become so entrenched in organisations that they come to be viewed as inevitable parts of human nature. Managers make self-fulfilling prophecies about what will happen at meetings, because they claim it is human nature; they indulge in the game playing, so confirming their belief in human nature. The defence routines, game playing and cover-ups can become so disruptive that managers actually avoid discussing contentious issues altogether. Even if this extreme is not reached, the dysfunctional learning behaviour blocks the detection of gradually accumulating small changes, the surfacing of different perspectives, the thorough testing of proposals through dialogue. When they use the control management model with the organisational defence routines it provokes, managers struggle to deal with strategic issues. They end up preparing long lists of strengths and weaknesses, opportunities and threats that simply get them nowhere. They produce mission statements that are so bland as to be meaningless, visions not connected to reality, and long-term plans that are simply filed. Or they may decide on an action and then not implement it.

Managers collude in this behaviour and refrain from discussing it. They then distance themselves from what is going on and blame others, the chief executive or the organisational structure when things go wrong. They look for solutions in general models, techniques, visions and plans. All the while the real causes of poor strategic management – the learning process itself, the political interaction and the group dynamic – remain stubbornly undiscussable.

People within an organisation collude in keeping matters undiscussable because they fear the consequences if they do not. Consultants too find themselves sucked into defence routines because they are nervous of the consequences of exposing them – they may be fired. The result of the defence routines is passive employees and managers, highly dependent upon authority, who are not well equipped to handle rapid change. In these conditions, managers produce vague, impractical prescriptions as a defence against having to do anything in difficult situations, such as 'we need more training' or 'we need a vision'. The organisation loses out on the creativity of people because of the management model it uses.

The way out of this impasse, proposed by Argyris, is for managers and managed to reflect jointly, as a group, on the processes they are engaged in. If this can be perceived as a challenge rather than a potential source of embarrassment and fear, then managers are able to engage in double-loop learning.

Double-loop learning, then, involves changing a mental model, a recipe, a mindset, a frame of reference or a paradigm. It is a very difficult process to perform simply because one is trying to examine assumptions one is not normally even aware one is making. People will therefore keep slipping into single-loop learning because that is easier. But it is important to encourage double-loop learning since it is this that produces innovation. Managers who would innovate need constantly to be shifting, breaking and creating paradigms – they must engage in double-loop learning.

4.4 Building a shared vision and team learning: humanistic psychology

The fourth discipline of the learning organisation is that of building a shared vision. A shared vision inspires people to learn. It is a lofty goal and requires the skill of identifying inspiring pictures of the future. It is important that this vision should not be dictated but developed by people working together. The humanistic foundations of this idea are evident.

The final discipline of the learning organisation is that of team learning. Senge maintains that teams can learn and when they do the intelligence of the team exceeds that of the individual members and produces extraordinary results. When this happens the individuals learn more rapidly too.

Teams and shared models

Managers do not act as isolated individuals but interact with each other in teams or groups. According to organisational learning theory, individuals learn to share the mental models they use simply by being part of a group. In this way they cut down on the communication and information flows that are required before they can act together. In particular, the more they share those implicit, expert models that have been rendered unconscious, the less they need to communicate in order to secure cohesive action. This sharing of implicit models is what is meant by the culture of the group or the organisation in learning organisation theory. Groups and organisations develop cultures, company and industry recipes or retained memories, as they perform together, in order to speed up their actions.

Individuals who are part of any group are put under strong pressure by group processes to conform, that is, to share the mental models of the other members. While this may have great benefits in terms of efficient action in stable conditions, it becomes a serious liability when conditions are changing rapidly. It then becomes necessary to question the implicit, unconscious group models that are being used to design actions. As conditions change, the unquestioned models may well become inappropriate. The powerful pressures that grow up within groups of experts to accept rather than question very fundamental values open up the strong possibility of skilled incompetence in group behaviour, of groupthink.

The kind of group that learning organisation theory focuses on is the team and the key question is what kind of team performs double-loop learning effectively. The basic premise is that this will happen when people can engage in true dialogue rather than in the kind of defensive conversational cover-ups discussed in the previous section. This requires that members of a group trust each other enough to expose their shared assumptions to public scrutiny. It is held that this is possible only when the team is cohesive, that is, when there is good team spirit. Today, organisations spend considerable sums of money to provide social and training events where teams can be together in the belief that this fosters the required team spirit. In addition, attention is paid to the composition of the team in terms of different personality types. It is believed that a balance of different personality types will enable a team to function and learn effectively.

The basis of team learning is said to be dialogue and Senge's discussion of dialogue is based on the views of Bohm (1965, 1983; Bohm and Peat, 1989). According to Bohm, dialogue means the free flow of meaning through a group of people, allowing them to discover insights not attainable individually. This is a collective phenomenon that occurs when a group of people becomes open to the flow of a larger intelligence. Bohm talks about a new kind of mind that comes into existence. People are said to participate in this pool of common meaning, which is not accessible individually. He talks about the whole organising the parts. The whole here is this common pool of meaning, a kind of transcendent mind analogous to the idea in quantum physics that the universe is an indistinguishable whole. This is Bohm's idea of an implicate order that is unfolded by experience. The parts in this way of thinking are individual mental maps that guide and shape individual perceptions. Here, Bohm is clearly thinking in terms of formative causality, in which the future is the unfolding of what is already enfolded as implicate order, rendering any true novelty impossible. This idea of an already enfolded implicate order is expressed in the notion of a common pool of meaning, a kind of transcendent whole or group mind that people access when they interact with each other in dialogue. Bohm takes a perspective in which there is *both* a collective pool of meaning *and* an individual mind that is shaped by the common pool, quite outside individuals, in dialogue.

For Bohm and Senge, then, dialogue is a special kind of collaborative conversation, quite distinct from discussion, which is primarily competitive. Dialogue, as special conversation with a life of its own, is said to be rare nowadays and the call is for a return to ancient wisdom, to ways characteristic of so-called 'more primitive' people who used to practise it. North American Indians are often given as an example of the few people who still practise it today. Senge says that when we do (rarely) experience dialogue nowadays, it is a chance product of circumstance. So he calls for systematic effort and disciplined practice of the art of dialogue, which we need to rediscover to satisfy a deep longing. If we do it right we will all win. In order to do it right, people have to participate in a particular way: they must suspend, that is, be aware of, their assumptions; they must regard each other as colleagues and friends; and there should be a facilitator present who holds the context. Resistance and defensive routines are then diminished and dialogue can take place. Bohm claims that in these circumstances people can become observers of their own thinking and that once they see the participative nature of their thought they separate themselves from it. Conflict then becomes conflict between thoughts and not conflict between people. Dialogue, therefore, offers a safe environment in which it can be balanced with discussion. Dialogue becomes a new tool and a prescription for management behaviour (Isaacs, 1999), although Bohm himself thought dialogue was virtually impossible in hierarchical organisations.

Team learning also requires skill in identifying factors that block true dialogue. These blockages must be recognised and surfaced. Senge claims that it is teams rather than individuals that learn. It is important to notice how Senge handles this question of the individual and the team. It sounds as though he is making the group primary to the individual. However, this is not so. Although he says that it is the team that learns, when he develops what he means by team learning it is clear that he is saying that an effective team provides the context within which a number of individuals together learn more than they could on their own. It is still the individuals who learn. They arrive to form a team and the atmosphere of that team then affects their capacity for learning together. Part 3 will take a very different view of the relationship between the individual and the group, arguing that individual minds are formed by the group while they form it at the same time. This perspective also takes a very different view of the nature of conversation, avoiding the positing of a special form called dialogue in the way that Bohm and Senge do.

The move to the mystical

For Senge, then, the notion of dialogue is an essential aspect of the learning organisation and it is understood as an activity enabling people to come into contact with a rather mysterious pool of 'common meaning'. This notion is greatly elaborated by one of Senge's collaborators, Scharmer, who outlines a theory of learning as the sensing and enacting of emerging futures (Senge *et al.*, 2005). Scharmer distinguishes between two different sources of learning and argues that both are required for organisations to succeed. He calls the first 'reflecting on the experiences of the past' and the second 'sensing and embodying emergent futures' *rather than* re-enacting the patterns of the past. One kind of learning is, therefore, relevant to the past and the other to the future.

The first kind of learning involves uncovering the past and bringing it into awareness as a process of 'presencing'. This occurs at the surface level of concrete experience. It is the cognitive process of downloading mental models and simply re-enacting old habits of thought. It also occurs below the surface level of action, involving the uncovering of common will and the changing of consciousness and then embodying the changes in the form of behavioural routines and procedures. In other words, this is close to single-loop learning. The second kind of learning, to do with the future, is called generative learning, which is understood as cognitive processes involving the reframing of mental models, that is, double-loop learning. This requires the special conversational process called dialogue. It also requires imagination, which is described as becoming aware through the redirection of attention from an object to its source. Scharmer talks about generative learning as the deepest level and presents it as an essentially mystical experience, the manifestation, or coming into awareness, of a deeper, hidden reality. Here, individual intention is at one with the intention of the emerging whole. It is a process of bringing the emerging whole into reality 'as *it* desires', rather than as the ego desires, and this is what he means by the coming into presence of the emerging future.

Presencing is a process of becoming aware that involves taking off one's self-created cognitive filters, turning inward to the source of oneself, redirecting attention from current reality to an emergent reality, and letting go, that is, emptying or surrendering to a deeper higher will. Scharmer then adds another stage, which he calls 'letting come'. For him surrender means switching from 'looking for' to 'letting come', a phase of quickening or crystallisation in which one allows the arrival of the highest possible future, the highest presence, the highest Self. What is received is an emerging heightened quality of will and a more tangible vision of what the individual and the group want to create. The language is strikingly mystical.

The key question for generative learning is how to access this level, for it is here that transformation occurs, where transformation is understood as the coming into presence of emerging futures. Scharmer emphasises that presencing is as much a collective phenomenon as it is an individual one and by this he seems to mean that individuals fuse together into the collective when they reach this stage. Scharmer describes presencing as a mystery and says that it is a mode of relating in which the individual relates to the collective whole of the community, team and organisation. In this state people become more 'selfless' and become aligned with their true selves and with the intention of the emerging whole. Scharmer's understanding of generative learning, therefore, is one of accessing, even immersing in, a transcendent whole. It is essentially a mystical process in which there is participation in a mystical whole. This amounts to postulating a transcendent system and ascribing to it an actual intention rather than the 'as if' intention to be found in Kantian thinking. Emergence means bringing into being what this transcendent system desires.

For Scharmer, transformation is the enactment of a deep spiritual process in which individuals fuse into a common will. The origin of transformation, and thus novelty, lies in a transcendent whole that is brought into being, is presenced, by the basically meditative practices of a group of people. Individuals and groups are simultaneously transformed but this is in no way paradoxical because the individuals and the group are fused. The process is the same and there is nothing contradictory in terms of individual and group. There is no mention of difference, conflict or power, which implicitly play no part whatsoever in the transformative process. The social is not thought of as a responsive relating of a co-operative/competitive nature but as fusion in a transcendent whole. Participation means individuals participating in a transcendent whole.

The theory of causality is clear. Individuals fuse together and submerge in the 'whole', the transcendent system. This system is the formative cause of action in that action is clearly understood as unfolding the enfolded will of the whole. Scharmer suggests that this is transformative causality, but if it is then it is of a mystical kind.

Scharmer says that it is the role of leaders to choose the learning level at which to operate. The key challenge for leaders is how to enable teams to uncover layers of reality that will move them from one level of learning to another. Scharmer defines leadership as the activity of shifting the place from which a system operates and he defines this as shifting the conversation from talking 'nice' and talking 'tough' to reflective and generative dialogues. Generative dialogues lead to an intentional quietness or sacred silence. The only sustainable tool for leading change is the leader's self as the capacity of the 'I' to transcend the boundaries of its current organisation and operate from the emerging, larger whole, both individually and collectively. The leader's role is to create the conditions that allow others to shift the place from which their system operates. The leader, then, is understood as an autonomous individual standing outside the system and choosing the level at which to operate. Causality here is of the rationalist kind.

This immediately exposes the dual causality typical of systems thinking. There is a transcendent system of which individuals become a part in order to transform and there is an autonomous leader standing outside this and deciding whether to operate at that level. This is clearly 'both . . . and' thinking that eliminates paradox. The 'both . . . and' nature of the thinking is evident in the postulation of *both* a system with an actual intention/desire *and* autonomous individuals who create conditions for shifting the system.

So far, this chapter has been describing the key features and assumptions of organisational learning theories, focusing in particular on what has been the most influential variant of these theories, at least in terms of the impact on organisational practitioners. It started by identifying the theory of human interaction on which organisational learning perspectives are built. This is a view in which an organisation is understood as a system interacting with other systems in a supra-system, all understood in terms of systems dynamics. The chapter then identified the cognitivist and constructivist theories of individual psychology as the basis for understanding how individuals, as aspects of the system, learn. The important concept here is that of mental models and how learning takes the form of either single-loop learning where mental models remain the same or double-loop learning where individuals consciously engineer changes in their own mental models. Organisational learning theories identify what the obstacles to such double-loop learning are and present prescriptions for overcoming them. In essence the prescription is to work in cohesive teams in a harmonious way using a special conversational form called dialogue. The chapter then went on to describe how easily this line of thought slips into mysticism, taking us back to what we started with, namely, the system, now understood as a mystical, transcendent whole into which 'good', selfless people submerge themselves. The reflection of humanistic psychology is clear.

Of course, not all organisational learning theorists make this move to the mystical. Others point to the importance of power, politics and vested interests in organisational learning. The next section looks at these perspectives.

4.5 The impact of vested interests on organisational learning

A previous section looked at how attempts to learn in a double-loop way can give rise to a number of fears, such as the fear of failing, of being embarrassed and of embarrassing others. These fears tend to trigger defensive routines, game playing and covert politics that block the learning. The whole point of double-loop learning is to bring about organisational change and it is highly likely that change of an important kind will alter power relations between people. Change threatens vested interests and the prospect of losing power is likely to trigger action to prevent this from happening. That action is also likely to block the process of double-loop learning. In other words, the nature of an organisation's political system, the way in which power is used, is likely to have an important impact on its capacity to learn.

Authoritarian use of power

The authoritarian use of power may be relatively benign when it is based on legitimate positions in the hierarchy and exercised according to the accepted procedures of the organisation. This is likely to be accompanied by a group dynamic of compliance, especially when followers strongly share the same ideology. Compliance amounts to the suspension of intellectual and moral judgement about the appropriateness of superiors' choices and actions. People then willingly do what the powerful want (Bacharach and Lawler, 1980). Clearly this is incompatible with double-loop learning. Where power is exercised as force over unwilling followers the dynamic tends to be much more volatile. It is characterised by sullen acceptance, covert resistance and at times outright rebellion. Again, this is inimical to double-loop learning.

Collegial use of power

Highly authoritarian political systems based on mechanistic rules are, however, rather rare in practice. There is far more likely to be a complex pluralistic political system in which power is already spread around an organisation in groups with vested interests (Greiner and Schein, 1988). Thus, the typical modern corporation does not have a political system in which one or two powerful executives at the top control what goes on throughout the company. Instead there are powerful subsidiary companies and powerful departments in many different parts of the organisation and those at the top have to sustain enough support to govern. Any change of notable significance is going to affect the balance of power, making one department, subsidiary company or management grouping weaker or stronger than it was before. Any sign of change will touch off fears that such power shifts might occur even before it is clear what they might be. People and groups will therefore start taking protective action as soon as they get wind of any possible change.

Any attempt to engage in double-loop learning, to change mental models, is likely to be just such a change, one that is directly concerned with changing power positions. It is therefore highly likely to touch off political activities that undermine and perhaps eventually destroy learning. The more people are persuaded to move to a consensus collegiate way of making choices, the more powerful groups with vested interests are threatened and the more likely they are to put a stop to the programme. The more managers try to head off this threat, the more they have to play by the rules of the political system they are trying to replace. If they do this they simply reinforce what they are trying to remove.

Power vacuums and organised anarchies

If managers do succeed in installing a collegial political system and the commitment management model, other behaviours may be activated by the shift in the distribution of power.

As authority and other forms of power are dispersed, as organisational structures are flattened, as job descriptions become looser and as the establishment of widespread consensus comes to be required before decisions are possible, so the likelihood of a power vacuum at the centre increases. It becomes more and more difficult for anyone to exercise much authority; more and more people have to be able to handle their own independence. In situations in which most people seek the comfort of dependence this could create serious difficulties. One way of understanding the consequences of changes in power distribution is provided by Greiner and Schein (1988).

Greiner and Schein relate changes in willingness to assert and to accept power to the consequent group dynamic. When both leaders and followers consent freely to the exercise of power, there is a high probability of active consensus. When the leader exerts power but the followers do not consent, then we get the behaviour of covert resistance. As the leader becomes less able or willing to exert power, while followers still look for a lead, then the behaviour is that of passive loyalty. If, in the same circumstances, the followers too become less willing to accept the exercise of power, the group's behaviour is characterised by peer rivalry. So the dispersal of power and the spread of participation could set off feedback loops in which declining central power leads to greater rivalry throughout the organisation, or to passive loyalty, both of which will block double-loop learning.

4.6 Knowledge management: cognitivist and constructivist psychology

The theory of the learning organisation discussed in previous sections is reflected in the more recent interest in knowledge management. Many argue that the global change towards the knowledge economy has major implications for the strategic management of organisations. First, professional knowledge workers need to be managed in different ways from manual workers in the industrial age. The argument is that to unleash the creativity of knowledge workers they must be empowered so that they can participate more fully in the development of the organisation and special measures need to be taken to ensure that individual knowledge becomes organisational knowledge. Many argue that this is to be done by codifying the knowledge held by key knowledge workers and by taking steps to retain their services. The new knowledge economy also has major implications for the nature of an organisation's assets. In the industrial age, accounting measures of asset values were close to the capital market valuation of the organisation because market pricing of the main assets, namely physical resources such as plant and equipment, enabled them to be measured. Managing the value of a corporation meant managing measurable physical assets and the 'human resources' who used them. In the new knowledge economy, however, knowledge is said to be the major asset and since it is not directly traded in markets, it is not measured and recorded in corporate balance sheets. As a result, enormous gaps have opened up between the asset values recorded by a corporation and the value that capital markets place on the corporation itself. This creates problems for managing assets to produce shareholder value. The response to this has been a call to measure the intellectual capital of a corporation and manage its knowledge assets.

Nonaka's writings (Nonaka, 1991a; Nonaka and Takeuchi, 1995) have exerted a major impact on the development of theories of knowledge creation in organisations (for example, Brown, 1991; Burton-Jones, 1999; Davenport and Prusak, 1998; Garven, 1993; Kleiner and Roth, 1997; Leonard and Strauss, 1997; Quinn *et al.*, 1996; Sveiby, 1997). Like Senge, Nonaka draws on the systems dynamics strand of systems thinking, including some concepts from chaos and complexity theories, which he treats as extensions of that thinking (*see* Chapter 8), and Argyris and Schon whose learning theories he traces back to Bateson (1972). In addition, he relies heavily on Polanyi's (1958, 1960) distinction between tacit and explicit knowledge.

Creating new knowledge

According to Nonaka (1991a), new knowledge is created when tacit knowledge is made explicit and crystallised into an innovation, that is, a re-creation of some aspect of the world according to some new insight or ideal. New knowledge, according to Nonaka, comes from tapping the tacit, subjective insights, intuitions and hunches of individuals and making them available for testing and use by the organisation as a whole. For him, tacit knowledge is personal and hard to formalise. It is rooted in action and shows itself as skill, or know-how. In addition to being in technical skills, tacit knowledge lies in the mental models, beliefs and perspectives ingrained in the way people understand their world and act in it. Tacit knowledge is below the level of awareness and is therefore very difficult to communicate. The nature of explicit knowledge, however, is easy to understand: it is the formal and systematic knowledge that is easily communicated, for example in the form of product specifications or computer programs.

Nonaka gives an example of how tacit knowledge is to be tapped. In 1985, product developers at Matsushita could not perfect the kneading action of the home bread-baking machine they were developing. After much unhelpful analysis, including comparisons of X-rays of dough kneaded by the machine and dough kneaded by professionals, one member of the team proposed a creative approach. She proposed using a top professional baker as a model, so she trained with a top baker to acquire his kneading technique and after a year of trial and error she was able to help her colleagues reproduce a mechanical kneading action that mimicked that of the professional. This example describes a movement between different kinds of knowledge, the tacit and the explicit:

- tacit to tacit as the product developer acquires the skill of the professional baker through mimicry;
- tacit to explicit as the product developer articulates the foundations of her newly acquired tacit knowledge to her colleagues;
- explicit to tacit as the colleagues internalise the knowledge and use it to alter their own tacit knowledge;
- explicit to explicit as the newly formulated product specifications are communicated to the production department and embodied in working models and final production processes.

Innovation then flows from a form of learning, that is, new knowledge creation, that in turn flows from moving knowledge between one type and another.

New knowledge starts with an individual, according to Nonaka. Tacit knowledge has to travel from one person to another, in a way that cannot be centrally intended because no one knows what is to travel, or to whom, until it has travelled. New knowledge can therefore be created only when individuals operate in empowered teams.

A key difficulty in the creation of new knowledge is that of bringing tacit knowledge to the surface of individual awareness, conveying tacit knowledge from one person to another, and finally making it explicit. This is so difficult because it requires expressing the inexpressible and this needs figurative rather than literal language. As new knowledge is dispersed through a group and an organisation, it must be tested, which means that there must be discussion, dialogue and disagreement.

The distinction Nonaka makes between tacit and explicit knowledge is derived from Polanyi (Polanyi and Prosch, 1975). Nonaka and Takeuchi maintain that 'knowledge is created and expanded through social interaction between tacit and explicit knowledge' (1995, p. 61) in the four modes of knowledge conversion described above. However, as Tsoukas points out, Polanyi was actually arguing that tacit and explicit knowledge are not two separate forms of knowledge, but rather that 'tacit knowledge is the necessary component of all knowledge' (Tsoukas, 1997, p. 10).

Another point to note is how Nonaka and Takeuchi (1995) talk about knowledge as embodied, rooted in experience and arising in interaction between individuals. They emphasise the importance of dialogue and discussion in this conversion process (p. 13), pointing to the importance of intuition, hunches, metaphors and symbols (p. 12). They see knowledge as essentially related to action and arising from a process in which interacting individuals are committed to justifying their beliefs. They talk about knowledge as justified belief closely related to people's values. They talk about the context of ambiguity and redundancy in which knowledge is created (p. 12). However, they then take their argument in a direction that leaves the importance of relationships and the social undeveloped and unexplored. Having emphasised the social, they locate the initiation of new knowledge in the individual when they argue that 'knowledge is created only by individuals' (p. 59).

In this way of seeing things, tacit knowledge is possessed by individuals and the knowledge creation at an organisational level is the extraction of this already existing tacit knowledge from individuals and its spread across the organisation by socialising processes. This leads to a rather linear sequential view of individuals passing tacit knowledge to others, primarily through imitation, then formalising and codifying it so that it can be used. The emphasis of Nonaka and Takeuchi on the individual as the origin of knowledge leads them to emphasise the organisation-wide intentional character of knowledge creation. Having emphasised the ambiguity of the situation in which knowledge arises, Nonaka and Takeuchi leave this behind and move to the strategic choice view of knowledge creation. Nonaka and Takeuchi do not pay much attention to the ever-present possibility of groups of people becoming stuck in some stable dynamic, or some fragmenting one that kills off the knowledge-creating process. What Nonaka and Takeuchi end up with, then, is a process for knowledge creation that can be managed and controlled.

Knowledge management writers focus attention on this process of translation but do not explain how completely new tacit knowledge comes to arise in individual heads.

4.7 Communities of practice

Another approach to organisational learning and knowledge creation that has attracted considerable attention from organisational practitioners is the notion of communities of practice (Brown and Duguid, 1991; Lave and Wenger, 1991; Wenger, 1998). Wenger (1998) regards engagement in social practice as the fundamental process through which people learn and so become who they are, thereby making a close link between social practice and identity formation. Not only do people form communities of social practice, they also are formed by the process of learning in which they engage in their communities of practice. From this perspective, then, one can think of an organisation as a community of practice, that is, as a collective identity that shapes and is shaped by individual identities. An organisation then becomes what it becomes, it forms strategies, in the learning process of a community of practice.

Wenger builds a theory of *community*, social *practice*, *meaning* and *identity*, in which learning is a process of social *participation*. Learning is not simply an individual process but the lived experience of participation in local situations in the world as the production and reproduction of specific ways of *engaging* in the world. Through *local interactions*, learning *reproduces and transforms* the social structure in which it takes place and the *identities* of those who participate. These are all matters that will be very much the focus of attention in Part 3 of this book. However, the explanation it will put forward is significantly different from that of Wenger.

First consider Wenger's definition of the key concepts in his argument. For him, practice is essentially an experience of everyday life, and meaning is located in the process of negotiating meaning. *Practice is essentially the process of negotiating meaning.* He closely associates practice with the formation of communities, defined as those engaged together on a joint enterprise. It is this joint enterprise that distinguishes communities of practice from cultures and social structures. Practice is the source of coherence in communities of practice and it has three dimensions: *mutual engagement* in actions whose meaning is being negotiated; *joint enterprise*, which is a collective process of negotiation creating relations of mutual accountability; and *shared repertoire* consisting of routines, words, ways of doing, stories, gestures, symbols and genres.

Wenger describes (1998, pp. 96–7) these three dimensions as 'interdependent and interlocked into a tight system' combining 'an open process (the negotiation of meaning) and a tight system of interrelations'. He talks about small perturbations rapidly having 'repercussions throughout the system' so that learning 'involves a close interaction of order and chaos'. Practice as a shared history of learning creates discontinuities between those participating and those not, and in so doing creates boundaries and also connections with other communities across boundaries. Wenger associates learning with *boundary* crossing. Furthermore, a practice is local but there are interactions between local and global *levels*. What I am stressing here is the way in which Wenger uses the terminology of systems thinking and its central concepts such as boundaries and hierarchical levels.

Running throughout Wenger's exposition there is the central role accorded to the negotiation of meaning. This is the centrepiece of his theory, so how does he understand this process?

The negotiation of meaning

Wenger understands the negotiation of meaning to be a process and distances his theory from functional, cybernetic or system-theoretical accounts. When he does this (Wenger, 1998, p. 286, n. 5), he means something quite specific. He wants to exclude things (like computers) from the status of participant in the negotiation of meaning. He does not want to think in terms of a total system in which both things and persons are actors. He wants to understand how meaning is negotiated, and only people can negotiate and recognise experience of meaning in each other. However, as I have already pointed to above, he does refer to the dimensions of learning as interlocked into a tight system, to interrelations between people as a tight system, and to the importance of boundaries. So it seems to me that while he mostly talks in terms of the process of negotiation, he does couple it with a notion of a system of interrelationship.

How does he think about the negotiation of meaning as a process? He argues that the negotiation of meaning is the interplay of two constituent processes that form a duality. He calls these processes participation and reification. Participation is an active process of human bodies, of human persons, engaging together in a practice. The actions are the personal and social acts of doing, teaching, talking, conversing, thinking, reflecting, feeling and belonging. Participation is a process characterised by mutual recognition, which is a source of identity.

Reification is also a process of engagement with the world but this time it has to do with things. Reification is the production of the artefacts of a practice and they embody a long diverse process of reification. It is a process in which people project meanings on to the world and then perceive those meanings as existing in the world and having a life of their own. In reification we project ourselves onto the world, do not recognise ourselves in our projections and attribute to our meanings an independent existence. Reification *gives form to our experience*, so creating points of focus around which negotiation is organised. An understanding is given form and the form becomes the focus.

They are *both* distinct *and* complementary in that they come about through each other. The negotiation of meaning is the seamless interweaving of these two distinct and complementary processes and the experience of meaning is this duality. A duality is a single conceptual unit formed by two inseparable and mutually constitutive elements whose inherent tension and complementarity give the concept richness and diversity. Taken together, participation and reification are inseparable elements of the duality of the negotiation of meaning. This is not a paradox because although they interweave at the same time in tension with each other, they are distinct processes in which there is no inherent contradiction. They are dual modes of existence through time because they exist in different realms (Wenger, 1998, p. 87). They continually converge and diverge, unfolding in different media. The duality operates as follows. Participation organises itself around reifications such as words. Conversation is said to be a powerful form of communication because it is the interweaving of participation, the action of talking to and mutually recognising each other, and of reification, the words or argument we are using. The words (reification) take advantage of shared participation to create shortcuts to communicational meaning, while participation produces and uses reification.

As I understand it, Wenger is saying that communities of practice are fundamentally social processes of negotiating meaning, which is the same as learning. Participation and reification are distinct processes, or modes of existence, operating in different realms, in different media with their own laws. However, they are also complementary and the process of negotiating meaning is the continuous interplay of the processes of participation and reification, which together constitute an inseparable, interwoven unity. The realm of participation is the actions and interactions of people. It is their doing, talking, thinking, feeling, reflecting and belonging. The realm of reification is another mode of existence, namely the process of projecting meaning on to objects, that is, artefacts, tools or abstractions treated as if they were things. In addition to material artefacts and tools, reifications are also all symbols, including language, and also any bodily expression of feeling, or communication such as glances and silences.

What Wenger is doing, I think, is moving from a micro-description of communities of practice to an abstract, macro-level explanation of the process. He provides a detailed description of the ordinary, daily experience of a woman engaged in a community of practice of claims processors. In constructing a theory to illuminate and explain their practice, he moves away from the daily lived experience and talks in terms of abstract (in the sense of removed from direct experience) macro processes called 'negotiation of meaning', 'participation' and 'reification'. In doing this he splits the experience of action and interaction into two distinct but complementary aspects constituting the unity of a duality. In other words he adopts a 'both . . . and' mode of thinking in that his view of experience as the negotiation of meaning consists of *both* participation *and* reification.

Wenger says that learning cannot be designed but that it is a response to design. For him, designs then lead to a learning response and he implies some degree of control exercised by the designer over at least the occurrence of learning. Wenger's move to talking about designing participation and reification implicitly suggests that someone can step out of the processes and design the whole, while others in the community of practice are subjected to the designed aspects of participation and reification. This, it seems to me, creates a problem for personal freedom because persons are subject to these macro processes of participation and reification which have a life of their own.

4.8 Key debates

As with strategic choice theory, the notion of organisational learning has generated much debate. Two key debates are briefly reviewed in this section: representation versus enactment; and the learning organisation versus organisational learning.

Representation versus enactment

This is the debate between cognitivist and constructivist psychology, which has been mentioned above. Cognitivism takes the representational perspective in holding that the human mind constructs accurate representations of an already given reality. These representations are then built into mental models that form the basis upon which people act into the real world. Cognitivists accept that mental models can become inappropriate in a changing world and therefore become inappropriate for action requiring the double-loop process of learning in which mental models are changed. They accept that people are interpreting their world and in a sense constructing it through their interpretation. What they are constructing, their interpretation, can be appropriate in that it is an accurate interpretation of the real world or it may be inappropriate in the sense of an inaccurate representation. This is a view in which thought comes before action. Constructivism goes further than this and takes an enactment perspective in arguing that the human body actively selects what it is able to pay attention to and so constructs the reality into which it acts. This is a view in which thought comes after action in that the world is first constructed in action and then understood. These differences will be returned to in Chapter 7.

Learning organisation or organisational learning: the individual versus the group

Do organisations learn or is it individuals and groups in organisations who learn? If one thinks that it is individuals and groups *inside* an organisation that learn then one focuses attention on individual and collective learning processes. If it is thought that it is organisations that learn then attention is focused on what it is about an organisation that makes learning possible. A distinction along these lines is used by Easterby-Smith and Araujo (1999) to identify two strands in the literature to do with organisations and learning. They distinguish between the literature on *organisational learning* and that on the *learning organisation*. They say that the former 'has concentrated on the detached observation and analysis of the processes involved in individual and collective learning inside organizations' (p. 2). The literature on the learning organisation, on the other hand, is concerned with 'methodological tools which can help to identify, promote and evaluate the quality of learning processes inside organizations' (p. 2) and in so doing this literature identifies 'templates, or ideal forms, which real organizations could attempt to emulate' (p. 2). Easterby-Smith and Araujo argue that there is a growing divide between the two strands. Those writing in the organisational learning tradition are interested in 'understanding the nature and processes of learning' (p. 8). Those writing in the tradition of the learning organisation are more interested in 'the development of normative models and methodologies for creating change in the direction of improved learning processes' (p. 8).

Easterby-Smith and Araujo distinguish between a technical and a social strand in the organisational learning literature. The technical strand takes the view that organisational learning is a matter of processing, interpreting and responding to quantitative and qualitative information, which is generally explicit and in the public domain. Key writers in this tradition are Argyris and Schon (1978) with their notions of single- and double-loop learning. The social strand focuses attention on how people make sense of their work practices (Weick, 1995). This strand utilises Polanyi's distinction between tacit and explicit knowledge (Polanyi and Prosch, 1975). It focuses attention on the socially constructed nature of knowledge (Brown and Duguid, 1991), the political processes involved (Coopey, 1995) and the importance of cultural and socialisation processes (Lave and Wenger, 1991). The literature on the learning organisation also displays technical and social interests. The former tends to focus on interventions based on measurement and information systems, while the latter focuses on individual and group learning processes in a normative manner (Isaacs, 1999; Nonaka and Takeuchi, 1995; Senge, 1991).

However, the claim that *organisations* learn amounts to both reification and anthropomorphism. We slip into thinking that an organisation is a thing, even an organism or living thing, that can learn. To sustain the claim that an organisation is in any sense a living organism, we would need to point to where this living *body* is.

Since an organisation is neither inanimate thing nor living body, in anything other than metaphorical terms, it follows that an organisation can neither think nor learn. But the alternative is not all that satisfactory either. To claim that it is only *individuals* who learn is to continue with the major Western preoccupation with the autonomous individual and to ignore the importance of social processes. One might try to deal with this objection by saying that it is *both individuals and groups* who learn. But that runs into the same objection as saying that organisations learn. The claim that *groups* learn is also both reification and anthropomorphism. Furthermore, to talk about individuals who learn *in* organisations or *in* groups is also problematic because, once again, this implies that the group and the organisation exist somewhere as a different 'place' or 'level' from people. If this were not so, how could people be *in* a group or organisation? Part 3 will suggest an alternative to thinking in these ways, namely, that learning is an activity of interdependent people, exploring in a different way the emphasis that writers such as Wenger place on the socially constructed nature of knowledge.

4.9 How learning organisation theory deals with the four key questions

At the end of Chapter 1, I posed four questions that I would ask of each of the theories of organisational change that this book is concerned with. They were:

1. How does the theory view the nature of interaction?
2. What view does it take of human nature?
3. What methodology does it employ?
4. How does it deal with paradox?

Then in Chapter 3, I examined the answers to these questions suggested by strategic choice theory. Consider now how they are answered from the organisational learning perspective.

The nature of interaction

Learning organisation theories see interaction in systemic terms just as cybernetics does. They are concerned with how components, entities or individuals interact to produce a system. They understand the system in the terms of systems dynamics, and this, like cybernetics, is a theory that focuses on the macro level. They identify the feedback structure of the system. It does not attempt to model the micro detail of the entities constituting a dynamic system. Two assumptions are implicitly made about these entities, events or individuals in systems dynamics (Allen, 1998a):

- First, it is assumed that micro events occur at their average rate and that it is sufficient to take account of averages only. Interactions between entities are then homogeneous.

- Second, it is implicitly assumed that individual entities of a given type are identical, or, at least, that they have a normal distribution around the average type. The entities, or events, are thus implicitly assumed to be homogeneous. Within a category, distinctive identities and differences are not taken into account.

These assumptions make it possible to ignore the dynamics governing the micro entities, events or individuals and model the system at the macro level. This is done by specifying the structure of negative and positive feedback loops that drive the system. For example, the beer distribution system, described earlier in this chapter, is specified in terms of damping and amplifying loops between orders, inventories and shipments between the different components of the system, namely customers, retailers, wholesalers and producers. Nothing is said about how customers, retailers, wholesalers and producers are organised or how they make decisions. This kind of model yields insight into the dynamics of the system as a whole and the possibility of unexpected outcomes. The way systems dynamics is used in learning organisation theory amounts to adding positive feedback loops to a cybernetic system.

However, there are also major differences compared with cybernetics. Because of the presence of positive feedback loops the dynamic is no longer an automatic movement towards an equilibrium state. Instead, the system is a non-equilibrium one with the dynamics of fluctuating patterns that create considerable difficulties for prediction over longer time periods. However, it is claimed that if the feedback structure of the system is understood, then leverage points can be located. Action at these leverage points makes it possible to control the system. In the end, however, the theory of causality underlying systems dynamics is formative cause just as it is with cybernetics. In systems dynamics, the system unfolds archetypes already enfolded in it. People are still thought to be parts of a system and so not free. Because of its theory of causality, systems dynamics cannot explain novelty or creativity.

The nature of human beings

Learning organisation theory draws on cognitivist, constructivist and humanistic psychology to understand the nature of human beings. The cognitivist assumptions are particularly clear in that individuals are understood to act upon the basis of mental models built from previous experience and stored in the individual mind. They are representations of the individual's world. Part of each individual's model is shared with others and this forms the basis of their joint action together. The focus on the individual nature of these models, their representation function, the claim that they are stored and shared, the belief that they can be surfaced and subjected to rational scrutiny, are all hallmarks of a cognitivist psychology. However, the way in which mental models select some aspects of reality for atten-tion and exclude others is a feature of a constructivist approach to psychology. The emphasis placed on individual vision and fulfilment, as part of the learning process, is evidence of the humanistic leaning in the theory of the learning organisation.

In all of these psychological theories the individual is held to be prior and primary to the group. Mental models are individual constructs that are shared with others. Effective teams are composed of a balance of different types of individual. Note, however, how differences between individuals do not feature in a fundamental way in the learning organisation theory. A small number of different categories may be identified but the difference is located between categories, while within those categories everyone is implicitly assumed to be the same. This is consistent with a systems dynamics approach in which micro entities are all assumed to be average and their interactions are assumed to be homogeneous. What I am trying to emphasise is this: cohesion and sharing are seen as the foundations of effective learning. There is no notion that deviant and eccentric behaviour might be essential to any creative and innovative thinking and behaving. In Part 3, I will be arguing that organisations change in novel ways through deviant behaviour.

The group is treated in a particular way. It consists of individuals and develops in phases, only some of which are conducive to members learning together as individuals.

So, learning organisation theory uses the same psychological theories as strategic choice theory but does place more emphasis on emotion and relationships between people. It also identifies more clearly what may block people from changing and learning. Perhaps the importance of power receives more attention but power is still located in the individual. However, there is no fundamental change in the view of human action as one moves from the one theory to the other.

Methodology and organisational learning

The methodological stance in learning organisation theory is similar to that in strategic choice theory in some respects. A realist position is sometimes implied in which managers are assumed to be able to stand outside the system of which they are a part and think systemically about it. They are also supposed to be able to stand outside their own mental models, rigorously scrutinise them and then rationally change them. However, at other times an idealist position is suggested in that managers are assumed to respond not to the real world but to their idea of the real world as represented in their mental models.

Dealing with paradox

The notion of paradox does not play a fundamental part in learning organisation theory. Tensions, contradictions and dilemmas are certainly recognised but they are thought to be obstacles to learning and hopefully in the end resolvable. As with strategic choice theory, learning organisation theory takes a position at one of the poles of what seem to me to be fundamental paradoxes of organisational life. This is very clear in the case of the individual and the group. I argue above that this is not seen as a paradox at all. The individual is given primacy and understood to be in fundamental conflict with the group. This conflict must be resolved through building relationships of trust in teams if learning is to take place. Sameness and difference are not held in mind at the same time. For example, individuals within a personality category are treated as if they were all the same and all different from individuals in another category. Although unpredictability is pointed to, it is predictability and the possibility of control that are emphasised. As with strategic choice theory, order, stability, consistency and harmony are all seen as prerequisites for success and the role that the opposites of these might play in creativity is largely ignored.

Making sense of experience

The focus on learning, and what blocks it, provides a rich addition to strategic choice theory when it comes to making sense of my experience. I certainly recognise my own involvement in defence routines and political struggles. I also recognise the difficulty of learning in a fundamental way. However, I think the theory holds out a rather idealised picture of what it is possible for people in an organisation to do.

For example, Argyris (1990) reports that he has worked with large numbers of managers in many countries, coaching them to engage in double-loop learning. He reports that they find it difficult and rarely engage in it when they return to their workplace. Instead, they carry on with their win/lose dynamics and their defence routines. I think this immediately raises a question mark over his theory of learning as a change in mental models. Many organisations clearly do change, often in quite creative ways. How does this happen if double-loop learning is such a rarity? Furthermore, I wonder whether it really is possible for people to surface their mental models and change them. Where are they located? It is far from clear that brains store anything that could be correlated with a map or a model. If it is possible for people to identify assumptions of which they are unaware and change them, then why is mental illness so prevalent and difficult to deal with? I greatly doubt my own ability to identify whatever it is that makes me think the way I do, and then simply change it.

In the hurly-burly of organisational life, with its political intrigues and the possibility of losing one's job, is it at all wise to expose the defence routines that one is taking part in? If it is so important to do so, why is it so rare to find people doing it?

When I ask myself questions such as these I have serious doubts about the practicality of the prescriptions this theory presents for successful organisational learning. For example, the kind of conversation that the theory of organisational learning presents is a special kind called dialogue which has the rather mystical tones of people participating in a common pool of meaning as if it were an already existing whole outside of their experience. There seems to be no constructive place here for ordinary conversation. Also participation has a special meaning – participation in some whole system outside of our direct experience of interacting with each other (Griffin, 2002).

4.10 Summary

This chapter introduced systems dynamics theory and clarified how it differs from cybernetics. The most significant difference relates to the introduction of nonlinearity and positive feedback. The way in which positive feedback processes have been used to understand life in organisations was reviewed. From this it can be seen that a systems dynamics perspective presents a richer, more complex insight into the dynamics of life in organisations.

This chapter has also reviewed learning organisation theory. According to this theory, organisations are systems driven by both positive and negative feedback loops. The interactions between such loops tend to produce unexpected and often counterintuitive outcomes. Perfect control is not possible but it is possible to identify leverage points where control may be exerted. Perhaps the most important loops relate to learning. Organisations learn when people in cohesive teams trust each other enough to expose the assumptions they are making to the scrutiny of others and then together change shared assumptions which block change. The theory identifies some important behaviours that block this learning process. Although learning organisation theory uses a different systems theory from strategic choice theory, its conceptualisation of that systems theory in terms of feedback loops keeps it close to cybernetics. Learning organisation theory is built on the same psychological theories as strategic choice theory. Control and the primacy of the individual are central to both.

Further reading

Richardson (1991) provides an account of the use of feedback thinking in human systems and Senge's (1990) book gives a summary of systems thinking. Rush *et al.* (1989) explain how personality types affect decision making, as do Belbin (1981) and Kiersey and Bates (1978). Argyris (1990) is important reading. Critiques of learning organisation theory from a system perspective are to be found in Flood (1999) and from a process perspective in Griffin (2002). Wenger's (1998) book on communities of practice is an important source for understanding the notion of communities of practice.

Questions to aid further reflection

1. What theory of causality is reflected in systems dynamics?
2. How is the conceptualisation of control different in systems dynamics from that in cybernetics?
3. What are the basic features of constructivist psychology?
4. What implications do theories of organisational learning and knowledge creation have for strategy?
5. Can organisations learn?
6. Do you think it is possible for people to change their mental models?
7. If double-loop learning is as difficult for people as some writers claim then how do organisations change?

Chapter 5

Thinking in terms of organisational psychodynamics

Open systems and psychoanalytic perspectives

This chapter invites you to draw on your own experience to reflect on and consider the implications of:

- The nature of unconscious group processes in organisational life and the part that they play in the activities of managing and strategising.

- How people in organisations deal with the experience of anxiety, particularly the social defences against anxiety that they employ and the effects these have on how an organisation evolves.

- The role of leaders and how this is co-created in groups, particularly in its neurotic form.

- The nature of groups and teams and the irrational processes that affect team formation and functioning.

This chapter is important because it draws attention to the unconscious, irrational and neurotic and the part that all of these play in the evolution of an organisation. It provides a fuller understanding of the leadership role and how it arises, particularly the negative aspects and the way leaders play a role in the fantasies of others, so providing a very different perspective from the charismatic hero view of leadership in learning organisation theory. This is a useful antidote to the generally idealistic view of teams taken in theories of the learning organisation.

5.1 Introduction

Chapter 3 explored the foundations upon which the theory of strategic choice rests: a theory of interaction to be found in cybernetic systems theory and a theory of human nature to be found primarily in cognitivism, but also in humanistic psychology. Then Chapter 4 examined the theoretical foundations of learning organisation and knowledge creation theories. Here there is some shift from a theory of interaction based on cybernetics to one based on systems dynamics. However, the way systems theory is used retains a link with cybernetics through the conceptualisation of systems dynamics in feedback terms. There is much less of a shift in the basic theory of human nature. This remains heavily cognitivist, although with the addition of a constructivist slant by some writers in pointing to the way that mental models select features for attention, so constructing rather than purely representing experience. The reliance on humanistic psychology is even stronger than it is in strategic choice theory. Some writers also develop a link with Eastern spirituality so that participation comes to be understood as participation in a mystical whole that is greater than the individuals comprising it.

This chapter reviews a theory of organisational change that is built on both a different theory of interaction and a different theory of human nature. Interaction continues to be seen in systemic terms but this time from the perspective of general or open systems theory. The theory of human nature is provided by psychoanalytic perspectives. The chapter first reviews open systems theory and then turns to relevant psychoanalytic notions, before showing how they can be combined to shed light on life in organisations, primarily the obstacles to strategic choice and learning arising from unconscious group processes.

5.2 Open systems theory

Around the same time as the development of cybernetics and systems dynamics, there also appeared the closely related ideas of general systems theory. In a number of papers and books between 1945 and 1968, the German biologist von Bertalanffy put forward the idea that organisms, as well as human organisations and societies, are open systems. They are systems because they consist of a number of component subsystems that are interrelated and interdependent. They are open because they are connected to their environments, or supra-systems, of which they are a part.

Each subsystem within a system and each system within its environment has a boundary separating it from other subsystems and other systems. For example, the sales department in an organisation is a subsystem separated by a boundary from the production and accounting departments. One organisation such as IBM is a system separated by a boundary from the other organisations and individuals that form its environment. Within each system or subsystem, people occupy roles, they conduct sets of activities, and they engage in interrelationships with others. They do this both within their part of the system and in other parts or other systems. Each subsystem within a system and each system within an environment is open. It imports materials, labour, money, information and emotions from other subsystems or systems. It also exports outputs, money and information to other subsystems and systems.

Open systems explanations of managing and organising therefore focus attention on:

- organisations, industries and societies as systemic wholes;
- the behaviour of people within a subsystem or system;
- the nature of the boundary around a subsystem or system;
- the nature of the relationships across the boundaries between subsystems and systems;
- the requirements of managing the boundary.

The open systems concept provides a tool for understanding the relationship between:

- the technical and the social aspects of an organisation;
- the parts and the whole organisation (e.g. the individual and the group, the individual and the organisation);
- the whole organisation and the environment.

Negative feedback

Changing one component in an open system has knock-on effects in many other components because of the prevalence of interconnection. Changes in the environment have an impact on changes in the subsystems of an organisation. What happens in one system will affect what happens in another system and that in turn will affect the first.

One can see the importance of the insight provided by open systems theory if one considers how the technical subsystem of an organisation is interconnected with its social subsystem (Trist and Bamforth, 1951).

Scientific rational management tends to concentrate on the technical subsystem. This system consists of the techniques, technology and sets of tasks required to achieve the organisation's purpose. The prescription for success put forward by scientific management is to make the task subsystem as efficient as possible. So, if you introduce the latest technology for mining coal, for example, together with rules and regulations about quality and efficiency to govern the work of coal miners, then you should succeed according to scientific management. Success here depends primarily on the technical subsystem. The behavioural school of management, on the other hand, focuses primarily on the psychosocial subsystem. Its prescriptions for success stress the establishment of a social system in which people are motivated and participate in making decisions about the nature of the tasks and the technology. To succeed you must consult those who perform the organisation's primary tasks, involve them in decision making, and introduce reward structures that will motivate them to operate efficiently. Success here depends primarily on the social subsystem.

The insight that comes from open systems theory is that the technical and social systems are so interconnected that it makes no sense to regard one as dominant and the other as subordinate. Both subsystems have to be handled together in a manner that takes account of their interdependence. The importance of this interconnection was demonstrated many years ago in a study of the coal-mining industry in the UK by Trist and Bamforth (1951). In the late 1940s, the British coal industry introduced the long-wall method of mining coal, which was more efficient than the previous method. The new technology, however, required changes in the set of tasks performed by coal miners. These changes broke up the co-operative teams in which miners were accustomed to working, teams that reflected their social arrangements in the coal-mining villages in which they lived. Because of the consequent resistance to working in the new way, the technology failed to yield its technical potential.

The message is that, if changes are to succeed, then they have to be based on a realistic understanding of the interconnection, or feedback, between the social and the technical subsystems. And that interconnection is not taken account of simply by introducing participation or reward schemes for individuals. Instead, general systems theory prescribes a match between the two subsystems, one that establishes stable equilibrium.

Like cybernetics and systems dynamics therefore, the general systems strand of thinking sees an organisation as a feedback system. It also sees that feedback system as one that maintains equilibrium with its environment, and between its parts, by utilising the mechanisms of negative feedback.

Conflicting subsystems

In general systems theory, open systems are thought of as having maintenance sub-systems to sustain orderly relationships between the parts of the system (Lawrence and Lorsch, 1967). In an organisation this would be the management information and control systems and the cultures that keep people working harmoniously together. However, it is recognised that these maintenance systems are conservative by nature. They are intended to hold the system together; to prevent it from chang-ing too rapidly; to keep it efficiently carrying out its main tasks. The inevitable consequence of this maintenance form of control is that the overall system and its subsystems become out of balance as time goes by and things change. They become out of balance with each other and with the environment.

But organisations also have adaptive mechanisms that promote change so as to keep them in dynamic equilibrium with the environment. These two subsystems, the maintenance and the adaptive, inevitably conflict, but successful organisations sustain a stable balance between them, according to general systems theory. Note that general systems theory recognises a fundamental conflict inherent in the struc-ture of the system, but assumes that successful systems deal with this by sustaining equilibrium.

General systems theory has made an important contribution to an understanding of the nature of managing and organising in a number of ways. It focuses attention on:

- interdependence, interaction and interconnection between parts of an organisa-tion and between organisations;
- the importance of the boundaries between parts of an organisation and between one organisation and others;
- the roles of people within and across the boundaries and the nature of leadership as management of the boundary.

These ideas are summarised in Box 5.1.

Box 5.1   **General systems theory: main points on organisational dynamics**

- An organisation is an open system: a set of interconnected parts (individuals, informal groups, formal groups such as departments and business units) in turn interacting with other organisations and individuals outside it.

- Interconnection means that a system imports energy and information from outside itself, transforms that energy and information in some way and then exports the transformed result back to other systems outside of itself.

- An organisation imports across a boundary separating it from other systems, transforms the imports within its boundary and exports back across the boundary. The boundary separates a system from its environment but also links it to its environment.

- Relationships across the boundary are always changing, the environment is always changing. The boundary therefore exercises a regulatory function: on the one hand it protects the system from fluctuations in the environment and on the other it relays messages and prompts changes within the boundary so that the system adapts to its environment.

- It is the role of leadership to manage the boundary, to regulate so that the system is protected and changes adaptively.

- Successful management keeps an organisation adapted to its changing environment through a process of negative feedback producing stable equilibrium.

- Adaptation to the environment determines the stable equilibrium balance between differentiation and integration, between maintenance control systems and change, required for success. Organisational paradoxes are thus solved in a unique way determined by the environment.

- Success is therefore a state of stability, consistency and harmony.

I now want to move on from open systems theory to some relevant psychoanalytic concepts. I will return to open systems theory in Section 5.4.

5.3 Psychoanalysis and unconscious processes

In developing psychoanalysis, Freud focused attention on the unconscious. He believed that people repress dangerous desires and painful memories but that this repression does not get rid of such desires and memories – they remain in the unconscious as determinants of behaviour. Repression is one of the major defences against anxiety, that is, a painful state of unease for which no clear reason can be found. It is also held that people's behaviour can be driven by unconscious group processes.

Unconscious processes in organisations

An unconscious group process is one in which a group of people engage without consciously agreeing to it or even realising that they are doing it. When groups of people are in this state they find what is happening to them both puzzling and upsetting and it makes it impossible for them to engage in rational decision making and learning. Covert politics is a defence against anxiety that people are more or less conscious of practising but unconscious processes are defences they indulge in quite automatically without being aware of what they are doing. A group of people can make rational decisions and learn only when they are able to contain the anxiety of organisational life, as opposed to avoiding it through covert politics, on the one hand, or becoming overwhelmed by it in the form of unconscious processes, on the other.

When ways of thinking are challenged, people become anxious. That anxiety may rise to such high levels that people swing into automatic basic assumption behaviour – an unconscious process (Bion, 1961). When groups are dominated by basic assumption behaviour they cannot learn and therefore their organisation cannot develop new strategic direction. On the other hand, if there is a good enough holding environment so that people can contain rather than submit to or avoid the anxiety, then insight and creativity may be generated by and accompany the anxiety of learning. Since all people behave in ways that are directed by unconscious as well as conscious processes, it is inevitable that, when they come together as a group, at least part of their behaviour in that group will be determined by those unconscious processes. In other words, unconscious group processes will inevitably be part of most decision-making processes in an organisation.

This proposition is not recognised in most explanations of managing, organising and decision making. The role of unconscious processes is also firmly denied any explicit attention by many management practitioners. Such considerations tend to be dismissed as peripheral concerns for mature managers who are supposed to make decisions in largely rational ways. When unconscious processes are discussed they are normally seen as peripheral influences on a decision, usually adverse influences, which must and can be removed.

More careful reflection, however, suggests that unconscious processes are so deeply embedded in human behaviour that it is only some completely inhuman, and therefore nonexistent, decision-making process that can occur in the absence of unconscious processes, or with those processes occupying a position of only peripheral importance. It is therefore a matter of importance for the effectiveness of strategic management to explore what impact these processes may have and how they come about. A psychoanalytical explanation is that, when humans are confronted by high levels of anxiety provoked by unfamiliar tasks and lack of leadership, they revert very easily to infantile mechanisms. They begin to behave according to patterns they learned as infants. So first look briefly at an explanation of how infants cope with their world provided by the object relations school of psychoanalysis (Klein, 1975).

Infantile mechanisms

According to Melanie Klein's explanation (1975), infants are born with two powerful drives: the libido, or life force, which is the drive to love; and the morbido, or death wish, which is the fear of death and destruction, the feeling of persecution. The inner life of the infant is very simple – it is dominated by these two extremes of love on the one hand and persecutory fear on the other. The infant's perception of its external world is also very simple, consisting of two part-objects: a good part of the mother that feeds and comforts it and a bad part that denies it food and comfort.

The infant copes with this simple and also powerfully distressing world by splitting its inner life into a loving part that is projected on to the good part of the mother. The infant then identifies itself with that good part and introjects it back into itself. The same thing is done with the persecutory feelings and the aggression and hatred they arouse. These are all projected on to the bad part of the mother, and the infant identifies its own violent impulses with that bad part – it then introjects that bad part of the mother back into itself.

The infant projects its feelings and then perceives those feelings as coming from the outside object. It therefore reacts to the object in a manner provoked by the feelings that originally come from itself. So it projects its own fears of persecution and then reacts to the object projected upon as if that object is actually persecuting it. This leads to a reaction of hate and aggression, strengthening the feeling of persecution. If the projection affects the behaviour of the object, then the whole process becomes even stronger. It is through these processes that the character of the infant is formed. If it experiences loving responses to its loving projections then the loving side of its character is strengthened. If the persecutory projections are reinforced by lack of love and actual persecution then this side of the character is reinforced.

This first stage of infantile development is known as the paranoid–schizoid position. It is schizoid because the infant splits the external world and it splits its own internal world too. It is paranoid because of the persecutory fears of the infant. The infant deals with these fears by using the mechanisms of splitting and projective identification, putting what is inside its own mind out into some external object or person and then identifying with and reacting to what it has projected and subtly influencing the one projected on to to behave according to the projection. The infant copes with harsh reality by creating a fantasy world of separate objects, some of which are persecuting it. It is idealising the good parts and denying its own bad parts by projecting them, so building the external bad into a demon.

The infant who develops normally works through this position and comes to realise that the bad and good objects in its external world are really one and the same whole person. But for the infant having learned how to defend against the earliest anxieties, these defences remain in the unconscious. In later life when people confront anxiety again, they are highly likely to regress to the infantile mechanisms of splitting the world and themselves into extreme and artificial categories of the good and the bad, projecting the parts of themselves they do not like on to others, so creating fantasies that have little to do with reality.

Once the infant realises that it loves and hates the same person it is filled with anxiety because of the feelings of anger and hatred previously projected on to the mother. This causes the depressive position. The normal infant works its way through this position too, developing strong feelings of love and dependence on the mother, while seeking to make amends for previous bad feelings. It experiences hope from the more mature relationship with the mother. Once the infant can hold the depressive position, that is, hold in the mind the paradox of simultaneously loving and hating, then that child can go on to make reparative acts and have reparative feelings. If these are responded to with love then a lifelong cycle of experiencing guilt, making reparation and receiving forgiveness is put in place. Melanie Klein saw this as the basis of all later creative behaviour. So, it is when people are in the depressive position, when they can hold in their minds the paradoxes and ambiguities of organisational life, that they are able to engage in rational decision making. When they regress from that depressive position to the paranoid–schizoid position they become trapped in primitive ways of thinking and behaving. And this, it is held, happens to all of us when we cannot contain the anxiety of learning and when our environment provides us with no anxiety containment either.

Groups and infantile mechanisms

When mature, competent managers come together as a group, each is said to bring along the infantile mechanisms of dependence, idealisation, denial, splitting, projection and fantasising that have been learned as an infant and laid down in the unconscious. Anything that raises uncertainty levels and thus anxiety levels could provoke regression to those infantile mechanisms. Bion has provided an explanation of how these mechanisms are manifested in group behaviour (Bion, 1961).

Bion distinguishes between two important aspects of any group of people. The first aspect is the sophisticated work group. This group focuses on the primary task that it has come together to perform. So a team of top executives has the primary tasks of controlling the day-to-day running of the business of the organisation and also the strategic development of that organisation. All groups are also at the same time what Bion called 'basic assumption groups'. A basic assumption group is one that behaves as if it is making a particular assumption about required behaviour. The assumption becomes most apparent when uncertainty and anxiety levels rise. What Bion is talking about here is the emotional atmosphere, the psychological culture, of the group. All groups of people have these two aspects: some task they are trying to perform together, accompanied by some emotional atmosphere within which they are trying to perform their task. That atmosphere can be described in terms of a basic assumption they are all making.

So, at any one time, a group of people may constitute a sophisticated work group characterised by a basic assumption on behaviour that occupies a kind of low-level background position, influencing the conduct of the primary task but not dominating or blocking it. Then when uncertainty and anxiety levels rise markedly the group can become suffused with and dominated by the basic assumption, a strong emotional atmosphere, or group culture, that blocks the group's ability to function as a sophisticated work group. The primary task will not be carried out, or it will be carried out in an ineffective manner.

Bion distinguished amongst three basic assumptions:

1. *Dependence*. Here the group behaves as if it has come together to depend on some leader. The members of the group seek a leader on whom they can depend. They abandon their individuality and critical faculties in favour of some kind of adoration of a charismatic leader. They actively seek a charismatic person who will tell them what to do. Charisma lies not in the person of the leader but in the interrelationship between the followers and the leader. In this state, members of a group will idealise the leader, expecting completely unrealistic performance from the leader. Groups working on this assumption are destined to be disappointed and will quickly denigrate and abandon the leader. This dependence is an infantile mechanism because the members of the group are projecting their requirements for something to depend upon on to someone else. This projection

will in effect select the leader. Note how this raises a possibility not normally thought of in organisations. When a group is behaving in this mode it is creating its own leader through projecting demands on to a person – it is not the leader who is creating the group. If the person selected for this projection does not co-operate or disappoints, then members of the group project their frustration and fear on to that person and begin to attack. This brings us to the second basic assumption.

2. *Fight/flight*. Here it is as if the group has come together for the purpose of fighting some enemy or for the purpose of fleeing from some enemy. Members project their desire for fight or flight on to someone to lead them in fight or flight. Once again they may rapidly become disappointed with and attack the leader. Groups in this state invent fantasy enemies in some other department or some other organisation. The energy goes into competition and win/lose dynamics or in scapegoating a member.

3. *Pairing*. Pairing is another mode in which a group might operate. Here it is as if the group has come together to witness the intercourse between two of their number that will produce the solution to their anxieties. The atmosphere here is one of unrealistic hope that some experts will produce all the answers.

Turquet (1974) added a fourth basic assumption:

4. *Oneness*. Here it is as if the group has come together to join in a powerful union with some omnipotent force that will enable members to surrender themselves in some kind of safe passivity. Members seem lost in an oceanic feeling of unity.

Once a group of people comes to be dominated by one of the basic assumptions, group members enter into volatile dynamics in which they switch, for apparently no reason, from one basic assumption to another. While people in a group are behaving like this they are incapable of performing the primary task or acting as a work group. They cannot remember what they have just discussed; they go around and around in incompetent circles; they suck unsuitable people into leadership positions; they create scapegoats; they act on untested myths and rumours; they build fantasies and lose touch with reality. Individuals sink their individuality in group uniformity and become deskilled.

What provokes the switch from a work group with some background basic assumption, being used in a sophisticated way to support their task, to a group dominated by a basic assumption? The provocation seems to have a great deal to do with levels of ambiguity and uncertainty on the one hand, and with certain styles of exercising power on the other. If leaders abandon groups in times of great uncertainty and ambiguity then they will develop into basic assumption groups and become incapable of handling the uncertainty and ambiguity.

But note that this is not clear-cut causality between a specific action, say the withdrawal of power, and specific outcomes in behavioural terms. All one can say is that, when the nature of power in a group is changed so that people's requirement for dependence is frustrated, they will display general patterns of behaviour that can be labelled as fight/flight or some other label. It will not be possible to say what form such fighting or such flight may take, or when it will occur. The key points about the dynamics and unconscious processes are summarised in Box 5.2.

Box 5.2	Unconscious group processes: main points on organisational dynamics

- Any attempt to change an organisation in a fundamental way upsets the balance and nature of power and raises the levels of uncertainty and ambiguity so increasing anxiety.

- Increased anxiety unleashes unconscious processes of regression to infantile behaviour. Work groups become swamped with basic assumption behaviour in which they are incapable of undertaking strategic developments.

- A group of managers facing strategic issues is turning up the levels of uncertainty and ambiguity since these are characteristics of strategic issues. Such issues threaten power positions. It is therefore inevitable that strategic issues themselves will raise anxiety levels which could trigger basic assumption behaviour.

- In these circumstances it is quite likely that long-term plans, mission statements, visions and the like are simply being used as defence mechanisms. Perhaps people cling to a dominant paradigm despite all the evidence to the contrary because it is their main defence mechanism against anxiety.

- The dynamics of any real-life organisation is inevitably unstable, unless it is completely dominated by rules, fears or force, in which case it will atrophy and die. Strategic management proceeds as part of this unstable dynamic.

- Success has to do with the management of the context or boundary conditions around a group. The main factors that establish the context are the nature and use of power, the level of mutual trust and the time pressures on people in the group. The purpose of managing the context, or the boundaries, is to create an emotional atmosphere in which it is possible to overcome defences and to test reality rather than indulge in fantasy.

5.4 Open systems and unconscious processes

The combination of open systems theory and psychoanalysis originated in the Tavistock Institute of Human Relations. This was set up London in 1946 by a group of psychoanalysts from the Tavistock Clinic and social scientists from other institutions. During the 1950s and 1960s a distinctive approach to understanding life in organisations was developed by members of this Institute, for example Trist, to whom I have already referred, and Rice and Miller (Miller and Rice, 1967).

As I have already said, an open system exists by importing energy/materials from its environment across a boundary, transforming them and then exporting them back across the boundary (Miller and Rice, 1967). This boundary is seen as a region in which mediating, or regulating, activities occur not only to protect the system from disruption due to external fluctuations but also to allow it to adapt to external changes (Miller, 1977). The boundary region must therefore exhibit an appropriate degree of both insulation and permeability if the system is to survive. This makes regulatory functions at the permeable boundary region of central importance. In organisational terms, these regulatory functions are performed by leaders/managers at the organisation's boundary with other organisations. It is the activities of leaders and managers at the boundary that are key to the process of change. It then becomes quite logical to think about change in terms of rational design and to look for what might inhibit such rational designing activity. Disorder is seen as an inhibitor that must be removed. The disorder is due to the unconscious processes described in the last section.

Miller and Rice (1967) used Bion's (1961) insights to see a group of people as an open system in which individuals, also seen as open systems, interact with each other at two levels. At one level they contribute to the group's purpose, so constituting a sophisticated (work) group, and at the other level they develop feelings and attitudes about each other, the group and its environment, so constituting a more primitive (basic assumption) group. Both of these modes of relating are operative at the same time. When the basic assumption mode takes the form of a background emotional atmosphere it may well support the work of the group, but when it predominates it is destructive of the group's work. So, individuals are thought of as open systems relating to each other across their individual boundary regions. In this way they constitute a group, which is also thought of as an open system with a permeable boundary region. Furthermore, Miller and Rice argue that it is confusing to think of organisations, or enterprises, as open systems consisting of individuals and groupings of individuals. So, an inter-systemic perspective is adopted in which an enterprise is thought of as one open system interacting with individuals and groupings of them as other open systems.

Enterprises are seen as task systems – they have primary tasks that they must perform if they are to survive. There are various definitions of the primary task. It may be the task that ought to be performed. It may be the task people believe that they are carrying out. It may be a task that they are engaged in without even being aware of it and this probably means that it is a defensive mechanism. The primary task requires people to take up roles in order for it to be carried out and the enterprise, or task system, imports these roles across its boundary with the system consisting of individuals and groupings of them. Roles, and relationships between roles, fall within the boundary of the task system. However, groups and individuals, with their personal relationships, personal power plays and human needs not derived from the task system's primary task, fall outside it: they constitute part of the task system's environment. So, there is one system, a task system, interacting with other systems, individuals and groups, and the groups are always operating in two modes at the same time: work mode and basic assumption mode.

When the individual/group system has the characteristics of a sophisticated group with basic assumption behaviour as a supportive background atmosphere, then it is exporting functional roles to the task system and the latter can perform its primary task. The enterprise, or task system, is thus displaying the dynamics of stability – that is, equilibrium or quasi-equilibrium. When, however, the individual/group system is flooded with basic assumption behaviour it exports that behaviour into the task system so disrupting the performance of the primary task. Miller (1993) argues that this inter-systemic view encourages one to focus on interdependence: people supplying roles to enterprises and those enterprises requiring performance in role from people in order to survive.

Part of the task system, a subsystem of it, might be set up to contain imported basic assumption behaviour such as fight. Its primary task is then to operate as an organisational defence that allows the rest of the task system to carry out its primary task. Without such organisational defences, the task system as a whole would import fantasies and behaviours that are destructive of the primary task – the dynamics of instability. These undesirable imports are to be diminished by:

- clarity of task;

- clearly defined roles, and authority relationships between them, all related to task;

- appropriate leadership regulation at the boundary of the task system;

- procedures and structures that form social defences against anxiety (Jacques, 1955; Menzies Lyth, 1975);

- high levels of individual maturity and autonomy.

Most of these factors seem to me to emphasise design and some joint intention relating to the system as a whole. Furthermore, there is, it seems to me, a strong implication that the dynamics of stability are a prerequisite for a functioning task system, while the dynamics of instability are inimical to that functioning. There is little sense in this formulation of the creative potential of disorder. I am making this point here because the theory to be presented in Part 3 takes a different view on these matters.

Shapiro and Carr (1991) employ the above model in their interpretation of the role of the consultant. The consultant uses counter-transference feelings to formulate hypotheses about the transferential and projective processes at work in an organisation, and about the impact of basic assumption behaviour on the work of that organisation. Shapiro and Carr see the function of the consultant as one of feeding back those hypotheses into the life of the organisation and so fostering a collaborative, negotiated understanding and verbalisation of the unconscious, irrational processes at play. It is believed that this process enables the reclaiming of projections and distorted impressions of reality, so restoring to the group its work function. The consultants engage with and understand the complexity of organisational life by adopting an interpretive stance. This stance is seen as the most important element in creating a holding environment and they draw an analogy with a therapeutic setting: 'containment and holding ordinarily refer to symbolic interpretive ways in which the therapist manages the patient's (and his own) feelings' (Shapiro and Carr, 1991, p. 112).

Another feature of the holding environment, one that interpretation aims to secure, is the clarity of task, boundary and role. This is seen as containing, for example, sexual and aggressive feelings. Empathic interpretation affirms individuals in their roles and the resulting containment establishes a holding environment. This provides for safe regression, a shift from rationally organised words to the primitive distortions of fantasy images and simple metaphors which can then be articulated and so disarmed. The aim of interpretation is to move people from states of irrational anxiety and fantasy that distort work to the more reality-based taking of roles that support it.

According to Shapiro and Carr, the aim of the consultant's work is to identify whether an organisation is functioning according to its design. This will happen when members of the organisation understand their tasks so that roles within and across parts of the organisation can be legitimately authorised and fully integrated. This, in turn, requires clarification of authorisation from one level to another in the hierarchy and a structure of meetings to promote effective communication. Shapiro and Carr stress the need to develop a culture in which people bring their work-related feelings to legitimate forums where they can be made available for examination in relation to the work rather than discharged in informal subgroups. What they mean by an interpretive stance, then, is a collaborative verbalisation of unconscious processes leading to withdrawal of projections that might be adversely affecting task performance. The objection to informal subgroups seems to be based on the belief that, since they are based purely on personal relationships rather than on task, they are fertile ground for projections and basic assumption behaviour. Note how this model of organisational functioning leads to a focus on the legitimate relationships in an organisation.

5.5 Leaders and groups

In both strategic choice and mainstream learning organisation theory, leaders are assumed to be perfectly healthy, balanced people, who set the direction of the organisation for others to follow. However, as soon as it is recognised that basic assumption groups can very quickly emerge from work groups, the possibility arises that leaders can also be the creations of the group. It is quite possible that leaders are vainly trying to act out the fantasies that those in the management team are projecting. Leaders affect what groups do, but groups also affect what leaders do through processes of unconscious projection.

Leadership

Bales (1970) identified the emergence of two kinds of leaders in small task-oriented groups: the task leader who gives suggestions, shows disagreement and presses the group to focus on task completion; and the social-emotional leader who asks for suggestions, shows solidarity and soothes tempers by encouraging tension release. These leadership roles are mutually supportive in that each helps the group solve different problems, provided that the role occupants can work together. Sometimes one person can combine both roles – the 'great man' leader (Borgatta et al., 1954). When specialist leaders of this kind do not emerge or cannot work together, then members begin to deal with their frustration in unconscious ways that lead to the emergence of scapegoat roles, enemy roles, messiah roles and so on. Bion (1961) distinguishes between different types of leader in the basic assumption group: the fight leader, the flight leader, the dependence leader and the leader who symbolises some unrealistic utopian, messianic or oceanic hope. Bion points to the precarious position these leaders occupy. The important point here is that the leader is sucked into that position by the group and is controlled by the group, not the other way around as we usually believe.

An important distinction is that between the leader of a work group and a basic assumption leader. An effective leader is one who maintains a clear focus on and definition of the primary task. That task determines the requirements of the leader, who must continually struggle to synthesise, participate and observe. The effective leader operates on the boundary of the group, avoiding both emotional immersion and extreme detachment. Leaders are there to regulate transactions between their groups and other groups. Both immersion and distance make this impossible. When a group is dominated by basic assumption behaviour it sucks into the leadership position one who is completely immersed in the emotional atmosphere, the basic assumption behaviour of the group. This leader is subjected to conflicting and fundamentally impossible roles – to provide unlimited nurturance, to fight and subdue imaginary enemies, to rescue the group from death and dissolution, to fulfil utopian or messianic hopes.

The kinds of roles that have been distinguished are those of the aggressor, the seducer who tries to seduce people into exposing their feelings and positions, the scapegoat, the hero, the resistors, the anxious participators, the distressed females, the respected enactors, the sexual idols, the outsiders, the prophets (Dunphy, 1968). These informal roles develop in order to contain and deal with internal conflict, the tension of fusion and individuation. Managers' choices and actions may have more to do with unconscious processes than any rational consideration.

Neurotic forms of leadership

Strategic choice and mainstream learning organisation theory focus on what leadership means when it is functioning well. However, leaders often do not function very well and quite often they are definitely dysfunctional. Such dysfunctional leadership has not attracted very much attention in most of the management literature, but it occurs frequently and it is therefore a matter of importance to understand something about it. Functional leaders assist in the containment of anxiety and thus help to create the possibility of learning, but dysfunctional, neurotic leaders may well become caught up, and drive others to become caught up, in neurotic defences that will block such learning.

Kets de Vries (1989) explains the nature of neurotic leadership in the following way. Everyone behaves in a manner that is affected by what one might think of as an inner theatre. That theatre consists of a number of representations of people and situations, often formed early in childhood, and those that have come to play the most important roles are core conflictual relationships. It is as if people spend much of their lives re-enacting conflicts that they could not understand in childhood, partly because they are familiar to them, and partly, perhaps, because they are always seeking to understand them. What they do, then, is project this inner play with conflictual situations out on to the real world they have to deal with. Leaders do this just as others do, the difference being that they project their inner conflicts on to a much larger real-world stage that includes their followers. A leader projects internal private dialogues into external public ones and these dialogues are about core conflictual themes from childhood. The particular neurotic style a leader practises will be determined by the nature of these core conflicts.

Followers also project their inner plays on to the leader and these leader/follower projections keep leaders and followers engaged with each other in a particular manner. Followers project their dependence needs on to leaders and displace their own ideals, wishes and desires on to them too.

The inner theatre in which leaders and followers join each other contains scenarios that are the basis of imagined, desired and feared relationships between them. There are typical scenarios that are found over and over again and they constitute typical dispositions, typical ways of defending against, repressing, denying and idealising particular leader/follower relationships. Everyone is said to use such devices and everyone has a number of prominent dispositions that constitute that person's neurotic style. This is quite normal and it becomes a problem only when people massively, compulsively and habitually use a rather small number of defences. This blocks their ability to relate to reality effectively and it is then that they might be labelled 'neurotic'.

Kets de Vries (1989) distinguishes amongst a number of such dispositions or neurotic styles as follows. Every leader will display a combination of some of these styles and it becomes a problem only when a rather small number of these come to dominate the behaviour of the leader and the followers.

- The *aggressive* disposition tends to characterise many who become leaders and rather fewer who are followers – aggression is often acceptable in leaders but creates problems for followers. Tough chief executives who are socially forceful and intimidating, energetic, competitive and power oriented fall into this category. People are not important to them and they want to dominate. They tend to be impulsive and to believe that the world is a jungle. They expect people to be hostile to them and they become aggressive in advance to counteract such expected hostility. Of course their behaviour may well provoke the hostility they expect. Such leaders probably experienced parental rejection or hostility.

- The *paranoid* disposition is found frequently amongst leaders and less amongst followers. Such people are always looking for hidden motives and are suspicious of others. They are hyper-vigilant, keep scanning the environment and take unnecessary precautions. They deny personal weakness and do not readily accept blame. They tend to be restricted and cold in relationships with little humour. They are fond of mechanistic devices to measure performance and keep track of people. Such people may have had intrusive parents and may feel uncertain of themselves.

- The *histrionic* disposition is characterised by a need to attract the attention of others at all costs. Such people are alert to the desires of others, they are sociable and seductive with their sense of self-worth heavily dependent on the opinion of others. They love activity and excitement and tend to overreact to minor incidents, often throwing tantrums. Such people may have had difficulty attracting the attention of parents.

- The *detached* disposition is displayed when people find it difficult to form close relationships. They tend to be cold and aloof and this may be a response to parental devaluation.

- The *controlling* disposition is high in leaders and low in followers and it is displayed by people who want to control everything in their lives. They have an excessive desire for order and control. This is a way of managing hostile feelings that may have arisen from the behaviour of controlling parents. The resultant hostility may emerge as tyrannical ways of behaving or its opposite of submission.

- The *passive-aggressive* disposition tends to be found more in followers than in leaders. Such people are highly dependent but tend to attack those they depend upon. They resist demands for performance, they are defiant, provocative and negative, complaining all the time and demanding much from their leaders. They tend to blame others all the time, they are ambivalent and pessimistic. This difficulty might arise because such people find it difficult to assess what is expected of them. They are likely to have parents who presented them with conflicting messages.

- Other dispositions are the *narcissistic* one when people see themselves as exceptional and special; the *dependent* disposition in which people are excessively dependent upon others; and the *masochistic* disposition.

It is not just the style of the leader or the style of the followers on their own that determines how their joint behaviour unfolds. It is how the styles engage each other that will create the environment within which they have to work. So, an aggressive, controlling leader interacting with dependent, masochistic followers will produce a rather different context and pattern of behaviour compared with such a leader interacting with, say, passive-aggressive followers. These patterns of interaction will have a powerful impact on how effectively an organisation learns. Such neurotically based interactions, therefore, have to be understood as central to processes of management.

5.6 How open systems/psychoanalytic perspectives deal with the four key questions

This chapter now turns to how open systems/psychoanalytic perspectives answer the four questions posed at the end of Chapter 1. These were:

1. How does the theory view the nature of interaction?
2. What view does it take of human nature?
3. What methodology does it employ?
4. How does it deal with paradox?

You can compare how the theories surveyed in this chapter answer the questions with the kind of answers found in strategic choice theory (Section 3.7). You can also make comparisons with learning organisation theory (Section 4.9). Consider now how open systems/psychoanalytic perspectives deal with the questions.

The nature of interaction

Interaction within and between organisations is understood in systems terms as with strategic choice and learning organisation theory. While cybernetics analyses a system in terms of self-regulating negative feedback loops and systems dynamics takes account of amplifying positive feedback loops, open systems theory focuses attention on regulatory functions at the system's boundary. Essentially, these functions regulate the flows of imports into, and exports out of, the system so that the system adapts to its environment. The dynamics, the way the system moves, is therefore the same as for cybernetics, that is, a tendency to move towards stable equilibrium when the system is succeeding.

Open systems theory pays more attention to the micro level than cybernetics and systems dynamics do. In other words, it pays attention to the subsystems of which the whole is composed. This is especially so when it is combined with psychoanalytic perspectives because they are very much concerned with the individuals and the groups that make up an organisation. The disorderly dynamics generated by individuals relating to each other in groups then become very important as an obstacle to the successful movement towards adaptive equilibrium. Those writing in the Tavistock tradition distinguish between the task/role system and the system of individuals/groups. The task/role system is a subsystem of the organisation, which is open to the other subsystem consisting of individuals and groups, and also open to the environment consisting of other organisations. When the imports from the individuals/groups subsystem are adequately regulated then the task/role subsystem can make rational choices about adapting to the environment of other organisations.

So, this is a theory that pays considerable attention to both macro and micro levels and it envisages both orderly and disorderly dynamics. The former is equated with successful adaptation to the environment and the latter as an obstacle to this process. The orderly operation of the task/role system is understood in much the same way as strategic choice or learning organisation theory. However, the attention to micro detail brings in very important processes that can disrupt the rational processes.

The theory of causality, however, is the same as that for cybernetics/strategic choice and systems dynamics/learning organisation, namely formative cause. The emphasis is on already enfolded archetypes that are unfolded as the system develops. The same problems to do with ordinary human freedom and novelty follow. This open systems/psychoanalytic approach cannot explain how novel, transformative changes come about in systemic terms. These are matters that rely on some kind of explanation in terms of the individual.

The nature of human beings

The theory reviewed in this chapter takes a very different view of human nature from the mainly cognitivist and humanistic perspectives on which strategic choice and learning organisation theories are built. The main difference is the emphasis it places on unconscious processes, the effects of anxiety and the ever-present possibility of defensive and aggressive behaviour. Human ability to behave rationally and altruistically is seen as highly problematic and the capacity for learning as very fragile. Attention is focused on power and dysfunctional behaviour in a similar way to that found in organisational learning theories which emphasise defensive routines but which other writers in this tradition as well as in strategic choice theory largely ignore.

However, there are also significant similarities. First, the notion of representation is as central in psychoanalysis as in cognitivism. In other words, in both of these theories it is assumed that individuals' minds are internal worlds consisting of mental representations of outer reality upon which the individual then acts. However, the nature of the representations and the processes through which they are formed are very different. Consider what representation means in most psychoanalytic theories:

- In classic, Freudian drive theory, a representation is a conscious or unconscious idea that represents an instinct and as such it is the expression of some basic, inherited body function. So, here there is no notion of a more or less accurate picture of a pre-given external world. Instead, there is a unique expression of general bodily functions internal to the individual body, developed from the interaction of inherited instincts and actual experience. In early object relations theory (Klein, 1975) the notion of representation is developed in a different way. Representations are of part-objects and objects encountered in relationships. Object here is mainly a person or some part of a person and the nature of the representation is highly complex. It is not at all a more or less accurate picture of an external reality but rather an internal construct developed through experience on the basis of inherent, inherited fantasies common to all humans. The earliest object is that of the mother's breast and what is being represented is not so much the object itself as the experience and fantasised relationship with the object. Later object relations theorists (Bion, Winnicott, Fairbairn) placed much more emphasis on the relationships, as did attachment theorists (Bowlby, Balint), self psychologists (Kohut) and relational psychologists (Sullivan, Stern), for all of whom representations are primarily of relationships with other human beings.

- As with cognitivism, representations are made up of symbols that form 'internal' templates (drive derivatives, forbidden wishes, objects, relationships) which are the basis upon which a human being knows and acts. 'Internal' here refers not to the brain but to a mental apparatus or process. This is described in terms of mental components or agents – the ego, the id and the superego, various object and self-object representations, relational interactions that have been generalised. The question of where such an apparatus might be located, or where the fantasies and other psychological processes might actually be, is never addressed.

- As with cognitivism, representations are built up through a process of symbol processing but in psychoanalysis there is no suggestion that this is like a computer. Indeed, the process through which the representations are constructed becomes highly complex. Freudian drive theory emphasises processes of defence and suppression. Object relations theory presents highly complex mental processes of splitting, projecting, introjecting, identifying, idealising, denigrating, making reparation and so on. Attachment theorists, self and relational psychologists talk about processes of evocation, resonance, mirroring, attunement and empathy. All of these processes build up representations of objects and relationships.

- As with cognitivism, representing is a process of recovering or reconstructing templates from a memory bank but these now take different forms. They could be drive-driven wishes that are permissible in terms of external reality or suppressed wishes expressive of the pleasure principle. Or, they could be recoveries of past object relationships. Representing, as a process of comparing new stimuli with past representations of external, environmental features, receives little emphasis. Instead the representations are used to interpret reality and may well distort it in various transferential and projective processes.

The above usage of 'representation' clearly carries with it substantial implications. It postulates that the individual human mind is formed by the clash of inherited drives and social constraints, out of which there emerges a mental apparatus that mediates the clash. Later developments in psychoanalytic theory increasingly see humans occupying a world formed by relationships with other human beings, with representations of these relationships emerging from them and coming in turn to govern them. There is a separate entity that does this representing, namely a mind or psyche of the individual. These separate individual entities cannot easily share the same representations because each individual uniquely constructs his or her own psyche. However, psychic processes are postulated that allow some degree of sharing of mental contents or states. These processes include projective identification, resonance, mirroring, empathy, attunement and, of course, talking.

There is a decentring of the individual in an inner sense in that the individual is not clearly in control of his or her mind, but, rather, is buffeted about by the id. However, in any external sense there is no significant decentring of the individual. It is true that the social prohibition is part of the process of structuring the psyche, particularly in the form of the superego, but groups arise when members identify with the same leader. There is no sense of individuals and groups co-creating each other. The social plays a part only in terms of the reality principle. This curbs the limitless drive for pleasure on the part of the individual, a drive that has to be mediated first by an ego and then by a superego. The process of mental structuring is essentially the feat of the individual infant as it copes with unconscious fantasy, proceeding from primitive dependence to autonomy. This is very much within the dominant Western paradigm of the autonomous individual.

To summarise, in cognitivism, constructivism, humanistic psychology and psychoanalysis, the individual is prior and primary to the group. With the exception of constructivism, all of the theories involve individuals building representations of reality. However, they do so in very different ways and build very different kinds of representations. Psychoanalysis, therefore, presents very different views on human nature and the ability of an individual to control his or her own mental processes. The impact of unconscious group processes on the individual's ability to think and act rationally receives a great deal of attention in this theory. The individual is primary in the sense that he or she is born with inherited drives and fantasies that are constrained by social forces.

Methodology

In strategic choice and learning organisation theory the researcher, consultant and manager are assumed to be able to stand outside the organisational system and to take the position of the objective observer. The perspectives in this chapter take a similar methodological stance but with an important difference. The consultant, researcher and manager are assumed to stand at the boundary of the organisational system. In this position one is not so immersed in the organisational culture that one loses a rational, objective perspective. However, one is immersed enough to experience how being in that culture feels. These feelings are part of the information that can be used to understand the organisation.

Paradox

While strategic choice and learning organisation theory do not recognise paradox, it is central to a psychoanalytic perspective. The struggle amongst ego, id and superego is never resolved. The capacity to think and learn requires an individual to take the depressive position where it is possible to hold ambiguity and paradox in the mind. Creativity requires the individual mind to occupy the transitional space. This is essentially paradoxical since it is both fantasy and reality at the same time.

Making sense of experience

The perspectives in this chapter are particularly useful when it comes to making sense of experiences that feel stressful or bizarre. It might be possible to understand them by paying attention to the effects of anxiety on people's behaviour and how people defend against it. It also offers ways of understanding the nature and impact of dysfunctional leadership and inappropriate applications of power. The argument presented is that the processes described in this section affect how an organisation evolves. They are as important as rational choice in determining what happens to an organisation.

5.7 Summary

This chapter has reviewed open systems theory and psychoanalytic perspectives, pointing to how they focus attention on aspects of life that do not feature much in strategic choice and learning organisation theories.

The open systems/psychoanalytic approach opens up insights like these:

- Charismatic leaders and the strong cultures of dependence they provoke in followers may well be extremely unhealthy for organisations. Researchers (e.g. Peters and Waterman, 1982) may therefore note the presence of charismatic leaders and superficially conclude that this is the reason for success, when it might well be a neurotic phenomenon that is about to undermine the company.

- A cohesive team of managers may not be a healthy phenomenon at all. It may be an unhealthy and unproductive reflection of the fantasy of basic assumption groups acting out dependence or oneness assumptions. Again, researchers not considering an organisation from a psychoanalytic point of view may well conclude that such neurotic cohesion is a reason for success.

- The idea of the group or the management team may itself be a defence mechanism. So, faced by high levels of strategic uncertainty and ambiguity, managers may retreat into the 'mother figure' of the team for comfort and in so doing fail to deal with the strategic issues.

- Groups clearly do not have to have a purpose or even a task to function very tightly as a group, even if it is a misguided one. Again, signs of close teams should provoke suspicion, not praise.

- Groups or teams are a two-edged sword. People need them to establish their identity. They need them to operate effectively. But they can also deskill people.

- The desire for cohesion may well be a neurotic phenomenon.

- Plans and rigid structures and rules may all be defences against anxiety instead of the rational way of proceeding usually considered.

- One aspect of culture is the emotional atmosphere, the basic assumption, that a group of people create as they interact.

Further reading

Hirschhorn (1990) provides an important exposition of the role of the informal organisation as a defence against anxiety. I would also recommend Shapiro and Carr (1991) and Kets de Vries (1989), as well as Miller (1993), Oberholzer and Roberts (1995) and Gould *et al.* (2001). They all give deeper insight into the psychodynamics of organisations. Winnicott (1971) is also well worth reading.

Questions to aid further reflection

1. How do open systems differ from cybernetic systems and systems dynamics models?

2. What are the similarities and differences between psychoanalysis, cognitivism, constructivism and humanistic psychology?

3. From a psychoanalytic perspective, how would you understand the notion of the charismatic leader?

4. How would you understand the move to the mystical in organisational learning theory from a psychoanalytic perspective?

5. How would you think about teams from a psychoanalytic perspective?

6. How would you think about power from the open systems/psychoanalytic perspective?

7. What does it means to contain anxiety and how does this happen?

8. What is the nature of the relationship between the individual and the social in psychoanalysis?

Chapter 6

Thinking about participation in systems

Second-order systems and autopoiesis

This chapter invites you to draw on your own experience to reflect on and consider the implications of:

- How, in second-order systems thinking, account is taken of the fact that humans cannot simply take the objective observer position in relation to human phenomena because they are themselves participants in such phenomena.

- How second-order systems thinking encounters the problem of infinite regress, which has to be either ignored or arbitrarily interrupted by an appeal to the mystical.

- The ideology reflected in the criticism of first-order systems thinking in the work of interactive, emancipatory, soft and critical systems thinkers.

- How the causal dualism of first-order systems thinking continues as a central feature of second-order systems thinking.

- The emphasis placed on the validity of different viewpoints and multiple meanings.

- The move from the realist position of first-order thinking to an idealist position in second-order systems thinking.

- How critical systems thinkers take a linear view of time and avoid notions of paradox.

- Intention and being in control remain central.

- The manner in which ethics are dealt with.

- The way in which living persons disappear when an organisation is thought of as an autopoietic system.

The ideas in this chapter are important because they constitute a much more sophisticated idea of systems and bring in the social dimension of human activity as well as ethics and power.

6.1 Introduction

Previous chapters in this part of the book have described the origins of modern systems thinking in the philosophy of Kant and how the idea of systems was significantly developed around the 1950s in what might be called the first wave of twentieth-century systems thinking. That first wave had three strands, namely, cybernetics, systems dynamics and general system theory and it also reflected a shift in psychological theories from behaviourism to cognitivism and later constructivism to some extent. So far, the chapters have reviewed how these theories of systems and psychology have formed the basis of three important theories of organisation and management. First, there is the theory of strategic choice and it was pointed out how it is built on theoretical foundations provided by cybernetics and cognitivist psychology. Here, an organisation becomes what it becomes through the strategies chosen by its dominant coalition in a rational manner. The second group of theories is that of the learning organisation built on the theoretical foundations of systems dynamics, humanistic and cognitivist psychology, and to some extent constructivist psychology. Here, an organisation becomes what it becomes through the processes of learning in which its managers and other members engage. Leadership, motivation, inspiration and widespread participation in a greater whole become important concepts. Discussion of this theory was followed by a chapter discussing the behavioural obstacles to strategic choice and organisational learning to be found in a theory combining general systems theory with psychoanalytic perspectives on human psychology. Here, an organisation becomes what it becomes through strategic choice and learning intertwined with complex unconscious processes. The manner in which anxiety is contained becomes very important.

In the last decades of the twentieth century, many presented criticisms of first-order, hard systems thinking (cybernetics, systems dynamics and general systems theory). Second-order thinking raised the problem of the observer of a human systems also being a participant in it (Bateson, 1972; von Foerster, 1984). Others were critical of early systems theories because they implied that organisations were physical entities like organisms with clear boundaries, structures and functions and this limited the domain of effective application. Allied to this was the criticism that hard systems theories presented individuals as deterministic, thinking machines and ignored the aspects of emotion, conflict, politics, culture and ethics. In other words, the critics of hard systems thinking were taking a much more social perspective. For example, Churchman (1968, 1970) focused on boundaries and ethics; Ackoff (1981, 1994) developed interactive planning; and Checkland (1981, 1983; Checkland and Scholes, 1990) developed soft systems thinking, arguing that very few real-world situations allowed one to think of them as systems with clearly defined goals and objectives. Later, critical systems thinking grew out of the critiques of Churchman, Ackoff and Checkland (Flood, 1990, 1999; Jackson, 2000; Midgley, 2000). Since the main approaches to strategic management are based on systems thinking, it is important to explain how systems thinking has been evolving and what the implications for strategic management are.

6.2 First- and second-order systems thinking

The general systems, cybernetics and systems dynamics strands of systems thinking all departed from mechanistic and reductionist approaches in that they stressed dynamic interaction between parts of a system and between systems in an environment. However, they did not make a major move away from the radical separation of the observer (the subject and rationalist causality) from the observed (the object and formative causality). Like mechanistic and reductionist thinking, the first wave of twentieth-century systems thinking, often called hard systems thinking, assumes an objective reality that is objectively observed by an individual. The assumption is that the world is made up of systems having a purpose, which can be objectively observed and modelled. The boundaries of a system are taken to be given by the structure of reality. In other words reality is held to consist of systems in a realist perspective. On the whole, most hard systems thinkers forgot the 'as if' of Kant's regulative idea in relation to systems (*see* Chapter 2) and reified the organisation as a real system. This approach allows managers to imagine that their organisation is a system that they can control in an optimal manner. First-order systems thinking is concerned with intervening in the system to define clear goals, identify problems and propose rational solutions. This involves characterising a situation in terms of identifiable objects with well-defined properties; finding general rules that apply to situations in terms of those objects and properties; applying the rules logically to the situation and drawing conclusions as to what is to be done. The approach is clearly scientific and it emphasises thought and its application as independent activities. It is concerned with transferable knowledge and it is based on the sender–receiver model of communication.

Second-order systems thinking, on the other hand, is built on the understanding that human beings determine the world they experience (constructivist psychology) and this requires that we reflect upon how we operate as perceiving and knowing 'observers'. Second-order thinking is the continual attempt of managers and researchers to be aware of their own framework of understanding. One key name associated with the origins of second-order systems thinking is that of von Foerster (1984) who said that he was part of the universe and whenever he acted he was changing both himself and the universe. Another key name is that of Bateson who explored how the observer could be included in the system being observed.

Bateson (1972) starts with the classic example of the cybernetic system, namely, the central heating system, to exemplify the three levels of learning: Level 1, which is single-loop learning where mental models stay the same; Level 2, which is double-loop learning where mental models are changed; and Level 3, examples of which are religious conversion and deep personal change.

Consider what happens as we move from one level of learning to the next. The boundary of the system is redrawn. Before Level 1, the system contains only the central heating device and no learning is possible – the device is a deterministic mechanism that responds to gaps between target and actual. To reach Level 1, the boundary of the system has to be redrawn to include the human operator of the central heating system because it is the human who sets goals for the system. The human operator sets such goals according to some mental framework in his or her mind, that is, a mental model. The system now includes a person who can detect an error, a gap, between what he or she experiences and what he/she wants as determined by his/her habits, or mental model. The human operator can respond to this error and set a new goal for the system without in any way changing habits, mental models, or way of understanding the world. In other words, the person's mental model, which remains the same, is now part of the higher-order system and this higher-order system can learn. This learning is itself a cybernetic process in that experience of an error triggers a change in the goal set for the lower-order system, that is, the central heating device.

Mental models, then, are higher-order cybernetic devices that change the goals for the lower-order cybernetic system. Learning Level 1, or single-loop learning, is therefore made possible by including the objective observer's fixed mental model in a widened system. Note that the process of changing mental models remains outside the definition of the Learning Level 1 system.

However, the system can now be widened to include this observer's observing of him/herself performing the single-loop learning. The observer may find that as he/she changes the temperature setting according to his/her habit, or mental model, this does not yield the satisfaction he/she is seeking. This error could trigger him/her into changing his/her habits, that is, mental model. The process for changing the mental model is now part of an even higher order system and the mental model can also change as a result of the choice of the human. When it does so, Learning Level 2, or double-loop learning, is achieved. The system is now widened to include the process of changing mental models and this too is thought of as a cybernetic system. However, the process that triggers the process of changing the mental model, something to do with satisfaction and dissatisfaction, or preference, is still outside the definition of the Learning Level 2 system.

This too is dealt with by redrawing the boundary of the system, widening it even further to include this observer observing him/herself changing his/her preferences that trigger the choice to change his/her mental model. The observer becomes aware of him/herself learning in a double-loop way and this is presumably made possible by a mental model of the process of changing the mental model. This process of changing preferences is now included in an even wider system. However, once again, there is now the problem of defining the process by which the observer becomes aware of the need to change his/her preferences. Bateson found he could not identify what this would be and fell back on mysticism, for example, religious conversion, and said that Level 3 was extremely rare.

The problem with second-order system thinking, then, is that it rapidly runs into an infinite regress and some kind of mysticism. It seems to me that this problem of infinite regress, which second-order systems thinking immediately runs into, is a key conceptual concern. It is a sign that second-order systems thinking is not addressing the paradox of the observing participant, or the participating observer, but eliminating it through the device of redrawing boundaries and changing levels of description. I will argue, later in this chapter, that systems thinkers in the second-order tradition of soft and critical systems thinking have not been able to overcome this problem either – their response is to ignore it, claiming that in practice it would come to an end. I think that failure to solve the problem of infinite regress leaves us with the necessity of appealing to some kind of mystical whole in order to account for transformative learning and knowledge creation. Of course, an appeal to the mystical is not an explanation and neither is simply ignoring the problem on practical grounds.

The problem of infinite regress is fundamental to all forms of systems thinking simply because systems thinking is built upon a conceptual spatial metaphor. It always involves postulating a whole separated by a boundary from other wholes. There is always an 'inside' and an 'outside'. Drawing a boundary creates an 'inside', which has to be different to what is 'outside'. This cannot be other than a dualism in which one kind of causality applies to the inside and another kind to the outside. There always has to be something outside the system that is drawing the boundary around it and what that something is must eventually be a mystery. Systems thinking is fundamentally Kantian 'both . . . and' thinking. This matters in practical terms because it ends up with an appeal to mysticism. Part 3 of the book will move from systems thinking with its spatial metaphor to responsive processes thinking, which makes no use of concepts such as 'inside', 'outside' and 'boundaries'.

6.3 Interactive planning and soft systems thinking

As examples of the critical attitude towards the first wave of twentieth-century systems thinking, consider the work of Ackoff on interactive planning and then that of Churchman and Checkland on soft systems.

Interactive planning

Ackoff (1981, 1994) holds that obstructions to change lie in the minds of the members of an organisation, that is, in their mental models. He believes that it is not practically feasible to surface these mental models and change them as many learning organisation theorists believe. Instead, he argues that members of an organisation should participate in formulating an idealised design of the future they desire and create ways of achieving it. They should seek to close the gap between their present situation and this desired future. The central message is to plan or be planned for. Ackoff developed a method of interactive planning to do this, one that focuses on the participative development of scenarios for desired futures. The first step in the rather detailed process he proposes is systems analysis, that is, the formulation of a detailed picture of the organisation as it is today in terms of process, structure, culture and relationships with the environment. He is concerned with what can be done now to create the future.

Ackoff presents a version of strategic choice theory that emphasises not just the roles of leaders but also the participation of members of an organisation in making the strategic choice. It seems to me, therefore, that his perspective represents a shift in ideology from 'command and control' to teamwork and democratic participation. Ackoff is not explaining how managers and others actually do behave. Instead, he is prescribing what they should do to act more effectively.

While Ackoff clearly continues within the theory of strategic choice, Churchman moves to a theory of organisational learning.

Churchman's critique

Churchman (1968, 1970) argued that human systems are best understood as systems of meaning (ideas, concepts, values) and learning. Churchman set out the

conditions required for a system to be purposeful. Purposeful systems are characterised by a decision maker who can produce change in performance measures, a
designer whose design influences the decision maker, a design aimed at maximising
value and a built-in guarantee that the purpose can be achieved. He stressed the
importance of critical reflection on system design and operation.

Notice here the distinction between decision maker/designer and the system of
ideas, concepts and values about which performance measurement decisions and
design changes are made. The decision maker/designer is clearly understood to be
rationally seeking to maximise value and achieve a purpose through the system
of ideas, concepts and values. The action of this decision maker/designer is thus
thought of in terms of Kantian autonomous individuals to be explained in terms
of rationalist causality. However, the systems of ideas, concepts and values, which
the autonomous individuals design and measure, must be subject to some other
causality for they are clearly not autonomous individuals. What causes the system's
movement has to be the formative process of interaction between the ideas, concepts
and values that produce the whole conceptual or value system. In other words,
the conceptual and value system unfolds what the designers and performance-
measuring autonomous individuals have designed into them. Furthermore, the decision maker/designer is a participant in the ideas, concepts and values of the system.
The decision maker/designer must think in terms of the ideas and concepts and act
in accordance with the values in order to count as relevant to the system. If they
deviate then they are no longer relevant to the construction of the social system of
ideas, concepts and values.

Churchman's thinking, therefore, has the same structure as that of all the other
systems thinkers so far reviewed in this part of the book, namely that human interaction is first understood in terms of the rationalist causality of the decision
maker/designer and then in terms of the formative causality of the conceptual and
value systems they have designed. In the former they are free to choose the design
of the system and in the latter they are not because they are subject to the formative
causality of the system they have designed. This is not sensed as a paradox and no
explanation is offered of how people manage to live with alternating between being
free and being not free.

Churchman also placed great importance on moral practice. For him, the first
step in systems thinking was to draw a boundary around the system, which is essentially a choice that opens up ethical questions because drawing a boundary always
includes some and excludes others, dominating some and liberating others. For
Churchman, the aim of systems thinking was to emancipate people from domination so that they could participate on a free and equal basis in the process of system
design, that is, in the design of their own thinking. The way in which particular views
are privileged over others was to be identified (Flood, 1990) and exposed so that
people could be liberated from dominant worldviews (Phelan, 1999). Churchman
also stressed participation, debate and trans-discipline and trans-function team-
working. The response to the criticism that systems are designed by technocrats,
who exclude people, is to focus on democracy and participation in the process of
design. What this move does is substitute a democratic group for the individual
designer of the system. The understanding of a system or the design of a system
is now a task for a team in dialogue with each other. The method of their thinking
and talking to each other is still supposed, however, to be systemic. So, the idea
of human systems as systems of meaning is closely linked to an emphasis on

participation as equality and an idealised, democratic freedom. The ideological basis of Churchman's thinking is thus quite transparent. It is based upon a belief in liberation and participation. It presents a prescription for better ways to manage human affairs. Churchman is not explaining what actually does happen but is calling for a better way of making decisions.

Notice, however, that although Churchman is deeply concerned with participative social interaction and human freedom, he employs a framework that has problems with freedom. The autonomous individuals who are designing and making decisions about the systems of ideas and values are clearly free because they are choosing the system design. However, what they are designing is their own systems of ideas and value. If these systems are to mean anything to them then they and others must adhere to the formative purpose and process of the system. The ideas, concepts and values of the system must also be their ideas, concepts and values. As such, they cannot be free and this is why Kant warned against thinking of human action in terms of systems. The problem of freedom applies as much to the idealist position of Churchman as to the realist position of earlier hard systems thinkers. In the realist position people are actually taken to be parts of a real system while in the idealist position the system is thought of as the mental construct of the people involved. However, even though the system is their own mental construction, the very act of this construction means that they must be thinking of themselves as parts of the system they are constructing, otherwise they are not really thinking in systems terms at all. Notice, also, a point already made about hard systems. Since the system, whether it be a real system or a system of ideas, is subject to formative cause, it cannot produce anything new. The source of novelty, therefore, lies in the individual and systems thinking does not explain how such novelty arises.

This feature of dual causality and the problems it brings to do with freedom and novelty are also evident in Checkland's thinking.

Soft Systems Methodology

Checkland (1983) was critical of the positivist, engineering view of systems to be found in the three strands of systems thinking discussed in previous chapters of this part of the book. These views of systems took the realist perspective, regarding the world as actually consisting of systems having an objective existence. Instead, Checkland proposed that systems were the mental constructs of observers, in effect bringing back Kant's idealist view of the regulative, 'as if' nature of systems. For Checkland, the notion of systems related to the process of enquiry, meaning and intention and he developed Soft Systems Methodology (SSM) as a reflection of this view. Notice how this approach implies the notion of the autonomous individual, the enquiring scientific observer who hypothesises about reality 'as if' it were a system.

SSM approaches a problem situation on the basis that people possess free will rather than being subjected to forces beyond their control and because of this they must be involved in any changes to the systems they create. Checkland is thus implicitly assuming some kind of rationalist causality, this time including emotion, as applying to human action. The implicit assumptions around human psychology are those of cognitivism. The aim of the methodology is to integrate multiple viewpoints of free participants in order to assist them *to predict and control the changes to their systems* in vague situations in which there are no agreed goals. The assumptions of rationalist causality and cognitivist psychology are again made clear.

The key phases of SSM are as follows:

1. An initial phase of analysis that should *not* be pursued in systems terms but should build up what Checkland calls a 'rich picture' of the problem situation. This is to avoid jumping too rapidly to conclusions about representing the situation in systemic terms.

2. In the next phase, a number of systems are drawn from the 'rich picture'. These are systems regarded as relevant to improving the problem situation and each system represents a particular viewpoint because it is not obvious which system design is appropriate to the particular problem situation. Notice here that Checkland is thinking in Kantian terms in that he posits a rich reality from which categories of the mind, called systems, are to be drawn to form understanding. Here, the autonomous individual is hypothesising systems as mental constructs just like Kant's regulative ideas, which impart 'as if' purpose to the system.

3. The third phase is the construction of a number of system models. These models are not blueprints for the design of an objective system but conceptual models contributing to a debate about change. This again is Kantian in that the conceptual models are subject to formative causality. The interaction of their parts, the concepts of which the system consists, produces the whole conceptual system, which unfolds the purpose ascribed to it by its designers. As soon as a designer defines a system in terms of the interaction of its parts, that designer enfolds in it that which is to be unfolded by it.

The second and third steps in Checkland's approach are essential if it is to qualify as systems thinking. One has to posit wholes formed by interacting parts within a boundary to qualify as thinking in systems terms. However, this very act of thought entails exactly the same causal dualism as that found in Churchman's version of systems thinking and brings with it the same problems to do with freedom and novelty. There are thus autonomous individuals, the designers of the system, who are subject to a causality of freedom of choice and there is the system they have designed, which is subject to formative causality. Soft systems thinking is thus clearly a form of thinking in terms of causal dualities. One implicitly thinks about oneself as designer in terms of a causality of autonomy and then one thinks of oneself as part of the designed system in some sense and so subject to formative causality.

In a later version of SSM Checkland identified two strands. The first was a cultural strand consisting of a view of the interventions and rules of clients, problems solvers and other stakeholders. This involves taking a cultural view of the social systems, roles, norms and values, as well as the politics and sources of power. The second strand is the logical analysis. Both strands are modelled as systems and compared to the real situation to learn from differences.

Checkland, therefore, did not stop at the level of the cognising individual. In developing soft systems thinking, he advocated (Checkland, 1981; Checkland and Scholes, 1990) an interpretive approach to systems in which account is taken of the social rules and practices of participants in a problem situation. He defined a model, a learning cycle, with a number of steps that constitute the SSM, which is a methodology for systems designers to follow when facing soft, ill-structured problems *that include social practices, politics and culture.* Intertwined with this designed intervention is an investigation of the process of designing the intervention itself and the culture and politics this process involves. In other words, Checkland is taking account of the need for second-order systems thinking, or reflexivity, in which people seek to understand their own processes of interaction in systemic terms. In short people are being advised to think of their interaction with each other as creating a system of values, culture, ideas, power interests, social relations and so on.

In SSM, the subjective aspects of decision making are brought into consideration and a number of different systems models are developed to make explicit the implications of different viewpoints so that the consequences of alternative courses of possible action can be compared. The purpose is to provide a systemic learning process in which participants can come to appreciate more fully their differing viewpoints and how they might come to some kind of consensus or accommodation as the basis of change. SSM does not seek to study objective facts or search for causal relations because it views systems as the creative mental constructs of the human beings involved in the problem situation. Researchers and practitioners, therefore, need to understand subjectively the viewpoints and the intentions of all involved in a problem situation. SSM is a way of probing alternative worldviews and it uses specific models of systems to explicate those worldviews in specific situations rather than tries to identify the 'truth' about the nature of systems.

Note how Checkland is not explaining how people actually do go about dealing with life in organisations. Instead he presents prescriptions for dealing more effectively with problem situations. This heavily prescriptive rather than descriptive stance points to the underlying ideology to do with participation and the validation of alternative viewpoints.

In putting forward SSM, Checkland moved from a paradigm of goal seeking and optimisation, as in hard systems thinking, to a paradigm of learning, understood as the maintaining and development of relationships. Unlike Ackoff, Checkland does not seek to define an ideal future and identify ways of achieving it. Checkland moves from a positivist, functionalist philosophy to a phenomenological and interpretivist one, in which social reality is constructed and reconstructed in a social process in which meanings are negotiated. For him, an organisation is not an entity but part of the sense making of a group of people engaged in a dialogue. *Action is the managing of change in a set of relationships rather than taking rational action to achieve goals* (Checkland and Holwell, 1998). SSM helps to *manage relationships by orchestrating a process* through which organisational actors can learn about accommodations to each other that are feasible and desirable. Checkland provides lists of constitutive rules prescribing what constitutes a genuine soft systems study (Checkland, 1981; Checkland and Scholes, 1990), which ensures that the soft systems philosophy is carried out in practice. Managers are supposed to step out of the hurly-burly of ongoing events to make sense of these events and apply structured, systemic thinking to them. The use of systems models is meant to facilitate social processes of enquiry in which social realities are constructed. Notice here how the underlying notion of autonomous individuals is subtly retained although Checkland distances himself from 'rational action to achieve goals'. There is still a straightforward causality of individual freedom as evidenced in the managing and orchestrating of relationships and the intentional use of systems models to facilitate social processes.

6.4 Critical systems thinking

In their critiques of the approaches of Checkland, Ackoff and Churchman, Jackson, Mingers, Flood and Midgley developed critical systems thinking. This section takes the work of Midgley and Jackson as examples of this development.

Midgley on critical systems thinking

Midgley (2000) is concerned with problem situations faced by people and his question has to do with how they may be assisted by systems thinkers to deal with those problem situations, understood in terms of wholes. As with all systems thinkers, Midgley's approach is based upon the assumption that people are facing a systemic problem or issue to which they must find a solution or answer in order to act.

Midgley argues that systems thinkers seek to be as comprehensive as possible in their analyses but, because everything is connected to everything else, it is impossible to be totally comprehensive. It therefore becomes essential to make boundary judgements. For him, the making of boundary judgements is the core of systems thinking; it is what he calls systems philosophy. Boundaries are social and personal constructs that define the limits of the knowledge to be taken as pertinent (first-order system) and the people who may legitimately be considered as decision makers or stakeholders (second-order system). It is the inclusion of stakeholders that yields the second-order system and this means that there are no experts and that far from being comprehensive, systems thinking highlights the bounded nature of understanding. However, systems thinkers need to widen boundaries so as to sweep in more information because, even though understanding will never be comprehensive, it can be greater than what we currently have.

The perspective Midgley seems to be writing from is that of an agent (individual or group) confronted with some situation in which that agent must make a decision or choose an action. He advocates a particular approach to such a situation called systemic intervention. This is an approach to analysing the situation by making boundary judgements and the creative design of systemic methods of intervention to enable agents to look 'outwards' at the situation understood as a first-order system and to look 'back' to the knowledge-generating system (biological organisms, mind, social group, society, etc.) in which the agents/stakeholders are embedded. He understands the latter to be a second-order level or system. The first-order boundary judgement is one of including all those relationships judged to be pertinent to the situation to be analysed and in relation to which action must be taken. The second-order boundary judgement is one of including legitimate stakeholders, that is, those who have the legitimate right to be involved in or be affected by the situation or action. Boundary judgements are therefore matters of values and ethics and particular attention has to be paid to who or what is being excluded or marginalised. The excluded or marginalised can only be identified or understood in terms of a further boundary judgement. Although this involves infinite regress in theory, in practice people will not go on making boundary judgements but will act so that this is not a practical problem.

Since everything is connected to everything there are multiple realities. It is therefore necessary to make many different boundary judgements in any situation and this requires using many different theories and methodologies. This underlies the prescription of the creative design of methods, which means tailoring a mix of methods (critical systems heuristics, viable systems model, etc.) to the situation and varying them during the work of systemic intervention. Systemic intervention is always purposive and the purpose is improvement, that is, the realisation of a desired consequence that can be sustained indefinitely.

This approach, it seems to me, has a number of key features:

- Thought in the form of reflection, analysis, determination of desired consequences, intervention design, all of which are either before or apart from action.

- How agents come up with creative boundary judgements and subsequent actions is not explained.

- Participation is systemic, that is, embedded in a knowledge-generating system. Despite moving to a second-order level – the knowledge-generating system – the whole implication is one of agents who step outside the first-order level when they look outwards at it and outside the second-order level when they look back at it. It is recognised that this involves infinite regress but this is not regarded as a problem. In my view it is a serious problem because in practical situations people are trying to understand how to act creatively. When they start asking questions about who draws the boundaries, for example, the explanation tends to end up in mystical terms. This shuts down thinking with very important practical consequences. The infinite regress of systems thinking thus avoids explaining how novelty and creativity come about and also does not deal with the contradiction of freedom when individuals become parts of knowledge-generating systems.

- Midgley's argument reflects 'both . . . and' thinking. There is both the first-order and the second-order system. There are both systems and autonomous agents drawing boundaries.

- He implicitly assumes cognitivist/constructivist psychology.

Jackson on critical systems thinking

Jackson (2000) says that systems thinking is a holistic way of thinking that respects profound interconnectedness and pays attention to emergent properties in reaction to the reductionism of positivist science. Jackson calls for systems thinking to put people, with their different beliefs, purposes, evaluations and conflicts, at the centre of its concerns. Systems thinking uses models to try to learn about behaviour and does not take for granted, or impose, boundaries on situations. Instead, it reflects upon and questions where the boundary has been drawn and how this impacts on the kind of improvement that can be made. It encourages different perspectives and values as contributing to holistic appreciation.

Jackson says that the core systems concepts are:

- Holism, which means either taking the whole into the models or continually reflecting on the inevitable lack of comprehensiveness in a system design.

- Knowledge as inevitably organised into cognitive systems, which are structured frameworks linking elements of knowledge into coherent wholes. System is the fundamental element in ordering human thinking. This indicates the basis of critical systems thinking in cognitivist psychological theories.

- Boundaries drawn in different ways according to different worldviews.

- Jackson seeks to re-establish the hegemony of systems thinking by developing a coherent multi-perspective, multi-methodological framework encompassing all strands of systems thinking.

Jackson wants to show that systems thinking is not confined to the functionalist thinking of the first wave of twentieth-century systems theories but can contribute to radical and interpretive discourses. He believes that systems thinking must offer theoretical and methodological coherence in a world of multiple paradigms and clear, noncontradictory advice on how systems thinking can be put to use. Jackson defines the essence of critical systems thinking as critical and social awareness. Critical awareness is the differentiation of different strands and paradigms of systems thinking and social awareness is the understanding of the social contexts that lead to the popularity and use of the different systems methodologies.

Critical systems thinking seeks to address the problem created by the strengths and weaknesses of any particular systems approach depending upon the paradigm from which it is observed. Jackson develops what he calls the System of System Methodologies (SOSM) to encompass all methodologies and indicate how they create particular problem contexts, that is, how they depend upon different sets of assumptions.

Jackson distinguishes between method, methodology and meta-methodology in an ascending hierarchy. The method is the specific systemic tool applied in a particular problem situation. Methodology is the principles underlying methods, encompassing a number of methods. Meta-methodology is the relationship between methodologies. This meta-methodology includes all systems thinking in a pluralist framework that can be used to select a particular form of systems thinking, or some combination of them, or some combination of parts of them, as being appropriate to a particular problem context.

The SOSM, which is at the heart of Jackson's critical systems thinking, is thus a meta-methodological framework relating all systems methodologies to appropriate contexts, that is, according to the assumptions made about the nature of the problem. It brings pluralism to systems thinking by defining ideal problem contexts that differ from one another in a meaningful way. The existence of these ideal problem contexts implies, says Jackson, the need for a variety of problem-solving methodologies. Important differences in context should be reflected in differences of methodology.

The final element of Jackson's critical systems thinking is what he calls Total Systems Intervention (TSI), which is described as a meta-methodology. This takes different views on the problem situation and combines different methodologies to address them in three phases: the creativity phase, where metaphors are used to stimulate thinking; choice of the appropriate systems-based methodology; and implementation, which is the use of a particular systems methodology to implement specific proposals. The tools of TSI, consisting of lists, metaphors and models, are available to assist this process and the outcome is co-ordinated change that brings about improvement.

The essentials of critical systems thinking are commitment, pluralism and emancipation or improvement. It aims to help individuals realise their potential. The point of pluralism is to enable the best use of methodologies, methods, models, tools and techniques in any intervention. Critical systems thinking is thus very clearly an ideology. It is not a description or explanation of what people in organisations are actually doing but a set of prescriptions for how people should approach problem situations. The ideology is the commitment to pluralism, emancipation and improvement.

The causal duality characteristic of all of the systems thinking so far reviewed is apparent in Jackson's thinking. He writes about someone choosing an appropriate systems-based methodology. This immediately implies autonomous individuals subject to the causality of free choice. The person(s) choosing between different types of systems thinking are exercising some kind of choice based on their observation of context and systems methodology. Someone, the researcher, consultant or manager, has to form a judgement about the nature of the context of a problem situation and select the appropriate methodology. However, once the person has selected a methodology, that methodology is then applied to interacting humans, including the person(s) choosing the methodology. They are then subject to the formative causality of the system they have chosen. This is the dual causality and 'both . . . and' thinking that eliminates paradox. There is no sense in Jackson's discussion of the inherent paradox of observing that which includes oneself as participant.

Critical system thinking, therefore, has in common with all other forms of systems thinking the employment of central notions of wholes and boundaries. Difficulties with the concept of the whole are recognised and it is argued that they are inevitably incomplete. Difficulties with the notion of drawing boundaries and the infinite regress to which this leads are also recognised. However, these difficulties, and the inevitable causal dualism that goes with them, are not regarded as practically important. It is suggested that in practice they are overcome by pluralism.

Pluralism means taking many different perspectives on a problem situation and selecting those that are most helpful in a specific situation. The metaphor of lenses is often used. It is claimed that individuals have the capacity to change perspectives rather in the same way that one changes lenses in a pair of spectacles. The belief is that decision-making processes in groups, organisations and societies can be greatly improved if those involved avoid commitment to a particular perspective. Instead, they should engage in dialogues, hold their assumptions in abeyance and explore with each other different ways of understanding their situation. I would argue that this is a highly idealised notion and I do not think that it is possible for people to follow this advice The perspective we take on the world is intimately tied up with our very identities and we cannot easily change who we are as if our identities were simply interchangeable lenses.

In Chapter 4, I examined Wenger's arguments that meaning and identity are interlinked. In Part 3, I will make much the same argument. If the way we together make sense of our world is so much a part of who we are, is in fact a vital aspect of our identities, then putting on one lens after another would mean frequently changing identities, and pluralism implies that this is as easy as changing our spectacles. This is an idealised way out of conflict. People do not simply alter perspectives as if they did not matter – they kill each other for them because they are aspects of collective identity. Despite the concern with the social, with political action, power and freedom, the systemic way of looking at these does not accommodate their ordinary conflictual nature and it retains the primacy of the individual.

6.5 Autopoiesis

The biologists Maturana and Varela (1992) developed the notion of autopoiesis to account for what was distinctive about living systems, starting with a living cell. An autopoietic system is one whose components participate in production processes that produce those components and the boundary that separates the system from its environment. In doing this, Maturana and Varela are taking up a notion that is very similar to that of Kant's self-organising wholes. The autopoietic system consists of a circular organisation of production processes that continually replace the components necessary for the continuation of that system. In other words, the system creates itself. What this means can be seen most clearly in relation to living cells, which have: *identifiable components*, such as the nucleus and mitochondria in a cell, which produce a cell as a cell produces the nucleus and mitochondria; *mechanistic interactions* between components, such as the general physical laws that determine changes that occur within a cell; and an *identifiable boundary* produced by the system itself, such as a plasma membrane around a cell.

These properties have a number of distinctive consequences. The boundary is not imposed from outside but determined by internal relationships, and in producing its own boundaries, an autopoietic system establishes its own autonomy, that is, its identity. The focus of attention is, therefore, on single, self-defined individuals as parts of organisms, populations and species operating in an environment.

Maturana and Varela distinguish between the organisation and the structure of an autopoietic system. The organisation is the nature of the components and the relations between them required for an entity to belong to a particular category or type. It is thus an abstract generalisation that determines the identity of a system and this identity must remain constant and invariant if the system is not to disintegrate. The organisation of the system prescribes the properties of its components and the relationships between them that permit them to enter into a limited, but large, number of relations to each other while still preserving the fundamental form of the system. Organisation is, thus, the dynamics of interaction within the system, the context within which the components interact. Structure is the mode of operation that produces the potential range of structural arrangements that retain identity. The structure, then, is an actual example of the organisation. In other words, the structure embodies the abstract principles that define the organisation, or identity, of the system. It is the specific arrangement of the components at any particular moment. So, the organisation of a prokaryote cell, that which gives it its identity as this kind of cell, is the abstract features of cell membrane containing nucleoid material. The structure of a prokaryote cell is some living example that has the features just described. The organisation emerges from component interactions, while those interactions flow from the organisation so that the circular, self-referential process functions to sustain the organisation.

Identity determined from within

Autopoietic systems are organisationally closed. This means that the system's organisation, or identity, is not determined by anything outside of it. It may import energy or information and export waste but its identity is determined by its own operations.

There are no instructive interactions with its environment so that it can receive no constructive instructions from outside of itself. This does not mean that it is isolated: it is structurally coupled to other systems in its environment. The structural coupling means that change in other systems can perturb the system in question and so trigger internal change, but the nature of the change itself will be determined entirely by the production processes within the system.

The structural coupling between systems leads to evolution as structural, or natural, drift rather than adaptation to the environment. Evolution is the history of structural coupling and it is this history that is referred to as structural or natural drift. It is the system's own nature, identity and operational processes that determine the structural shape it takes, not the particular environmental perturbation it experiences. In this sense the system does not adapt to a unique pre-given environment. However, because it is structurally coupled to other systems, they together determine the history of structural coupling. Evolution is thus codetermined or co-created. Evolution is a reciprocal adjustment between structurally coupled entities that continually trigger changes in each other but these changes are always internally driven. Those changes that facilitate the process of autopoiesis, that is, the maintenance of identity, are maintained and conserved. The loss of identity is the destruction of the system. This leads to natural drift, which is change in the total population of species due to the success of some groups which maintain their identity and the dying out of others through the loss of their identity.

Comparisons with other systems theories

General systems theory is concerned with open systems. It explains how living systems function through importing energy from a pre-given environment, across the system's boundary with that environment, transforming the imports into a form of functioning, and then exporting waste to the environment. The boundary is a given and its formation is not due to the functioning of the system. The theory explains how the system sustains homeostasis, or equilibrium, through adaptation to the environment. The history of the system is not important in that what matters is the process of adaptation to the current environment. The principle of equifinality means that the state of homeostasis can be achieved from a large number of starting points and it is this that renders history unimportant.

Autopoietic systems are substantially different in that they produce their own boundaries. They are organisationally or operationally closed, which means that the state of the system is determined by its own operations, triggered by changes in other systems constituting the environment. This means that the system cannot be said to be adapting to a current state of the environment but, rather, that its current state reflects the history of its structural couplings with other systems. There is a similarity with homeostasis in that all structural changes must be consistent with the conservation of system identity. The only alternative is system destruction. While general systems theory understands the dynamics as simple movement to stability, autopoiesis theory understands the dynamic as wide variations consistent with identity. Open systems are self-regulating but they are not self-organising or emergent in the Kantian sense, while autopoietic systems are.

The cybernetic branch of systems thinking explains system stability in terms of negative feedback applied to information about the external environment with the system structure playing little part in the nature of change. A cybernetic system functions with reference to some state in its environment, adapting to that environment. Again, history is not important as far as the current adapted state is concerned, although it plays a part in movement towards that state. The internal structure of the cybernetic system is not considered to be important, only the gap between current state and the environmental state to which the system must adapt. An autopoietic system is substantially different in that it is the internal structure that determines how it changes in a way consistent with the conservation of its identity. History is important in the form of a history of structural coupling with other systems. Again, while cybernetic systems are self-regulating, they are not self-organising or emergent, while autopoietic systems are.

The systems dynamics branch of systems thinking understands systems change in terms of damping and amplifying feedback loops. Here the internal dynamic of the system determines the pattern of change. This is similar to autopoiesis, the difference being the emphasis the latter places on the conservation of identity, a concept lacking in systems dynamics. In systems dynamics, the system is self-influencing but not self-organising and emergent in the way an autopoietic system is.

Despite the significant differences between autopoietic systems theory and these other three systems theories, there is one important matter that they all have in common. This is the underlying causal framework, namely that of formative causality (*see* Chapter 2). They all assume that the future is the unfolding of what is already enfolded in the system or its environment. So, in general systems theory, an open system moves towards its homeostatic state of adaptation to the current environment. In cybernetics, the system moves towards the stable state specified in the external reference point. In systems dynamics, the system realises archetypal patterns of damping and amplifying feedback. Although autopoietic systems co-construct their environment rather than adapt to it, they also unfold an already enfolded identity. Autopoiesis quite explicitly excludes transformation of identity. As with other systems theories, autopoiesis cannot explain the emergence of novelty as the transformation of identity – the system either survives or it does not. Indeed, it quite explicitly excludes this possibility in its insistence on the conservation of identity.

This inability to explain the origins of novel identities is revealed in the concept of structural or natural drift. Natural drift is the history of structural coupling between systems, where either each system conserves its identity or that identity is destroyed. Natural drift discards systems that do not manage to conserve their identities. It explains the history of the destruction of species but does not explain new speciation. Evolution is understood as variations on a central theme, some of the variations being destroyed as they lose their identity. This is a view that understands evolution not as the transformation of identity, as the emergence of the truly novel, but as a continuing unfolding of an already enfolded central theme.

Autopoiesis and organisations

Those taking up the theory of autopoiesis to understand human action also apply the notion of autopoietic systems to groups and organisations. An organisation, for example, is thought of as a higher-level autopoietic system and often as a living autopoietic system. An organisation then is a self-contained entity functioning according to the principles of its own identity. It is an organisationally closed system but it is perturbed by changes in other organisations, which are also autopoietic systems. These perturbations trigger change but the change itself proceeds according to its own internal dynamics, its identity. It can receive no constructive instructions from outside. Instead organisations co-evolve, reflecting the history of their structural coupling.

Industries and societies can then also be understood as autopoietic systems (Luhmann, 1984). In Luhmann's formulation, a social system is a system of communicative events in that one communicative event produces another. This satisfies the condition of an autopoietic system that it should produce the components that constitute it because communications always refer to previous communications and lead on to others. Communicative events are not thoughts, behaviours or actions. They are utterances of information by one individual that have meaning for another individual. This system of communications is at a different level to people and their thoughts. In fact, people are the environment of a social system. The communicative events are separate from the people, who come and go, while the self-referring communication goes on.

Mingers (1995) critiques the work of Luhmann, pointing out that he does not adequately solve the problem of boundaries because his system of communicative events cannot be said to produce a boundary between communicative events and people. Secondly, he does not demonstrate how communicative events could emerge from the interactions of humans and yet constitute a domain independent of them. Communications require people to make them but in Luhmann's theory people disappear into the environment of disembodied communicative events.

Novelty and infinite regress

Earlier on, this chapter pointed to the problem encountered in the first wave of systems thinking, often called hard systems thinking. The problem was twofold. First, as soon as a system of the general, cybernetic and systems dynamics kinds is specified by an observer that system can only unfold what the observer has specified or enfolded in it. In other words, the causality is of the formative kind. The source of any transformative change, therefore, has to be the functioning of the observer. The observer is understood in terms of cognitive psychology as an individual who can choose to change. This is rationalist causality. The second problem is that the observer of the human system is also always a part of that system. The observer, therefore, is subject to two quite different kinds of causality. Second-order systems thinking sought to deal with this problem by incorporating the observer into the system. However, this immediately means that there is then no explanation of how the system can transform, simply because the source of that transformation, the observer, is now subject to formative causality, which cannot explain transformation. This leads to the problem of infinite regress in which there is first the mental model outside the system, then the learning model that changes the mental model. This exposes the inability of the cognitivist position to explain transformational change and the only way to stop the infinite regress is to appeal to some transcendent whole. The source of transformation is then of a mystical kind. The question now is whether the shift to autopoietic systems and constructivist psychology escapes this problem. It does not for the following reasons.

An autopoietic system changes when triggered by perturbations in its environment but the change itself is entirely determined by the internal dynamics of the system. Nothing outside it causes the change so it looks as if the problem of infinite regress does not even arise. However, the change that takes place can be one of only two possibilities. Either the change is such as to conserve the identity of the system or the system ceases to exist. There is no possibility of transformation in identity. The infinite regress does not get going because there is no question of the transformation of identity. However, a collection of autopoietic systems, in which each is triggering others, is co-creating the environment. That collection could then be understood as a higher-level autopoietic system that evolves through natural drift. This means that some of the lower-level systems survive while others become extinct. The higher-level system, therefore, changes. However, because it too is autopoietic it can only either sustain its identity or become extinct. Again there is no possibility of the higher-level system transforming its identity. However it too could be one of many autopoietic systems co-creating an environment as a higher-level system. That higher-level system could change because some of the lower-level systems are surviving while others are becoming extinct. However, it too can only sustain its identity or become extinct. In the end there is the same problem of infinite regress in order to explain the transformation of identity. Perhaps this is why Varela *et al.* (1995) also appeal in the end to Eastern mysticism.

Many believe that the notion of autopoiesis is useful in understanding the nature of single cells, but there is considerable disagreement as to whether other living systems are autopoietic. Maturana and Varela have not given definite or consistent views on whether multicellular organisms are autopoietic. Varela claims that the human nervous and immune systems are operationally closed. Both he and Maturana have said that they do not believe that social systems are autopoietic.

Some (Morgan, 1997) suggest that autopoiesis provides one of many possible metaphors for organisations, while others claim that social systems are autopoietic. Some have incorporated the work of Maturana and Varela into their thinking about knowledge creation and the management of intellectual capital (for example, Roos *et al.*, 1997). They draw on this work to conclude that knowledge is always located in the individual and created within autopoietic brains. For them, knowledge is always tacit and what is called explicit knowledge is data that help individuals to create their own knowledge.

6.6 Summary

This chapter provided a brief description of second-order and critical systems thinking and pointed to the conceptual problem of dual causality and the infinite regress associated with it. This problem is either ignored or eliminated in an appeal to some kind of mysticism. However, the move to second-order and critical systems thinking does present a much fuller account of social processes, conversation and narrative. It shows considerable concern with matters of participation and inclusion based on a view of the co-construction of the realities into which organisational members act. The chapter also looked briefly at the theory of autopoietic systems, which has been taken up by many organisational writers, and argued that it does not provide an adequate theory of change for organisations.

In the course of describing these systems theories a number of key debates have been pointed to. The first is concerned with whether organisations actually are systems or whether they are to be thought of 'as if' they were systems. The second debate has to do with the explicit incorporation of ideology into systems thinking, one that expressed emancipation and democracy. The third is the postmodern emphasis on a pluralism of viewpoints versus the modernist position in which claims to some kind of fundamental generality are made.

Further reading

Flood (1999), Midgley (2000) and Jackson (2000) all provide thorough accounts of the more recent developments in systems thinking described in this chapter. Mingers (1995) provides an important review and critique of autopoiesis.

Questions to aid further reflection

1. How does second-order systems thinking deal with the problem of infinite regress?
2. What ideologies do soft and critical systems thinking reflect?
3. What role does the notion of pluralism play in critical systems thinking?
4. What are the main differences between interactive planning, soft systems and critical systems thinking?
5. How are social processes understood in soft and critical systems thinking?
6. How would you think about strategic management from a second-order systems approach?
7. What theory of causality is reflected in autopoietic systems?
8. How do the systems theories reviewed in this chapter deal with the four key questions posed in Chapter 1?

Chapter 7

Thinking about strategy process

This chapter invites you to draw on your own experience to reflect on and consider the implications of:

- The way of thinking reflected in systemic notions of process, practice and activity in organisational life.

- How the notion of rationality has been increasingly problematised over a number of decades.

- The possibility of choosing, shaping or influencing particular processes, practices and outcomes in organisational life and the possibility of remaining in control.

- The manner in which the concept of emergence is used in systemic views on process.

- The manner in which the activity-based view of strategy draws attention to the ordinary everyday activities of managers.

- The theory of time, which is reflected in systemic views on organisational processes and practices.

- The key debates in the process and activity-based literatures concerning the relative importance of macro and micro levels; formal versus informal processes; and the tension between deliberately intended and emergent processes.

This chapter provides the basis for comparisons to be made with an alternative view of process to be explored in Chapter 10 below and begins to bring into focus matters that will be further developed in Part 3 of this book, namely, the importance of ordinary everyday activities of managers in processes of managing and strategising, which include conversation, political activities, emotion, improvisation and the connection with individual and collective identities. The concept of emergence, which is touched on in this chapter, will become central to the chapters in Part 3.

7.1 Introduction

Chapter 3 reviewed the theory of strategic choice and its intellectual foundations in economics and systems thinking. The main focus of attention in this theory is on choosing the optimal market position and resource base required to gain competitive advantage and so produce successful performance for the organisation. The choice of the strategy and the effectiveness of its implementation are taken to be the cause of successful performance. This focus of attention, therefore, is on the *content* of strategy, that is, on *what* the strategy *should be*. The approach is highly prescriptive and it tends to take for granted the *processes* through which the strategy is said to be chosen and then implemented, that is, the *how* of strategy. The taken-for-granted processes are those of technical rationality, which tend to be regarded as unproblematic. The review of strategic choice theory ended with a brief look at some key debates provoked by this theory. The first was firmly within the theory itself and had to do with whether the market position was more or less important than the resource base in determining performance. The second debate amounted to a direct challenge to the theory and those taking up the challenge argued that managers did not actually work in the technically rational manner assumed by the theory. For example, Mintzberg influentially argued for taking a more descriptive approach to strategy based on what managers actually did (Mintzberg, 1973, 1998) and his research into this led him to propose that while some strategies were the result of *deliberate* choices made in a more or less rational manner, many others *emerged* (Mintzberg, 1987; Mintzberg and Waters, 1985). What he and others were calling for was the focusing of attention on process, how strategies came about, rather than simply on content.

Chapter 4 then explored organisational learning processes, concentrating on the particularly influential theories of the learning organisation, while Chapter 5 considered how one might think about the psychological obstacles to learning in organisations from a psychoanalytic perspective. The emphasis these chapters placed on strategy process was continued in Chapter 6, which was concerned with later developments in systems thinking that took account of human participation in a human system, attending, in particular, to processes of dealing with problem issues in organisations. The intellectual foundations of these ways of thinking about strategy are to be found more in psychology and sociology than in economics, although the importance of systems thinking as foundational continues. All of these approaches to process in organisations drew attention to the political nature and practical difficulties involved in strategising, learning, creating knowledge and dealing with problem issues to do with cognitive, psychological and emotional factors, as well as uncertain, even turbulent environments. However, mainstream writing primarily responds to the prevalence of uncertainty, ambiguity, unconscious motivation, emotion and conflict in organisational life with calls for some form of conscious design at both the individual and organisational system levels. There is very little exploration of the notion of emergence which Mintzberg drew attention to but did not develop.

This chapter looks more explicitly at how influential writers have dealt with issues of uncertainty, ambiguity, emotion and conflict in the move from strategy content to strategy process. To begin with, consider the critique that has been made of process as technical rationality.

7.2 Rational process and its critics: bounded rationality

The word 'rational' can be used in different ways and its use can cause confusion in discussions about management processes. It is important, therefore, to distinguish one meaning from another. The notion of 'rationality' can be thought about in two ways:

1. Rationality is a method of deciding that involves setting clear objectives, gathering the facts, generating options, and choosing one that maximises or satisfices (i.e. approximately satisfies) the objective. Irrationality here is any behaviour that is not preceded by fixing objectives and weighing up options based on observable facts. It involves rejecting that which cannot be tested by reason applied to objective facts. Rationality here is behaving and deciding only on the basis of propositions that can be consciously reasoned about, rather than on the basis of customs, norms, emotions and beliefs. Irrationality here consists not only of fantasy but also of behaviour driven by emotions and beliefs even if they are connected to an emotional and ideological 'reality'. We can refer to this meaning of rationality as 'technical rationality'.

2. Alternatively, rational could be a method of deciding and acting in what seem to be sensible ways which are reasonable in the circumstances and sane, rather than foolish, absurd or extreme. Rationality here is behaving and deciding in a manner connected to 'reality' in some sense and judged likely to bring about desired consequences. Irrationality consists of fantasy-driven behaviour, while rationality involves testing for reality where that reality may well be of an emotional, ideological or cultural kind.

It is quite possible, indeed highly likely, that thinking rationally in its broader sense will lead to the conclusion that technical rationality should be avoided, that is, it may be quite 'rational' in sense 2 to avoid being rational in sense 1. So, in a totally unpredictable environment, under strict time pressures, it would not be logical or sensible to try to make decisions in a painstaking manner that could never anyhow succeed in meeting all the criteria of rationality in its sense 1 meaning. You may achieve a better response from others if you base your behaviour on emotion and belief in certain circumstances. To do so would therefore be rational in sense 2 but not in sense 1.

When managers know what their objectives are, agree upon them and find themselves acting in highly stable, predictable situations, it could well be effective to make decisions and act on the basis of processes akin to technical rationality. I say 'akin' because, even in these circumstances, the limits to human cognition, as well as the inevitability of human emotion, make purely technical rationality impossible for the following reasons.

Given clear agreed objectives in relation to clear-cut problems, pure rationality requires the decision maker to perceive the relevant objective facts in a direct manner. To perceive in a direct manner means to perceive without some kind of subjective interpretation that could open up the possibility of distortion. Having perceived the facts directly, the purely rational person would then have to store them in an exact form so that they could be processed later on without distortion. This would mean storing facts in categories that are precisely defined. Having memorised the facts in this fashion and having memorised the processing techniques required to manipulate them in much the same way, the rational person would then process the facts in a step-by-step fashion according to the rules of logic and select the action option that maximises the objective. The choice is predetermined by the facts and the problem is simply one of calculation.

However, as was recognised decades ago, humans do not perceive in this manner and they cannot therefore decide using a purely technically rational mode. Some kind of interpretation is always involved and it is highly questionable to think of the human brain/mind as some kind of information-processing device.

Bounded rationality, bureaucracy and dominant coalitions

Recognising the restrictive circumstance in which pure technical rationality could be applied, Herbert Simon developed the concept of bounded rationality (Simon, 1960). Bounded rationality is what might be called the weak form of technical rationality. Simon argued that managers could be rational only within boundaries imposed by resource availability, and by experience and knowledge of the range of options available for action. The collection, analysis and exchange of information all use resources, impose costs and are time consuming. It will therefore never be possible, or even sensible, to gather all the information and examine all the options. Instead of screening all the facts and generating all the action options before making a choice, managers, in common with all humans, take shortcuts. They employ trial-and-error search procedures to identify the most important bits of information in particular circumstances; they identify a limited range of the most important options revealed by the search; and then they act knowing only some of the potential outcomes of their actions. This means that they cannot take the action that maximises their objective. Instead they satisfice: they achieve the first satisfactory outcome they can in the circumstances. What they do then depends upon the sequence in which they discover changes, make choices and take actions.

Limited resources and the nature of the brain's processing capacity are also compensated for by the use of bureaucratic procedures (Cyert and March, 1963; March and Simon, 1958; Simon, 1960). As managers act together they develop rules of action and standard operating procedures in order to cut down on the need to make decisions afresh each time. Precedents are established and subsequent decisions are taken without having to repeat the search process anew. Decisions and actions come to be outputs of standard patterns of behaviour, that is, routines. For example, next year's budget is often determined largely by up-rating this year's spend. New alternatives tend to be sought only when a problem is detected: that is, some discrepancy between what is expected and what happens. Once such a discrepancy is detected, a trial-and-error search for a new solution is undertaken. Since all possible outcomes are not known, the tendency will be to make incremental decisions, that is, decisions with consequences as small and containable as possible. By relying on bureaucratic roles and incremental decision making, managers are able to reduce the levels of uncertainty they have to face. What they learn will be embodied in rules and procedures and these are used not to optimise outcomes, but to reduce uncertainty.

The lack of realism of the pure rationality model was recognised in other ways as well (Cyert and March, 1963). Although decisions and actions may flow from bureaucratic rules and precedent for most of the time, there are numerous occasions on which objectives and interests conflict. Which objectives are pursued will then depend on what the most powerful coalition of managers wants so that strategising becomes a political process.

The above paragraphs indicate how and why bounded-rationality/bureaucratic modes of deciding explain how managers actually strategise. However, like pure technical rationality, bounded rationality is still about solving problems, even though they may not be as clearly framed. The processes described are still step-by-step or algorithmic procedures, differing from those of technical rationality only in that they are routinised or heuristic, that is, involving rules of thumb to interpret and proceed by trial and error. An organisation is still seen as searching for satisfactory attainment of known objectives according to known criteria for success and failure.

What the bounded-rationality/bureaucratic explanations do is recognise economic constraints and take a more complicated view of human cognition; they recognise the limitations of human brain processing capacity. There is also some recognition of managing as problematic because of the need to interpret facts through some frame of reference. However, since this view of decision making assumes that the outcomes of different possible action options are roughly known, it provides an explanation that is useful only in rather restrictive conditions.

7.3 Rational process and its critics: trial-and-error action

The previous section has described how one response to the problems identified with thinking about decision making as technically rational is to say that decision making in practice is a form of trial and error. For some this process amounts to a form of muddling through, while for others it does have a logic to it.

Muddling through, organised anarchy and garbage-can decision making

Lindblom (1959) describes the process of strategic decision making as incremental, taking the form of 'muddling through'. His observations are derived from decision making in state sector organisations, but they are relevant to private sector organisations too. Since it is not possible, in complex situations, to identify all the objectives of different groups of people affected by an issue, policies are chosen directly. Instead of working from a statement of desired ends to the means required to achieve them, managers choose the ends and the means simultaneously. In other words, two different managers may choose the same policy or solution for different reasons.

This means that a policy cannot be judged according to how well it achieves a given end. Instead it is judged according to whether it is desirable in itself or not. A good policy is thus simply one that gets widespread support. It is then carried out in incremental stages, preserving flexibility to change it as conditions change. The policy is pursued in stages of successive limited comparisons. In this approach, dramatically new policies are not considered. New policies have to be close to existing ones and limited comparisons are made, making it unnecessary to undertake fundamental enquiries. The procedure also involves ignoring important possible consequences of policies, a necessary evil, perhaps, if anything is to be done. But serious lasting mistakes can be avoided because the changes are being made in small steps.

Cohen *et al.* (1972) have carried this kind of analysis of state sector organisations further. They described many of these organisations as organised anarchies and their decision-making processes as garbage-can decision making. In their research, they found that universities and some state bodies were characterised by widely distributed power and complex, unclear hierarchical structures. The hierarchical structure was such that just about any issue could be taken to just about any forum, by just about anyone. According to Cohen *et al.*, these institutions were noted for widespread participation in decision making, for ambiguous and intersecting job definitions, and a lack of shared cultural values across the whole organisation. What was found in the conditions prevailing at universities and some state bodies was said to be the following:

- Individuals and subunits do not have clear goals.
- No individual has much power and the distribution of power is not stably determined by sanctions, interdependence or contribution, but fluctuates with the context within which decisions are being made.
- Consequently, the distribution of power over time is not constant.
- The distribution of power over issue is also not constant.
- Furthermore, choices are often avoided, deferred, made by oversight, or never implemented.

Such organisations face high levels of uncertainty not only, or even primarily, because their environments are changing but because of the uncertainty of their technology. It is far from certain what good teaching is, for example, or what good medical care is. Such organisations therefore have to be collections of relatively free professionals, or at least this is what was thought at the time of this research. Over recent decades this view has been completley countermanded by managerialism in the public sector. However, these authors argued that a collective of relatively free professionals consituted what they called an organised anarchy. Here decisions and their outcomes occurred largely by chance. The flow of choices over time was erratic and haphazard. There was a continuing flow of problems, opportunities, solutions and choices coming together in a largely haphazard manner. This happened because there was no simple and clear hierarchy and because the distribution of power was close to equality. Note how this description of collegial processes of decision making reflects a particular ideology in which orderly rationality is impicitly valued while messier, more participative approaches are denigrated even though they may be regarded as neccessary.

Cohen *et al.* suggest that where power is widely dispersed so that there are no powerful actors who can enforce their wills; where power is therefore unstable over time and issue; where there is little sharing of values; where there are heavy workloads on individuals and meetings; where participation in decision making is open and fluid; where access to choice situations and participation structures is open and unclear; then choice will be determined largely by chance. The choice will depend entirely upon the context in which it is attended to; the level of attention paid to it in the light of all the other issues; who was present and participated; how they participated and how others interpreted that participation. Looking back it will not be possible to say that the choice occurred because some individual or group intended it. In this sense, intention or purpose is lacking in the choice process. There is no overall rhythm to the process and the specific sequence of choices is random and without any pattern. The sequence of specific choices can shoot just anywhere because important constraints provided by unequal power, clear hierarchies and job descriptions have been removed. Action is then the result of habit, custom or the unpredictable influence of others. It is impossible to predict the choice without knowing all the small details of the context. Intention is lost in the flow of events and goals are the product of sense-making activities after the event.

What they are talking about here is emergence but they ascribe it entirely to chance and assume that clear hierarchy, clear roles and clear tasks would prevent decisions 'just emerging'. When emergence is referred to in the organisational literature it is frequently equated with the kind or organised anarchy presented by Lindblom and others, that is, as decision making without intention where outcomes arise by chance. This view will be critically examined in Chapter 10, particularly the taken-for-granted view of emergence as chance and so the opposite of intention.

The search for error

Others took a less damning view of processes of trial and error. For example, Collingridge (1980) argued that effective decision making in conditions of ambiguity and uncertainty amounted to a search for error and a willingness to respond to its discovery. Instead of searching for the right decision as you would when using a technically rational mode, you need to choose an option that can most easily be found to be in error, error that can most easily be corrected. In this way fewer options are closed off; you get more opportunities to adjust what you have done when the circumstances change.

For example, if you can forecast future electricity demand reliably, the right solution to increased demand may be to build one large power station now. If, however, the future demand for electricity is highly uncertain, it would be better to build a number of small power stations, spread over a few years. That way you will find it easier to check for error in your forecast of future demand and easier to correct for mistakes. You may only have to close a small power station instead of running a large one at low capacity.

This kind of approach requires a considerable psychological adjustment. Most of us are used to being judged on whether we made the right choice. If it turns out to be wrong we devote much energy to concealing this fact, or in justifying our original decision. Applying technical rationality in conditions of great uncertainty leads us intentionally to avoid the search for error and to delay its recognition. If we abandoned technical rationality in these circumstances and searched for error instead, we would have to admit mistakes as soon as possible and avoid trying to justify them. Here we are talking about a mature recognition that being wrong is a valuable learning exercise, and this is a very difficult proposition in modern organisations.

Trial and error – logical incrementalism

Quinn (1978, 1980) argued that there was a degree of logic to trial-and-error processes. His research into the decision-making process of a number of companies revealed that most strategic decisions are made outside formal planning systems, that is, outside the bounded-rationality mode of decision making. He found that managers purposely blend behavioural, political and formal analytical processes together to improve the quality of decisions and implementation. Effective managers accept the high level of uncertainty and ambiguity they have to face and do not plan everything. They preserve the flexibility of an organisation to deal with the unforeseen as it happens. The key points that Quinn made about the strategic decision-making processes are as follows:

- Effective managers do not manage strategically in a piecemeal manner. They have a clear view on what they are trying to achieve, where they are trying to take the business. The destination is thus intended.

- But the route to that destination, the strategy itself, is not intended from the start in any comprehensive way. Effective managers know that the environment they have to operate in is uncertain and ambiguous. They therefore sustain flexibility by holding open the method of reaching the goal.

- The strategy itself then *emerges* from the interaction between different groupings of people in the organisation, and different groupings with different amounts of power, different requirements for and access to information, different time spans and parochial interests. These different pressures are orchestrated by senior managers. The top management level is always reassessing, integrating and organising.

- The strategy emerges or evolves in small incremental, opportunistic steps. But such evolution is not piecemeal or haphazard because of the agreed purpose and the role of top management in reassessing what is happening. It is this that provides the logic in the incremental action.

- The result is an organisation that is feeling its way to a known goal, opportunistically learning as it goes.

In Quinn's model of the strategy process, the organisation is driven by a central intention with respect to the goal, but there is no prior central intention as to how that goal is to be achieved; the route to the goal is discovered through a logical process of taking one small step at a time. In logical incrementalism, overall strategy emerges from step-by-step trial-and-error actions occurring in a number of different places in an organisation; for example, some may be making an acquisition while others are restructuring the reporting structure. These separate initiatives are pushed by champions, each attacking a class of strategic issue. The top executives manage the process, orchestrating it and sustaining some logic in it. It is this that makes it a purposeful, proactive technique. Urgent, interim, piecemeal decisions shape the organisation's future, but they do so in an orderly logical way. No one fully understands all the implications of what they are all doing together, but they are consciously preparing to move opportunistically.

Quinn (1978) illustrates his concept of strategies being developed through a process of logical incrementalism as follows:

When Exxon began its regional decentralization on a worldwide basis, the Executive Committee placed a senior officer and board member with a very responsive management style in a vaguely defined 'coordinative role' vis-à-vis its powerful and successful European units. Over a period of two years this man sensed problems and experimented with voluntary coordinative possibilities on a pan-European basis. Only later, with greater understanding by both corporate and divisional officers, did Exxon move to a more formal line relationship for what became Exxon Europe. Even then the move had to be coordinated in other areas of the world. All of these changes together led to an entirely new power balance toward regional and non-US concerns and to a more responsive worldwide posture for Exxon.   (Quinn, 1978, p. 10)

Processes of innovation

In more modern studies of the strategy process, this interest in trial-and-error decision making continues. For example, Dougherty (1992) studied the *processes of innovation* arguing that they are processes of creating and exploiting knowledge, which involve exploration, research, strategic scouting, and the advice of a council of elders. It is these processes that link technological opportunities and markets. Garud and Van de Ven (1992) studied processes of trial and error in product innovation in one organisation over a period of twelve years and argued that, when ambiguity is high and resources are slack, managers avoid trial and error and simply carry on with their strategy even if it is producing negative outcomes. Here they are pointing to how organisations often lose the capacity to change and remain stuck in a strategy that once served them well but no longer does so. However, when ambiguity is low and there is little slack in resources then managers engage in processes of trial and error and so develop new strategies for their organisations.

7.4 A contingency view of process

In taking account of how uncertainty impacts on decision-making processes a number of authors have related the appropriate decision-making processes to the context in which the decision has to be made. The process then becomes contingent on the situation.

Thompson and Tuden

Thompson and Tuden (1959) related the mode of decision making to:

- the lack of clarity in causal relationships;
- the lack of agreement over objectives.

Where causal connections are clear and objectives shared, the conditions are said to exist for managers to take decisions in a rational–logical way. As they move away from these conditions it is thought that it becomes impossible to apply rational logic and so they have to use some other approach. Thus, when causal connections are clear but managers conflict, then the decision has to be made in a political manner – those with the greatest power will prevail. The decision-making process here will be one in which managers build coalitions (Child, 1972, 1984; Cyert and March, 1963; Pfeffer, 1981). When managers are agreed on what they should be trying to achieve but the causal connections make it unclear how to do so, then they will have to use judgemental, or intuitive, modes of making a decision. They will have to reason by analogy; they will have to think laterally and use trial-and-error decision-making processes. The most difficult situation is where causality is unclear and objectives conflict. Here managers will have to decide in a way that combines intuitive individual judgements with political interactions in a group.

Duncan's approach

Other writers have also highlighted the connection between levels of uncertainty and modes of making decisions. Duncan (1972), for example, related modes of decision making to degrees of environmental complexity and stability.

He distinguished environments that are static from those that are dynamic, where dynamic means that the frequency, rate and extent of change are all high. He also categorised environments into those that are simple and those that are complex. In simple environments there are only a small number of variables that may change, while in complex environments there are many interconnected variables that may change. The two measures create four archetypal environments. The simplest archetype is the static and simple environment where the appropriate organisational system is the mechanistic one with its technical/boundedly rational modes of decision making. In the most demanding of these environmental archetypes, the complex dynamic one, it is only organic organisational systems that will survive, that is, those with flexible, political, intuitive modes of making decisions. In between, some pragmatic combination of the mechanistic and the organic is required.

Perrow's model

Perrow (1972) provided a model of the technology appropriate to different conditions, which makes much the same point. He posited a spectrum of problem-solving procedures. At one end of the spectrum there are problem-solving procedures available that are analysable: they can be broken down into prearranged steps or rules of a logical kind. At the other end the only procedures available in a particular situation are unanalysable or unprogrammable. This means that the problem is such that one has to use some unique method of solving it, unique to that particular problem. Then he classified problem-solving situations in terms of the number of exceptions. Few exceptions mean that there is little variability in the situation in which decisions have to be made. Actions and responses required are familiar and repetitive. At the other end of the spectrum there are many exceptions calling for different, unique responses.

In situations where there are few exceptions and analysable problem-solving techniques are available, then routine technology is appropriate. The decision-making mode here is the bounded rational one. As the situation and the problem-solving techniques become more complex the required technology has a higher skill content – engineering and craft skills are required. The corresponding decision-making mode calls for more judgement, but can still be reduced to step-to-step rules and procedures even though they may become very complex. But when the situation becomes complex and the techniques for solving problems become non-routine and unique, then the required technology is that of research and development. Here the decision-making mode involves unique methods of identifying new problems and finding unique solutions.

What emerges from all these analyses of decision situation and appropriate decision-making mode is this: making a decision in a technical/bounded rational manner is only a possibility in the most restrictive of conditions. It will not be possible in conditions of disagreement, ambiguity and uncertainty where decision making has to involve routines, judgements and politics and it is quite possible that organisations will show very little capacity for change. The implicit assumption throughout the work presented in this section is that managers are able to identify archetypal, typical situations and then rationally select appropriate processes, almost like tools, to use in making decisions. This is classic thought before action. It is common to present these theories of decision making using Cartesian diagrams with the implication that process can be moved around. One process then is assumed to be required to move around or change another process – Chapter 10 will take up this issue of the doubling of process. It will also be argued in Chapter 10 that the thinking in this section takes a 'both . . . and' form, which eliminates paradox (*see* Chapter 2). The writers in this section present a manager as being in control of the decision-making mode to be employed.

Now consider in more detail the political and routinised forms that decision making in organisations may take.

7.5 Institutions, routines, politics and cognitive frames

The literature on what has come to be known as strategy process research (which includes the writers already described in this chapter) pays particular attention to the internal dynamics of organisations and their internal politics, thereby humanising the strategy process to some extent. More recently, the process view has been linked (Chakravarthy and Doz, 1992) to the resource-based view (*see* Chapter 3), which emphasises the importance of resources and competences, including practices and procedures, in determining competitive advantage. There is also a link to institutional economics (DiMaggio and Powell, 1991; Tolbert and Zuckner, 1996), which is concerned with the behaviour of organisations as entities seeking legitimacy rather than competitive advantage. These writers seek to understand organisations in terms of routines, norms and rules.

Other writers in the strategy process tradition emphasise the frame of reference of managers. In doing this, the understanding of the limitations of technical rationality as strategy process is expanded. The notion of bounded rationality sees decision making as being mainly limited by the scarcity of time, resources and brain processing capacity. However, it is not just the capacity of the human brain that is relevant here because the way in which strategists think has the effect of filtering attention – managers only notice features and issues that their frame of reference, mental model or mental map predisposes them to notice. This point was made in Chapter 4 on the learning organisations. What might be called the *interpretive view*, therefore, takes cognitive limitations further to look at the limitations imposed by historically evolved ways of understanding and sense making. As mentioned in Chapter 4, Weick ([1969] 1979) argued that how managers scan and interpret their environment affects an organisation's strategic actions. Barr *et al.* (1992) explored the *process of managerial cognition* by comparing changes in the cognitive maps of top management over a 25-year period in a number of railway companies and related these to performance. They concluded that survivor companies were characterised by processes of continuous first- and second-order change (single- and double-loop learning) in the cognitive maps of top managers. When top managers make timely adjustments to their mental models they are able to make linkages between environmental change and corporate strategy and then organisational renewal is possible. Ginsberg and Venkatraman (1992) studied the *process of managerial interpretations* of technological innovations in 291 organisations and concluded that interpretations play a role in initiating strategic change while existing competitive posture influenced the implementation. Huff *et al.* (1992) explored the processes of inertia and stress in organisations using a simulation model and concluded that it is the initial level of inertia and stress rather than the external characteristics of stressors which influence strategic change.

Cognitive limitations, therefore, can lead to strategic drift. Here managers resist changes that conflict with their predominant way of understanding their organisation and its environment, until some crisis makes it impossible to continue doing so (Greiner, 1972; Johnson, 1987; Miller and Friesen, 1980; Mintzberg, 1989; Tushman and Romanelli, 1985). Before that, an organisation is driven down the same path by its own momentum, becoming more and more out of line with its environment. This gives rise to strategic drift. In other words, managers are caught in a fixed way of thinking. When that drift has taken an organisation too far from its environment, it then makes sudden revolutionary adjustments, rather than the incremental change Quinn talked about (see earlier in this chapter). These inevitably involve breaking the old frames its managers were working within and establishing new ones.

In his research into what managers actually do, Mintzberg (1973, 1998) challenged what he called the folklore of managerial activity:

- Instead of being reflective, systematic planners, managers work at an unrelenting pace, moving rapidly from one task to another.
- Instead of having no regular duties to perform because these are delegated, leaving room for planning, managers have to perform regular duties including rituals, ceremonies and negotiations.
- Instead of using aggregated information provided by formal management information systems, managers favour verbal communication and direct contact with people.
- Instead of being a scientist, managers rely on judgement and intuition.

Mintzberg (1987) talks about strategy as an activity of crafting and argues that strategies arise from the grass roots wherever people have the capacity to learn and the resources to support this. He talks about umbrella strategy where senior managers deliberately provide broad guidelines and deliberately leave others to interpret and act upon them so that the strategy emerges in its specifics. He talks about the strategy being *deliberately emergent*. He also says that process strategy is deliberately emergent in that senior mangers deliberately control the process of strategy formation but leave the content to others. Sometimes, emergent strategies need to be uprooted while those that prove useful can be made deliberate and incorporated into formal strategy. Notice here how the process of emergence is thought to be one over which managers can exert some degree of control. A different view of emergence will be provided in Chapter 10.

An early expression of how politics, routines and cognitive limitations impact on strategy process is to be found in the work of Mintzberg.

The Mintzberg decision process model

Mintzberg *et al.* (1976) analysed 25 decision-making processes and formulated a descriptive model as follows. The decision-making situations they analysed were characterised by novelty, complexity and open-endedness. The research showed that a final choice was made in such situations only after lengthy periods that involved many difficult discontinuous and recursive steps.

They divided the decision process into three basic stages:

1. identification;
2. development;
3. selection.

Within each of the stages a number of routines were identified as described in the following subsections.

The identification stage

It is a feature of high levels of uncertainty that the issues which have to be attended to, the problems and opportunities requiring a decision, are not at all obvious or clear. The need to make a decision therefore has to be identified or prompted by signals from the environment or from the working of the organisation. The stimulus for a decision may be the voluntary recognition of a problem or an opportunity, or the result of some pressure or mild crisis, or the consequence of a major crisis that forces a decision. Many small stimuli may need to build up to some threshold before a decision need is identified and a decision triggered. In this regard the frame of reference of the manager is important. So, if the stimuli for a decision fall outside the currently shared wisdom on what the business is about and how it should be conducted, then managers will ignore the stimuli. It will probably require a crisis to force a decision. Where managers identify a problem to which there is no clear solution there will be a tendency to ignore it. Problems for which there are matching solutions will tend to be dealt with.

Note how the routine for recognising a problem depends upon the behaviour of individuals, is culturally conditioned, and involves political interaction.

Once managers have recognised a problem, the diagnosis routine is activated. Old information channels are tapped and new ones opened. The diagnosis may be formal or it may be very informal. It may be skipped altogether. What managers are said to be doing here is trying to shape or structure the problems so that they may decide how to deal with them.

The development stage

The development stage takes up most of the time and resources in the decision-making process. It involves search routines and design routines.

The search routine is an attempt to discover a ready-made solution. These routines include simply waiting for an alternative to materialise, searching the memory of the organisation, that is, the solutions to problems that have worked before, scanning alternatives, hiring consultants and so on. Search is a step-by-step or incremental process beginning with the easiest search routine.

The design routine consists of the steps taken to design a solution to the problem. Mintzberg and colleagues found that organisations avoid custom-made routines for making a decision because they are expensive and require many steps. In other words, they tend not to consider large numbers of alternatives but to select one promising alternative, one that they have tried before. There is then a natural tendency to avoid innovative approaches to strategic decision making.

Selection

Selection is often intertwined with the development stage and involves the routines of screening, evaluative choice and authorisation. The screen routine is used to screen out options that are clearly not viable. It is a superficial routine. The evaluation choice routine was not found to be one that involved the use of analytical techniques. The evaluation criteria were normally based on judgement and intuition. Managers dealt with information overload by using precedent, imitation or tradition. They made judgements on a proposal according to the reliability of the proposer rather than the project, on the track record of the manager.

The final routine is that of authorisation and legitimation of the choices that individuals and groups have made.

The decision-making process identified here is a number of routines that have behavioural, political and learning aspects. The routines are affected by interruptions caused by environmental factors, by scheduling and timing delays as well as speed-ups generated by those involved in the process, by feedback delays as people wait for information and authorisation, and by cycling back to earlier stages in the process.

The writers in this section reflect a trend over the past few decades in which simplistic views of strategic choice and organisational learning are problematised, so challenging taken-for-granted views of managers being 'in control'. They point to how routinised strategising tends to become, so trapping managers into repetition leading to strategic drift. These views bring in the importance of interpretation and politics, judgement and evaluation. They continue, however, to present processes of decision making in stages or phases and they also continue to sustain an ideology of being 'in control' despite implying how difficult this is.

7.6 Process and time

So far, this chapter has reviewed some key writings focusing on the strategy process where process refers mainly to the *cognitive activities of managers and the decision-making techniques* involved in formulating and implementing strategy. Process, however, always involves time in that it is concerned with sequences of changing events, that is, with history. In the views presented so far, what is being assumed about time is not made explicit. Van de Ven (1992) points to four perspectives on the nature of time implicit in the literature on strategy process: life cycle, teleological, dialectic and evolutionary.

Time as life cycle

An example of the life-cycle theory of time is provided by the work of Greiner (1972) who presented a model of the life stages of an organisation in which the stages change in an incremental rather than a revolutionary way. He held that if companies are to sustain acceptable levels of performance then they must pass through five phases of growth, each of which is punctuated by a crisis. These phases and their related crises are as follows:

1. *Growth through creativity.* In the early stages of its life, when it has simple structures and is small, a company grows through the creative activity of small close-knit teams. At some point, however, the company faces the crisis of leadership. As the company increases in size it can no longer be managed in highly personal, informal ways.

2. *Growth through direction.* If the leadership crisis is successfully resolved through 'professionalising' the management, specialising its functions and setting up more formal systems, the company proceeds to grow in a centrally directed way. This leads to the crisis of autonomy. As the organisation gets bigger and bigger, employees feel restricted by the hierarchy and the top finds it more and more difficult to maintain detailed control.

3. *Growth through delegation.* If the autonomy crisis is successfully resolved through changing formal structures and decentralising, then growth proceeds through delegation. This brings with it a crisis of control. The top feels it is losing control and parochial attitudes develop in the divisions of the company.

4. *Growth through co-ordination.* If the control crisis is successfully resolved through installing systems to bring about greater co-ordination and co-operation, then the growth of the company proceeds. As it grows larger and more complex it is brought to the crisis of red tape. Increasingly bureaucratic controls create sharp divisions between head office staffs and operating divisions.

5. *Growth through collaboration.* Here the crisis of red tape is resolved through strong interpersonal collaboration and control through cultural sharing rather than formal controls. Greiner thinks that this growth stage may lead to a crisis of psychological saturation in which all become exhausted by teamwork. He thinks there may be a sixth growth phase involving a dual organisation: a 'habit' structure for daily work routines and a 'reflective' structure for stimulating new perspectives and personal enrichment.

Life-cycle theories point to the institutional rules or programmes that require development to proceed in the prescribed sequence. Note how the resolution of each crisis is itself a strategic choice made by individuals and how Greiner describes the resolution to each crisis in terms of more and more elaborate cybernetic systems. Life-cycle theory clearly assumes that the developing entity contains within it an underlying logic, programme or code that regulates the process of change and moves from a given origin to a mature stage. This theory, therefore, is an expression of Kantian systems thinking where the causality is formative (*see* Chapter 2). Time here is thought of in terms of a linear sequence with a clear beginning in an embryonic state proceeding step by step into the future to an already given end state. The present does not feature in any important way.

Teleology and time

Teleology refers either to purpose or to an end state or to both. It is an answer to the question of why a phenomenon is doing what it does, in order to do what. It involves a theory of time in which it is assumed that the developing entity is purposive and adaptive either in itself or in interaction with others. Models of planning and goal setting are obviously of this kind. This does not assume a necessary sequence of events but does imply standards by which change can be judged. There is no assumption of historical necessity and instead it is rational choice of objectives and actions that drives the development. This theory is, therefore, a reflection of Kant's notion of the autonomous individual where causality is rationalist (*see* Chapter 2). Here, too, time is thought of in linear terms. Through a rational understanding of the past, autonomous individuals are able to choose a future and move to that future through step-by-step actions. There is a linear movement from the past to the future in which the present is simply a point separating the future from the past.

Dialectic and time

In this theory of time the developing entity is assumed to interact with other entities in an essentially conflictual manner. According to Van de Ven, stability and change within this model depend upon relative power between opposing forces. Stability follows from struggles that sustain the status quo while change occurs when opposing forces go out of balance. The antithesis overthrows the thesis to produce a new thesis as synthesis. Schwenck and Thomas (1983) provide a description of the kind of dialectical enquiry that Van de Ven is referring to, identifying three procedures for formulating problems and selecting outcomes:

- *Brainstorming*. Here a small group of people work together to produce as many ideas as they can on what problems they should be addressing and how they should deal with them. The ideas generated can then be ranked and subjected to further study and consideration.

- *The devil's advocate*. Here one or more persons play the role of trying to tear a proposal apart. They are performing the important function of identifying and questioning the tacit assumptions that are being made.

- *Dialectical enquiry*. This is similar to the devil's advocate approach but involves groups of people. Two opposing groups enter into a debate on a proposed solution to a problem. Again, this focuses attention on tacit assumptions being made. From the two conflicting options being debated, a third, a synthesis of the two, may emerge.

I will be taking up the argument about dialectics and its implications for a theory of time in Chapter 10 but here I want to point out that Van de Ven and Schwenk and Thomas seem to regard dialectic as a debate and they use the language of Kantian dialectic to describe it. As I pointed out in Chapter 2, the essence of Kantian thinking is the dualism in which opposites are resolved in a way that eliminates paradox. What is being described above is a dualism of thesis and antithesis which is resolved by the formation of a synthesis. This implies a linear view of time in which there is a past consisting of an opposition of thesis and antithesis and a future in which they will be synthesised, creating an impression of closure in which there is no paradox. In Chapter 10, I will be describing how Hegel views dialectic as essentially paradoxical and therefore leads to a nonlinear understanding of time.

Evolution and time

In the evolutionary theories taken up in the organisational literature, chance variations in routines and other actions are held to create novel forms of behaviour (Aldrich, 1979), which are then competitively selected for survival (Hannan and Freeman, 1979). A key question in evolutionary theories of organisations has to do with whether traits can be inherited only through intergenerational processes, as held by social Darwinists such as Hannan and Freeman (1979) and Nelson and Winter (1982), or whether traits can be inherited within a generation through cultural evolution, mimicry and learning, as held by social Lamarkians such as Weick ([1969] 1979) and Burgelman (1991). Another key question has to do with whether evolution is continuous and gradual or revolutionary in the sense of punctuated equilibrium.

This view of evolution, imported directly from biology to constitute a theory of organisational development, implies a particular view of causality, which we might call adaptionist (Stacey *et al.*, 2000). The cause of change is chance, which is adapted to an environment through the process of competitive selection. This theory allows very little, if any, room for human agency. The process through which organisations become what they become is essentially one of chance. The implicit theory of time is once again linear in which a system moves from its past to an unknown future, changing through chance variations and competitive adaptation to an environment. Here too there is little significance attached to the present.

I will be referring back to the linear theories to time implicit in systemic views of organisations and their strategies when I come to an alternative understanding of process in Chapter 10.

7.7 Strategy process: a review

In reviewing the development of the process view of strategy so far described in this chapter, Chakravarthy and Doz (1992) argue that it is concerned with

> how managers can continuously influence the quality of the firm's strategic position through the use of appropriate decision processes and administrative systems. By the term administrative systems we mean the organizational structure, planning, control, incentives, human resource management, and value systems of a firm. The strategy process research subfield is concerned with how effective strategies are shaped within the firm and then validated and implemented efficiently. Moreover, the strategies of a firm must change in keeping with both new opportunities and threats in its environment and changes in its own competencies and strategic intent. The strategy process within a firm influences such adaptation and self-renewal. (p. 5)

The process subfield is thus distinct from the content subfield in that the latter focuses exclusively on *what* strategic positions lead to optimal performance. Both are interested in improving performance but the emphasis is different. While content research is concerned with the rationally chosen interaction of an organisation with its environment, the process subfield is concerned with interactions between people and groups of them within an organisation where that interaction could be rational, boundedly rational or even irrational. Process research is concerned with *how* an organisation achieves, maintains and modifies effective relationships between administrative systems and decision process, on the one hand, and competitive/resource positions, on the other hand. For example, Rajagopalan and Finkelstein (1992) explore the conditions under which an organisation's reward systems change and the linkages between such systems and strategic orientation. Floyd and Wooldridge (1992) researched the process of management involvement in the strategy process.

In commenting on the above quote from Chakravarthy and Doz, Schendel (1992) says that since processes inevitably affect performance there is an indirect causal connection so that both content and process researchers are interested in causal linkages to performance. He goes on to make the following points. The process researchers explore how effective strategies are shaped, validated and implemented where these are seen as separate activities. Shaping has to do with finding strategy and implementing has to do with using strategy, that is, with developing the administrative activities necessary to use strategy. Shaping need not engage the whole organisation but implementing does. However, some process researchers do not regard shaping and implementing as separate activities. Schendel argues that they then have to argue that strategy *merely emerges* from collective, random action in the everyday activities of an organisation. Schendel holds that this creates a problem of validation in that the only test of a particular strategy is its use – an essentially *ex post* view. He then says that without an *ex ante* prediction to be tested by *ex post* results there is no role for the management of strategy and no opportunity for the accumulation of knowledge. This is why process must include the validation step involving prediction in terms of what is expected to work. Validation of strategy found is thus essentially concerned with content. So, content and process can never be separated. The challenge is to select and use winning administrative processes to shape and use strategy to gain winning positions. He rejects any alternative as meaning that winning positions depend simply on luck.

Schendel's argument is based on the notion that thought comes before action. He also understands emergence purely in terms of chance. I mention these points here because they are commonly held views that will be critiqued from an alternative perspective on process to be developed in Chapter 10.

I want now to turn to more recent developments in researching the strategy process known as the activity-based view.

7.8 The activity-based view

In a special edition of the *Journal of Management Studies*, Johnson *et al.* (2003) argue that the process literature reviewed in previous sections of this chapter has defined process in terms of systems and processes of organisational wholes, which does not encourage probing into what goes on inside these wholes as practical activity and tools. In other words, the process literature takes a macro view of the organisation as a whole at the expense of the practical activity of the people involved. It follows that this literature does not pay much attention to managerial agency, tending to exaggerate its possibilities, on the one hand, and tending to place insufficient emphasis on how managers may become trapped in belief systems, on the other hand. Johnson *et al.* also say that the process literature has tended to be prescriptive, focusing on the overarching design of strategy and decision-making processes, remote from what managers actually do. In addition it sets up too sharp a dichotomy between content and process and lacks specific links between process and strategy outcome. Johnson *et al.* also question whether process research really helps managers in their strategising activities, such as how to run a strategy meeting. They call for a shift in the strategy debate towards a micro perspective, and by this they mean an emphasis on the detailed processes and practices of the day-to-day micro activities of organisational life that have to do with strategy. For them, practice is what goes on inside the process.

Whittington

In taking up such a challenge, Whittington (2002a) focuses on the formal activities of strategising rather than the informal processes that produce the emerging outcomes that Mintzberg has emphasised. The formal work of strategising encompasses data gathering and analysis, preparation of documents and presentations, project meetings, board meetings, conferences, workshops and away-days. It is performed by senior and middle managers, strategic planners, organisational development experts, management consultants, communication specialists, lawyers and investment bankers. Whittington distinguishes this work of formulation from that of implementation. He is concerned with where and how the work of strategising, both formulation and implementation, is done, who does it, what skills are required and how they are acquired, what the tools and techniques are, how the work itself is organised and how the products of this work are communicated and consumed. He argues that his interests are in tune with the interest in practice and communities of practice (*see* Chapter 4) in the literature (Brown and Duguid, 2001). For Whittington, practice has to do with the skills that people exercise in making do with the resources they have in their everyday lives and how this means focusing on people, their routines and their situated activities rather than abstract processes. The concern is with the local effectiveness of people and only indirectly with the performance of organisations as wholes. He is interested in the ability to enter strategic conversations and his practice perspective emphasises the creative improvisatory nature of the production and consumption of strategy.

Whittington (2002b) defines strategy content as the relationship between strategic choices and performance and strategy process as the activity in which strategies are formed and implemented (Rumelt *et al.*, 1994). He proposes an integrated model of strategic practice, consisting of three aspects, to complement the process and contents perspectives:

1. Strategy praxis (work), which is what strategisers actually do in a specific situation as distinct from general practices (*see* 3 below).

2. Strategy practitioners (workers), who participate in many activities, the praxis, and in doing so draw on a set of established general strategy practices (*see* 3 below).

3. General strategy practices (tools), which consist of what is done legitimately and what is done in a well-practised way through repeated doing. Practices refer to the social heritage of traditions, norms, rules and routines of a community, thought of as tools.

Whittington argues that there are those in the process perspective who emphasise strategy systems and decision processes in a fairly static sense (Chakravarthy and Doz, 1992) and those who emphasise change over time (Langley, 1999; Pettigrew, 1992; Van de Ven, 1992). For all of these writers, the analytical unit is the firm leading to a concern with the source of competitive advantage and performance in terms of superior financial outcomes. The practice perspective, however, is concerned with the relative diffusion of various technologies for doing strategy, focusing on practices, that is, tools. The question of performance has to do with a particular practice that performs well in terms of diffusion.

Salvato

Another writer in this field, Salvato (2003), starts with evolutionary models, developed by *economists*, in which organisations are understood to be collections of routines that are recombined in various ways over time (Nelson and Winter, 1982), so generating the variances upon which evolution depends. Some of these new combinations are selected, so providing new strategic configurations. This process of recombining routines provides the link between the micro and the macro. Salvato suggests that individual skills, rules of thumb, best practices and resources, as well as routines, are also drivers of strategic evolution. His main critique of evolutionary theory to date is that it lacks guidance on the interplay between managerial agency and organisational and environmental structure. To address this he proposes a *micro-sociological* account of strategic evolution in which strategic evolution is generated by *intentional* recombinations of what he calls core micro-strategies with new resources and organisational routines. A core micro-strategy is an established *system* of interconnected routines, micro-activities and resources that characterise most of the organisation's strategic initiatives.

This model focuses attention on the importance of managerial leadership, micro-level processes and the resource base. He points to a tension between coherent organisational-level strategy (the *whole*) and the many fragmented activities (the *parts*) to be found in daily organisational life. When the whole is emphasised it becomes difficult to implement strategies in daily activities, but when the parts are emphasised people engage in the generation of variance in micro terms to the exclusion of higher-meaning processes and so the organisation tends to drift. Salvato attaches central importance to the maintenance of balance between micro- and macro-activities. He also attaches great importance to managerial agency in guiding evolution. It is top management that continually recombines core micro-strategies in a process he calls the evolutionary engineering of knowledge. Here he differs from the earlier evolutionary models, which attach little importance to managerial agency. For Salvato, managers can shape and engineer micro-strategies. While the building blocks of core strategies emerge from the routinisation of micro-activities across an organisation, the gradual recognition of an emerging meta-project by top managers allows them to formalise its emergence, for example through appointing project managers and organising workshops.

Regner

Regner (2003) argues that strategy process research has shown that the strategy literature provides broad descriptions of aggregates involved in strategy making such as culture, politics and individual cognitive processes. In doing so it makes clear that strategy making involves a variety of actors and contextual influences. However, it provides only an imperfect understanding of particular situations because it does not pay attention to the micro level, particularly the practices of the actors involved. Although there is some writing on micro-politics, routines and interpretation modes, the practices of managers are usually described in vague terms such as artistic, creative, intuitive and crafting. Regner proposes the study of different categories of strategic activities in terms of their direction and the balance between exploration and exploitation. Regner is concerned with how managers inform themselves about strategies and how they make sense of them in terms of cognitive knowledge structures. This involves exploring the linkages between activity, understanding and strategic outcome.

Regner distinguishes strategy making at the centre of an organisation from that at the periphery. Strategy-making processes at the centre tend to be deductive, with a focus on industry levels and exploitation activities such as planning, analysis and standard routines. However, strategy making at the periphery tends to be inductive, with exploration activities such as trial-and-error, experiments, informal noticing and heuristic approaches. Regner's empirical work showed that strategies emerging in the periphery tended to be imprecise, vague and undefined in conditions of great uncertainty. Here strategies are impelled forward, often in secret, as the periphery tries to keep the centre away. They rely on knowledge rather than reports and forecasts and their activities are characterised by explorative enquiry. In the centre, however, activities are based on exploitation rather than exploration and tend to be confined to the existing organisation and industry. They rely on inference from history and emphasise the current knowledge structure.

Other writers

Jarzabkowski (2003) draws on activity theory according to which strategy *emerges* in the interaction of four components: the collective structures of an organisation; the primary actors, often equated with the top management team; the practical activities by means of which the actors interact; and strategic practices through which the interaction is conducted. She focuses on the formal practices of direction setting, resource allocation, monitoring and control. Such practices may distribute shared interpretations so contributing to continuity or they may mediate between contested interpretations leading to reinterpretation and change. She is therefore making a distinction between practice and practices, where the former is the *pattern of interaction* and interpretation *from which strategic activity emerges* over time (which is what Whittington calls praxis), and the latter is habits, artefacts and socially defined modes of strategic activity through which strategic activity is constructed (which is what Whittington also calls practices). Practices are the infrastructure generating the strategic activity which is practice (praxis). She seeks to explain continuity and change at the *activity system level* by focusing attention on practical activity. She draws on Vygotsky (1978) to argue that psychological development is a process of social interaction in particular historical and cultural contexts. Individuals attribute meaning to their own and others' actions through the interpretive interaction which enables them to engage in shared activity, which is practical because it is engaged in with an outcome in mind. She defines the context of such activity as an activity system, indeed the organisation is an activity system in which the components are actors, organisational structures (history, culture) and practical activities.

Maitlis and Lawrence (2003) argue that organisational strategising results from the interplay of organisational discourse and organisational politics and that there are certain forms of these that lead to strategic failure. They seek to understand the specific episodes of strategising, which they see as having four elements: an episode begins with the politics of taking a position in response to a specific strategic issue; then organisational members define a call of solutions; then the politics of assigning responsibility and accountability follow in which a specific instance of the general concept is developed; and the episode ends with the discursive construction of the strategic object, a specific strategy.

Brundin and Melin (2003) argue that the individual is central to the micro-activities of strategising but that individuals are essentially interactive when it comes to strategy and that emotions are highly important in such interaction. Brundin (2002) holds that emotions are socially constructed in relationships and that they evolve in institutional and organisational contexts. As such, emotions are important in all organisational operations including the activities of strategising. Emotions are important in processes of change as is the organisational ability to acknowledge, recognise, monitor, discriminate and attend to emotions. The ways in which emotions are expressed and communicated by strategic leaders will affect the evolution of strategy.

Samra-Fredericks (2003) focuses attention on the practices of strategists and how they do social and political life through talking as an essentially relational–rhetorical process (Shotter, 1993). Samra-Fredericks observes and records the talk-based interaction of strategists, including the way they express emotions and speak of morals in lived experience. She draws on ethnomethodology and conversation analysis to highlight the linguistic skills of strategists. In such activity they build a shared definition of the future. It is in language that strategists establish a 'discourse of direction'. Her research points to how the effective strategist is one with the skills of persuading others in a community to take his or her own view of the past and the future as the basis of making decisions. This is accomplished in the skilful use of metaphor and the ability to articulate complex and tacit forms of knowledge. Language is taken as the dominant symbolic system for the accomplishment of social reality. She is concerned with showing how the micro, as human interaction, is linked to the macro, as social structure. She describes how this is done in conversation using rhetorical devices. The appropriate display of emotion is a key tacit resource in persuading others. In such processes, people's identities are invoked and contested.

Having summarised the criticisms of the strategy process perspective made by writers in the activity-based view, and having described the approach of the latter, I now want to go on to explore the underlying assumptions of both perspectives.

7.9 The systemic way of thinking about process and practice

This section explores the way of thinking underlying the process and activity-based views of strategy. While they differ in terms of the level of analysis, with the process view focusing on the macro level and the activity-based view focusing on the micro level, in my view they both the reflect the same underlying way of thinking in that they both take a systemic perspective on process and practice. They are systemic in that they are concerned with what processes or activities produce a better whole or are diffused more effectively through the whole. In their interaction with each other, members of an organisation are assumed to be using processes, practices and activities, together thought of as an integrated system, to produce the position of an organisation, where the organisations is also thought of as a system. Consider, first, how the notion of process is presented in the process view.

Macro view of process

In the process view, process is taken to be specific categories of managerial action, namely, decision-making techniques/procedures and administrative systems. These may be formal, such as the approved planning and policy-making activities that produce deliberate strategies, or they may be informal, such as the political activities managers engage in, which are said to produce emergent strategies. Section 7.5 above gave further examples of the kind of processes writers in this tradition refer to: managerial cognition, interpretation and judgement; emotions of stress and inertia; innovation and the creating and exploiting of opportunities involved in this; reward systems; and management involvement. The process view seeks to explain *how managers use* processes such as these to adapt their organisation to its environment. There is a difference of view, however, as to how the decision-making techniques and administrative systems come about in the first place. Most writers in this field hold the view that the administrative systems and decision techniques are deliberately designed by managers, or at least that it is possible to do so if managers so choose and this extends even to their own cognitive frameworks. Other writers argue that at least some of the systems and techniques emerge in the ongoing activity of managers and, by and large, they take this to mean that those systems and techniques evolve largely through chance, as in garbage-can decision making and the evolutionary school. Alternatively, Mintzberg sees strategy and processes as deliberately emergent, that is, managers allow emergence to occur. However, emergent and deliberate are usually seen as polar opposites although they may be layered on to each other in the view of some, amounting to a doubling of process. From the deliberate perspective, design is a process being used to form processes of decision making and administration, even of emergence. Of course, processes of designing processes of decision making would themselves have to be designed, which is an even higher level process, suggesting an infinite regress of processes. From the evolutionary perspective, evolution is a process producing chance variations in processes of decision making which are subjected to another process: competitive selection.

Those taking the evolutionary or emergent perspectives naturally also hold the view that strategies emerge in what, for some, amounts to a form of muddling through, as in Lindblom's writing, or a form of garbage-can decision making in the writing of Cohen *et al.* (1972). Many find this a 'no hope' situation because it excludes the possibility of managerial agency and influence. Those taking the deliberate design perspective say that managers *use* the administrative systems and decision-making techniques they have designed to shape, validate and implement strategies. The activity of shaping is the finding of strategies, validating is the activity of predicting what shaping and using will work, and implementing is the activity of using the strategy through developing administrative systems, for example. It is in using the strategy in this way that the organisation is adapted to its environment and renewed in what amounts to a life cycle, designed evolution or deliberately chosen emergence.

There are three important points to note about the deliberate strategy process being suggested here. First there is a further layering of process on process. The designed administrative systems and decision-making techniques, which are processes, are used to shape, find, validate, predict and implement, all of which are themselves processes. Then the latter layer of process is used to adapt the organisation to its environment and this adaptation is itself also a process. The second point to notice is the theory of time underlying this view of process. Time takes a linear form moving from the past through the present towards the future, with the present as a point separating the past from the future. Managers inherit decision-making techniques and administrative systems from the past and then predict what processes will work in the future as the basis of designing the processes in the present. This is a view of phases through time in which managers first shape or find, then select the best design and then implement so that the organisation is then adapted to the environment. The third point to note is how process is equated with system. Managers are designing and using systems to adapt and change the organisation, which is also understood to be a system operating in a supra-system, the environment. The parts of the process/system are designed to be integrated, to fit together to produce an effective whole.

Micro view of process

Next consider the micro-, or activity-based view. Writers in this tradition are concerned with the practices and activities that go on *inside the process* understood as a whole. They, or at least some of them, are therefore making a distinction between process, practice and activity and declare their interest in exploring practice and activity. So, Whittington (2002b) defines practices as the social heritage of traditions, norms, rules and routines that managers draw upon and use as tools in their strategising activities (praxis), which encompass data gathering and analysis, preparation of documents and presentations, project meetings, board meetings, conferences, workshops and away-days. Jarzabkowski (2003) makes a similar distinction although using slightly different terminology. So, for her, strategic practices are the means through which management interaction is conducted, such as habits, artefacts and socially defined modes of strategic activity, which include direction setting, resource allocation, monitoring and control. Strategic practices are the infrastructure that generates strategic activity as in Whittington. Strategic activity, which Jarzabkowski calls practice as opposed to practices, is the pattern of interaction and interpretation from which strategies emerge. The practices these authors talk about are often defined as skills, routines, norms, rules and tools.

What I find striking is that all of these activities fall within the definition of process used in the process literature subfield, the difference being that process is viewed from a macro perspective in that subfield while the activity-based writers talk about process from a micro perspective. Do they then also layer process on process as the macro-process writers do?

To answer this question, consider the distinction between practices and activities (praxis). It seems to me that this distinction reflects, to some extent, Giddens' (1976, 1979, 1984) sociological theory of structuration. According to this theory, as individuals interact with each other, Whittington's activity (praxis) and Jarzabkowski's practice, they build up a fund of knowledge that is largely tacit and embodied in institutions as rules of conduct, social structures, procedures, routines and so on, which constitute practices. Institutions, social structures, or practices, embody the previous experience of a community of people and form the framework within which individual agents will make subsequent choices. Giddens refers to this as a duality of structure and agency in which, in their ongoing dealings with each other as agents, that is, in their activities or practice, individuals draw on the resources provided them in the form of social practices that evolve in their use. Here we do not get layers of process but one recursive process in which activity as process is drawing upon process as practice while sustaining and changing that practice. In Giddens' theory there are no levels with individual action at one level, the micro, and social structure at another, the macro. Instead they are on one level at which they recursively form each other. However, the writers in the activity-based tradition reviewed above do not go as far as Giddens because they retain the micro–macro split. In effect their notion of practice can be understood as micro processes while their notion of practices is the same as that of the macro process of the process school. There are, therefore, two layers of process in which the lower level draws on the higher level for tools. What the activity-based writers do is provide a link between the micro and the macro in that they together form the organisation understood as a system.

It is clear that the activity-based view falls firmly within systems thinking just as the process view does. Jarzabkowski (2003) wants to explain continuity and change at the activity system level and understands an organisation to be an activity system whose parts are collective structures, primary actors, practical activities and strategic practices. Strategic activity emerges in the interaction of the parts of the organisations. Salvato (2003) argues that organisations evolve through the intentional recombination by managers of what he calls core micro-strategies, which he defines as a system of interconnected routines, micro-activities and resources. He regards organisation-level strategy as the whole that exists in tension with the many fragmented activities, the parts, in organisations. He uses the concept of emergence but argues that top managers can formalise emerging projects by appointing project managers and organising workshops. What is striking, for me, in this activity-based literature is how intention and emergence are no longer polarised as they are in the process literature. Instead, evolution and emergence themselves become subject to intention. This involves layering a process of intentional design on top of a process of emergence. Given the systemic and deliberate nature of processes in the activity-based view, the implicit theory of time remains the linear one to be found in the process literature.

I am arguing, then, that the activity-based writers have not departed in any essential way from the understanding of process to be found in the process literature. If process is the 'how' of strategy then, since both groups of writers are describing how strategy is done, they are both talking about process. Both are systems in which process basically means the interaction of parts to produce wholes. Both have the same view of time. Both make the psychological assumptions of cognitivism in which the individual is the primary unit with a mind inside and society outside.

However, in focusing attention on the local, daily, practical activities of managers, the activity-based writers bring a much richer perspective on process. Some of the writers focus attention on emotion (Brundin and Melin, 2003), and discourse and politics (Maitlis and Lawrence, 2003) as well as conversation (Whittington, 2002a). They draw attention to the detail of rhetorical skills of effective strategists (Samra-Fredericks, 2003) and the creative, improvisatory nature of daily managerial activity. The moral aspects of strategising and the connection with identity are also brought out (Samra-Fredericks, 2003). These are all aspects of managerial life that are central to the perspective to be presented in Part 3 of this book.

There are two other points to note about the systemic view of practice. The first has to do with causality. In the deliberate view of process, whether it is considered to be micro or macro, there is the same duality as in all the other systems theories so far considered in this book. There is the formative causality of the system itself and the rationalist causality of the individuals who design it. The theory of causality is different in the evolutionary process view where we might call the causality adaptionist in that what drives the evolution is adaptation of chance variations to the environment.

The second point I want to draw attention to is a consequence of the linear view of time. As soon as one takes a linear view of time, it seems natural to hold that sensible people first think and then act – thought comes before action. However, some authors, such as Weick, argue that thought comes after action. Yet others talk about thought, or reflection, in action. The argument is really about whether, in separating thought from action, one is to be placed in the past and the other in the future or whether to locate thought in action. In all of these cases, the argument is based on the selection of an arbitrary beginning at which point either thought or action is located and both are attributed to autonomous individuals who may well be interacting with each other but are nevertheless autonomous. I make this point here because I will be returning to it in Part 3, which will introduce a different notion of time in which it is purely arbitrary to place thought before, after or at the same time as action.

7.10 Summary

The theory of strategic choice is primarily concerned with the content of strategy and implicitly assumes a technically rational process for formulating and implementing strategies. This chapter has reviewed the process view of strategy, which focuses on how strategies come about rather than what their content is. This literature critiques the technically rational mode of strategic decision making by pointing to the information-processing limits of the human brain and by taking an interpretive view in which the cognitive frameworks of managers, their mental models, restrict what they attend to, so making it possible for organisations to simply repeat old strategies and thus experience strategic drift. The process view focuses attention on the routines managers use in making decisions and the often trial-and-error nature of the strategy process.

The process view focuses attention at the macro level of an organisation as a whole and this has led to the critique presented by the activity-based view of how strategies arise. This view takes a micro perspective and attends to the daily practical activities of managers in their local situations. When this is done it becomes apparent that emotions play a part in strategising and other factors such as conversation and politics become important. The creative improvisational nature of strategising is emphasised.

The key debates in this literature can be summarised as follows:

- Should the process of strategising be understood at the macro or the micro level?
- Does strategy determine organisational structure or the other way around?
- Do individual agency or organisational structures and routines take primacy in the strategy process?
- Should attention be focused on formal decision-making processes or on informal ones?
- Are strategy and strategy processes primarily deliberate or emergent and can the latter be deliberately chosen, shaped or influenced?

Further reading

The 1992 special issue of the *Strategic Management Journal* edited by Chakravarthy and Doz provides a good overview of the process perspective on strategy. The 2003 special issue of *Journal of Management Studies* edited by Johnson, Melin and Whittington provides a good overview of the activity-based view.

Questions to aid further reflection

1. What do the concepts of process and practice mean in the process and activity-based views of strategy?
2. What traditions of thought and taken-for-granted assumptions are reflected in the notions of process, practice and activity in the process and activity-based views of strategy?
3. In your own experience, what do you find practical in the writings of the strategy process and activity-based views?
4. What are the similarities and differences between process and activity-based views of strategy?
5. Why is it problematic to think of strategising as a rational activity?
6. How do writers in this chapter use the concept of emergence?
7. What does it means to say that the writers reviewed in this chapter double process and why might this be problematic?

8. How do the views on the strategy process expressed in this chapter deal with the key questions posed in Chapter 1? These key questions are as follows:

    (i)   How does the theory understand the nature of human interacting and relating?

    (ii) What theory of human psychology, that is ways of knowing and behaving, does each theory of strategy and organisational change assume?

    (iii) What methodology underlies the theory?

    (iv) How does the theory deal with paradox?

Part 2

The challenge of complexity to ways of thinking

Part 1 of this book has described how the 1940s and 1950s saw the development of a number of closely related ideas. At much the same time, engineers, mathematicians, biologists and psychologists were developing the application of systems theories taking the form of open systems, cybernetics and systems dynamics. These systems theories were closely related to the development of computer languages, cognitivist psychology and the sender–receiver model of communication. Over the decades that followed, all of these theories and applications were used, in one way or another, to construct ways of making sense of organisational life. The central themes running through all of these developments are those of the autonomous individual who is primary and prior to the group, and the concern with the control of systems. This first wave of twentieth-century systems thinking raised a number of problems that second-order systems thinking sought to address. One of these problems had to do with the fact that the observer of a human system is also simultaneously a participant in that system. This led to soft and critical systems thinking, which shifted the focus of attention from the dynamical properties of systems as such to the social practices of those using systemic tools in human activities. Ideology, power, conflict, participation, learning and narratives in social processes all feature strongly in these explanations of decision making and change in organisations.

The 1970s and 1980s bear some similarities to the 1940s and 1950s in terms of the development of systemic theories in that mathematicians, physicists, meteorologists, chemists, biologists, economists, psychologists and computer scientists worked across their disciplines to develop new theories of systems. Their work goes under titles such as chaos theory, dissipative structures, complex adaptive systems, and has come to be known as nonlinear dynamics or the complexity sciences. What they have in common is the centrality they give to nonlinear relationships. Unlike the development of second-order, soft and critical systems thinking in the social sciences, this new wave of interest in complex systems has been very much concerned with the dynamical properties of systems as such. This has brought new insights into our understanding of systems functioning. Let me explain why this matters.

Part 1 explored the way of thinking reflected in the currently dominant discourse about organisations and their management. The dominant discourse is that way of talking and writing about organisations that is immediately recognisable to organisational practitioners, educators and researchers. It sets the most acceptable terms within which debates about, and funded research into, organisations and their management can be conducted. As such, it reflects particular, fundamental, taken-for-granted assumptions about organisational worlds that constitute 'common sense' ways of thinking. If one is to be readily understood and persuasive in organisational and research communities then one must argue within the dominant way of thinking, or at least in ways that are recognisable within its terms. The aim of the chapters in Part 1 was to identify the different strands of the currently dominant discourse, including its critics, so as to clarify the differences and similarities in the ways of thinking that they reflect.

The strands of thinking about organisations identified in Part 1 were described as the theory of strategic choice, the theory of the learning organisation, open systems–psychoanalytic perspectives on organisations, and second-order systems thinking. Common to all of them is the assumption that organisations are systems, or at least that they are to be thought of 'as if' they are systems. The different strands of thinking assume different kinds of system with consequent important implications. In strategic choice theory the main assumption is that organisations are to be designed and managed as cybernetic, that is, self-regulating, systems. In theories to do with organisational learning it is mostly assumed that organisations are to be managed in recognition of their being systems of the systems dynamics type. In open systems–psychoanalytic perspectives, the system is assumed to be an open system. Second-order systems thinking, in contrast to the strands so far mentioned, draws on all these systems theories but usually does not regard any system as actually existing in the real world – they are all mental constructs.

Since organisations have to do with people there always has to be some explicit, or quite often implicit, assumption about human psychology. Common to all of the strands of thinking in the dominant discourse is the psychological assumption that the individual is primary and exists at a different level from a group, organisation or society. Individuals, with minds inside them, form groups, organisations and societies outside them, at a higher level to them, which then act back on them as a causal force with regard to their actions. The different strands of the dominant discourse express this common assumption by drawing on different psychological theories which have important implications. Strategic choice and learning organisation theories draw heavily on cognitivist and humanistic psychology and to a much lesser extent on constructivism. The open system–psychoanalytic perspective reflects the assumptions of psychoanalysis. Second-order systems thinking could draw on all of the mentioned psychological theories.

The chapters in Part 1 explored the differences between the ways of thinking of these different strands consequent upon their different assumptions about psychology and the nature of systems. Just as important, however, are the entailments of what is common to all of them. They all make the following assumptions:

- There is some position external to the system from which powerful, rational individuals can, in principle, objectively observe the system and formulate hypotheses about it, on the basis of which they can design the system to produce that which is desirable to them and, hopefully, the wider community. Usually this is quite taken for granted, although second-order systems thinking does grapple, unsuccessfully I argue, with the problem created by the fact that the external observer is also a participant in the system. Where the problematic nature of the assumption that individuals can design human systems is recognised it is normally resolved by arguing that 'you', the powerful, rational individual, can at least set a direction or present a vision so that the system will produce reasonably desirable outcomes, or, failing even this, 'you' can design the conditions or shape the processes within which others will, more or less, operate the system to desired ends. If even this watered-down assumption is questioned, the immediate response is that the only alternative is pure chance, which leaves no role for leaders or managers.

- This first assumption amounts to one that rationalist causality is applicable to human action, although all of the strands of thinking in the dominant discourse recognise, in one way or another, the severe limitations to human rationality.

- The first assumption also immediately entails a further assumption about system predictability. A system can only be designed and operated to produce a desirable outcome set in advance if its operation is reasonably predictable. The purpose of the design and operation is to reduce uncertainty and increase the regularity and stability of system operation so as to make possible the realisation of the purposes ascribed to it by its designers. Success is equated with stability.

- Stability of system operation requires a reasonable degree of consensus between the individuals who are, or at least operate, the systems. What is required therefore is agreement on purpose and task and this is aided by strongly shared cultures and values. It is the role of leaders and managers to inspire, motivate and persuade others to act in the best interests of the 'whole'.

- The assumptions about predictability and stability immediately imply a particular theory of causality as far as the system is concerned and these are either efficient 'if–then' or formative causality.

- Causality is thus dual, with rationalist causality ascribed to designing individuals and formative causality ascribed to the system they design.

- The primary task of leading and managing is to be in control of the direction of the organisation, whether in a 'command and control' way or in some other more facilitative way in which others are empowered and invited to participate.

The way of thinking reflecting the above assumptions was primarily developed in relation to the private sector of Western economies. However, over the last two decades there has been a major shift in the form of public sector governance. Marketisation and managerialism have been imported into the public sector, and also into non-governmental organisations (NGOs), from the private sector. The private sector way of thinking about organisations now dominates these sectors too.

The assumptions common to the different strands of the discourse now dominant across all organisations reflects much more than the basis of intellectual argument. Even more importantly and more powerfully they reflect dominant ideologies. At the centre of this ideology is the belief in the possibility of, and the necessity for, *control*. This ideology has a long history in the West. It justifies the use of the natural sciences to control the resources of nature and the central concern with efficiency in organisations even if people experience this as oppression. The domination of nature and the oppression of people in the interests of efficiency have, of course, been fiercely contested for some considerable time. This is evident in the ecological movement with its ideology of preserving the planet, in the human relations movement and humanistic psychology and its motivational ideology within organisations, in the call for empowerment, democracy, emancipation, pluralism and participative decision making, for example in second-order systems thinking, and in the move to the mystical and the spiritual, for example in learning organisation theory.

However, all of these ideological responses to the domination and oppression that can flow from of an ideology of control are themselves dependent upon control. At issue is not control itself but the manner in which the control is to be exercised and the consequences it has. So, the ecological movement expresses its ideology in a call for the control of industry and consumers in the interests of preserving the planet. The ideology of democracy, emancipation, pluralism and empowerment expresses the manner in which control should be exercised rather than its abandonment. Indeed the ideology of progress and improvement, more recently expressed in the pubic sector as modernisation, depends very heavily on the ideology of control. To question the ability of humans to be 'in control' is to question a belief that groups of well-meaning people can devise ways of improving whole sectors of human activity such as healthcare. Much the same point is true of those who call for more attention to be paid to the spiritual and the mystical in organisational life in the interests of securing simpler, better ways for organisations to operate so that people can find fulfilling lives.

In challenging the dominant way of thinking about organisations, therefore, one is engaging in far more than an intellectual debate. To question a way of thinking is to question the dominant ideologies underpinning it and throw into confusion the sense people make of what they are doing and who they are at a very deep level. To question the ideology of control is not simply to question domination and oppression but also to question the nature of our ability to preserve and improve the world we live in. It is to question some of the deepest beliefs people have about what it is possible for them to do for the good.

To claim, then, that the development of what have come to be called the natural complexity sciences potentially presents a major challenge to ways of thinking, not just in the natural sciences but also in relation to human actions and organisations, is a claim of major importance which can be experienced as deeply threatening. Although they have their origins over a century ago, it is only since the 1960s that the complexity sciences really began to develop and only over the past two decades that they have attracted significant attention in both the natural and social sciences. They represent the most significant advance in the understanding of the nature of systems since the middle of the twentieth century. Since the currently dominant discourse on organisations is so heavily dependent on the first wave of system ideas it is important to consider in what way the new systems theories support or contest those developed in the middle of the twentieth century.

For this reason the first chapter in this part, Chapter 8, briefly reviews some of the main ideas in the complexity sciences and the one after that considers how these ideas have been taken up by some writers on organisations. Chapter 8 also points to the different understanding different natural scientists have of complex systems. For some, complexity does not amount to science at all. Amongst those who do argue that their complexity work is scientific, there are some, perhaps the majority, who do not regard the insights of complexity theories as a major challenge to the natural science project of the past few hundred years to do with certainty and control. However, there are others who rigorously argue that complexity insights do present a major challenge to currently dominant ways of thinking and call for a radical re-thinking of the scientific project. So, what are the insights that might lead one to such a radical re-thinking?

First, complex systems display spatial patterns called 'fractals' and patterns of movement over time that have been described as 'chaos' or 'the edge of chaos'. These terms may be suggestive of fragmentation or utter confusion but in fact they refer to the discovery of *coherent patterns* in what might have looked random and so without pattern. However, these patterns are not what we are used to. Fractals, for example, display a regular degree of irregularity so that within each space of stability there is always instability. Movement over time called 'chaotic' or at the 'edge of chaos' is movement that is regular and irregular, stable and unstable, at the same time. Such systems operate far from equilibrium where they have structure but the structure is dissipating. In other words, complex systems are characterised by paradoxical dynamics. Most phenomena in nature, and all living phenomena, are held to be characterised by these paradoxical dynamics. This challenges the assumptions about stability and equilibrium in previous systems theories, the ones previously imported into the dominant way of thinking about organisations, which equate stability with success. If paradoxical dynamics have anything to do with organisations then the dominant discourse's equation of success with stability would be open to question and we would have to explore the ways in which instability is vital in organisational life.

Second, systems operating far from equilibrium, in chaos or at the edge of chaos are radically unpredictable over the long term. They are characterised by predictability and unpredictability at the same time in the present and over the long term their futures are unknowable when they are evolving in the presence of diversity. This challenges the assumption of previous systems theories that the movement of systems is predictable, or at least follows given archetypes. It is these latter assumptions that were imported to form the basis of the currently dominant way of thinking about organisations. If radical unpredictability is a characteristic or organisational life then we clearly need to re-think the most taken-for-granted prescriptions for managing organisations.

Third, the future of complex systems is under perpetual construction in the self-organising, that is, local interacting, of the entities comprising them. The long-term future of the whole system, that is, the pattern of relationships across whole populations of agents, emerges in such local interaction. Emergence means that there is no blueprint, plan or programme for the whole system, the population-wide pattern. In other words, the whole cannot be designed by any of the agents comprising it because they collectively produce it as participants in it. This challenges the assumptions made in previous systems theories about the possibility of taking the position of external observer and intervening in, even designing, the whole system. If the development of an organisation emerges in the local interaction of its members then we will have to re-think all the approaches which suppose that powerful or well-meaning people can directly change the 'whole'.

Fourth, complex systems can evolve only when the agents comprising them are diverse. Evolution, the production of novelty, and creativity are possible only where there is diversity and hence conflicting constraints. Evolution as emergence occurs primarily through the self-organising, that is, local conflictual interacting, of the agents rather than by plan or central design, which inspires harmony. This challenges the assumption of previous systems theories that functioning, developing systems are characterised by harmony where the pieces fit together. Again this challenges the previous systems theories imported into thinking about organisations.

If these four insights from the complexity sciences were to replace the assumptions of earlier systems theories in thinking about organisations, they would lead to a very different way of understanding organisational life. We would need to understand how people together are coping with fundamental unpredictability, how organisations as population-wide patterns are evolving in many, many local interactions, and what role diversity, conflict and non-average behaviour play in all of this. We would have to reconsider what we think we are doing when we formulate and implement strategic plans and design organisations, re-engineer processes, plan culture changes, install values, develop policies for the 'whole', and so on. In other words, we would have to re-think what we mean by control because under the new assumptions no one would be 'in control'. It follows that no well-meaning group of people could directly improve the whole. One consequence of taking the radical insights of complexity theories seriously, then, would be the serious undermining of dominant ideologies.

However, others have a different take on what the complexity sciences mean for human action. Ecologists might take the challenge to the control paradigm as supporting their ideology on the basis of which they can resist the folly of treating nature as humans do. Others may see in the emphasis on local interaction support for their ideology of more caring relationships between people. Yet others may resonate with the unknowability of complex system futures and link this with something spiritual, while regarding emergence as linked to something mystical. And others may find in the study and modelling of complex systems a different way to control systems and so sustain the control ideology.

In view of all of these possibilities it seems important to me to devote some effort to trying to understand just what different complexity scientists have to say and just how writers on organisations are using their work. That is the purpose of this part of the book.

Chapter 8

The complexity sciences

This chapter invites you to draw on your own experience to reflect on and consider the implications of:

- Whether the traditional scientific project of certainty is undermined by the complexity sciences.

- The role of conflicting constraints in the functioning of complex phenomena.

- The relationship between local interaction and population-wide pattern.

- The different theories of causality implicit in models of complexity.

- The different ways in which theories of complexity are interpreted.

- Whether developments in the complexity sciences present key challenges to the fundamental assumptions previously imported from the natural sciences into thinking about organisations.

- The challenge that notions of self organisation and emergence present to the possibility of whole system design to be found in mainstream thinking about organisations.

- The importance of diversity, difference and non-average behaviour in the generation of novelty and what challenge this presents to mainstream thinking about organisations.

It is important to understand the ideas presented in this chapter because all of the theories of organisation reviewed in Part 1 rely on ideas that were originally imported from the natural sciences, and the complexity sciences could present significant challenges to these older imports. It is important, therefore to consider the challenges presented by these more recent ideas for taken-for-granted ways of understanding organisations. The key ideas in this chapter will serve as analogies for the alternative way of thinking about organisations to be presented in Part 3. This chapter is thus an important transition from Part 1 to Part 3.

8.1 Introduction

For some 400 years now, since the times of Newton, Bacon and Descartes, scientists have tended to understand the natural world in terms of machine-like regularity in which given inputs are translated through absolutely fixed linear laws into given outputs. For example, if you apply a given force to a ball of a given weight, the laws of motion will determine exactly how far the ball will move on a horizontal plane in a vacuum. Cause and effect are related in a straightforward linear way. On this view, once one has discovered the fixed laws of nature and gathered data on the inputs to those laws, one will be able to predict the behaviour of nature. Once one knows how nature would have behaved without human intervention, one can intervene by altering the inputs to the laws and so get nature to do something different, something humans want it to do. According to this Newtonian view of the world, humans will ultimately be able to dominate nature.

This whole way of reasoning and understanding was imported into economics, where it is particularly conspicuous, and also into the other social sciences and some schools of psychology. This importation is the source of the equilibrium paradigm that still today exercises a powerful effect on thinking about managing and organising. That thinking is based on the belief that managers can in principle control the long-term future of organisations and societies. Such a belief is realistic if cause-and-effect links are of the Newtonian type described above, for then the future can be predicted over the long term and so can be controlled by someone – they can get organisations and societies to do what they want them to do.

The basis of this approach to both nature and human action is that of determinism in that there are fixed laws causally connecting an action and a consequence and also reductionism in that the laws governing the movement of phenomena can be discovered by identifying their smallest components and the laws governing the movement of these small components. One comes to understand the whole phenomenon through understanding the smallest components in the belief that the whole is the sum of its parts. It follows that in this approach the micro aspects of phenomena are of crucial importance.

The notion of systems, first put forward by Kant, represents a very important addition to this way of thinking in that it focuses attention not simply on the parts but on the *interaction* between them. The whole then becomes more that the sum of its parts and functioning wholes are stable. This represents a major move away from simple reductionism and the chapters in Part 1 of the book have traced how the notion of systems has been taken up in thinking about organisations and their management. The move from reductionism is thus a move from the micro to the macro. The systems theories represented in Part 1 model phenomena at the macro level of the whole.

However, this movement from reductionism to systems, from micro parts to macro wholes, did not amount to a move away from determinism. Cybernetic, general systems and systems dynamics models are all deterministic so that nature and human action are both still understood to move according to fixed laws but now the laws take account of interaction. The same idea about the possibility of human control persists both in relation to nature and human action. Stability continues to be the key characteristic.

The move to systems thinking is also not necessarily a move away from linear causality. Cybernetic and general systems models continue to be based on linear relationships, although they do envisage the possibility of a linear connection between cause and effect being followed by a linear connection between the effect acting back on the cause, so leading to circular connections. In the review of the systems dynamics model, however, Chapter 4 pointed to how it differed from both cybernetics and open systems theory in the emphasis it placed on nonlinearity and non-equilibrium states. In other words, systems dynamics took account of relationships where the effects of a cause could be more or less than proportional to that cause and where there could be more than one effect for a single cause, or more than one cause for an effect. When systems dynamics came to be used in learning organisation theory, the nonlinearity was incorporated by adding positive feedback loops to the negative feedback that formed the basis of cybernetic systems. As a consequence of this non-linearity, links between cause and effect can become distant and hard to identify, prediction becomes more difficult and so systems dynamics models can produce unexpected outcomes. Control, therefore, becomes more problematic but it is held in learning organisation theory that control over the whole system is still possible if one recognises archetypal behavioural patterns and acts at leverage points.

The next two sections of this chapter are concerned with much the same kind of nonlinear relationships that systems dynamics was originally concerned with. These sections introduce two branches of what have come to be called the complexity sciences, namely, the theories of mathematical chaos and dissipative structures. Both of these theories have been developed since the 1950s and provide models that are essentially an extension of systems dynamics. Just as in systems dynamics, the models of chaos and dissipative structure theory focus on the macro level and both are nonlinear and deterministic. Because they are deterministic, the relation-ships in the models do not themselves change, develop or evolve, although the system they produce does develop as that which is enfolded in the relationships is unfolded by the interaction of its components. It follows that it is problematic to apply these theories in any direct way to human relationships since humans do learn and evolve. However, the theories of chaos and dissipative structures may have some value as metaphors and they do significantly extend the insights into systems dynamics.

These insights can be claimed to be so fundamental as to challenge the scientific project of control, based on predictability and certainty, which has prevailed in the West now for hundreds of years. Both of these theories demonstrate the fundamental unpredictability of nonlinear interaction in conditions required for change, render-ing long-term forecasting impossible. Both of these theories identify a paradoxical dynamic, a paradoxical movement through time, in which stability and instability cannot be separated. Instead they constitute a new dynamic that one would have to call stable instability or unstable stability. Uncertainty becomes a basic feature of nature and the possibility of control is seriously compromised. Furthermore, dissi-pative structure theory shows that a system can only move from one pattern of behaviour to another of its own accord if it operated far from equilibrium. Here the system can amplify irregularities in its interactions with the environment called 'fluctuations', break symmetries and spontaneously produce a shift from one pattern of behaviour to another which cannot be predicted from the previous pattern. Instability is shown to be fundamentally necessary for a system to change of its own accord. The preoccupation with equilibrium and stability in both the natural and social sciences is thus severely challenged by theories of chaos and dissipative struc-tures. The manner in which systems models have been applied to organisations and the prescriptions deduced from them are thus severely challenged by the develop-ment of chaos and dissipative structure theory.

Section 8.4 takes up another branch of the complexity sciences, namely, the theory of complex adaptive systems developed by scientists working at the Santa Fé Institute in New Mexico, who formulate systemic behaviour in agent-based terms.

Here there are no equations at the macro level. Instead, the system is modelled as a population of agents interacting with each other according to their own local 'if–then' rules. This theory of systems differs from all of those so far surveyed in that it focuses attention at a lower level of description, namely the micro level of the individual agents that form the system. The models demonstrate how local, that is, self-organising, interaction yields emergent order for the whole system and also, in certain conditions, evolution in the form of emergent novelty. These models focus on a system's internal capacity to evolve spontaneously because of micro diversity. Here self-organisation refers to local interactions between agents in the absence of a system-wide blueprint, rather than the collective response of the whole system as in dissipative structure theory.

Consider first what is meant by mathematical chaos theory.

8.2 Mathematical chaos theory

Chaos theory (Gleick, 1988; Stewart, 1989) is concerned with the dynamical properties of the same kind of models as systems dynamics. It can, therefore, be regarded as an extension of systems dynamics. A systems dynamics model consists of a set of interrelated nonlinear equations which model the movement over time of some phenomenon at the macro level. The concern is with how the whole phenomenon is changing over time. The model is such that the calculated output of one period is taken as the input for the calculation of the output of the next period. The model is thus *iterated* over time and the pattern of movement of these iterations is studied to identify dynamical properties. This description applies to the models used in chaos theory too. Those studying systems dynamics models showed how, for particular parameter values, the model produces perfectly stable, predictable movement over time. The model produces one pattern of equilibrium behaviour. In the language of chaos theory this is referred to as a point attractor in that the model settles down at one equilibrium point. At other parameter values, the model produces perfectly stable, predictable cycles of movement from a peak to a trough and back again. In the language of chaos theory this is a cyclical, or period two, attractor. At yet other parameter values, a systems dynamics model can produce explosively unstable behaviour. In the language of chaos theory this might be referred to as high-dimensional chaos, a pattern of fragmentation.

It is important to note that these attractors of stability and instability are a consequence of the internal structure of the model itself, not due to changes occurring in the environment. Those using systems dynamics models in organisations have explained the changing dynamics of the model in terms of feedback where negative feedback produces the stable equilibrium of a point attractor and positive feedback produces instability. However, strictly speaking this is not feedback in the cybernetic sense because there is no comparison with an external reference point which is then used as an input to the next calculation so that system change is due to environmental change. However, in the systems dynamics models, the whole output of one calculation is 'fed back' into the calculation for the next period without any comparison with an external reference point so that systems change is due to the internal structure of the model.

What has so far been said about systems dynamics models applies to chaos theory models too. What chaos models reveal is an important property of these models that had not been noticed before. Between parameter values at which the system is stable (point or cyclical attracts) and values at which it is unstable (high-dimensional chaos), there are values at which the system moves in a manner that might appear to be random but on closer examinations a pattern is revealed. This pattern is regular irregularity, or stable instability, and this means that it is predictably unpredictable. In other words, the dynamics, the pattern of movement, is paradoxical and it has been given the name of strange attractor or fractal or low-dimensional chaos. It is tempting to understand this pattern as a balance between stability and instability, or as a flipping back and forth between negative and positive feedback, or as a tension between stability and instability. However, descriptions such as these lose the paradoxical nature of the dynamic. The strange attractor called mathematical chaos is not a little bit of stability and a little bit of instability, but a completely different dynamic in which instability and stability are inextricably intertwined so that in every stability there is also instability and they cannot be separated out. Taken together in this way, stability and instability no longer mean what they did in their separate states. Note that chaos here does not mean utter confusion but pattern that we are not used to noticing or thinking about.

When a system moves according to the chaotic pattern of the strange attractor, it is highly sensitive to initial conditions. Precisely where the calculation starts matters a great deal. This means that a tiny difference, an error or fluctuation, in the input of one period can escalate over subsequent periods to qualitatively change the pattern that would otherwise have occurred. This creates enormous practical difficulties for long-term prediction; in fact it is impossible to make long-term predictions when a system's movement is mathematically chaotic.

Models of mathematical chaos have been used to explain many natural phenomena, for example, the earth's weather system. Models of weather systems consist of nonlinear relationships between interdependent forces such as pressure, temperature, humidity and wind speed that are related to each other by nonlinear equations. To model the weather system, these forces have to be measured at a particular point in time, at regular vertical intervals through the atmosphere from each of a grid of points on the earth's surface. Rules are then necessary to explain how each of the sets of interrelated measurements, at each measurement point in the atmosphere, moves over time. This requires massive numbers of computations. When these computations are carried out they reveal that the weather follows a strange attractor, which is the technical term for a mathematically chaotic pattern.

This means that the weather follows recognisably similar patterns, but those patterns are never exactly the same as those at any previous point in time. The system is highly sensitive to some small changes and blows them up into major alterations in weather patterns. This is popularly known as the butterfly effect in that it is possible for a butterfly to flap its wings in São Paolo, so making a tiny change to air pressure there, and for this tiny change to escalate up into a hurricane over Miami. You would have to measure the flapping of every butterfly's wings around the earth with infinite precision in order to be able to make long-term forecasts. The tiniest error made in these measurements could produce spurious forecasts. However, short-term forecasts are possible because it takes time for tiny differences to escalate. Chaotic dynamics means that humans will never be able to forecast the weather at a detailed level for more than a few days ahead because they will never be able to measure with infinite precision. The theoretical maximum for accurate forecasts is two weeks, one meteorologists are nowhere near reaching yet.

Although the specific path of behaviour in chaos is unpredictable, that behaviour does have a pattern, a qualitative shape. So the specific path of the weather is unpredictable in the long term, but it always follows the same global shape. There are boundaries outside which the weather system hardly ever moves and, if it does so, it is soon attracted back to the pattern prescribed by the attractor. Some weather conditions do not occur – snow storms in the Sahara desert or heat waves in the Arctic. There is a pattern to weather behaviour because it is constrained by the structure of the nonlinear relationships generating it.

Because of this, the system displays typical patterns, or recognisable categories of behaviour. Even before people knew anything about the shape of the weather's strange attractor, they always recognised patterns of storms and sunshine, hurricanes and calm and seasonal patterns. These recognisable patterns are repeated in an approximate way over and over again. They are never exactly the same, but there is always some similarity. This means that it is not possible to identify specific causes that yield specific outcomes, but the boundaries within which the system moves and the qualitative nature of the patterns it displays are known. The very irregularity of the weather will itself be regular because it is constrained in some way – it cannot do just anything. The resulting self-similar patterns of the weather can be used to prepare appropriate behaviour. One can buy an umbrella or move the sheep off the high ground. People can cope with the uncertainty and the lack of detectable causal connection because they are aware of self-similar patterns and use them in a qualitative way to guide specific choices.

Throughout the 1970s and 1980s the principles of chaos were explored in one field after another and found to explain, for example, turbulence in gases and liquids, the spread of some diseases and the impact of some inoculation programmes against some diseases. The body's system of arteries and veins follows fractal patterns similar to the branching pattern generated by the mathematical models. The growth of insect populations has chaotic characteristics. The leaves of trees are fractal and self-similar. The reason for no two snowflakes ever being the same can be explained using chaotic dynamics. Water dripping from a tap has been shown to follow a chaotic time pattern, as does smoke spiralling from a cigarette. One of the most intriguing discoveries is that healthy hearts and healthy brains display patterns akin to mathematical chaos. The heart moves into a regular rhythm just before a heart attack and brain patterns during epileptic fits are also regular. It seems that chaos is the signature of health.

The properties of low-dimensional deterministic chaos have been found to apply to nonlinear systems in meteorology, physics, chemistry and biology (Gleick, 1988). Economists and other social scientists have been exploring whether these discoveries are relevant to their disciplines (Anderson *et al.*, 1988; Baumol and Benhabib, 1989; Kelsey, 1988). There are some indications that chaos explanations may give insight into the operation of foreign exchange markets, stock markets and oil markets (Peters, 1991).

It is important to note that chaos theory models of systems, just as with systems dynamics models, do not have the internal capacity to move spontaneously from one attractor to another. It requires some external force to manipulate the parameters for the system to move from a point attractor to a cyclical one and then to the strange attractor. Finally it is important to note a related point about causality. Causality continues to be formative, just as it is in systems dynamics. The chaos model is unfolding the pattern already enfolded in its mathematical specification. Such systems are incapable of spontaneously generating novelty.

The conclusion, then, is that very simple nonlinear relationships, perfectly deterministic ones, can produce highly complex patterns of behaviour over time. Between stability and instability there is a complex 'border' that combines both stability and instability. Note that although the word chaos is being used, it does not mean the utter confusion, the complete randomness it usually means in ordinary conversation. On the contrary, mathematical chaos reveals patterns in phenomena previously thought to be random. It is just that the patterns are paradoxically regular and irregular, stable and unstable.

The central insight from chaos theory is that, in certain circumstances, iterative, recursive, nonlinear systems operate in a paradoxical dynamic which makes it impossible to make long-term forecasts for practical reasons. The next section continues the exploration of deterministic dynamical systems by briefly describing the theory of dissipative structures.

8.3 The theory of dissipative structures

Prigogine (Nicolis and Prigogine, 1989; Prigogine and Stengers, 1984) has demonstrated in laboratory experiments how nonlinear physical and chemical systems display intrinsically unpredictable forms of behaviour when they operate far from equilibrium. He identified a fundamental relationship between fluctuations, or disorder, on the one hand, and the development of orderly forms, on the other. A nonlinear system far from equilibrium escalates small changes, or fluctuations, in the environment, causing the instability necessary to shatter an existing behaviour pattern and make way for a different one. Systems may pass through states of instability and reach critical points where they spontaneously self-organise to produce a different structure or behaviour that cannot be predicted from knowledge of the previous state. This more complex structure is called a dissipative structure because it takes energy to sustain the system in that new mode. Consider what happens when a system moves from equilibrium to a far from equilibrium state.

A liquid is at thermodynamic equilibrium when it is closed to its environment and the temperature is uniform throughout it. The liquid is then in a state of rest at a global level, that is, there are no bulk movements in it, although the molecules move everywhere and face in different directions. In equilibrium, then, the positions and movements of the molecules are random and hence independent of each other. There are no correlations, patterns or connections. At equilibrium, nothing happens and the behaviour of the system is symmetrical, uniform and regular. This means that every point within the liquid is essentially the same as every other and at every point in time the liquid is in exactly the same state as it is at every other, namely, at a state of rest at the macro level and randomness at the micro level. However, when the liquid is pushed far from equilibrium by increasing the heat applied to it, small fluctuations are amplified throughout the liquid. So, if one starts with a layer of liquid close to thermodynamic equilibrium and then begins to apply heat to the base, that sets up a fluctuation or change in the environmental condition in which the liquid exists. That temperature change is then amplified or spread through the liquid. The effect of this amplification is to break the symmetry and to cause differentiation within the liquid.

At first the molecules at the base stop moving randomly and begin to move upward, those most affected by the increase in temperature rising to the top of the liquid. That movement eventually sets up convection so that those molecules least affected are displaced and pushed down to the base of the liquid. There they are heated and move up, in turn pushing others down. The molecules are now moving in a circle. This means that the symmetry of the liquid is broken by the bulk movement that has been set up because each point in the liquid is no longer the same as all others: at some points movement is up and at other points it is down. After a time, a critical temperature point is reached and a new structure emerges in the liquid. Molecules move in a regular direction setting up hexagonal cells, some turning clockwise and others turning anti-clockwise: they self-organise. What this represents is long-range coherence where molecular movements are correlated with each other as though they were communicating. The direction of each cell's movement is, however, unpredictable and cannot be determined by the experimenter. The direction taken by any one cell depends upon small chance differences in the conditions that existed as the cell was formed.

As further heat is applied to the liquid, the symmetry of the cellular pattern is broken and other patterns emerge. Eventually the liquid reaches a turbulent state of evaporation. Movement from a perfectly orderly, symmetrical situation to one of some more complex order occurs through a destabilising process. The system is pushed away from stable equilibrium in the form of a point attractor, through bifurcations such as the limit cycle, and so on towards deterministic chaos. The process is one of destruction making way for the creation of another pattern.

What I have been describing is a laboratory experiment used to explore the phenomenon of convection. When it comes to that phenomenon in nature, rather than in the laboratory, there is an important difference. In the case of convection in nature there is no experimenter standing outside the system objectively observing it and turning up the heat parameter as there is in the laboratory experiment. Instead, the patterns of convection in the earth's atmosphere and oceans are caused by variations in the earth's temperature, which are in turn partially caused by the convection patterns. Outside of the laboratory, the system itself is changing the parameters and it is this that the experiment is trying to model.

So, self-organisation is a process that occurs spontaneously at certain critical values of a system's control parameters and it involves the system organising itself to produce a different pattern without any blueprint for that pattern. Emergence here means that the pattern produced by self-organisation cannot be explained by the nature of the entities that the system consists of or the interaction between them. What is important is that there should be fluctuations, that is, non-average impacts from the environment, otherwise the system cannot spontaneously move to a different attractor. The different pattern that emerges is a dissipative structure in that it easily dissolves if the system moves away from critical points in its control parameters. An equilibrium structure requires no effort to retain its structure and great effort to change it, while a dissipative structure requires great effort to retain its structure and relatively little to change it.

Prigogine (Nicolis and Prigogine, 1989; Prigogine and Stengers, 1984) has established that nonlinear chemical systems are changeable only when they are pushed far from equilibrium where they can become dissipative systems. Dissipative systems import energy and information from the environment that then dissipates through the system, in a sense causing it to fall apart. However, it also has structure and it is capable of renewal through self-organisation as it continues to import energy and information. A dissipative system is essentially a contradiction or paradox: symmetry and uniformity of pattern are being lost but there is still a structure; dissipative activity occurs as part of the process of creating a different structure. A dissipative structure is not just a result, but a process that uses disorder to change, an interactive process that temporarily manifests in globally stable structures. Stability dampens and localises change to keep the system where it is, but operation far from equilibrium destabilises a system and so opens it up to change.

It is important to note here that the kind of system described in the section on chaos theory cannot spontaneously move of its own accord from one attractor to another. Something outside the system has to alter the parameter for this to happen. However, with the kind of system described in this section such a spontaneous move is possible because the system is sensitive to non-average interaction with its environment (Allen, 1998a, 1998b).

Note, however, that these are deterministic systems modelled at the macro level just as is the case in chaos theory and that neither of these systems evolve. Formative causality still applies but now the dissipative system can move spontaneously from one enfolded attractor to another. The suggestion is that a spontaneously changeful system is one that is constrained from settling down into equilibrium, a completely different finding from that usually assumed.

When Prigogine (1997) considers the wider implications of his work, he poses an important question: 'Is the future given, or is it under perpetual construction?' One could express the question thus: 'Is causality to be understood as formative or is it to be understood as transformative?' Prigogine sees the future for every level of the universe as under perpetual construction and he suggests that the process of perpetual construction, at all levels, can be understood in nonlinear, non-equilibrium terms, where instabilities, or fluctuations, break symmetries, particularly the symmetry of time. He says that nature is about the creation of unpredictable novelty, where the possible is richer than the real. When he moves from models and laboratory experiments to think about the wider questions of evolution, he sees life as an unstable system with an unknowable future in which the irreversibility of time plays a constitutive role. He sees evolution as encountering bifurcation points and taking paths at these points that depend on the micro details of interaction at those points. Prigogine sees evolution at all levels in terms of instabilities with humans and their creativity as a part of it. He pronounces the end of certainty for the scientific project and the intrinsic uncertainty of life, calling for a new dialogue with nature.

So a key discovery about the operation of deterministic iterative nonlinear systems is that stable equilibrium and explosive instability are not the only attractors. Nonlinear systems have a third possibility: a state of stable instability far from equilibrium in which behaviour has a pattern, but it is regularly irregular and intrinsically uncertain. That pattern emerges without any overall blueprint through self-organisation. It is important to note how the nature of self-organisation and emergence is conceived in these theoretical developments. Self-organisation and emergence are thought of as the collective response of whole populations. These are properties of the system itself, not the consequences of some external agent first applying positive feedback and then applying negative feedback.

When it operates in the paradoxical dynamic of stability and instability, the behaviour of a system unfolds in so complex a manner, so dependent upon the detail of what happens, that the links between cause and effect are lost. One can no longer count on a certain given input leading to a certain given output. The laws themselves operate to escalate small chance disturbances along the way, breaking any direct link between an input and a subsequent output. The long-term future of a system operating in the dynamic of stability and instability at the same time is not simply difficult to see: it is, for all practical purposes, unknowable. It is so because of the structure of the system itself, not simply because of changes going on outside it and impacting upon it. Nothing can remove that unknowability.

If this were to apply to an organisation, then decision-making processes that involved forecasting, envisioning future states, or even making any assumptions about future states, would be problematic in terms of realising a chosen future. Those applying such processes in conditions of stable instability would be engaging in fantasy activities. It follows that no one can be 'in control' of a system that is far from equilibrium in the way that control is normally thought about, because no one can forecast the specific future of a system operating in stable instability. No one can envision it either, unless one believes in clairvoyance, prophecy or mystical visions. No one can establish how the system would move before a policy change and then how it would move after the policy change. There would be no option but to make the change and see what happens.

Prigogine's theory of dissipative structures takes a radical step from systems dynamics and chaos theory. Like systems dynamics, Prigogine's models are cast in nonlinear equations that specify changes in the macro states of a system and like systems dynamics and chaos the system is assumed to be a non-equilibrium one. In addition, however, the assumption that micro events occur at their average rate is dropped. In other words, the 'noise', or 'fluctuations', in the form of variations around any average are incorporated into the model (Allen, 1998a, 1998b). Prigogine's work demonstrates the importance of these 'fluctuations', showing how fluctuations impart to a nonlinear system that is held far from equilibrium the capacity to move spontaneously from one attractor to another. He calls this 'order through fluctuations' and shows how it occurs through a process of spontaneous self-organisation.

8.4 Complex adaptive systems

A complex adaptive system (Gell-Mann, 1994; Holland, 1998; Kauffman, 1995; Langton, 1996) consists of a large number, a population, of entities called agents, each of which behaves according to some set of rules. These rules require each individual agent to adjust its action to that of other agents. In other words, individual agents interact with, and adapt to, each other and in doing so form a system which could also be thought of as a population-wide pattern. For example, a flock of birds might be thought of as a complex adaptive system. It consists of many individual agents, perhaps thousands, who might be following simple rules to do with adapting to the movement of neighbours so as to fly in a formation without crashing into each other, a population-wide pattern called flocking. The human body might be thought of as a complex adaptive system consisting of 30,000 individual genes interacting with each other to produce human physiology. An ecology could be thought of as a complex adaptive system consisting of a number of species relating to each other to produce patterns of evolving life forms. A brain could be considered as a system of ten billion neurons interacting with each other to produce patterns of brain activity across the whole population of neurons. Complexity science seeks to identify common features of the dynamics of such systems in general.

Key questions are these: how do such complex nonlinear systems with their vast numbers of interacting agents function to produce orderly patterns of behaviour across a whole population? How do such systems evolve to produce new orderly patterns of behaviour?

The traditional scientific approach to answering these questions would be to look for general laws directly determining the population-wide order and governing the observed evolution of that population-wide order. The expectation would be to find an overall blueprint at the level of the whole system, the whole population, according to which it would behave or to identify some global process governing the evolution of the system. This is the kind of macro approach common to all the branches of systems thinking reviewed so far in this book, including chaos and dissipative structure theory. Scientists working with complex adaptive systems take a fundamentally different approach. They do not look for an overall blueprint for the whole system at all but, instead, they model individual agent interaction, with each agent behaving according to its own local principles of interaction. The interaction is local in the sense that each individual agent interacts with only a tiny proportion of the total population and it is local in the sense that none of them are following centrally determined rules of interaction. In such interaction, no individual agent, or group of agents, directly determines the rules of interaction of others or the patterns of behaviour that the system displays or how those patterns evolve and neither does anything outside of the system. This is the principle of self-organisation: agents interact locally according to their own principles, in the absence of an overall blueprint for the system they form.

A central concept in agent-based models of complex systems is that this self organising interaction produces emergent population-wide pattern, where emergence means that there is no blueprint, plan or programme determining the population-wide pattern. What happens is the emergence and maintenance of order, or complexity, out of a state that is less ordered, or complex, namely, the local interaction of the agents. Self-organisation and emergence can lead to fundamental structural development (novelty), not just superficial change. This is 'spontaneous' or 'autonomous', arising from the intrinsic iterative nonlinear nature of the system. Some external designer does not impose it, rather, widespread orderly behaviour emerges from simple, reflex-like rules.

Since it is not possible to experiment with living systems in real-life situations, complexity scientists use computers to simulate the behaviour of complex adaptive systems. Some scientists argue that computer simulations are a legitimate new form of experiment but others hold that they show nothing about nature, only about computer programs.

How complex adaptive systems are studied

In the computer simulations, each individual agent is an individual computer program. Each of these programs is a set of operating rules and instructions concerning how that program should interact with other individual computer programs. It is possible to add a set of rules for evaluating those operations according to some performance criteria. It is also possible to add a set of rules for changing the rules of operation and evaluation in the light of their performance. Another set of rules can be added according to which each individual computer program can be copied to produce another one. That set of replicating rules could take the form of a rule about locating another computer program to mate with. Another rule could instruct the first to copy the top half of its program and the second to copy the bottom half of its program and then add the two copies together. The result would be a new, or offspring, program. This is known as the genetic algorithm, developed by John Holland of the Santa Fé Institute.

You can see how such a procedure could model important features of evolution in that a population of individual computer programs interact with each other, breed and so evolve. The result is a complex adaptive system in the computer consisting of a population of agents, each of which is a computer program. Each of the agents in the simulation, that is, each individual computer program, is made up of a bit string, a series of ones and zeros representing an electric current that is either on or off.

The inherent patterning capacity of interaction

Those who have developed the study of complex adaptive systems have been most interested in the analogy between the digital code of computer program agents and the chemical code in the genes of living creatures. One of their principal questions has been this: if in its earliest days the earth consisted of a random soup of chemicals, how could life have come about? You can simulate this problem if you take a system consisting of computer programs with random bit strings and ask if they can evolve order out of such random chaos. The answer to this question is that such systems can indeed evolve order out of chaos and this chaos is essential to the process.

Contrary to some of our most deep-seated beliefs, disorder is the material from which life and creativity are built and it seems that they are built, not according to some overall prior design, but through a process of spontaneous self-organisation that produces emergent outcomes. If there is a design, it is the basic design principles of the system itself, namely a network of agents driven by iterative nonlinear interaction. What is not included in the design is the emergent outcomes, the emergent pattern, which this interaction produces. There is inherent order in complex adaptive systems which evolves as the experience of the system, but no one can know what that evolutionary experience will be until it occurs. In certain conditions, agents interacting in a system can produce not anarchy but creative new outcomes that none of them was ever programmed to produce. If this has anything to do with human action then even if no one can know the outcome of their actions and even if no one can be 'in control', we are not doomed to anarchy. On the contrary, these may be the very conditions required for creativity, for the evolutionary journey with no fixed, predetermined destination.

According to this view, evolution is, then, not an incrementally progressive affair occurring by chance as in neo-Darwinism, but a rather stumbling sort of journey in which a system moves both forwards and backwards through self-organisation.

Fitness landscapes

You can see why this is so if you think in terms of fitness landscapes, a concept Kauffman (1995) has used to give insights into the evolutionary process. Picture the evolution of a particular species, say leopards, as a journey across a landscape characterised by hills and mountains of various heights and shapes, and valleys of various depths and shapes. Suppose that movement up a hill or mountain is equivalent to increasing fitness and moving down into a valley is equivalent to decreasing fitness. Deep valleys would represent almost certain extinction and the high peaks of mountains would represent great fitness for the leopards. The purpose of life is then to avoid valleys and climb peaks.

The shape of the landscape

What determines the shape of this landscape, that is, the number, size, shape and position of the peaks and valleys? The answer is the survival strategies that other species interacting with leopards are following. So, leopards could potentially interact with a large number of species in order to get a meal. They could hunt elephant, for example. However, the elephant has a survival strategy based on size and if leopards take the elephant-hunting route they will have a tough time surviving. Such a strategy, therefore, is a move down into a rather deep and dead-end sort of valley. Another possibility is to hunt rather small deer. In order to achieve this the leopard might evolve the strategy of speed, competing by running faster than the deer. To the extent that this works it is represented by a move up a fitness hill. Or, the leopards may specialise in short-distance speed plus a strategy of camouflage. Hence their famous spots. This strategy seems to have taken them up a mountain to a reasonably high fitness peak.

The evolutionary task of the leopard species, then, is to journey across the fitness landscape in such a manner as to reach the highest fitness peak possible, because then the leopard stands the greatest chance of surviving. To get caught in a valley is to become extinct, and to be trapped in the foothills is to forgo the opportunity of finding one of the mountains.

Moving across the landscape

So, how should the leopard species travel across the landscape to avoid these pitfalls, given that leopards cannot see where the high peaks are? They can only know that they have reached a peak when they get there. Suppose the leopards adopt what strategy theorists call a logically incremental strategy (*see* Chapter 7). That is, they adopt a procedure in which they 'stick to the knitting' and take a large number of small incremental steps, only ever taking a step that improves fitness and avoiding any steps that diminish fitness – they are driven by efficiency. This rational, orderly procedure produces relatively stable, efficient, progressive movement uphill, consistently in the direction of success. Management consultants and academics in the strategy field would applaud leopards following this procedure for their eminent common sense. However, a rule that in essence says 'go up hills only and never downwards' is sure to keep the leopards out of the valleys, but it is also almost certain to get them trapped in the foothills, unless they start off with a really lucky break at the base of the highest, smoothest mountain, with no crevices or other deformities. This is highly unlikely, for a reason I will come to.

The point to note here is that the rational, efficient way to move over the short term is guaranteed, over the longer term, to be the most ineffective possible. What is the alternative? The alternative is to abandon this nice, neat strategy of logically incremental moves and travel in a somewhat erratic manner that involves sometimes slipping and tumbling downhill into valleys out of which a desperate climb is necessary before it is too late. This counterintuitive and somewhat inebriate method of travelling across their fitness landscape makes it likely that the leopards will stumble across the foothills of an even higher mountain than the one they were climbing before. So, cross-over replication, sex to us, makes it more likely that we will find higher mountains to climb than will, say, bacteria, which replicate by cloning, precisely because of the disorder of mixing the genetic code rather than incrementally improving it.

The whole picture becomes a great deal more interesting when you remember that the fixed landscape I have been describing for the leopard is in fact a fiction, because the survival strategies of the other species determine its shape and they are not standing still. They too are looking for peaks to climb and every time they change their strategy then what was a peak for the leopard is deformed and could become a valley. So, if the leopard increases its short-distance speed and improves its camouflage then it moves up towards a fitness peak on its landscape. But, if the deer respond by heightening their sense of smell, then that peak certainly subsides and may even turn into a valley.

The evolutionary journey for all species, therefore, is across a constantly heaving landscape and it is heaving about because of competition. Competition ensures that life itself never gets trapped. Species come and go but life itself carries on, perhaps becoming ever more complex. It is this mess of competitive selection that is one of the sources of order, the other being the co-operative, internal process of spontaneous self-organisation. This possibility occurs in a dynamic known as 'the edge of chaos', which is the pattern of movement which is both stable and unstable at the same time. One property of the edge of chaos is known as the power law, which means that many small perturbations will cascade through the system but only a few large ones will. In other words, there will be large numbers of small extinction events but only small numbers of large ones. It is this property that imparts control, or stability, to the process of change at the edge of chaos.

Systems characterised by dynamics that combine order and disorder, which operate at the edge of chaos, are capable of evolving while those that are purely orderly, those that operate well away from the edge of chaos, cannot evolve. At the edge of chaos, systems are capable of endless variety, novelty, surprise – in short, creativity. Systems that get trapped on local fitness peaks look stable and comfortable, but they are simply waiting for destruction by other species following messier paths. Kauffman gives precise conditions which generate the dynamics of the edge of chaos. The dynamic occurs only when the agents are numerous enough and richly connected to each other. Agents impose *conflicting constraints* on each other and it is these that provide control to the movement of the system.

Kauffman is arguing, then, that the manner in which competitive selection operates on chance variations depends upon the internal dynamic of the evolving network, that is, upon the pattern of connections, the self-organising interaction, between the entities of which it is composed. The fitness landscape is not a given space containing all possible evolutionary strategies for a system, which it searches for fit strategies in a manner driven by chance. Rather, the fitness landscape itself is being constructed by the interaction between agents. The notion of fitness landscape, its ruggedness, becomes a metaphor for the internal dynamic of a system, not an externally given terrain over which it travels in search of a fit position. These internal properties of the network are the connections between its entities and these connections create conflicting constraints. The internal dynamic is thus one of enabling co-operation and of conflicting constraints at the same time, a paradoxical dynamic of co-operation and competition at the same time. Notice how connection, constraint and conflict are all essential requirements for the evolution of a system.

While no agent is 'in control' of the evolution of the system, it is nevertheless evolving in a controlled manner and the source of this control lies in the pattern of conflicting constraints. This is a very important point because it is the conflicting constraints that sustain sufficient stability in a network at the edge of chaos.

However, the interests of complex adaptive systems modellers are not confined to such major questions as the evolution of life. The complex adaptive system model has been applied to many other phenomena too.

Simulating populations of homogeneous agents

Take a simple example of a complex adaptive system, namely a flock of birds. Reynolds (1987) simulated the flocking behaviour of birds with a computer program consisting of a network of moving agents called Boids. Each Boid follows the *same* three *simple rules*:

1. Maintain a minimum distance from other objects in the environment including other Boids.
2. Match velocities with other Boids in the neighbourhood.
3. Move towards the perceived centre of mass of the Boids in the neighbourhood.

These three rules are sufficient to produce flocking behaviour. So, Boids, each interacting with a relatively small number of others according to its own local rules of interaction, produce an emergent, coherent pattern for the whole system of Boids. There is no plan, or blueprint, at the level of the flock. There is no overall intention in relation to the flock, for the population as a whole, on the part of any Boid. Each does what it is required to do in order to interact with a few others and orderly behaviour emerges for the whole population. Flocking is an attractor for a system in which entities follow the three rules given above.

Note how all agents follow the *same rules*. Each agent is the same as every other agent and there is no variation in the way they interact with each other. Emergence here is therefore not the consequence of non-average behaviour, as was the case with dissipative structures in the last section. Instead, emergence is the consequence of local interaction between agents. Unlike dissipative structures, and because of the postulated uniformity of behaviour, these simulations cannot spontaneously move, of their own accord, from one attractor to another. Instead, they stay always with one attractor and show no evolution.

However, more complicated simulations of complex adaptive systems do take account of differences in agents or classes of agents and different ways of interacting. These simulations do then show the capacity to move spontaneously from one attractor to another and to evolve new ones. This is demonstrated by the simulation called Tierra (Ray, 1992).

Simulating populations of interacting heterogeneous agents

Organic life utilises energy to organise matter and it evolves, developing more and more diverse forms, as organisms compete and co-operate with each other for light and food in geographic space. An analogy to this would be digital life in which central processing unit (CPU) time organises strings of digits (programs) in the space of computer memory. Computer programs are then used as the analogue of living organisms. Would digital life evolve as bit strings and interact and compete for CPU time?

This is the question explored by Ray (1992) in his simulation. In this simulation, Ray, the programmer, designs the first digital organism, which he calls a creature, consisting of 80 instructions on how to copy itself. The first creature is thus a string of digits of a particular length. The programmer also introduces a mechanism to generate variety into the replicating process, taking the form of random bit flipping to simulate random mutations in evolution. It follows that, as the creature copies itself, the new copies will differ from the original one and, as they copy themselves, each subsequent copy will differ from them. The programmer also introduces a constraint in the form of scarce computer time, which works as follows. Agents are required to post their locations in the computer memory on a public notice board. Each agent is then called upon in turn, according to a circular queue, to receive a slice of computer time for carrying out its replication tasks. The programmer introduces a further constraint on agent life span. Agents are lined up in a linear queue according to their age and a 'reaper' lops off some of these, generally the oldest. However, by successfully executing their programs, agents can slow down their move up the linear queue whereas flawed agents rise quickly to the top.

The only task agents have is that of replicating in a regime of scarce CPU time and what happens is that new modes of doing this evolve. In other words, different categories of replication method appear. These changes can be observed in numerical terms by watching changing patterns of dots on a computer screen. An analogy is then drawn between this digital interaction and the biological evolution of species and the simulation is described in these biological terms. For example, categories of agents are said to develop their own survival strategies. It is important to remember that this is an analogy drawing attention to changes in categories of agent in the digital medium and changes in categories of species in the biological medium.

What happens in the simulation?

The simulation was set off by introducing a single agent consisting of 80 instructions. Within a short time, the computer memory space was 80 per cent occupied by these agents but then the reaper took over and prevented further population growth. After a while, agents consisting of 45 instructions appeared, but they were too short to replicate. They overcame this problem by borrowing some of the code of longer agents in order to replicate. This strategy enabled them to replicate faster within their allocated computer time. In other words, a kind of parasite emerged. The use of the term 'parasite' is obviously an analogy.

Although the parasites did not destroy their hosts, they were dependent on them for replication. If the parasites became too numerous in relation to hosts then they destroyed their own ability to replicate and so declined. In the simulation, the parasites suffered periodic catastrophes. One of these catastrophes occurred because the hosts stopped posting their positions on the public notice board and in effect hid so that the parasites could no longer find them. Some hosts had, thus, developed an immunity to parasites by using camouflage as a survival strategy. But, in hiding, the hosts had not retained any note of their position in the computer memory. So, they had to examine themselves to see if their position corresponded to the position being offered computer time, before they could respond to that offer. This increased the time they needed for replication. However, although not perfect, the strategy worked well enough that the parasites were nearly wiped out.

Then, however, the parasites developed their own memories and did not need to consult the public posting board. Once again, it was the parasites' turn to succeed. Later, hyperparasites appeared to feed off the parasites. These were 80 instructions long, just like the hosts, but they had developed instructions to examine themselves for parasites and feed off the parasites by diverting computer time from them. These hyperparasites worked symbiotically by sharing reproduction code: they could no longer reproduce on their own but required co-operation. This co-operation was then exploited by opportunistic mutants in the form of tiny intruders who placed themselves between replicating hyperparasites and intercepted and used hyperparasite code for their own replication. These cheaters could then thrive and replicate although they were only 27 instructions long. Later, the hyperparasites found a way to defeat the cheaters, but not for long.

How the simulation is interpreted

I would like to emphasise, once more, what is happening in this simulation. After the simulation has run for some time there are a number of bit strings, each arranged into operating instructions requiring them to replicate in a particular way, often in interaction with other bit strings. These bit strings fall into categories and all within a category replicate in the same way while bit strings in another category replicate in a different way. In complexity language, each of these categories is an attractor and there are a number of different attractors in the system. To put it another way, there is microdiversity in the total population of bit strings. During one round of replication, that is, during a given short time period, the bit strings carry out their instructions, one after the other, and as they do so bits in some of the strings are randomly flipped. Over a series of runs the bit flipping and the interaction between the bit strings result in rearrangements in the bit strings themselves. In other words, new arrangements of bit strings appear, that is, new categories of replicating instructions. At the same time older categories disappear because of the procedure of competitive removal of some of them. Once begun, this evolution continues even when the random bit flipping, that is, chance, is turned off. Self-organisation is then the driving force of evolution.

In summary, the population of bit strings is a population of algorithms, or logical procedures. What running the simulation demonstrates is the logical properties of iteration (replication) and local interaction of algorithms (self-organisation in the absence of a blueprint for the whole) in the presence of random mutation and competitive selection. The simulation shows that it is logically possible for self-organisation, mutation and selection operating iteratively to display evolution – that is, emergent novelty that is radically unpredictable. This evolution is characterised by both destruction of some categories and emergence of new ones.

Anything more that is said about the simulation is an interpretation by way of analogy. So, Ray uses the simulation as an analogy for biology and calls the bit strings creatures. One category of bit strings is called hosts and another is called parasites. If the interpretation is done carefully, it may provide insight. For example, it may indicate that new biological forms can emerge from a process of self-organisation, not just chance. If done carelessly it could produce unwarranted claims. It is, therefore, important to take great care in using insights about self-organisation and emergence in relation to organisations. The question becomes one of how to interpret, in organisational terms, the logic of iterative, nonlinear interaction between replicating algorithms and their self-organising and emergent properties. Even more fundamental is the question of whether it even makes sense to try to do this.

Some major insights

It seems to me that this simulation provides some major insights into the nature of complex adaptive systems.

First, this system produces evolving population-wide order that comes about in a spontaneous, emergent way through the local interaction of diverse agents. The evolving population-wide order has not been programmed and there is no blueprint, grand design or plan for it. Furthermore, this spontaneous self-organising activity, with its emergent order, is vital for the continuing evolution of the system and its ability to produce novelty. However, what form that order takes – that is, the population-wide pattern of behaviour, the system-wide strategies – cannot be predicted from the rules driving individual agent behaviour. The strategies are emerging unpredictably in co-evolutionary processes. First the strategy is small size, but then parasites change the rules and the most successful strategy becomes feeding off others. Then the hosts change the rules and the better strategy is camouflage. But the parasites change the rules of the game again and the best strategy becomes the development of a local memory. Competition and conflict emerge and the evolution of the system is driven by agents trying to exploit each other, but the game can go on only if neither side succeeds completely, or for long, in that exploitation.

From this perspective, the evolution of life in the universe occurs primarily not through random mutations selected for survival by the forces of competition as in Darwinism, but through an internal, spontaneously self-organising, co-operative process that presents orderly forms for selection by the forces of competition. Selection is not made by freely operating competition that chooses amongst random little pieces, but by a competitive process constrained to choose amongst new forms emerging from a co-operative process. Life in the universe, and perhaps life in organisations, arises from a dialectic between competition and co-operation, not from unconstrained competition.

Causality

In Kant's philosophy, the scientist understands organism in nature as wholes consisting of parts. It is in the self-organising interaction of the parts that those parts and the whole emerge. The scientist understands the development of such a system by hypothesising that it is developing according to some 'as if' purpose, usually that of the whole realising a mature form of itself – formative causality. Although the first wave of twentieth-century systems thinkers did not develop Kant's idea of systems as *self-organising* wholes, emphasising self-regulation and self-influence instead, they did implicitly adopt the formative theory of causality. In the more recent wave of complex systems theories, chaos and dissipative structure theorists also produce models of systems which unfold attractors already enfolded in the equations specifying them, although dissipative structure models do bring back the notion of self-organising wholes that can spontaneously move from one enfolded attractor to another. Homogeneous complex adaptive systems model self-organising processes at the micro level but, because the agents are all the same, the theory of formative causality continues to apply.

However, heterogeneous complex adaptive systems, where the agents differ from one another, do what none of the other systems can. They display the capacity for spontaneous evolution to new forms, the unknown. Causality, therefore, is transformative. In other words, such systems take on a life of their own. This creates a problem for the notion of the 'whole' because here the 'whole' is never finished but always evolving. One then has to talk about incomplete or absent wholes, notions that make rather dubious sense. It amounts to saying that there is something that is a whole but is not yet a whole and never will be. Heterogeneous complex adaptive systems then begin to point to a problem with one of the central concepts of systems thinking, namely 'wholes'. The notion of a system with a life of its own brings other problems. If the system model has a life of its own how can we be confident that it actually models what it is supposed to? Surely the model and what it is trying to model would diverge as each takes on a life of its own? Also, what would it mean for individual members of an organisation to think of themselves as parts of an organisational system that had a life of its own?

Models of complex adaptive systems differ significantly from all of the system models so far reviewed in this book. All the other approaches model phenomena at a macro level, paying little or no attention to the nature of the entities comprising the system, while complex adaptive systems model agent interaction at a micro level. In all of the other macro-system models, with the exception of dissipative structures, interactions with the environment are assumed to be average or distributed around an average. It follows that only the dissipative structure models and complex adaptive systems with homogeneous agents have the internal capacity to move spontaneously from one given pattern of behaviour to another given pattern of behaviour. In all of the other system models, including dissipative structures and some complex adaptive system models, agents are implicitly or explicitly assumed to be homogeneous, or average. Such systems have no internal capacity to spontaneously evolve and so are incapable of novelty. All of these models can move only within one attractor and novel change has to come from outside the system. It is only when agent diversity is introduced, for example in heterogeneous complex adaptive system models or in Allen's complex evolutionary models to be referred to in the next chapter, that the system can produce novel forms, that is, evolve.

The new emerges in these models when the system displays the dynamics of the edge of chaos, where the differences between entities, microdiversity, are amplified. Here the system produces not only the new but avalanches of destruction as well, with many small and few large extinction events. In the review of all of these systems theories there has been a move from models that are linear, equilibrium seeking and lacking in any microdiversity to those that are nonlinear, far from equilibrium and full of microdiversity. The most striking change in the properties they display is the capacity for spontaneously developing new forms.

So far in this chapter, I have described my interpretation of what some branches of the complexity sciences mean and why I think it is important to take account of them with regard to organisations. However, the complexity sciences are in their infancy and there is by no means one monolithic view of what they mean. In this chapter I have drawn heavily on what I see as one important strand of thinking in these sciences exemplified by the work of Prigogine, Kauffman and Goodwin. However, there are natural complexity scientists who take a different view. The next section will therefore consider the nature of these differences. In the next chapter I will explore how those differences appear in the way researchers and writers are using the concepts in relation to organisations.

8.5 Different interpretations of complexity

It seems to me that there are at least four important matters on which those working in the field of complex systems take different positions. These four matters are:

- The significance of self-organisation.
- The nature of emergence.
- The importance of unpredictability.
- The implications for the scientific method.

To illustrate how views on these matters differ (Griffin *et al.*, 1998; Stacey *et al.*, 2000), consider the views of some leading figures in the field of complexity, namely, Langton (1996), Gell-Mann (1994), Holland (1998), Kauffman (1995), Goodwin (1994) and Prigogine.

Langton

Langton (1996) specifies the simple rules of interaction that each agent in his system will follow and then observes the behaviour that emerges, stressing the radical unpredictability of the pattern that emerges. The inability to provide a global rule, or algorithm, for changes in the system's global state makes it necessary to concentrate on the interactions occurring at the local level. It is the logical structure of the interactions, rather than the properties of the agents themselves, which is important.

He retains the notion of processes of information manipulation, of computation, found in the field of artificial intelligence (AI) but locates them at the level of the agents rather than at the global level as AI does. This establishes a strong link with cybernetics and cognitivism. In both of the latter, the manipulation and processing of information is a central concept. For Langton, the system as a whole is no longer a cybernetic one but it is composed of cybernetic entities which function in a cognitivist manner in that they process information. Algorithms drive the behaviour of the agents, although no algorithm can be identified for behaviour at the global level. This retention of an essential cognitivist view of the world has important implications for the ease with which the insights generated by Langton's work can be assimilated into management discourses based on systems thinking.

Langton holds that his approach is both mechanistic and reductionist, but in a new sense (Langton, 1996). What Langton appears to mean by this is that the old mechanism is one in which the components could be added to arrive at the whole in a linear manner. Parts have functions that fit together uniquely to determine the whole. The new mechanism he is talking about is one in which the parts interact according to recursive rules to produce a whole that is radically unpredictable. However, the system remains mechanistic in the sense that the recursive rules are computed and it is this running of the program that yields the resultant whole. The mechanism is the rules and the reduction is to the rules, so that there is nothing left unexplained. Intervention at local levels gives rise to global-level dynamics and this affects the lower levels by setting the local context within which each entity's rules are involved. The behaviour of the whole system does not depend upon the internal details of the entities, only on the details of the way they behave in each other's presence.

So, Langton's position on methodology is one that stays close to scientific orthodoxy. The methodology remains deterministic, reductionistic and mechanistic. However, he stresses the radically unpredictable nature of emergent order. For him, self-organisation is an algorithmic interaction of a cybernetic kind and emergence is a fundamentally important phenomenon.

Gell-Mann

Gell-Mann (1994) says that all complex adaptive systems acquire information about their environment and their interactions with it. These systems identify regularities in their environments and their interactions, which they condense into models on the basis of which they then predict and act (p. 318). The cognitivist frame of reference and its cybernetic underpinnings are, in his view, therefore clear.

Gell-Mann does not talk a great deal about self-organisation and emergence, at least not in the book that most now use when importing his ideas into organisation theory. When he does, he relates these concepts very much to structures emerging from systems characterised by very simple rules (p. 100). He uses the word 'apparently' to limit the notion of the complex and describes self-organisation as a process of following *simple rules*. This makes it very easy to assimilate what Gell-Mann says into systemic perspectives on the nature of organisations. What Gell-Mann is doing is downplaying the importance of self-organising process and emergence and focusing on competitive selection as the driver of evolution in complex adaptive systems. This is made clear by the importance he attaches to 'frozen accidents'. Evolution occurs by chance, but once a new form has emerged as an accident, it is frozen and so characterised by regularities which make it predictable (p. 229).

So, like Langton, Gell-Mann stays with orthodox scientific methodology. He emphasises the importance of chance in the evolution of complex adaptive systems. Although this implies long-term unpredictability, Gell-Mann seems to me to downplay the implications of this and focuses instead on regularities and predictability.

His emphasis on 'frozen accidents' and competitive selection is close to the ortho-dox ideas of neo-Darwinism, as is his lack of emphasis on self-organisation and emergence, which he clearly does not see as radical concepts. Despite talking about the importance of interaction, he retains the primacy of the autonomous individual in the sense of agents and systems that individually represent a world and then act autonomously on those representations. For me, the potentially radical implications of complexity theory are readily assimilated by Gell-Mann into scientific orthodoxy. Complexity theory, in his version, is an interesting extension of orthodoxy. This, and the explicitly cognitivist frame of reference he works within, makes it almost inevitable that the importation of his work for theorising about organisation will not pose any radical challenge. Also, the kind of emphasis he places on simple rules has proved to be very popular amongst many of those who have applied the theory of complex adaptive systems to organisations. The validity of doing this will be explored in Chapter 9.

Holland

Holland (1998) is particularly concerned with nonlinear agent-based models and he sets out the procedure for designing such models. The first step is to shear away irrelevant detail because the model must be simpler than that which it models – he is looking for simple laws (p. 46). He then talks about specifying the mechanisms through which entities, or agents, relate to each other and how these mechanisms form the building blocks of the model. The configuration of the building blocks determines the state of the model at any particular moment and transition functions determine how it changes state. These building blocks make predictability and plan-ning possible (p. 11).

Holland's cognitivist frame of reference is quite explicit, as is his deterministic and reductionist approach to science. He clearly takes the position of the indepen-dent observer of a system and talks about models needing to follow the designer's intent. Repeatedly he talks about focusing on the time spans and the levels of detail that allow the uncovering of regularities and unchanging laws. He stresses how *simple rules* of interaction yield emergent pattern, how rules generate perpetual novelty. However, he rapidly follows such statements with others in which he says a phe-nomenon is emergent only when it is recognisable and recurring, although it may not be easy to recognise or explain. So, he points to chance, unpredictability and novelty and then rapidly backs away from these notions to advocate concentrating on time spans and levels of detail where predictability is possible and 'novelty' is regular.

The emphasis he places on the autonomous individual also comes out very clearly when he describes the individual agents in his models. He says that these agents must have strategies, that is, prescriptions telling them what to do as the game unfolds, approximating a complete strategy that tells them what to do in all possible situations. For Holland, emergent patterns are predictable and regular. He points to how chaos theory is used to explain why it is that the long-term future of nonlinear systems is unpredictable. He accepts this but then takes the example of the weather system and says that because meteorologists do not know all the relevant variables, they simply do not work at the level at which chaos would be relevant. They simply start their forecast afresh each day and chaos does not matter (p. 44).

What Holland does, then, is to dismiss the importance of long-term unpredictability and holds that it is possible to get by through focusing on the short term. What I see here is someone pointing to radical unpredictability, emergent novelty through a radical notion of self-organisation and then immediately assimilating it into orthodox science and so neutering its implications. Again, I would argue that the principal route through which this is achieved is the retention of a cognitivist perspective on human knowing. As with Gell-Mann, I would argue that, in the hands of Holland, complexity theory represents an interesting development of orthodoxy in the natural sciences. I am not trying to say that this is unimportant. I am simply pointing to the reasoning process being employed. Holland's views, even more so than Gell-Mann's, are immediately and easily assimilated into systems-based management thinking.

Kauffman

Kauffman's (1995) work has much in common with that of Gell-Mann and Holland but in some important respects it is radically different. The similarity is in his method. He simulates abstract living systems consisting of large numbers of autonomous adaptive agents in terms of information-processing systems. What he does is quite close to Langton's work. Once again, the agents and their *rules of interaction are simple* and, from this simplicity of interaction, complex novelty emerges. As with the others, his agents are cybernetic entities, cognitivist in nature. His methodology and the underlying cognitivist assumptions make it just as easy to import his modelling approach into systems-based theorising about organisations. However, the conclusions he draws from his work are radical. He emphasises the importance of self-organisation in evolution, calling it a second-ordering principle and attaches greater importance to it than to random mutation or natural selection. He places emergent novelty at the centre of life and as a consequence accepts that one has to give up the dream of predicting the details. Instead, one has to pursue the hope of explaining, understanding and, perhaps, predicting the emergent generic properties of a system.

The radical position Kauffman takes up here is contrary to management orthodoxy in many ways and it is this kind of perspective I will be interested in exploring in relation to organisations in Part 3.

Goodwin

Goodwin (1994) also holds the radical implications of complexity theory, particularly emphasising relationship and participation. Like Kauffman, Goodwin rejects the neo-Darwinian view of evolution. Goodwin takes the organism, rather than the gene, as the fundamental unit in biology. He thinks in terms of a network of interacting genes located within an environment, or context, which he calls the morphological field. This context is a constraint on the possible patterns of expression by the genetic network. By ensuring that parameter values fall within certain domains, genes contribute to the stability and repeatability of a life cycle, the biological memory, or heredity. But, organisms are entities organised dynamically by developmental and morphogenetic fields. Fields are wholes actively organising themselves. Goodwin relocates agency away from interacting individual components and places it at the level of the whole.

Prigogine

Prigogine sees the radical potential more than anyone, perhaps, as he speaks of a new dialogue with nature in which the purpose of science would not be that of dominating and controlling nature.

A review

On the one hand, there is what seems to me to be an orthodox perspective, typified by the views of Holland and Gell-Mann and to some extent by those of Langton. From this perspective, a complex system is understood in somewhat mechanistic, reductionist terms and is modelled by an objective observer in the interests of predicting its behaviour. Self-organisation is not seen to be a new ordering principle in the evolution of the system. Evolution occurs through random mutation and competitive selection. The radical unpredictability of emergent new forms is not emphasised. The system is modelled as a network of cybernetic and cognitivist agents: they represent regularities in the form of schemas, the equivalent of mental models; they store those representations in the form of rules and then act on the basis of those rules. Complexity is reduced to simplicity and much emphasis is placed on complex patterns emerging from simple rules.

On the other hand, there is what seems to me to be a radical perspective on the nature of complex systems. This is typified by the views of Kauffman and Goodwin, and, even more so, Prigogine. From this perspective, self-organisation, rather than random mutation, plays the central role in the emergence of new forms. Those new forms emerge and they are radically unpredictable.

The more orthodox viewpoint can be brought to bear on organisational issues within a cognitivist view of human psychology and a systemic perspective on interaction. The result, I hope to show in the next chapter, is a theory of organisation that uses the terminology of complex systems but stays firmly within dominant systems-based thinking about organisations. Potentially radical insights from complexity theory are easily assimilated into the orthodox discourse. This is done by selectively concentrating on time periods and levels of detail that are predictable and talking about self-organisation and emergence as if they could be controlled by managers. When this is done, what is lost is the invitation to explore what managers do when time spans and levels of detail are radically unpredictable. In the next chapter, I will be exploring how some writers have been doing just this, in my view. In Part 3, I will be exploring the consequences for organisational theory of the radical perspective on complexity within a framework of human psychology that is different from cognitivism, constructivism, humanistic psychology and psychoanalysis. I will be reviewing a responsive processes rather than a systemic way of making sense of life in organisations, a way that draws on analogies from the more radical expositions of complex adaptive systems with heterogeneous agents.

8.6 Summary

This chapter has reviewed a number of developments in theories of systemic behaviour, namely chaos, dissipative structures and complex adaptive systems.

Chaos theory is a theory of systems that focuses on the same level of description as systems dynamics; that is, both focus on the level of the system as a whole. They both make assumptions about the entities comprising a system and their interactions, particularly with the environment. The assumption is that both the entities and their interactions are average, or normally distributed around an average. Dissipative structure theory develops the notions of self-organisation and emergence. It models the system of interest in terms of nonlinear mathematical equations governing state changes at the macro level of the system, just as systems dynamics and chaos theory do. However, unlike these last, dissipative structure models incorporate fluctuations, or variety, in exogenous variables, or micro events. In other words, fluctuations in the sense of non-average behaviour in the system's environment are incorporated in the former and not in the latter. The result is the phenomenon of self-organising order through fluctuations and, given the presence of non-average behaviour, the system has the internal capacity to move spontaneously from one attractor to another. Note also that self-organisation in dissipative structure theory is a collective response of the whole system. It takes the form of correlations and resonances between the entities comprising the system that emerge as new patterns or order.

Complex adaptive systems theory models interaction between many agents comprising a system. It sets out the logical structure of algorithmic, that is, digital-code-based, interaction and derives the properties of such interaction through the method of computer simulation. The digital code interaction is then used as an analogy for some other kind of interaction. For example, digital code is used as an analogy for the genetic code of biological organisms. The properties of digital code interaction are then taken to apply to biological code. In other words, an act of interpretation is required in order to utilise the insights derived from the logic of digital code interaction in relation to some other kind of interaction.

Further reading

On chaos there is the classic account of how chaos was discovered and what it means by Gleick (1988), and also Briggs and Peat (1989) and Kellert (1993). A more mathematical but accessible treatment is Stewart (1989). On self-organisation it is useful to read Prigogine and Stengers (1984), Davies (1987) and Nicolis and Prigogine (1989). Useful reviews of complexity theory are provided by Waldrop (1992), Casti (1994), Cohen and Stewart (1994), Goodwin (1994), Kauffman (1995) and Levy (1992). Boden (1996) provides a useful review of the philosophy and methodology of complex adaptive systems.

Questions to aid further reflection

1. What do the terms self-organisation and emergence mean?
2. What is meant by conflicting constraints and what part do they play in the functioning of complex adaptive systems?
3. In what way might the theory of complex adaptive systems present an alternative to the neo-Darwinian theory of evolution?

4. What theories of causality are reflected in different theories in the complexity sciences?

5. What do you see as the major differences between alternative interpretations of complexity theories?

6. How might notions of self-organisation and emergence challenge mainstream theories of organisation?

7. In what way do the dynamics of stable instability and the possibility of radical unpredictability challenge mainstream theories of organisational change?

8. What role does diversity play in theories of complexity and what implications does this have for thinking about life in organisations?

Chapter 9

Systemic applications of complexity sciences to organisations

This chapter invites you to draw on your own experience to reflect on and consider the implications of:

- The different quantitative and qualitative ways of applying the complexity sciences to organisations.

- How the application of the complexity sciences to organisations may simply continue to reflect the position of the external objective observer of a system and so lose the potentially radical insights coming from the natural complexity sciences.

- How many applications retain the central concern of organisational theorists with control.

This chapter is important because it invites reflection on how insights coming from the complexity sciences are being taken up by some writers on organisations and how these insights may be easily subjugated and absorbed into the dominant discourse on organisations. Understanding the material in this chapter aids in understanding the distinction to be made in the approach to management in Part 3 of the book which draws on relevant insights from the complexity sciences in a different way.

9.1 Introduction

Chapter 8 argued that during the 1970s and 1980s the complexity sciences developed further the thinking about the fundamental dynamics of systems. These new systems theories, like the first wave of twentieth-century systems theories, have been developed largely by natural scientists. I have argued that they are potentially radical in that they point to the self-referential, self-organising capacities of such systems. What this means is that agents in a complex system interact locally with each other on the basis of their historically evolved capacities, and this local self-referring, self-organising interaction itself generates emergent new forms of the whole system in the absence of any blueprint or programme for that whole. These insights are a radical departure from earlier systems theories in that new forms are now seen to emerge from local interaction, but only in the presence of diversity. The emphasis is placed on the local, differentiated, evolving relationships between entities rather than on some view of the whole and its properties. This potentially displaces the externally observing cognising individual from the central position occupied in the application of the earlier systems theories to human organisations. Furthermore, the creative novelty that emerges in this fashion is fundamentally unpredictable. This raises question marks over the nature of control, another central feature of the application of earlier systems theories to organisations.

However, in the last chapter I also tried to show how some interpretations of the theory of complex systems in the natural sciences do not depart from cybernetics in many ways. This is because, in some formulations, the agents making up a complex adaptive system are defined in cybernetic and cognitivist terms. Furthermore, complexity theories continue, of course, to be systems theories. Despite the radical potential of some complexity theories, stressed by a few, most of the natural scientists working in this area seem to me to remain, more or less, within a basically orthodox perspective on science and, of course, all of them continue to think within the systems paradigm. Organisational theorists using chaos and complexity theory also continue to think in terms of systems and, I suggest, most of them focus on those expositions of the natural complexity sciences in which agents are cybernetic entities. They therefore continue with an individual-based psychology drawn from cognitivism, constructivism or humanistic perspectives. With the notable exceptions of the work of Allen and Marion discussed below, most organisational complexity writers avoid exploring the implications of radical unpredictability and so retain conventional notions of control. They therefore continue to argue within the dominant ideologies of control, harmony and conformity. I will illustrate what I mean by looking at some books and papers that use notions from complexity theory.

9.2 Modelling industries as complex systems

One approach to applying theories of complexity to organisations is to use the mathematical and modelling techniques of the natural scientists to model the dynamics of whole industries. This section looks at three examples of this. The first uses chaos theory, the second makes considerable use of fitness landscapes and the third draws on Prigogine's work.

The application of chaos theory to industries

Levy (1994) simulates an industrial supply chain using nonlinear equations of the type that can produce mathematical chaos and concludes that the model can be used to guide decisions concerning production location, sourcing and optimum inventory levels. Levy focuses his analysis on the macro level, arguing that industries can be modelled as dynamic systems that exhibit both unpredictability and underlying order. He notes the point that human systems are not deterministic and that human agency can alter social system but believes that 'chaotic models can be used to suggest ways that people might intervene to achieve certain goals' (p. 169).

He concludes that, although short-term forecasting is possible, long-term planning is impossible and says that this has 'profound implications for organisations trying to set strategy based on their anticipation of the future' (p. 170). He concludes that strategic plans should take account of a number of scenarios and that firms should not focus too narrowly on core competences. For him, strategy becomes a set of *simple* guidelines that influence decisions and behaviour. This is the notion of '*simple rules*' so popular amongst those applying complexity theories to organisations. Furthermore, firms need to change these guidelines as industries and competitors change. Levy also says that the system as a whole must be understood if one is to understand indirect and counterintuitive means to an end.

Notice how this argument proceeds. It recognises the impossibility of long-term prediction. However, instead of asking how managers are actually now proceeding in the absence of reliable forecasts or foresight, Levy says they should foresee a number of scenarios and set simple guidelines. The notion seems to be that complex systems can be managed if one can identify the right set of simple rules. He also recommends, just as the systems-dynamics-based theory of the learning organisation does, that organisations must be understood as a *whole* and that this can be done by computer simulation. For him, goals are to be achieved through indirect means. So, here chaos theory is being used to model an operational system at the macro level in order to aid decision making. Levy clearly equates the manager's role with that of the model builder or programmer who stands outside the system and controls it.

I think that the radical potential of theories of complexity for organisational theory tend to be obscured by simulations of this kind because of the direct application of concepts from the natural sciences with no interpretation of what they mean in the human domain. This is a problem if you are interested in the nature of organising and managing in terms of human relationships. Attempts to model people as an impersonal collective driven by rules immediately loses the rich texture of emotional and embodied relating. The idea that an organisation can be modelled and then influenced and controlled is implicitly cognitivist and cybernetic. What is lost here is the question of what it is like for a manager to be a member of a complex system, interacting at a local level, when it is not possible to see the organisation as a whole or know where it is going.

How industries explore fitness landscapes

Marion (1999) describes the development of the microcomputer industry and uses it to illustrate his perspective on organisational complexity. He describes how mainframe computers became commercially available in 1952 and how, in the mid-1960s, microprocessors were developed and incorporated in hand-held calculators. Small packets of technology were, therefore, emerging in a moderately coupled network of industries over the 1950s and 1960s. Then, in 1975, MICS produced the first microcomputer, the Altair, which was cheaper and more accessible to a wider market than mainframes. Microcomputers had a different architecture from mainframes and calculators and during the initial stage of market development, competition in the microcomputer sector had more to do with architectures than with anything else. There were, and still are, only two architectures. One is based on the Intel chip and the other on the Motorola processor. A number of operating systems were built around these chips: CP/M; the Apple system; IBM DOS; and systems for the Commodore, Tandy, Texas Instruments, NCR, NEC, Olivetti, Wang and Xerox microcomputers. The early market niche for microcomputers was thus crowded with architectures and operating systems when, in 1981, IBM entered the micro-computer market. The entry of IBM immediately put the fastest growing operating system, CP/M, out of business. By the mid-1980s, IBM's architecture was dominant and others adopted it in order to survive. At the same time, Apple introduced the Mac, which was not as cumbersome or as difficult to learn as DOS. Later, Microsoft brought some simplicity to DOS but it is still not able to match the elegance and simplicity of the Mac. During this period, microprocessor technology was also developing: the earliest processors were 4 bit and were soon replaced by 8- and then 16-bit processors. By the mid-1990s, 32-bit technology was dominant.

Marion describes a development, then, in which there were a few people dream-ing of microcomputers in 1974, a great many people wanting one by 1976 and explosive growth in the ensuing two decades. It looked as if microcomputers had suddenly appeared out of nowhere. However, the pieces were coming together long before microcomputers were ever envisioned: microcircuits, microprocessors, ROM and RAM memory chips were being used in calculators, while computer language logic was being documented in mainframes. The microcomputer was built from these pieces.

Marion uses the Kauffman framework described in Chapter 8 to make sense of these developments. He argues that bits of already existing technology come together as emergent microcomputers just as Kauffman argued that emerging connections between molecules became the chemical basis of life. He continues with Kauffman's framework to argue that the early microcomputer niche was occupied by a large number of architectural species. These early producers were small organisations driven by a few engineering personalities. They were relatively simple organisations, lacking much internal complexity and having few internal connections. They also displayed relatively few connections with other players in the niche, since producers specialised in sub-niches, for example, Apple in the education market and Com-modore at the low end of the home market. Competitive interaction was thus limited. Kauffman's models show that such patterns of connection produce highly unstable, chaotic dynamics and this was evident in the rapid and unpredictable development of the microcomputer market in the early days. The industry was characterised by frequent and strong shocks, or large avalanches of extinction.

Then, in the 1980s, the number of players in the architecture field diminished until IBM DOS and Mac dominated that field. In addition, the entry of an internally complex organisation, IBM, and the rapid growth and development of Apple, meant that internal complexity rose, that is, there was a greater number of connections between agents within the competing organisations. At the same time, the number of connections between organisations in the niche increased because both of the main players competed with each other in all of the market niches. In Kauffman's models, this pattern of connections produces the dynamic at the edge of chaos. Marion argues that the intertwining of stability and instability at the edge of chaos was also characteristic of the microcomputer industry at the end of the 1980s and on into the 1990s, when changes became much smaller and more incremental, with large extinction events a rarity. IBM DOS came to dominate the architecture niche, despite the technical superiority of the Apple Mac. This is technological 'lock-in', which occurs as more and more users come to rely on a particular technology so that the costs of change become too high and users stay with the technology they have, even if it is inferior. However, there was still change as the number of microcomputer producers increased, IBM lost its market dominance and Microsoft increased its power. The changes, of course, continue to this day.

Marion is showing how an industrial network evolves through its own internal dynamic to the edge of chaos. He emphasises the radical unpredictability of such evolution and the continuing unpredictability when a network operates at the edge of chaos. He draws on three characteristics to reach this conclusion. The first is sensitive dependence on initial conditions (*see* Chapter 8), which he argues can be seen in the sensitivity of human interaction to small events. Unpredictability here is due to human inability to monitor and observe infinite detail. Second, he refers to Prigogine's work on potential energy and Poincaré resonances to argue that intrinsic unpredictability is also a feature of complex systems. Third, he brings in the power law (*see* Chapter 8) to argue that, despite its great stability and robustness, a network at the edge of chaos will be subject to many small, and a few large, extinction events and that these are impossible to predict.

He argues that all of these factors are sources of radical unpredictability in the evolution of human networks that makes it impossible for an individual to be in control of such a network. In other words, no single organisation in the industrial network chooses the future direction of the industry, and this means that it cannot choose its own evolution either. This suggests that managers who claim to be planning the future of their organisation will not actually be doing so. Furthermore, no single organisation can choose the dynamics of the industry as a whole and therefore no organisation can choose its own dynamic either. In the early stages of the development of the microcomputer industry, the dynamics were chaotic because of the large number of simply structured competitors, loosely connected to each other. None of them chose this. It flowed from the nature of the interaction between them. The entry of IBM was a deliberate choice but the reduction in the number of competitors and the increase in the range of competitive interaction between the survivors was not simply IBM's choice. It depended upon what the others did too. The evolution to the dynamic at the edge of chaos was co-created through the interaction of the organisations, not chosen by one in isolation. Outcomes and dynamics continued to change in unpredictable ways, outside the power of individual organisations to choose, as the number of microcomputer producers increased and Microsoft gained greater power over the market. More recently, the power of Microsoft was challenged by lawsuits and freely available operating systems on the Internet.

Marion is making an important point here because many who take up complexity theory in relation to organisations may accept that organisations cannot choose future outcomes but then claim that they can deliberately choose the dynamic in which they operate.

However, Marion also repeatedly stresses that unpredictability does not lead to the conclusion that it all happens by chance or that there is no control. Attractors at the edge of chaos are bounded and demonstrate a family-like similarity. Therefore, it is not possible for just anything to happen. He also argues that the power law is itself a form of control because, at the edge of chaos, the numbers of extinction events both large and small are smaller than they are in the dynamics of stability, on the one hand, and instability, on the other. Because of the relatively small number of large extinction events, change spreads through a network in a controlled manner. In the other dynamics, change spreads through the network in a highly destructive, continuous manner.

Marion, therefore, focuses at the macro level of a whole industry and talks about a population of impersonal organisations (IBM and Apple for example) interacting with each other in a self-organising manner, driven by an urge to survive. He is talking about this population and the organisations of which it consists as if they were no different from a population of organisms. However, what are these organisations? They are not organisms, or anything like organisms, but, rather, patterns of joint human action. Marion reifies organisations and treats them as if they are things, or organisms, apart from, or outside of humans, interacting according to principles that apply to them at a macro level, split off from the humans that constitute them. The principles governing these systems are taken to be the same as those governing non-human systems.

To this Marion adds the deliberate purposefulness (teleology) of human beings, by which he means what has been called rationalist causality in Part 1. The result is that humans, acting according to rationalist causality, find themselves having to act within a system that is somehow independent of them, operating according to the causal principles of self-organisation. The latter considerably restricts the scope humans have for realising their intentions. Patterns in human action, then, emerge as the 'both . . . and' paradigm of both human choice and a system with a life of its own.

Marion's assumptions about human psychology are clearly individual centred and cognitivist. He argues that social behaviour arises from the selfish needs of the individual. Selfishness is local and personal, an individual trait that does not depend upon any external force. Humans are said to co-operate because that is the best way of achieving individual goals. In addition, he says that humans assign meaning to symbols and mental constructs that catalyse human action to create complex social structures. This clearly places the individual as fundamental and thought before action. Before there can be the social there have to be individual humans with their selfish interests and before they act, they think and make selfish choices.

However, another part of Marion's argument does pick up on a radical insight coming from complexity theory. He argues that the very nature of the irrational and the random is essential to the emergence of novel structures. He ties creativity and the emergence of novelty firmly to the unpredictable aspect of the dynamic at the edge of chaos. He argues that without irrationality there would be stagnation. He sees irrationality as the social equivalent of the Poincaré resonances that Prigogine regards as essential to the emergence of new structures in nature. Diverse and surprising order in the world arises because life takes unexpected directions. Marion thinks about human learning as a process of tinkering, often without much thinking. People tinker, and as they do so they sense patterns. These patterns organise their perception and understanding, and as they tinker further those perceptions and understandings restructure, which in turn affects what people observe. He claims that learning occurs because humans are irrational. Perfectly rational decision makers have nothing to discover and hence nothing to learn. Heroic leaders do less than we think they do, but they do act as symbols of a cause and they do rally unified behaviour. However, having taken a radical position on causality, predictability, equilibrium, limits on human ability to change social processes through deliberate action alone, and so in many ways decentring the individual, Marion ends up with a view of human psychology and social relating that is not particularly radical, apart from the way he stresses the irrational and the need for deviant behaviour.

Complex evolutionary models of industries

Allen and his colleagues (Allen *et al.*, 2006), who work in the tradition of Prigogine (*see* Chapter 8), argue that change in organisations occurs through an ongoing process of co-evolution in which behavioural types interact with each other. Alan argues that the underlying mechanisms of such evolution involve microdiversity within a system and it is this that drives ongoing, emergent, qualitative changes in systems and structures. He draws on Darwinian theory in saying that there are selective effects of interaction and also mechanisms that discover new strategies or niches. He also says that human intention, calculation and belief may channel diversity into a narrower range than that which the random microdiversity of nature would produce.

Diversity is defined in terms of the number of qualitatively different types of individuals, each type having different attributes. As an organisation evolves, changes occur in both the attributes internal to each type and the configuration of interactions between types. Individuals are thought of as bundles of attributes reflecting a type and organisations are thought of as bundles of these individual types, with societies being bundles of organisations. These levels of individual, organisation and society co-evolve and the diversity of each level emerges in the co-evolutionary process, driven by diversity at the level below. Evolution requires the invasion of a population by new behaviours which grow to a significant level in the system.

This conceptualisation allows the construction of a mathematical model consisting of differential equations where each equation generates growth rates for a different type in a population and where the growth rate of each type depends to some extent on the growth rates of competing types. The model shows that a new type can only invade the system, the system can only evolve, if it is unstable – stability makes invasion by a new type, and thus evolution, impossible. The model is used to demonstrate that evolution generates coherent diversity and that microdiversity at one system level drives the evolution of the system level above it.

So, a model of macroscopic equations of population dynamics is used to describe how evolution works. This model starts with the assumption that each agent in a type is the average across that type. Errors are then introduced into the replication of the behaviours, or strategies, of agents within a type, amounting to a relaxation of the assumption of averages across a type. This takes account of microdiversity within a type, that is, of non-average agents. Then the model shows how error making, or ignorance, is a robust way of exploring for new strategies.

Failure

The conclusion is that when agents are in a new domain then learning/exploration leads to better overall performance, despite the opportunity cost of error making. But in a domain which is not new, exploitation rather than exploration produces better overall performance. Allen suggests that industries display similar dynamics to the model as they gradually switch from exploration to exploitation. The models show that there is no such thing as an optimal strategy because as soon as one strategy becomes dominant then it will be vulnerable to the invasion of some other strategy.

The model is developed to explore the dynamics of economic markets. Potential customers are modelled in terms of their revenue, recognising that this means ignoring different desires and needs of individuals. The model shows how an ecology of strategies emerges indicating that agents are not susceptible to adopting the same strategy, contrary to the prescriptions for best practice or benchmarking to be found in the organisational literature. Diverse behaviours and learning rules lead to more rapid evolution of market structure at a lower cost than benchmarking. However, the explorations/innovations tried out at a particular time cannot be logically deduced because their overall effect cannot be known ahead of time.

The conclusion is that a system of co-evolving agents with underlying micro-diversity, or idiosyncrasy, automatically leads to the emergence of new structures, and the general implications are that:

- error-making diffusion leads to successful performance and innovation;
- the whole process leads to the evolution of a complex community of types of agent;
- successful and sustainable evolutionary systems are those in which there is freedom and encouragement of exploration – they are more co-operative than competitive;
- uncertainty about the future allows actions that are exploratory.

The same authors (Allen *et al.*, 2005) use a macroscopic model to show how non-linear responses can generate new (false) information which can break symmetries and lead to evolutionary change. They take the problem of policemen trying to catch criminals. In the first model they assume that the policemen carry out the random 'stop and search' of people when they seem to be acting suspiciously. Microdiversity is introduced by assuming that there are two types of people – pink and blue. These two types commit exactly the same average rate of crime. However, in actuality there are fluctuations, small deviations around the average, so that in one period pinks commit a higher rate of crime and in others the blues do. On average the rate is the same but for particular sampling periods there is some purely chance variation around the average. Over a long period, the deviations around the average will cancel out if the police stop and search pinks and blues randomly. The statistics they collect on their arrests will reflect the underlying real rates of crime over a reasonably long sampling period.

However, to improve performance the police authorities introduce targets for arresting criminals and reward policemen according to target achievement. The police gather statistics on crime rates over a particular sampling period during which it just happens that more pinks than blues are arrested. So, policemen form a theory that crime rates are higher in the pink population and so focus more attention on stopping and searching pinks. This turns into a self-fulfilling prophesy because the greater police effort in relation to pinks does lead to the arrest of more pinks than blues. Also, the blues may come to feel that they can more easily escape detection and so actually commit more crimes than the pinks, but this fact escapes detection by the police because they are focusing their attention on the pinks. The statistics the police collect will then show that pinks commit much more crime than blues when in fact the opposite is the case. This false information will lead to even more effort being directed at the pinks so leading to the vicious circle of a self-fulfilling prophesy. Complex systems evolve into an unknowable future sometimes with unwanted consequences. The authors argue that uncertainty and surprise are essential features of life itself.

This kind of macro modelling yields important insights which are often counter-intuitive. For example, the models show that following best practice benchmarks actually harms strategic exploration and that apparently rational strategies developed to meet targets can have highly distorting effects on activity. The models can therefore be used to generate provocative generalisations. The interesting question then becomes just how people in organisations use such articulations of *generalisations* in their context-specific situations. However, I argue that macro models cannot capture the detail of unique, context-specific detail of human interaction and so cannot explain how people actually make particular such generalisations in their specific situations. This will be a matter of concern in Part 3 of the book. Also, while the models considered above make an important move to explore the consequences of diversity, mathematical models cannot deal with the full diversity of human behaviour. For example, in modelling markets, the models mentioned above cannot capture differences in the preferences and tastes of individual consumers. Part 3 will also be concerned with the actual diversity of human action in our experience.

Although Allen's models are extremely useful in generating provocative insights, they can quite easily be subtly reproduced as theories of strategic choice and the learning organisation, cast in a new vocabulary. I suggest that this happens because of the continued employment of the language of systems and the adoption of an essentially cognitivist view of human psychology, emphasising the primacy of the individual who knows through making representations of reality and behaves on the basis of these representations. This is an essentially cybernetic view of human knowing and behaving, one that is entirely compatible with systemic management and organisational theory. The result is that the potentially radical implications of the models may not be realised in relation to the management of organisations.

To illustrate what I mean, take Allen's (1998a) analysis of the fishing industry. He contrasts the conclusions produced by equilibrium (cybernetic system), systems dynamics, self-organising, and evolutionary models of that industry. The equilibrium model produces a policy recommendation to constrain fishing effort at, or just below, the maximum that yields a sustainable fish population. However, the dynamics of the fish population and fish markets rapidly render any selected sustainable level of fishing highly inaccurate. A systems dynamics model allows for variations in fish populations and in economic conditions. However, the model uses average data for all of these factors and so cannot capture spontaneous change.

Allen then introduces 'noise' into the equations to represent random fluctuations in fish populations to construct a model of the systems dynamics kind. This model produces boom-and-bust oscillations in fishing fleet catches. On the basis of this model, management should concern itself with overcoming this cyclical behaviour rather than discussing fishing quotas. Allen then introduces a variable to represent the rate of response of the fleet to fish availability, another for the level of technology and yet another for price responsiveness to construct a model of the self-organising kind. Now there is still a boom-and-bust attractor, but in addition, another attractor emerges, one of a small high-priced niche where fish becomes a luxury food.

Allen also incorporates different levels of information acquired by each fishing fleet and different attitudes to risk into the self-organising model. He assumes that fishing fleets are boundedly rational decision makers and so imports cognitivism as his theory of human psychology. The model demonstrates that optimal use of information increases profit in the short term but not necessarily in the long term. Cautious optimisers get locked into the existing situation while more adventurous risk takers open themselves to the possibility of finding new strategies. The model identifies a tendency to follow short-term profit-maximising strategies at the expense of the long term.

Finally, Allen specifies what he calls an evolutionary complex model, which introduces different types of boats and fleet behaviours. The result is a model that can be used to explore the relative effectiveness of different strategies (1998a, p. 33). From this analysis, he reaches the conclusion that sustainability lies not in efficiency, or in allowing free markets, but in creativity. Creativity is rooted in diversity, cultural richness and the will and ability to experiment and take risks. Another conclusion is that uncertainty is inevitable.

Allen very clearly demonstrates the importance of diversity in generating new forms as he moves from one way of modelling the fishing industry to another. He clearly identifies the radical nature of models that incorporate high levels of diversity. However, what he suggests as application in terms of management falls quite easily into the systemic management discourses reviewed in Part 1. For example, his whole methodology implies a cognitivist view of human beings who use rational constructs to explore scenarios with the intention of gaining insight. This easily allows one to sidestep the possibility that management itself is an evolving process. The implication is that managers can step outside their system and model it as the basis of making decisions to manipulate it. The insights he produces are radical but the prescriptions are not. However, in saying this I do not in any way diminish the importance of the generalised insights that complex evolutionary models generate. I am simply arguing that they need to be taken further in terms of the detail of actual human experience in organisations.

9.3 Understanding organisations as complex systems

In this section, I will look briefly at a number of publications that import theories of chaos and complex adaptive systems into theorising about organisations in a qualitative way, as opposed to the quantitative modelling of whole industries explored in the last section.

Thietart and Forgues

Thietart and Forgues (1995) review chaos theory and conclude that mathematical chaos can be found 'when there is the simultaneous influence of counteracting forces' (p. 23). The authors then review relevant literature on organisations to show that organisations are characterised by counteracting forces. Some of these forces push an organisation to stability, namely the forces of planning, structuring and controlling. Other forces, however, push an organisation towards instability and disorder. These forces include innovation, initiative and experimentation. They argue that when these forces are coupled they produce the chaotic organisation. On this basis, Thietart and Forgues present a number of propositions based on the theory of chaos, such as:

- Organisations are potentially chaotic.
- Organisations move from one dynamic state to another, namely stable equilibrium, periodic equilibrium or chaos.
- Forecasting is impossible, especially at a global scale over the long term. Change, therefore, has an unpredictable long-term effect.
- When in the chaotic state, organisations are attracted to an identifiable configuration.
- Similar actions taken by the same organisation will never lead to the same state.

They conclude that the interaction of forces of stability and change can create chaotic dynamics, which they define literally as 'deterministically induced random behavior' (p. 28), which they say has an underlying order and so leads to new stabilities. The prescription then becomes to 'let chaos develop because it is the only way to find new forms of order' and 'look for order but not too much, because it may be a source of chaos' (p. 28).

There are a number of points to note about this kind of analysis. First is the level at which the analysis is conducted, namely the macro level of the organisation as a whole. Second, it adopts the position of the objective observer. Third, there is a hint of an underlying cognitivist perspective in that organisations, presumably those who manage them, are assumed to be able to choose how much chaos or order to have. There is the notion that the role of managers is to move their organisation between different dynamic possibilities. I would like to sound a note of caution in pursuing this kind of analysis. Chaos theory is a theory of deterministic systems but human action is not deterministic. The behaviour of people is not driven by unchanging rules. The 'rules', if that is what they are, change as people learn.

Morgan

Morgan (1997) uses chaos and complexity theories as the basis of one of his metaphors for organisations, namely the organisation as flux and transformation. He points to the order that can emerge from interaction governed by a few *simple rules* and equates these simple rules with his notion of 'minimum specs': that is, avoiding a grand design and specifying a small number of critical variables to attend to. He says the minimum specs define an attractor and create the context within which the system will move to it.

There are problems with this idea of 'simple rules'. If the requirement is some new form then the rules, or the context, that will produce that form do not exist yet. If emergence depends critically on small changes then there is no way to specify what they are in advance. You could not ensure that you have detected all of them or measured them accurately enough. Morgan passes over this and recommends that managers should manage the context and allow self-organisation to do the rest. Here again there is the notion of manager not as participant in a difficult-to-understand complex system but as one who stands outside it, identifies the minimum specs and then creates the context for it to produce self-organisation. Note the talk about a manager 'allowing it to happen'. This seems to assume that self-organisation is some new form of behaviour an individual can choose rather than a different way of understanding how people have always behaved.

Morgan also recommends identifying the small changes, or leverage points, that will transform the system. I have already explained why I think that this does not fit with the notion of a complex system. He also recommends identifying the existing attractor that is locking an organisation into a stable position and identifying whether it should be changed. If it is to be changed, then managers are supposed to work out how the transition is to be achieved and how small changes can be used to do so. In advance, they are supposed to identify what the new ground rules are supposed to be. They must consider how they are going to manage through the 'edge of chaos'.

For me, the essentials of cybernetics and cognitivism are all firmly in place in this argument. The focus is on the autonomous individual who stands outside the system and in effect controls it, even if in a much looser way than is often supposed. The reasoning remains, I think, firmly within the systemic tradition and the invitation to explore a radical perspective is passed by.

Nonaka

Nonaka (Nonaka, 1988, 1991a; Nonaka and Takeuchi, 1995) also uses chaos theory in his perspective on creation of knowledge in organisations (*see* Chapter 4). Nonaka and Takeuchi use the words 'self-organising' but in a very different way from my understanding. They see self-organisation not as the local interaction of agents that produces emergent patterns, but rather as the unconstrained activity of autonomous or free individuals. They describe a self-organising team as a structure in which individuals can be free to diffuse their ideas (p. 76). They link this with Morgan's (1997) 'minimum critical specifications'. In complexity theory, self-organisation is a process in which agents interact locally on the basis of their historically evolved identities. They are constrained by the need to interact and this does not imply the kind of freedom that Nonaka talks about.

A key insight from complexity theory is that of the paradoxical dynamics of stability and instability at the 'edge of chaos'. Again Nonaka and Takeuchi use similar words but they equate chaos with crisis and assign to top management the role of injecting it into the organisation in order to break down routines, habits and cognitive frameworks. I cannot see any justification for equating mathematical chaos with human crisis.

Sanders

Sanders (1998) claims that chaos and complexity are everywhere in organisations and talks about the need to master them, claiming that the complexity sciences provide a way to 'anticipate, respond to, and influence change as it is emerging and before a crisis arises' (p. 7). She talks about observing the system, so implicitly taking the position of manager as objective observer rather than participant, and moves immediately to prescriptions for success.

She says that it is possible to identify any system's initial conditions because systems are deterministic, but that it is difficult to predict their future states because they are nonlinear. This statement is clearly wrong. It is in practice impossible to forecast the long-term state of the kind of system she is talking about precisely because it is not possible to identify the initial conditions to the infinite exactness required. Infinite precision is required because the nonlinear structure of the system may amplify even the tiniest failure to identify and precisely measure the initial conditions. Without this, long-term prediction would be possible *because* the system is deterministic. Determinism is a theory of causality and it implies nothing whatsoever about the ability to measure initial conditions.

She then says that despite an inability to make predictions of long-term states it is possible to provide qualitative descriptions of whole system behaviour over time. This is true, but only for the attractor the system is currently drawn to. It would not be possible to describe any new attractor that some system was capable of spontaneously jumping to, until the jump occurred. Furthermore, human systems are not deterministic because even if there are 'rules' governing them, these rules change over time. If one is to think of the human in terms of systems then one at least needs to think of them as learning, evolving and producing new forms. In other words, they have to be thought of as moving to entirely new attractors, the 'shape' of which cannot be 'seen' before the move is made. So, you can only 'see' the shape of the attractor you already know about. To the extent that strategy is about producing creative, innovative new forms of business, it would not be possible, in terms of complexity theory, to 'see' that form before it emerges.

As far as I understand it, what I have summarised above is the conceptual core of the whole book and underlies all the prescriptions it makes. Sanders clearly takes the stance of external objective observer who sees an organisation as a chaotic system. Implicitly, she is prescribing this as the stance that a manager should take too. Managers are supposed to look at the system as a whole and then identify the pre-existing order, the strange attractor, hidden in apparent disorder. Then they are supposed to detect new initial conditions and take hold of them, master them she says, before they do something that is unexpected. Not only is the manager to be the objective external observer but also the heroic individual who can master chaos and find hidden order. Unpredictability is mentioned and then, in effect, ignored. The words are from complexity science but the concepts are from cybernetics and cognitivism. In the process, any new insight is lost and orthodox prescriptions are simply presented in different language.

Consider now how Shona L. Brown and Kathleen M. Eisenhardt (1998) apply complexity theory to management in their book, called *Competing on the Edge: Strategy as Structured Chaos*.

Brown and Eisenhardt

Brown and Eisenhardt appeal to a central concept from complexity theory, namely, the 'edge of chaos', which they define as being only partially structured. This immediately loses the paradoxical notion of contradictory forces that can never be resolved, replacing it with a simple balance: too much structure gives stability and too little produces chaos. Being at the edge also means *letting* a semi-coherent strategy emerge from the organisation, that is, one that is not too fixed, nor one that is too fluid. They turn to that favourite of organisational complexity writers, the notion that a few simple structures 'generate enormously complex adaptive behaviour – whether flock behaviour among birds, resilient government (as in democracy), or simply successful performance by corporations' and argue that the 'critical management issue at the edge of chaos is to figure out what to structure, and as essential, what not to structure' (p. 12).

These authors take the notion of the edge of chaos across into organisations and immediately collapse it into one of organisational structure, which then becomes a choice for managers to make. The choice is to install just enough structure to move their organisation to the edge of chaos where it can experience relentless change. Self-organisation is equated with adaptiveness and the notion of local interaction amongst agents producing emergent outcomes is lost. The analogy of the birds is used and then quite effortlessly coupled with successful organisations.

However, flocking is one attractor for bird behaviour, one that already exists. The few simple rules that produce it will not produce spontaneous jumps to new attractors. Surely, success for corporations over the long term requires just such a move to new attractors. Furthermore, a key feature of the edge of chaos is the power law. This means that small numbers of large extinction events occur periodically while large numbers of small extinctions occur. There is no guarantee of survival at the edge of chaos, only the possibility of new forms emerging that might survive. Nowhere do the authors mention this power law. Instead, they make a simplistic equation between being at the edge of chaos and success.

They reduce human behaviour to a few key rules and assume that these can ensure success. The authors provide a questionnaire that managers can use to identify whether they are at the edge of chaos or trapped in one of the other dynamics (pp. 30–1). They give examples from their research of a company in each of these states and, of course, the only successful one is reported to be at the edge of chaos. They then give prescriptions for moving to the edge, if they are not already there. Managers should foster frequent change in the context of a few strict rules. They should keep activity loosely structured but at the same time rely on targets and deadlines. They should create channels for real-time, fact-based communication within and across groups.

So, the strategic choice now relates less to outcomes and more to a few simple rules, frequent changes to keep people on edge and fact-based communication channels. Why is it necessary to appeal to complexity theory for these prescriptions?

I think I have said enough to show that, once again, researchers have made some very loose interpretations of what complexity theory means and quite easily subsumed it into orthodox organisational theory. The prescriptions and the descriptions rely implicitly on cybernetics and cognitivism, even though the language is drawn from complexity theory. The result is a watered-down strategic choice theory.

Wheatley

Griffin (2002) provides a critique of Wheatley's (1999) reliance on chaos and complexity theory. He points out how she sees chaos and complexity theories providing an insight into the simplicity of all living systems in nature. If leaders come to understand their organisations as living systems then they will be able to use the insights from chaos and complexity theories to find a much simpler way of organising human affairs. For her, it is by recognising and working with the living system, by participating in a higher-level whole, that leaders can achieve a more human and a more creative organisation. She also attaches much the same importance to the notion of vision as learning organisation theorists do but she understands vision as a field of real but unseen forces influencing human behaviour. Having conceived of an organisation as a living whole in which people participate, Wheatley argues that those people exhibit a self-organising capacity just as in nature's living systems. Wheatley suggests that organisations are quite literally alive and must be understood, using the complexity sciences, just as other living systems in nature are thought of.

For Wheatley, the essence of living systems is the *simple rules* according to which they function. If leaders of organisations are to lead in a simpler way then they must identify the simple rules and they can do this by turning to the complexity sciences, which she sees as the rediscovery of ancient wisdom. In her thinking about leadership, Wheatley clearly displays the 'both . . . and' thinking of causal duality. There is a living system having it own purpose and an autonomous individual, the leader, also having purpose, and what she is arguing for is for leaders to align their individual purpose with that of the greater living whole. For her, it is an overriding system that assures the emergence of order and she often refers to this in mythological terms, for example, as the order of Gaia emerging from Chaos. Wheatley affirms the mysterious nature of this level of system, and being a part of such a system is what participation is about. She speaks of finding the self in participation in higher wholes. Not to participate, she says, leaves one isolated as an individual. Those who participate in the whole are 'healthy'. Ethical action is equated with conforming and submission to harmonious wholes (*see* Griffin, 2002, for extended critique). Note how her view of organisational life is essentially the same as learning organisation theory and emphasises the rather mystical aspects of that theory (*see* Chapter 4).

Lewin and Regine

Griffin (2002) discusses the work of Lewin and Regine (2000), who also state that organisations are living systems, which they understand as complex adaptive systems, drawing on the work of Stuart Kauffman. They are concerned with the individual's soul being allowed to be present in the workplace and with the emergence of the collective soul of the organisation, thereby displaying the same kind of dualistic, 'both . . . and' thinking as Wheatley. Individuals are *both* agents in complex adaptive systems, where the simple rules governing their interactions have to do with ensuring *caring* relationships, *and* have souls, that is, they are autonomous individuals responsible for their actions in a way that is independent of the self-organisation of the complex adaptive system. There is a distinction between individuals as agents in the system making choices that are caring and participative, so contributing to the health of the system (organisation), and individual agents making other choices which are selfish and make the system (organisation) an unhealthy place to work in.

For Lewin and Regine, the implication of the complexity sciences is that leaders must come to a new understanding of themselves, putting aside their egos to serve others. The new form of leadership requires nothing less than a personal conversion, which is a painful process of learning to let go of the illusion of control. However, they also talk about the leader as the one who changes the culture. The leader, on the one hand, is capable of changing the culture and, on the other hand, must give up the illusion of control.

Just as Wheatley did, so Lewin and Regine emphasise the 'few simple rules' idea, arguing that rich, creative, complex behaviour emerges from a few simple guidelines. They, along with so many others, cite the Boids simulation (*see* Chapter 8), which reproduces flocking patterns on the basis of only three simple rules of interaction among individual agents. They argue that when leaders formulate a few simple rules and leave the rest to self-organisation they will unleash human creativity. However, as Chapter 8 made clear, simulations based on a few given rules produce no creativity whatsoever. What the simple rules thinking represents is simply a different form of control (Stacey *et al.*, 2000).

Lewin and Regine express the source of commitment and ethical action in terms of idealised wholes. Individuals must give up themselves in order for this whole to emerge, which then becomes the basis for the action already taken. This means that the participants are not focused on the everyday potential emerging from conflict and difference, but rather on an idealised and harmonious whole. Again, what Lewin and Regine present is little different from the more mystical aspects of learning organisation theory.

Pascale

Pascale (Pascale *et al.*, 2000) also claims that organisations are living organisms, and that, as such, they are complex adaptive systems. It is not just a metaphor for organisations. Nevertheless, he uses the terminology in both metaphorical and literal senses. For example, he views the mathematical term 'attractor' as a key concept in understanding complex adaptive systems but also uses it in the metaphorical sense of a 'vision' drawing the organisation forward. In a manner that is very similar to that of Lewin and Regine, Pascale describes the leader as being in a 'both . . . and' position. Operational leadership is to be applied in conditions of relative equilibrium. Adaptive leadership, on the other hand, makes happen what would not otherwise have happened. The individual leader must choose the appropriate form of leadership. It is taken for granted that the leader can observe the system from outside and choose amongst possible alternatives to apply to the system.

However, Pascale differs significantly from Wheatley and Lewin and Regine in his focus on conflict as the most important quality of relationship in looking at the organisation as a complex adaptive system. The leader, again from a position external to the system, judges when adaptive leadership is necessary and then considers how much the system needs to be disturbed. Pascale says that this is achieved by communicating the urgency of the adaptive challenge, establishing a broad understanding of the circumstances creating the problem, clarifying why traditional solutions will not work and keeping up the stress until guerrilla leaders come forward with solutions. Leaders intentionally generate anxiety and tension when an adaptive style is called for. They push their organisation to the edge of chaos. Social interaction is driven by conflict but the leaders introduce the source of the conflict into the team.

Griffin (2002) argues that Pascale and his co-authors present a view of leadership that is unethical in Kant's sense. To induce crisis into human teams in order to take advantage of 'productive' self-organisation for the survival of the whole is using humans as a means to an end and so contravenes Kant's ethical imperative.

The problem with 'living systems' and 'simple rules' as a theory of organisation

Griffin (2002) makes a number of criticisms of those who present a theory of organisations as living systems. First, those proposing this view frequently make emotive appeals for a return to ancient wisdom, supposedly now made scientific by the complexity sciences. However, it is far from clear that the ancients were any wiser than we, or that the complexity sciences are rediscovering this ancient wisdom, including Far Eastern spirituality. These are simply assertions. Second, the suggestion that an organisation is a living system sets up a whole outside of the experience of interaction between people, a whole to which they are required to submit if their behaviour is to be judged ethical. This distances us from our actual experience and makes it feel natural to blame something outside of our actual interaction for what happens to us. It encourages the belief that we are victims of a system, on the one hand, and allows us to escape feeling responsible for our own actions, on the other. Or it alienates people. They come to feel that they are insignificant parts of some greater whole and that there is nothing much they can do about it. The third difficulty is that organisations are not things at all, let alone living things. They are processes of communication and joint action. Communication and joint action as such are not alive. It is the bodies communicating and interacting that are alive.

Those prescribing 'simple rules', as the new way to manage complex organisations, hope to accomplish two rather attractive states. On the one hand, they hope that simple rules will replace complicated procedures, plans and other forms of bureaucracy, so freeing people to act creatively. On the other hand, they implicitly hope that this replacement of a bureaucracy by autonomous people freely following a few simple rules will not erode the control of the leaders. What these writers tend not to notice is the ideological basis of their prescription. This is an ideology of harmony in which people voluntarily submit themselves, often somewhat mystically, to a greater living whole in which they display caring behaviour and get in touch with their true selves, their souls. Griffin (2002) points to how this distracts our attention from the essentially conflictual nature of human interaction and so covers over inevitable power relations. Griffin draws on Mead's (1923) distinction between cult and functional values (*see* Chapter 13). Cult values are idealisations in which real-life obstacles to what we want to achieve are ignored. Cult values provide a feeling of enlarged personality. Functionalised values are interpretations of cult values in ordinary, real-life situations. On the rare occasions in which humans do directly follow the simple rules (cult values) without functionalising them, they form a cult. However, organisations are rarely cults. Mostly, they are collectives of people who are interpreting or functionalising the cult values in their interactions with each other.

Those prescribing 'simple rules' in this way usually draw on the Boids simulation (*see* Chapter 8) to justify their view that simple rules can generate complex behaviour. This demonstrates a complete misunderstanding of the Boids simulation. In that simulation, all the Boids are the same – they are homogeneous. They each precisely follow the same three simple rules and only those three rules. They do not interpret or functionalise them. They are the equivalent of cult values directly applied to conduct and they can only produce one pattern of complex behaviour, namely flocking. The Boids are in no sense free, just as the members of a cult are not free. If they were free, then each Boid would be interpreting or functionalising the three rules in their own unique way and they would then not flock. They would produce some other pattern and we cannot know what that pattern is until we see it.

If the leaders of an organisation do prescribe a few simple rules (cult values) for the members to follow, then it is highly likely that the members will interpret or functionalise the values in many different ways. The overall pattern of behaviour they would produce would be unpredictable. The simple rules prescription can, therefore, not be a means for retaining control and as the leader tries to influence the interpretations, more and more rules must be added. If, on the other hand, people did slavishly follow the simple rules then they would constitute a cult, which is incapable of creativity.

I am here emphasising the need for a careful study of what the complexity simulations are actually doing before jumping to simplistic prescriptive conclusions.

9.4 How systemic applications of complexity sciences deal with the four key questions

The above sections have briefly reviewed some of the literature taking a complex systems view of organisations. Some employ the simulation methods of complexity scientists to model organisational processes at the macro level of the industry or the organisation as a whole. Others use the theory of complex systems as a metaphor that gives insight into the management of organisations. The analysis here is usually at the macro level, but sometimes at a more micro level. In the latter case, the emphasis tends to be on prescription rather than analysis.

I would like now to do what I did in relation to the main theories of organisation reviewed in Part 1 of this book and examine how the theories surveyed in this chapter deal with the four questions posed at the end of Chapter 1.

The nature of interaction

As with strategic choice, organisational learning, knowledge management and psycho-analytic perspectives, the writers in this section understand interaction in organisations in systemic terms, this time in terms of chaotic or complex systems. Analysis of these systems may be at a macro level in which diversity in agents and their interactions is not postulated. In that case, the system may follow equilibrium attractors or some strange attractor, but it does not have the internal capacity to move from one attractor to another. In this regard, there is relatively little difference from systems dynamics. What is different is the identification of strange attractors and the use of the concept of self-organisation to explain how movement around the strange attractor emerges. Alternatively, the system may be modelled on a macro level but also take account of some microdiversity. In this case, the system does display the internal capacity to move spontaneously from one attractor to another or to evolve new ones. Self-organisation is then understood as the process that produces emergent novelty. This is a major difference from all of the other systems models reviewed in this book because here the system takes on a life of its own.

It seems to me that the literature reviewed in this chapter mainly uses the first of the above complexity models, namely the one that does not place microdiversity at the centre. This is evidenced by the focus on identifying a few simple rules and on someone operating on the conditions, or model parameters, to move the system to the edge of chaos. Apart from Allen and Marion, it is rare for those utilising complexity theory to talk about the importance of diversity, which in human terms amounts to deviance and eccentricity, as central to that kind of self-organisation that might produce emergent novelty. As a result, the causality of the system is always formative. Those who do focus attention on diversity point to transformative causality but do not develop the implications of this move.

Complex systems at the edge of chaos display the dynamics of order and disorder, stability and instability, regularity and irregularity, all at the same time. When this is interpreted in organisational terms, by the authors reviewed in this chapter, it is often translated as 'crisis'. I suppose that from an orthodox perspective it might be crisis. However, the dynamics of the edge of chaos are not at all the dynamics of crisis, but rather, of paradox and ambiguity. For me, this connotes a mature ability to hold a difficult position, not a state of crisis. Those who equate the edge of chaos with crisis then prescribe the injection of crisis into an organisation. Surely, this is a misinterpretation of what complexity might mean in human terms.

The nature of human beings

The applications of complexity theory to organisations reviewed in this chapter all make implicit assumptions about human psychology. These are drawn from cognitivist and humanistic psychology. This is evident in the emphasis placed on the individual. This means that the notion of a complex system is being interpreted in organisational terms from the same psychological perspective as those theories based on cybernetics and systems dynamics. Given the tendency also to interpret complex systems from the orthodox perspective, it would be surprising to find enormous differences between the theories surveyed in this chapter and those of strategic choice, organisational learning and knowledge management. Again, the exception is provided by the work of Marion and Allen who, although implicitly retaining individual-centred psychological theories, emphasise unpredictability and diversity as generalised insights.

Methodology and paradox

The methodological position of the theorists reviewed above is no different from that of those proposing strategic choice, learning organisation and knowledge management theories. They all take the position of the objective observer, understood in terms of rationalist causality, who stands outside the system and models it in the interest of controlling or, at least, influencing it. The prescriptions derived from these theories all implicitly place the manager in the same position. It is the manager who must produce and impose the few simple rules that will produce the desired attractor. It is the manager who must alter the parameters, or create the conditions, that create the edge of chaos dynamics. This is then simplistically equated with success.

Although paradox seems to me to be at the heart of what the dynamics at the edge of chaos means, it does not feature at the centre of the theories described in this chapter. The paradox of observing participant is eliminated in the 'both . . . and' thinking of dual causality (Griffin, 2002).

Focusing attention

The approaches using chaos and complexity theory reviewed in this chapter focus attention on much the same factors as the systemic theories reviewed in Part 1 of this book, apart from Allen and Marion. There is the same emphasis on the agency of the autonomous individual. There is the same concern with control. There is the same downplaying of the importance of unpredictability and diversity. There is the same belief in the possibility of an organisation moving according to some organisation-wide intention.

It seems to me that what is happening is this. Complexity theories, particularly those modelling systems with a life of their own, have potentially radical implications for thinking about organisations. The most radical potential implication, it seems to me, is to question systems thinking itself. Continuing to think of human interaction as 'system' makes it impossible to move away from all the other systemic theories and the problems with them that Kant identified so long ago. Added to this, the theories of complex systems are combined with a cognitivist theory of human behaviour. Cognitivism has close links with cybernetics and systems dynamics and as soon as the cognitivist perspective is brought to bear, cybernetics and systems dynamics assumptions come with it. The result, I think, is theoretical developments that start off with radical promise but then rapidly slip back into the same systemic theories as those reviewed in Part 1. It seems to be very hard to hold on to the radical perspectives of complexity theory while retaining the perspective of systems, the assumptions of cognitivism and the methodology of the objective, external observer.

9.5 Summary

This chapter has reviewed the way in which a number of writers are interpreting chaos and complexity in organisational terms. It has suggested that the common approach is to retain a systems view of interaction and a cognitivist approach to human psychology and to interpret chaos and complexity from that perspective. This amounts to retaining the assumption of the autonomous, even heroic, individual and the prescription of the manager as the objective observer of the organisation as a system. I have argued that the result is the re-presentation of strategic choice, learning organisation and knowledge management theory in a different vocabulary. The emphasis on control and organisation-wide intention remains intact. For me, this means that the opportunity to explore what it means to operate as a participant in a setting in which the future is unknowable is lost. No further understanding of the process of how strategy might emerge from local interaction is obtained. The interpretation of chaos and complexity thus remains within management and organisational theory orthodoxy. The essentially dual causality, formative and rationalist, remains.

Part 3 of this book reviews a very different way of interpreting the insights of the complexity sciences for organisations. This moves from systems thinking to thinking in terms of responsive processes.

Further reading

For further reading I suggest Axelrod and Cohen (1999), Goldstein (1994), Wheatley (1999) and Zimmerman (1992). In addition to those reviewed in this chapter, other recent publications you might want to refer to are: Wood (2000); Ralls and Webb (1999); Lissack and Roos (1999); Rycroft and Kash (1999); Baets (1999); Petzinger (1999); Stickland (1998) and Kelly and Allison (1999). An in-depth critique of the use of complexity theories can be found in Griffin (2002). There is also a journal called *Emergence: Complexity and Organization*.

Questions to aid further reflection

1. How are organisational complexity writers using the notions of self-organisation and emergence?

2. How does the property of unpredictability feature in the work of organisational complexity writers?

3. How is the notion of the 'edge of chaos' taken up by organisational complexity writers?

4. What are the consequences of emphasising the 'simple rules' idea?

5. What is the implicit ideology in the work of many of the organisational complexity writers?

6. How does the notion of diversity feature in the work of organisational complexity writers?

Complex responsive processes as a way of thinking about strategy and organisational dynamics

When organisational practitioners and researchers talk and write about an 'organisation', no matter what perspective they take, they are all basically talking about groupings of people engaged in some kind of joint activity that has some purpose – which could be to search for some purpose. Fundamental questions immediately arise which have to do with *what* an organisation is and *how* it is becoming *what* it is *becoming*. As soon as we try to enquire into these questions of what and how, the controversy begins. To introduce Part 3 of this book, I first give a brief summary of the position taken in the dominant discourse in relation to this controversy in order to clarify how the chapters in Part 3 will provide a different perspective.

Part 1 of this book explored how those engaged in the dominant discourse, including most of those critical of it, explicitly or implicitly assume that the people comprising an organisation are independent, autonomous individuals, or at least come close to this position when they are acting rationally. In other words, human action is understood in terms of the individual-centred psychologies of cognitivism, constructivism, humanistic psychology and psychoanalysis in which individuals are understood to have minds inside them which either represent or select the world outside them. It is, therefore, assumed that an organisation exists, or at least is thought of 'as if' it exists, outside of the individuals comprising it. In their joint activity individuals create, choose, design, shape or give direction to an organisation which is understood to be a system of one kind of another. An organisation is thought of as a system, at a higher level than the individuals, having properties of its own and acting back on the individuals as a cause of their actions. Once taken, this view leads to particular ways of answering the fundamental organisational questions posed above of what and how.

All strands of the dominant discourse on organisational strategy are concerned, if only implicitly, with *how* an organisation is *becoming* – this is the concern with *strategy as process*. Process refers to the administrative systems and decision-making procedures managers use to formulate and implement strategy *content*. It refers to the routines, habits, frames of reference, interpretive schemas, cultures, political activities, learning activities, norms and values of the organisation. It can also refer to informal conversation, storytelling and engagement in communities of practice. There is debate around which of these aspects of how an organisation is becoming are more important than others. All the perspectives in Part 1 were also concerned with *what* is becoming, usually referred to as *strategy content*. Strategy content is taken to mean a description of an organisation's position in a market and of the resources, competences, skills, information and knowledge that the organisation uses to take that position. There is debate about which aspects of content are more or less important than others and whether the content should be expressed in formal plans or in vaguer visions, missions and directions. All of this, both content and process, is what strategy means in the dominant discourse.

Underlying this understanding of strategy is the ideology of control. From the strategic choice perspective, leaders and dominant coalitions choose the process and the content of strategy for an organisation in order to ensure acceptable performance. From the learning perspectives, this ability to simply choose in rational ways is questioned and, instead, leaders and managers are understood to shape and influence the learning process that produces strategy content. The argument between the two approaches is not about *whether* leaders and managers can be 'in control' of an organisation but *how* they are able to exert such control. This possibility depends crucially on the nature of organisational dynamics. It is possible for someone to be 'in control' only if the dynamics, the patterns of movement over time, are reasonably stable and thus predictable. This possibility has been vigorously contested, as described in some of the chapters in Part 1. The critics argue that strategy content and process are not simply deliberately chosen, shaped or influenced by leaders and managers because they emerge to a significant extent. This argument holds that, in a sense, strategy is being chosen for leaders and managers by chance changes in the environment and their role is to fit into these changes. For me, this critique remains firmly in the dominant discourse because it takes the same view on the importance of predictability. If it is possible to predict then we can choose and if we cannot predict then we have no choice but to adapt to chance. Here deliberate choice and emergence are seen as polar opposites. We either choose in orderly ways because we can predict the consequences of our actions or when we cannot predict the consequences of our actions we are reduced to inertia or some form of organisational anarchy, muddling through and garbage-can decision making. Neither side in this debate questions whether predictability is indeed a prerequisite for order.

The dominant discourse is conducted primarily at the macro level of the whole organisation or the whole industry. Strategy process is concerned with how process and content are to be chosen, shaped or influenced for the organisation as a whole. The link to the micro level of the ordinary everyday activities of organisational members is understood to be provided by the inspirational, motivational, target setting and performance-monitoring activities designed or influenced by leaders so that their strategies will be implemented by the organisational membership. There are those who are critical of top-down, command-and-control approaches to strategic management and they call for those at the top to arrange for, or at least allow, involvement, democracy, empowerment and bottom-up forms of strategic management. Empowerment is understood as the top giving away some of their power. However, in order to prevent the immediately feared anarchy this could lead to, bottom-up proposals are quickly accompanied by the requirement that those at the top should set some direction, guidelines or logic within which the empowered must act. So here the link between the macro and the micro is partially reversed, with the micro activities now shaping and influencing the macro level but only within guidelines set at the macro level. However, in my view, this critique does not depart from the dominant discourse because the relationship between micro and macro is still understood in terms of different levels and it is only a very few who advocate bottom-up management without any top-down management – most call for some balance between the two. Chapter 7 in Part 1 did draw attention to the recent call made by activity-based strategy theorists for attention to be focused on the micro level of ordinary, everyday management activity. These writers identify the need to explain the link between this micro activity and the macro level but, as far as I can see, have not yet provided a satisfactory explanation of this link. Just as the dominant discourse takes for granted polarised distinctions between intention and emergence, between unpredictability and order, so it takes for granted the opposition between micro and micro levels. All of these distinctions are ultimately reflections of the separation of the individual and the organisation as system.

The dominant discourse reflects a way of thinking that has its origins in the natural sciences, particularly in the importation of systems thinking after the 1950s. Part 2 of this book explored more recent developments in understanding the dynamics of systems in the form of the complexity sciences. A radical interpretation of these sciences leads to the following conclusions. Complex systems display the capacity to change and produce new forms only when they operate in a paradoxical dynamic of stability and instability at the same time. The properties of this dynamic are such that small differences can escalate into major, completely unpredictable changes, so creating new forms and destroying others at the same time. This creative destruction emerges in processes of self-organisation. Self-organisation means local interaction between the agents comprising the complex system, and what emerges is the form of the system where emergence means that the form arises in the complete absence of any plan, blueprint or programme for it. The emergent form is due entirely to the self-organising activity of the agents. New forms can emerge only if the agents differ from each other enough – diversity is essential for the evolution of the new. In Chapter 8 I suggested that it is possible to understand these properties in terms of local interaction between agents producing emergent patterns across a whole population.

These findings are of major importance, in my view, because they challenge the dominant discourse's most fundamental assumptions. From a complexity perspective, stability, harmony and consensus cannot be equated with success and unpredictability is fundamentally unavoidable, making it impossible to talk about being 'in control'. The 'whole' is not designed or chosen in advance because it emerges in local interaction. Such emergence is in no way a matter of chance because what emerges does so precisely because of what all the agents are doing or not doing. There is nothing mysterious about emergence. Orderly global forms, which I will usually call population-wide patterns, do not come about by chance or mystery but as basic properties of local interaction. The cause of the global order is the connections between the agents, where connections mean that agents impose conflicting constraints on each other. It is constraint and conflict in local interaction that impart order to the 'whole' so constituting a mode of control. The cause of new global form, new population-wide patterns, is the diversity of the locally interacting agents. This explanation of emergence challenges the equating of emergence with chance and some form of anarchy or muddling through to be found in the dominant discourse. It supports the call for an activity-based perspective on strategic management which focuses attention on the micro, local interactions of people in an organisation. Furthermore it offers a different understanding of the link between micro and macro – the macro emerges in the micro. In fact, the distinction between the macro and the micro as different ontological levels dissolves and with it further taken-for-granted distinctions between intention and emergence, unpredictability and order, individual and organisation also dissolve.

Part 2 then reviewed how a number of writers are interpreting the finding of the complexity sciences in terms of human organisations. Some writers apply some aspects of the complexity sciences to the macro level of the whole organisation or industry. I argued that mostly they do so in a way that does not take seriously enough the radical challenge presented by insights from the complexity sciences and so slip back into the dominant discourse. Chapter 9 referred to two exceptions to this conclusion in the work of Allen and of Marion. Both of these writers emphasise fundamental unpredictability and how essential microdiversity is for the emergence of new forms. In doing this they present major challenges to the dominant discourse on organisations and strategic management and, particularly in the case of Allen's work, point to the limitations of systems models themselves. However, in focusing on the macro level, their work does not reach the ordinary, everyday human diversity of organisational life. Many writers do focus on the micro level but, as I argued in Chapter 9, they tend to apply the less radical interpretations of the complexity sciences and so mainly re-present the dominant discourse in a different language.

The purpose of Part 3 of this book is to explore how we might interpret the radical insights of the complexity sciences in terms of human action. Human agents differ from those studied in the natural complexity sciences in fundamentally important ways. Human agents are unique and therefore diverse persons who are conscious, self-conscious, emotional, rational, irrational, often spontaneous beings capable of some choice. Furthermore, in their local interaction, human agents are capable of perceiving and articulating something about the population-wide patterns they are implicated in and even of desiring different population-wide patterns. This is something that the agents of complexity models cannot do. Any interpretation of complexity insights must be firmly based on these attributes of human agents and that is what the chapters in this part will seek to do. This requires returning to the most basic assumptions we make when we talk about organisations.

I started this introduction to Part 3 by stating that an organisation is groupings of people engaged in joint activity having some purpose. The dominant discourse assumes that those people are independent, autonomous individuals. The argument of this part departs immediately from this position by claiming that such independence and autonomy is a fiction because human persons are always fundamentally and inescapably interdependent. This shift in assumption from autonomy to interdependence leads to a move away from the individual-centred theories of cognitivism, constructivism, humanistic psychology and psychoanalysis to a view of the individual self as thoroughly social through and through. Individual selves are formed by social interaction as they form such social interaction at the same time. There is no possibility of human society without human minds and there is no possibility of human minds without human societies. The distinction between psychology and sociology dissolves. Mind is no longer thought of as existing inside a person and nor is society thought of as existing outside a person as a system. Instead both mind and society are thought of as the actions of human bodies and this way of thinking has no need for concepts such as 'system'. Instead, the focus of attention is directly upon the responsive manner in which human persons interact with each other, hence the label 'complex responsive processes of relating' which will be applied to the perspective taken in this part. A caution is necessary at this point. In talking about human relationships I am not just talking about something 'good' simply because human relationships are frequently very 'bad'. The term 'complex responsive processes of relating' refers to both the good and the bad and is concerned with how we might understand them.

Once taken, this view leads to very different ways of dealing with the fundamental question posed at the start of this introduction which has to do with *how* an organisation is becoming *what* it is *becoming*. In the dominant discourse, process (the how becoming) refers to the administrative systems and decision-making procedures managers use to formulate and implement strategy content. From the complex responsive processes perspective, process refers to the fundamental processes of human interaction, namely, communicative interaction between interdependent persons taking the form of the conversation of gestures. The very fact of interdependence means that this ongoing conversation is at the same time processes of power relating which are sustained by ideologies. Furthermore, in their ongoing conversational power relating, persons are always forming intentions and making choices evoked and provoked by each other and these intentions and choices always have an ideological basis. Processes then refer to conversation, power, choice and ideology, which may be patterned as routines, procedures and so on. However, what it is important to focus attention on is not simply the routine or the procedure but the complex responsive interactions between persons which may have a routine pattern. Strategic processes are then understood as basically conversational forms of power relating based on ideology and reflected in intentions and choices.

Since the persons comprising an organisation are interdependent it follows that none of them can simply choose what is to happen to all of them. What happens to all of them will emerge in the interplay of their intentions and no one can be in control of this interplay. The shift from the assumption of autonomous to interdependent persons immediately challenges the whole basis of strategic choice theory. Strategy as a population-wide pattern of action cannot be chosen by anyone but rather emerges in the interplay of individual intentions and choices in local interactions. Here there is no polarisation of deliberate intention and emergence and emergence has nothing to do with chance. Instead emerging patterns are becoming what they are becoming because of the interplay of many, many intentions in many, many local situations. This presents radical challenges to the dominant discourse in all its forms because it questions the ability of leaders and others to change the 'whole' in any direct manner. They may be articulating desires for the population-wide pattern, the 'whole', but this will be a gesture into the ongoing conversation and what happens will depend upon the responses evoked in many, many local interactions. All *anyone* can ever do, no matter how powerful, is engage intentionally, and as skilfully as possible, in local interaction, dealing with the consequence in an ongoing manner as they emerge. Many practical activities such as organisational change programmes, strategic planning, the nature of leadership, the meaning of control, and so on, need to be re-thought if one takes this perspective.

In fact, the shift in the focus of attention to the basic forms of human interaction leads one to reformulate the fundamental question of how an organisation is becoming *what* it is becoming. The question changes to one to do with *how* a group of interdependent people are becoming *who* they are *becoming*. The strategy process (how becoming) has already been referred to above as basic human interaction. But now for strategy content we ask about *who* instead of *what* simply because we are talking about people and not abstract systems.

When we talk about organisational strategies, we are taking about what kind of joint action people are undertaking, about what purpose it is meant to achieve and what the actors desire it to be. When we talk about organisational dynamics, we are talking about patterns of movement in this activity and its purposes over time and how the actors involved are engaged in, and thinking about, this movement. In other words, we are talking fundamentally about who people think they are and what they think they are doing together; who they want to be, what they want to do together and what they desire to achieve. Put this way we can immediately see that organisations and their strategies are fundamentally about the identities of people. Identity is the answer we give to the question, 'who are you and what are you doing?' and when asked this question we usually reply with some description of the groups or organisations we belong to and what kind of work we do in them. At strategy 'away-days', groups of managers talk about what kind of business they are in and how they might want to change it; what kind of image their organisation has, how they might wish it to change and sometimes how they are thinking about all of this. In doing this, they are talking about identity; their own identities. From a complex responsive processes perspective, then, strategy content is dynamic patterns of emerging continuity and potential transformation of collective identities which are inseparable from individual identities. Put like this the distinction between content and process dissolves.

Chapter 10 will explore what I mean by responsive processes and how this notion differs from systemic process reviewed in Chapter 7. Systemic process is interaction between parts that produces a system or whole outside of the parts. For example, the human individual may be thought of as a cognitive system consisting of interacting mental models and the group is then a supra-system of interacting individuals. In the notion of responsive processes, there is no 'inside' or 'outside', no 'whole' or 'boundary'.

Chapters 11 to 13 will explore the communicative, power relating, ideological and choice aspects of complex responsive processes of relating between persons. Chapter 14 will explore how thinking in responsive process terms focuses attention in relation to strategy and organisational dynamics. Moving from systems thinking to responsive processes thinking about strategy and organisational dynamics has a number of important consequences. Strategy ceases to be understood as the realisation of someone's intended or desired future state for the whole organisation. It ceases to be understood as the intentional design and leveraging of whole organisational learning and knowledge-creating systems. Instead, strategy is understood as evolving patterns of simultaneously collective and individual identities. Evolving identities are understood to emerge in the local communicative interacting, power relating and ideology based choices of the people who constitute an organisation.

The focus of attention is then not on some abstract systemic whole but on what people are actually doing in their relationships with each other in the living present. It is in these relationships that strategy as evolving identity continually emerges.

It is in interaction, particularly ordinary, everyday conversation, that members of organisations perpetually construct their future as continuity and potential transformation at the same time. The Reflective Management narratives that follow some chapters in this part indicate how some practitioners make sense of the complex responsive processes perspective in their organisational work.

Chapter 10

Responsive processes thinking

This chapter invites you to draw on your own experience to reflect on and consider the implications of:

- An alternative to systemic ways of thinking about process in human action. I call this alternative view 'responsive processes' in order to distinguish it from the notion of systemic process discussed in Chapter 7.

- The fundamental assumptions upon which this alternative notion of process is based and its location in the historical tradition of Western thought.

- The concepts of self-organisation and emergence in human action.

- The key differences between the notions of systemic process and responsive processes of human action.

This chapter provides foundational concepts required to understand the theory of complex responsive processes of human relating and the explanation it provides of strategising and organising, which will be developed in later chapters. I believe it is very important to understand the nature of responsive processes and how this notion differs from systemic process because it leads to a very different way of thinking about what an organisation is. As soon as one takes one view rather than the other, one inevitably goes down a particular path of thought and action. From a systemic process perspective it is easy to think of an organisation as a thing separate from people, a thing that managers can give direction to, and move about in time and conceptual space. As soon as one takes a responsive processes view one goes into a way of thinking about organisations as nothing more or less than patterns of interaction between human persons. These two different starting points lead to very different ways of thinking about what it means to manage, strategise and lead, which will be explored in some detail in Chapters 11 to 13. In broad terms, the difference is as follows. If you think from a systemic process perspective about what you are doing as leader or manager then you will believe that you can and should take an objective viewpoint from outside of your organisation as a whole or the part of it that you are responsible for. From this viewpoint you will be concerned with designing, or at the very least, shaping, influencing or conditioning organisational process. You will understand process in terms of administrative systems and decision-making procedures. You will be concerned with changing the whole system and the whole process. However, if you take the alternative perspective on process, you will understand what you are doing as leader or manager as participating in relationships with other people. You will understand that there is no objective, external position in relationships, only the subjective–objective, involved–detached, participation in relating to others. You will understand your work as influencing, perhaps even manipulating, other people, not some abstract system or process, in order to get things done. You will understand what you are doing as processes of communication with others, as patterns of power relations between you, as choices based on ideological criteria. From the systemic perspective one's thinking is abstracted from the direct experience of relating to others while in the responsive processes perspective that relating, both good and bad, is at the centre of one's attention. Moving from the systemic to the responsive perspective challenges the belief that 'you' can be 'in control' and directly change the whole. Instead, it invites you to reflect on what you are actually doing in the ordinary, everyday activities of leading, managing and organising.

10.1 Introduction

Social, responsive processes thinking developed in reaction to Kantian philosophy, so by way of introduction I will first briefly summarise some points made in Chapter 2 about Kant's thought. Kant thought in terms of dualisms:

- On the one hand, there is reality, the noumenal, which is unknowable, and on the other hand, there is the appearance of reality, the phenomenal, which is knowable.

- On the one hand, there are subjects, that is, autonomous individual humans, who can freely choose goals and actions through their reasoning capacity and are therefore subject to rationalist causality. On the other hand, there are objects, the natural phenomena, which human subjects can know because they have innate mental categories by means of which they can classify and causally connect phenomena.

Kant argued that humans come to know phenomena by means of the scientific method, which means that they take the position of the objective observer external to the phenomena to be known, formulate hypotheses about them and then test the hypotheses in experimental action. These hypotheses can take the form of mechanistic 'if–then' rules, that is, efficient cause, in the case of inanimate matter, or they can take the form of regulative ideas in relation to organisms, which means that the objective observer ascribes an 'as if' purpose to organisms, understood as systems. Kant defined a system as a self-organising whole consisting of parts which interact with each other to form both themselves and the whole. Furthermore the whole develops over time in a purposive manner as it moves from its embryonic to its mature form in developmental stages. The system is understood as unfolding the purpose or mature form ascribed to, or enfolded in, the idea of the system.

What Kant was doing here was *presenting a particular notion of process, systemic process, involving a particular notion of time*. Process here is the interaction of parts to form a whole and time takes a linear, life cycle form. Chapter 7 explored just how this systemic notion of process pervades the literature on the process and activity-based views of strategy. According to Kant, then, organisms in nature are understood to move according to the formative, systemic process of the system, that is, formative cause, and the human subject can take a rational, external position. The result is another dualism:

- Human action is understood to be subject to *rationalist* causality and nature is understood to be subject to either *efficient* or *formative* causality.

The essence of Kantian thinking, therefore, is the dualism. This way of thinking has a 'both . . . and' structure in which one side of the dualism applies at one time or place and the other side of the dualism applies at another time or place. First one side is the figure and the other the background and then this is reversed. The effect of this dualistic, figure–ground way of thinking is to eliminate paradox. Locating the opposites of the dualism in a sequence avoids the need to hold the two together *at the same time*, which is the essence of paradoxical thinking (Griffin, 2002).

Although Kant had cautioned against thinking about human action as a system because this was incompatible with the autonomy of the individual, all of the systems thinkers of the twentieth century have ignored this caution and applied systems thinking not only to nature but to human action and interaction as well. The *how* of strategy, the process, is then thought to be designing, shaping and influencing the system as a whole and its process. The content of strategy is thought of as the pattern of intended movement of the system and intended changes in the process over time by a regulator or controller standing outside them. Strategy, here, is all about moving systems and designing process.

This chapter explores an alternative to systems thinking about organisations. The philosopher Hegel argued against Kant's dualisms and their elimination of paradox. Instead, for him, thought was essentially paradoxical. Unlike Kant, who located human knowing in the innate capacities of the individual mind, Hegel presented a view of human knowing that is essentially social and, as later chapters will explain, this immediately signals a move away from individual-based views of human psychology. In doing this, Hegel was in effect developing a notion of processes that differed fundamentally from Kant's notion of systemic process. Hegel's notion of processes is a social one, essentially involving the interaction of human persons in what I would call *responsive* processes of struggling for mutual recognition as participants. Here there is no external viewpoint and everything any of us does is as a participant in some interaction with others. This alternative view of processes indicates a different notion of time from the linear one of Kant's systemic process, a matter I will take up later in this chapter. From a responsive processes perspective, the *how* of strategy is thought of as social processes of interaction between conscious and self-conscious persons in which their very identities emerge. The content of strategy is thought of as patterns of interaction, that is, as iterated identity. Strategy, here, is all about sustaining and changing identity, that is, who we are and what we are doing together.

The next section of this chapter briefly reviews Hegel's thinking and how the sociologists Mead and Elias thought in essentially the same terms. The section after that suggests that the insights of the natural complexity sciences can be interpreted in human terms using the kind of social, responsive processes thinking that derives from Hegel and Elias, rather than the dominant systemic process theory implicit in the writings of most others who appeal to the complexity sciences (*see* Chapter 9).

This chapter seeks to clarify the sense in which systemic and responsive processes thinking provide two incompatibly different ways of understanding human organisations. Later chapters in this part will point to some of the consequences of thinking in responsive processes terms about strategy and organisational dynamics.

10.2 Responsive processes thinking

In the late eighteenth and early nineteenth centuries, the philosophers known as Romantic idealists (Fichte, Schelling and Hegel) moved from Kant's split between the knowing subject and the object to be known and argued that the object of knowledge was constituted by the *process of knowing* performed by the subject or self. Subjects, then, were together mentally creating their knowledge of the world of objects and of themselves at the same time. The Romantic idealists were particularly concerned with self-consciousness where the subject is an object to itself. It is the self that is real and all experience is carried back to this immediate experience of the self so that the reflexive position becomes central. This immediately challenges the external objective position and claims instead that knowledge is socially constructed in the interaction of interdependent, conscious and self-conscious persons. Kant held that the mind encountered contradictions when it attempted to go beyond the phenomenal world to the noumenal and these contradictions were warnings of a mind going beyond its limits. For the Romantic idealists, however, contradictions were inherent in the movement of thought. The Romantic idealists moved away from a Kantian innate logic, with already given forms of thought outside of experience (transcendental), to a dialectical logic in which human consciousness and self-consciousness as experience are central to knowing. Furthermore, individual selves and social relations were understood to be intimately interconnected and *experience was understood as historical, social processes of consciousness and self-consciousness*. This represented a powerful break with the notion of the autonomous individual and innate, transcendental, pre-given knowing. From the Kantian perspective it is possible to take a position external to social interaction and objectively observe it. From the perspective of the Romantic idealists, this is not possible because all self-conscious persons are always participating in social activity even when they think they are observing it from an external position.

Hegel

In Hegel's philosophy, the development of thought takes place through *conflict* between persons and the world of *our experience is the world we are creating in our thought*. Hegel held that one cannot begin, as Kant had done, with an isolated individual subject experiencing the world and then ask how a world of objective experience gets built up out of the inner world of purely subjective, individual representations as in systems and mental models. Rather, one must begin with an already shared world of subjects making judgements in the light of possible judgements by other subjects, in other words interacting responsively. Hegel also emphasised the notion of *mutual recognition* to argue that there was an intersubjective unity of mutually recognising agents, in other words, agents acting responsively. He argued against any separate realm outside of experience. In this, he moved decisively away from the Kantian notion of a system, which others had directly applied to human interaction, lying outside of direct experience of such interaction and causing it.

For Hegel, the notions of person and subject are historically specific and are given content only by the social institutions in which each individual achieves social identity through interdependence and mutual recognition. Mind or consciousness is manifested in social institutions, that is, ways of life, which give identities, self-concepts, to individuals. Each person is self-consciously, purposively directing herself or himself but each is also dependent on others at the same time. How we come to understand our own desires, interpret their intensity and priority, how we categorise objects to satisfy our desires, is not fixed or determined by our natures or the real world but depends on the concepts we employ and these are socially evolved. Self-determination by a free subject can only occur through other persons who are also self-determining subjects and are doing the same. Another self-conscious subject offers resistance to the realisation of my desires by testing or challenging me and my self-world conception. It is inevitable that two self-determining, self-conscious subjects will conflict and struggle.

Hegel argued that individuals are fundamentally social practitioners and what they do, think or say takes form in the context of *social practices*, while these practices provide the required resources, objects of desire, skills and procedures. In contrast to Kantian thinking, where there is a duality of the individual and the social, Hegel presents a perspective in which they cannot be separated. Indeed, individual consciousness and self-consciousness arise in the social relations, which they are simultaneously constructing. This is clearly a paradoxical perspective in which individual minds are simultaneously forming and being formed by social relations. This presents a different notion of causality, which we may call *transformative* causality (Stacey *et al.*, 2000).

The move from systemic to responsive processes thinking is, therefore, fundamentally a move from a dualistic theory of rationalist–formative causality to one of transformative causality. These different notions of causality are summarised in Table 10.1.

Table 10.1 Comparison of different ways of thinking about causality

	Nature of movement	Cause of movement
Efficient cause	Corrective repetition of past in order to realise an optimal future state	Universal, timeless laws of an 'if–then' kind
Rationalist cause	Towards rationally chosen goals for the future in order to realise a designed, desired state	Human reason
Formative cause	Unfolding of enfolded mature form in order to realise that form in the future	Self-organising systemic process of unfolding in developmental stages
Transformative cause	Iterated interaction perpetually constructing the future in the present in order to express continuity and potential transformation in identity at the same time	Responsive processes of local interaction between entities in the present

The Kantian and Hegelian ways of thinking have continued to influence sociologists, psychologists and organisational theorists up to the present time. The sociologist Mead continued in the Hegelian tradition and worked out in detail how one might think of mind, self and the social in a responsive processes way, and this will be explored in Chapter 11. First, however, consider how another sociologist, Elias, who was also influenced by Hegel's thought, reflects the notion of social, responsive processes in his sociology.

Elias

Following the tradition of Hegel, Elias did not think about the relationship between the individual and society in terms of any spatial distinction between inside and outside, as in systems thinking. He argued that while the notion of a receptacle containing something inside it might be applicable to the physical aspects of a human being, it could not be applied to the personality or the mind (Elias, 1991, p. 480). In rejecting the notion of the individual mind as an 'internal world', he also argued against thinking of the social as an organic unity or supra-individual with a 'group mind' developing through stages of youth, maturity and old age to death (pp. 5–6). Instead, he pointed to the essential interdependence of people. Elias also usually avoided any kind of systemic formulation, arguing that such formulations abstract from experience. Instead, he understood both individual and social purely in what I am calling responsive processes terms. He did not think of the individual and society first existing and then subsequently affecting each other (p. 456). He suggested that we can see the connection between individual and social more precisely if we refuse to abstract from the processes of their development, of their becoming. Elias also argued against concepts of society as some kind of 'whole', arguing that the social life of human beings was full of contradictions, tensions and explosions rather than being more or less harmonious as the concept of a 'whole' implies. Furthermore, while the concept of a 'whole' implies something complete in itself, societies are always more or less incomplete, remaining open in time as a continuous flow (p. 12). What Elias is doing here is moving completely away from any notion of human interaction as a system and any notion of some 'whole' existing outside of that interaction and causing it. Instead, he is focusing entirely on the processes of interaction between human bodies. Elias argued that the concept of the whole applied to human action simply created a mystery in order to solve a mystery.

In order to understand the nature of human interaction, Elias made a detailed study of changes in the way Western people have experienced themselves over hundreds of years and pointed to how social order *emerges* in interactions between people.

The emergence of social order

Elias argued that what we now call Western civilisation is not the result of any kind of calculated long-term planning. Individual people did not form an intention to change civilisation and then gradually realise this intention through rational, purposive measures. It is not conceivable that the evolution of society could have been planned because that would suppose that modern rational, calculating individuals with a degree of self-mastery already existed centuries ago, whereas Elias's research shows that such individuals did not exist then but were, rather, themselves the products of social evolution. Societal changes produced rational, planning kinds of individuals, not the other way around. In medieval times, people experienced their self-consciousness in a completely different way, in a completely different kind of society, compared with the way we experience our self-consciousness in modern society. Elias concluded that the development of a society was not caused by 'mysterious' social forces but was the consequence of the interweaving, the *interplay* of the intentions and actions of many, many people. He talked about the moves of many interdependent players intertwining in ways that none of them could control no matter how powerful they were. However, despite the development of a society being unplanned and outside the immediate control of its members, the interplay of individual plans and intentions nevertheless produced an orderly pattern of development, tending in a particular direction (Elias, 1991, pp. 146–7)

So, Elias argued that change in society occurred in an unplanned manner but nevertheless displayed a specific type of order. His research demonstrated how the constraints imposed by others were converted into self-restraints and how many human bodily activities were progressively pushed behind the scenes of communal social life and invested with feelings of shame. Elias explained how the growing interdependence of people caused by the increasing division of labour and specialisation of tasks could only be sustained by the increasing self-control of those interdependent people. In other words, increasing interdependence, taken together with the increasing state monopolisation of violence, came to be reflected in the very personality structures of people. The 'civilising' process is one of increasing self-control bringing with it the benefits of social order but also the disadvantages of neurotic behaviour associated with such self-control and increasing anxiety of contravening social norms. Furthermore, this civilising trend is easily reversed by any threat to, or breakdown in, social order. Although this transformation of societies and personality structures could not have been planned and intended, it was not simply a sequence of unstructured changes (Elias, 2000, p. 365). Elias looked for an explanation of how it was possible that orderly population-wide formations, which no human being had intended, arose in the human world:

> *It is simple enough: plans and actions, the emotional and rational impulses of individual people, constantly interweave in a friendly or hostile way.* This basic tissue resulting from many single plans and actions of men can give rise to changes and patterns that no individual person has planned or created. From this interdependence of people arises an order sui generis, an order more compelling and stronger than the will and reason of the individual people composing it. *It is the order of interweaving human impulses and strivings, the social order, which determines the course of historical change; it underlies the civilizing process.*
> (Elias, 2000, p. 366)

Although it is highly unlikely that Elias was ever aware of the complexity sciences, what he is describing here is what complexity scientists call self-organisation and emergence. Elias is arguing that individuals and groups are interacting with each other, in their local situations, in intentional, planned ways. However, the widespread, population-wide consequences of the interplay of these intentions and plans cannot be foreseen by any of them – long-term population-wide patterns emerge without an overall plan or blueprint. Elias explains that long-term consequences cannot be foreseen because the interplay of the actions, plans and purposes of many individuals constantly gives rise to something that has not been planned, intended or created by any of those individuals. Elias pointed to the important fact that individuals pursuing their plans are always in relationship with each other in a group or power figuration. While individuals can plan their own actions, they cannot plan the actions of others and so cannot plan the interplay of plans and actions. The fact that each person depends on others means that none can simply realise their plans. However, this does not mean that anarchy, or disorder, results. Elias talks about a trend or direction in the evolution of the consequences of the interweaving of individual plans and intentions. In other words, he is talking about self-organisation and emergence. Consider how we might understand recent developments at British Airways from Elias's perspective of the interplay of intentions.

The interplay of intentions in the airline industry

Gate Gourmet is a catering company in the UK owned by a corporation in the United States. Some years ago, a group of executives at British Airways (BA) chose to outsource the provision of all of its in-flight meals and chose Gate Gourmet as its sole provider because this was the least-cost solution. Here, in their local interaction, executives form BA's plan to outsource while another group of executives at Gate Gourmet interact locally to plan their bid for the contract and in the interplay of these plans a different population-wide pattern of supplying in-flight meals emerges. So far, it looks as if the interplay of plans produces the population-wide pattern that all had intended. However, by mid-2005, executives at Gate Gourmet were coming under pressure from another group of locally interacting executives at their parent company to stem the large losses they were making from supplying BA meals. Notice the local interaction on both sides of the Atlantic. In August 2005, in response, the directors of Gate Gourmet decided to reduce costs by making 670 employees redundant, intending to replace them with cheaper labour from Eastern Europe. And here we have another Gate Gourmet plan emerging in the interplay with the intentions of executives on the other side of the Atlantic. The 670 staff who packed meal containers for the in-flight services were predominantly Sikh women who lived in a close-knit community, organised around a Sikh temple near to Heathrow airport. When these women were abruptly dismissed, they angrily informed members of their families and the wider community. That night there was a meeting in the temple. Notice the population-wide pattern emerging in the interplay of the intentions of executives and workers. Many of the husbands of the dismissed women happened to work for BA as luggage handlers at Heathrow. At the meeting in the temple they agreed to form picket lines outside Gate Gourmet to interrupt the delivery of meals to BA flights and also to call a wild-cat strike of BA luggage handlers. So here we have the workers' plans arising in their local interaction. On the next day, within hours, managers at BA found that the only way to deal with the escalating situation was to ground all of their flights around the world. Here another BA plan emerges in response to the interplay of the plans of Gate Gourmet's executives and workers. For days after this, thousands of passengers were stranded at airports around the world and even months later meal services on BA flights were still not back to normal and a large dent had been made in BA profits. Another population-wide pattern has emerged.

Here we have an example of the interplay of intentions that Elias talked about. Executives at BA intended to outsource the provision of meals. Executives at Gate Gourmet intended to reduce its labour force. The affected members and others in their community intended to take action against this. In response, executives at BA intended to ground all its flight. However, the overall, widespread pattern of the interaction between all the players was not intended by anyone but, rather, emerged in the many local interactions between all of those involved. If we think of strategy as a widespread pattern of actions over time, we can see the emergent nature of the individual strategies, that is, intentions of all involved. Instead of thinking about strategy in terms of an isolated organisation making choices, we can see from this example how the choices, intentions, decisions, strategies of all are all responses to what the others involved are doing. Together they are creating the ongoing processes of local interaction, aspects of which could be described as strategising, and it is in the interplay of these local actions that population-wide patterns emerge and we could call these strategies.

Intention and emergence are not polarised

It is important to note how Elias does not polarise intention and emergence. I pointed out in Chapter 7 how writers in the process and activity-based strategy traditions polarise intention and emergence. They argue either that emergence means that everything happens by chance or that emergence is such that it can be designed, conditioned or at least influenced by powerful, effective individuals with intention. Elias takes a completely different view. People interact with intentions but their intentions will differ – indeed, each of these intentions is a response to the intentions of others – and so what happens emerges in the interplay of all of their intentions. Intention and emergence are thus in play at the same time without either being opposed by or subordinated to the other. No one can get outside of the interplay and so there is no doubling of process in the sense of someone using a process called influencing to shape a process called interplay or emergence. All that *everyone*, no matter how powerful, can do is to continue participating with intention and continually negotiate and respond to others who are also intentionally doing the same. It is in this ongoing, intentional, local interaction of strategising that the population-wide patterns of strategy emerge.

Elias talked about essentially paradoxical processes in which individuals form groups while being formed by them at the same time. This is a fundamentally different way of thinking compared with the dualism of individual and social to be found in systems thinking. In Elias's process theory, change occurs in paradoxical transformative processes – change is self-organising, emergent processes of perpetually constructing the future as continuity and potential transformation at the same time. Elias argued that we cannot identify self-organising social order with the order of nature, or with some kind of supra-individual. Instead the order arises in specific dynamics of social interplay in particular places at particular times.

If it makes sense to think of societies and their 'strategies' in this way, then there is no reason why we could not think about organisations in this way too and this is what the rest of the chapters in this part of the book will be doing. We can come to understand how organisational strategies emerge unpredictably in the interplay of many different intentions and, as such, emergence is not a matter of chance. What emerges does so precisely because of what all involved do and do not do. This notion of emergence presents a serious challenge to the dominant discourse on strategy and organisation, which assumes that leaders or others can directly change some whole system, process or population-wide pattern in an intentional manner.

The whole notion of planned global change programmes 'rolled' down organisations begins to look rather like a fantasy.

Elias developed his process sociology during the 1930s and 1940s well before the emergence of the complexity sciences. He continued to develop his theories until his death in 1990 but it is unlikely that he knew anything about the developments in the natural complexity sciences. However, these sciences provide considerable support for what Elias was arguing. What these sciences are pointing to is the ubiquitous presence in nature of the unpredictable emergence of order in disorder through processes of spontaneous self-organisation or, to put it another way, the emergence of population-wide patterns in local interactions. The sociology of Elias, and some others in the Hegelian tradition, therefore provides an alternative to systems thinking for interpreting the insights of complexity theories into human terms.

10.3 Chaos, complexity and analogy

The complexity sciences present an ongoing, rigorous exploration of what self-organisation and emergence mean and in doing so represent a departure from some of the scientific foundations long ago imported into organisational thinking. They offer an important source of understanding the concepts of self-organisation and emergence and since these concepts are central to the responsive processes perspective, it becomes important to draw on what the natural complexity scientists have to say. The purpose of this section, therefore, is to explore how the abstract relationships studied in the complexity sciences might provide analogies for human interaction understood from the perspective of Elias's process sociology and also the work of Mead. This will involve taking abstract relationships from the domain of natural science complexity theories and interpreting them in the human domain by taking account of the distinctive features of human agents. Unlike agents in the natural sciences or in the computer simulations described in Chapter 8, human agents are conscious and self-conscious, they form intentions and have some freedom of choice, they display emotion and spontaneity, and they have the capacity to articulate the population-wide patterns emerging in their local interactions, even desire different ones, and these desires and articulations affect their local interactions at the same time as they are being articulated and desired. These are all matters to be taken up in subsequent chapters.

First, however, consider whether it is reasonable to regard chaos and complexity theories as source domains for analogy with human interaction.

Chaos theory

Chaos theory (*see* Chapter 8) is concerned with the properties of iterative, deterministic, nonlinear mathematical relationships (i.e. algorithms) in which the output of one iteration becomes the input of the next. In other words, the current state is determined by referring, through a deterministic nonlinear algorithm, to its own previous state. At some values of a control parameter, such models display a strange attractor called chaos, a paradox of stability and instability, predictability and unpredictability, at the same time. However, the pattern of movement takes one, and only one, form, namely that of the particular strange attractor generated by the particular algorithmic relationship specified. Furthermore, mathematical models are not reality but simply logical structures created by mathematicians. The physicist, meteorologist, chemist, biologist, or any other scientist in any other field, then has to interpret how these abstract logical structures might apply to the field they are interested in. They do this by calling upon what is already known, through scientific experiments, about the phenomena in their field of study. They also perform new experiments suggested by chaos theory in order to provide empirical support for the claim that the abstract mathematical models they have developed do apply to the phenomena in their field of interest.

In Chapter 9, I referred briefly to the work of some economists and organisational theorists who adopt exactly the same approach. They use data on macro events, such as foreign exchange rates, to explore whether the mathematical equations of chaos theory fit the data. As soon as they do this, they make implicit assumptions about the nature of human interaction. They assume that human beings are such that patterns in their interaction can be described at the macro level in terms of deterministic equations. Alternatively, some organisational theorists use the properties revealed by the mathematical models of chaos as metaphors to describe organisations. For example, Chapter 9 reviewed the work of a number of researchers who describe an organisation as chaotic. As soon as they do this, they too are making the implicit assumptions about the nature of human interaction just described.

It is very important not to jump straight from a mathematical model to an application in a particular field without examining how the model is being interpreted in that particular field. In other words, the implicit assumptions being made about human action when chaos theory is applied to organisations need to be made explicit if one is to think rigorously. If one applies chaos theory directly to any form of human action, including organisations, then one is assuming that human interaction is deterministic or, at least, can be thought of 'as if' it is. This immediately means that one is assuming away any form of human freedom, that is, any possibility of individuals making any kind of choice or learning from experience. Since this is so directly contrary to our experience, it follows that chaos theory cannot be directly applied to human action. Furthermore, chaos theory cannot offer analogies for human action. In *reasoning by analogy*, we take relationships, without any attributes, from one domain and argue that these relationships apply in some other domain. The relationships in chaos theory are abstract relationships between mathematical symbols of a deterministic kind yielding abstract patterns in those symbols, for example patterns called strange attractors, fractal or mathematical chaos. I have already argued that we cannot take abstract deterministic relationships as analogous to real human relationships because that would amount to assuming that humans do not exercise choice. However, we might still want to reason using metaphor. When we *reason by metaphor* we take the attributes of phenomena in one domain to another domain without taking the nature of the relationships. So, one could use chaos theory to provide metaphors for human interactions. For example, one might want to say that human interactions are patterned like the paradoxical patterns of mathematical chaos, strange attractors or fractals. Chaos theory, then, can only ever provide what might be experienced as provocative metaphors, which might give us some kind of poetic insight into patterns of human action. The same conclusion applies to dissipative structure theory because it too is based on deterministic models.

Complex adaptive systems theory

The theory of complex adaptive systems differs from chaos and dissipative structure theory in that it reveals the properties of iterating the interaction between separate algorithms representing entities comprising a system, rather than those of iterating algorithms modelling the system as a whole. The former focuses at the micro level while the latter focuses at the macro level. Chapter 8 distinguished between two substantially different kinds of complex adaptive system simulation. The first is where the algorithms, or agents comprising the system, are all the same as each other, as for example in the Boids simulation (Reynolds, 1987), and the second is where the agents differ from each other, as for example in the Tierra simulation (Ray, 1992).

Complex adaptive systems with homogeneous agents

In some simulations of complex adaptive systems, the agents are algorithms, or computer programs, that are all the same as each other. For example, Reynolds' simulation of Boids consists of a number of computer programs, each comprising the same three instructions that organise the interaction of each computer program with other programs. Furthermore, the algorithms or computer programs are cyber-netic entities. This is so because one of the algorithms, for example, requires each agent to keep a target distance from its nearest neighbours. The actual distance from a neighbour is compared with the target and the difference is fed back so as either to increase or to decrease the distance. The agents in complex adaptive systems of this homogeneous kind are deterministic, cybernetic algorithms.

The simulation then reveals that this interaction between each individual algo-rithm with some others, that is, local interaction between them, yields a population-wide pattern in the relationship between all of them. They clump together. When each algorithm is represented as a dot on the computer screen, the clumping pattern can be seen and the programmer can observe how it persists in various forms over time. Reynolds then makes an interpretation. He calls each individual algorithm a 'Boid' and he calls the population-wide pattern they produce 'flocking'. He makes a further interpretation when he suggests that the Boids are logically equivalent to real birds and that the model points to how real birds produce flocking behaviour. He then points to how a few simple rules of local interaction can yield emergent population-wide patterns of a very complex kind, without the need for any overall blueprint to determine the population-wide patterns. Each algorithm interacting with a few others at their own local level of interaction is sufficient to produce a population-wide pattern of relationships between all of them. What the iteration of their interaction reveals is the *emergence* of a coherent collective pattern, that is, an attractor for the whole system.

There is a very important point to note about simulations, such as the Boids one, where each interacting symbol pattern, or agent, is the same as all the others. This is interaction where there is no diversity amongst the symbol patterns, no non-average interaction between them, no noise, no fluctuations in Prigogine's terms. Because of this lack of diversity, the simulation cannot display spontaneous moves from one attractor to another, nor can it spontaneously generate a new attractor (Allen, 1998a, 1998b). The symbol patterns, or rules, always yield the same attractor and change can occur only when the programmer changes the individual algorithms. Furthermore, each of the agents is a deterministic cybernetic system, a set of rules, a blueprint. In other words, such a model cannot explain novelty because it has no freedom of choice and does not evolve of its own accord, and because it is deterministic it cannot be applied to human action other than metaphoricaly.

Each individual Boid is itself a blueprint, doing only what its programme enables it to, and it is constrained by that programme from doing anything else. These agents cannot be said to be organising themselves in some kind of individual manner with connotations of doing whatever they please. They are constrained by the need to interact locally with each other. In fact, self-organisation does not mean that something is organising itself. It means local interaction. Furthermore, emergence does not mean that some pattern arises by chance. Emergence means that population-wide patterns arise in local interaction in the complete absence of a blueprint, program or plan for that population-wide pattern. The global pattern is what it is because of the manner in which the agents interact locally and this is not a matter of chance. The overall pattern of interaction is said to be emerging because there is no blueprint for it.

Organisational interpretations

Some organisational theorists interpret simulations like the Boids to suggest that if a manager wants his or her organisation to produce an overall pattern, or strategy, of a highly complex kind then it is not necessary to formulate and implement an overall strategy. Instead, the manager should establish a few simple ground rules and this is held to unleash the power of self-organisation and allow emergence to happen. In this interpretation, the manager is, without any explicit justification, equated with the programmer. Reynolds, the programmer, took the position of the objective observer, standing outside the pre-given reality of birds flocking, and induced rules that might produce flocking. He then simulated them in the computer and showed that they do produce the equivalent of flocking. This is what the manager is now supposed to do. Implicit in the prescription to formulate a few simple rules that all in the organisation are to follow is the notion that the manager must first choose which attractor he or she wants the organisation to be drawn to. The manager then has to induce the few simple rules that will produce it.

However, note the consequence of this. Assuming for the moment that an organisation is a system and that people do follow rules, then if the manager succeeds in identifying the *right* set of rules and people do follow them, the required attractor will emerge. However, this is all that will emerge. The organisation will follow this attractor until the manager changes the rules, because a system in which the separate entities are all following the same rules does not possess the capacity for spontaneously moving to another attractor, nor does it possess the capacity to generate new attractors spontaneously. The prescription ensures that the organisation will not be creative. The only change from strategic choice theory is that the manager is now relieved from having to formulate detailed overall plans. This is not a radically different insight since it was long ago concluded that detailed long-term plans were not very helpful in turbulent times and that what managers needed to do was set the direction in the form of a few guidelines or a vision.

Now consider whether complex adaptive systems, such as the Boids one where all the agents are the same, can provide a source domain for analogies with human behaviour. The abstract relationships in such systems are relationships between cybernetic entities defined as deterministic, simple rules. It follows that such complex adaptive systems cannot provide analogies with human interaction for exactly the same reasons as chaos and dissipative structure theories cannot: humans are not cybernetic entities. In addition, if people really are to follow rules then they will need rules to interpret the rules in a particular contingent situation. And then they will need rules to select the appropriate rules of interpretation and so on in infinite regress. Furthermore, if people following rules keep altering their interpretations even according to rules, rather than following them rigidly, then they are no longer following a given set of simple rules and so they will not produce the attractor enfolded in the first rule set. It follows that simulations with homogeneous agents can only ever provide metaphors that may or may not provoke thinking about human interaction. The most immediately obvious metaphor is the human cult or fascist power structure – here people do follow simple rules, for a time at least.

Complex adaptive systems with heterogeneous agents

Now consider another simulation in which the interacting algorithms (agents) do not all follow the same rules and can change from one iteration to another. This means that the algorithms in the population fall into different categories, so that difference is located between categories and sameness within a category. An example of this kind of system is provided by the Tierra simulation in Chapter 8. In the Tierra simulation, each agent is an algorithm consisting of 80 instructions specifying in detail how the algorithm is to copy itself. The programmer then introduces a mechanism to generate diversity, namely, random mutation in the copying of an algorithm, and selection criteria, namely, limited computer time available for replicating and a limited total time period over which an individual algorithm has the opportunity to replicate. The programmer then runs the program and observes what happens.

A population-wide pattern rapidly emerges in the form of an increase in the number of algorithms. The attractor is one of exponentially increasing numbers, which eventually impose a constraint on further replication. The population-wide pattern is continually moving from sparse occupation of the computer memory to overcrowding. The algorithms are also gradually changing through random mutation and so they are gradually differing from each other – increasing diversity is appearing. Before long, a new attractor appears in the form of shorter algorithms with only 40 instructions. Now there are distinctively different kinds of algorithms, namely, long ones and short ones. The constraints on computer time favour smaller ones and the emerging population-wide pattern is now decline in the number of long algorithms and increase in the number of short ones. The system has spontaneously produced a new attractor. Later, another kind of algorithm emerges, taking the form of instructions to read the replication code of neighbouring algorithms. Another new attractor has emerged, which is usually understood to be a system where agents are at one level and the global system is at a higher level.

However, we could think about what is happening in this simulation in another way. We could say that new forms of individual algorithm and new overall patterns of the population have emerged at the same time. There can be no population-wide pattern of increase and decline without simultaneous change in the length of some individual algorithms. There can be no sustained change in individual algorithms without the population-wide pattern of increase and decline. Individual algorithms and the population-wide pattern can be said to be forming and being formed by each other, at the same time. Here we do not need to say that the agents are forming a system at a higher level. Instead, we could argue that agents and population-wide patterns are emerging at the same time and that neither constitutes a system. This is very much the argument presented by Elias in relation to individual human agents and populations in the previous section.

The important point is that the programmer has not programmed the new attractors in advance. They emerge because overall, global, population-wide pattern is emerging through the local interaction of the agents (self-organisation) within the constraints that the programmer has set, but the programmer is not able to predict what the global patterns will be before they emerge. The new emerges through self-organisation (local interaction), not prior design of the whole. Here, again, I am avoiding an interpretation involving systems and levels because I want to explore a responsive processes perspective, rather than a systemic one, for the reasons provided by Elias and outlined earlier in this chapter.

This simulation is very different from the Boids one. The latter displayed only one population-wide pattern and could not spontaneously move to another or generate a novel one. The programmer would have to change the individual agents for this to happen. In the Tierra simulation, however, there are spontaneous moves to emergent new individual algorithms and population-wide patterns. The programmer did introduce a mechanism for generating diversity in the replication process in the first place, but once diversity has appeared the random-generating device can be turned off and the evolution continues without it.

Note how the agents are not feedback mechanisms in that they do not compare their actual state with some target; instead, each refers back to itself as it interacts locally with others, as when some use the code of others. The key point here is that the agents are different from each other and the nonlinearity of the iterating interaction can amplify tiny differences into major qualitative changes in population-wide pattern. This microdiversity is what enables both the population-wide pattern and the individual algorithms to simultaneously evolve in the sense of producing emergent, unpredictable, novel forms (Allen, 1998a, 1998b). Note that the agents and the interactions between them are not deterministic but evolving and that the capacity for evolution arises because of the presence of microdiversity in the interaction between diverse entities.

Important points to note

With models of the heterogeneous kind just discussed there is the possibility of reasoning by analogy about human action. This is because the agents in these models are not deterministic or cybernetic but evolving. One can, therefore, explore the transfer of abstract relationships from the model domain to the human domain and this will require some kind of interpretation that adds human attributes. While agents in the models interact in the medium of digital symbols, humans interact in the medium of other kinds of symbols, particularly those of language.

The computer simulations demonstrate the possibility of digital symbols arranged as algorithmic rules interacting locally (self-organising) in the dynamics at the edge of chaos to produce emergent attractors of a novel kind, provided that those symbol patterns are richly connected and diverse enough. Natural scientists at the Santa Fé Institute and elsewhere then use this demonstration of possibility in the medium of digital symbols as a source of analogy to provide explanations of phenomena in particular areas of interest such as biology. My argument is that the abstract, nonlinear, iterative relationships of heterogeneous complexity models are analogous to the interactive processes of social evolution proposed by Elias.

Analogies

I suggest the following analogies:

* *There is **no** analogy between the programmer of the complex adaptive system model and anything in human interaction.* There is no possibility of standing outside human interaction to design a program for it since we are all participants in that interaction and cannot control the interplay of our intentions. When Ray and others use a model of complex adaptive systems to simulate life they are quite clearly trying to simulate the evolution of a process where there is no outside programmer or designer. They are trying to model self-organising and emergent phenomena in nature, that is, phenomena that evolve without design. Since, they are using a model for this purpose, they naturally have to design the model, at least initially. But they do not propose any analogy in nature for the modeller of the system – on the contrary they argue that there is no designer outside nature. If one is trying to understand human organisations as self-organising and emergent phenomena then one cannot find an analogy for the programmer.

* Furthermore, following the arguments of Elias, I suggest that *there is no analogy between systems and humans*. Throughout Part 1, I pointed to the ways in which it is inappropriate to think of human interaction in systems terms, since that perspective reifies what are ongoing processes and ascribes a causality to human action that does not take account of individual capacities to choose actions and that does not explain the possibility of novel forms. Furthermore, the simulations of heterogeneous complexity models begin to pose problems for systems thinking, even though they are models of systems. For example, as I have explained above, these simulations can be understood in a way that does not involve hierarchical levels, which is a central concept in systems thinking. Then there are problems created for that other central concept in systems thinking, namely the 'whole'. Heterogeneous complexity models take on a life of their own, that is, they evolve in unpredictable and novel ways. It follows that the 'whole' is not there until it has emerged and since it is always evolving it is never complete. One then has to talk about incomplete or absent wholes and this begins to undermine the usefulness of the very concept of the whole itself. The explanation for the unpredictability and the novelty has nothing to do with the 'whole'. It lies in the *intrinsic properties of the process of interaction between diverse entities*. The notion of a model that takes on a life of its own also creates problems for the use of the models. If one is modelling a phenomenon with a life of its own then the

phenomenon and the model will soon diverge from each other. The usefulness of the model is then restricted to the insight it gives into the general nature of the dynamics. The points I have been making above apply to all systems, whether one thinks of a system as mechanistic or as a living organism.

- With regard to human action, the *analogy begins with the interaction* of agents in the complexity models. This interaction is analogous to the kind of interplay of individual human intentions and plans described by Elias earlier in this chapter.

- Furthermore, the *digital symbols of the complexity models are taken as analogies* for the symbols humans use to interact with each other. In other words, it is the aspects of responsive processes in the complex adaptive system models that I suggest provide analogies for human interaction, not the systemic aspects of those models. From a responsive processes point of view *there are no levels of operation*, only degrees of detail in which the phenomenon of interest is examined. Elias's description of societies forming individual minds while being formed by them at the same time is analogous to populations of algorithms forming individual algorithms while being formed by them.

- Finally, the *transformative causality* displayed by interaction between heterogeneous entities in the complexity model is analogous to the transformative causality that Elias posits in relation to interaction between people. This represents a move away from the dual causality of the theories described in Part 1 to the paradoxical transformative causality of 'forming and being formed by at the same time' that will be the basis of the theory developed in the subsequent chapters of this part.

What I hope to do in the subsequent chapters of Part 3 is to explore the implications of taking a responsive processes view of human action rather than a systemic one. I want to explore what happens when organisational analogies are sought for in simulations in which there is agent diversity and hence the spontaneous capacity to change. Instead of thinking about the manager as the analogue of the programmer I would like to consider the consequences if the manager is a participant in responsive processes of relating, and human interaction is thought of not as a system or a network but as responsive processes. Since humans do not always adapt to, or fit in, with each other, it might then be useful to think of human relating not as adaptive but as responsive. I will suggest that the human analogues for complex adaptive systems in the simulations are *complex responsive processes* of relating in organisations.

Table 10.2 summarises the different ways in which complexity theory is used as a source domain for systems and responsive processes thinking.

What is to be gained by drawing analogies between complex adaptive systems and human interaction is a clearer understanding of self-organisation and emergence and a strong argument that coherent, population-wide patterns can emerge from many, many local interactions. Other insights of importance have to do with unpredictability, the importance of diversity and conflicting constraints and the paradoxical dynamics in which novelty can emerge.

Having explored how analogies might be drawn and what insights they might give about human processes of interaction, I want to turn to another key aspect of process, namely, time.

Table 10.2 Human analogues of simulations of heterogeneous complex systems

Computer simulations	Systemic analogue in organisations	Responsive processes analogue in organisations
The programmer	CEO	None
The whole is a complex adaptive system	The whole is a complex adaptive system	None
Consisting of locally interacting (self-organising) algorithms	Consisting of interacting individuals said to be organising themselves, with minds	Complex responsive processes of relating between persons interacting locally (self-organising) in the medium of symbols (see Chapter 11) where the symbols are
Arranged as rules and called agents	Arranged as schemas and mental models as basis of individual as agent	Arranged as narrative and propositional themes that organise experience (see Chapter 13)
Reproduced through replication with random mutation	Reproduced through individual choice to change mental models	Reproduced through interaction with conflict, negation, misunderstanding and deviance as source of transformation (see Chapters 11 and 12)
What emerges is forms of algorithm and population-wide patterns at the same time	What emerges is the organisational system and the detail of action which can be shaped from an external position	What emerges is population-wide patterns as themes in conversations that are individual mind and group at the same time as well as figurations of power relations (see Chapters 11 to 13)
Novelty emerges at the edge of chaos, i.e. paradox of stability and instability in processes of self-organisation	Edge of chaos defined as crisis and stress in which self-organisation and emergence can be intentionally unleashed to produce novelty	Novelty emerges as re-patterning of conversational themes in paradoxical processes of human interaction simultaneously predictable and unpredictable, continuity and transformation (see Chapters 11 and 13). Self-organisation is local interaction between persons
Radical unpredictability	Unpredictability played down	Radical unpredictability
Attractor	A vision, etc., as something that draws the system towards it	A population-wide pattern such as a routine, habit, some generalisation or idealisation such as a social object or cult value (see Chapter 11) which has to be made operational in local interaction
Boundaries set by programmer	Boundaries set by CEO, i.e. simple rules	Emerging constraints of power relations and dynamics of inclusion and exclusion (see Chapter 12)

10.4 Time and responsive processes

From a responsive processes perspective, people interact with each other locally and in doing so produce population-wide patterns for which there are no global blueprints or programs. Furthermore, local interactions are iterative, that is, they are perpetually reproduced, and they are nonlinear, which means that differences, even very small ones, from one iteration to the next are potentially amplified to produce novelty. One consequence of thinking in these terms is that *time* is immediately of the essence because one is thinking of iteration or reproduction from one period to the next in which the patterns of interactions in the present depend upon the history of interactions in the past and expectations of the future.

Mead (1932, 1938) distinguished between two ways of thinking about the past. First, the past may be thought of as real events that are independent of any present. On this view, the investigation of the past is a reconstruction, belonging to the past, of real events that unquestionably occurred in the past. Our investigation of the past is a process of slowly and imperfectly deciphering what actually happened. This past is then the background for, the constraint on, dealing with the issues we face in the present. We refer to a given past out of which the issues we are now dealing with have arisen. However, we know that a particular reconstruction of the past is questioned and reinterpreted at some later date – each generation rewrites history, indeed each of us tends to reinterpret our own past from time to time. Any present interpretation of the past is therefore open to doubt. This leads to the second view of the past, not as a given to be discovered but as a meaning to be formulated anew. Here, the significance or meaning of past events is to be found in, that is, belongs to, the present rather than to the past. In other words, we know the past through the present. Furthermore, the future is implicated in that the knowledge we gain of the past, the hypotheses we form about the past, depend upon the viewpoint of the present, which will change in the future. In other words, the future will change the meaning of the past. In this way we *construct different pasts* and one past displaces and abrogates another. There are coincidences and events that are relatively permanent and this makes possible a translation from one historical account to another but these coincidences are not the object of our knowledge.

Mead, then, is arguing that each present has a different past in that in each present we interpret the past differently because we have a different viewpoint and so construct different meanings of past events. The reality of the past that gets into our experience is thus different depending upon our present standpoint. Mead says that the only alternative is to think of our experience in terms of being a reflection of a transcendental reality. The perspective he suggests is one in which the past can only reach us though our own current frame of reference within which we are interpreting our own present and determining our future.

What Mead is doing here is pointing to iteration, that is, the reproduction and potential transformation of the past in the present. He is pointing to the time structure of the present in which the movement of present experience is that of forming and being formed by our reconstruction of the past while forming and being formed by our expectation of the future, all at the same time in the present. In complexity terms we might say that it is the nonlinear nature of this iteration that makes possible both continuity and potential transformation at the same time. Mead explicitly links this time structure of the present to the notion of emergence as the appearance of unique events.

Clearly, human experience is also experience of what Prigogine (1997) called the arrow of time, in the sense that we all know that what has been said cannot be unsaid, and what has been done cannot be undone. We cannot go back in time and unsay or undo. We can only go forward in time and elaborate on what we have said or done. It is also our experience that interacting with each other in one way immediately precludes all alternative ways of interacting and that what happens next will be different from what might have been if we had interacted in one of these alternative ways. It is because the past is not a given but a perpetual construction in the present that we cannot go back to the past. It is because of the potential for small differences to escalate that we cannot retrace our steps. In other words, it is because time has the structure of the living present that we also experience the arrow of time.

Human interaction in the present is thus simultaneously forming and being formed by the past and the future. In other words, the arrow of time means that time moves only from the past through the present to the future because of the iterative nonlinearity of interactions and the bifurcations they encounter. In relation to human action, the arrow of time has an important temporal implication. It means that the present has a circular time structure in that the present both forms and is formed by the past and the future at the same time. The arrow of time then means that the movement of human experience in the present has the circular self-referential time structure of reconstructed pasts and imagined futures. We may call this the living present, which is very different from the notion of the 'here-and-now', which explicitly excludes the past and the future in focusing entirely on present feelings.

10.5 The differences between systemic process and responsive processes thinking

In dictionaries, the word 'process' is defined as 'going on, being constructed over time, a series of changes, a series of operations, or a course of action'. For the philosopher Whitehead (1978), process refers to *how entities become* what they become. Process, then, refers to some kind of movement over *time* in which entities are *becoming*. I think that there is a further implication, given a universe of interdependent entities, and this is that the movement of process always involves some kind of interaction between entities. So at its most basic, I take process to be the ongoing, interactive movement (the *how*) of entities over time through which these entities become, individually and collectively, the coherent patterns of activity (the *what*) that they are. Process is interactive movement, the *interaction* of entities, and what these interactions are continually producing or creating is the coherent *pattern* of the entities themselves both individual and collective.

Consider how systemic and responsive processes perspectives interpret the key terms of this general definition of process in substantially different ways.

The *entities* in systemic process are defined as parts of a system. These *parts interact* over time, *the process*, to produce a bounded whole, the coherent *pattern*, which actually exists, or is thought of 'as if' it exists, at a higher hierarchical level than the parts. In other words, the whole is more than the sum of the parts, has additional properties and can act back on the parts as a causal force in their interaction, giving meaning to the parts. In the organisational literature on systemic process, reviewed in Chapter 7, the parts were defined as routines, core micro-strategies, micro-practices, procedures and many similar concepts. In their interaction, sometimes called re-combination, these parts are said to produce an activity system, or an organisation as a system, which is a coherent pattern. The parts themselves may also be thought of as subsystems produced by the interaction of sub-parts. For example, the sub-parts could be individuals or the mental models through which individuals interpret the nature of the organisational whole and its environment. In this systemic process view it is some kind of system which is *becoming* what it becomes.

From the perspective of responsive processes, however, the *entities* are embodied human persons and the movement, the *how*, is the *interacting*, the relating, *between persons* in their ongoing responding to each other. *Process* is understood as responsive acts of mutual recognition, where recognition is not simply good since persons may recognise each other and themselves as superior or inferior, as attractive or repugnant. The coherent *patterns* that are being produced in such interaction are not 'wholes' outside of the interaction but the coherent patterns of the interaction itself, of the process itself. Nothing is being produced above, below, behind or in front of the patterns of interaction, of the process. Patterns of interaction simply produce further patterns of interaction, individually and population-wide. What are *becoming* are the individual and collective identities of the persons interacting. Furthermore, in the responsive processes view, categories of pattern such as routines are instances of more fundamental patterns, namely the thematic patterning of communication (*see* Chapter 11), the patterning of power relations between people (*see* Chapter 12), and the patterning of the ideologically based choices people make (*see* Chapter 12). So in firmly grounding the notion of processes in interaction between human persons, the responsive process perspective makes central the iterative processes of communication, power and ideologically driven choice. This perspective, then, focuses attention not on abstract wholes or administrative procedures but on the actual micro, local interaction between people in the living present in which people may imaginatively construct 'wholes' felt as the unity of experience, especially the experience of value (*see* Chapter 12).

Second, notice how the systemic perspective on process is based on a spatial metaphor of 'inside' and 'outside'. The parts of an organisational system are inside the whole system, which is outside the parts, and outside the system there is its environment. Of course, the activities of the parts take place in a physical, spatial setting but in a systems view they also take place in conceptual space, that is, the system itself is thought of as a space. Furthermore, process itself is often thought about conceptually as spatial. This can be seen in Chapter 7 when writers refer to what is going on 'inside' the process. This conceptual spatial distinction immediately leads to the notion of an observer who can perceive the system or the process from the outside, as it were, and so can shape or influence the process and what goes on inside it. This leads to talking about a process called shaping which shapes another process called routines (*see* Chapter 7). In systemic process thinking there is a doubling of process – some process shapes, influences or conditions another process.

In the responsive processes view, although the activities of interdependent people obviously take place in a physical setting, space, there is no notion of the activities themselves being inside or outside of anything – mental activity, for example, is not thought of as being inside a person as it is in systemic process thinking. Responsive processes thinking is not based on a notion of conceptual space. Furthermore, there is no external objective observer, only participants. Participation also means something completely different in the two approaches. In systems thinking, people are thought to participate in a system, a whole. In responsive processes thinking, participation means direct interaction between persons in local situations in the living present. So the methodological position is a participative one rather than one based on the objective observer. In responsive processes thinking there is no doubling of process – there is only one process, namely interaction between persons which is creating the patterns in their interaction. Since persons can only participate in their interaction with each other there is no outside position from which anyone could use another process to shape or influence the processes of interaction – any influence is exerted through relations between people in the interaction itself.

Third, the spatial metaphor and the taken-for-granted linear theory of time renders time itself a relatively unimportant aspect of systemic process. Instead, the systemic perspective focuses attention on routines, procedures and analytical tools. Systemic process thinking is built upon a linear notion of time in which the past is factually given, the future is yet to be unfolded and the present is simply a point dividing the two. It is based on linear phases or stages of development.

Responsive processes thinking, however, takes a circular, paradoxical view of time. This means that the past is not actually given but is being reiterated, retold in the present in the light of the expectations people are forming in the present for the future. Expectations for the future are affecting how the stories of the past are being retold and those stories are affecting expectations for the future, all in the present. In a sense the future is changing the past just as the retelling of the past is changing the future, all in the present. The present is thus living in the sense that it has a time structure incorporating both the past and the future. The *living present*, the present we actually live in, implies the arrow of time because you cannot tell the same story twice – you cannot return to the past. Systemic perspectives look for how the system moves over linear time, while the responsive processes approach asks about the narrative patterns being created in each living present, how narrative patterns are moving over time.

Fourth, in systemic process thinking, causality takes a dual form. The individuals designing the system, with its routines and values, are subject to rationalist causality, which means that the cause of their actions lies in their rationally chosen objectives. The system itself is subjected to formative cause, which means that the operation of the system unfolds the form already designed into it in a move from an embryonic to a mature state.

Responsive processes thinking is based on a different theory of causality. In responsive processes thinking, the theory of causality is unitary and transformative in that patterns of interaction emerge as continuity and potential transformation at the same time in the iteration of interaction itself. The future is thus under perpetual construction in the interaction between people and it is the processes of interaction between differences that amplifies these differences into novelty. The explanation of novelty lies in the properties of the processes of interaction.

Fifth, it can be seen immediately that systemic and responsive processes thinking make completely different assumptions about human psychology. The former is based on the individualistic psychologies of cognitivism, constructivism, humanistic psychology or psychoanalysis, while the latter takes a relational, social perspective on individual psychology, a point that will be explained in Chapter 11.

Sixth, in systemic process thinking, practice means the system of routines, cultural traditions and so on that individuals use as tools in their practices or praxis. From the systemic view, experience is the formulation and testing of hypotheses about an objective world understood in terms of systems, where the system is outside of experience, a hidden reality or given categories such as mental models.

In responsive processes thinking, individuals are social practitioners through and through in that their very selves emerge in social practice. Practice is the local activity of bodily interaction as communication, power relating and evaluative choice.

Generalisations such as routines and cultural traditions are to be found only in their particularisation in local interaction (*see* Chapter 11). As for Hegel, experience is the historical, social processes of consciousness and self-consciousness, the world we are creating in our thought.

Seventh, the systemic view places thought before action while from the responsive processes point of view there is no necessary sequence because interaction is continuous over time.

Eighth, from the perspective of responsive processes, population-wide pattern emerges in local interaction rather than being intentionally created by a plan. The systemic process perspective takes the view that population-wide pattern, understood as a system, can be intentionally planned or at least the process producing it can be shaped from some external position.

The differences between systemic process and responsive processes are summarised in Table 10.3.

10.6 Summary

This chapter has presented arguments for interpreting the relevance of complexity theories for organisations from a responsive processes perspective rather than the systemic process point of view discussed in Chapter 7.

Systems thinkers use the word 'process' to mean the interaction of parts of a system to produce that system, whether that system be real or a mental construct. In human terms this amounts to the assumption that, in their interaction, people either actually are a system or that they understand their interaction as if it were a system. Here a macro perspective is taken, which I have signalled by using 'process' in the singular when referring to systems views. It is easy then to reify 'process' and talk about shaping and choosing it. In responsive processes thinking, the interaction between persons is understood to produce further interaction between them. In responsive processes thinking, people are thought of not as parts producing a system but as interdependent persons producing patterns of relationships, which produce them as selves at the same time. In the kind of responsive processes thinking I am talking about there is no notion of system at all. In talking about this perspective I have used 'processes' in the plural to indicate the micro perspective being taken, in which the macro emerges not in one monolithic process but in many local processes of local human interaction which cannot be reified and talked about as if they could be influenced from the outside.

From a responsive processes perspective, there is also no notion of hierarchical levels in human action. Instead of thinking that individuals produce organisations as another level, which shapes their identities, individual identities and the organisational are thought of as the same responsive processes. In responsive processes thinking, people interacting are intrinsically social and what they produce is further interaction with widespread, population-wide patterns, not some higher-level system or whole. In systems thinking, emergence relates to levels in that interaction at one level produces an emergent system at another level. In responsive processes thinking, relationships are emerging in relationships and the question of levels does not even arise.

Table 10.3 The differences between systemic process and responsive processes

	Systemic process	Responsive processes
Entity	Parts of a system, which could be individuals, routines, etc., and which can be thought of as subsystems, such as mental models. Psychological assumptions are those of individual-centred cognitivism, etc.	Embodied interdependent human persons. A social, relational view of human psychology is taken
Process	Interaction of parts	Responsive acts of mutual recognition by persons
What is becoming	The system, a bounded whole which exists at a higher level than the parts, has properties of its own, and acts causally on the parts	Coherent patterns of interaction, of the process itself. Patterns of interaction produce further patterns of interaction and nothing else. These constitute individual and collective identities
Causality	Dual causality of the rationalist, objectively observing autonomous individual and the formative cause of the system unfolding a mature form of itself imputed by the observer	Transformative causality in which continuity and potential transformation emerge at the same time. The potential for transformation arises in the capacity of nonlinear interaction to amplify difference and in the inherent possibility of spontaneity in human agents
Theory of time	Linear view of time where past is factually given and future is yet to be unfolded in developmental stages	Time as the living present in which both accounts of the past and expectations for the future are formed in the perpetual construction of the future in the present
Conceptual space	Spatial metaphor of parts inside the system and the system outside the parts	No spatial metaphor in that human action itself is not inside or outside of anything. So there is no society or organisation at a level higher than human interaction
Emergence	Not central to the process and, where used, equated with chance happenings as the opposite of intention	Central to the process of human interaction where emergence is understood in terms of the interplay of human intentions. Emergence is not seen as the polar opposite of intention and what emerges does so because of the interplay of what people intend to do, not by chance
Doubling of process	Autonomous individuals can stand outside a process, such as strategising, and shape it, that is, use another process to shape a process	No doubling of process since there are only the processes of human interaction and no one can take an external vantage point in relation to this
Practice	Practice is a system of routines, etc.	Practice is the local, social activity of communication, power relating and evaluative choice
Experience	The use of tools and techniques to make decisions and act	Historical, social processes of consciousness and self-consciousness in interaction with others. The world we together create in our thought
Organisation	A thing to be moved around	Patterns of relating in which one can only participate

Responsive processes thinking involves moving away from any form of systems thinking when it comes to human action and focuses on:

- The detail of local interaction between diverse people in the living present as patterning of experience, emergent identity and transformation.
- Interaction in the form of conversation and how it patterns experience in narrative-like forms. This emphasises the importance of the informal and the narrative rather than the prescriptive and instrumental.
- Ideology as the basis of evaluative choices made by persons.
- The importance of conflicting constraints emerging as power and the dynamics of inclusion and exclusion and the links to how people deal with anxiety.
- The emergence of population-wide patterns in the local interaction of inter-dependent persons.
- The simultaneous emergence of continuity and novelty, creation and destruction, in the iteration of nonlinear interaction and its amplification of small changes.

By patterns of interaction, then, I mean the activities of interdependent people and these activities can be categorised in many different ways. For example, such patterns may take the form of routines as in the process and activity-based literature but now they are thought of not as systems but as the patterns of activities of human persons iterated over time.

I will be arguing that a perspective along these lines forms a coherent way of thinking that directs attention to the narrative forms of human experience. The focus is on lived experience in local situations in the present, paying particular attention to the diversity of relationships within which individual and organisational identities emerge. The practical implication of such a move is that we focus attention directly on patterns of human relating and ask what kind of power relations, ideology and communication they reflect. We ask how themes such as planning or routines are becoming in ordinary daily life. We look beyond the already given, beyond the tools, to the ordinary everyday nature of human interaction in organisations.

Further reading

The arguments presented in this chapter are explored in Stacey et al. (2001) and Stacey (2003, 2005). Further information on the differences between Kantian and Hegelian thinking can be found in Ameriks (2002).

Questions to aid further reflection

1. What do the terms systemic process and responsive processes mean and what are the key distinctions between these notions?
2. How would you articulate different notions of process, practice and experience in human action generally and in organisational life in particular?

3. In what traditions of thought are the notions of systemic process and responsive processes located?

4. What does it mean to reason by analogy?

5. On what analogies with the complexity sciences does the notion of responsive processes draw?

6. What do the concepts of emergence and self-organisation mean to you and how would you take them up in thinking about human action?

7. Elias argued that change in societies is unplanned and emerges in the interplay of intentions. Would it make sense to think of organisations in the same way?

8. What difference would it make to thinking about the nature of organisations and the strategising of managers if you think in terms of responsive processes? For example, would it be possible for a leader to change the culture or values of an organisation?

9. In your own experience, can you trace out how what actually happens in organisations emerges in the interplay of many intentions?

Chapter 11

The emergence of organisational strategy in local communicative interaction

Complex responsive processes of conversation

This chapter invites you to draw on your own experience to reflect on and consider the implications of:

- Thinking of organisations not as things or systems but as dynamic patterns of relationships between people.

- Understanding patterns of relationships in terms of ordinary, everyday conversation between people in their local interaction with each other in which they form their intentions to act.

- How the attributes of being human persons – consciousness, self-consciousness, spontaneity, choice – arise in the social conversation of gestures and what difference this makes to thinking about the activities of strategising in organisations.

- The difference between the sender–receiver model of communication found in the dominant discourse and the understanding of communication as conversation in the complex responsive processes perspective.

For more than 50 years now a vast literature on strategy and organisation has been explaining organising and strategising in a particular way and presenting prescriptions for success based on these explanations. This dominant discourse, described in Part 1 of this book, is based on the assumption that an organisation can be thought of as a system for which leaders and managers can more or less choose the strategic direction and/or design, influence or condition the process which will determine that direction. Over this period there has been an enormous expansion in management education delivered both by business schools and expensive training and development programmes for leaders and managers. The great majority of these educational programmes operate firmly within the dominant discourse. To present anything else is dismissed as theoretical as opposed to practical. Over much the same period there has been a significant, research-backed critique of the explanations and prescriptions of the dominant discourse, but this has not, by and large, questioned the fundamental assumptions of that discourse, nor has it dented the still common belief amongst organisational practitioners that they should be able to do what the dominant discourse prescribes even if they may not really be doing it properly yet. Although at first mainly confined to the private enterprise sector, over the past two decades this dominant discourse has now taken over public sector governance in the form of managerial systems to improve performance. This too has attracted criticism which has had very little effect in deflecting or modifying managerialist forms of governance. What is striking, however, is that after more than 50 years of research, the approaches found in the dominant discourse have not delivered what they promise. Commercial organisations still fail as much as they did in the 1960s and the debates about public sector performance and the more and more frenetic calls for improvement are all replays of what one could hear in the 1960s. Limited research indicates that mergers and acquisitions fail 80 per cent of the time. It is widely known that culture change programmes, business process re-engineering, quality improvement programmes, and many others, come and go without producing what they promised. And yet commercial organisations have grown and proliferated, expanded across the globe and delivered ever more varied and advanced products and services as their activities have contributed to growing pollution and cultural clashes across the globe. In many countries, public sector services have expanded rapidly and increased in sophistication as healthcare and education become more widely available. It seems that improvement and deterioration come about at the same time, despite the huge question marks over the impact of the prescriptions of the dominant discourse. The question this raises for me has to do with the adequacy of dominant ways of thinking about what is happening. On the one hand, we have the surprising, unpredictable but recognisable, creative and destructive evolution of organisational life, and, on the other, we have a dominant way of thinking according to which it all ought to be happening in a stable, orderly and purely progressive way according to some leadership choices, otherwise it is all a matter of chance. I think the ideas presented in this chapter are important because they offer a way of escaping this dichotomy between order and disorder, predictability and unpredictability, choice and chance, and so provide a way of thinking about what people in organisations already do in all its creative and destructive aspects. This perspective does not present prescriptions for some new, more successful form of organisation. It is concerned with how we might *think* more usefully and more satisfyingly *about what we already do*.

11.1 Introduction

Chapter 10 suggested a move from systemic ways of thinking about organisations to one in which organisations are understood in terms of responsive processes of interaction between human persons. It drew on complexity sciences to suggest that we might think of organisations and their strategies as population-wide patterns that emerge in the interplay of local, responsive interaction. It was suggested that complex adaptive systems with heterogeneous agents could provide a source domain for analogies with human interaction but that this would involve an interpretation grounded firmly in the attributes of human agents, such as consciousness, self-consciousness, spontaneity and choice. The purpose of this chapter is to carry out that task of interpretation using the work of Mead.

Mead (1934) cogently argues that human consciousness and self-consciousness emerge in the conversation of gestures. He holds that mind, self and society all arise simultaneously in the same social, conversational processes. His work, therefore, explains in detail how the attributes of being human arise in social interaction, so providing a way of interpreting the analogies from the complexity sciences as far as human action is concerned. It is in communicative interaction, in conversation with each other, that humans accomplish whatever it is that they accomplish. Organisation is conversation and organisation and strategy emerge through conversation. Furthermore, in exploring the work of Mead, this chapter will be arguing that it is far more than organisational strategies which emerge in local conversational interactions – what also emerges is the ongoing iteration of the selves of the interdependent people who are members of the organisation.

If one adopts this approach, then one comes to think about organisational communication and strategy in very different ways from the theories described in Part 1. Communication is understood as ongoing, responsive conversation and strategy comes to be understood as the evolving patterns of individual and collective identities. Strategy is about what people in organisations do and who they are and this is exactly what identity means. Strategy is about the evolution of what people in an organisation do and how they become who they become. One then takes a very different position in the debates about: intention versus emergence and the meaning and consequences of organisational planning activities; macro (population-wide) versus micro (local) with its implications for top-down and bottom-up strategy processes; formulation (thought or theory) versus implementation (action or practice). Dominant ways of thinking about what it means to lead and control, to manage change and knowledge, to manage improvement in quality and performance, to design organisations and change values, are all brought into question. This chapter and the next three will outline the basis of this challenge; its implications will be dealt with more fully in Chapter 15.

An important general point about the responsive processes perspective to be explored in this and subsequent chapters is that *it is a way of thinking about what we already do*. It is not about prescribing what people ought to be doing or about labelling what they are doing as futile or foolish. The point is to try to understand and explain what we are already doing in an uncertain world of experience that we are creating in our interaction, some of which might look foolish and futile but may nevertheless be serving a purpose. The importance of a different way of thinking, a different explanation of what we are already doing, is not that it immediately leads to another prescription but that it focuses attention on aspects of what we are doing together that have been invisible to us, especially that made invisible by determined efforts to be 'rational'. In focusing attention differently we may find ourselves doing things differently. So what does this chapter focus attention on that is not often taken seriously? It focuses on the ordinary, everyday local interactions, particularly conversational interactions, which are mostly ignored when talking about organisation and strategy and dismissed as 'just talk'. The purpose of this chapter is to focus on conversation as the basic activity of local interaction, leading in the next chapter to an exploration of the interplay of intentions, in which emerge population-wide patterns of relating called strategy. The claim is that conversation is *the* activity of organising. Organisational change is change in conversation.

This chapter now turns to complex responsive processes of human communication.

11.2 Human communication and the conversation of gestures: the social act

Mead (1934) proposed a way of thinking about communication which differed markedly from the cybernetic sender–receiver model discussed in Chapter 3. According to the latter model, a thought arises in one autonomous individual's mind which is encoded in language and transmitted to another autonomous individual who then decodes the language so that, when communication is good, the thought in one mind is transferred to the mind of another. If there is a gap between what was transmitted and what was received, then further transmissions are required to close the gap. Here meaning lies in the word, that is, in the vocal gesture of the one making the gesture; the part played by the receiver is simply one of translation until the same meaning is received as was transmitted. It becomes very important, then, to get the communication 'right'. This model is reflected in the dominant discourse when people in organisations talk about insufficient, good and bad communication. When people in organisations complain about poor communication they are usually thinking in these terms. In this model, communication begins with the sender and ends with the receiver, implying a linear view of time.

Mead, however, did not think in terms of a sender and a receiver. Instead he thought of one body making a gesture to another body where the gesture calls out, or evokes, a response from that other body. That response is itself a gesture back to the first body which, in turn evokes a further response. What we have, then, is ongoing responsive processes, which Mead called *the conversation of gestures*, where beginnings and endings are purely arbitrary. The conversation of gestures is temporal, social processes in which the fundamental unit is the social act consisting of gesture and response, where these are phases of the social act and cannot be separated from each other because together they constitute meaning in the following way.

Mead gave an example of a very simple act of communication between two dogs to explain this point about the social constitution of meaning. One dog makes the gesture of a snarl and this may call forth a counter snarl, which means fight; or the gesture could call forth flight, which means victory and defeat; or the response to the gesture could be crouching, which means submission and domination. Meaning, therefore, does not lie in the gesture alone but in the social act as a whole. In other words, meaning arises in the responsive interaction between actors; gesture and response can never be separated but must be understood as moments in one act. Meaning does not arise first in each individual, to be subsequently expressed in action, nor is it transmitted from one individual to another but, rather, it arises in the interaction between them. Meaning is not attached to an object, formed as a representation, or stored, as in cognitivism, but is created in the interaction. Imme-diately, knowing becomes an aspect of interaction, or relationship. Here meaning is emerging in the action of the living present (*see* Chapter 10) in which the imme-diate future (response) acts back on the past (gesture) to change its meaning. Meaning is not simply located in the past (gesture) or the future (response) but in the circular interaction between the two as the living present. In this way the present is not simply a point but has a time structure. Communication is then a social, relational process so that poor communication means inadequate interaction.

The process of gesture and response between biological entities in a physical con-text constitutes simple co-operative, social activity of a mindless, reflex kind. At this stage, meaning is implicit in the social act itself and those acting are not conscious of that meaning.

Consciousness

For consciousness to arise, Mead argued that our mammal ancestors must have evolved central nervous systems that enabled them to gesture to others in a manner that was capable of calling forth in themselves the same range of responses as in those to whom they were gesturing. This would happen if, for example, the snarl of one called forth in itself the fleeting feelings associated with counter snarl, flight or submissive posture, just as they did in the one to whom the gesture was being made. The gesture now has a substantially different role. Mead described such a gesture as a significant symbol, where a significant symbol is one that calls forth the same response in the gesturer as in the one to whom it is directed. Significant symbols, therefore, make it possible for the gesturer to 'know' what he or she is doing. If, when one makes a gesture to another, one is able to experience in one's own body a similar response to that which the gesture provokes in another body, then one can 'know' what one is doing.

Possessing this capacity, the maker of a gesture can intuit, anticipate and to some extent predict, the consequences of that gesture. In other words, he or she can know what he or she is doing, just before the other responds. The whole social act, that is, meaning, can be experienced in advance of carrying out the whole act, opening up the possibility of reflection and choice in making a gesture. Furthermore, the one responding has the same opportunity for reflecting upon, and so choosing, from the range of responses. The first part of a gesture can be taken by the other as an indication of how further parts of the gesture will unfold from the response. In this way, the two can indicate to each other how they might respond to each other in the continuous circle in which a gesture by one calls forth a response from another, which is itself a gesture back to the first.

As individuals interact with each other in this way, the possibility arises of a pause before making a gesture. In a kind of private role-play, emerging in the repeated experience of public interaction, one individual learns to take the attitude of the other, enabling a kind of trial run in advance of actually completing or even starting the gesture. Will it call forth aggression, fright, flight or submission? What will be the consequences in each case? In this way, *rudimentary forms of thinking develop, taking the form of private role-playing*, that is, gestures made by a body to itself, calling forth responses in itself. Mead said that humans are fundamentally role-playing animals.

Consciousness, therefore, arises in interaction and the body, with its nervous system, becomes central to understanding how we 'know' anything. I want to stress how Mead is arguing that individual human consciousness, mind, arises in the social act, in communicative interaction, so that there cannot be the one without the other.

Language

Mead then argued that the gesture that is particularly useful in calling forth the same attitude in oneself as in the other is the vocal gesture. This is because we can hear the sounds we make in much the same way as others hear them, while we cannot see the facial gestures we make as others see them, for example. The development of more sophisticated patterns of vocal gesturing, that is, of the language form of significant symbols, is thus of major importance in the development of consciousness and of sophisticated forms of society. Mind and society emerge together in the medium of language. However, since speaking and listening are actions of bodies, and since bodies are never without feelings, the medium of language is also always a medium of feelings.

As soon as one can take the attitude, the tendency to act, of the other, that is, as soon as one communicates in significant symbols, there is at least a rudimentary form of consciousness. The nature of the social has thus shifted from mindless co-operation through functional specialisation to mindful, role-playing interaction made more and more sophisticated by the use of language as silent conversation with oneself. Meaning is now particularly constituted in gesturing and responding in the medium of vocal symbols but these vocal symbols are always aspects of a process that always includes the 'symbols' of feeling. Mind, or consciousness, is the gesturing and responding action of a body directed towards itself as private role-play and silent conversation, and society is the gesturing and responding actions of bodies directed towards each other. They are thus the same kind of process.

It is important to note here that the conversational processes of communication described by Mead are not some kind of social determinism and they do not function in some perfect manner. Although I have the physiological potential for calling forth in myself similar responses to my gestures as those evoked in others, there is no guarantee that I will 'get it right', certainly not at the first attempt. This is because there is no fixed causal connection between my gesture and the response evoked in you, which is why Mead's theory is not a form of social determinism. There is no fixed causal connection because at the same time as your response is evoked by my gesture it is also selected by you in a manner that reflects your experience of a lifetime of interacting with others. Although I may be able to anticipate something of the kind of response you may make, I can never be sure because I can never know your life history in full and, even if I could, there is always the possibility of some surprising, spontaneous response from you. Furthermore, the response that my gesture to you evokes in me is also, at the same time, selected by my own lifetime of experience so that what is evoked in me may have to do more with me than with you. The possibility for miscommunication is thus substantial and can only be dealt with in ongoing conversation as we try together to clarify what we mean. This is not a cybernetic feedback process, as in the sender–receiver model, but an ongoing, conversational negotiation of meaning.

Comparison with the sender–receiver model of communication

Mead's mode of communication is thus profoundly different from the sender–receiver one. The sender–receiver model encourages us to believe that good communication will enable us to 'get it right'. So if I translate my thought clearly into language, if there is no 'noise' in transmission caused, for example, by distorting emotions, and if you translate my clear words clearly into thought, then our communication will be good. Or if the communication does not succeed at first then 'feedback' from the receiver will enable the sender to provide a more precise communication. On this view, a leader or manager who is a good communicator will be able to send a message to all the members of an organisation and they will immediately understand it. However, people in organisations frequently complain that communication is not good enough and the response is to blame the sender or the receiver. This leads to a call for improvement in communication skills, involving the development of language and presentational skills and the development of detached attitudes to objective communication. This, it is believed, will lead to improved communication in an organisation. In terms of strategy it then becomes important to formulate clear plans and communicate them clearly so that people will implement them. Implementation problems are frequently blamed on poor communication.

However, in Mead's model of communication, when I make a gesture to a number of people, I can rely on its calling forth many different responses from others, all of whom have different life histories. Since the meaning does not lie in my words alone but emerges in the words and the responses they evoke in others taken together, it follows that I can only know the meaning of what I say in your responses to them. There is no point in blaming you, or your blaming me, because we are having to carry on exploring just what it is we mean – this is the very nature of communication. Sending me for training in communication skills can, therefore, have only a very limited effect in terms of improving the communication between us because you are implicated too. From this alternative perspective on communication it is no use for a leader, or manager, to imagine that they have sent a clear message and leave it at that. Communication ceases to be a one-off event that someone can get right and becomes instead an ongoing conversational process in which meaning is being clarified and, in the course of such clarification, is actually evolving in potentially novel ways. From this perspective, one can no longer think of the strategic plan as a one of communication which must be got right. Instead, one comes to see the activities of strategising as ongoing conversational processes, essentially involving emotion and fantasy, as well as reason and all the other aspects of conversation.

I think leaders, managers and others will act differently with regard to communication and communication skills training if they take this different perspective on communication.

The generalised other

Mead takes his argument further when he suggests how the private role-play/silent conversation of mind evolves in increasingly complex ways. As more and more interactions are experienced with others, so more roles and wider ranges of possible responses enter into the role-playing/silent conversational activities that precede the gesture, or to be more accurate, are continuously intertwined with, public/vocal gesturing and responding. In this way, the capacity to take the attitude of many others evolves and this becomes generalised. Each engaged in the conversation of gestures can now take the attitude of what Mead calls the *generalised other*. Eventually, individuals develop the capacity to take the attitude of the whole group, or what Mead calls the game or the social attitude. The whole of society, in a generalised form, then enters the mental processes of each interdependent person. In a fundamentally important way, this constitutes a powerful form of social control through self-control. The result is much more sophisticated processes of co-operative interaction. There is now mindful social behaviour with increasingly sophisticated forms of co-operation. The next chapter will continue with the exploration of the nature of the generalised other, while the rest of this chapter looks at how Mead explains self-consciousness and then considers further points on the nature of conversational activity in organisations.

Processes of self

In understanding self-consciousness Mead talked about processes in which a person takes the attitude, the tendency to act, of the generalised other, or the group, to himself as an 'I', where that attitude is the 'me'. It is important to bear in mind that Mead was saying something more than that the self arises in the attitude, the tendency to act, of specific others towards oneself. Mead was talking about social, generalising processes where the 'me' is generalised tendencies across a whole community or society to act to me as a person. For example, what it means to be an individual, a person, a man or a woman, a professional, and so on, does not arise in relation to a few specific people but in relation to a particular society in a particular era. We in the West think of ourselves now as individuals in a completely different way from how people in the West thought of themselves four hundred years ago and in a different way from people in other cultures. In what Mead called the 'I–me' dialectic, then, we have *processes* in which the generalising of the 'me' is made particular in the responses of the 'I' for a particular person, at a particular time, in a particular place. For example, I may take up what it means to be a man in my society in a particular way that differs in some respects from how others see themselves as men in my own society, in other societies and at other times.

What is happening here is the linking of the attitude of generalised other, of the whole group, organisation or society, with a 'me' in becoming an object to oneself. The 'me' is one's perception of, one's feelings towards, the configuration of the gestures–responses of the others/society to one as a subject, or an 'I'. A self, as the ongoing relationship between 'me' and 'I', as well as an awareness of that self, that is, self-consciousness, emerges in a life history of social interaction, which includes organisational interaction, and continues to evolve throughout life. Mead argues, very importantly, that the responses of the 'I' to one's perception of the attitude of the group to oneself (the 'me') are not givens but are always potentially unpredictable in that there is no predetermined way in which the 'I' might respond to the 'me'. In other words, each of us may respond in many different ways to our perception of the views that others have of us. Mead's argument, therefore, is not a form of social determinism because the possibility of individual spontaneity means that the response of the 'I' is not given. The response is simultaneously called forth by the gesture of the generalised other and selected or enacted by the responder on the basis of past history reconstructed as the present, always with the possibility of spontaneous variation. In other words, the response of the 'I' is both being called forth by the other and being enacted, or selected by the history, biological, individual and social of the responder. Society's gesture, as 'me', calls forth an 'I' response, but only a response I am capable of making and that depends upon my history. There is a tension of movement in the response, a tension of selection/enactment and evocation/provocation at the same time. The process is one of emergence in which the future of my self is being perpetually constructed and it does not ultimately locate the source of personal change in the individual alone.

Mead's concept of the 'I' is sometimes interpreted as the spontaneous impulse of the body (Joas, 2000). However, in complex responsive processes terms, the 'I' is no less social than the 'me' simply because they cannot be separated from each other. The dialectical 'I–me' process evolves – it has a history. This means that in any present, the 'I' response reflects a history of social engagement. It is the capacity for imagination and reflection that brings small differences in the 'I' response to the 'me' gesture from one present to another and it is the amplifying propensity of nonlinear interaction that escalates these small differences into transformations of the self.

It is essential, if we are to understand the important point Mead makes, not to split the 'I' and the 'me'. They are inseparable phases of one act. The self then is understood as an ongoing activity, an ongoing temporal process of 'I' responding to 'me'. It is not that there is a true self called 'I' which is seen in the mirror of the social 'me' or that the 'I' engages in some kind of conversation with the 'me' as the voices of other people. In Mead's formulation there is no given, true self. Instead a self is continually iterated, continually emerges in interaction with others and oneself. This self is truly social through and through (Foulkes, 1948). Mead is not denying unique individuality but explaining how such uniqueness emerges in social processes of interaction. What he is clearly denying is any notion of an autonomous self. Elias said much the same when he claimed that the individual was the singular of inter-dependent people while the social was the plural.

The social, in human terms, is highly sophisticated processes of co-operative and competitive interaction between people in the medium of symbols in order to undertake joint action. Such sophisticated interaction could not take place without self-conscious minds but neither could those self-conscious minds exist without that sophisticated form of co-operation. In other words there could be no private role-play, including silent conversation, by a body with itself, if there was no public interaction of the same form. Mind/self and society are all logically equivalent processes of a conversational kind. The result is self-referential, reflexive processes of sophisticated co-operation and competition in the medium of symbols that constitute meaning. These processes, always involving the body and its feelings, both enable and constrain human actions. All of these interactions, private and public, are processes in which humans act within a physical, non-human environment using tools and technology in a co-operative manner. In so acting within the context, humans affect that context, which simultaneously affects them, enabling them to do what they do, and constraining them from doing other things. Individual selves/minds emerge between people, in the relationship between them, and cannot be simply 'located' within an individual. In this way of thinking, individual minds/selves certainly exist, and very importantly so, but they emerge in relationships between people as iterated processes rather than arising within an individual. The notion of conceptual space with a mind inside a person and society outside is completely avoided in this way of thinking.

What relevance does this view of mind and self have for organisations and the activities of strategising? Organisations and the work activities of their members are social activities which play a very important part in the lives of all of their members. Organisations are ongoing patterns of relating between people in which their very minds and selves are sustained and continue to evolve in important ways. If one thinks in this way then it becomes very difficult to regard people in organisations as *its* 'human resources', on the one hand, or as autonomous individuals for whom the organisation should provide special opportunities for their self-actualisation, on the other. People's selves are sustained and evolve in the ordinary, everyday work activities they undertake in their local interactions with each other. Changes in hierarchical reporting structures, divisional or subsidiary company groupings, procedures for accountability, control systems, objectives and targets, performance appraisal systems, to name but a few, will all have implications for how people experience their selves. Changes in how one experiences one's self are bound to be highly emotional and anxiety provoking and this is highly likely to lead to responses which are difficult to understand and may even seem to be bizarre. There are many practical questions which this view raises for managing change and managing people which I will return to later in this chapter and in Chapter 14. First, however, consider a further development of Mead's argument.

Having set out Mead's basic theory of human consciousness and self-consciousness as social processes of conversation, we now turn to a more detailed exploration of ordinary conversation in organisations.

11.3 Ordinary conversation in organisations

Ethnomethodologists (Garfinkel, 1967; Goffman, 1981) study the finely ordered detail of local interaction, including an analysis of the detailed flow of ordinary conversation (Jefferson, 1978; Sacks, 1992; Shegloff, 1991).

The turn-taking/turn-making nature of conversation

Conversation analysts have used recordings of ordinary conversations to build up a picture of how conversation is patterned and how it produces orderly interactions between people. What they point to, as the fundamental organising principle of conversation, is the process of turn taking. Turn taking is at the heart of all social activity in that it establishes a temporal and spatial location for social interaction. From it flows the back-and-forth rhythm of social relationships. Turn taking

> creates the rhythms of daily life, from the formal, public rituals and ceremonies of ancient religions and national states to the most intimate of human intercourse.
>
> (Boden, 1994, p. 66)

Sack's (1992) research pointed to the way in which turns to speak are valued, distributed across speakers, competed for, abandoned and held on to. Turn taking is, thus, one of the important ways in which power differentials are established and sustained in conversations, very much a reflection of the processes to which Elias points (*see* Chapter 13). Turn-taking processes are self-referential as participants respond to each other in a back-and-forth way with reference to their own histories and the history of the communities they are embedded in. The response of one calls forth a further response from another, in turn calling forth a response from the first, always simultaneously selected on the basis of the life histories of all involved. The processes of turn taking are also reflexive processes since who takes turns reflects each person's individual history and the history of the community they are members of.

There is no objective position external to the conversation from which someone can control, shape, influence or condition the conversational processes of turn taking and turn making. All are participants and none of them can get outside the conversation, observe it and control it, at least without destroying its very nature as ordinary, everyday conversation. Each participant can, of course, reflect on the emerging pattern of the conversation and its turn-taking, turn-making processes but each reflection is always itself an activity within the ongoing conversation. Elias (1987) drew a distinction between involved and detached participation. By involved he meant highly emotional, rather unaware participation and by detached he meant a less emotional, more aware, more reflective participation. He also made clear that neither form of participation is ever encountered in pure form. Conversational participation is always a paradox of involved detachment or detached involvement where the emphasis may shift from more to less detachment or involvement, but never completely. The point is that there is no process external to the conversation. Anyone's influence can only be exerted through participating in the conversation in some involved-detached way. There is no possibility of the doubling of process from this perspective (*see* Chapter 7 and 10).

Furthermore, conversational processes are ones of local interaction in the sense that each participant is acting on his or her own local organising themes. This local interaction produces emergent patterns of meaning for participants in the sense that there is no blueprint for that meaning. I am suggesting, then, that conversations are complex responsive processes. Speakers take turns that are organised by certain principles that have themselves emerged out of the history of interaction in the community to which the speakers belong.

The principles of turn taking have to do with how one person speaks at a time; how it may, or may not, be permissible to interrupt or talk over others; how the number and order of speakers varies; how turn sizes vary; how turn transition is accomplished; what kind of gaps and overlaps occur in turn taking; how the turns themselves are allocated. These organising principles evolve, and so come to differ from one historical period to another and from one locality to another. For example, in many organisations the most senior executive is automatically granted more and longer turns than anyone else, and in others one may notice that men take more turns than women.

Sacks and others have also pointed to the manner in which turns tend to be organised into what they call 'adjacent pairs'. So conversational exchanges may be organised into greeting–greeting, question–answer, invitation–acceptance (rejection), summons–answer, request–response and so on. Speakers create turns with recipients in mind and listeners are motivated to hear their turn, all in local interaction. Speakers tend to pursue a response until they are acknowledged and those being addressed are under pressure to respond to the meaning emerging between them. This requirement to respond does not mean that grammatical sentences are always used. In fact, ordinary conversation is characterised by grunts, other noises such as 'mm', pauses and fragments of sentences. The listener is thus co-creating the meaning by a constructive process of filling in. The result is the highly associative nature of ordinary, everyday conversation.

Boden talks about different kinds of conversation:

> From the basic elements of conversational turn taking, what Sacks and his collaborators proposed was that other speech exchange systems such as meetings, classrooms, interviews, debates, and even the most ritual of ceremonies would span a kind of continuum. The central differences between casual, freely occurring conversation and the kinds of exchanges listed depend primarily upon such issues as: allocation and duration of turns, selection and order of potential speakers, and designation and order of topic, as well as a specific method for ensuring that each speaker is heard and that discussion does not break down into mini conversations. In meetings and on conference calls, the structuring methods of turn-taking are indeed modified . . . but the core of organizational communication remains this simple, reciprocal and self organizing system.
>
> (Boden, 1994, pp. 72–3)

In their sophisticated, associative turn taking, participants in conversation co-create meaningful patterns over time which can be described as themes.

The thematic patterning of ordinary conversation

Each member of a group has his or her own personal organising themes that have been taken up in the silent conversation, or mind, of that individual. They reflect his or her own personal history of relations with, and between, others in the community he or she lives in. As soon as members of a group meet each other, they all actively, albeit largely unconsciously, select, and so organise, their own subjective experience of being in that place, with those people, at that time. However, what those particular themes are at that particular moment will depend just as much on the cues being presented by others as upon the personal history of a particular individual. Each is simultaneously evoking and provoking responses from others so that the particular personal organising themes emerging will depend as much on the others as on the individual concerned. Furthermore, since everyone is also, largely unconsciously, taking the attitude of the generalised other in all their interactions, particular organising themes of individuals also depend on the wider communities of which they are members. Put like this, it becomes clear that no one individual can be organising his or her experience in isolation because all are simultaneously evoking and provoking responses in each other and simultaneously taking up the attitude of the generalised other. Together they immediately constitute intersubjective, recursive processes. These are continuous back-and-forth circular processes in which themes emerge that organise the experience of being together out of which further themes continuously emerge.

Relationships between people in a group can then be defined as continuously iterated patterns of *intersubjective themes that organise the experience of being together*. These themes emerge, in variant and invariant forms, out of the interaction between group members as they organise that very interaction. I want to stress, however, that I am not suggesting that these themes are disembodied interactions.

Although the themes emerge between people, and therefore cannot be located 'inside' any individual, the experience is nevertheless always a bodily experience. I am suggesting, then, that both personal and group themes always arise between people in a community but are always at the same time experienced in individual bodies as changes, marked or subtle, in the feeling tones of those bodies.

From this perspective, themes interact in many, many local situations in which patterns of relating continuously emerge both locally and across populations. These patterns are changes in the themes organising local interaction as group members seek to negotiate with, and respond to, each other in some way as members of a community. The patterns of organising themes are continually iterated in self-referential, reflexive ways.

Another important point to be made here about organising themes is that they arise in a particular place at a particular time. The bodies interacting with each other in a group are located in a wider context of a community and a society that has a history. This means that the group/individual themes are resonating with wider themes that organise the experience of being in a community and a society at a particular point in its history. The themes arising in a particular group, at a particular time, will thus be influenced by the figuration of power relations in the wider grouping (see Chapter 13). They will also reflect the pattern of control over economic resources and, therefore, the material, technological and physical nature of the place at a particular historical moment.

So, organising themes are continuously arising in the interaction between people, while simultaneously being experienced in their bodies, located in a particular community, in a particular place, at a particular point in the history of the community and the group. Note that this is very different from saying that members of a group share the values of the community and the society in which they are located. It is saying that at a particular time there will be salient themes organising the experience of being together in a community. They will evoke themes organising the experience of being together in a particular group. The theme evoked in the group might be quite different from group to group. For example, a theme organising the experience of being together in a community might have to do with condemning asylum seekers. Groups of established residents and groups of asylum seekers in the community will not be sharing a common theme. However, both groups will be responding to the same theme in a different way.

The thematic patterning nature of ordinary, everyday conversation can be very easily seen by asking a group of people to play a word game. One member of the group is asked to start with any word he or she chooses and the others are asked to respond. What always happens is this. One word almost always triggers a response, usually by association, from another person and that response triggers yet another and so on. Within a very short time, a theme emerges. For example, the theme may have to do with the weather, with body parts, with places, with moods, or whatever. Some people may try to break the associative links and if they succeed another theme begins to emerge. Even when people try very hard not to associate but to keep breaking the links, it turns out to be rather difficult to keep it going. This is exactly what happens in ordinary conversation: a theme emerges and the talk swirls around this theme, until some remark triggers the emergence of some other theme. The dynamic, the pattern of movement over time, has the paradoxical characteristics of regularity and irregularity at the same time. What themes will emerge and how they will change are not predictable. However, there are coherent themes, order, even though there is no plan or blueprint for them. And the themes do not come about by chance. They emerge in what people are doing and not doing both intentionally and unconsciously.

Intention

Intention is a communication between people, and like any other communication it is expressed in conversation. It is a particular kind of theme and it organises experience just as any other theme does. Intentional themes may also be expressed explicitly or implicitly in a narrative theme (*see* Chapter 14). All of these intentional themes are gestures that provoke or evoke responses in others. Those articulating the intention then find that these responses, in turn, evoke or provoke responses from them and they will not be able to know in advance just how these responses, and response to responses, will evolve. The theories of strategic choice and organisational learning, as well as psychoanalytic perspectives on organisations, take intention for granted. They assume that the formation of an intention is the starting point of action, as thought before action. Intention is not problematic. People simply decide as autonomous individuals because of an innate capacity to do so. However, when one comes to regard intention as a theme that organises the experience of being together it becomes clear that intentions emerge in relationships just as any other organising themes do. Intention, then, emerges in the conversational life of a group of people. A single individual does not simply 'have' an intention. Rather the intention an individual expresses has emerged in the conversational interaction with others. Intention and choice are not lonely acts but themes organised by and organising relationships at the same time. Everything that everyone does, or does not do, matters in what is always local conversational interaction. So what are we doing and not doing in organisational conversation?

Rhetoric

Shotter (1993) talks about experience being organised in what he calls the rhetorical-responsive conversations of ordinary, everyday life. What he means by this is that people continually account for themselves to each other. They continually respond to what others are doing and try to persuade others to take the position they want. This conversational activity organises experience. Shotter explores how groups of people come to a more articulate grasp of their practices from within their ongoing conduct of them. Shotter and Katz (1997) talk about a relational-responsive form of understanding between people in their ordinary everyday conversation. In their ordinary forms of language they:

> deconstruct the routine links and relations between things once constructed and then taken for granted. In this way, new possibilities are revealed. People do this in the directive use of words: by saying 'Look at that', 'Look at this', people can lead others and themselves to notice important features of their circumstances. In ordinary conversation, people arrest or interrupt each other in order to deconstruct and destabilise so that they can make new distinctions and so create new knowledge. They also use analogies, metaphors, and other ways of making comparisons to develop new ways of talking. It is in talk like this that people are moved.
> (Shotter and Katz, 1997, p. 5)

Here Shotter is pointing to the *rhetorical* nature of ordinary conversation. This is a very important point: new knowledge can emerge in ordinary, everyday conversation as people go on together and seek to persuade and negotiate with each other. As mentioned in Chapter 7, Samra-Fredericks (2003), arguing in the emerging tradition of activity-based strategy, has drawn on Shotter's work and on an analysis of the conversational activity of strategising to indicate how the rhetorical skills of the strategiser are key to the influence exerted.

Rhetoric is the art of persuasion and Springett (1998) categorises rhetorical ploys as follows:

- Those that influence the direction of conversation. Under this heading, he includes statements that invoke a sense of purpose, as when someone says, 'these are *the* objectives'. Then there are silencing moves such as not responding to a point made but rapidly raising another. There are also moves that block a direction, such as 'this is really Stone Age stuff'. Some moves contract the line of conversation, such as 'let's concentrate on the key points'. Other moves expand the line of conversation, such as 'there must be other ways to think about this'. Yet other moves give emphasis, such as 'this is the way we must go'.

- Those that provide frames of reference. This takes place when someone uses other companies as examples of the successful application of their ideas.

- Those that make claims to be the truth, such as 'the latest research shows', or 'customers feel'.

- Those that destabilise, such as 'Does that really add anything?'

- Those that influence beliefs about what is real and possible. Examples are making the intangible seem tangible, such as talking about a merger as a 'marriage', referring to a company as if it were a person and using statements like 'let me walk you through this'. Another example is a move that implies pre-existence, such as talking about unlocking a company's potential.

- Those that construct urgency, such as 'there is a short time window'.

The point is this: without even being aware of it, people in ordinary conversation may be using conversational devices to dismiss the opinions of others and close down the development of a conversation in an exploratory direction. If this way of talking to each other is widespread in an organisation, it will inevitably keep reproducing the same patterns of talk. The use of some rhetorical device is therefore one of the most important blockages to fluid conversation and thus the emergence of new knowledge. Other rhetorical devices, however, could have the effect of freeing these blockages. The use of rhetorical devices is thus of major importance in influencing what people talk about and do. This is how strategy happens and what change is about.

Conversation, strategy and change

Shaw (2002) draws attention to the importance of ordinary conversations in organisations as the processes in which change emerges. In such ordinary conversations, what is being talked about is often unclear in many respects and the lack of clarity is the very reason for having the conversation. We come to know what we are talking about from within the development of the conversation itself, even when a topic has been agreed in advance. Shaw argues that ordinary conversations do not take the form of one person saying something, others listening in order to understand what is said, and then formulating a response. Instead, people speak into one another's responses, so responsively shaping what they say in the very process of conversing. When people understand what they are doing in conversation as clarifying information, reaching shared understandings, developing orderly agreements and plans and capturing outputs, they lose awareness of the ongoing mutually constructive nature of what they are doing together. Shaw argues that the widespread demand that management meetings should be carefully planned and prepared actually kills the spontaneity of ordinary conversation in which new meaning can emerge. She points out how consultants and managers try to agree, in advance of starting a conversation, on the ground rules for good communication, such as listening carefully, respecting the views of others, suspending judgements and surfacing assumptions. The result is a set of idealised rules that change the nature of the conversation and limit its ordinary spontaneity.

As a consultant, Shaw seeks to foster fluid, more spontaneous conversation through the way in which she participates in ordinary conversations in organisations. She does not decide in advance what role she is going to take at a meeting. Instead, she joins the meeting and leaves unspecified what the rules of interaction should be. After the meeting she does not try to abstract what was learned, nor does she make summaries and action plans to provide feedback to anyone anywhere. She argues that as people continue to meet and talk with others in other settings they will remember what was relevant in previous conversations. She does all this to avoid the rigidity that people impose on meetings in organisations and to restore something of the ordinary spontaneity of conversation.

What Shaw is drawing attention to is those aspects of processes of change that are excluded in orderly accounts of organisation change initiatives. She is drawing attention to the importance of ordinary conversation in processes of change and such ordinary conversation is characterised by random as well as intended encounters. As people go about conversing in an ordinary manner, they purposefully make connections with others but often without a set of clearly defined objectives. They participate in situations where they have only an incomplete grasp of what is happening. In doing this ordinary process of relating, they are forming and transforming, they are perpetually constructing their future in the living present.

The point, then, is that whatever people do is accomplished in local conversational interaction which always has some thematic pattern that organises the experience of being together. Themes trigger other themes that trigger yet others in repetitive ways that often have some potential for transformation given that any small difference from one iteration to another could be escalated into a different theme. In talking about ordinary conversation in this way, I am saying something about the dynamics of conversation, that is, the patterns of movement over time.

11.4 The dynamics of conversation

As argued above, the thematic patterning of conversation is iterated over time as both repetition and *potential* transformation at the same time. However, this potential need not always be realised. When it is not, the themes emerging in and organising the conversation become highly repetitive and, when this happens, conversation loses its lively, energising characteristics as a group of people may get stuck in repetitive, emotionally dulling exchanges (Foulkes, 1948). Change can only emerge in fluid forms of conversation. However, it is important to understand that fluid conversation is not some pure form of polar opposition to repetition. Rather, 'fluid' conversation refers to thematic pattering, which is paradoxically repetitive and spontaneously transforming at the same time. The repetitive aspects of conversational patterning promote continuity, imparting the stability to social relations required to enable people to go on together. This kind of stability is what is meant by the term 'social structure'.

Social structure is usually defined as the repetitive and enduring patterns of recurring relations between people in their ongoing dealings with each other. Examples of social structures are economic phenomena such as patterns of relationships between the owners of capital and the providers of labour. Markets are patterns of relationships between suppliers and demanders of goods and services and as such constitute social structures. Other examples of social structures are state and government functions; legal relationships; technological development; the family; religious practices; language; demography. Institutions and social structures are characterised by repetition and endurance reflected in widely accepted discourses. Organisations may be thought of as institutions with a significant element of formal description of roles, relationships between members and the tasks they perform. Closely linked to the ideas of social structure, institutions and organisations are the notions of habits, customs, traditions, routines, mores, norms, values, cultures, paradigms, beliefs, missions and visions. These are all ideas about the repetitive, enduring practices of people in their ongoing dealings with each other in institutional life.

From a complex responsive processes perspective, these are all social acts of a particular kind. They are couplings of gesture and response of a predictable, repetitive kind. They do not exist in any meaningful way as a thing in a store or artefact anywhere. Social habits and routines, values and beliefs are emerging aspects of the thematic patterning of interaction between people. Habits here are understood not as shared mental contents but as history-based, repetitive communicative interactions, both private and public, reproduced in the living present with relatively little variation. They are aspects of the continually iterated interactions between people. In other words, they are habitual themes organising the experience of being together. However, even habits are rarely exactly the same. They may often vary as the contexts and participants in interactions change. In other words, there will usually be some spontaneous variation in the repetitive reproduction of patterns called habits and it is this that creates the *potential* for transformation. An important factor sustaining habitual, repetitive conversation, one which blocks more fluid, spontaneous conversation, is anxiety.

Anxiety

Anxiety is a generalised form of fear. While fear has a known cause, anxiety is a very unpleasant feeling of general unease, the cause of which cannot be located. Chapter 5 on psychoanalytic perspectives reviewed the important contribution that psychoanalytic perspectives make to an understanding of the organisational effects of anxiety. First, there are the defences people use to avoid feeling anxious. These may take the form of structures and procedures having the ostensible purpose of enabling some rational task, but actually operating as defences. For example, people may prepare forecasts of future states that are impossible to predict and develop strategic plans on the basis of these forecasts. Such plans may then have little impact on what is actually done but by creating a sense of certainty defend people against the anxiety of feeling uncertain. The result is stable, repetitive conversational dynamics around strategies that are simply a continuation of what is already being done. An alternative form of defence is what Bion (1961) called basic assumption behaviour. Here people in groups are overwhelmed by volatile fight, flight, dependence and other dynamics that disable their thinking capacity. Conversations are organised by fantasy themes that produce highly unrealistic conversational stability or conversational disintegration. The former are present when the basic assumption is dependence and the latter when it takes the form of fight–flight.

Chapter 5 also introduced the important psychoanalytic concept of 'good enough holding'. Here conditions are such that people are able to live with the simultaneous excitement and anxiety of conversations that test the boundary of what they know. The 'good enough holding' of anxiety is an essential condition for the fluid, spontaneous conversational dynamics that are the analogue of the edge of chaos. I suggest that 'good enough holding' is a quality of the themes organising the experience of relating. When these take the form of trusting interaction, they are themselves then forms of 'good enough holding' that enable people to live with anxiety. In other words, when the quality of relating is characterised by trust, conversation can take more fluid forms. This interpretation of 'good enough holding' differs from the psychoanalytic interpretation in that it does not locate the 'good enough' in a leader or a consultant (Stapley, 1996) but in the quality of conversational interaction itself.

Closely related to the 'good enough holding' of anxiety is the matter of the quality of power relations (see Chapter 13). Themes organising relating between people may be highly constraining so that power relations have the qualities of force, authoritarianism, dictatorship and so forth. The responses that these qualities evoke are either submission or rebellion. The former produce highly repetitive, stable conversational patterns, while the latter produce disintegration in communication. Sometimes, the themes organising the relating between people impose very little constraint. This is equivalent to saying that relational ties are very weak and, therefore, patterns of conversation are likely to be disrupted. The conversational dynamics are disintegrative. It is a critical range that is associated with fluid conversation, this time a critical range in the constraining qualities of relating.

The crucial distinction I am making here is that between more fluid conversation and patterns of conversation that take on a repetitive, stuck form. This is crucial because it is only in the former that potential creativity, that is, emergent new patterns of conversation, lies. A healthy, functioning organisation is one in which its members continually respond to each other and to members of other organisations – they provoke and evoke responses from others and react to the provocations and evocations of others so as to survive in an uncertain world of experience. For this to happen, communication must flow freely and not get caught in repetitive themes. This means that the themes organising experience must interact so as to flow continually along new pathways. An ailing organisation is one in which communication is blocked.

The capacity for emergent new ways of talking is fundamental to organisational creativity. If this is so, then it is a matter of considerable strategic importance to pay attention to the dynamics of ordinary conversation. The purpose of this attention is not to control the conversation or somehow produce efficient forms of it but to understand it so as to participate more effectively. The dynamics of more fluid, spontaneous conversation rely on enough trust and ability to live with anxiety, as well as power relations that are both co-operative and competitive at the same time and rhetorical conversational practices that do not block exploration. Key questions become: What conversational practices block fluid, exploratory conversations? What practices trap groups of people in highly repetitive conversations?

11.5 Leaders and the activities of strategising

So far, this chapter has argued that organisations are patterns of interaction between interdependent persons. Processes of human interaction are fundamentally conversational in nature. Not only do people accomplish and change their joint activities in these processes, their very identities are sustained and potentially transformed in them too. Conversational dynamics in organisations are thus of primary importance. Whether such conversational dynamics take the form of stuck, repetitive patterns or of more fluid, spontaneous ones depends upon the nature of power relations between people, the way they find it possible to deal with the inevitable anxieties of organisational life and the conversational practices, particular rhetorical practices, they have together evolved. Repetitive conversations block the emergence of innovative strategies while more fluid forms of conversation create the possibility but by no means the guarantee that creative strategies will emerge. The activity of strategising is also, on this view, fundamentally conversational.

A particular view of the role of leader follows from the claim that creative organisational strategies are more likely to emerge in more fluid, spontaneous forms of conversation. Instead of understanding the role of leadership purely in terms of directing and exhorting followers, one comes to see leadership in perhaps humbler but no less skilful or important terms. Given the power relation of the leader to others, he or she is in a particularly well-placed position to create opportunities for conversation that may foster greater spontaneity. Such spontaneity is likely to be fostered through the manner in which the leader handles a situation, encouraging others to create and shape the situation rather than simply giving instructions. The founder of group analysis, Foulkes (1964) took the view that it was the primary role of the therapy group conductor to deepen and widen communication in the group through the manner of his or her participation in the group. What Foulkes has to say could just as easily be applied to leaders in other situations where it is important to help create fluid forms of conversation. Foulkes called upon the leader to apply the

minimum of instructions, of program or of rules, and maximum of freedom in self expression, a maximum of active participation in what is going on. The keynote . . . is informality and spontaneity of contributions which leads to what I have described as 'free-floating discussion'. The conductor gives a minimum of instructions and there are no set topics, no planning. While he is in the position of a leader, he is sparing with leading the group actively. He weans the group from wanting to be led – a desire which is all too strong – from looking upon him as an authority for guidance.   (Foulkes, 1964, p. 40)

This situation promotes active participation that awakens interest and communication in an atmosphere enabling people to search for meaning for themselves. The group provides support by sharing anxiety and the leader lets his or her own contributions come in response to the members of the group. The leader is a participant, whose his aim is to encourage others towards taking responsibility. He or she resists the inevitable idealisation of the leader and seeks to replace submission with co-operation and explorative conflict. For Foulkes, the leader has self-confidence that comes from modesty, courage, social responsibility. The leader *participates* in the simultaneously social and individual processes of exploring together our way of life as members of our organisation. However, although he or she participates as others do there is also a very important difference, namely, that he/she is more powerful. This power difference is a very important part of the relationships between every one in the group. The leader almost always comes to occupy an important part in the fantasy lives of others, no matter how much he or she tries to resist this. The skilled leader pays particular attention to the unconscious aspects of the communicative interaction between group members and seeks to avoid taking for granted or exacerbating power differentials, all in the interests of encouraging more fluid forms of conversation. This does not involve abdicating power in any way nor does it mean that the leader never moves into highly directing roles where appropriate.

11.6 Summary

This chapter started by looking at Mead's explanation of how the important human attributes of consciousness and self-consciousness emerge in local social interactions. He argued that such interactions take the form of the conversation of gestures in which the very selves of interdependent people are constituted. Local interaction between people in organisations can, then, be understood to be fundamentally conversational in nature. Drawing on ethnomethodological studies the chapter pointed to the turn-taking and turn-making structure of conversations. It went on to describe how meaningful themes emerge in ordinary conversation which organise the experience of people being together. Organisational strategies can be understood as such emerging themes. On this view the dynamics of ordinary everyday conversation become of crucial importance for the qualities of the activities of strategising. The emergence of novel strategies depends upon the practice of more fluid, spontaneous forms of conversation. The possibility of such conversational dynamics occurring depends up the conversational practices that have evolved in an organisation, on the manner in which anxiety is dealt with and on the nature of the power relations between people.

Further reading

Useful further reading is provided by Burkitt (1991), Shotter (1993), Steier (1991), Stacey (2001, 2003), Shaw (2002) and Shaw and Stacey (2005). Also refer to Boden (1994) and Samra-Fredericks (2003).

Questions to aid further reflection

1. In what ways does Mead's theory of communication differ from that to be found in the dominant discourse on organisations?
2. What does self-consciousness mean in Mead's theory?
3. Why would fluid forms of conversation be important in strategising?
4. What role does anxiety play in strategising?
5. If fluid conversation is important for the emergence of novel strategies then what is the role of the leader?
6. How would you understand your own involvement in the strategising activities of your organisation?

Reflective management narrative 1

At the time of writing this reflective narrative, Nol Groot was the managing director of a division of a large services company. He tells the story of what begins as a very general strategy to cut costs and how one suggestion for doing this is the merger of the National and International sales offices of two divisions of his company. It takes over two years before the merger is accomplished and, as he reflects on how this was done, he comes to question his taken-for-granted assumptions about what strategy actually is. When he compares his experience of strategy in these events over two years he finds a mismatch between this experience and the usual view of strategy as a systematic plan of action formulated by top executives and then implemented by others. Instead, the experience was one of ongoing conversations involving not only top executives but many other members of his organisation, all of whom had interests in, and views on, what was happening and what should happen. The process was exploratory and political, characterised by personal relationships, people falling ill or retiring, personal rivalries and anxiety. It became clear to him that strategy emerges in the social interweaving of (different) intentions and actions by all groupings involved. New strategic issues were emerging, leading to actions not at all related to the original intention of management. The points that stand out for me in his account are as follows:

- How strategies emerge in the interplay of many intentions (*see* Chapter 10) in conversational processes (*see* Chapter 11).

- How the initial strategies of senior executives arise in their local interaction and take the form of gestures to others in the organisation, which evoke responses from others in many, many other local interactions. Strategies emerge in the interplay of gestures and responses (*see* Chapter 12).

- How patterns of power relations shift during the strategy process, reflecting the dynamics of inclusion and exclusion which are constitutive of identity (*see* Chapter 13).

- How strategy is patterned as narrative (*see* Chapter 14).

Strategic development of a merger: formulating and implementing at the same time

by Nol Groot

This reflective narrative describes a two and a half year merger process between the sales and distribution offices of the International and National divisions of a large services company. Approximately 1,500 people and 40 regional sales offices were directly involved in this merger. I focus attention on micro-strategising activities and leadership, exploring how thinking in terms of complex responsive processes (Stacey, 2003) affected how I worked in this situation. I point to how groupings of different departments play a part in the merger process through their changing positions and shifting power relations, reflected in the dynamics of inclusion and exclusion and the effect this has on their identities (Elias, 1978, [1939] 2000; Elias and Scotson, [1965] 1994; Iterson *et al.*, 2002; Soeters and Iterson, 2002). If, from a complex responsive perspective, I see organisations as patterns of interaction between people who have to live and work with the outcome of strategic developments, it becomes important to work with strategic questions in this community. I invite people to co-develop strategic answers in diverse settings and groupings as part of their day-to-day work, leading most of the time to new unexpected outcomes. Asking strategic questions can also surface insider and outsider relations (Elias and Scotson, [1965] 1994), in which diverse groupings develop or damage their co-operation, making this an important point in strategic development. The following narrative describes the trial-and-error process of formulation and implementation of strategy at the same time and my own shifting of thinking about strategy as the interplay of intentions in conversational processes.

Organisational background: established–outsider relations

The National and International divisions both operated through the same sales and distribution department unit until five years ago, when the International Division decided to develop its own sales and distribution department. The National offices were then separated from the International offices and staff had to choose where they wanted to work. Although they continued to be located next to each other, and often shared back office facilities, a psychological divide arose between the people involved in which they came to regard each other and themselves as the 'International elite' and the 'workers'. The people working at the International desks were paid on higher grades and this led to some envy.

This situation did not attract my attention when I became responsible for the division in which the national sales and distribution activities were located but it was later to become very important. Looking back and reflecting on the way these group formations played an important role in what subsequently happened, I find it helpful to turn to Elias and Scotson ([1965] 1994). They describe 'established and outsider relations' in a small community in England which led to people thinking about themselves as being superior or inferior to each other, so establishing power differences between two interdependent groups. The only real difference in this community was that people in one area had been there longer than the others. This small difference was used to establish major differences between groups through labelling in streams of blame and praise gossip (Soeters and Iterson, 2002). For Elias, power was not something pos-

sessed by one group or person and not by another but, rather, a structural characteristic of all human relationships in every situation (Elias, 1978). Elias held that people are not autonomous but always live in figurations of power relations taking the form of 'we' and 'them' (Elias, 1978). The difference between the groups of International and National were pay grade and the feeling that International sales were more complicated. In gossip terms they were called the 'ladies with the pearl necklaces'. The real differences, however, were relatively small. Personal identity is connected to these 'we' and 'them' relationships. Such group dynamics do not feature much as important factors to take into account in most approaches to strategy but, as I will explore later, they can be very influential.

Round one: cost reduction through co-operation as strategic choice

With all of this in the background, the Executive Board, of which I am a member, had budget meetings to investigate ways of improving the company's financial results. The management of the International Division was not present at this meeting. So even though that division had budget problems because of low-cost operators entering their markets, attention was nationally focused where we sought to identify areas where we could perform more effectively and efficiently. My colleague Gerald, managing director of the Commercial Department, and I proposed developing co-operation between the National and International desks with a view to increasing efficiency and lowering costs, or increasing service levels for our clients. This was not a worked-out plan but emerged as a possible intention worth following up. So after we had discussed the idea with the others present, we decided that the two of us should meet the management of International and share our ideas with them. Knowing that they had financial problems and were looking for more efficiency too, we expected that the idea would find a warm welcome. We also knew that some of the members of the management group at International were going to move to other positions soon and that a new managing director was preparing to take over.

The national sales and distribution department was part of my division but the Commercial

Division was responsible for sales and marketing strategy and they financed the offices in which we worked, playing an important role in decisions about the layout and image of the offices as well as the presentation of our staff. Two weeks later, Gerald and I informed the management of International about the meeting we had and the idea we wanted to discuss with them. They did not explode with enthusiasm, which often happens when colleagues start introducing ideas concerning your business, but they listened carefully. In the end they followed our argument and we decided to ask the responsible directors and personnel managers of both divisions to investigate whether this approach could lead to an acceptable form of co-operation between our sales offices and reduce costs enough to make it worthwhile putting the energy in. Four of the directors and managers had their first two meetings in December, two months after the board meeting, and agreed to meet again the next January.

In the meantime I confidentially informed our Staff Council about the plans we were starting to develop. I did not want to surprise them and was curious about their initial reaction. They liked the idea and I promised them I would involve them the minute it became serious business. Some European countries have a two-tier board structure, consisting of a Supervisory Board and a Management (Executive) Board, and in addition they have introduced a Staff Council structure by law. This law ensures that the rights and interests of employees are respected by management in relation to matters of labour conditions and company strategy. The Staff Council has to approve a request for change in labour conditions and they have a right to give advice on company strategy. Both parties have the right to appeal to a labour court if one feels that the other did not follow the proper rules. In most companies, the Staff Council has a right to appoint one or more Supervisory Board members. This structure reduces the direct influence of unions in the company, as happens in the UK and the USA, because it is the Staff Councils that have a direct interest in the success or failure of a company. Based on the size of the company, the number of elected members of a Staff Council ranges from 3 to 21 and elections take place every two or three years. In large companies with several structural levels, such as divisions, each division will have its own Staff Council with representatives of these Councils forming a central Staff Council at the top level to meet with the president of the company. During the election process unions play a role in proposing and supporting union member candidates.

Under normal circumstances, management builds up a good working relationship with the Staff Council and part of this involves informing its chairman when new developments appear on the horizon but have not yet reached formal discussion status. In general, the Staff Council structure creates more balanced relations between workers and management, which results in fewer strikes than in many other countries. On the other hand, international companies mostly hate this 'talk culture', as they call it. However, I think co-operative talks can solve many issues before they become problems.

The plan stops: strategic decision making in isolation

In the second week of January, my colleague Genevieve, one of the directors of sales and services in my division called me. Anxiously she said, 'The new managing director of International, Robert, is going to call you in a few minutes to tell you that they have changed their strategy and will present a recovery plan for their division which involves shifting most of their sales activities to the Internet while maintaining telesales and reducing the workforce by 250 people, including almost all the 150 staff members of the International sales offices.' She had also heard that they had consulted union leaders and their Staff Council and planned to release a press statement soon. However, the former managing director had suddenly fallen ill so that Robert, who had not even started his new job yet, had to take over and was about to inform all employees of the changes. It was Genevieve who had urged him to call the managing directors of the other divisions and tell us what his plans were. I was speechless when I heard the news, especially since colleagues from his and my division were investigating a possible merger of the sales offices. However, the only concern Genevieve and I had at that point was the effect this message would have on our 1,000-plus sales and information people who were working in close proximity to International sales staff and had originally been one team who all knew each other well. We decided to inform our site managers about what was going to happen and assure them that this would have no effect on our operation.

That afternoon there were no international sales – all the International offices were closed because staff members were engaged in emotional meetings. After a while I explained to our Staff Council what had happened.

Back to business as usual

We then had to look for other opportunities to improve our performance and lower our costs. We also had to visit all our offices to regain the confidence of our own teams and reduce the fear of 'today it is them, tomorrow it is us'. Despite the assurances, however, the doubts remained and it took us some time to get everybody back to normal. Even more surprising was the fact that after a few days the International sales staff went back to work and took up their daily activities as if nothing had happened. However, we heard that they had little confidence in what was going to happen and no idea how rapidly the shift from personal selling to Internet sales would be. At the time of the decision, 6 per cent of International sales went through the Internet and the plan was that this would be increased to more than 60 per cent over two years. The Staff Council of the International Division withdrew in protest, leaving management without any means of formally communicating the change in strategy.

It was also surprising that none of this was discussed at the Executive Board. During this period International was not in the mood to seek co-operation and my Executive Board colleagues and I just let it go, since we thought it was not crucial to the short-term developments of the whole Group. Furthermore, it was in accordance with the overall strategy of increasing Internet sales and electronic ticketing. After Robert took his new place at the Executive Board, we started to work together and I developed a better understanding of how he was trying to restore results in his division. However, he did not ask anybody for help, so he was very much on his own. Also, at that time I started to prepare for negotiations with the unions about a new labour agreement for the Group and so had many other things to do.

Renewal of personal acquaintance and restart of co-operation

In October, twelve months later, I was interviewing my colleagues on their ideas about the coming labour agreement negotiation. Robert and I decided to have lunch together to exchange our views. We both had the feeling that it would be a wise idea to get to know each other better, since we were sitting together around the same table at every board meeting. My attitude was still one of keeping a certain distance. After exchanging formalities, I tried to explain why I had kept my distance. I asked why they had not only stopped the talks at the end of the previous year but had also chosen not to inform us in advance. Robert gave two reasons: first, the former management had told him that we could not be trusted and acted only to serve our own interests; and, second, they wanted to be sure that none of their ideas would leak out before they were ready to present them.

After continuing our conversation, he understood that I felt offended and did not want to have anything to do with the developments of the International Division. He also admitted that if he had the chance to do it again he would make different choices, including carrying on with our talks about integrating the sales offices. The development of Internet sales was unlikely to meet the original expectations of an increase to 60 per cent in two years because after one year it had only moved up to 8 per cent, which meant that the International sales offices would have to remain open. From a personal point of view, I liked Robert, and so after a while I accepted his suggestion to restart the integration talks. I knew that our division had some extra financial resources that would enable us to absorb part of his staff and that the rest could come from his reorganisation funds. Together we would be able to raise sufficient funds to integrate and so cut costs while developing the future of electronic ticketing. A complete restructuring of tasks and responsibilities would take place for all our operational staff, which would enable us to save a great deal of money without incurring any job losses and so, we hoped, avoid any unacceptable social conflict. We decided to reopen talks with the same people who were present ten months earlier.

Reflections on strategy

The events I have described so far affected the whole of the International Division, as well as large parts of the National Division, and they had potential long-term consequences for the whole Group. They are, therefore, what most people would call strategic. How can I make sense of the strategising activities in this story? Or better, how can I understand strategy and strategic management in the light of the above events and my long working experience? What is the role and influence of all the people working in this strategy process, apart from continually being surprised? To develop a better understanding of what was happening, I first want to focus on the broad notion of strategy.

A few years ago I would have defined 'strategy' as an 'elaborate and systematic plan of action'. When I now look back at the events of the last two years and compare my experiences with this statement, I am struck by a number of points. You could say that the story so far displays elaborate patterns of action but they hardly constitute a systematic plan. A systematic plan would normally take the form of a clear decision reached after analysis of the facts, followed by a clear sequence of implementation steps, which all concerned follow. This clearly did not happen – it was all much more exploratory and political, characterised by personal relationships, people falling ill or retiring, personal rivalries, and possibly the anxiety of Robert when he suddenly discovered that he was on his own, leading him to forget to involve his colleague managing directors. Instead, when I reflect on the above events, it becomes clear to me that through the social interweaving of (different) intentions and actions by all groupings involved (Elias, [1939] 2000, p. 436), new strategic issues were emerging, leading to other actions not at all related to the original intention of the management of the International Division. On the first day of the announcement, all International sales offices were closed and staff members were engaged in emotional meetings. Pretty soon after the emotional reaction of staff, the question took over whether management had made the right decision to move in the direction of totally automated sales and whether our clients had the ability to use these new technologies. People were worried whether this new system would lead to the loss of a great number of customers. The reactions of staff and customers caused doubt in the minds of International's management, making this a story of stopping and starting, where the demarcations between formulating and implementing strategy are far from clear.

I now see that my earlier, taken-for-granted, clear statement about strategy does not describe what happened. Robert and I, seeing the outcome of the processes so far, could say that our strategy processes had failed. Were we incompetent? On the other hand, it could be that simple definitions of strategy are unrealistic in practice. Perhaps strategy needs to be looked at in different ways. But what different ways are there?

The definition of strategy in standard textbooks runs along the following lines: 'top management's plan to attain outcomes consistent with the organization's missions and goals' (Wright *et al.*, 1992, p. 3). However, many authors do not consider the definition of strategy to be a simple matter and provide a broad spectrum of views. For example, Mintzberg *et al.* (1998) present a complete guide to nine 'strategic schools of thought'. They focus on two major lines of thinking. The prescriptive schools are built around planning and design, reflecting the above standard definition of strategy, and are more concerned with how strategies *should be* formulated than with how they *are actually* formed. The descriptive schools are developed around the learning aspects of strategy and more concerned with ideal strategic behaviour than prescribing how strategies should be formulated. Volberda and Elfring (2001) link to the work of Mintzberg and take a 'Synthetic Approach' that incorporates all of the nine schools. A synthesising school of thought in strategic management consists of more than one base discipline and one set of problem-solving techniques to deal with a specific range of strategic problems. They have analysed three emerging schools of thought with synthesising characteristics: the configuration school, the dynamic school and the boundary school. Volberda and Elfring see these classifications as an improvement on some previous attempts which simply distinguish between 'content' versus 'process' and 'strategy formulation' versus 'implementation', leading to more fragmentation in the field of strategy instead of contributing to strategy synthesis and bringing schools of thought together.

▶

The confusing conclusion so far is that strategy is a complicated matter and that all approaches seem useful in one way or another, providing choices that, taken on their own, do not really help practitioners such as me to go further. We can conclude that our knowledge of strategy and management is fragmented, unstructured and inconsistent, even self-contradictory (De Wit and Meyer, 2005). Whittington (2001) does not give any answers, but encourages managers to start thinking differently about strategy. Members of the academic community increasingly argue that the concepts and tools of analysis that have formed the backbone of the strategy literature during its major growth period need a basic re-evaluation in order to pave the way for new ideas (Volberda and Elfring, 2001). I could continue with a longer list of statements by other authors, all telling us practitioners that there is no general recipe for strategy and all encouraging us to use our own brains and senses in developing our strategic awareness.

As we created a second chance for ourselves in the merger of the two sales and distribution departments, we needed to ask ourselves whether other approaches might be useful in helping us to develop new ways of strategising, which included our own awareness of our day-to-day practice. The complex responsive processes view of organisations and their strategies is that they are continually iterated processes of relating and communicating between people. The central argument of complex responsive processes perspective is that strategy is the evolving pattern of collective and individual identities and intentions, emerging in the ordinary, everyday local interactions between people (Stacey, 2001). These local interactions lead to population-wide processes that give form to emerging strategies in organisations. It is not the exclusive domain of a few top managers to create their strategy and pass it on to the rest of the organisation. Frequently, strategising activities lead to confusion and opposition which require the ongoing involvement of people in top hierarchical positions in organisations like mine.

Looking at the narrative so far and taking the events of the merger between the sales and distribution offices of International and National into account, it becomes clear that without emphasising the detailed approach and introduction of another level of participation, we would not have been able to finalise the merger with a positive outcome. The strategic world changes, and strategic innovation increasingly involves managers at the periphery, rather than just at the centre. Strategy making then becomes a continuing feature of organisational life and there is an increasing pressure for a more micro perspective and to involve people in the daily strategising process. In our case, the total separation between management formulating the new strategy and staff blocking the implementation is a good example of the necessity to rethink how to involve people performing the daily working process in strategic developments. With this in mind the missing link in the developments of International so far is the bridge between the formulation of strategy and the way a company can actually make its strategies work.

At this stage it became clear that my view on how to develop strategy had changed from the traditional top-down approach to a broader perspective in which many people play many roles, sometimes without even realising it. Small events influence the way in which the outcome is formed. Many patterns were emerging showing examples of the interplay of intentions and coincidences, leading to mostly small, but some big, steps in the strategic process when it moved forward. What looks like a systematic approach is in reality largely influenced by unexpected events. Traditional literature focuses on prescriptive schools such as the planning and design schools, advocating this systemic approach. More recent literature describes other strategic approaches in which less absolute choices are made and developed through thesis and antithesis, ending in a synthesis for that specific strategic question. The real strategic world is much more messy and unpredictable and is influenced by small incidents that have important effects. Who is present and who is absent at a meeting affects what happens afterwards. Many groupings like the Staff Councils are part of the strategising activities in which personal relationships, personal agendas and shifting coalitions are important to reach goals. During our process the effect of people not informing each other or trying to manipulate each other had great influence on progress at certain stages. Conversations, including gossip, at formal and informal meetings (Soeters and Iterson, 2002) are vital to what happens in terms of the strategic outcome.

Different groupings develop different intentions and they clash in their interplay, which leads to strategic patterns emerging across the organisational population. The interdependence of these groupings makes it very clear that one cannot live without the other. During one period the Executive Board was left out, which later turned out not to be very sensible when you need the co-operation of other colleagues. People in operations of the International Division did not play any role of importance in the top-down strategic thinking process. Their real influence, however, was significant as they were able to make the process stop or go when they wanted, making developments not very smooth and linear. Formulating and implementing in this example can be seen as one activity and top management has to remain involved.

Let us now move on to the next episode in this story of a merger.

Round two: interplay of intentions in strategic development

At the first meeting of the second round of talks with our four managers, in November after thirteen months, Robert and I shared our feeling that we had not explored all the possibilities for integrating jobs and operational responsibilities in such a way that the 150 people earmarked to leave the company could keep a job related to their experience and even maintain their same wage level. We discovered that we needed to invest more time and energy to bring our colleagues to the same level of co-operation that Robert and I were slowly approaching. Change was happening through the conversational nature of the interaction (Shaw, 2002; Shotter, 1993), formulating and implementing were happening at the same time (Pettigrew and Whipp, 1991; Stacey, 2001; Whittington, 2001) and politics was involved to convince each other and balance individual positions. At the end of the meeting everybody was ready to proceed again and appointments were made.

During the next regular Staff Council meeting, I announced that we were starting discussions again, which could mean that a greater part of the sales staff of the International Division would have jobs. They again reacted positively. Shortly after this announcement it became clear that during the period of unrest in the International Division,

people had started to move to other jobs without waiting to see how future developments would look. At three locations this was leading to a staff shortage and the management of International proposed a quick merger at these locations. My Staff Council accepted this on condition that the people coming back from International to our division would be placed at the bottom of the seniority list in each location, which meant that they would have the last choice when jobs had to be transferred to other locations. The interplay of different intentions became very obvious at this point as did the shift to the new relative positions of the established (National sales) and the outsiders (International sales).

Although one might have thought that the most important matter for the International staff would be to move from the category of 'being redundant' to 'having a job', the condition to do with seniority generated much emotion and led both the National and International groups to label the latter as 'second-class citizens' and 'rubbish'. I suddenly realised that some of the old envy felt by National staff was still there. I could understand the way of thinking of the National staff, who felt that helping others was fine provided it did not lead to higher risks of relocation, but I did not expect these strong emotions. Power relations were shifting as the International staff felt their increasing dependence on the National staff (Elias and Scotson, [1965] 1994, p. xlv).

For me, the story is one of ongoing local interactions taking the form of formal and informal conversations between small numbers of people in which they were relating to each other in ways that reflected their histories of being together, as well as their own individual histories. These local interactions are conversational and political in nature. Various intentions emerge in these conversations and those intentions interact with each other, so interweaving human activities (Elias, 1978, p. 441). The management of International decided to close their sales offices to reduce increasing losses. People in operations opposed this decision, not only because their own jobs were at stake, but also because they thought such a drastic decision dangerous for client continuity and in the long run for the continuity of the company. They also seemed to have enough power to make these developments really come to a standstill. However, on their own

▶

they were not able to reach an agreement on a new strategy without management co-operation. Small decisions, such as the pre-merger of three offices, were blocked by other groupings from National; they just would not let them in. All these events led to other outcomes, which in their turn influenced new (global) outcomes, determining the future of the company. Patterns of local interactions of (small) groups led to the emergence of global (that is, population-wide) patterns. Discussions in all sectors of the divisions concerned, and even outside of them, led to a global outcome that could not be influenced by one single grouping in the field of operation and management. These processes, however, still develop under generalised restrictions set by company management, such as 'We have to find a solution, otherwise financially we will not be able to continue to serve our clients in the same way we do today.' In other words, it is not a completely free process and it can not end anywhere with any outcome.

Robert, the managing director of International, and I were expecting to do the right things. We reopened our merger discussions, involved our Staff Councils and made a pre-merger decision solving capacity problems at three locations. Again it came to a standstill. What was going wrong? What were we doing wrong this time? We could have forced our decision on to the organization, but we didn't know what effect that would have on our plans for the near future. I consider myself a participative manager, but when I think it is necessary I will not hesitate to use power. People in operations have their own power position, influencing co-operation and the outcome of your ideas. The same power relations make people feel included or excluded in the development of strategy and the links with identity and recognition (Elias, 1978, p. 93; Elias and Scotson [1965] 1994; Griffin, 2002, pp. 197, 200). During the process up till now several things became very clear: people were taking positions, airing their ideas, wanting to be heard, using their power in closing the offices. Different groupings were more or less forcing their way into the discussion. From a complex responsive processes perspective I started to understand this form of strategy as the iteration and emergent change of the identities of various groupings and the interplay of intentions. These considerations convinced us and opened up our minds to investigate other options. Closing all the sales offices ceased to be the main target of the management of International.

Round three: exchanging new ideas with the Staff Councils

At the beginning of a new year, after fifteen months, Robert and I sat down again to think about what to do next. What had first looked like a very rational process was turning out to be far from that as the emotional conflicts between the National and International sales groups became more evident. One option to deal with this situation would be to stop the discussions and go back to the original plan of keeping the sales offices separate. However, at this stage it would mean great social instability again and, given the labour agreement negotiations at that time, could hurt more than help. So we decided against this option. Instead, we had to carry on with a full merger between the two sales and distribution departments. As stated before, we also started to understand strategy as the iteration and emergent change of the identities of various groupings and the interplay of intentions, and therefore organised another meeting with our directors and personnel managers to exchange ideas about how to take the next step. International had made their director Holger responsible for sales and marketing and he joined us for the first time. The new Staff Council of the International Division was almost reinstalled so we agreed to prepare an official letter to them to present our ideas for the full merger and ask their advice. At the same time, directors would inform staff groups of National and International at various locations and present the ideas. Robert and I would join the presentations at the biggest locations to give moral support and show that we were really serious this time.

We invited both Staff Councils to a joint presentation to exchange our ideas and present our plans. We invited them to join us during presentations to staff of both divisions on location in the country and see what kinds of questions were coming up. The meeting itself was not a great success because the Staff Council of International was new and showed mistrust regarding our intentions. I intervened one time when they doubted my trustworthiness, reacting very personally to one of their members. You could see that they were not used to a personal reaction like that. Luckily, the effect was that the atmosphere went back to normal, making the result of the meeting more or less acceptable. Everybody, however, seemed to have forgotten that the current plan was still to fire a great number of people. Due to all kinds of personal initiatives the number had been reduced to 150, but it was still substantial. Part of the discussion was about what kind of International products were going to be sold and where, despite the original intention of the management of International to stop physical sales activities. People tend to hold to their original ideas about their working situation as long as possible, so blocking any awareness of any threats, such as, in this case, the real threat of their losing jobs. In practice this means that people do not start being creative and look for new solutions in view of the changing circumstances, but strongly hold on to their idealised situation of the old structure, which in practice was not so ideal at all and had the same working problems as everywhere else.

It was our obligation to make it clear to the Staff Council of International that if no solution was found it would mean that the International sales offices would cease to exist. In the end we agreed to do our presentations personally on location and then move forward to the official part of the merger in co-operation with the Staff Councils.

Presentation(s) in the country: shifting established–outsider positions

In March, some seventeen months after the start of this story, Genevieve and Holger visited one of the smaller locations in the countryside. There were separate presentations to National and International workers, about twenty people in all. The presentations did not go very well but nor did they go badly – people reluctantly waited for things to happen. The members of the Staff Council were the ones trying to light the fire, but also with little success. The same thing happened at another smaller location with the same result. Then the first big group, about 80 people, was on the list. Robert and I would join our colleagues to show our commitment.

We started our presentation in the kitchen of the International team. This idea about the kitchen was not so bad at all, because it created a homely at-mosphere which helped the flow of the discussion. People still had many questions about their personal situations, wages, hours and future positions, but, to my surprise, they spent a long time discussing sales, disappointed clients and many other sales-related strategic subjects, which were not actually part of the discussion. During this meeting in which we expected to talk about personal expectations of people moving to another division it was a surprise to enter into discussions about the strategy of the International Division and the effects this had on customers. Even when management has made a decision, this does not mean that people dealing with this decision on a day-to-day basis will accept this as a given situation.

The presentation for the National team was in a meeting room, which was really full. The atmosphere was hostile. The possible impact of the seniority listing was blown up to gigantic proportions and our colleagues at International were taken completely off balance at so much aggression from the National sales staff. I must say I was somewhat off balance too, not really knowing what to do next. We collected all the arguments and told them we would come back to them as soon as we could.

The next day I asked Brent, one of Genevieve's colleagues who was responsible for this group, what had happened? His answer astonished me. He had stayed a little longer and talked to the group and some individuals. They told him that they had a marvellous time, that it was good to see the managing director and that they were very relieved. My experience, however, was that of going nowhere. A member of the learning group in my Doctor of Management programme suggested looking for an explanation about what happened in *The Established and The Outsiders* by Norbert Elias and John L. Scotson. Reflecting today on what had happened, it becomes clear that there had been a shift in the established–outsider relation between International and National. The identity of the last group had changed and they saw what happened as an attack on their new power superiority (Elias and Scotson, [1965] 1994, pp. xlv, xlvi).

Round four: involving people on operational levels in strategy development

What became clear during these meetings was that people working in operations do have views on how strategy should be developed in our divisions and how co-operation between our divisions could help us perform better. What does it mean to involve people in strategy making and how should it be done? Mintzberg (1987) compares strategic planning by one or more senior managers sitting in an office formulating courses of action that everyone else will implement on schedule, with someone crafting strategy. Crafting is not so much about thinking and reasoning as about involvement with the materials at hand, with feelings of intimacy and harmony developed through long experience and commitment. Formulating and implementation merge into a fluid process of learning through which creative strategies evolve.

When they talk about strategy, many managers have in mind what Mintzberg (1987a) calls deliberate strategy based on intention, formal plans and pronouncements. But can we trust these plans? Do we not often fool ourselves by denying unconscious motives? Mintzberg puts emergent strategies at the other end of the spectrum to deliberate strategies. He describes emergent strategies as strategies without clear intentions, actions simply converging into patterns (Mintzberg, 1987, p. 69). He argues that strategists have to take into account the many actors in an organisation and the 'interplay' of their actions which he understands in terms of chance. Elias (1978) also talks about emergence but as the emergence of pattern in the interplay of intentions rather than chance. He links the interplay of intentions with the development of identity and power relations.

Having had good earlier experiences in asking managers and co-workers to get involved in finding solutions for future next steps in our organizational development, I suggested to my colleagues that we ask the two responsible managers, National and International, at the ten different locations to organise a series of meetings with all their people. They would take to these meetings our basic problem: how to develop a full merger of our sales and distribution offices, taking into account the new commercial parameters of the International Division. We would help them in facilitating the meetings when required and would ask them to come back with their ideas in three month. We hoped that this would allow new patterns of interaction and intention to emerge. I did not see many other options so I phoned Robert about this idea. It did

not really surprise him that I suggested another approach, he had been at the previous emotional meetings too. He answered that he would discuss it with his team and come back to me in 24 hours.

The next day he said he embraced the idea. We also agreed to invite a member of both Staff Councils to the meetings on location to keep everybody at the same pace. Our teams started organising the joint meetings and the facilitation. The reception in the country was positive and everybody was ready to go to work. Then there was a surprise: the Staff Council of International was against the plan. They thought it was their job to give advice on this subject and that their position was undermined when the whole country started to influence the discussion. After a short deliberation Robert and I decided that we could make a management decision on the approach because this was not part of the legal rights of the Staff Council. We still gave them the possibility to team up on location, which in the end they did. The personal involvement of top management, playing an active part in these meetings, enables implementation and formulation of strategy to take place at the same time, and in the end this became one of the key success factors. If you cannot separate the processes of formulation and implementation you cannot play a distant role as a leader as this will immediately split this process into two different actions, one following the other. Influenced by the power of decision-making capacities, the managing director can speed up the development of ideas. Initiatives of middle management to involve their groupings in a strategy discussion followed by a meeting where results of these middle managers groups can be exchanged with top management creates an acceptable mixture of middle management and top management involvement, making strategy formulation and implementation possible at the same time. Top management also has the power to alleviate identity conflicts within the different groupings participating in the process of the information exchange. Again the importance of conversation is emphasised, as it is through conversation that identities are formed.

If strategising is not a top-down one-way street and we accept the alternative that strategy is developed in local interaction leading to novel global patterns, it is important to create an atmosphere that enables participants, as serious players, interactively to contribute to these processes (Stacey, 2005). The constraint for leadership is to create this atmosphere, realising that power is at play in all relations, but certainly also knowing that hierarchy is always present when opening up these non-hierarchical discussions. The need for co-operation with the Staff Councils, during the merger, shifted power relations substantially in their direction. Power relations form figurations, or groupings, in which some are included and others excluded and where power balance is tilted in favour of some groupings and against others (Elias, [1939] 2000). However, it is these groupings that will play an important role in the final outcome of the process we have initiated. Belonging to a group establishes powerful feelings, constituting each individual's 'we' identity. These 'we' identities derived from the groups we belong to, cannot be separated from the each of our 'I' identities (Stacey, 2005). Mead (1934) explains that processes of human relating form and are formed by the individual and collective identities. These processes reflect complex processes of power relating as part of the processes of interaction. When the ideas to organise the meetings were emerging there was a large difference in identity between the International and National groups. I developed the idea that bringing people of both groups together and stimulating conversation about a common problem would bring both groups closer together. During the next phase of the process this turned out to be the case. Top management's responsibility is also to alleviate identity conflicts that will emerge during these processes of interaction. Initiating the strategy meetings between the groups of International and National brought people closer to each other through conversation. These meetings led, especially after the exchange of ideas in the big meeting, described below, to new strategic ideas and plans applicable to the whole (population-wide) organisation working on the merger.

The big meeting: formulation and implementation of strategy at the same time

The communication manager of my division took responsibility for organising the big presentation event, which was to be held in October. She hired a top facilitator to lead the day and the large-group discussions and prepared the feedback sessions for the people of the ten different locations. When the day started one could feel the difference compared with the last sessions. National and International colleagues from different parts of the country had prepared their presentations together and walked in together, chatting loudly.

In retrospect, the invitation accepted by participants to develop intentions on a local level through conversation, good facilitation and the assurance that management would take their contributions seriously helped in bringing down the boundaries between groups. In addition to bringing people together and stimulating conversation about what has to be done, a trust in the leadership helped the process move forward. My personal feeling is that a lack of trust will increase the positional bias of the participants because they will focus discussions on their own responsibilities and the local environment in which they work, instead of joining the invitation to participate in a wider-scale discussion.

After coffee, our facilitator introduced the two representatives of our Staff Councils, as well as Robert and me, to the more than 100 people present and briefly gave us the opportunity to express our hopes for a fruitful day. Today's goal was to be able to write the legal request for advice to the Staff Councils based on the requirements and practical input of the groups from the country offices who would have to do the real work.

During the first half of the morning, five groups presented the combined ideas of each of their locations to the other five, who were free to move around at ten-minute intervals. During the second half of the morning the roles were reversed, giving everybody the chance to absorb the information of at least six groups, but with some intelligent shifting of presentation responsibilities, this could be even more. It was good to see that National and International people from all locations had joint ideas on how they saw their co-operation. Some had worked this out in great detail as it was not necessary that every location had to follow the same standards, as their markets were quite different. Everybody had the chance to ask questions, and show doubt or confirmation. The remarks were added to the flipcharts to be used in later presentations.

During lunch, the facilitator discussed the questions of the morning with management and some of the Staff Councils' members. We extracted six to eight major subjects to be discussed in the afternoon by mixed groups of both divisions. We hoped that this would lead to suggestions on how to handle the request for advice and the next steps. One remark came back from all groups: please let us get going and finalise these discussions as soon as we can. This was, in fact, good news.

After lunch we presented the general questions. This led to a small interruption, when one of the participants accused us of bringing in subjects that had not been discussed that morning. Although they were related, he had a point. The Staff Councils also had a suggestion on one of the subjects not presented that morning, so we had a common problem. Genevieve saved the situation by mentioning that everybody could sign up to participate in any of the discussions. If nobody was interested then the slots would remain empty, which actually did not happen.

The big group split into all kinds of smaller groups like an open-space session (Owen, 1992), discussing the most important questions that should lead to the next steps on how to organise the follow-up. The level of participation was high. Everybody had this feeling of responsibility; as if people were crafting and designing their own future (Johnson et al., 2003; Mintzberg, 1987). At the end of the day all the groups presented the outcome of their discussions and Robert and I assured them that all their suggestions would find their place in our plan and the legal request for advice to the Staff Councils.

People were really influencing each other that day. When people meet, start working together and exchange information a form of generalisation takes place, influencing the process into a global outcome. Two weeks later Robert and I presented the combined legal request, prepared by our colleagues, to our Staff Councils, with an answer expected within six weeks of the meeting.

Micro-strategy in retrospect

Looking back at what had happened, it became clear that the moment we asked our staff members to participate in the project it suddenly gained speed. It involved the methodology of asking middle management (Nonaka, 1988) to take up responsibility for local interaction, based on the open questions we formulated: 'what do we have to do to make this merger work?' and 'what are the consequences for all people involved?' We looked for a meeting design which offered the possibility of a high exchange rate of information with a high degree of participation in the shortest possible time and followed the suggestions of our facilitator.

The information exchange session helped bring all ideas and views together in a way that allowed us to formulate a strategy beneficial for the company with the input and support of all employees. In implementing the next phases of the merger we could relate our findings to the outcome of the Ketovi and Castener (2004) research on joint reduction of managerial position bias. When people were asked to participate in the strategy process in the various sessions of the meetings described above, they found that their interactions with each other tended to reduce their highly personal focus on their own local situations and enable them to see the connection to company-wide developments.

The way our managers in the offices in the country developed their strategic input, based on our questions, can also be compared with the results presented by Regner (2003), who describes strategy making in the periphery, our offices, as inductive, including externally oriented and exploratory strategy activities like trial-and-error, informal noticing, experiments and the use of heuristics. Strategy making in the centre is more deductive, involving an industry and exploitation focus and activities like planning, analysis, formal intelligence and the use of standard routines. We actually introduced our micro-strategy (Johnson et al., 2003) and periphery approach (Regner, 2003) the moment we got stuck in the original deductive approach (Mintzberg et al., 1998). During the process we chose our different approaches as a trial-and-error run. Views I developed during my Doctor of Management programme resulted in the move away from the centre of power, looking for other forms of participation and enabling other forms of communication and patterning. It is only now through reflection that I am able to explain what happened and change future ways of thinking.

Balogon et al. (2003) focus in particular on the importance of working with organisational members as research partners, rather than seeing them as passive informants. When working with larger groups to gather data, facilitation skills and the knowledge of group settings need special attention.

We were supported by skilled facilitators who helped us to make this process a success. In a way, studying strategy and performing strategy is comparable in its action to studying 'the know-how' and 'the know-what', bringing strategy back to its day-to-day function in organisations.

Being aware of the established–outsider circumstances and the shift between positions (Elias and Scotson, [1965] 1994, p. xlv) we introduced different platforms of conversation between International and National, leading to new (global) patterns. Original intentions, even negative ones, disappeared and were replaced by new intentions of groups formed by other people not having worked together before (Elias, [1939] 2000). The people of International felt superior in the beginning, continuing to hold this point of view even during the period in which their jobs were planned to disappear. It took some time before they realised what was at stake and, even then, more than once they shifted discussions back, leading to denial of what was really happening (Elias and Scotson, [1965] 1994). Very slowly the people of National discovered their power position through being at the receiving end of the merger, and power positions changed, leading to highly repetitive patterns of thinking. Only after management started to enable different patterns of conversation during the local meetings and the big meeting were new plans formed that led to new strategic outcomes, again emphasising the importance of direct top management involvement during the whole process.

Questions to aid further reflection

1. The author starts the story with a meeting at which it is judged desirable to cut costs. Do you think this was the beginning?

2. The author focuses attention on one sequence of events but clearly this is not all that the top executives and others were engaged in. What effect do you think this has on strategy?

3. What part do you think personal relationships, ambitions and agendas play in strategy?

4. What role do you think leaders play in what happens in events such as those recounted in this narrative?

5. In what sense could one say that strategy and implementation were taking place at the same time?

6. What form did the actual strategising activities take?

7. How would you think about intention and emergence in the above narrative?

© Nol Groot

Chapter 12

The link between the local communicative interaction of strategising and the population-wide patterns of strategy

This chapter invites you to draw on your own experience to reflect on and consider the implications of:

- Thinking of organisations as social rather than physical objects.

- Thinking of organisational strategies as generalised population-wide patterns of activity that emerge in many, many local interactions.

- Thinking about the interplay of intentions as the connection between local inter-actions in organisations and population-wide patterns of activity called organisational strategy.

- The meaning of emergence in human activity.

- Control as social processes rather than anyone being 'in control'.

The last chapter looked in some detail at the nature of local interaction in organisations, arguing that it is fundamentally communicative. The argument was that all the activities of organising, including those of strategising, are conversational processes. It is in local conversational processes that the population-wide patterns of strategy emerge. However, people in organisations also have the ability to notice and interpret emerging population-wide patterns, and what they notice and how they articulate their interpretations have an impact on how they interact locally with each other. Strategising, as patterns of local interaction, forms population-wide patterns of strategy while being formed by them at the same time. The ideas in this chapter are important because they constitute a way of thinking about the paradoxical processes of strategising and strategy which in the dominant discourse would be described as the link between micro and macro. The way of thinking presented in this chapter reverses the usual connection made between strategy and change. In the dominant discourse, a population-wide pattern is formulated first and then implemented as the cause of population-wide change. If one argues that emergence applies to human action then this causal link from a global plan to local change is impossible. In the approach adopted in this chapter it is in local change that new population-wide patterns of strategy emerge. If a plan for a population-wide pattern cannot be the cause of it, if local interaction is the cause of it, then what effect does the population-wide pattern have on local interaction? This is the question explored in this chapter.

12.1 Introduction

Chapter 10 explored a responsive processes way of thinking about *how* organisational strategies, understood as population-wide patterns of activity, arise. It drew on traditions of Western thought exemplified by the philosophy of Hegel and the sociology of Elias, who both emphasised the essential interdependence of human persons and how their patterns of activity could only be understood in terms of the history of responsive interactions between them. The key point made in this chapter is that individual persons and groupings of them make choices and act with intention in expectation of realising some future population-wide pattern of activity which they desire. However, the fact that they are always interdependent means that there can be no simple realisation of such desire. The population-wide patterns of activity will always *emerge* in the *interplay* of the desires and intentions of all of them. Since it is extremely unlikely that all will have the same desires and intentions, the interplay of intentions is an essentially conflictual process, in the sense of ongoing exploration and negotiation, taking the form of co-operation or manipulation, and sometimes hostility, aggression, competition, revolution or war. While each person or group may, *perhaps*, be more or less able to control their own desires and intentions, none of them will be able to control the desires and intentions of everyone else all of the time. It follows that no one can be 'in control' of the interplay of desires and intentions or even fully understand that interplay. Clearly, then, no individual person or grouping of persons, no matter how powerful, can choose the population-wide patterns of activity that will continuously materialise. Instead, the actual, realised ongoing population-wide pattern of activity will continually emerge, where this means that the ongoing realised pattern of activity is not caused by any plan or blueprint for it – the pattern that emerges is not the pattern that anyone planned. That pattern is caused by the ongoing responsive adjustment of the individual plans and actions of persons to each other. It is caused by the interplay of desires and intentions.

Chapter 10 also argued that this view is supported by the properties of complex adaptive systems consisting of heterogeneous agents. Using this idea, serious natural scientists have shown that evolving, coherent, population-wide patterns do emerge in local interaction between agents (self-organisation or interplay) when those agents are richly connected to each other, so imposing *conflicting constraints* on each other, and when they differ sufficiently from each other, so displaying *diversity*.

When these conditions are met, the dynamics, the patterns of movement over time, of both local interactions and population-wide patterns, take the form of regular irregularity (edge of chaos), which has the property of *amplifying small differences* into novel patterns. So, there is nothing mysterious or inexplicable about the emergence of population-wide pattern in local interaction, nor is it due to chance. Emergence is caused by what agents do as they impose conflicting constraints on each other in which their diversity, the small differences between them, is amplified. Elias's painstaking research provides us with a means of understanding how these abstract ideas from the complexity sciences can be understood in terms of the evolution of human communities and this is, of course, what organisations are.

In the dominant discourse, strategy is mostly defined in terms of the desire and intention of some individual person, or group of persons, and the definition stops there. It is then the obvious next step to ask what process persons do or should employ to formulate and implement their chosen desire or intention, or at least to learn together how to do so, in order to realise their desire or intention. What materialises is, here, by and large, thought to be caused by the intention when carried out competently. Where such realisation of strategic intention fails and something else happens it is ascribed to chance and called emergent. The responsive processes perspective does not stop the definition of strategy at the point of individual, or collective, desire or intention because it is concerned with the interplay of different desires and intentions. The realised strategy is caused, not by individual or collectively shared desires and intentions, but by their interplay. This is in no way to diminish or downplay the importance of individual or collective desires and intentions because without them there could, obviously, be no individual or joint actions and so no interplay with the individual or joint actions of others. The interplay is not some abstraction but the embodied interaction of human persons acting with intention and also often quite unconsciously without intention.

If one is *not* to stop the definition of strategy at the point of individual intention then how are we to use the word 'strategy'? I will be using the word 'strategy' to mean *generalised articulations* of the ongoing *pattern of activity* that people in an organisation are engaged in. For example, they may be engaged in a pattern of activity to which the label 'outsourcing' could be attached. Or, they could be engaged in a pattern of activity called 'wildcat strikes'. Furthermore, the ongoing pattern of activity of people in an organisation clearly also includes what intentions they are forming, how they are forming them and what *thinking* they are *doing* as they desire and intend. In other words, the distinctions between thought and action, planning and implementation, doing and thinking, all dissolve.

In the following chapters, then, strategy refers to generalisations about the ongoing, population-wide patterns of activity of interdependent people and those population-wide patterns continually emerge in the ongoing local strategising activities as the interplay of the desires and intentions of all involved, both as members of a particular organisation and as members of other organisations they interact with. What now becomes important is to explore just what is meant by the interplay of intentions, that is, by the local interaction of persons, just what is meant by the emergence of population-wide patterns, and just how such patterns are related to local interactions. That is the purpose of this chapter and the next one.

Chapter 11 focused on local interaction as communicative interaction. People accomplish whatever they accomplish in communicating with each other. That chapter explored how such communication might be understood from the perspective of Mead who understood communication as the conversation of gestures, by which he meant ongoing everyday, local activities of bodies gesturing to each other in the process of which they are evoking and provoking responses from each other. Meaning, or knowledge, emerges in these iterated social processes of gesture and response, that is, conversation. What I mean by local interaction, therefore, is fundamentally these complex responsive processes of conversation between human bodies, whether in each other's presence or using technologies such as writing and e-mail.

This chapter is concerned with the extension of Mead's argument to understand how the local interaction of conversation is linked to population-wide social patterns. Mead also argued that such conversation was social process and as such always reflected the history of the communicators' communities. In other words, human local communicative interaction always involves the population-wide patterns that have evolved over time in the many, many local interactions of the past. These population-wide patterns are present in all current actions as generalisations and idealisations, also referred to by Mead as social objects and cult values, which are continually taken up by people in their local interactions. In other words, in local communicative interaction, local patterns of interaction are being formed by population-wide patterns – generalisations and idealisations – while at the same time forming them. Pattern is emerging locally and globally at the same time, all in local communication in which the interplay of intentions means making particular to a particular situation that which is general and idealised. This chapter will be exploring just what the meaning might be of this possibly unfamiliar way of thinking about the meaning of the relationship between the local and the global, the micro and the macro.

To say that both local and population-wide patterns *emerge* at the same time is to say that both are arising and evolving into the unknown without any plan or blueprint. In other words, the emerging patterns are paradoxically predictable and unpredictable at the same time and over the long term fundamentally unknowable in their important detail. If this is so, then people can certainly articulate these patterns in generalised and idealised terms once they have occurred and we know that they do – these hindsight articulations are the stories about the past that we take up in the living present (*see* Chapter 10) as a basis for forming our next intentions.

But what of foresight? If the world of experience we create in our interactions with each other is stable and regular enough, then foresight can mean predicting future local and population-wide patterns in general. However, if the world of experience we create in our interactions is paradoxical and fundamentally unknowable in the long run, as the perspective being discussed here claims, then foresight cannot be equated with prediction. However, this does not mean dismissing foresight or any form of discussion about possible futures as futile. What it does mean is reflecting more deeply on what foresight means in a fundamentally uncertain world of experience. It could mean desiring, imagining, fantasising about, dreaming of, having premonitions of, speculating about, having expectations for, even omnipotently claiming certain knowledge of, future population-wide patterns. These are all fundamentally important human motivations to act and no theory trying to explain what we actually do could possibly dismiss them. Such 'foresight', taking the form of stories about dreams or expectations for the future, will have no less impact on action taken in local interaction as the living present than the stories told with hindsight.

Chapter 10 referred to the circular structure of the living present in which stories about the future affect the stories told about the past which affect stories about the future, all as the basis of the intentions we form and the actions we take in the present. This notion of the present does not dismiss either the past or the future but indicates how both are aspects of the living present, the present in which we always live.

Consider now how, according to Mead, local communicative interaction and population-wide patterns are interconnected.

12.2 Human communication and the conversation of gestures: processes of generalising and particularising

As we saw in the last chapter, Mead sought to understand the complex social acts in which many people are engaged in conversation through which they accomplish the tasks of fitting in and conflicting with each other in order to realise their individual and collective objectives and purposes. People do not come to an interaction with each other afresh each time because they are born into an already existing, socially evolved pattern of activity and they continue to play their part in its further evolution. This leads Mead to his concept of the *generalised other*. In order to accomplish complex social acts, it is not enough for those involved to be able to take the attitude of the small numbers of people they may be directly engaged with at a particular time. They need to be able to take the attitude of all of those directly or indirectly engaged in the complex social act. It would be impossible to do this in relation to each individual so engaged but humans have developed the capacity to generalise the attitudes of many. In acting in the present, each individual is then taking up the attitude of a few specific others and, at the same time, the attitude of this generalised other, the attitude of the group, the organisation or the society. These wider, generalised attitudes are evolving historically and are always implicated in every human action. In play, the child takes the role of another. But in the game the child must take on not only the role of the other but also that of the game, that is, of all the participants in the game and its rules and procedures. The generalised other is the taking of the attitude of all other participants in general.

We learn early on in life to take the attitude of the generalised other as, for example, when one's mother says, 'What will *people* think of you if you do this or say that?' Here one's mother is not warning one to take account of how particular people will respond to us, but how people in general in our society will respond to us. We care about what others think of us and about the consequences of their not thinking well of us – ongoing existence requires the recognition of others simply because we are all interdependent persons. We continue throughout life to care and this provides a powerful constraint on what we do and so a powerful form of social control. We begin to see here how, despite the inability of anyone to be in control, there are powerful forms of social control expressed most effectively as socially acquired self-control so that the only alternative to someone being in control is not anarchy, muddling through or garbage-can decision making. It is only when social habits break down, as for example in the recent flooding of New Orleans or the aftermath of the Iraq war, that anarchy ensues.

Taking the attitude of the generalised other

It is important here to note what Mead means by '*attitude*'. He does not mean simply an opinion; he means a 'tendency to act'. In taking the attitude of the generalised other we are therefore taking into account the established tendencies to act towards us and each other of people in general in our group, organisation and society. However, we are always having to interpret what these generalised tendencies to act might mean in the specific, contingent situations we find ourselves in. We cannot simply, directly apply the generalisation because in each present time period, in each contingent situation, we will find it necessary to make the general particular to that time and situation. This will inevitably lead to conflict in that we will differ from each other on just how to make the generalisation particular in each present time period and situation. Such conflict requires us to carry on exploring with each other just what our differences are and negotiating the meaning of the generalisation. And it is this conflictual, explorative process of particularisation that makes possible the further evolution of the generalisation as tiny variations in the particular way the generalisation is taken up are amplified across a population over time. We can immediately see the superficiality of the notion, taken by some from the complexity sciences (*see* Chapter 9), that people should follow simple rules. Simple rules are generalisations and there is nothing simple at all about the processes of making particular such generalisations.

To see what the above argument means in terms of human action, consider the activity of smoking cigarettes. A person who undertakes this activity inevitably affects others in the immediate vicinity and so, in order to carry on in an ordinary way with those others, has to take the attitude of those specific others, that is, the tendency of those specific others to act towards the smoker and they too find they have to take the attitude of the smoker. We are talking about what the parties directly involved have to take account of in each other's actions in order to go on being together. If we are dining together at a restaurant and I want to smoke at the table, I have to take account of how you might react and you will have to take account of how I might react if you protest. To go on together we each have to take the attitude of the other. However, there is more to it than this because people in general in the wider society have a generalised tendency to act towards each other with regard to the activity of smoking. What can we say about the attitude of the generalised other here? Well, if we go back some 70 years to the period of the Second World War, the attitude of the generalised other could be described as permissive, even encouraging of the activity of smoking. For example, the military authorities gave cigarettes to members of the armed forces in the belief that smoking calmed people down in very difficult circumstances. In lighting a cigarette in a specific situation, say a restaurant or cinema, a person would take account of the attitude of the specific others in the vicinity and, at the same time, quite unconsciously take account of the permissive attitude of the generalised other at that time, and others in the vicinity who were not smoking would do the same. So in a specific restaurant or cinema a smoker would probably feel perfectly entitled to light up and most others would feel that it was quite acceptable for this to happen.

However, as the years went by, the attitude of the generalised other with regard to smoking evolved and became more complex. Groups of people in the medical research community produced evidence of harmful effects of smoking, not just on smokers but on those around them. Other groups of people entered into the discussion, particularly over the past twenty years, accelerating over the past five years. Gradually over these years, and increasingly so over the past few years, the tendency of people in general to act in relation to smokers has shifted to one of prohibition, even hostility, and this shift in the attitude of the generalised other has been codified in the law. Now a person lighting a cigarette has to take the attitude of those in the immediate vicinity and the attitude of the generalised other and in doing so knows that he or she is acting in a way condemned by people in general. Non-smokers now feel perfectly justified in condemning the practice of smoking and refusing permission for others to smoke near them. How is the smoker going to deal with the attitude of the generalised other in specific situations, for example while waiting for a bus near a bus shelter? I might feel quite justified in lighting a cigarette in the open air but those nearby might feel that it is quite unjustified. We are both accepting the general attitude of prohibition but conflicting around what this means in the specific situation of the area around a bus shelter.

This is an example of how people take up the attitude of the generalised other across a whole society, indeed across many societies, and of how the generalised other evolves. However, the processes in this case are just as much in operation in all of the ordinary, everyday activities of people in any organisation. So, for example, a manager arrives at the office on Friday to find that a member of his staff has not reported for work and, furthermore, has not telephoned to explain the absence, as required by company policy. Some hours go by and the manager telephones her to find that her mobile phone is switched off and he cannot contact her. In deciding what to do next, he will find himself taking account of the attitude of the absent staff member and the attitude of other staff members. Will they be supportive of her or, given that she frequently fails to attend work on a Friday, will they be annoyed by any failure to take action against her? He will also, largely unconsciously, be taking the attitude of the generalised other – in general, people in this society do not approve of people who stay away from work for no good reason and do not explain why they are doing so. This attitude is codified in company policies and, since she has done it before, the generalisation would be to take disciplinary action.

However, in this specific, contingent situation, on this particular Friday morning, in this particular office, how is this generalisation to be made specific? For example, the absent staff member is a single mother abandoned by her partner who has great difficulty caring for her young daughter and furthermore she has produced letters from her doctor saying that she is suffering from depression. These contingent aspects of the situation call out other generalised attitudes to do with protecting single mothers, not discriminating against those with mental problems, and so on. In deciding what to do, then, this manger is making particular to this situation the generalisations so far mentioned. Furthermore, over the past few years all of these generalisations have been evolving as new specific situations are encountered and many have been codified in law.

Mead's theory of the evolution of groups and societies in processes of communicative interaction between persons provides us with a way of understanding organisations that focuses upon the ordinary, everyday activities of people, rather than abstracting from them and regarding people as the resources of an organisation, which is what most other explanations of organisations do. I want to stress that this focus on people is in no way an idealisation of people and their relationships with each other nor is it a fundamentally ideological position, although of course it has ideological implications. This is because no claim is being made that relationships between people are essentially good. Mead's theory of the conversation of gestures, in which generalisations are made particular, is as much an explanation of war, corruption, abuse and all the other terrible ways people relate to each other, as it is of caring, loving relationships.

From Mead's perspective we come to understand organisations as patterns of interaction between people which evolve over time in those processes in which people are making particular the generalisations, and in the course of which those generalisations evolve. The strategies of an organisation are those generalisations and the strategies therefore evolve in the ordinary, everyday processes in which people interpret and negotiate with each other what the strategies as generalisations mean in specific contingent situations and what implications these meanings have for what to do next. For example, consider a commercial organisation where the strategy is described as one of delivering, to customers, mobile telephones of a quality consistently higher than the competition, on time, and at competitive prices, while generating acceptable profit without compromising the safety of staff or customers. It may also be part of the strategy to do all of this in an ethical, socially responsible and environmentally aware manner. All of this may well have been codified in the form of strategy documents, procedural manuals and administrative systems such as financial budgeting and quality monitoring. However, what we are talking about here are generalisations that have emerged from numerous past conversations, including formal meetings, as well as actual production experiences. Now, at a particular time, on a particular day, particular people in the assembly operation encounter a quality problem with a particular component. To sustain quality they should stop the assembly operation but then they will not meet time deadlines and profits will suffer. This is, of course, a common problem encountered when strategy requirements conflict as they inevitably do. It will be necessary for those involved to make particular decisions about these generalisations. Would it be better to take a small risk on quality and meet the time deadline, or not? If similar problems are more frequently encountered, the manner in which they are dealt with in particular situations may well come to be expressed in a reformulation of the generalisation. It is in this way that the generalisations evolve in further conversations on how to deal with the conflict.

Conflict

This perspective, then, brings conflict to the fore. It is not just that the generalisations may conflict with each other but that the particular people involved in the particular, contingent situation may well conflict with each other on how to interpret the generalisations and how to take them up at this particular moment. The movement of strategy occurs in the negotiation of such conflict. Groot (2005) draws a conceptual distinction between explorative conflict and polarised conflict. Conflict is usually understood as the polarised form. Here people take up opposed positions and hold on to them in an overt power struggle in which one side holds out to win at the expense of the other. When Mead is emphasising conflict he does so in its explorative sense. Explorative conflict is conversational, negotiating processes in which people explore how to interpret generalisations and negotiate different inter-pretations with each other to make them particular. Such explorative conflict always has the potential, but not the necessity, of polarisation.

In the evolution of organisations, then, many generalisations emerge which are taken up, or particularised in people's local interactions with each other and in the course of which the generalisation evolves. This is a point of major importance. Mead draws attention to paradoxical processes of generalisation and particularisa-tion at the same time. Mental and social activities are processes of generalising and particularising at the same time. Individuals act in relation to that which is common to all of them (generalising) but responded to somewhat differently by each of them as each living present (particularising).

Social objects

Mead's (1938) discussion of what he called a social object is yet another formula-tion of the generalising and particularising processes discussed in previous sections. Mead distinguished between a physical object and a social object. A physical object exists as a thing in nature and is the proper object of study in the natural sciences, while a social object is the proper object of study in the social sciences and this object exists only in human experience. While the physical object can be understood in terms of itself as a thing, the social object has to be understood in terms of social acts. Mead referred to markets as an example of a social object. When one person offers to buy food this act obviously involves a complex range of responses from other people to provide the food. However, it involves more than this because the one making the offer can only know how to make the offer if he is able to take the attitude, the tendency to act, of the other parties to the bargain. All essential phases of the complex social act of market exchange must appear in the actions of all involved and appear as essential features of each individual's actions. The activities of buying and selling are involved in each other.

As another example, take a National Health Service trust in the UK. From a complex responsive processes perspective this organisation is the iterated patterning of communicative interaction between large numbers of interdependent persons and groupings of them – when asked what they do their answer is that they work in a hospital. Some are employees and belonging to the trust is an aspect of their identities, the 'we' aspect of each of them. Furthermore, they are not simply members of the trust because each of them also belongs to groupings of doctors, nurses, porters, managers and so on – when asked who they are, their answer is that they are doctors, hospital porters and so on. Even in these grouping there are subgroupings, for example sur-geons, and even within that there are groupings, say, heart surgeons – when asked who they are they reply that they are heart surgeons. All of these groupings give rise to the 'we' identities of their members, providing them with a powerful sense of identity or self. Others are receiving attention as patients and so belong to the group of the 'sick'. Yet others are relatives of the 'sick' and so belong to yet another group, perhaps, 'carers'. And of course each of these groups consists of subgroups, such as the diabetics, the mentally ill, the Aids patients and so on. They too take aspects of their identities, albeit often more temporarily, from belonging to these groups. For all of those mentioned, such identities constitute how they are recognised by others in the wider society. All of these people continually interact with each other in a coherent manner, moment by moment, every day, because each has the largely unconscious capacity to take the attitude, the tendency to act, of all the others in the hospital game. We have some expectation of what will happen when we enter a hospital as a patient. We have some expectation of how doctors, nurses, administrators and porters will act. And so do all of them of us and each other. What we are all doing is taking up the attitude of the 'game'. We are all taking up, in our interactions, the social object that is the hospital organisation. As an organisation, the hospital does not exist as a thing. Rather, it is only to be found as patterns of interaction in our experience. This must be so if we are to interact coherently. Try to imagine what it might be like to be rushed to a modern hospital in London from a remote jungle village somewhere in South America.

However, taking up the social object in our interactions is not a perfect process because it is not the actualisation of something given and the expectations of all involved will not therefore fit in easily with each other. As generalisation, the social object will have to be made particular in each particular, contingent situation and this will inevitably lead to some kind of conflict. Nurses and physicians, for example, might well take up the social object in their actions in different ways so that they will conflict and there will be complaints.

Social objects, as generalisations, can also be idealised, becoming what Mead called a cult value, a matter to be discussed in Chapter 13. I mention this concept here in relation to the hospital example because nowhere will the conflict caused by making some generalisation particular be greater than when this generalisation is also a cult value. For example, how will the cult value 'treat all patients equally' be taken up in Ward A at the Royal Free hospital at 15.25 on 14 May 2006 in relation to patients X and Y by doctor L and nurse M? And it is more complicated than this because there will be more than one cult value and they may well conflict with each other. Nowadays, hospitals take up cult values to do with performance, quality assurance, risk management and evidence-based treatment. These frequently clash with other cult values such as vocation, collegiality, causing no harm, professional freedom and personal responsibility. People then have to negotiate their way through inevitable conflicts in ways that inevitably transform their identities. This becomes especially pressing when the scope for particularising the generalised cult values is more and more severely restricted by shifts in power relations, as in the concentration of policy making, monitoring and control in the hands of central government. People must comply, or at least be seen to comply, to avoid public humiliation, shame and even annihilation of identity. Identities, which can only be sustained in the recognition of important others, may come to be characterised more by appearance and spin than substance. Compliance may mean submerging values that may feel more important leading to feelings of alienation and inauthenticity because to survive we may have to deceive. All of this will have enormous implications for the strategy of hospital improvement. As is now very evident, it is by no means guaranteed that formulating a strategy of health improvement and implementing it through administrative systems of monitoring will have sustainable effects. This is hardly surprising when one takes account of the local particularising of generalised strategies such as 'healthcare improvement'.

It is important to notice how Mead used the term 'object' in a social sense as a 'tendency to act' rather than as a concept or a thing, which are meanings appropriate to physical objects. In a social setting, then, Mead used the term 'object' in tension with the usual understanding of object as a thing in nature. The pattern, or tendency, which Mead calls an object is in a sense an object in that it is what we perceive in taking it up in our acting but this is a perception of our own acting not a thing. We seem to have a strong tendency to reify patterns of acting and this makes it important to emphasise that Mead's social object is not a thing.

Mead, therefore, defined a social act as one involving the co-operation of many people in which the different parts of the social act undertaken by different individuals appear in the act of each individual as a social object. The tendencies to act as others act are present in the conduct of each individual involved and it is this presence that is responsible for the appearance of the social object in the experience of each individual. A social object is only to be found in the conduct of the different individuals engaged in the complex social act. The social object appears in the experience of each individual as a stimulus to a response not only by that individual but also by the others involved – this is how each can know how the others are likely to act in general situations and it is the basis of co-ordination. A social object is thus a generalised gesture taken together with many tendencies to respond in particular ways. Social objects are common plans or patterns of action related to the future of the act. Social objects have evolved in the history of the society of selves and each individual is born into such a world of social objects. Individuals are forming social objects while being formed by them in an evolutionary process.

What Mead is talking about here is the manner in which population-wide patterns of action are generalisations that can only be found in the particular local interactions between people. Generalising is the same as both articulated and unconscious population-wide patterning and particularising is the same as local interacting.

Social control

Mead linked social objects to social control. Social control is the bringing of the act of the individual person into relation with the social object. The social act is distributed amongst many but the social object appears in the experience, the selves, of all of them. Social control depends upon the degree to which the individual takes the attitude of the generalised other, that is, takes the attitude which is the social object. All institutions are social objects and serve to control individuals who find them in their experience. So the social tendencies to act feature as key aspects of the individual selves comprising a group, organisation or society as the basis of self-control.

Mead's notion of social object has something in common with the notions of social structure, habit and routine. What was distinctive about Mead's approach to these matters, however, was how he avoided positing social structure as a phenomenon that exists outside individuals. Social objects are generalisations that only have any existence in their particularisation in the ordinary, everyday interactions between people as the living present. Box 12.1 summarises the key points about social objects.

Mead's view of control stands in contrast to how control is thought about in the systemic perspectives underlying the theories reviewed in Part 1 of this book. From the systemic perspective, control is usually equated with someone being 'in control' and this control is effected by cybernetic system forms of monitoring where actual outcomes are compared with targets and action is taken to close the gap. From this perspective the only alternative to someone being 'in control' through the

Box 12.1	**Key points about social objects**

- Social objects are *generalised tendencies*, common to large numbers of people, *to act in similar ways in similar situations*.

- These generalised tendencies to act are iterated as each living present as rather repetitive, *habitual patterns of action*.

- In their continual iteration, these general tendencies to act are normally *particularised* in the specific situation and the specific present the actors find themselves in.

- Such particularising inevitably involves *conflictual processes* of interpretation as the meaning of the generalisation is established in a specific situation.

- The possibility of *transformation* of social objects arises in this particularising because of the potential for *spontaneity* to generate variety in human action and the capacity of nonlinear interaction to *amplify* consequent small differences in their particularisation.

- While physical objects are to be found as things in nature, social objects can only be experienced in their particularisation in complex social acts as the living present. Social objects do not have any existence outside of such particularising social acts.

- The self is a social object and since social objects appear in the actions of individual people, the processes of particularising the general constitute social control.

use of monitoring procedures is anarchy or some form of muddling through. What Mead is making clear is that there are far more widespread and powerful forms of social control which do not involve any individual or powerful group of individuals being in control. The only alterative to someone being in control through operating monitoring process is not anarchy or muddling through simply because humans are social animals, that is, they are dependent upon each other, which requires each to unconsciously take up the generalised other, the social object, in their particular interactions with each other as aspects of their very selves. It is only when normal social relations break down that social control is disrupted, for example in the aftermath of a war, during riots or in the aftermath of major natural catastrophes such as hurricanes and flooding.

12.3 The relationship between local interaction and population-wide patterns

In all his formulations of human communicative interaction, Mead presented the same paradox: gesture and response are inseparable phases of one social act; generalising and particularising are inseparable phases of social objects; the 'I' and the 'me' are inseparable phases of the social self. It is in the ongoing activity of gesturing and responding, of generalising and particularising that meaningful patterns of interaction between people arise, including their very selves. I suggest that these meaningful patterns take the form of iterated, emerging, narrative and propositional themes that organize the experience of being together (*see* Chapters 11 and 14). Such themes are iterated as each present taking the paradoxical form of habit, or continuity, and potential transformation at the same time. The essentially reflexive nature of human consciousness and self-consciousness means that we have the capacity to reflect imaginatively on these patterns, both local and population-wide, articulating both the habitual and the just emerging transformations and in doing so either sustain the habitual or reinforce the transformation of habit.

Imaginative constructs

In our reflection we generalise the tendencies we experience across many present situations, creating imaginative 'wholes' that have never existed and never will (Dewey, 1934). What we are doing in creating these imaginative 'wholes' is constructing in our interaction perceptions of unity in the patterning of our interactions. That imaginatively perceived unity is then a generalised tendency to act in similar situations in similar ways. What is emerging is the imaginative generalisation that is one phase of what Mead calls social object. The other phase, which is inseparable from the generalisation, is the particularising of the general in the specific contingent situations we find ourselves in. The general population-wide pattern can only be found in its particularisation in our local interaction and that particularising inevitably involves conflict. In reflecting upon our patterns of interaction, in generalising those patterns and in imaginatively constructing some kind of unity of experience, we employ the tools of writing to codify habits or routines, for example as law, and even design changes in them. However, any intentionally designed change can only ever be a generalisation and what that means can only be found in the particularisation, that is, in the interplay between the intentions of the designers of the generalisation and the intentions of those who are particularising it.

Given the points made above, we can now understand what we mean by local interaction and population-wide pattern and how they are related to each other. Population-wide pattern is the imaginatively created unity across a whole population that we perceive in our patterns of interaction – it is the activity of generalising as one phase of social object. Local interaction is the particularising of the general, of the imaginatively constructed unity of our experience across the whole population we are part of. However, these are phases of one social act and can never be separated. The general is only to be found in the experience of the particular – it has no existence outside of it. The processes of particularising are essentially reflective, reflexive, emotional, imaginative and potentially spontaneous. It is possible for individuals and groups of individuals, particularly powerful ones, to intentionally articulate and even design a desired generalised pattern but the particularising involves an interplay of many intentions and values and this interplay cannot be intended or designed, except temporarily in fascist power structures and cults (*see* Chapter 12). Furthermore, the generalisations will further evolve in their particularisation. In short, the population-wide and the local are paradoxical processes of generalising and particularising at the same time.

This point about the particularisation of generalisations is of great importance and reinforces, for me, the inappropriateness of simply applying the notion of complex adaptive systems, or any notion of systems for that matter, to human interaction. In complex adaptive systems, the agents follow rules, in effect, they directly enact generalisations. If humans simply applied generalisations in their interactions with each other then there would be no possibility of individual imagination and spontaneity and hence no possibility of creativity. We would simply be determined by the generalisations. It is in the essentially conflictual particularising of the generalisations, which have emerged over long periods of human interaction, that socially constructed, interdependent persons display spontaneity, reflection, reflexivity, imagination and creativity as well as conflict.

Spontaneity

Spontaneity, it seems to me, should be distinguished from impulse. In humans, impulse is an unreflective compulsion to do something, on the 'spur of the moment', as it were. Impulsive actions, however, are still socially formed and reflexive. Humans are reflexive in that their actions are formed by their own histories. Whatever we do, whether impulsive or not, depends upon who we are, upon identity/self, which is socially formed. Humans are also socially reflexive in that what they think and what they do is formed by the group, community, society they are part of, which have histories. This social reflexivity is also shaping whatever we do, impulsive or not. Spontaneity is often spoken of as if it were the same as impulse and the opposite of reflection in that spontaneous action also has that 'spur of the moment' quality. However, this is to chop out one event from an ongoing flow of interaction. I would argue that if we pay attention to the interactions preceding the arbitrarily selected moment of spontaneous interaction, we find people exploring the situation they face in ways that are reflective and it is because of this 'preparation' as it were that someone takes spontaneous action, having the appearance of 'on the spur of the moment'. What distinguishes this kind of spontaneous interaction from mere impulse is that it is a skilful performance, not just a historically, socially conditioned reaction. Spontaneity is what makes it possible for people to deal with the unique contingencies of the situations they always face. Spontaneity generates variety in responses, often as small differences that have the potential for being amplified in interaction. In other words, human spontaneity is closely associated with the possibility of transformation and novelty in human interaction (Friis, 2004; Larsen, 2005). Spontaneity in humans, I would argue, is reflexive, just as impulse is but unlike impulse, the spontaneous act emerges in a history of skilful, reflective performance. Furthermore, spontaneity is never simply located in the individual, or the 'I', because the 'I' can never be separated from 'me', the social.

This perspective leads to ways of understanding what organisations are and what form the strategising activities of managers takes. Our understanding of organisational life might be enhanced by the notion of social object as generalised tendencies on the part of large numbers of people to act and the notion that such generalisations must be particularised in essentially conflictual processes in specific situations at specific times.

Organisations as social objects

What Mead presents is a complex, nonlinear, iterative process of communicative interaction between people in which mind, self and society all emerge simultaneously as the living present. Mead is concerned with local interaction as the present in which population-wide patterns emerge as social and personality structures. If one takes the complex responsive processes view then one thinks of the emergence of long-term, widespread, coherent patterns of relating across a population emerging in the local processes of relating. It follows that there is no need to look for the causes of coherent human action in concepts such as deep structures, archetypes, the collective unconscious, transcendental wholes, common pools of meaning, group minds, the group-as-a-whole, transpersonal processes, foundation matrix, the personal dynamic unconscious, internal worlds, mental models and so on. Instead, one understands human relating to be inherently pattern forming – it is its own cause.

Consider what organisations are usually thought to be. From a legal point of view, an organisation is a legal person. It is legitimised, under the laws of the land, by a legally recognised and binding constitution specifying purpose, procedures to be followed, hierarchical offices to be taken up, authority to be granted, and membership criteria and categories. This legal person has legal rights and obligations and it can be sued and punished. However, it is by no means necessary, and certainly not sufficient, to posit an organisation as a *legal* person. Some organisations are not legal persons at all. Indeed they are illegal, as is the case, for example, of a terrorist organisation or a drug smuggling ring. Furthermore, the *person* part of the definition is highly problematic, although very useful because without it we would have extremely ambiguous, cumbersome and muddled laws of contract and this would obstruct our joint activities. It is, therefore, a convenient *fiction* to think of an organisation as a person for legal purposes but it does not really get us to what an organisation is in our experience.

If we listen to how people talk about an organisation and read how the word 'organisation' is used in the now vast literature on the subject, it is striking how frequently the word 'it' is used in referring to an organisation. There is a powerful tendency to reify an organisation as an 'it' that somehow has a separate existence from the individuals who comprise it. We tend to talk about an organisation as actually existing as a thing, as a system. However, when we come to look for this 'thing' I think we are hard put to find it. People go even further than this and talk about an organisation as an organism, as a living system. They anthropomorphise it, treat it as actually being a person in ascribing purposes and direction to it. They claim, for example, that organisations learn. However, when we come to look for this organisational organism or person, we are hard put to find a body that qualifies as living. Organisations are not things because no one can point to where an organisation is – all one can point to is the artefacts used by members of organisations in their work together. In our experience of ordinary, everyday life, we do not encounter organisation as a thing, let alone a living thing with purposes of its own.

What we are doing in thought when we talk in the way just outlined is treating an organisation 'as if' it were what Mead called a physical object and often we forget the 'as if' nature of our construct. An alternative way of thinking would be to regard an organisation as a social object. In other words, we then think of an organisation as the ongoing patterning of the relationships between those who are members of the organisation and indeed between them and members of other organisations. The organisation is nothing more or less that the iterated ongoing processes in which people are together particularising the generalisations in terms of which they perceive their organisation. An organisation then exists as an emergent phenomenon taking the form not only of practical activities, but also, very importantly, the form of an imaginative construct emerging in the relationships between the people who form and are formed by organisation at the same time. Patterns of relationships and imaginative constructs are as 'real' as anything to be found in our lives, indeed, they are essential to the meaning of our lives. It is for this reason that I am using the term *imaginative construct* to distinguish what I am talking about from a mere 'fiction', however useful that may be, and from the notion of 'fantasy' with its connotations of some individual experience that stands in contradiction to 'reality'. We together construct the imaginative, not in some individual process of introspection or fantasising, but in our continually iterated local relationships with each other. This immediately brings us to the fundamentally social nature of imagination and so of organisation. We understand organisations as emerging patterns of communicative interaction between people, as ongoing 'conversations' in which emerge themes that organise our experience of being together. As people interact locally with each other, moment by moment, they form patterns of activity. They iterate, in a sense repeat, these patterns of communicative interaction as the living present and it is this activity of communication across the population of members that constitutes the experience of organisation.

Organisations are the ongoing patterning of conversations so that changes in conversations are changes in organisations. Usually, when talking about organisations, people refer to procedures, roles, tasks, and the activities of monitoring, planning and budgeting. They talk about organisations in terms of technologies, bundles of resource and positions in markets and dismiss ordinary conversation as 'just talk'. I think that in doing this they are focusing attention on what are only the tools we use in our ongoing local interactions with each other. If we think of organisations as social objects we avoid mistaking the tools for the organisation and see them for what they are, namely, the tools we use in the activities of organising.

Mead's notion of social object as generalised tendencies to act is the same as the population-wide patterns I have been referring to and his notion of particularising such generalisations is the same as the processes of local interaction I have been referring to. Drawing on analogies from the theory of heterogeneous complex adaptive systems I have suggested that population-wide patterns, or social objects, emerge in many, many local interactions. Mead explains the processes by which social objects, as generalisations, are made particular in many, many local interactions. This is what the activity of management is all about – it is the activity of making generalisations particular. The processes of management as particularising are interpretive and conflictual and it is in such local interaction that social objects continue both to be reproduced and to evolve, that is, population-wide patterns are iterated in local interactions as continuity and potential transformation at the same time. So, it is not simply that population-wide patterns emerge in local interaction but also that population-wide patterns are themselves taken up as particulars in local interactions – they are mutually constitutive. Furthermore, humans can articulate and even codify the population-wide patterns emerging in their local interactions and these articulations are themselves important aspects of local interaction.

This leads to a different way of thinking about formulation, or thought, and implementation, or action. This is a distinction widely made in the ways of thinking about organisations and strategy reviewed in Part 1 of this book. From the above discussion one concludes that such a distinction is purely arbitrary. The activity of particularising the general cannot be described simply as either formulation (thought) or implementation (action). This is because the activity of making the general particular involves interpretation, conflict and negotiation, all of which are actions that involve thinking. Generalising also cannot be simply categorised as formulation or implementation because the generalisation is emerging in the local interactions of particularising and the activities of articulating and codifying the general are themselves actions requiring thought. Instead of an arbitrary beginning described as formulation and an arbitrary end described as implementing we have ongoing processes of formulation and implementation, thinking and acting, at the same time.

Analogies from the complexity sciences

In the last chapter I took local interaction between human persons to be analogous to the concept of self-organisation in the theory of complex adaptive systems. To recapitulate, self-organisation in heterogeneous complex adaptive systems means that:

1. each agent interacts with only a small fraction of the total population of agents and in that sense agents only ever interact locally;

2. each agent interacts with others on the basis of its own historically evolved local organising principles rather than according to population-wide general rules set for each agent by some designer external to their interaction;

3. agents in their diversity are thereby locally constraining each other in conflicting ways and such constraining is an important source of order.

So I am arguing that local interaction between human agents as conversation, as in Mead's thought, and the interplay of intentions, as in the thinking of Elias, is fundamentally self-organising in the sense of points 1 to 3 set out above with an important addition in the case of human agents, namely, their ability to particularise generalisations of population-wide patterns in their local interaction. Then by further analogy I am arguing that just as global, population-wide patterns of interaction emerge and evolve in self-organising interaction in abstract models of complex systems so population-wide patterns of interaction between people emerge and evolve in local human interaction. In both cases, emergence means that the global or population-wide patterns are not the consequence of any plan, programme or blueprint for that population-wide pattern. Simulations of complex adaptive systems demonstrate that this is possible in principle and the work of both Mead and Elias indicates just how this happens in the case of human agents. And, by yet another analogy, I am arguing that, just as global and local patterns in complex adaptive systems both evolve together when the agents are diverse, so in human interaction both local and population-wide patterns evolve together because of human differences which inevitably bring with them conflict, just as both Mead and Elias argue.

It may be argued that the way I have draw the analogies in the previous paragraph ignores the following aspects of human interaction:

1. Some human agents, namely leaders, might be said to interact with a whole population of agents in an organisation or society.

2. While most other agents may be interacting with only a small fraction of the total population, they do not do so simply on the basis of their own historically evolved local organising principles but also, to a significant extent at least, on the basis of generalised, population-wide rules such as the laws of society, and the

visions, objectives and norms of an organisation, as well as its plans, routines, procedures and administrative systems.

3. Agents are constrained not simply by the conflicting constraints they place on each other but by the need to conform harmoniously to the population-wide rules specified in 2 above.

However, if we take account of the arguments about the social act of gesture and response, and of the relationship between the general and the particular as social object, it becomes clear that points 1 to 3 in the above paragraph present too simplistic a picture of human interaction for the following reasons:

1. When we look at how leaders or dominant coalitions interact with whole populations of people in an organisation or society we find that they can only do so in essentially the same way as anyone else. All any of us can do, including leaders and members of powerful coalitions, is gesture and respond to others. When the powerful and the charismatic are said to be interacting with a whole population what they are doing amounts to only one phase of the social act, namely, the gesture – the responses of all the individual members of the population are required to complete the social act. As Mead cogently argued, the meaning does not lie in the gesture taken on its own. The meaning emerges only in the gesture of the powerful take together with the second phase of the social act, namely, the responses of the many to whom the gesture is made. Such responses can only be made in many, many local interactions in which those gestured to discuss what the gesture of the powerful means and since there are many, many local interactions there will be many, many conflicting responses and accompanying meanings. The responses all occur in local interaction on the basis of local organising principles to do with, for example, emotion and individual histories as well as the generalised other/social object, which is always involved in local interaction. The powerful will then find that they must in turn respond to these many, many responses and meanings. What they thought their gesture meant might turn out to provoke surprising, unpredictable responses, which they will then have to deal with. Furthermore, both their original gesture and their responses to the responses to that original gesture will all arise in their own local interaction. No matter how powerful a person is, that person always interacts directly with a small number of close colleagues and their intentions emerge in such local interactions. So the powerful do not interact directly with large numbers of people after all because all they can do is undertake one phase of the social interaction, namely, the gesture, while the response arises indirectly in many other local situations. Human interaction remains fundamentally local despite the enormous differences in the visibility and power of different human agents.

2. The gesture made by the powerful can only ever be some articulation of a generalisation, perhaps one which is just emerging or one which is desired, wished for, or dreamt of. So the powerful are articulating the nature of social objects or their desires for it. Such generalisations or social objects must be made particular in many, many local, contingent situations. So people in an organisation are not simply following generalised rules but are continually interpreting and negotiating them with each other in local situations. This involves the spontaneity of the 'I' and the interplay of intentions.

3. People rarely conform harmoniously to general principles. Instead they make them particular in conflictual processes of the interplay of intentions.

Then when we take account of other organisations, or populations, with which people in any organisations have to interact, there is a further interplay of intentions. In a fundamental sense we are talking about local interaction (self-organisation) and emergence when it comes to human interaction.

I find that there is a typical response whenever I suggest to a group of managers that they might think of themselves, and also their chief executive officer (CEO), as participants in essentially self-organising processes, that is, local interaction from which population-wide patterns and imaginatively constructed unities of experience emerge. They claim that if they cannot be the designer of the whole and if they cannot know the outcomes of what they are doing in terms of directly causing the whole then they have no role. They claim that they would simply give up if they thought that population-wide patterns emerged and the 'whole' was an imaginative construct. Alternatively, they point to examples of CEOs who do form overall intentions for their organisation, who set out compelling visions and missions and do thereby transform their whole organisation. They conclude that the notion of self-organisation as local interaction does not apply to them. Why do they think this?

It seems to me that they are immediately understanding self-organisation in terms of the individual: the unquestioned assumption of the primacy of the individual. Self-organisation is taken to mean that it is the individual members of the organisation who organise themselves without the direction of their leaders. This then leads to the view that self-organisation is all or some of the following:

1. Something that happens no matter what anyone does. This means that there is no point in doing anything. One should simply sit back and just wait for fate or destiny.
2. Full-blown democracy in which all agents are equal and nothing is done without complete consensus.
3. Anarchy in which everyone does whatever they please.
4. The empowerment of the lower echelons in the organisation and then leaving them to get on with it.
5. The disempowerment and incapacitation of the higher echelons who no longer have a role.

It is important to stress that the notion of self-organisation as it is employed in complexity theory does not mean any of these things. People think it does because they hear these words from the perspective of the autonomous individual and think that it means that individuals are organising themselves without any constraint. However, if you look carefully at the simulations intended to demonstrate the nature of self-organisation you will notice two points.

First, there are conditions that simultaneously enable and constrain the interactions between agents. Take the Tierra simulation (Ray, 1992) discussed in Chapter 8. Agents are enabled to replicate because computer time is allocated to them, but this is also a constraint because they only have limited time. In organisations, all members are both enabled and constrained by the availability of resources. In the simulation, agents are constrained by the mode of replication and by the competitive selection applied to them. In the simulations, the programmer imposes all of these constraints but in the reality the programmer is trying to model, they all emerge in evolving interaction. So self-organisation is certainly not a constraint-free form of behaviour. In organisations, people constrain each other (*see* Chapter 12 on power) and they are constrained by each other and the generalised other/social object, which constitutes key aspects of their very selves.

Second, that which is organising itself is not the separate individuals on their own. In fact, self-organisation does not involve anything organising itself – it means local interaction. Population-wide patterns of relationships are emerging at the same time as the nature of the agents is changing, all in local interaction. The agents are forming and being formed by population-wide patterns of relationships. Once this perspective is taken there is no justification for making any of the interpretations of self-organisation in points 1 to 5 above. Instead:

1. Far from there being no point in doing anything, everything one does in one's local interactions, including nothing, has potential widespread consequences. Far from population-wide patterns being a matter of fate or destiny, they are the co-creation of all locally interacting agents.

2. There is no reason at all why agents should be interacting in a democratic way. They might, but they might not. Indeed, what it means to interact democratically, as a generalisation or idealisation, will need to be continually negotiated in local, contingent situations. Furthermore, they are not all equal in a simulation such as Tierra. Some are pursuing more powerful strategies than others, in terms of survival. There is certainly no requirement for consensus but, rather, the tension between competition and co-operation is expressed as conflict.

3. There is no anarchy because no agent can do whatever it pleases. There are a number of constraints, not least those provided by the actions taken by other agents.

4. There is no connection whatever between empowerment of the lower echelons in an organisation and self-organisation, a matter I will explore next.

5. There is also no connection whatever between disempowering the higher echelons and self-organisation, also to be explained in the next section.

12.4 The roles of the most powerful

Understanding organisations and their strategies as social objects that emerge in local communicative interaction immediately raises questions about the role of leaders. Since many equate emergence with chance they immediately conclude that it implies no role for leaders. This section will argue that this is not so.

To repeat, self-organisation means that agents interact locally with each other according to their own local principles of interaction, where those local principles have evolved in a life history and include the historically evolved generalisations of their community that have become aspects of their personality structures. This means that as agents they respond to each other according to their own historically evolved capacity to respond. They are enabled to respond in certain ways and constrained from responding in others by that capacity, which has emerged from their histories of interacting with others in which social objects have become aspects of their very selves. Some agents will have developed wider-ranging capacities for taking the attitude of others and of the social object than others. Some will have evolved capacities that enable them to respond more effectively and more success-fully than others do. In organisational terms, some members will have more knowl-edge and more understanding than others and so the power ratio will be tilted toward them. Some agents interact with more agents than others. Some are able to stand back and understand something of the larger processes in which they are par-ticipating, which does not mean that they are stepping outside those processes and understanding them from the perspective of the objective observer. Instead they are reflecting, as participants, on the nature of what is happening in the situations in which they are participating.

In organisational terms, then, the top executives have more power than others, that is, a greater capacity to instruct, persuade or even force others to do what they want. Furthermore, those top executives interact with a great many more people than the less powerful. A CEO may communicate with, and issue instructions to, hundreds of thousands of others in his or her organisation through e-mail, for example. A CEO might form certain views about the nature of his or her organisa-tion, the nature of leadership, the direction the CEO would like it to go in, a vision or a mission for it and so on. These are all actions the CEO is taking that are likely to call forth some kind of response from many others in the organisation. A small group of powerful people at the top of an organisation might, after many local inter-actions, take a decision to enter a new market or to negotiate with a small group of powerful people in another organisation to merge with it. All of these actions would evoke and provoke multiple responses from others, both within and outside the affected organisations. If the pattern of these responses were simply the expression of some overall blueprint then we could not talk about self-organisation or emerg-ence. However, if others were responding according to their own local capacities to respond, we would be talking about self-organisation and emergence.

The point I am making is this. Small groups of very powerful people at the top of an organisation allocate resources and in so doing both enable and constrain other members of the organisation. They design sets of procedures and hierarchical reporting structures but always in local interactions in which they are responding to what has just been happening. They legitimise some actions and not others. They gesture to very large numbers of others. They make statements about visions and missions. They make decisions and take actions that greatly affect a great many others. What they cannot do, however, is program the responses those others will make. They cannot control the interplay of intentions. The powerful may identify what kind of responses they would like by making statements about values and required cultures and behaviours. They may try to motivate others to adopt all of this. They may have desires and dreams. However, people will still only be able to respond according to their own local capacities to respond and the most power-ful will find that they have to respond to the responses that they have evoked and provoked. This is what I think self-organisation means in human terms. It is a process of interaction that is ever present in all human situations and would only cease if people really did respond like automatons to statements about the values and behaviours they were supposed to display.

For example, suppose the chief executive of a major multinational corporation announces his new vision of the 'corporation as global leader in network solutions'. Perhaps one hundred thousand people around the globe hear the gesture and a great many feel called upon to respond in some way. However, the meaning of the vision, like the meaning of all gestures, does not lie in the gesture taken on its own. What it means will be created in the responses. Will most just pay lip service to it and carry on doing what they were doing before? If they do not, just what will they do? The gesture may call forth the response of many meetings around the globe as people discuss what it means and what they are supposed to do about it. The meaning of the chief executive's gesture, and its impact on the organisation, will emerge in many local situations, including his or her own, in the living present of conversations around the globe.

From a complex responsive processes perspective, no one can determine the dynamic of interaction within an organisation because that dynamic depends upon what others both within that organisation and in other organisations are doing. In other words, an individual, or a group of individuals, powerful or otherwise, can make gestures of great importance but the responses called forth will occur in local situations in the living present and from these there will emerge the population-wide patterns of strategic activity that perpetually constructs an organisation's future.

The focus of attention, in trying to make sense of what happens, shifts from the chief executive's statement, or new tool, to the processes in which the statement or tool arises and to the many, many local situations in which they have their effects. Instead of taking it for granted that powerful chief executives actually individually change organisations directly through their intended actions, the complex responsive processes perspective focuses attention on the communicative processes in which the mere presence of, the images of and the fantasies about leaders all affect local processes of communicative interaction in the living present from which emerge the population-wide patterns that are organisations. Emergence, then, has very little, if anything at all, to do with chance. No one can shape, influence or condition emergence.

12.5 Summary

The key question addressed in this chapter had to do with understanding the basic structure of the local (self-organising) interaction between human agents as persons and the connection between such local interaction and the emergence of population-wide patterns, an organisation being an example of such a pattern.

Mead's work provides an explanation of human interaction in which such interaction is understood to be communication between human bodies, taking the form of the conversation of gestures where the fundamental unit is the gesture–response as inseparable phases of the social act. What is profound about Mead's thought is that it explains how the basic attributes of being human emerge in such social communication. His theory is also able to provide a convincing explanation of how population-wide patterns emerge in local, human communicative interaction. Local interaction always occurs in a social situation which has evolved to its present through a history. The social is generalised tendencies on the part of large numbers of people to act in similar situations in similar ways through taking the attitude of the generalised other/social object. These generalisations must be made particular in contingent situations and it is this particularising activity that constitutes the local, communicative interaction of negotiating meaning which always involves explorative and sometimes polarised conflict. It is in this conflictual negotiation, involving spontaneity, that small differences can occur and be amplified across a population.

The consequence of thinking in this way is that we come to understand organisations as social objects, as iterated patterns of interaction. The key argument is that strategies and organisational changes emerge in local interaction understood as conversation. This requires us to re-think what we mean by most organisational activities such as strategising, leading and many more. The next chapter will turn to the power and ideology aspects of local interaction and the consequences for emergent population-wide patterns.

Further reading

Useful further reading is provided by Stacey (2005) and Shaw and Stacey (2005).

Questions to aid further reflection

1. What do you understand 'population-wide pattern' and 'local interaction' to mean and how are they related to each other?

2. In what ways does Mead's idea of control differ from that to be found in the dominant discourse on organisations?

3. What is a social object in your experience?

4. Can you think of population-wide patterns that have emerged in local interaction?

5. What happens in your organisation when leaders issue statements on visions, missions and values?

Reflective management narrative 2

In this narrative, Nicholas Sarra describes his experience as an internal consultant engaged in an Organisation Development project. The mental health trust where he works is part of the UK National Health Service and was formed by a merger of a number of smaller trusts a short time before the start of his account. As in all mergers, a major problem facing the managers of the new organisation was the integration of people from a number of disparate institutions into one functioning organisation. All organisations dealing with post-merger problems seem to have found this problem of integration to be extremely difficult to deal with and Sarra's organisation was no different. What little research there is indicates that most integration attempts produce very disappointing results. Most approaches to such integration problems take a macro perspective in which the problem is identified as one of creating a new unified culture to replace the cultures of the organisations that have merged. Planned culture change programmes are designed and 'rolled down' the organisations with the aim of instilling new values and behaviours and exhorting people to sign up to the new 'vision'. The idea is to create some kind of harmony in which all share the same values and visions. The way of thinking reflected in this approach is that of the dominant discourse reviewed in Part 1 of this book. I have include Sarra's narrative at this point to provide the reader with an opportunity to reflect on how thinking in an alternative way, provoked by a complex responsive processes perspective, led him to approach the post-merger organisational problems in a rather different way. The points that stand out for me in his account are as follows:

- He makes clear the intention he formed for his Organisation Development (OD) work and the design that he and his colleagues prepared for an interpersonal learning programme as a form of OD. These intentions and designs arise in the local interaction of all involved and he expresses his awareness that what happens subsequently will emerge in the interplay of intentions of colleagues and others directly or indirectly involved in the programme (*see* Chapters 10 and 12). This is a narrative of the interplay of different intentions, not only of the middle managers involved directly in the programme but of the senior executives to whom they report and who find that they too are being affected by the programme. This brings out the nature and importance of conflict in organisations.

- In understanding communication as conversation (*see* Chapter 11), Sarra focuses his OD activities on creating a forum for interaction and increased connectivity between people. His programme is a 'live' experience of integration. The participants are not talking about integration as something to be accomplished later but are actually engaged in integrating through participating with each other on this interpersonal learning programme.

- Sarra stresses how the interactions of programme participants are relations of power, reflecting wider relations of power throughout the organisation. He tells us how the activities of the programme actually shift power relations across the organisation. He links power relations to inclusion–exclusion dynamics, ideology and identity, all matters to be explored in Chapter 13.

- The narrative brings out the constructive nature of explorative conflict, rather than attempting to impose some kind of harmony (*see* Chapter 13).

- The narrative brings out the relationship between local interaction and population-wide patterns discussed in Chapter 12. Sarra describes how government policies for the NHS across the country, which can be understood as the generalisations/idealisations of social object, are expressed in local interactions where, in fact, they find their meaning.

Organisational development as interpersonal learning

by Nicholas Sarra

I work in a mental health trust, partly as a therapist and partly as an internal organisational consultant. This trust had only recently been formed by a merger between a number of smaller trusts. The problem confronting us was that of undertaking organisational development in a meaningful way in a complex organisation struggling with post-merger problems. At the time I was doing research for a doctoral degree at the University of Hertfordshire and I decided to develop an organisational change programme that would explicitly attempt to engage the theory of complex responsive processes in pragmatic terms. I set out to explore how a theory of complex responsive processes might inform a programme of professional and organisational development. I stress the word 'inform' at this point because I did not see this programme as a formula or as the application of a concept but, rather, as a way of thinking about my work.

I designed what I called the Artemis programme as an interpersonal learning process to provide opportunities for developing the organisation through the interaction of its members. Artemis was a Greek goddess, daughter of Zeus and Leto, and sister of Apollo. She was associated with places of transition, the bearing of children, the bringing of light, and with journeys and roads. She had an unpredictable and sometimes dangerous nature and she was as capable of destruction as she was of creativity. Her name was used for this programme because these qualities evoke the uncertainty and unpredictability of the programme as well as its potential to develop organisational connectivity and creativity. I also hoped that the programme would address some of the professional development needs of the participants. At a personal level I thought that it would allow me to maintain influence at a time when my role as an internal consultant was being challenged as counter cultural. This narrative will explore the development of the Artemis programme and its impact upon both the participants and the wider organisation.

The objective of the Artemis programme was to form a group of about 40 middle managers and take them through a year-long process to develop their interaction with each other. I should emphasise the notion of forming this group because prior to Artemis there was no such cohesive entity. The managers were geographically separated across the county and few had regular opportunity for face-to-face contact. Many of them felt isolated and overwhelmed by the complex dynamics in which they found themselves operating. Support structures were often limited to those provided by line managers who were themselves often too busy to provide the support required. Therefore, one of the primary purposes of the Artemis programme was to provide opportunities for this peer group to make sense of their various tasks and roles within an organisation that is continually changing. They could then help each other in the work of understanding this shifting organisational context. This seems fundamental given that they are tasked with making operational the strategies of the senior management team.

However, this work of understanding cannot be predetermined nor preconceived. There is no predictable outcome and in this way it differs from other Organisation Development (OD) methodologies, which place an emphasis on a paradigm of preconception and control. The underpinning idea is that this group of middle managers is ideally placed to maximally influence the wider organisation. They are ideally placed because of their access (and this means opportunities for interaction) to different tiers of the workforce (approximately 2,500 staff). Each of these managers is able to express an understanding of the organisational process in a unique way, is in touch, so to speak, with different facets of organisational life. Their voices represent not only their own perspectives but also those of all the people with whom they relate and, importantly, of whom they manage. Artemis aimed to help managers find these voices in situations where power relations may tend to silence them. The use of a large group meeting on the programme was designed to replicate the psychological pressures of power relating within a complex organisation so that, through this activity, managers might find themselves better equipped to use their voice and thus influence the conversation around them.

The three-day event: Artemis begins

After much preparation the day arrived for the beginning of the programme; a three-day experiential event. Over 40 middle managers assembled on a bright December morning at a hotel in a small market town. The National Health Service trust, for which they work, serves a predominantly rural community across one of Britain's largest counties. Together with Harold, my co-convenor, we had formed a further team of four facilitators who would work alongside us on the year-long programme. We also had a researcher, Bob, who would come to play an important role, and our own consultant, David, whom we had brought in specifically to support us during the process. This team, which I shall refer to as the convenors, had spent the previous day at my house, preparing for the event.

Those three days were indeed anxious ones. I slept poorly and seemed to be living on adrenalin. The amount of material produced by the group seemed enormous and, as convenors, we worked hard amongst ourselves to make sense of what was arising both between ourselves and with the managers. Apart from David, our consultant, and Bob, the researcher, the situation was further complicated by our being members of the organisation whose programme we were convening. This meant that some of us had line management relationships with other participants so that the power relations extended beyond the parameters of the programme and into the workplace.

We took the participants through a process of small, large and inter-group experiences. We sought as convenors to make links between the emergent experience of these groups and the life and dilemmas of our host organisation and even with organisations in general.

At first there was a marked degree of aversion to the programme, even of overt hostility. Several participants complained of being 'told to' attend the

programme and their resentment at having to comply. This feeling, however, once openly expressed, seemed to dissipate and to become replaced with a growing interest in their own opportunities as a group and what we might achieve together. Initially they appeared as a collection of disparate individuals and subgroups which were disconnected through geographical location. Their initial response to being brought together appeared to me as one of a defensive, sometimes hostile, wariness mingled with a growing curiosity and excitement.

As they developed in cohesiveness over the three days, they seemed to shift from a need to see 'otherness' and difference as located in the convenors' group to the blaming of senior managers for the organisation's woes and finally to a perspective that included responsibility for their own interaction. It was as if their sense of identity as a group, and their sense of belonging to it, were being achieved by the creation of perceived outsiders. These outsiders were then invested with qualities, usually unwanted ones, such as aggression or incompetence, which group members were not yet able to explore within their own cohort. The displacement of conflict and difference on to other groups therefore enhanced their sense of being insiders and of belonging. This protected them from a feared fragmentation with consequent anxieties of isolation and vulnerability and especially of being 'picked off' or scapegoated by the rest of their group.

On the first day of the programme, the participants engaged in an afternoon of inter-group activities. These were designed to highlight, and get people talking about, issues about insiders and outsiders in organisations. We asked the small groups, which had self-selected in the morning, to send delegates to the other groups and to report back on what they discovered. This provoked at least two dilemmas. First, how would individuals cope with the process of both choosing and being chosen as delegates and second, how would the groups respond to any visitors who might arrive? The result was a powerful learning experience for many of those involved. The exercise exposed how groups bond together in the presence of outsiders and tend to render any internal differences invisible. This may then help protect them from potential attack or exploitation. In addition there was a marked increase in social display when visitors arrived so that elaborate greeting rituals and body language seemed to be used to reduce the possibility of conflict. The visitors tended to act in more appeasing and submissive ways as if there was a real possibility that they might be attacked. Those receiving, however, had a tendency to be haughty and even rude to the visitors as if they were basking in the new-found feelings of security and power from the cohesion of their group. Some overcompensated by displays of elaborate social courtesy.

In the plenary meeting, many of the participants behaved as if this particular exercise had opened their eyes to relevant situations at work in which they were coming in as outsiders or receiving colleagues from external agencies. This would become particularly relevant the following morning when Vera, the chief executive, met with the participants and, along with some of her directors, sat in the plenary meeting. I had asked her to do this by way of underwriting and visibly putting her authority behind the Artemis programme. Her arrival, however, brought new difficulties.

A deteriorating relationship

My confidence in convening the Artemis programme had been affected by worsening relations with Vera. I felt that she had been avoiding me for some time. I had previously had a lot of contact with her and would usually see her or hear from her several times a week, including when I was abroad. Within the organisation I was directly accountable to her. She had confided in me about a number of delicate organisational situations and taken risks in doing so. There was thus a degree of intimacy in this working relationship that I knew she felt uneasy about but also had required. Suddenly there was nothing and I felt that I detected an icy avoidance as if she were making a strategic withdrawal. Without her support, both Artemis and I would be potentially endangered.

I found myself in a difficult position. Support from my immediate line manager appeared to have been withdrawn and yet here I was, attempting to deliver a major organisational development programme. I felt very let down by Vera and assumed that if anything went wrong, I would have little backup from her. To add to my anxieties, Vera had called out one of the convenors to a meeting on the first morning of Artemis. This seemed to me an intensely unhelpful act and it was immediately picked up by the other convenors as a signal of ambivalence towards the programme. Having to take the helm through what seemed like increasingly rough seas, I chose to remain quiet about my true feelings to the other convenors lest they grew anxious and passed their anxiety through to the participants. I was, however, able to talk things through with our consultant and my co-convenor Harold.

The turbulence that I experienced within myself at this time, this complexity of embodied feeling which is commonly referred to as emotion, mirrors the anxieties and tensions that form and are formed by the surrounding organisational interaction. I suggest that in convening a programme of this nature, I inevitably enter into iterated patterns of interaction generated from and through the wider organisation. However, in my role as convenor, I am in effect entering a patterning of emotional construction similar to that being experienced by people in the wider organisation, including Vera.

On the second morning of Artemis we began with a plenary that Vera and two directors of the trust attended. Rather irritatingly they were a few minutes late in arriving and thus made a special entrance that seemed to draw attention to the power relation. The room fell silent. This type of unstructured large group meeting was a new experience to most of the participants and there were corresponding levels of anxiety. I felt that, at least in these initial stages, I had some responsibility to help people with these anxieties. Everyone looked at Vera and the directors and then at me. I felt tense and anxious and concerned that my difficulties with Vera had affected my confidence. Someone to my right whispered, 'I don't know which one Vera is'. I took this as a sort of cue and said aloud to the group that there were people here who were unsure who the visitors were. I looked at Vera assuming that this was an obvious opportunity for her to introduce herself but she said not a word. The directors, looking extremely uncomfortable and presumably unable to speak because Vera had not spoken, also remained silent. I felt angry with Vera. Why was she making things so difficult? Was she panicking and couldn't think? Did she think it impossible that staff in the organisation might not know her? Was she emphasising her importance and authority? I had no idea and her body language gave no clue. Finally I broke the silence and invited the group to reflect on their experience of Artemis so far. There was an audible sigh of relief.

Further into the plenary, Vera's input continued to be minimal and this was especially disappointing since everyone had expected her to say something about Artemis. Eventually one of the participants said he would like to know what Vera's expectations of the programme were, after all it was she who had commissioned it. She ignored the question. After her departure I and the other convenors struggled to make sense of her behaviour. One of the facilitators thought she was keeping her distance in case things went badly on the programme in which case it could be quietly forgotten. Others wondered whether she had changed her mind about the programme but felt that it was now too late to prevent it because it had acquired its own momentum.

Whatever Vera's strategy had been, it failed to impress the participants who were now angry and confused by what they experienced as unsupportive behaviour. Paradoxically this helped to bond the group, although at Vera's expense. However, a group of 40 participants holds a lot of diversity and collusion to maintain a particular worldview inevitably comes under pressure so that the preoccupation with Vera led in time to wider exploration. By the end of the three days, most participants were enthusiastic about the programme and looking forward to its continuation. So what had they learnt about? Artemis, in contrast to many development programmes, set no prior learning objectives. The programme was based on the premise that the participants' own process of interaction would yield the necessary experiences for organisational learning and development. Learning objectives could not be identified in the same way as the future of the organisation could not be determined other than perhaps in very short term or general terms. Learning therefore was emergent in the sense that participants would discover, as they went along together, what it was they wanted to understand more about. This was important because the continual process of change shifted the organisational frame from day to day so that participants were always in the act of working out just what kind of corporate landscape they were operating in.

This flexibility of approach therefore allowed for all kinds of unexpected discoveries and for learning to take place. This was because the programme explicitly worked with the emergence of multiple discourses rather than restricting them *a priori* by means of a fixed agenda. Thus the focus on Vera gradually gave way to an understanding that not all responsibility and blame could be located with the chief executive and her board of directors but that they too could affect outcomes through the quality of their interaction. There was a movement over the initial three days, from talking about the trust as meaning the board of directors to one of talking about the trust as inclusive of all its participants. This was a major shift in attitude from one of simple projection to a more integrated view based on a growing awareness of the impact of themselves as managers on those around them.

Not long after the above I had a difficult meeting with Vera. She had redirected my line management to Anne, head of Human Resources and Organisational Development who was also present at the meeting. This made sense to Vera because she saw me as being directly engaged with organisational development. In the context of my difficulties with Vera, however, I experienced it as a rejection and thought it was an attempt to reduce my authority in the organisation.

Furthermore, I found Anne very difficult to work with. She had never attended any of the events that I had put forward and had talked about my work to others in a disparaging way, calling it 'weird, touchy feely, navel gazing, not my kind of thing'. I had tried to have meetings with her to move things on but they were always cancelled. Now she was to be my line manager. I felt disappointed with Vera who I knew had doubts about Anne's competence as a director of organisational development. I felt she was trying to make me peripheral or even eliminate my role. At the same meeting, Vera informed me that she had commissioned an external review of organisational development and that my role as an internal consultant would be reviewed in that process. I thought I detected a look of triumph from Anne.

In retrospect, I believe I had come to operate in a way that threatened to undermine particular power structures within the organisation, those configurations at a senior management level which are legitimised through the mechanics of bureaucracy and over which the CEO holds court as a kind of monarch. There is a strong valency within organisational working relations towards a type of fealty to line managers. This is perhaps amplified

▶

at senior management level and culminates in ritualised displays of obeisance to the figure at the apex, the CEO. As Jackall puts it:

> In short, the subordinate must symbolically reinforce at every turn his own subordination and his willing acceptance of the obligations of fealty. In return, he can hope for those perquisites that are in his boss's gift – the better, more attractive secretaries, or the nudging of a moveable panel to enlarge his office.   (Jackall, 1988, p. 159)

Violation of these fealty obligations, like going around the boss or contradicting them in public, constitutes what Jackall terms

> a kind of death wish in business and one who does so should practice what one executive calls 'flexibility drills,' an exercise 'where you put your head between your legs and kiss your ass goodbye'.   (Jackall, 1988, p. 158)

The monthly events

The initial three-day event of Artemis was to be followed by nine further days occurring at regular intervals with spring and summer breaks so that the whole process would take a year. The managers had so far engaged more whole-heartedly with the process than expected. I thought there would be more antipathy from the participants as they found that their patterns of interaction were being exposed but so far the problems lay more outside the programme than within it. Artemis tended to amplify organisational concerns and proved to be a useful forum for working these through. This was true for both issues that could be explored usefully with any context in mind and those that were specific to the trust at this particular time.

An example of the former arose in the February meeting that coincided with some schools' half-term holidays. There were consequently a number of absences and, predictably, conversation in the plenary initially revolved around those that were not present. We then made connections with the perennial organisational dilemma of how meetings progress in the face of absences and their potentially paralysing influence. This led to an exploration that was new to many of the participants, namely, their own experiences of having to be in several places at the same time and also their experiences of moving meetings forward in the absence

of key players. The result was the turning around of a potentially destructive situation into a creative and helpful conversation.

An example of how Artemis amplified current issues specific to the organisation follows. First, I will describe how I was drawn into a particular situation.

The axe falls

About a year before the programme began, there had been a serious incident on one of the psychiatric wards, Fairport. Three patients left the ward and leapt off a cliff top together, killing themselves. I was asked to debrief the staff who had been involved with them and play a role in getting senior managers alongside the team, visiting them on their ward to talk events through rather than looking for who was to blame. The search for someone to blame is a familiar dynamic to those working with the aftermath of people who have killed themselves. It is as if a quality of anger and persecution permeates the relationships of those formerly involved with the care of the deceased. Everyone seems concerned that the finger of blame will be pointed at him or her and with good reason, since scapegoats are frequently sought. The finding of a scapegoat alleviates everyone else of the anxiety of bearing guilt for the suicide. In the event the situation was handled well and staff felt very supported. Vera and several senior managers went to Fairport ward and spent time talking to staff, some of whom were quite traumatised from such a shocking event. This event attracted the attention of the national press and many of the staff underwent multiple interviews with the police.

Time went by and we were working towards the inquiry and preparing staff for that event when a number of other incidents occurred on Fairport. Principal amongst these, a patient absconded from the ward and went to London to join a peace rally. This patient was supposed to be observed every fifteen minutes and yet it was two hours before his absence was noticed. He had a history of setting fire to himself. Although nothing untoward had occurred, staff could almost read the headlines: *Stop Press – 'Mental Patient Dies In Flames At Peace Rally – How could this happen again?!'*

Obviously the break in observation was a serious breach of protocol at a sensitive time. Nobody wanted further suicides and bad publicity at the time of a major triple inquest. However, events such as these happen frequently on psychiatric wards, and the incidents were being dealt with by both the director of nursing and the medical director, when events took a turn for the worse.

One morning I sat with the director of nursing, Sally, in my office. She burst into tears. She had had a letter from Vera saying that she may be facing disciplinary action as a result of her handling of the recent incidents on Fairport and advising her to contact her professional representatives. What had annoyed Vera was that she had discovered about the recent absconding by chance in a conversation in the corridor. Sally was upset and angry. She had spoken to Vera in the last few days and apologised for not informing her directly and been assured that 'these things happen', so something had changed dramatically. Various stories spread immediately around the organisation about Sally being disciplined. The charge nurse on Fairport was replaced and a manager with a nursing background brought in 'to change the culture'. To many, including myself, it seemed like a huge over reaction, but there was to be more.

In an apparent effort to contain the rumours that were spreading, the board decided on a damage limitation exercise that became a public relations disaster. I was sitting in my office one afternoon when a colleague rushed in to ask if I was going to a special meeting in which Greg, one of the directors, would be reading out an important statement. I was rather irritated by this since the Artemis learning groups were meeting and I learned that some of their members had been called out to these 'special meetings', thus undermining the learning groups. I had also had difficulties with Greg and he had difficulties with Artemis. He had complained that senior management should be steering Artemis and not the participants. So I went along to the meeting. Greg saw me and said in a double-edged way that he had not expected me but was glad I was there. He looked very angry and then read out a rather pompous statement in a solemn tone. The gist of it was that, following serious incidents on Fairport ward, there would be an internal review and that no one was being disciplined but that the director of nursing was being seconded to another trust while the review was in progress. We learned that at that precise moment,

around the organisation, senior managers would be reading exactly the same statement.

To me this was rather like someone saying, 'What ever you do, don't think about elephants.' This was clearly an attempt to dampen down speculation over the fate of the director of nursing but it only served to raise further questions and anxieties. I also knew that his version was very different from the one I had heard from the director of nursing. Greg finished his statement and looked around the room. He asked for any comments in a manner suggesting that none would be welcomed. There was an obsequious silence. I learned later that this was his directorate management group and that I had gatecrashed the meeting. I said something like 'Isn't this all a bit over the top?' Greg rounded on me in cold fury. 'Did you not hear?', he spat. 'Did you not hear the seriousness of the statement I just read, Nick? Are you saying that you didn't understand it, Nick?' I was taken aback by the vehemence of his response and his brutal condescension. I felt myself blushing as if I had committed some heinous *faux pas*. However, I was determined neither to be silenced nor to silence myself. I then raised all the concerns I had about the statement and its mixed messages, saying that it risked drawing further attention and speculation. In doing so I challenged the rhetoric evolved for the occasion by the senior management team and therefore confronted that particular power structure.

The following morning I was told to report to Anne, the head of personnel who was now my line manager. Greg had complained. Greg had found my behaviour destructive. Greg was not pleased, etc. In these circumstances I kept coming across people who were similarly confused about the situation but could only voice their doubts privately. Artemis was about to prove its worth.

The next Artemis meeting

The programme convened shortly after the above event. In the morning plenary there was a brief silence and then someone asked about the director of nursing. For the next hour and a quarter there was a great deal of expressed emotion on the issues around Fairport. The conversation was intense and volatile as those in the room gave their different perspectives and spoke of their feelings. There were those who were outraged on Sally's behalf and those who put forward Vera's perspective. There were people enquiring, people protesting, people crying, people leaving the room to 'make a really important phone call'. It was as if all of the organisational turbulence from the previous fortnight was being expressed by the participants. By the end of that meeting, everyone was feeling drained, but the issues were all out on the table and being openly discussed and people were finding ways of moving forward.

Something was happening in the room that allowed new ways of making sense of the situation to occur. This was the making available of a variety of different discourses and points of view. By discourse I mean socio-historically specific ways of making sense that organise the emergent narratives produced through interaction. The notion of discourse implies a postmodern constructionist standpoint. This questions empirical and absolutist notions of truth as discovered in language. Discourses are created through power relations in a particular socio-historical frame. It can be difficult to discern the inherent power issues within particular discourses that can be experienced as unquestionable truth claims. As Gergen puts it:

> the very idea that there is a single set of propositions that will accurately reflect the nature of the condition (or its 'causal' underpinnings) is grossly misleading . . . Competing realities are suppressed in the name of 'scientific' authority.
>
> (Gergen, 2001, p. 166)

This idea of discourse is important because the senior managers had imagined that they could communicate their intentions in such a way that only one meaning (their meaning) would be construed. This restricted conversation with those managers to one particular discourse. Alternative points of view were not to be tolerated and were actively suppressed. However, this strategy inevitably failed because alternative discourses were then driven underground where the managers were unable to influence them. Artemis provided a forum in which diversity could gain some legitimacy and, although painful, it helped move things forward. There was a great deal of anger around. It seemed that Sally was not seconded to another trust, but that she was sitting unhappily in her garden at home. The directors also had interpreted their instructions to read the statement in different ways. Some had read

it out like Greg but some had more informally had a discussion with their staff. Their staff, however, had interpreted it in all kinds of different ways.

This raises for me an important question concerning communication. If one adopts a sender–receiver model of communication then one might assume that information can be transmitted, intact as it were, from person to person. Meaning in this case is assumed to remain constant. There is one true meaning and all others are false. Such assumptions about communication, however, miss the complexity of human relating. Meaning, for example, takes place in the context of power relating so that 'the truth' may be a particular construction favoured by those with greater power chances and imposed upon those with fewer chances. This I believe is what Greg had resorted to with me in his managers' meeting. He had tried through the use of rhetoric, aggression and finally hierarchical structure to silence me and thus restrict the meanings ascribed to the situation. Communication is a reciprocal process and meaning is constructed in the iterative action of relating. It cannot be assumed that one's gestures will be interpreted in the way one intends them.

There is also, in the above scenario, the question of what happens to the wider organisation when someone at the top falls. The conversation on the Artemis programme suggests to me that a reduction in the power chances of a senior manager affects not only that individual, but all those who identify with them. So, when Sally was perceived as being attacked, all the nurses in the organisation also felt under threat. The actions towards Sally therefore affected a large subgroup. Alienate an influential individual and you also potentially alienate everyone who identifies with them. In the stormy plenary meeting just described, it was noticeable that those who would count themselves as nurses, albeit managers as well, and those who came from Sally's pre-merger locality were amongst the most distressed and affected by her apparent demise. Also, interestingly, the head of communications, who is very close to Vera, was in tears. This was because she was shocked at the extent of anger towards Vera and had not realised the intensity of feeling in the workforce; it placed her in the painful position of questioning her own sense of reality. This raises a further question about communication and power, namely, that the flow of communication in management lines is always censored as a means of attempting to manage the power relations. This is particularly true of the upward flow, where there is often a tendency to tell those above what they want to hear in order to preserve (keeping one's head below the parapet) or even enhance one's status quo.

An exploration of intention

So what am I intending to do in the above programme? How does Artemis compare with other organisational programmes and processes of enquiry, both in method and ideology? First, there is the question of intention. This question relates also to my role as an internal consultant from which Artemis is generated. My confrontation with Greg as described above can be understood as a conflict of intentions within our respective roles. My intentions as a consultant are complex and emergent. I intend to help counter tendencies for 'groupthink' in organisational discourse, to open up diversity of view when such diversity may be compromised through the vested interests of power configurations. This activity is undertaken to find ways of moving forward and of bearing the stresses of a difficult environment. Such intentions are inherent within my task of helping make sense of organisational experience, for sense making of any kind takes place in the context of power relating. Greg's intention is to implement the board's strategies and tactics, to represent and further the interests of those involved in his power configuration. This brings us into conflict because the credibility and integrity of my role demands a questioning rather than compliant attitude.

Both Greg and I have intentions to further ourselves independently of the overall organisation's requirements. This means that, for the time being, I can reconcile my personal ambitions with the overall requirements of the organisation for which I work but that I may leave if this changes and as and when other opportunities present themselves. My intention, therefore, is to develop in such a way that my interests and those of my family are not jeopardised in any potential fall from grace so that I have a viable exit strategy. This is important since my role inevitably brings me, at times, into conflict with a variety of organisational power structures and configurations that may then act to suppress or even remove me from position. I stress the phrase 'overall requirements of the organisation' since it is important that I resist identifying too closely with any particular power structure since this would then raise problems of collusion and inhibit the expression of difference necessary for the role. There is something of a paradox here, given that the role is sanctioned by the board who then may find its interests in conflict with work undertaken on its behalf. However, the latent creativity inherent in any conflictual situation depends on the capacity of those involved to work through problems together.

Our intentions for the Artemis programme develop and differ as the project moves forward and are being reconstructed in an ongoing way. They are thus emergent in the sense of discovering how we, as participants, move forward at any given time. Therefore, Artemis was originally conceived as an induction for new managers to the trust. As relationships developed around the programme, it became apparent that we were providing personal and organisational development. As these working relations grew, we found ourselves forming intentions through the contingencies and constraints that arose through our interaction.

For me, Artemis, as a programme, was concerned with maintaining a process that could allow the exchange and potential transformation of multiple stories and points of view concerning the organisation. In this way, it provided a forum for an active engagement with the process of organisational diversity. This diversity is crucial both for the creativity of the organisation and the sense-making capacities of its participants. The programme helps to counter the collapse of the (legitimate) organisational conversation into a monolithic discourse permitted by politicians in central government. It was also, for me, a strategy to simultaneously maintain position organisationally and create a passport for myself beyond that organisation.

There are similarities in the above methodology to that taken by Reason and Heron (1995) in the development of the approach they term co-operative inquiry. Both processes bring people together in iterative cycles of interaction. Both harness local interaction through group work as a means of developing ways forward for the participants. Both aim at the amplification of meaning and interactive sense making within those processes.

However, there are important differences. Reason separates out action and reflection as if they were discrete from each other. He talks of alternate

►

cycles in which 'agreed actions' arise from the group's reflections. These are initiated and applied in 'every day life and work'. He and others such as Traylen (1994) separate the co-operative enquiry (reflection within the group) from the action research, 'being up and doing'. Action research is seen as ideas generated from the group being applied and tested in the work environment. I argue that this creates a misleading dichotomy that negates the interaction within the co-operative enquiry group and reduces it to something called reflection. The interaction within the group is as significant in terms of 'action' as are the activities of the participants outside of it. The difference between Reason's way of thinking and that of Artemis is that his concept of action sounds like something that has an existence outside of interaction as if one could exist separately from the other as separate procedural entities. The latter then justifies the former. Owen (1992) adopts the same dichotomous position in his approach to organisational development, 'Open Space Technology'. Owen places much emphasis on participative interaction through the creation of 'open spaces' but seems to validate this process in terms of 'the proceedings', written accounts and action plans arising from the work. This again suggests that these 'proceedings' have a life of their own outside of interaction. Owen writes:

> In the course of the two-day meeting, that diverse group created, and totally self-managed, an agenda built around some 52 different task groups . . . [who] produced about 150 pages of proceedings in 36 hours. Thanks to the wonders of modern computers . . . copies of the final proceedings rolled hot off the press in time for the departure of all participants.
>
> (Owen, 1992, p. 1)

What, one wonders, was the fate of all that paperwork and was it serving any purpose other than to alleviate an anxiety that interaction in itself was purposeless without a reified outcome? Again Owen states:

> Although Open Space Technology is powerful and effective, never use it for the sake of the process alone, only for the potential results.
>
> (Owen, 1992, p. 17)

The supposition here is that the results are in some way outside of the process and legitimise it. By contrast, the ethos of Artemis was not to place anything outside the ongoing process of living interaction and this included planning as an emergent part of the process.

The Artemis programme, in terms of enquiry, aimed to explore the emergent interaction of the participants in the light of organisational issues. At the same time we were seeking to develop the quality of this local interaction in such a way as to influence the wider organisational conversation. This is crucial in terms of the dynamics of power relations currently prevalent in the public sector. As previously described, these dynamics tend to elevate a particular discourse driven from the centre and aimed at performance management. The implicit threat behind much performance management is that inability to reach targets will result in removal from role and, for some, the loss of their income. This anxiety thus strikes at the heart of the worker's sense of identity and in addition potentially threatens his or her dependents. The aim is to maximise the efficiency and profitability of the organisation. The means, however, are coercive and this has the effect of evoking fear and resentment throughout the workforce. The resulting fear silences people and pushes underground the exchange of experience so that the only legitimate conversation is one that relates to performance. The result is a closing down of available discourses upon which people could draw to move their various departments forward.

This phenomenon that I am describing as the closing down of available discourses happens in a number of ways. In the attempt to reach operational targets through optimisation of performance, complexity of purpose may be reduced. This is especially the case when performance is evaluated purely in terms of ability to hit targets in a linear and predictable fashion. When purpose is reduced to this type of performance, power relations develop that tend to rigidify the legitimated lines of organisational communication so that only a narrow range of meanings may be ascribed to interaction. For example, in the meeting with Greg when he was reading out his statement regarding the director of nursing, there was a strong move towards restricting the meanings that might have been ascribed to that situation. Greg, through the use of rhetoric and hierarchical position, attempted to establish a dominant discourse to the exclusion of others. In the attempt to equate lines of communication with line management relations, interaction patterns itself on the type of power relating that predicates dominance–submission dynamics. This essentially means that people have a marked tendency to tell their superiors what they imagine that they want to hear. Also, as Gramsci (1971) points out, people internalise particular power relations and take on attitudes as if they were their own opinions. This makes it difficult to think freely in particular power relations and since they appear natural, part of how things are, they can feel like 'common sense'.

The above, I believe, has implications for the potential of creativity within the organisation, or rather the lack of it. If discourse is overly constrained or reduced to performance, then diversity of view similarly suffers and this may prevent novelty from arising in the organisation. This novelty amounts to people finding new ways forward together in an ever changing landscape. It represents the ability for the organisation to develop and ultimately survive. By way of contrast, people fall into patterns of interaction that reiterate power relations where there is a lack of counter-constraint. It is not as if the constraints that we present to each other are undesirable; they enable us to progress. Rather it is the lack of counter-constraint in organisational and political life that represents a danger. This may lead to the worst excesses of inhumane behaviour. Thus the availability of a multiplicity of discourses also represents the movement of thinking within a field of activity characterised by mutually constraining influences. Artemis was an attempt to develop this multiplicity of discourse. This enabled managers potentially to find personal meaning and purpose within their work rather than to feel that they are on some kind of treadmill in which they are little but a mechanistic cog.

Pursuing perfection

Serious attention to local interaction is often lacking in major organisational change initiatives, of which I shall discuss 'Pursuing Perfection', a programme currently in vogue in the health service. It is not so much that the importance of local interaction is denied as that it becomes reified through system design. This in effect means that people imagine that they have dealt with relational issues through the design of a system. Thus processes that might prove effective when dealing with machines with clear linear relationships can prove less adequate when applied to human relating. 'Pursuing Perfection' is a programme designed by the Boston-based Institute for Healthcare Improvement. It had a contract with the National Health Service worth some £2 million annually to badge 'Pursuing Perfection' for the United Kingdom.

The programme arose from two reports commissioned by the American Institute of Medicine. *To Err is Human* (published in 1999) explores errors in healthcare within the USA and makes recommendations for what it terms radical change within the healthcare industry, while *Crossing the Quality Chasm* (Lohr, 2001) extends the agenda beyond safety for patients and strives to expound a methodology for transforming health care systems. 'Pursuing Perfection' aims to dramatically improve outcomes for patients in all their major care processes (Dugdale, 2002). It does this by small increments in specific locations. Teams are asked to make 'promises' to deliver radical 'improvements' to clinical outcomes within very short time frames. Underpinning this drive for improved outcomes is a framework for quality improvement that is designed through the use of rules, aims and guidance to stimulate beneficial change. Perfection in this context is defined as the delivery, without waiting and without risk, of efficient, evidence-based healthcare to the patient and preferably in such a way that the patient will notice and be happy with the quality of service on offer. The ideology corresponds well with the political agenda to produce tangible 'evidence' of improvement in public sector services and it is not difficult to see why it has been so well supported.

This approach has an evangelical, inspirational quality to it that seeks through devices such as the 'promises' to effect the solution beloved of many cults, namely, the subjugation of individual participative responsibility to a higher moral or even transcendent authority. Attention is focused upon the reification of a process, for example a system or a structure, rather than upon the ongoing interaction necessary to effect the desired outcomes. Of course there is also the question of the desirability of targeted outcomes and the effects these have upon interdependent services that may suffer as a result. This may be why 'Pursuing Perfection' tries to implement change in short bursts because

▶

anything more long term would inevitably meet the counter-constraints of interdependent services affected by rapid change. However, this then raises the question of whether the effects of such programmes are sustainable.

There is also a strong rhetoric about the elimination of redundancy. Under the aegis of efficiency, we are exhorted to unceasingly apply ourselves to the reduction of waste and total cost of care. The care system is supposed to reliably match care to science, avoiding overuse of ineffective care and underuse of effective care (Dugdale, 2002).

The difficulty with this relentless efficiency and reliance on evidence is that it is difficult to see how the conditions might be created for people to enter the murky state of confusion and uncertainty so necessary for creative endeavour. This aspect of the creative process that gets mistaken for redundancy is something that causes discomfort and gets called 'a waste of time' or 'navel gazing' but may be crucial for the emergence of new patterns of relating. Let us return to Artemis to see how this might be so.

Polarities of discourse

Artemis had been assigned a steering group appointed by Vera. It comprised Harold and me as co-convenors and four service directors as well as a chair who was to be Anne. This group had a great deal of trouble in meeting up. It was supposed to have convened monthly but there were only two occasions on which we met and on the first of these only Harold, Anne and I had been present. However there had been an increasing number of e-mails, particularly from Greg, indicating that resentment and misunderstanding about the programme had been building. The tenor of these communications was to the effect that Artemis was out of control and being steered by the participants rather than by the senior managers on the steering group. It was suggested that the programme was indulging in something called 'navel gazing' and not addressing 'real and pressing organisational issues'. It sounded to Harold and me that Artemis was threatening the status quo of power relations within the organisation and that some of the senior managers were worried about not being able to set the agenda. In this way the programme differs significantly from mainstream organisational

development whose general purpose is to align the organisation with its operational goals. Rather Artemis set out to work with the ongoing process of interaction in which people, in their cycles of gesturing and responding to one another, make sense and negotiate how to move forward together as an organisation, as subgroups and as individuals, all at the same time.

The steering group finally met and began to address some of the concerns. There was a push to make the programme 'more useful'. Could we not give them tools such as teaching them 'process mapping'? Should we not be telling them in advance what they should be expecting on each day with some kind of agenda? If Artemis was informed by complexity then should we not be teaching them how to manage complex adaptive systems? And lastly could they have a regular report as to what had been covered on the programme? Somehow we managed to work through most of the above issues in a way that left the programme uncompromised. Essentially I felt we were struggling with an ideological conflict over the nature of management and how issues of power and control are dealt with. There was a tendency to collapse the experience of the programme into polarities so that they had heard Artemis was 'pointless, a waste of time' or 'amazing, a fantastic experience'. I encouraged people to think about the programme in a more complex way and to resist reducing it to narrow and polarised realms of experience.

Appraisal

On one of the Artemis days, we decided to focus upon the 'three-sixty-degree' appraisal process. The participants were asked to work in the pairs that they had chosen for their received feedback. We also wished to put the programme itself through this process and therefore we invited the large group to reflect upon their experience of the programme so far. I was struck by the way the group responded. It seemed like a shifting conflict of ideologies, So that whatever someone said, another would attempt to negate that view and often through the polarised expression of their own experience. We witnessed, for example, a debate between the values of psychiatric diagnosis on the one hand and the diametrically opposed philosophy of social care upon the other. This was followed by a conflict between those who advocated action on the programme and those who wanted reflection. Then there was a discussion on the merits of the 'human touch' versus those who valued target setting. Finally we heard from those who 'don't want to be told what to do' as against those who wanted to accept authority. This was all punctuated by not particularly long silences, which were experienced variously but again had a tendency towards polarity, such as 'What's the point of all this? This is a waste of time' to 'The silence is really helpful and gives me a chance to think'. Now, in many ways the process illustrates a broad dichotomy of ideologies present in public services such as the ethos of performance versus what might be termed an ethos of connectivity. It also illustrates the tendency of groups to polarise their discourse so that not only conflict and irritation arise but also, potentially, engagement of the kind that leads to shifts in perspectives and a deepening understanding of one another.

What was particularly interesting about the above process was the way that the group was moving from this position of sequential polarity to the exploration of some sensitive work issues. This happened towards the end of the day as the group began to slowly realise and then to use its capacity to exchange and make sense of information relating to the organisation. It emerged that a major and costly piece of work on clinical policy was being duplicated by different parties within the organisation and that neither one knew of the other. This revelation caused a flurry of excitement in the group as a number of those present undertook to take 'action'. Although this could be understood as a kind of flight from the anxious uncertainties of the large group, it can also be thought about as a helpful fruition born of increased connectedness, itself the eventual result of the labour of silences and conflictual, polarised tensions. In other words, the apparent periods of redundancy were a necessary precursor and gestation for effective action.

Conclusion

The Artemis programme set out to provide processes whereby people could explore their emergent organisational dilemmas in a live way. The programme raised anxieties not only for the participants but also for senior managers. These anxieties seemed frequently to be based upon threatened changes to familiar patterns of relating within the organisational power structures. The changes to patterns of power relating were brought about by increased interaction in which a multiplicity of discourse was facilitated. This multiplicity of discourse represented the diversity necessary for creativity and novelty to arise. As a result, people's views and perspectives on organisational life began to shift and develop. This helped to counter the rigid patterning of conversation developed by subgroups within the constraints of their power relations. Artemis allowed a greater possibility for people to develop their sense of purpose and meaning within their roles. This is essential in a culture that has elevated performance to a totalitarian level. In other words, the primacy of performance reduces complexity of purpose and threatens to subjugate and mechanise the individual through covert and profound threats to their identity.

Artemis as a programme set out to explore the emergent values of the organisation as they develop in interaction. The cult values of Artemis could be described as open communication and reflexivity in professional practice in the context of emergent interaction. In this way the programme suggests an ideal in terms of interaction but an ideal that we seek to explore, as it becomes fuctionalised within interaction. This therefore inevitably leads to conflict with the said cult values as people find themselves constrained by power relations in and around the context of the programme. Specifically we are attempting to work with the ongoing cycles of gesture and response as suggested by Mead and formulated by Stacey (2001) in terms of complex responsive processes. So Artemis seeks to engage with the whole range of human relating and this means staying with and exploring conflict and other ways in which we constrain and enable each other at the same time. This is different from other participative approaches such as Appreciative Inquiry and Owen's (1992) Open Space Technology that explicitly set out to create conditions of safety through a variety of behavioural prescriptions.

This in effect means that we are not attempting to control or predict outcomes as in Schein's (1988) paradigm of organisational cultural development or to rely in our sense making upon underlying dynamic causal structures, as in the writers of the Tavistock tradition. Rather it is a question of how people find ways of moving forward together through their iterative patterns of interaction and of exploring where they find themselves in this process. As participative facilitators and researchers in this process we, like everyone else, can influence the conversation and play our part in the emergent movement of thought in action. This is to say that we do not see ourselves as neutral observers commenting upon an unfolding process but rather as actively involved as co-participants with particular roles of leadership in this particular programme.

Artemis appears to have helped to develop a sense of organisational connectivity and the importance of direct communication. As one manager put it at a recent meeting: 'I had this problem and just rang up a colleague on Artemis. I was able to sort it out because we had developed a better relationship through being on that programme together. I would never have done that before.'

Questions to aid further reflection

1. How do you understand intention and emergence in this narrative?

2. Would you describe what people are doing in this narrative as practical?

3. Does this narrative resonate with actions and events in your experience and, if so, does it lead you to think differently about them?

4. Would you describe the Artemis programme as Organisation Development or not? Why?

5. How are the local interactions of people in the narrative related to population-wide patterns of development of this trust and of government policy?

6. Sarra clearly thinks that conflict and anxiety are central aspects of creative organisational development. What do you think of his argument?

© Nicholas Sarra

Chapter 13

The emergence of organisational strategy in local communicative interaction

Complex responsive processes of ideology and power relating

This chapter invites you to draw on your own experience to reflect on and consider the implications of:

- The processes of idealisation in forming the cult values of an organisation and interpreting them in specific, contingent situations.

- The ideological basis of choice and intention in organisations.

- The nature of power relations in organisations and the ideologies that sustain them.

- The impact of the inclusion–exclusion dynamics of power in organisations.

- The role of inclusion–exclusion processes in identity formation.

- The part that gossip plays in sustaining ideologies and power relations in organisations.

- The implications of power relations and ideology for the local activities of strategising and the population-wide patterns of strategy that they produce.

This chapter carries further the exploration of processes of local interaction understood as conversation, drawing attention to how figurations of power relations emerge in ongoing communicative interaction and how these patterns of power relations are sustained by ideologies. It points to an understanding of choice, decision making and intention in organisational life as all fundamentally ideological in nature and reflective of power relations. This chapter is important because it introduces two further key aspects of complex responsive processes of relating in addition to conversation. In doing so it makes power and ideology central to an understanding of organisational life, aspects of experience that do not receive this prominence in the dominant discourse on organisation and strategy. We come to understand strategy as the evolving collective identities of people in organisations reflecting the pattern of power relations between them and the ideologies that sustain these patterns. We come to understand local interaction as not just the particularising of generalised population-wide patterns but also the functionalising of idealisations of these patterns understood as values and ideology. We come to understand population-wide patterns, that is, strategies, as generalisations and idealisations.

13.1 Introduction

Chapters 11 and 12 described how Mead drew attention to the human capacity to generalise the attitude, the tendency to act, of people in groups and societies and how each person takes up such generalisations, or population-wide patterns of action, in each specific local situation in which they interact with other people. General tendencies to act are thereby made particular in each specific situation, through interactive processes of essentially conflictual negotiation and compromise. They do all of this in conversation with each other. And it works primarily because, through the life histories of the individuals involved and through the history of their communities, these generalised tendencies to act have become central aspects of their very selves. Socialising processes have instilled self-control in persons and this is the basis of modern social order. Socially instilled self-control is a far more important source of the controlled behaviour of people in groups, organisations and societies than the instructions of the more powerful, the procedures of an organisation or even the law. However, individual persons do not act in ways that are simply socially determined because of the human capacity for choice and spontaneity.

This chapter is primarily concerned with the processes of human choosing reflected in the formation of intentions and the processes of decision making. Central to understanding processes of choosing, intending and making decisions is the nature of ideology. This chapter will, therefore, be concerned with how we might understand the formation of values and norms and the implications they have for power relations, and the impact they have on choices, intentions and decision making in organisations. The argument will be that ideologies and the power relations they sustain are central to the local communicative interactions of strategising in which the population-wide patterns of strategy emerge.

This chapter draws on the work of Mead and Dewey to understand ideology and on that of Elias to explore the nature of power relations. Chapter 12 drew attention to Mead's explanation of how the generalisations of social objects are made particular in ordinary everyday, specific, contingent situations in which people in organisations find they have to act. Mead also drew attention to another important human capacity: humans have a powerful tendency to idealise social objects, that is, to idealise generalisations of population-wide patterns. He argued that in idealising social objects people form cult values, an idea to be explored in the next section.

13.2 Cult values

Mead (1923) held that people not only generalise habitual patterns of interaction to imaginatively construct some kind of unity of experience, usually understood as some kind of 'whole', they also inevitably idealise these imaginatively constructed 'wholes'. Mead pointed to how people have a tendency to individualise and idealise a collective and treat it 'as if' *it* had overriding motives or values, amounting to processes in which the collective constitutes a 'cult'. Mead described such idealisations as cult values that emerge in the evolution of a society and said that they were the most precious part of our heritage. Cults are maintained when leaders present to people's imaginations an idealised future for the 'whole' that is free of conflicts and constraints, evoking in individuals who belong to it a sense of enlarged personality in which they can accomplish anything simply through their belonging to an idealised group in which they participate and from which they derive their value as persons. For example, a collective consisting of supporters of a football club displays the tendencies Mead was talking about. Simply belonging to the club and watching the team playing generates feelings of euphoria in fans, of belonging to the 'best', even though they are sitting in front of a television screen miles away from the very small number who are actually playing the game. The same kind of feeling of enlarged personality is experienced when one's country is selected to host the Olympic games or wins a war. Belonging to a major corporation elicits the same feeling of enlarged personality in many people. The visions articulated by leaders of countries and corporations are examples of idealisations of the 'whole' which promise a utopian future shorn of all obstacles to its realisation – 'we will be number one'.

It is important to stress immediately that cult values can be good or bad or both. Cult values would include 'ethnic purity' and 'loving your neighbour'. Mead points out that the processes of idealisation are far from unproblematic and could easily lead to actions that others outside the cult will come to regard as bad, even evil, as in 'ethnic purity'. On the other hand, cult values to 'end poverty' could lead to actions that others will come to regard as good, even saintly.

If cult values are applied directly to action, without allowing for variations contingent on a specific situation, then those undertaking such action form a cult in which they exclude all who do not comply. Members of 'cults' forget the 'as if' nature of their constructed unity of experience, the 'whole', and act in a manner driven by the cult's values. Mead was pointing to the dangers of focusing on the cult values themselves, on the values of the personalised institution or system, and directly applying them as overriding universal norms, conformity to which constitutes the requirement for continuing membership of the institution.

Normally, however, idealisation is accompanied by functionalisation. Idealisations, or cult values, can become functional values in the everyday interactions between members of an institution rather than being simply applied in a way that enforces the conformity of a cult. For example, the cult value of a hospital might be to 'provide each patient with the best possible care'. However, such a cult value has to be repeatedly functionalised in many unique specific situations throughout the day. In other words, specific healthcare professionals, in specific places, at specific times will have to decide how to interpret the meaning of 'best possible care' in the face of competing demands for time and other resources. As soon as cult values become functional values in real daily interaction, conflict arises and it is this conflict that must be negotiated by people in their practical interaction with each other as they act on present interpretations of cult values. For example, a cult value to do with the sacredness of life may be directly and rigidly applied by people in an anti-abortion group who deny that there are any circumstances whatsoever in which abortion is to be allowed. Such cult members have been known to murder doctors who defy this cult value. However, for many people the cult value of the sacredness of life is not directly applied, leading to conflict regarding the circumstances in which abortion may be permissible – the conflict may be around whether abortion should be allowed up to 20 weeks after conception or up to 24 weeks. Functionalising of values is the enactment of values in the ordinary, local interactions between people in the living present.

In many healthcare organisations today, the notions of 'modernisation', 'improvement' and 'performance' have taken on the status of cult values. Government ministers present to people's imagination a future for healthcare in which such care is of a continuously improving quality, and equally available on demand to everyone with very little waiting time. This 'vision' is presented in such a way that the difficulties in achieving it go unmentioned. However, when practitioners try to functionalise such cult values they are confronted with shortages of resources and many other relational problems which mean that they find it impossible to deliver the idealised future. They find they have to functionalise the undoubtedly worthy cult values and this gives rise to conflicting priorities.

Mead presented a paradoxical formulation in his distinction between cult and functional values. The idealisation must be functionalised in specific contingent situations – the meaning of the idealisation is only to be found in the experience of its functionalisation. In its functionalisation the ideal inevitably become less than ideal.

We may employ the tool of writing to articulate and codify our idealisations in the form of ethical propositions, myths and inspiring narratives. They may be presented as intended, crafted vision statements for a corporation, for example. However, although someone can design and intentionally present statements about values, they can only ever be cult values that have no meaning on their own. In other words, the cult value is the first phase of a social act that can never be separated from the other phase, namely, functionalising the cult values.

As well as being generalisations, then, social objects may also take the form of *idealisations* or cult values. Such values have the effect of *including* those who adhere to them and *excluding* those who do not, so establishing collective or *'we' identities* for all of the individuals in both groupings. Social objects/cult values are thus closely linked to *power*, a matter to be discussed later in this chapter. Social objects as generalised/idealised tendencies to act in similar ways both enable and constrain the actors at the same time. Social objects/cult values are thus forms of *social control* reflected in figurations of *power relations* between people.

Furthermore, cult values provide the evaluative criteria people use to make choices. We normally do not choose our actions in a technically rational manner but on the basis of what we believe, often unconsciously, to be 'right'. And we derive these beliefs from the social milieu in which we have grown up and live. The ideological basis of out choices of action have become so ingrained in who we are that we are mainly unaware of just what this ideological basis is. This point about the ideological basis of choice is of great importance because ideology deeply conditions the way we think about what we do, or should do, in organisations. For example, the ideology of control underpinning the dominant discourse about organisations goes largely unremarked. The demand for control ceases to be examinable as a belief and becomes taken for granted as 'reality', so closing down explorative processes of new thinking. The manner in which personal experiences of value arise is not explored and, instead, leaders of organisations are called upon to provide appropriate values for people and to inspire them with 'compelling visions of the future'. When they do this, leaders are actually articulating cult values, which may or may not be 'good'. What is overlooked, however, is the need to functionalise the cult values. On the contrary, the prescriptions usually call for the conversion of people so that they all share and act upon the same values. It is not realised that this is in fact a prescription for the formation of a cult through processes that can easily amount to propaganda, even brainwashing. Fortunately, visions, missions and value statements are usually simply acknowledged in public while privately people express their cynicism. What is also not questioned is how experiences of value arise and whether it is indeed possible for leaders to provide genuine value experiences for other people in an instrumental manner.

Recognising that many of today's prescriptions for leaders could amount to the potential formation of cults, that actually it is impossible to prescribe genuine values for other people except through intense propaganda and brainwashing, thus has considerable practical implications for currently dominant ways of organising, leading and strategising.

The question then is how cult values arise and how they evolve.

13.3 Desires, values and norms

The work of Joas (2000) is helpful in understanding how cult values arise and evolve. He draws on the thinking of the American pragmatists (Dewey, 1934; James, 1902; Mead, 1934) to make a distinction between desires/preferences, values/ideals and norms.

Turning first to desires, a distinction can be made between first- and second-order desires (Frankfurt, 1971). First-order desires or preferences are:

- fluid and particular bodily impulses expressed as unreflective action;
- experienced as compulsive motivations for actions;
- lacking in evaluative criteria and so not intrinsically linked to ethics or morals.

However, humans also have desires that are directed to their desires and could be called second-order desires. In other words, humans can desire to have desires, or not, and they can desire that their desire be strong enough to influence their will. We can desire to be different to who we are. Desires directed to our desires arise in reflective self-evaluation so that human desiring is essentially reflective and self-evaluative and so essentially social because the self is social. For human action it is not possible to take desire (bodily impulse, or first-order desire) on its own because of the human capacity, essentially social, to formulate the desirable and the judgement or evaluation that this always involves. Only in the rarest of circumstances, I would argue, do humans simply act on bodily impulse – there is almost always some kind of discrimination arising in a history of social interaction, although that discrimination could quite easily have become unconscious. This discrimination inevitably implicates norms and values. So what are they and how do they arise?

Norms are:

- evaluative in that they provide criteria for judging desires and actions;
- obligatory and constraining. They therefore restrict opportunities for action. We experience them as compelling in a restrictive sense;
- intimately connected with morals in that they provide criteria for what *ought* to be done, what is *right*.

Norms, then, provide a basis for evaluating and choosing between desires and actions. Elias ([1939] 2000) was particularly concerned with how norms emerge and evolve as people in a society become more and more interdependent and as the use of violence is monopolised by the state. He explained how desires are taken more and more behind the scenes of daily life as more detailed norms emerge about what can and cannot be done in public. These norms become part of individual personality structures and adherence to such norms is sustained by the social process of shame. Norms, therefore, are constraints arising in social evolution that act to restrain the actions and even desires of interdependent individuals, so much so that the constraints become thematic patterns of individual identities. In complex responsive process terms, norms are themes organising experience in a constraining way. However, norms are inseparable although different from values. First, consider how values differ from norms and then how inseparable they are, despite the differences.

Joas uses the words 'values' and 'ideals' interchangeably and identifies their characteristics as:

- evaluative in that they provide general and durable criteria for judging desires, norms and actions;
- attractive and compelling in a voluntary, committed sense. They motivate action and open up opportunities for action. Values attract us, giving life meaning and purpose, and so are not experienced as restrictive. They are the highest expression of our free will, presenting a paradox of compulsion and voluntary commitment at the same time;
- intimately connected with ethics in that they provide criteria for judging what *is* the *good* in action, differentiating between good and bad desires, good and bad norms.

Values are essentially concerned with what it is good to desire. When we reject a perfectly realisable desire because we believe it is unacceptable then we are distinguishing between higher and lower virtues or vices, profound and superficial feelings, noble and base desires. Such evaluations indicate a life we hold to be of higher value, a view of the kind of person we want to be.

Joas drew on Dewey (1934), a friend and colleague of Mead, to argue that values, as inspiring, attractively compelling motivations to act towards the good,

are continually arising in social interaction as inescapable aspects of self formation. Values are continually arising in our ongoing negotiation with each other,
and ourselves, in our going on together. It follows that values are contingent upon
the particular action situations in which we find ourselves. Although values have
general and durable qualities, their motivational impact on action must be negotiated afresh, must be particularised, in each action situation. Dewey combines such
an intersubjective understanding of self and value formation with experiences of self
transcendence. The communicative interaction in which self is formed is more than
a means to co-ordinating action; it opens human beings up to each other, making
possible the experience in which values and commitments to them arise. Shared
experiences overcome self-centredness producing altruism, which is a radical readi-
ness to be shaken by the other in order to realise oneself in and through others. This
opening, or transcending, of the self is the process in which genuine values arise.

Dewey also brings the role of imagination and creativity into the genesis of
values and value commitments. Imagination idealises contingent possibilities and
creates an imaginary relation to a holistic self. While imaginary, this relation is not
an illusion or a fantasy. Idealisation allows us to imagine a wholeness that does
not exist and never will but seems real because we have experienced it so intensely.
This is not a solitary but a social process. The will does not bring about the
imagined wholeness; rather, the will is possessed by it. The voluntary compulsion
of the experience of value and value commitment feels to come from outside of
ourselves, to be not of our own positing but of something higher than us.

The description of values and value commitments in the last section may easily
be taken as meaning that values are unequivocally good. However, as indicated in
the discussion above, this is not so. The notions of cult values, the power dynamics
of inclusion and exclusion they involve, and the way in which groups of people may
get caught up in destructive unconscious processes of self loss, focus our attention
on the darker aspects of values/ideals and value commitments. These processes point
to the particular problems that arise from the tendencies to idealise imagined wholes
and submerge oneself in imagined participation in them.

Notice the paradoxical nature of the theory of values so far outlined. Values arise
in processes of self formation and self transcendence at the same time. Values arise
in critical reflection and in experience beyond conscious deliberation at the same
time. Values arise in intense actual experience of interaction and in idealising acts
of imagination at the same time. Values may be good or bad or both, depending
upon who is doing the judging.

Values do not arise either from conscious intentions or through justification and
discussion, although such intention, justification and discussion may be applied
later. Genuinely experienced value commitments cannot be produced rationally
and authentic values cannot be disseminated through indoctrination. A purpose
in life cannot be prescribed. Instead, the subjective experience of values arises in
specific action contexts and types of intense experience. Values and value commitments arise in the process of self formation through processes of idealising key
intense experiences and through the imaginative construction of a whole self to
yield general and durable motivations for action directed toward what is judged
as the good. These generalised idealisations must always be particularised in
specific action situations as people negotiate their going on together if they are to
avoid a cult.

Values cannot be prescribed or deliberately chosen by anyone because they emerge, and continue to be iterated, in intense interactive experiences involving self formation and self transcendence. To claim that someone could choose values for others would be to claim that this someone could form the identity, or self, of others and form the self transcendence of others.

If one takes the above view of what values are and how they arise then the prescriptions of the dominant discourse that require leaders to form an organisation's values become highly questionable. Such approaches could not create authentic experiences of value and value commitment involving a mature capacity to functionalise them in contingent situations. All they could do, when effective as propaganda, would be to create the dangerous conformity of a fundamentalist cult. Alternatively, leadership activities claiming to be formulating values may only amount to the prescription of norms as obligatory restrictions rather than the voluntary compulsions of values. Even these norms would have to be functionalised in contingent situations unless people felt so threatened and afraid that they could do not other than rigidly comply in what would then be a fascist power structure. The less harmful consequence of attempts to instil values is the cynicism usually provoked by such attempts. The way one thinks about values and norms thus has profound consequences for what one does in organisations.

Now consider how norms and values together constitute ideology.

Norms, values and ideology

In complex responsive processes terms, values are themes organising the experience of being together in a voluntary compelling, ethical manner, while norms are themes of being together in an obligatory, restrictive way. Furthermore, in complex responsive process terms, norms and values constitute a paradox. When humans interact, they enable and constrain each other at the same time. It is the actions of human bodies that enable and constrain. However, in their ongoing negotiation of these enabling–constraining actions, all are taking the attitude of others, specifically and in a generalised/idealised way. In other words, they are continually negotiating the evaluations of their actions. The criteria for evaluation are at the same time both obligatory restrictions, taking the form of what they ought and ought not to do (norms), and voluntary compulsions, taking the form of what they are judging it good to do (values). The evaluative themes forming and being formed by human interaction are norms and values at the same time, together constituting ideology.

Ideology can be thought of as an imaginative 'whole' that is simultaneously the obligatory restriction of the norm and the voluntary compulsion of value, constituting the evaluative criteria for the choice of actions. As such it is largely habitual and so unconscious processes of self and social at the same time. If people in a group rigidly apply the ideological 'whole' to their interactions in all specific, contingent situations they co-create fascist power relations and cults which can easily be taken over by collective ecstasies. The result is to alienate people from their ordinary everyday experience and so create a false consciousness. Alternatively, if the ideological 'whole' is so fragmented that there is little generalised/idealised tendency to act, then people will be interacting in ways that are almost entirely contingent on the situation, resulting in anarchy. Usually, however, people particularise/functionalise some ideological wholes in contingent situations and this is essentially a conflictual process of negating the 'whole', which always involves critical reflection.

From a complex responsive processes perspective, there are no universals outside of human interaction, but this does not mean that norms and values are purely relative in an 'anything goes' kind of way because generalisations and idealisations can only be found in their particularisation in specific interactive situations. This always involves negotiation of conflict; power relating, in which 'anything goes' is impossible.

From a complex responsive processes perspective, desires, values and norms are all understood to be particular narrative and propositional themes emerging in inter-action and at the same time patterning that interaction. Norms are constraining aspects of themes, providing criteria for judging desires and actions. Emotions, such as shame and fear of punishment or exclusion, provide the main constraining force. Values, on the other hand, are highly motivating aspects of themes that arise in particularly intense collective and individual experience, involving imagination and idealisation, serving as the basis for evaluating and justifying desires and actions, as well as the norms constraining them. Emotions such as altruism, gratitude, hum-ility self-worth, guilt and outrage provide the attractive, compelling force of value experiences. For each person, these intense value experiences are particularly linked to interactions over a life history with important others, such as parents, who are perceived to enact values ascribed to them. These important others cannot unilater-ally prescribe such values because they emerge in the relationship. However, while the separation of values and norms is an aid to understanding, it is an abstraction from lived, practical experience in which norms and values are inseparable aspects of the evaluative themes, the ideologies, which are the basis of our choices of actions.

Ideology and healthcare

Consider the points made above in relation to government policy on the National Health Service in the UK. The NHS can be thought of as a collective identity, a 'we' identity that is inseparable from the 'I' identities of all who work for it and all con-cerned with its governance. Such an identity is a social object, that is, generalised tendencies to act in similar ways by large numbers of people in similar situations. On closer inspection, however, there is not one monolithic identity, one social object, but many linked ones. Each hospital, for example, has a distinctive identity, as do the groups of different kinds of medical practitioners and managers who are its members. There are, therefore, many social objects, many generalised tendencies by large numbers of people to act in similar ways in similar situations. Furthermore, the medical profession, the NHS and the many different institutions and group-ings the NHS composed of are all idealised. Cult values, such as 'providing free healthcare', 'doing no harm', 'providing all with the highest standard of care' and 'providing the same standard of care in all geographical locations to all classes of person', are essential features of what the NHS means. 'Performance' and 'quality' are recent additions to these cult values. The generalisations and idealisations can all be recorded in written artefacts, sound recordings and films as propositions and/or narratives. These artefacts may take the form of policy documents, legal contracts, procedures, instructions from the Department of Health, and so on. Such artefacts are then used as tools in the communicative interaction and power relating between members within the NHS and between them and those concerned with its governance. However, the artefacts recording the generalisations and idealisations are just artefacts, not the generalisations and idealisations themselves. Whether recorded or not, the generalisations and idealisation only have any meaning in the local interactions of all involved in each specific situation – they are only to be found in the experience of local interaction.

So, for example, when groups of policy makers in the Department of Health and each of the main political parties get together to decide what to do about the NHS, they are clearly interacting locally. What they will be reflecting upon and discussing are the generalisations and idealisations of the NHS or parts of it. They may issue a consultation document to large numbers of people for comment. This is then taken up for discussion in the professional bodies representing different groups in the NHS. Again the discussion is local interaction, as is the subsequent negotiation of changes in any of the policies. What they are discussing and negotiating in this local interaction is changes to population-wide patterns, to the generalisations and idealisations. Eventually a policy statement is produced and instructions sent to, say, all of the hospitals in the country, setting out what new targets they must meet in order to demonstrate quality and performance and in what way they will be punished if they do not. What I have been describing is processes of local inter-action, local negotiation, in which emerge articulations of the general and the ideal as far as the NHS is concerned. The processes are ones in which people have been trying to design the general and the ideal, and in the way they currently do this in the UK they reflect a particular way of thinking about the NHS. In setting targets and establishing monitoring process they display a way of thinking derived from cybernetics systems. They are trying to design and install a self-regulating system.

However, the NHS is not a self-regulating system, but many local patterns of interaction in which the general and the idealised are continually emerging as con-tinuity and change from one iteration of the present to the next. What then becomes important is how people are taking up, in their local interactions, the generalisations and idealisations articulated in the artefacts of written instructions and procedures. The meaning cannot be located simply in the gesture that these artefacts represent but only, at the same time, in the myriad responses this gesture calls forth. In a specific situation on a specific day, there may simply not be the physical capacity to achieve the targets set. In each specific situation there will always be conflicts on what the targets mean and how they are to be adhered to. The target might then become something that has to be avoided, manipulated and even falsified. For ex-ample, a specific decision might be to meet, say, a target of reducing waiting lists, by sending people home too early after an operation, leading to a rise in re-admissions. The global generalisation that the policy makers designed is thus being transformed in the local interaction so that it comes to mean something different – instead of uni-form high performance it might come to mean 'cover up' and 'deceit'.

As the unexpected emerges in many, many local interactions, the population-wide pattern is transformed and of course, in their local interactions, the policy makers are reflecting upon this. They may then conclude that the now burgeoning number of targets is proving too much of an embarrassment and should be scrapped. How-ever, still thinking in system terms, they feel that they must design some other form of generalisation to stay in control and secure adequate performance. The proposal is then that 700 targets should be abandoned, only to be replaced with 22 qualitative standards. Once again, however, the meaning does not lie on the generalisation alone but in its particularisation in many local situations.

The argument I am presenting here has an immediate implication for processes of policy making and strategising. This is that the almost exclusive focus on the design of a generalisation/idealisation in policy making will lead to continual cycles of surprise. Greater attention needs to be paid to processes of particularising if policy makers are to avoid some of the endless policy reversals that characterise policy making, at least in the NHS.

What is the part a leader plays in all of this? Leadership arises in social processes of recognition (Griffin, 2002) in which, in imagination, the leader can be recognised as embodying the idealised whole. The leader is not actually designing the values and persuading others to commit to them, although this is how it might appear. Instead, the leader is actually participating in the intense experience in which the values are arising and in which he or she comes to be imagined as embodying them. He/she and others may be so caught up in the process that they all lose sight of the imaginative nature of their construct. The leader is then idealised as a person and denigration is never far away. Leadership as a social object and cult value will be explored in the next section.

13.4 Ethics and leadership

Griffin (2002) argues that, from a systemic perspective, leaders are understood as autonomous individuals who formulate visions and values to be directly applied to an organisational or cultural system. In other words, the whole system is reified in thought and ascribed intentions or qualities such as 'harmonious', 'caring' or 'soul'. They are then understood as idealised wholes, which provide leadership to those individuals participating in them. The result is a dual notion of leadership being provided *both* by individual leaders, who define the values and purpose of the whole system, *and* by a system, which incorporates those values and purposes as the leading principles its members are to follow. Individuals following the principles of the whole are regarded as 'good' or 'compassionate', while those who do not are characterised as 'bad' or 'selfish'. In other words, leadership and ethics become matters of explicating the rules or qualities of the harmonious whole and of individuals conforming to it. Griffin is drawing attention here to how notions of leadership are inextricably interwoven with questions of ethics.

Griffin argues against this view of leadership and ethics because he says that it eliminates paradox and mystifies leadership, abstracting ethics from direct experience and locating it in some kind of external, idealised whole. As a result, people experience themselves as the victims of the systems they think they have created.

Griffin traces systemic thinking on ethics and leadership back to Kant's categorical imperative. By this, Kant meant that the principles behind an ethical action would reflect a universal law. Autonomous individuals could objectively observe their own conduct, just as they could objectively observe nature, and judge their actions, which could be understood 'as if' they were actions that could be performed by everyone. As people proceed in this way, different formulations of the categorical imperative emerge, for example, 'treat others as you want them to treat you' and 'do not treat other people as means to an end since all people are ends in themselves'. These imperatives have the character of universals but they do not dictate what to do in any specific situation. In specific situations people have to choose what to do by formulating hypothetical imperatives and then, in their acting, testing them against the categorical imperatives, also using such a procedure to justify what they have done. In this way it is thought that, just as we can progressively build up a body of knowledge about the timeless universal laws governing nature, so we can progressively build up a body of knowledge on timeless, ethical imperatives for human conduct. Ethics here is firmly based on the reasoning capacity of the autonomous individual who can discover the universal principles of good conduct through what amounts to the scientific method.

Kant, then, presented a notion of ethics as a body of universal imperatives that already exist, just as natural laws do, to be discovered by autonomous individuals, just as natural laws are, and expressed in a body of timeless ethical imperatives, just as natural laws are timeless and universal. From this perspective, the principles of actions do not depend upon social or natural contingencies, nor do they reflect the bias of the particulars of individuals' plans for their lives, the particular desires, aims or aspirations that motivate them. It is this notion of ethics that forms the basis of traditional business ethics today – a notion of universal codes of conduct discovered or formulated by autonomous rational individuals as the basis upon which they are to judge their own and each other's conduct. In this way of thinking, the leader is an autonomous individual, as is everyone else, charged with developing ethical behaviour.

Contrary to Kant (*see* Chapter 2), however, systems thinkers today apply the notion of systemic wholes to human interaction. This leads to an ethics that is quite contrary to Kant in that now autonomous individuals are required to participate in, submit themselves to, some larger whole or greater good. No longer are the autonomous individuals trying to discover in their actions what the ethical imperatives reflecting the not-to-be-defined whole are. Instead they are required to submit themselves to the visions and values revealed to them by their leaders. In doing so, they lose their autonomy. In the Kantian sense of autonomy, the endorsement of the vision statements of top management by others is in effect the surrender of autonomy. In organisational theory of this kind, it is only senior managers who are leaders in the Kantian sense of being fully autonomous individuals and they allow others to share in this autonomy. Participation becomes participating in the leadership of the leaders, where that leadership is the values ascribed to the organisational system.

Griffin suggests that the theory of complex responsive processes of relating provides an alternative way of thinking about leadership and ethics. Here participation is the direct interaction of persons with each other, not participation in some whole. This is an approach that stays with our experience of interaction and regards the ethics of action as processes of perpetual negotiation that do indeed depend upon personal desires, aims and aspirations as well as natural contingencies. These processes of communicative interaction are ones in which we together create what happens to us and they are such that small differences can be amplified to transform population-wide patterns. What each of us does matters even though we cannot know what the outcome of our actions will be. Griffin regards this as an empowering perspective that also makes it impossible for one to escape the responsibility for one's own actions by ascribing the causes of what happens to some whole system outside of our direct experience of interacting with each other. He argues that instead of leading us to feel hopeless, victimised or rebellious, this perception encourages us to pay attention to what we are doing and to believe that this is effective in some way, even though we cannot know how.

Griffin draws on Mead (1934) to develop this argument. For Mead, those who emerge as leaders are those who display a greater spontaneity and have a greater ability to deal with the ongoing purpose or task for which others are interacting. The leader is an individual who is able to enter into the attitudes of others, so enhancing connection and interaction between group members. Notice how this notion of a leader does not simply locate leadership in the individual by ascribing leadership purely to the personal attributes of the leader. This is because the leader is actually constructed in the recognition of others. It does not matter what leadership attributes one has if no one recognises them. And, of course, one cannot be a leader if one does not recognise the recognition of others and so recognise them. Leaders, therefore, emerge in complex responsive processes of mutual recognition.

Mead refers to the way in which groups tend to recognise the leader role in those who have acquired a greater spontaneity, a greater ability to deal with the unknown as it emerges from the known context. Mead argued that the ethical interpretation of action is to be found in the action itself, in the ongoing *recognition* of the meanings of actions that could not have been known in advance. In other words, ethical meaning does not reside in external universals to be applied to interaction but continually emerges in the interaction itself. Ethics are being negotiated in the interaction. Moral advance, for Mead, then consists not in adapting individuals to the fixed realities of a moral universe, but in constantly reconstructing and re-creating the world as individuals evolve.

The distinction between cult and functional is relevant to understanding leadership (Taylor, 2005). One aspect of a leader is his or her idealisation as cult leader. This idealisation is functionalised in the role of the leader in the everyday conflicts of interaction. The functionalised role of leader emerges in the interaction and those participating are continuously creating and re-creating the meaning of leadership themes in the local interaction in which they are involved. However, there always remains a strong tendency for a group to idealise the leader, who thereby becomes a cult leader, that is, leader of a group of people directly enacting idealised values, cult values, to which they are subtly pressured to conform to. This blocks the functionalising of the ideals, which is what an organisation needs in order to come alive in the present.

Chapter 9 referred to the way in which many people are using complexity theories to justify the formulation of simple rules and their application to an organisational system as an alternative to detailed plans. The hope seems to be that through specifying simple rules, we can still get the whole to do what we want it to. From the complex responsive perspective, these simple rules are cult values and what really matters is how they are functionalised in daily life. It is this functionalising that brings in the conflict and uncertainty, which will defeat our hope of controlling the whole unless it is indeed a cult.

The next section turns to the matter of how ideologies sustain relations of power.

13.5 Power, ideology and the dynamics of inclusion–exclusion

In order to go on together, people have to account to each other for what they do. In other words, the maintenance of relationship imposes constraint. However, at the same time, relationship enables. Elias (1991) argues that power is not a thing that someone possesses and is not simply force or violence but, rather, power is a structural characteristic of all human relationships in that it reflects the fact that we depend on each other and so enable and constrain each other. Power is this activity of enabling and constraining each other. The basis of power is need so that when we need others more than they need us for love, money, status, or whatever, then they have more power over us than we have over them. However, this is never absolute because the power of the more powerful depends upon the recognition of the less powerful that this is indeed so. Furthermore, if those others come to need us more than we need them then the power ratio shifts in our favour – power relations are dynamic. Elias expresses his relational view of power as ongoing processes of configuring power relations between people. Communicative co-operation arises in the process of people holding each other accountable for their actions in some way. They act towards each other in a manner that recognises their interdependence and so negotiate their actions with each other. Without this, relating breaks down.

The immediate consequence of such interdependence is that the behaviour of every individual is both enabled and constrained by the expectations and demands of both others and themselves. To carry on participating in the communicative interaction upon which an individual's very life depends, that individual has to rely on the enabling co-operation of others. At the same time that individual has to respect the wishes of others and those wishes will frequently conflict with his or her own. Communicative interaction is, thus, power relating as the patterning of enabling and conflicting constraints.

The dynamics of inclusion and exclusion

Power differences establish groupings in which some people are 'included' and others are 'excluded'. Power is thus felt as the dynamics of inclusion and exclusion. These dynamics feature prominently in Elias's process sociology.

Elias and Scotson ([1965] 1994) studied events following the influx of a working class group into a new housing estate in the UK, adjacent to an older estate that was also occupied by working class people. Although there was no recognisable difference between the two groups, hostility soon appeared, and persisted for a very long time, in which the older, established inhabitants denigrated the newer ones. The simple fact of having been there longer meant that the established group had a degree of group cohesion and collective identification that the newcomers lacked. The established community had developed norms and values that gave them the gratifying consciousness of belonging to a group of higher value with the accompanying contempt for the other groups. The established group had come to think of themselves as a 'we', a group with common attachments, likes, dislikes and attributes and this had emerged simply because of their being together over a period of time. They had developed an identity. The new arrivals lacked this cohesive identity because they had no history of being together and this made them more vulnerable. The more cohesive group therefore found it easy to 'name' the newcomers, to categorise them, and ascribe to them hateful attributes such as being dirty or liable to commit crimes. The two groups were unconsciously bound to each other in such a way that the members of one of them felt impelled, and had sufficient power resources, to treat those of another group collectively with a measure of contempt and the other group accepted it because they lacked cohesion.

So, although there was no obvious difference between the two groups, one group unconsciously used the fact that the other was newly arrived to generate hatred and so maintain a power difference. Furthermore, this was, in a sense, 'accepted' by the newcomers who took up the role of the disadvantaged. The established group ascribed the 'bad' characteristics of the newcomer group's 'worst' section to the group as a whole while ascribing to themselves the characteristics of their 'best' section. Population-wide ideological patterns had emerged in the conversation within and between both the established and the newcomer groups and this ideology established, and continued to reinforce, membership categories and differences between those categories.

One of the principal ways that power differentials are preserved, then, is the use of even trivial differences to establish different membership categories. It is not the difference itself but rather the ideological form that stirs up hatred in the interests of sustaining power positions in a dynamic of inclusion and exclusion. Dalal (1998) points out how this as an unconscious process in that the hatred between the groups emerges essentially in local interaction as patterns that no one is really aware of or actually intends. It should also be noted that what I have been describing is an everyday occurrence in less dramatic ways in all organisations. For example, when we debate differences in our theories, or when we talk in particular ways in ordinary, everyday life we are often using differences to sustain power relations.

There are other aspects of ideological themes that also serve to preserve power differentials in essentially unconscious ways in local interactions. A key aspect of ideology is the binary oppositions that characterise it and the most basic of these is the distinction between 'them' and 'us'. Ideology is thus a form of communication that preserves the current order by making that current order seem natural. In this way, ideological themes organise the communicative interactions, the conversation, of individuals and groups. As a form of communication, as an aspect of the power relations in the group, ideology is taken up in that private role play, that silent conversation, which is mind in individuals. So while diversity is essential for the evolution of novelty, such diversity can easily become polarised and stuck, so blocking the emergence of novel patterns of relating.

Note that ideology here is thought of as being mutually reproduced in ongoing communicative action rather than anything shared or stored. Here, ideology is not some fundamental hidden cause located somewhere. It is not stored anywhere, transmitted and then shared. Rather, it is patterning processes, that is, narrative themes of inclusion and exclusion organising people's experience of being together in perpetual reproduction and potential transformation. Ideology, as population-wide pattern, exists only in the speaking and acting of it in local situations.

The processes so far described in this section are ubiquitous in organisations and are key aspects of local interactions of managing and strategising. People working in, say, the finance department of an organisations experience themselves as a 'we' and may regard those who work in, say, the public relations department as 'them', ascribing lesser value to what they do. People working in an operating subsidiary of a large corporation regard themselves as 'we' who earn profits while 'them' at the head office are pen-pushing parasites. When people are reorganised into new departments or subsidiaries they normally experience feelings of loss of identity, which can lead to resistance, even sabotage. When a large corporation makes an acquisition the 'them' and 'us' dynamics become very powerful and often constitute the main reason for the failure of attempts at integration. The power dynamics of inclusion–exclusion and the ideological processes underlying them thus have a profound impact on emerging population-wide patterns of realised strategy.

It becomes important, then, to understand how ideological themes and the power relations they justify are created and sustained in organisations. How this happens is a crucial aspect of the local interactions of strategising. Gossip is a potent means of sustaining ideological patterns and power relations in organisations.

Gossip

Elias and Scotson pointed to how ideology emerges in local interactive processes of gossip. Streams of gossip stigmatise and blame the outsider group while similar streams of gossip praise the insider group. The gossip builds layers upon layer of value-laden binary pairs such as clean–dirty, good–bad, honest–dishonest, energetic–lazy, and so on. Gossip plays a significant role in maintaining identity. The same point applies to the 'inclusion–exclusion' dynamic created by particular ways of talking, for example talking in terms of complexity, in terms of psychoanalysis, in terms of making profit, and so on. Such gossip and other ways of talking attribute 'charisma' to the powerful and 'stigma' to the weak, so reinforcing power differences. In established, cohesive groups, streams of gossip flow along well-established channels that are lacking for newly arrived groups. The stigmatisation, however, only sticks where there is already a sufficiently large power difference. Again these are social relations that are reflected in the private role-play of individual minds, conferring feelings of superiority on the powerful and feelings of inferiority on the weak. Eventually, however, the weak or marginalised groups will probably retaliate with what may be thought by others to be unreasonable vigour.

Elias stresses the importance of streams of gossip in sustaining the group fantasy, showing how closely praise–gossip and blame–gossip are interlinked. A close-knit group, with its high power ratio, has more opportunities for effective gossip, and the more people feel threatened or insecure, the more gossip becomes fantasy of a rigid kind. Thus gossip of praise for the charismatic and blame for the disgraced becomes part of the individual personality structures of both groups.

I am drawing attention to Elias's explanation of gossip as the means by which people sustain ideologies, which in turn sustain relations of power and patterns of inclusion–exclusion, because gossip is an essential feature of local interactions in all organisations. Many managers tend to dismiss gossip as 'idle chatter' that has no connection with the activities of strategising. They think gossip is only harmful and steps ought to be taken to minimise it. Gossip is undoubtedly often harmful but it can never be removed from human relating and it is not just harmful because it serves a purpose in organisations. It is in activities of gossiping that ideologies and figurations of power relation are sustained but also potentially transformed, in making sense of strategising activities and how these play a part in the emergence of population-wide patterns of realised strategy, it is important to understand the effect that gossiping is having on what is happening in an organisation in terms of patterns of inclusion–exclusion which powerfully affect local activities of strategising. The dynamics of inclusion and exclusion are accompanied by powerful emotions that also impact on local strategising activities.

Emotional aspects of inclusion and exclusion

Any change in the processes of communicative interaction must at the same time constitute a shift in power relations and, therefore, a change in the pattern of who is 'included' and who is 'excluded' and so shifts in ideology. Such shifts generate intense anxiety and communicative interaction is recruited in some way to deal with this anxiety. These ways may be highly destructive of effective joint action and may even completely disrupt the reproduction and creative transformation of coherent communication. All of this is understood, from a complex responsive processes perspective, to be essential to the strategising activities of managers.

Elias and Scotson argued that inclusion–exclusion processes are expressed as differentials of cohesion and integration, which are sources of power differentials. There is a complementarity between one group's charisma and another's disgrace and this sets up emotional barriers on the part of the former to any contact with the latter, as well as processes within each group, as follows. All belonging to an established group participate in its charisma in return for which they have to conform or else suffer the humiliation of exclusion. The charismatic group uses language that deeply hurts the members of the disgraced group and this has a paralysing effect on the latter's members. Stigmatisation involves a person's image of his/her group's standing amongst others and therefore of his/her own standing. The silent voices of members of the disgraced operate as the ally of the dominant group because the disgraced have come to believe what is said about them.

The power differential with which the disgraced comply, even agree, is essential to enable the stigma to be driven in. The disgraced often act out the aspersion cast upon them, such as being dirty and noisy, because they know they can annoy the established in this way. Power confers on a group much more than economic advantage because the struggle is about the satisfaction of needs to do with esteem and identity. The outsiders suffer deprivation of identity and of meaning. Elias talks about the peculiar helplessness of groups unconsciously bound together in these dynamics of inclusion and exclusion. The processes that keep the disgraced in place are those of humiliation and shame.

Shame, panic and anxiety

According to Elias (Smith, 2001) the roots of civilisation are firmly planted in the soil of shame, which includes self-disgust, inhibition, isolation and fear. Shame is produced by any kind of transgression against the rules of society that others can 'see'. As people become more self-disciplined and self-aware, their thresholds of repugnance rise. Shame is in turn rooted in the body and because human metabolism cannot be easily controlled (blushing, sweating), people feel vulnerable in a civilised society, which pushes such bodily expressions behind the scenes of social life so that when the body plays its tricks the person gets blamed for infringing norms. Ironically, feelings of shame trigger many of the bodily responses that cause shame in the first place. Threats of exposure and exclusion involved in organisational surveillance techniques and in organisational change trigger feelings of insecurity and shame that can have a big impact on what people do in organisations.

Aram (2001) links shame with panic, which is a response to the fear of potential embarrassment. She argues that panic is simultaneously relationally constructed and individually experienced, and may be thought of as a response to anxiety that serves the purpose of not dealing with the situations provoking that anxiety. The fear of the fear is translated into panic. She also links panic to waiting for something to happen, dreading it and avoiding it until it 'arrives'. Panic is, then, an investment of energy into not feeling and not knowing that leads to exactly that which is being avoided. Panic is associated with strong desires to be with others, with avoiding being alone and ascribing great importance to what others think, so that withdrawing from interaction with others is experienced as particularly difficult. The fear of being on one's own, out of control and in constant need of support makes it extremely difficult to relax. It is not necessarily any change itself that leads to panic because when that which is being unconsciously avoided does happen, the panic symptoms diminish and the capacity to manage is found. It is the phase before a change, namely, the waiting period, which is experienced as panic. This waiting is felt to be an unconscious immobilising fear that past experiences are about to recur. People who suffer panic usually end up feeling exactly that which they are actively trying to avoid. They are highly invested in trying to maintain a strong, 'in control' sense of self and they feel humiliated when they realise how affected they are by others and how important others are in helping them maintain a sense of self. They fear dependence, yet are highly dependent. They long for relationships yet are often intimidated by them and tend to have fractious and unsuccessful ones.

Aram regards this interlinked process of panic and shame as a response to deeprooted fears to do with inclusion and exclusion and the consequent potential for being humiliated and shamed. Panic arouses feelings of shame and humiliation because it is taken as a sign of weakness and immaturity. Anxiety generated by endlessly waiting and preparing to be abandoned and rejected, reflecting past experience, is replaced with panic, anger, rivalry and fear of closeness.

The points about the emotional aspects of power relations and inclusion–exclusion dynamics and the role that gossip plays in them are highly relevant to the local interaction of strategising. These processes are ubiquitous and rarely paid much attention. They become particularly relevant during reorganisations, mergers and acquisition but they feature in all processes of decision making.

13.6 Complex responsive processes perspectives on decision making

This section will consider how the dynamics of power and ideology affect decision making processes in organisations. First consider the key arguments presented so far in this chapter.

Earlier in this chapter, I referred to Elias's understanding of power as a central characteristic of every human relationship which flows from the fact that people are interdependent and so need each other, some more than others. Power, therefore, arises in the relative difference of need, in an irremovable inequality between people. More specifically, power is those aspects of human activities through which people are continually enabling and constraining each other's actions. Drawing together the discussion in this chapter on power and its ideological basis, we could identify the nature of this enabling–constraining activity in the following terms:

- Forming and continuing to belong to groups are essentially activities of including some people and excluding others and much of this activity is unconsciously motivated. Such activity is experienced by people as feelings of inclusion and exclusion. Accompanying and inseparable from these activities are the activities, primarily gossiping, of labelling groups of people in terms of polarised attributes so as to differentiate 'us' and 'them'. These differentiating activities express ideological themes that organise the experience of being together, so defining the 'we' identities of all. All of these activities are enabling in that they create feelings of belonging which make it possible for people to co-operate more easily with each other within a particular group. At the same time these activities are constraining in that to continue to belong to a particular group it is necessary for members to conform to the group ideology. Activities of inclusion and exclusion also enable competition between groups while at the same time constraining co-operation between them. These activities are emotionally highly charged. The experience of inclusion and belonging generates feelings of affection and loyalty towards other members of the 'in' group and any criticism or threat to one's group quickly arouses aggression. The mere threat of exclusion, and so loss of identity, arouses feelings of shame and humiliation, anxiety and even panic. People unconsciously defend themselves, individually and collectively, in the mostly unconscious manoeuvres of what psychoanalysts have referred to as basic assumption behaviour, scapegoating and other forms of fantasy-driven behaviour (*see* Chapter 5).

- The activities of enabling and constraining can also be described in terms of co-operation and competition and this immediately directs attention to human motivations of altruism, empathy, compassion and acceptance, on the one hand, and self-centredness, envy, jealousy and rivalry, on the other hand. Some emotions and motivations are enabling of co-operation and others constrain interaction into competitive forms. There can be no pure form of enabling co-operation with its attendant emotions or of competition with its attendant emotions. Both are always present at the same time and which is more evident fluctuates over time. Of particular importance in organisational terms is the co-operation and competition around which discourse, and the ideology it reflects, is to dominate because this is the largely unconscious basis of power figurations.

- Other aspects of enabling activities are fantasising and imagination, while acting and thinking in defensive ways may well be constraining.

- Activities of enabling and constraining are inevitably conflictual activities. Explorative conflict may well be enabling, while polarised conflict may be constraining.

In making these distinctions it is necessary to stress that each describes a paradox. Human relationships are enabling and constraining, including and excluding, co-operative and competitive, imaginative and defensive, at the same time. This chapter has also argued that enabling and constraining activities always reflect some ideology, some interplay of norms and values. Enabling and constraining activities also always reflect the choices people are continually making as they select one action rather than another in response to the actions of others. They make these choices, often unconsciously, on the basis of evaluative criteria provided by ideology. Such evaluative choice is simply another term for decision making.

From the perspective of complex responsive processes, then, decision making is understood primarily in terms of the ideological, power, emotional and social processes briefly summarised in the points above. This way of thinking about decision making stands in contrast to that of the dominant discourse as described in the chapters of Part 1. In the dominant discourse, a decision is normally thought of as preceding an action and the making of a decision is usually thought of in terms of the step-by-step thinking activities of rational, autonomous individuals. Despite the continuing critique of rationality in the dominant discourse, decision making continues to be described as a programmatic activity. There are stages leading to the making of a decision that can be identified with a specific point in time. Action then follows. From the complex responsive processes perspective, choices, decisions and intentions are inseparable from other forms of action. Indeed they continually emerge in response to all forms of action in ongoing ways that make it arbitrary to select a particular point in time when the decision was actually made. A particular point in time when the decision is legitimised by some authority in the hierarchy can, of course, be identified, but this is not the same as deciding, which is an ongoing emotional, conversational activity of enabling and constraining reflective of ideology.

13.7 Summary

Ideology can be thought of in paradoxical terms as the simultaneous voluntary compulsion of value and the obligatory restriction of norm. Ideology provides criteria for choosing one action rather than another – decision making – and it serves as the unconscious basis of power relations, making it feel natural to include some and exclude others from particular groups, thereby sustaining the power difference between those groups. Ideology is the ideal made functional in specific situations always involving conflict.

We start from the position that humans are fundamentally social beings where this means that they survive and get done whatever they need or wish to get done in relation to each other. To relate to others is to communicate with others. By social, then, we essentially mean ongoing activities of communication between bodies in which they together accomplish whatever they accomplish. The social is the patterning of communicative interaction. To understand communication we turn to Mead and his notion of the conversation of gestures. Human communication takes the form of gestures calling forth responses from others and at the same time calling forth similar responses from oneself. In other words, communication takes place in significant symbols. Furthermore, in communicating, people take not only the attitude of the other but also always the attitude of the generalised other (group or game) and of the 'me', all encapsulated in the concept of social object as generalisation which is only to be found in the activity of particularising. This amounts to saying that consciousness and self-consciousness are social phenomena. Here communication, consciousness and self-consciousness are all social activities rather than individual representations. This is so in another sense too, namely, the tendency to idealise collectives, ideas, concepts, theories, physical objects, other people, etc. This leads to the notion of cult values which must be functionalised. The generalisation (social object)/idealisation (cult value) are major aspects of the consciousness and self-consciousness of everyone so that mind and self are patterned as social processes while they pattern social processes at the same time. Another way of talking about the enabling/constraining nature of social object and cult value is to talk about power. Elias points out that power is a characteristic of all human relating and is felt as the dynamics of inclusion and exclusion in which identity is formed. Ideology sustains patterns of power relations. Ideology, power relations, inclusion–exclusion forming identities and processes of gossip are all essential features of the local inter-action of strategising and decision making.

Further reading

Joas (2000), Griffin (2002), Stacey (2003) and Griffin and Stacey (2005) provide more detailed treatment of the points made in this chapter. Elias and Scotson ([1965] 1994) is important reading.

Questions to aid further reflection

1. How would you describe the cult values of the organisation you work for and what do you notice about the ways in which they are functionalised?

2. Do you experience values as voluntary compulsions and norms as obligatory restric-tions? Give examples from your own experience.

3. Where in your work do you notice the power dynamics of inclusion–exclusion and what effects do you think they have?

4. Do you think that factors to do with identity affect your work in organisations?

5. How do you think about the connections between organisational strategy and power, ideology and identity?

6. What part do you think gossip plays in organisations?

Reflective management narrative 3

Sheila Marriott is an independent consultant to healthcare organisations. In this reflective narrative she describes a consultancy assignment she took on at a children's unit, part of a health trust in the UK's National Health Service. The initial consultancy brief called for the preparation of a comprehensive business plan relating to a move to a new building. However, it soon became clear that the issues of greatest concern centred on the patterns of interaction within and between particular professional groupings within the trust that were impacting on its performance. Marriott came to understand the concern with plans and systemic procedures both in terms of the real need for planned ways of improving performance and, at the same time, as a means of avoiding difficult actions to deal with ongoing conflict and the emotions this aroused, all closely associated with patterns of power relations and differences in values. It would be easy to dismiss the events in this narrative as examples of poor leadership and ineffective management practices in one poorly performing organisation. However, this would be far to simplistic because, on the one hand, this unit was functioning even though it was not perfect, and, on the other hand, those working in other healthcare organisations in the UK and in other countries will immediately be able to recognise similar patterns in their own experience – it is just these patterns that have led to widespread national policies of healthcare quality improvement in many countries. Furthermore, ongoing power struggles and attendant conflict are not specific to healthcare organisations but central features of everyday life in all organisations. The points that stand out for me in this reflective narrative are as follows:

- The way in which the immediate focus of attention on rational planning, implementation and monitoring procedures diverts managers from dealing with their own patterns of interaction in which they actually use, or corrupt, the rational procedures. Taking a complex responsive processes perspective immediately focuses attention on the conversational processes in which people in the organisation actually co-operate and compete with each other.

- This focus of attention on communicative interaction between people leads to the exploration and greater understanding of the patterns of power relations between different grouping in the organisation and how these patterns are affecting what actually happens.

- Deeper exploration of power relations directs attention to the patterns of conflicts between different power groupings and the value differences these conflicts represent.

- Marriott draws our attention to the impact of population-wide patterns of planning and monitoring across the National Health Service and how these are being taken up in a particular, contingent, local situation. We can see how what happens to the health service as a whole will emerge in the way national policies are being taken up in many local situations.

- The importance of emotion in organisational life is brought out in this narrative, which particularly takes account of the emotional aspects of conflict.

- The narrative questions the possibility of 'managing conflict' and simplistic distinctions between 'good' and 'bad' conflict.

Making sense of power and conflict in a healthcare organisation

by Sheila Marriott

In what follows, I describe the conflict that emerged during the first day of the consultancy work I undertook in a children's unit. The initial consultancy brief was for a comprehensive planning exercise but it was soon agreed that my work should focus on the dynamics of a group of Clinical Nurse Managers who were being criticised for what was regarded as their ineffective management of nursing services against nationally set targets. They appeared to avoid challenging their subordinates when targets were not met so as to avoid conflict, forming a pattern of working that had become institutionalised. They seemed to be working very hard to preserve a harmonious working atmosphere in what was otherwise an aggressive and antagonistic environment reflected in the aggressive and assertive style of other medical staff, the physicians, which created an atmosphere of paralysis and fear at times, as less powerful groups were intimidated. The Clinical Nurse Manager group was being taken to task by their manager about their lacklustre performance but less action was taken about the behaviour of the other medical staff.

In relation to this situation, I explore different types of conflict as an inevitable part of everyday organisational life rather than simply thinking of conflict as a negative, anxiety-producing force that, it is usually thought, must be 'managed'. I also make a link with the pattern of power relationships between various staff groups. I discuss my role as a consultant in providing a forum for the Clinical Nurse Managers to relate to each other and reflect upon their anxieties about the day-to-day conflicts of their working lives. In this chapter, I consider how I might help clients to make meaning of the conflicts and power relationships which are inevitable aspects of human interaction so that new, rather than stuck, patterns can emerge. In reflecting on the narrative that follows, I have come to realise that conflicting constraints on relationships are just as important as enabling qualities if novel patterns

of relating, and so organisational change, are to occur. I found that the forum of action learning was a vehicle both for bringing attention to the organisational defensive routines causing people to remain stuck in unproductive patterns of relating and for enabling them to examine their behaviour and make changes.

What the assignment was really about: a 'full business case' or staff conflict

I received a letter from Hannah, the Business Manager of a large children's unit. She requested that I undertake a piece of work to 'realise the full business case for the new children's unit'. The letter outlined a great many tasks to be accomplished by the consultant, including: a transition plan for the move to the new children's unit; a phased workforce plan consistent with budgets for the new children's services; a recommended workforce profile to suit future needs benchmarked against other units of similar status; an assessment of the current profile of the skill mix against future requirements; a robust workforce planning model; and an educational framework to support staff in the transition. I felt quite bewildered by the project brief. I did not understand some of the jargon, even though I had worked in the National Health Service (NHS) for my entire career. There appeared to be a number of years' work outlined and I was not interested in working 200 miles from home for this length of time. I was, however, curious to explore the brief further because I felt that I had the skills to undertake some of the work and was interested in extending my expertise. I had met Hannah, the Business Manager, during my previous work and liked and admired her.

Hannah telephoned to discuss the work further. She said little about the full business case but told me that she managed the Lead Nurse, Liz, who managed the four Clinical Nurse Managers responsible for nursing in the children's unit. Hannah expressed concern about the Clinical Nurse Managers' lack of managerial control over their pay budgets and the poor co-ordination of nurse recruitment and retention. She suggested that I visited the unit to discuss the brief further with Liz and herself.

At the meeting, the topic of the Clinical Nurse Managers soon came up again. Hannah felt they supported each other too well, resulting in a lack of challenge. For example, when there was a staffing shortage, they all became involved in solving the problem rather than letting the accountable Clinical Nurse Manager resolve it. When there was a staffing shortage, the Clinical Nurse Managers worked the shift, rather than challenging reluctant ward staff to change their shifts, and were then not available for operational management work. Hannah described the Clinical Nurse Managers as expert clinical nurses who took refuge in clinical work because it was familiar and rewarding. She felt that they avoided the business side of their roles, which they found more difficult and demanding. Liz described the Clinical Nurse Managers as a powerful group with a reputation for being rather formidable, on the one hand, but avoiding confrontation, on the other. There was one Clinical Nurse Manager who was working well, Beth, a new appointment with a different management style which caused difficulties with the other Clinical Nurse Managers. Apparently, Beth had a more commanding style of management and was willing to challenge norms and question decision-making rationales – a style of interaction that her peers were unused to. Perhaps the other Clinical Nurse Managers were threatened by her.

Hannah also described the relationship between different professional groups at the unit. There was conflict and antagonism between medical and managerial staff and at times the relationship between doctors and nursing personnel was strained. She felt that the conflicts between the groups inhibited change and increased what was already a very stressful environment. Hannah saw her role as one of calming the situation and supporting the 'injured parties'. She was interested in my thoughts on how to 'manage' the conflict between the groups. I felt anxious about this request. I did not have experience in conflict management, but said that I would feed back my thoughts on how I saw the groups

working together. I have reflected on this 'lack of experience of conflict management' statement and recognise that I actually have been working with conflict in organisations for most of my career. My concern related to a lack of confidence because I had not studied conflict management frameworks. My own experience felt inferior to formal frameworks. This led me to explore the theoretical literature about conflict, which I will consider later.

I asked Hannah to describe her top priorities from the list of issues in the brief she had sent me. The work Hannah had described felt unfocused and I suggested that I could begin to work with the Clinical Nurse Managers since this is what they had spent most of the time talking about. Further work could then progress once their poor performance was addressed. Hannah agreed and asked me to help the Clinical Nurse Managers to understand their staffing budgets and agree staffing templates to recruit the right numbers of trained and untrained staff. I was intrigued that I was being asked to undertake this type of work, which should have been the remit of Liz. I suggested that the Clinical Nurse Managers would benefit from working together in an action learning set. They appeared to be struggling with their operational duties and needed the opportunity to reflect on why they were behaving in this manner. I wanted the Clinical Nurse Managers to reorganise their operational management systems so that they could then focus on the creative planning that was required for the unit move. Hannah and Liz agreed and I immediately contacted the Clinical Nurse Managers to explain my role and said that I wanted to work with them individually and as a group. They were very responsive and agreed to meet me after the next directorate meeting.

The directorate business meeting

I agreed to attend this directorate meeting two weeks later. As I listened to the discussions, I noticed that Liz and the directorate Financial Manager sat silently, leaning back in their seats as though they were on the edge of the meeting. The Head of Anaesthetics said little, as the main conversation seemed to be between Hannah, Frank, the quietly spoken Clinical Director, Ted, the junior manager, and David, the Head of Surgery.

As I drank coffee and looked around the room I wondered what Hannah had said to the group about the work I had been hired to do. I was concerned that she might have been vague and I was practising a short, succinct résumé of what we had agreed. The team continued to discuss the unacceptable number of cancelled operations. As I contemplated what I was going to say, I noticed that the discussion had become increasingly heated. The conversation had moved on to the shortage of parking places and Ted, responsible for the Facilities Department which included car parking, said that car parking spaces should not be saved for medical staff visiting the unit to undertake specialist outpatient clinics. The Clinical Director (a doctor) and David both felt that car parking space was a contentious issue and could lead to visiting clinicians refusing to travel to the unit. I was surprised that the discussion was escalating into a heated argument. David leaned forward, pointing his finger at Ted and said 'this issue is not for negotiation – you need to reserve the car parking places and that is an end to it'. Ted responded aggressively and said 'just stop wagging your finger in my face and stop threatening me – just back off.'

I felt uncomfortable about witnessing such an outburst between people I did not know. I wondered if this type of exchange usually took place at this meeting. If so, it was not surprising that a number of people sat quietly and did not enter into the debate. I noticed that everyone appeared to shuffle in their seats and Hannah immediately intervened, asking everyone to calm down. She suggested that they explore a local agreement with a car park near to the unit. David looked almost stunned that the problem could be solved so easily and relaxed. Ted, however, appeared to be very angry and tense as he clutched his papers and glared at everyone. The telephone then rang and Hannah took the call as the car park discussion continued. I noticed that the call sounded very one-sided and she became increasingly flushed as the call progressed. On returning to the meeting she briefly described her conversation with an angry surgeon who threatened to involve his lawyers in the negotiations of his new employment contract. The Chief Executive had become involved and was annoyed that the problem had been elevated to his level. I later discovered that this problem should have been managed by the Head of Surgery or the

Clinical Director but both had ignored the problem, according to Hannah, expecting 'management' to sort it out.

I was then invited to discuss the work that I intended to undertake with the Clinical Nurse Managers. The atmosphere seemed to change, as the group appeared pleased that the work was going to be undertaken. I was relieved by their response. David expressed frustration about the shortage of nurses, which resulted in the closure of beds, and hoped that the work would help solve this problem. He then had to leave the meeting, and I noticed that the tension in the room reduced further as people changed positions in their seats, sat back and appeared more relaxed as more humour was introduced into the conversation. I was struck by the (female) Head of Anaesthetics commenting, 'Well, I feel intimidated by the surgeons at times, so no wonder the nurses find it tough.' David's behaviour at the meeting appeared to mirror the manner in which the surgeons generally conducted themselves, and on this note the meeting finished.

I had planned to have lunch with Liz and then meet the Clinical Nurse Managers but Liz had to take a telephone call from a very angry and tearful ward sister who had been challenged about the number of beds that were empty. She felt she had been called 'a liar' by Beth, the Clinical Nurse Manager who had responsibility for bed management that day, and Liz hastily left the meeting to sort out the problem.

So instead, I had a long conversation with Ted. He felt very unhappy about being continually in conflict with one group or another. He had responsibility for reaching some of the performance targets and felt that the Clinical Nurse Managers were not managing their budgets or recruiting staff efficiently. This impacted on achieving some of the performance measures and he felt angry that they did not appear to make this a priority. He gave the example of allowing too much flexibility in the implementation of staff retention policies. Many part-time staff with families 'dictated' that they could only work weekends resulting in too many staff employed at the weekends. This was expensive since weekend workers at this time were paid more and this contributed to the pay overspend. He felt that the whole nursing service appeared to be out of control. He appeared to respect Liz but was frustrated that she never brought the Clinical Nurse Managers to task when they did not implement the actions agreed at their regular management meetings. Ted thought that some of the doctors were bullies and he was determined not to become their victim. I asked how he coped with such an unenviable role. He said that he had a job to do. Performance management was unpopular with both nursing and other medical staff and, although Hannah was very supportive, he was looking for another job. He felt that the degree of conflict he encountered from the different professional groups was intolerable and spent most of his time at work feeling anxious, angry and resentful at the lack of personal respect that he received.

I was intrigued by the level of conflict I had witnessed at the directorate meeting. What was my role going to be in such a dysfunctional group? The whole team seemed to be 'held together' by Hannah who appeared kind and respectful to her colleagues and was able to solve problems in a calm and energetic manner. She was concerned about the level of anxiety and conflict. She admitted that she was uncomfortable with confronting aggressive behaviours and so regularly acted as peacemaker. One conversation with Hannah and Ted made a particular impact on me and I wrote down Hannah's exact words: 'We all want the best care for the children, but we need to describe the systems – who does what – and more importantly, the output, then we can decide what people we need for the system, review what they do, and measure our success.' Rather than bring the Clinical Nurse Managers to task about their performance, Hannah and Ted opted for a rational, systemic approach to solving the problems, almost as if this would make all the conflict and poor performance disappear. This way of thinking is common in the NHS and is powerfully reinforced by central government policy on public sector governance.

The NHS Plan and performance

In 2000, the UK government published *The NHS Plan* (Department of Health, 2000), which outlined plans to invest in the NHS and reform it. National standards were set and monitored by the Commission for Health Improvement (now the Healthcare Commission). The NHS was to be redesigned around the needs of patients rather than run centrally.

However, the monitoring of centrally set standards and the power to intervene when organisations were seen to be failing was left with central government, who could intervene, and name and shame, when they perceived that organisations were failing.

The Healthcare Commission monitors the key targets and balanced scorecard indicators. According to the Healthcare Commission (2005), performance ratings for an acute and specialist trust include twelve key targets. Some of these targets are as broad as 'Unit Cleanliness' and 'Financial Management'. Others are more specific, for example, 'Total time in A/E: four hours or less'. The balanced scorecard indicators comprise three sections: Capacity and Capability with six indicators ranging from data collection indicators to staff satisfaction surveys; Clinical Focus with ten indicators ranging from Child Protection Indicators to Stroke Care; and Patient Focus with sixteen indicators ranging from 'Better unit food' to 'Breast Cancer: one-month diagnosis to treatment'. As can be seen, the indicators are broad, with the measurements ranging from a simple yes or no answer about waiting time achievements to more complex measurements such as assessing 'unit cleanliness'. Health trusts are awarded 'stars' according to how well they perform against all these targets and indicators.

Davies (2004) reports that health service staff detests the 'star' ratings as simplistic and distorting of clinical judgement and that people's own experience is often wildly at odds with their trust's own star ratings assessment. Bosanquet *et al.* (2005) conclude that in giving priority to elective care, targets had made it difficult to attend to other areas of service. The doctors' trade union, the British Medical Association (BMA, 2004), takes the view that performance indicators do not measure interpersonal care, which is an important attribute of the efficiency of care and an important aspect of the healthcare system for patients. They recommend that measurement of both structure and process should be linked to outcomes and that measures need to be combined with a culture of trusting healthcare professionals to find innovative solutions to local problems. These types of measures, they suggest, are less likely to produce dysfunctional behaviour.

There is, therefore, unrest and conflict in relation to performance targets at a national level, which

▶

was clearly reflected in the children's unit I was consulting to. Furthermore, the poor performance of the children's unit affected the results of the whole unit trust, leading to even more conflict. The argument about car parking probably reflected a deeper conflict and rebellion by the medical staff against the use of performance management systems, and an exercise of power against managers at a local level. On reflection, I think that the Clinical Nurse Managers were also rebelling against the pressure to focus on the centrally driven targets. Hannah wanted the Clinical Nurse Managers to organise their work around the targets by opening beds to meet the waiting list targets. The Clinical Nurse Managers were more interested in the clinical care of all children regardless of whether their diagnosis had a performance target attached to it.

As described earlier I was struck by the aggressive exchanges that I had witnessed in the directorate meeting and the lack of challenge within other groups. I will now consider how the notion of conflict is dealt with in the organisational literature.

Different perspectives on conflict in organisations

As members of an organisation interact with each other, their differing goals, values, styles and situations inevitably create tension and conflict (Bolman and Deal, 1997; Edelman, 1993) and traditional organisational structures with their functional silos and technical specialisations can themselves promote conflict (Shelton and Darling, 2004). The professional groups at the children's unit stayed in their silos with the nurses being blamed by other medical groups for not recruiting enough nursing staff and the managers being blamed for the 'loathsome' waiting list targets. The managers in turn blamed the nurses for the staff shortages leading to bed closures and the other medical staff for not arranging flexible operating lists. This resulted in a lack of shared meaning about how the problems could be solved. Kolb and Bartunek (1992) describe organisational conflict in terms of three bi-polar opposites: public/private, formal/informal and rational/non-rational. They suggest that most writers on management conflict tend to focus on public conflicts understood in rational terms because private, non-rational disputes usually take the form of covert conflicts, often obscured by other activities, rather like the car parking dispute

described earlier. Informal norms govern such private conflicts, which may include gossiping, sanctioning hidden agendas and ignoring requests.

Conflict may provide a healthy incentive for action, generating creative solutions and high levels of work satisfaction, but when it becomes the dominant feature of a culture it can be highly damaging, provoking ill feeling, stress and unhappiness (Edelman, 1993; Lewis *et al.*, 1997), as seemed to be the case at the children's unit. Writers on conflict in organisations frequently make this kind of distinction between aggressive, combative conflict and conflict which provides a more healthy non-destructive exchange, strengthening relationships as people recognise their differences and work towards resolving them, increasing trust and self-esteem if the differences are resolved and enhancing creativity and productivity. However, these positive effects of conflict at work tend to be less well-documented than the negative aspects, and working with conflict to encourage the positive aspects is generally not regarded as central to the work of managers or consultants. Instead, most of the writers on organisational conflict call for conflict to be 'effectively managed', in the sense of providing some kind of harmonious resolution, and provide frameworks for conflict resolution. For example, Crawley says:

> Constructive conflict management will enable you to transform the interaction between the ingredients so that when the sparks occurs, there will be heat generated, but it will not last, destroy the ingredients or damage the surroundings. Constructive conflicts are not easy to achieve.
>
> (Crawley, 1992, pp. 10–11)

Crawley writes as though the conflict manager has the power to 'transform the interactions' of others, as though constructive conflict management has a life of its own enabling the manager to be creative and effective. It seems to me that writers such as Edelman and Crawley describe people as if they were objects or ingredients to be 'managed', without feelings or memories. The many conflict management frameworks focus on the way that disputes should be handled in a rational manner (Kolb and Bartunek, 1992, p. 20).

What strikes me is the importance of acknowledging the significant emotional impact that conflict may have even though conflict may also be a catalyst for change. After participating in the directorate meeting described earlier and seeing the anxiety experienced by many of the staff, it is unsurprising that managers may try to control conflict. However, Shelton and Darling (2004) were critical of managers who avoided or tried to control conflict without acknowledging the stress, fear, anger and sometimes humiliation generated by conflict. Without this acknowledgement, it would be too easy to idealise conflict with the argument that it challenges the status quo and promotes innovation (Shelton and Darling, 2004). Schermerhorn *et al.* (1991) also acknowledge the emotional aspects of conflict when they differentiate between substantive conflict and emotional conflict, acknowledging the anxiety that emotional conflict generates. For them, *substantive conflicts* arise in disagreements about ends and means, such as resource allocations, rewards, roles and divisional versus organisational objectives. *Emotional conflicts*, on the other hand, arise in personal clashes with attendant feelings such as aggression, mistrust, dislike, fear and resentment. While Schermerhorn *et al.* acknowledge that it may be difficult to separate these forms of conflict, and although they acknowledge the stress and anxiety involved, they nevertheless regard substantive conflict as helpful and emotional conflict as harmful. It is as though the 'ends and means' type of conflict can occur without emotion. Surely, however, disagreements relating to ends and means are bound to be generated by, and intertwined with, emotion. Glasl (1999) takes a more integrated view, arguing that conflict affects the whole personality, threatening to corrupt thought and dominate actions. However, he sees conflict in negative terms as an existentialist issue for the individual.

The tendency is to think of a spectrum of conflict. At one end is the day-to-day conflict that involves diversity but is expressed in an environment of regard for the other people involved. At the other end of the continuum is behaviour fuelled by anger, mistrust, dislike, anxiety and resentment, where conflict becomes more difficult to handle at best and avoided if possible. Mastenbroek (1987) suggests that there needs to be a balance between these tensions. If the ratio tips to one extreme then behaviour becomes too aggressive and if it is tipped the other way then behaviour becomes too indulgent. This seems to be a rather simplistic way of

viewing conflict. It is not clear how the balance will be achieved or what types of interventions are required to 'control' behaviours within a linear continuum of aggression at one end and indulgence at the other.

Many of the conflict models (for example, Edelmann, 1993; Glasl, 1999; Isenhart and Spangle, 2000; and Mastenbroek, 1994) appear to take a rational, linear, problem-solving approach to dispute management, briefly noting the emotional elements contained within the disputes. The models focus on providing a cognitive step-by-step approach to managing conflict. In contrast, the non-rationalist approach to conflict emphasises the unconscious or spontaneous aspects of disputes, driven by impulse and by the feelings of participants and not simply by their cognition. Emotional reactions such as venting feelings, expressing displeasure and feeling hurt become a means of conflict management. Irrational displays that hinder logical thinking are said to be unhelpful (Morrill, 1991), rather like David's outburst at the directorate meeting. Non-rational conflict may be denigrated as bad behaviour by those who have not learned appropriate social responses (Kolb and Bartunek, 1992). However, it is problematic to separate the cognitive and emotional aspects of conflict and then attend primarily to the cognitive. According to Damasio (2000), neuroscience research shows that when certain parts of the brain are damaged the result is a loss of both emotion and the ability to make rational decisions. He concludes that:

> selective reduction of emotion is at least as prejudicial for rationality as excessive emotion. It certainly does not seem true that reason stands to gain from operating without the leverage of emotion. On the contrary emotion probably assists reasoning especially when it comes to personal and social matters involving risk and conflict.   (Damasio, 2000, p. 41)

So, Damasio suggests that emotion supports the ability to make rational decisions especially in conflictual situations.

I felt dissatisfied with the way that many of the authors acknowledge the presence of emotion in conflict situations but focus on problem-solving, rational frameworks alone. Although these approaches may be helpful, there seems to be a lack of exploration of the emotional impact arising within these circumstances. So, I decided to move towards the more social psychology and philosophy oriented literature to explore a different way of thinking about conflict. Mead (1908, 1934) suggests that conflict is an inevitable aspect of human behaviour. He argues that the main impulses leading people to organise themselves into societies take the form of co-operation, on the one hand, and antagonism, on the other. He holds that we continuously develop and re-create our world through conflict.

If conflict is a fundamental aspect of human behaviour, as many of the writers suggest, a different way of looking at it is to consider its paradoxical nature. In this sense, conflict can be creative and destructive at the same time. Stacey et al. (2000) argue that creativity and destruction, order and disorder, are inextricably linked in the same creative process. Stacey also suggests that the dynamic of interaction is determined by the nature of relationships. As the diversity increases, the energy within the relationship rises. The properties of the relationship then shift from stability and predictability towards randomness and disintegration. At some critical range in information/energy flow, connectivity and diversity, the dynamics of bounded instability appear, that is, the simultaneous presence of stability and instability, order and disorder. It is in this dynamic that novel forms of relationship may emerge. Stacey is suggesting that too little access to information or diversity within the relationship results in repetitive patterns of behaviour. Too much difference, however, results in the disintegration of the relationship. However, the dynamic of stability and instability at the same time, in which there is agreement and conflict at the same time, is a different way of thinking from that of writers such as Mastenbroek, who talks of 'balancing the tensions', suggesting that behaviour can be controlled by particular interventions to reduce the degree of conflict.

Hannah saw conflict as being destructive, and tried to control and stifle it. She seemed to hold an idealised notion of working in a harmonious team where conflict was eliminated through systems and procedures and creativity would materialise. Yet I had been told that the Clinical Nurse Managers appeared to have a harmonious relationship, but were criticised for being uncreative. The conflict within the directorate team was never discussed or confronted. There was no acknowledgment of, or attempt to work with, the conflict which may have allowed creativity to emerge. Of course there is no way of predicting that positive outcomes will emerge from working with the conflict, making the roles of general managers like Hannah difficult and anxiety provoking. It appeared that the surgeons had a long history of being aggressive and adversarial. The Head of Anaesthetics' comment at the directorate meeting suggested that it was not just managers and nurses who were fearful of the surgeons. The nurses avoided getting into conflict with the surgeons because of the anxiety that the conflict caused. Although the Clinical Nurse Managers group seemed to lack the conflict to motivate a healthy incentive for action, at the other extreme there was an ethos of damaging conflict perpetrated by other staff groups. Ted was often preoccupied with the degree of conflict that he encountered, and the conflict affected his actions. If units are to participate in high quality patient care, Skjorshammer (2001) suggests that organisations need mechanisms to handle the disputes and conflict, which will emerge between the different groups of 'actors'. He says that there are few empirical studies in healthcare which deal with these challenges.

Returning now to my consultancy assignment, I had been briefed that the Clinical Nurse Manager group avoided challenge and conflict but I felt anxious that they might be reluctant to work with someone from outside the trust. I was aware that they might not agree with the perception that they were stuck in unproductive ways of working.

Meeting the Clinical Nurse Managers

According to Hannah, the Clinical Nurse Managers appeared to be locked into patterns of conduct that they had set up amongst themselves, which had become institutionalised ways of behaving (Argyris, 1990). In my role as an external consultant I wanted to provide a forum in which they could reflect on their behaviour and convince themselves that they needed to change. I could help them to set up systems to improve the organisation of their work but unless they agreed to participate in the changes they would continue to work as before. We gathered in a dilapidated old house across the road from the main unit. I introduced my previous experience as a children's nurse and said that I had been asked to help them review their skill mix, the budgets, and also recruitment and retention issues. I asked them how they felt about my being asked to undertake the work. To my relief they said that they felt that they knew they were in a muddle. However, they felt resentful that Ted, the junior manager, was critical about the way that they managed their services. One of them said, 'He is only interested in budgets and targets. I have a responsibility to maintain a safe service and he does not care about this. He is aggressive and at times I refuse to speak to him because I get so upset. He is not our manager but thinks he is – all he does is criticise me and I am fed up with it. Life is difficult enough without him shouting all the time.' They said that no one understood how difficult it was. They had to work clinical shifts due to staff shortages, had difficulty recruiting staff due to national shortages, and had to manage budgetary constraints. They felt anxious about being pulled in different directions, which made their working environment very stressful.

The most recently appointed of the Clinical Nurse Managers, Beth, said that her service had different problems. She did not have a shortage of staff. She had challenged the way that her service was configured and had made changes. This had been very tough but she was pleased with the way that the changes were progressing. She worked across two unit sites and, at times, felt estranged from her Clinical Nurse Manager colleagues. I noticed the sideways glances between some of the other team members as she said this and I asked her to say more about her discomfort. Beth began to speak but was unable to complete her sentence because her colleagues interrupted her. They said they were concerned that she felt estranged since this was not their intention. At the time I felt excited that she was able to raise her issues with the group and noticed how the group immediately attempted to support her. Reflecting on this conversation now, I am challenging my interpretation of the Clinical Nurse Managers' intervention as being 'supportive'. Although I believe that there was a genuine concern, Beth's experience of feeling estranged challenged the notion of the harmonious Clinical Nurse Manager group. As she voiced her concern the group immediately attempted to return to their sense of harmony. I had a sense that gener-

ally Beth would not collude with the desire to maintain harmony. She had been the Clinical Nurse Manager who had challenged the ward sister earlier in the day when Liz rushed off at the end of the directorate meeting. As I consider this conversation between Beth and the other Clinical Nurse Managers I now have a sense that something new and exciting happened. Beth broke the pattern of collusion that suggested that harmony was the only acceptable behaviour between the Clinical Nurse Managers.

I then asked them what the main areas of difficulty appeared to be. Recruitment and budgets was their reply. We went around in circles, as they appeared to defend a position of helplessness, working within an environment of hostility, lack of funding and staff shortages. I felt split between a longing that *they* would come up with a way forward and a growing desire to direct them. I had read Shaw's (2002) description of the term 'facilitation' as helping human engagement flow more easily in conflictual situations, pointing to how habitual patterns can creatively transform. I was disappointed that this was not my experience in this situation and did not feel that the conversation was evolving at all. I had limited time and felt that the conversation was stuck. I then asked the Clinical Nurse Managers if co-facilitating a working group about skill mix, budgets, recruitment and retention might be a way forward. I wanted them to lead the projects but agreed to work with them, providing administrative and research support. I felt the tension reducing as they smiled and nodded in agreement. Although I felt confident about my ability to work with them on designing systems and processes to manage the work, my concern lay with how we could maintain continuity so that they would be able to continue to develop improved ways of working when I left. I voiced my concerns and volunteers agreed to lead the groups with me.

I felt that I had now established a rapport with the group and we discussed how we might create a forum to reflect on how they worked as a team, on how they engaged in unhelpful patterns of interaction and on how they might challenge each other in a constructive manner. I suggested that we might follow the principles of action learning. I explained how this is a process of learning and reflection with the support of a group or 'set' of colleagues working on real problems with the intention of

▶

getting things done (McGill and Beaty, 2001). I suggested that the learning set could be made up of the four Clinical Nurse Managers and the Professional Development Nurse. We agreed that one of the Clinical Nurse Specialists would also join since she worked closely with them. We also agreed that the group would meet monthly. At the meetings, time would be allotted for each person to describe their issue or story and others would not interrupt until the story was finished, after which they would ask open-ended, probing questions such as 'What do you really think is going on? What do you think would happen if . . . ? How would you know if . . . ? How does that make you feel?' Such questions are aimed at prompting a person to reflect more deeply and try to make sense of their world in ways that they are unlikely to encounter in their everyday relationships. They would also be encouraged to look at the process of what was happening during the learning set meeting. This means noticing how they felt about the questions that were asked, what they observed about body language, what physical responses they noticed in themselves during the interactions, and why the particular questions were asked. At the end of their allotted time, each member would agree the actions that they were going to take to deal with their problem. I also described my role within the learning set as demonstrating different ways of asking questions. My other role was to ask the 'difficult questions' to encourage them to own some of their unspoken emotions and to encourage them to explore what was happening between them.

I asked what they thought of the idea. The energy in the room changed as they laughed and joked about knowing each other and their inadequacies as the majority of them had worked together for years and knew each other well. This was useful but resulted in difficulties in challenging each other as they did not want to upset their friends and colleagues. The thought of being allowed to take time out in a safe environment to think about how they worked was appealing. One of the group said, 'I think it is a great idea and feel positive that the trust is willing to invest this time in helping us develop'. I hoped that action learning might be a way of confronting the passive behaviour of the Clinical Nurse Managers and the tendency to blame others rather than take responsibility for their performance.

I facilitated five action learning sets in total, the sixth and final set being cancelled by the trust's Director of Operations due to a lack of resources. Over time, the Clinical Nurse Managers said that they noticed that they were becoming more aware of how their behaviour and the behaviour of others impacted on each other. During the learning set meetings they dealt with difficult issues in relation to styles of management behaviour by describing specific problems. They reflected on what had happened, why they thought it had occurred and how they contributed to the situations they described. They appeared to become less anxious about the situations after they had named their anxieties and reflected on ways of dealing with the circumstances. Issues relating to power, conflict, support and challenge continually arose. This provided the opportunity to explore the notion of power and conflict in relation to their work. At times this was uncomfortable, difficult and emotional. They felt that the learning set was useful because they were challenged to find creative solutions to their problems. They agreed the actions they decided to take, what resulted and how they felt they had changed. Sometimes they felt that they experienced a real shift but at other times they were disappointed that the changes they made did not appear to help the situation. The action learning gave them one day per month to reflect and try to make meaning of their work environment in a way that they had never experienced before.

Since, in our discussions, the issue of conflict was so often linked to power, the next section looks at how we might think about power.

Power and complex responsive processes of human interaction

According to Isenhart and Spangle,

> If conflict only involved a decision between two choices, most of us would compromise or negotiate. But often conflict involves a struggle for power, the way decisions are made, the way we talk to each other, or unresolved problems from past interactions. Several of these factors may be occurring at the same time, so we are not sure what the real problem is.
>
> (Isenhart and Spangle, 2002, p. 2)

Power is most often defined in the organisational literature as the influence one person or group has on another so that one has power and the other does not (for example, Mastenbroek, 1987). Elias (1978), however, describes power in a different way in terms of a figuration or patterning of competitive and co-operative relationships between people that reflects their interdependence. No one possesses power as a thing because power is an aspect of every relationship in the sense that all parties in a relationship constrain and enable each other. Power ratios are created within the relationships, not simply by one person exercising their will over the other. The notion of power ratios is not about one person having power over the other because the ratios are co-created within the relationship. One of the central themes patterning communication between the doctors, managers and nurses had to do with power. Although the directorate meeting felt as though the medical staff were exercising their will over the managers, the power ratios were co-created by the two groups as the aggressive behaviours were ignored by those to whom they were directed thus maintaining the power ratios in the interdependence between the Clinical Nurse Managers, other medical staff and managers. The doctors held that they could not meet management's performance measures, which they did not agree with anyway, because the nurses were not organising their own work. There appeared to be some kind of unconscious collusion between the two groups to rebel against the culture of performance management. According to Coser, 'conflict involves a struggle over values and claims to scarce status, power and resources in which the aim of opponents is to neutralise, injure, or eliminate rivals' (Coser, 1967, p. 8). These comments resonated with the exchange I had witnessed between David and Ted. There was a struggle for power about who could decide whether visiting consultants could have a parking space, probably as a proxy for more important issues. The way that they addressed each other was a result of unresolved past interventions in a struggle for power.

The power relationships within the directorate were complex. If, as Elias suggests, power relations are co-created in interaction, the Clinical Nurse Managers allowed the medical staff to behave aggressively. This patterning of behaviour had been allowed to develop over a long period of time and had never been confronted. The issue of the consultant contract, which Hannah had to deal with, was an example of a problem that should have been dealt with by the medical staff but had been left to the managers to resolve. However, no one confronted the Head of Surgery or the Clinical Director about their accountability for resolving the problem. Similarly, the Clinical Nurse Managers appeared reluctant to confront their junior staff over issues such as the management of beds because they did not wish to upset their colleagues. Whether power was exercised or avoided, conflict appeared to be an issue within the team. The medical staff exaggerated power differences by behaving in an autocratic manner, evoking compliance, as in the case of the Clinical Nurse Managers, or rebellion, as in the case of Ted. Liz did not confront the behaviour of the Clinical Nurse Managers, leaving a power vacuum. I did not wish to fill the power vacuum left by Liz's lack of leadership. I needed to be continually aware that my suggestions may have a particular influence because of my experience as a senior children's nurse and my position as a management consultant.

According to Stacey, complex responsive processes constitute a theory of human psychology which takes as fundamental the processes through which people relate to each other. Rather than thinking of organisations as systems, complex responsive processes theory posits that they are ongoing processes of interaction between people in which patterns of interaction produce further patterns of interaction rather than a system. An organisation is the ongoing conversational processes in which people relate to each other and changes in organisations are changes in conversation. Stacy and Griffin (2005) suggest that the thematic patterning of conversational interaction takes a complex form which is

complex in that it refers to a particular dynamic or movement in time which is paradoxically stable and unstable, predictable and unpredictable, certain and uncertain, known and unknown, all at the same time.

(Stacey and Griffin, 2005, p. 7)

This is a very different view from how many in the NHS view organisations. The NHS is thought of as a system and the introduction of performance management tries to ensure that the NHS is stable, predictable, certain and known. Measuring is taken to be necessary for setting targets against which predicted outcomes can be controlled.

Stacey and Griffin (2005) go on to argue that thematic patterning of conversational processes are self-organising in the sense that people interact with one another on the basis of their own local organising principles rather than centrally set, pre-conceived blueprints. They also hold that what an organisation becomes emerges in this local inter-action rather than as a consequence of central blueprints. Drawing on Mead, they argue that centrally set blueprints amount to cult values where cults arise when leaders inspire people to imagine a future free from obstacles that could prevent them from being what they want to be. Hannah tried to convince the Clinical Nurse Managers that the cult value of 'the best care for the children' involved sorting out their systems, suggesting that if they organised their work better the performance targets would improve, as would the care of children. However, the Clinical Nurse Managers did not think that performance targets improved the care. They rebelled against the blueprint that Hannah wanted to impose because they did not advocate the performance management values that she promoted.

Finally, Stacey and Griffin suggest that the thematic patterning of interaction is understood to be evolving, and this inevitably involves choice and conflict. Hannah believed that implementing her particular types of system would improve the performance targets and that conflict would be reduced. In fact it seems that functionalising or implementing the notion of the 'best care for children' brought conflict, uncertainty and anxiety. This is because the Clinical Nurse Managers did not agree with her stance on what constitutes 'best care' and chose to focus on their clinical rather than managerial work.

This complex responsive processes way of thinking about organisational development was beginning to influence the way that I worked on the children's unit assignment. I was challenging my thinking about organisations as spatial metaphors of systems that people create in their interactions, which in my experience is the way of thinking that dominates the NHS. I was coming to the view that change is brought about through ongoing local interactions and patterning of conversations in which people contribute to the patterning and are also shaped by it. I am interested in the notion of how local interaction could shape what an organisation becomes, rather than being shaped by performance management targets or the strategic direction and business plan written by the executive directors. I used action learning sets to think about the patterning of relationships. The manner in which the Clinical Nurse Managers related within the learning set reflected their day-to-day relationships. The learning sets offered the opportunity to reflect on these patterns, and the power and conflictual relationships that constrained and enabled their abilities to get things done. It also provided an environment where they could discuss ways of containing their anxieties. There was an opportunity to use action learning as a vehicle for new ways of thinking and novelty to emerge. Although I have focused on the action learning aspect of my work within the children's unit there were a number of meetings about recruitment and skill mix where I challenged what they were doing and my assumptions were challenged in return. The discussions were sometimes robust and heated. However, the opportunity for all levels of staff to have an open forum to discuss these issues had not been available before. Some positive outcomes emerged, such as a process for staff recruitment. Other issues such as the clarity of the ward sister roles were not taken forward at this time. I see my role as helping staff to use conversational processes to notice what they are actually doing within their day-to-day working lives and make changes that will foster growth and novelty.

Conclusion

The issues emerging from the directorate meeting and the Clinical Nurse Managers meetings relate to power, conflict and anxiety. If conflict is an essential part of human behaviour as Mead argues, then, at times, work relationships are likely to be both creative and destructive. Conflict is often hidden and usually not discussed, making it difficult for staff to grasp the notion that work will inevitably contain conflict that is both enabling and constraining and that destructive behaviours need to be dealt with rather than avoided. Similarly, if all human relating is power relating as Elias argues, then people inevitably constrain and enable each other through competitive and co-operative relationships that reflect the interdependences between individuals and groups. Nurses and managers often see doctors as a highly educated, better-paid group with innate power intrinsic to their roles. The doctors' authority and decision-making capacity are greater than those of most other clinicians and managers. This issue becomes one of how other groups are to challenge the power of doctors in an environment that appears to value the role of doctors more than that of other groups.

If staff are able to discuss hidden conflicts and recognise the constraining and enabling patterns of relationships, they might be better able to contain the anxiety that working life often generates, making for greater possibilities of change. Part of 'making meaning' is being able to discuss the patterning of relationships and how to find a 'good enough' way of containing anxieties so that novelty and change can occur. The question for me as a consultant is how I can help clients make meaning of the conflict and power relationships that exist as part of human interaction.

Questions to aid further reflection

1. Do you think it is possible to manage conflict? If so, how do you think this can be done? If not, then how are we to think about conflict and what are we to do?

2. How does the view you take on power affect how you think about the events in this narrative and what you might do?

3. What further insight might you gain into what is happening in this narrative if you take account of processes of identity formation?

4. How does the issue of ideology arise in this narrative and what implications does it have for what happens?

5. What role do you think gossip is playing in this narrative?

© Sheila Marriott

Chapter 14

The emergence of organisational strategy in local interaction

The narrative patterning of everyday experience

This chapter invites you to draw on your own experience to reflect on and consider the implications of:

- How people construct experience together as narrative.

- How organisational strategy can be understood as continually iterated and potentially transformed identity narratives.

- The role played in the iteration and potential transformation of strategy narratives by the tension between legitimised and shadow ideologies expressed in local conversational interactions.

- The role of formal and informal conversations in the construction of narrative strategy.

- The part that conscious and unconscious processes play in ongoing strategy narratives.

This chapter develops an understanding of what people in organisations are doing in their strategising activities. Strategising activities are not confined to formal meetings with agendas specifically identified as 'strategic' and devoted to discussing propositions about markets and resources. Wider ranges of communicative interactions are involved as people talk together in informal, shadow ways about who they are and who they are not, who they want to be and who they do not want to be, what they are doing and not doing, and what they desire to do and not do. As they talk together in a whole variety of ways, they actually co-create their experience in the form of strategic narratives. This chapter seeks to understand ordinary, everyday activities in organisations as the iterated and potentially transformative narrative of strategy.

14.1 Introduction

Chapter 1 identified the primary concern of strategy as that of understanding how and what an organisation becomes whatever it becomes. For some, what it becomes is defined in terms of its resource base and its position in a market and whether or not it is successful in terms of some performance criteria. This leads to a debate about how an organisation becomes a successful performer. Some argue that this 'how' is a process of rational, strategic choice, while others point to how problematic such rational choice is for human beings and answer the 'how' question in terms of processes of organisational learning, which encompass politics, culture, cognition, emotion and many other factors. While these views may question straightforward strategic control by top managers, their proponents largely retain some claim for managerial ability to shape, influence or condition these processes of learning. The only alternative put forward seems to be some form of muddling through in which an organisation becomes what it becomes largely through chance.

Chapter 1 also proposed a wider definition of the primary concern with how and what an organisation becomes whatever it becomes. This wider definition regards strategy as fundamentally a matter of identity. Identity answers the questions 'who are we?' and 'what are we doing?' What identity an organisation comes to have and how it comes to have it can be thought about in terms of the dominant discourse just described. Or the matter of identity can be thought about in the terms suggested in Chapter 10 as the interplay of many, many intentions of individuals and groupings within and between organisations. This interplay of many intentions always occurs in local inter-actions between people from which emerge population-wide patterns of relationships between people called organisations. Strategy is then understood as the evolution of the iterated and potentially transformed patterns of identity emerging in local inter-action. Chapters 11 and 13 have explored in some detail how we might understand local interaction as conversational processes forming and being formed by ideologic-ally based figurations of power relations and ideologically based choices and intentions. Chapter 12 explored the paradoxical links between local interaction and population-wide patterns where the latter are thought of as social objects and cult values.

This chapter takes a further step in understanding what is meant by population-wide patterns. It argues that human persons are continually co-creating their ex-perience in essentially narrative forms. Ask anyone who they are and they respond with a narrative. Each of us is an autobiography. Ask people in an organisation what it is all about and how they come to do what they do and they tell you a story. Ask them what the strategy has been and they tell you a story of expansion, acquisi-tion, downsising, or whatever. In an ordinary, everyday way, therefore, strategy is a narrative of identity co-created by people in an organisation. The purpose of this chapter is to explore some facets of strategy as identity narrative and how people co-create it. Consider first the nature of narrative.

14.2 Narrative and knowledge

Tsoukas (1997) draws a distinction between propositional and narrative knowl-edge in organisations. Propositions make causal and prescriptive statements about experience, such as *if* you shout *then* people will get angry or *if* you improve the quality of your product *then* the volume of sales will increase. Narrative knowledge is more complex, taking the form of stories and evaluations of these stories which convey knowledge of how tasks are done. The point is that experience is organised by both narrative and propositional themes in conversations and that the narrative themes are of enormous, although much underplayed, importance. From a complex responsive processes perspective, narrative and propositional *themes* emerge in conversations, both the public/vocal conversations of the social and the private/silent conversations of mind. These themes can take a number of forms, for example fantasies, myths, rituals, ideologies, cultures, traditions, routines, habits, gossip, rumours, discourses, speech genres, dialogues, discussions, debates and presentations. In all of these forms, narrative and propositional themes are organising the experience of relating in a number of ways, for example by: selecting what is to be attended to; shaping how what is attended to is to be described; selecting who might describe it; accounting by one to another for their actions; articulating purpose in the form of themes expressing intentions; justifying actions in the form of themes that express ideology. *Ordinary, everyday conversation* is human activity in which experience emerges as themes organising the experience of being together mainly into stories and narratives.

Stories and narratives

A story is an account of a sequence of specific actions, feeling states and events, while a narrative is a storyline linked by reflections, comments upon, and categorisations of, elements of the storyline. So, a narrative contains within it a story but it is a more complex form of communication than a story because it involves some kind of evaluation. It seems to me that the associative, turn-taking processes of ordinary, everyday conversation produce emergent, co-created narrative. One person tells an anecdote that evokes some evaluative comment from another and an associated anecdote from a third as together they spin narrative themes. These narrative themes structure their historical experience and their current experience of being together, so creating personal and group realities (Gergen, 1982; Shotter, 1993).

Bruner (1986, 1990) has identified some of the key features of narrative processes of constructing experience. Narratives create a sense of temporality in experience, linking present experiences to past ones and pointing towards the future evolution of the experience. They focus upon departures from what is expected, from what is taken for granted as ordinary and acceptable, and thereby they reinforce cultural norms. Stories that simply recount expected routines are not particularly interesting, but those that describe the unexpected are, and such stories usually have a 'moral' that reinforces the culture or ideology of the group. Stories also impart something about the subjectivity of the narrator or about the subjectivity of the characters in the story. In other words, they disclose some aspects of individuals' silent conversations and provide the means for people to experience each other's subjectivity.

People also use stories to describe and deal with ambiguity. Bruner (1990) points to the essential ambiguity of stories themselves in that it is quite difficult to tell just what is fact and what is fiction in a story, thereby opening up the possibility of the fantasy potential to which Elias attached so much importance with regard to human interaction. An essential aspect of narrative, therefore, is the scope it offers for the exercise of imagination and the spinning of fantasy. Bruner also emphasises the constructive role of the listener in storytelling, because people do not just listen to stories. They select and fill in meanings and indeed storytelling techniques employ devices to encourage this active participation in the co-construction of meaning in narratives. Bruner talks about stories as 'trafficking in human possibilities rather than settled certainties' (1986, p. 28).

Sarbin (1986) points out the link between narrative and feelings: emotional states are located in narratives and passions are 'storied'. McCleod (1996) emphasises the problem-solving function of stories in that they are used to put chaotic experiences into causal sequences and explain dilemmas and deviations:

> In co-constructed narratives, the listener or audience may feed their own alternative accounts into the story that emerges, or may seek clarification by asking questions. So, the act of telling a story makes available a communication structure that not only conveys a sense of a world of uncertainty and ambiguity, but also provides a means of reducing dissonance and re-establishing a sense of control and order, by assembling an account that becomes more complete or ordered through the process of being told. (p. 37)

One can read the above description of stories and narratives and easily slip into thinking about them as special activities in which literature or folklore is constructed. What I want to draw attention to, however, is the narrative patterning of ordinary, everyday conversation. In such ordinary conversation, we are together constructing our experience as narrative. Our social interactions are patterned as narratives and each self in such interaction is an autobiographical narrative. Narratives, sometimes including propositional statements within them, are always constructed in local conversational interaction, and population-wide narratives emerge in many, many local interactions. Furthermore, as they iterate particular narratives in their local interaction, people are taking up the population-wide narratives that have already emerged and in so doing further evolving these narratives. The generating of the population-wide narratives, including the cult values they reflect, are being particularised in the local creation of particular narratives. Chapter 12 discussed social objects and here we can see the narrative form that social objects take. Strategy, then, can be thought of as narrative.

Strategy as narrative

Every organisation is a population of persons co-operating and competing with each other in performing some joint activity in order to accomplish some purpose, and such accomplishment always involves co-operating and competing with other persons in other organisational populations. The accomplishment of purposeful joint activity is possible only because all involved communicate with each other, and my argument is that such communication takes the form of local conversational interaction with its characteristics of power relations and ideologically based choices. All organisational activity, therefore, can be understood as conversational interaction, and this includes the activities of strategising.

Take the typical strategy away-day for example. A typical strategy away-day takes the form of a small number of the most powerful executives of an organisation staying together at some venue away from their offices. The occasion may begin in the evening with a dinner and much informal conversation, patterned primarily as narrative – the executives tell stories of a successful development here, a concern there, and a failure elsewhere. They are certainly interacting locally and their informal conversations are themselves creating narratives that are surely strategising activities in that the stories told may well have an impact on what the executives attend to when they return to the office. The next day, they assemble in a meeting room and the chief executive goes through a PowerPoint® presentation giving the key results for the past year. He takes the major turn, others may occasionally take a turn but only to ask for clarification, and the formal, presentational conversation is patterned mainly through propositional themes. However, the conversation soon shifts to narrative mode as the executives begin to discuss how and why the particular results presented came about and what this reflects about their strategy, that is, about their intentions for the future of the organisation. They may start talking about whether they are on track or not in strategic terms and telling stories of what has been happening to justify their positions.

When they start talking about strategy they are actually taking up a population-wide, generalised narrative that emerged at last year's away-day and was conveyed to others in the organisation. This strategy was in fact a narrative describing what activities would be continued, how some might be changed and how new ones might be developed. It was a story about purpose. Indeed it was an identity story, one articulating some kind of answer to the questions: Who are we? Who are we striving to be? What are we doing together? What do we want to be doing together? People in many, many local interactions across the organisational population have already taken up that narrative and, in many of these, the narrative will have undergone some subtle, and some not so subtle, changes. It is this evolving narrative that is now taken up by the powerful executives in the conversations at their away-day meeting and in their conversations the narrative also continues to evolve. And how it does so depends upon their conversational processes, the turn-taking and turn-making patterns, the figurations of power this reflects, the ideological themes supporting these figurations and the rhetorical ploys people are employing in their talking together.

Strategy here is being understood as the iteration and potentially emergent transformation of population-wide narratives that will again be taken up in many other local conversational interactions. If we are to understand just how this is happening, we need to explore further the forms in which ordinary experience in organisations is thematically organised.

14.3 Narrative themes organising ordinary experience

If one takes the perspective that an organisation is a pattern of conversation (relational constraints), then an organisation changes only insofar as its conversational life (power relations/ideology) evolves. Organisational change is the same thing as change in the patterns of conversation and therefore of the patterns of power relations and ideology. Creativity, novelty and innovation are all the emergence of new patterns of conversations, patterns of power relations and ideological themes. In other words, the strategic direction an organisation follows emerges as a pattern in the way people talk and in their talking configure power relations. Note that public, vocal conversations (group relationships) and private, silent conversations (individual minds) are both aspects of the same phenomenon. Change in one means some kind of change in the other at the same time. Organisations and their individual members change together. It is not a matter of changing the people first and then changing the organisation. Change is possible when conversational life is fluid and spontaneous and impossible when conversational life remains stuck in repetitive themes. The key questions then become: How do themes organise the narrative experience of organisational life? What facilitates and what blocks the emergence of new patterns, new narratives, of conversation?

I now want to explore how themes organise experience of life in organisations, starting with how they organise what can, and what cannot, be talked about.

Legitimate and shadow themes

In organisations it is not possible to talk freely and openly to just anyone, in any situation, about anything one likes, in any way one chooses, and still survive as a member. Relationships impose powerful constraints on what it is permissible to say, to whom and how. Sometimes it is quite acceptable to act but quite unacceptable to discuss freely and openly the reasons for acting. Alternative reasons that cover up the 'real' reason are disclosed instead. This is the basis of the distinction I make between *legitimate* and *shadow* themes that organise the narratives called organisational strategies.

Legitimate themes organise what people feel able to talk about openly and freely. They organise conversations in which people give acceptable accounts of themselves and their actions, as well as imputations about the actions of others. They are the kinds of conversation you readily engage in with others, even if you do not know them well. Shadow themes organise conversations in which people feel able to give less acceptable accounts of themselves and their actions, as well as of others and their actions. They are the kinds of conversations you would engage in only informally, in very small groups, with others you know and trust. Shadow themes organise what people do not feel able to discuss freely and openly and so construct narratives as gossip.

The distinction between legitimate and shadow themes is intimately related to ideology, which can be either official or unofficial. It is ideology that legitimises a conversation. In particular, it is the ideology sustaining current power relations that makes conversation feel natural, acceptable and safe – that is, legitimate. One would normally expect that ideology to be official, that is, the values that are publicly pronounced as those people are to live by. This official ideology may well exert a powerful influence on what may or may not be freely spoken about. However, it need not necessarily determine what may or may not be done. Despite the official ideology, people may act in ways consistent with unofficial ideologies, even though they cannot talk about how their actions are justified by their unofficial ideologies. Instead, they will have to find some other, plausible reason consistent with the official ideology. When people engage in shadow conversations, they also do so on the basis of some unofficial ideology that makes it feel natural and justifiable to talk as they do, but this time secretly. Shadow narratives then emerge as strategies organising experience.

Legitimate conversational themes are legitimate, then, because they conform to official ideologies. The opposite of legitimate is, of course, that which is illegitimate or illegal. This is not what I mean by the organisational shadow. Shadow themes form conversational narratives, that is, power relations, that are not legitimate but also not illegitimate or illegal. Shadow themes/power relations are shadow because of the manner in which they are expressed in conversation. Such conversations always take place informally between small numbers of people and their distinguishing feature is that they do not conform to the official ideology. Some unofficial ideologies may collusively support current power relations whereas others seek to undermine them and both can be taking place at the same time. This does not mean that such conversations only take place between the less powerful. The most powerful participate in them too and indeed skilful participation in shadow conversation plays a major role in sustaining the relations that render them more powerful.

In using the term 'shadow', I am connecting to Elias (1989) when he talked about people challenging the official ideology from the margin. Conversations in the shadow are conversations at the margin. I am also trying to capture the point Bakhtin (1986) makes about 'carnival'. Frequently, conversations in the shadow take humorous forms. Conversations in the shadow are a form of play. It is in the complex interplay of legitimate and shadow themes that ordinary, everyday conversations create the narrative of strategy.

Let me give an example to clarify the distinction. Although the organisation I am about to describe is fictional, it is nevertheless constructed from experiences in a number of real organisations.

Equal opportunities

This company's board of directors consists of eight men. The group of 30 senior executives who report to them also consists entirely of men. There are some 150 senior managers reporting to them, and, of these, 12 are women, mostly in the human resources, public relations and marketing functions. For the past ten years, the directors have emphasised the company's formal equal opportunities policy for recruitment and promotion and its policy on the harassment of women and minorities. Virtually everyone in the organisation is aware of this official ideology of equality, for example between men and women, and it exercises a powerful constraint on what may be talked about freely and openly. It is widely felt to be unacceptable to talk freely and openly about whether women, for example, are in general suitable for the most senior positions. It is also unacceptable to ask openly why there are no women in the upper echelons despite the equal opportunities policy. Even the twelve senior women managers in the company do not feel that it would be wise to talk to directors about this matter. The fear seems to be that such comments would be interpreted as accusations of hypocrisy. The organising theme has to do with its being unwise to point to openly, let alone question, the policies of equal opportunities and harassment in any way. What all are doing here is co-creating an official strategic narrative, an identity narrative, of transparency and equal opportunities.

This is what I mean by themes organising the legitimate experience of being together. Some of these themes are formal, propositional and quite conscious in nature, such as the policy statements on equal opportunities and harassment. Others are narrative, informal and possibly unconscious in nature. The unconscious aspect may lie in the reasons why the women managers do not challenge top executives. For example, it might be a fantasy that the latter would interpret any comment as an accusation of hypocrisy. It is legitimate in this organisation to talk openly and freely only in terms of the equality that is part of the official ideology but it is also quite legitimate to appoint only men to the upper echelons. In other words, it feels right and natural to appoint men only, but it does not feel right to talk openly about this. Note here how the ideology and underlying current power relations are a mixture of official ideology of equality and unofficial ideology of inequality.

However, people do talk about inequality in private, but only to those whom they trust and expect to agree with them, or in the form of a joke. For example, some of the directors and senior managers can be heard to tell disparaging jokes about women, occasionally in the presence of one of the twelve female managers. Female managers also sometimes make disparaging remarks about men, often in their presence. Because the exchanges take place in the form of jokes, any serious intention underlying them can be denied if need be. Privately, a few men express their unwillingness to report to a woman. Although women are sometimes interviewed for director and senior executive posts, a good reason has so far always been found for not appointing them. In each separate case, the reasons produced are indeed plausible but the pattern over a long period of time is curious. The senior women managers also talk in private, often amongst themselves but also with male colleagues who are known to be sympathetic. They talk about glass ceilings and hypocrisy.

These are all examples of what I mean by shadow themes that organise the experience of being together. These conversations express the organisation's unofficial ideologies. Unofficially, some have an ideology that does encompass discrimination and yet others believe that the top executives are hypocrites. Note how the themes organising shadow conversations are mainly narrative in nature. Also, note the unconscious aspect. Those making decisions not to appoint women are usually not cynically ignoring the equal opportunities policy and most of them would strenuously, and probably quite genuinely, deny that they are discriminating. After all, they provide very careful and convincing reasons why they have not appointed a woman in each separate case. The female managers may not be aware of how they are colluding in maintaining the situation by their public silence.

Clearly, unofficial ideologies are undermining official ideology. It is also easy to see that one powerful unofficial ideology, in part unconscious, is sustaining current power relations in which men get the top jobs. It can also be argued that the unofficial ideology of the women and some of the men who support them contributes to sustaining current power relations. It looks as if official ideology is about changing current power relations and unofficial ideologies are resisting this. However, a different argument can be made. In today's social climate, it would be unacceptable not to have public policies about equal opportunities and harassment. It is also probably helpful to have them from a legal point of view as a protection in the event of litigation. The policies may well be providing an official ideology that meets the requirements of public opinion and in the process covers up the unofficial ones that really make action feel right. This interpretation is strengthened when one of the human resources directors recounts how he raised the topic of equal opportunities over two years before it was incorporated in personnel policies. He did so privately with a few of his colleagues to get the necessary support to take it to the board. His most persuasive argument was the weight of public opinion.

I am using this example to argue that it is neither the official nor the unofficial ideologies on their own that are sustaining current power relations. Rather, it is the complex interplay between them, between legitimate and shadow organising themes, that sustains current power relations. I am also using it to point to how what is the officially stated ideology today in fact emerged from shadow conversations some time ago.

I want to take this example one step further. A few of the female managers become increasingly frustrated and begin to talk privately about how they can influence the situation. Some of them talk, as people do, at dinner parties about their experience of discrimination in the workplace. A guest at one of these dinner parties is an influential journalist, well known for her championing of women's rights. She interviews the chairman and writes a sarcastic piece in a major newspaper about the all-male management cast at this particular company. Most people in the company talk about the article and they now feel able to talk more openly and freely about why there are so few women in top management. What was a shadow conversation has now emerged into the legitimate arena. A few months later two women are appointed to the senior executive ranks and a prominent business-woman is appointed to the board as non-executive director. Clearly, the meaning of the equal opportunities policy has changed and with it the pattern of power relations. There has been some kind of transformation in the strategy narrative.

Again, what I am illustrating here is the complex interplay between shadow and legitimate themes organising experience in an organisation and how new themes, new meanings, can emerge in this interplay. This interplay has generated greater diversity and variety in the management of the company.

The distinction between legitimate and shadow is important because the tension between the two is the potential source of the diversity that is critical to the capacity to change spontaneously in novel ways. The organisational shadow, then, is those organising themes/power relations that are in some sense deviant and this deviance encompasses the despicable and the destructive, on the one hand, and the heroic and the creative, on the other. Shadow communications take the form of ordinary, everyday conversations, gossip, rumour, inspirational accounts, stories that express humour and the grotesque, tales that take the form of elaborate social fantasies or touching personal experiences. Shadow communications shape and are shaped by power relations, some of which collusively support, and others of which covertly undermine, the legitimate. I am suggesting that the potential for the emergence of new organisational direction arises when legitimate and shadow themes are in tension. In other words, creative potential arises from the subversion of legitimate organising themes by shadow themes. What emerges then is new forms of conversation, that is, shifts in power relations, new strategy narratives.

Unofficial innovation

Consider another example of the interplay between legitimate and shadow themes. Fonseca (2001) reports a development in a water utility in Lisbon. The manager and his colleagues in the Operations and Maintenance Department talked about the waste involved in having to consult many different maps showing the location of utilities in the streets before they could carry out any repairs on the water supply system. They decided that it would be a good idea to digitise all the existing maps so that repair crews would only have to consult one up-to-date map. However, the manager of the department knew that investment priorities lay elsewhere and that any request for funds for the digitisation project would be turned down. Without approval, the manager nevertheless started the project, freeing up some time for the four engineers who were enthusiastic and finding small amounts of funding from other budgets.

The project could not be talked about openly and freely to anyone because it was not in the legitimate arena. This did not mean that no one else knew about it. Senior managers did know about it and tolerated it. However, it still could not be talked about openly. Conversations about it were organised by shadow themes. The reason is obvious. The official ideology on control was one in which the use of resources had to be approved by senior executives. It is immediately evident how such a control ideology sustains current power relations and how going around the approval procedures subverts them. After some time, the project reached a stage at which there was enough evidence of its potential usefulness to seek and obtain official approval. As it further developed, it led to significant shifts in power re-lations between different departments in the organisation. The complex interplay of shadow and legitimate themes led to the emergence of a new technology. This sequence of events clearly takes the form of strategy narrative.

The distinction between legitimate and shadow themes is not one that is made in the organisational theories reviewed in Part 1. The distinctions made there were between formal and informal, conscious and unconscious aspects of organising. Consider how they are defined and then how they differ from the legitimate–shadow distinction.

Formal and informal

All of the theories reviewed in this book draw much the same distinction between the formal and the informal aspects of an organisation. The formal is identified in terms of an organisation's purpose, its mode of fulfilling its purpose, that is, its task, and the individuals who are assigned roles in carrying out the task. The formal organisation is defined in terms of the role it promises to fulfil in its larger com-munity and it is defined in terms of those formally authorised to be its members. The organisation's identity here is defined in terms of formal propositions as to mem-bership, roles and relationships between roles, tasks and purposes.

The informal organisation consists of all relationships not formally defined by people's roles or clearly related to their tasks. All personal and social relationships fall within this category. These personal relationships extend into other organisa-tions, making it difficult to define the membership. As everyone knows, no organ-isation can function without these informal relationships and an organisation, therefore, has to be understood in terms of both formal and informal relationships.

In the terms I am using in this chapter, some of the themes that organise the experience of being together, and therefore some aspects of power relations, may be described as formal. These are often propositional themes, frequently expressed in written form setting out reporting structures, procedures and policies of various kinds. The propositions model the hierarchy and the bureaucracy and set out the official ideology. However, the formal organising themes also encompass some of a more narrative kind. For example, there are unwritten understandings of how people should conduct themselves at formal meetings and the kind of deference they should display in conversations with those more senior to them in the hierarchy. The themes that organise informal experience almost always take a narrative form as the informal strategy narratives of an organisation.

Note that this distinction between formal and informal is very different from the distinction between legitimate and shadow. The former distinction relates to the degree of formality and the latter to the degree of legitimacy.

Conscious and unconscious

Learning organisation theory distinguishes between assumptions people are aware of and those that they are not aware of. The concept of mental models used in this theory postulates that most of the content of the models is below the level of awareness. A distinction is also drawn between tacit (unconscious) and explicit (conscious) knowledge. Psychoanalytic perspectives distinguish between what members of an organisation do consciously and what they do unconsciously and it attaches particular importance to the notion of unconscious group processes. This theory pays attention to the impact of unconscious fantasy on how people experience being together, particularly the unconscious deployment of defences against anxiety. A complex responsive processes perspective also draws attention to the unconscious processes in which people are unaware of how they use ideology to justify power relations and patterns of inclusion and exclusion (see Chapter 13).

People are usually conscious of the formal propositional statements that organise their experience of being together. Reflective members of a group are also usually aware of a number of the narrative themes that are organising their experience of being together. However, most of the themes organising experience are likely to be unconscious. It is unusual for people to struggle publicly to identify what these themes are. Certain categories of themes are particularly likely to be unconscious and will be linked with other themes that protect them from exposure to consciousness. In Chapter 13 one such category was identified around the unconscious preservation of power relations through talking and acting on differences that are used to stir up hatred. This is the dynamic of those who are 'in' and those who are 'out'. While people will be aware of who is 'in' and who is 'out', what they tend to be unaware of is the purpose this categorisation is serving. People in groups also unconsciously categorise experience into binary opposites that become entrenched as ideologies, which make their behaviour seem right and natural. Here the ideology may be conscious but its dubious basis will be unconsciously excluded from consideration. Then the very categorising and logical procedures of language work to highlight certain differences and obliterate others in what is ultimately an arbitrary way. The difference is conscious but what it obliterates becomes unconscious.

How organising themes interact

This section examines how organising themes of the formal–informal, conscious–unconscious and legitimate–shadow type relate to, and interact with, each other in the formation of narratives of experience. Although, for explanatory purposes, I have focused attention on categories of themes taken separately, they are always simultaneously operating in any organisation – together they constitute the complex responsive processes of relating that are the organisation and in which its strategy emerges as identity narrative. All of the categories have to do with the reproduction and potential transformation of power relations. I have already described how the complex interplay between legitimate and shadow organising themes, or official and unofficial ideologies, either supports or undermines current power relations. The following subsections examine other important interactions and the strategy narratives they form.

Legitimate interactions

From the definition given above, it is obvious that all formal themes organising experience are also conscious and legitimate. These are the organising themes that strategic choice theory focuses attention on. The organising themes here are primarily propositional in nature and are arranged in models and maps of one kind or another. Plans and budgets, management information and control systems, reward systems and all the other systems and techniques discussed in the chapter on strategic choice theory, all take this form.

However, the formal–conscious–legitimate themes never interact in isolation from the others. Consider an account of a perfectly normal formal meeting to review a budget submission that is to be made to senior executives.

The budget meeting

Streatfield (2001) describes a meeting to review a programme budget. The original budget had been for £12 million but now looked like amounting to some £50 million. The ten managers who formed the programme team met to assess the situation, each with their own motives in assessing the budget. For example, the directors of Information Resources and Supply Operations wanted the programme to standardise global systems. The former was behind schedule in delivering his part of the project and had spent £2.5 million above plan so he wanted to get the budget number accepted at the highest possible level to cope with increasing resource requirements. Another director was pushing project planning methodology and yet another was trying to extricate himself from the project. This was a group, then, consisting of people with varying degrees of commitment to the success of the project and with their own anxieties about their reputations, credibility and career prospects.

They struggled together to make sense of what they called 'this damn thing'. They all knew that they had to put forward a sensible new budget proposal that would be acceptable to the chief executive. The chairman emphasised the need to reduce the budget but cautioned against creating an impossible situation for themselves later on. They started to review the excess Information Resources development costs, which now included an extra £6 million for a new approach to communications software. There were knowing glances exchanged as the Finance representative pressed the Information Resources team. Old differences emerged as people took positions. It seemed that there was no other way forward than to spend the £6 million. If the project were to be achieved then the communications software had to be budgeted at the higher figure. There were sighs of relief in the Information Resources corner. There was also more ammunition for the future for the Finance team who promised to come back to look at any potential overspends. They then turned to another systems installation on which £400,000 had already been spent without results so far. The Finance team wanted to get rid of it and develop another one but the Information Resources team resisted this.

Old scores came to the surface and new opportunities appeared from the background. Sometimes there was logical argument and then some raw emotion and frustration. Various experiences were introduced to support the arguments. Sometimes there was a complete lack of structure when everyone tried to talk at once. There was laughter at a sudden joke and the humour of the situation. All desired to maintain credibility and power. The interactions were very real and filled with emotion. There was fear and desire to make a difference. There was resentment when one felt that one was being taken advantage of.

Eventually, the group somehow arrived at a figure of £42.8 million that seemed to be acceptable to those present in that it did not make it impossible to continue with the project. The arguments practised during the review were to be written up to support the decision arrived at. The anxiety abated as the satisfaction of knowing that they had got somewhere, almost in spite of themselves, settled on the group.

So, the first striking point is how personal ambitions and interpersonal rivalries are all part of the process. This immediately brings in organising themes of an informal and even a shadow nature. The story reveals the emotional undercurrent and the anxiety, first of not knowing just how realistic the figures are, and, second, of not knowing how senior management will receive them. This points to the probability of unconscious organising themes as a response to anxiety. The story also points to the way in which interaction between various organising themes supports or threatens current power relations. The point is that even as routine and rational an activity as reviewing a budget cannot be understood purely in terms of formal, conscious, legitimate interaction. What emerges from the budget meeting emerges from the interaction of all the categories of themes as strategy narrative.

This example also helps to clarify the nature of intention and control. All arrive at the meeting with an intention, namely, to reduce the budget estimate. This is their response to the gesture made by senior management. Each participant also arrives with an individual intention, namely, to reduce his or her part of the budget as little as possible and with the hope of even increasing it. Whether this intention materialises, or not, depends upon the responses it evokes from the others. These intentions and the responses they evoke are all themes organising their experience together. It is relatively predictable that they will reduce the budget estimate. However, what they are all well aware of is that they might find themselves in a similar position next year. After all, when they prepared the original estimate some time ago they did not intend that it should quadruple. What happens over the next year will emerge, just as what happened to the detail of the estimate emerges in this meeting.

A prime requirement of the manager's role is that of controlling activities and the expenditure they generate. It is the purpose of this meeting to carry out that requirement. However, the managers are well aware that they have not succeeded in controlling the expenditure since the last estimate and they clearly realise that this might happen again. Nevertheless, they do not take this as a cause of despair and abandon the whole attempt. They, and the situation they are in, cannot be described as out of control. This is what Streatfield (2001) refers to as the paradox of control. In situations of great uncertainty managers are in control and not in control at the same time.

Consider some other interactions between organising themes.

Covert politics

In learning organisation theory, reviewed in Chapter 4, Argyris (1990) identifies behaviour in organisations that blocks learning. He calls it organisational defence routines. For example, people make certain issues undiscussable, and they also make undiscussable the fact that they are undiscussable. They do this, according to Argyris, because they fear embarrassing, and being embarrassed by, others. He ascribes this behaviour to a defective mental model of the learning process located in the minds of individuals. This model is one in which a person enters a discussion with assertions about others that are not disclosed, knowing that others are doing the same. Each also assumes that they are engaging in the discussion to win and not to lose. His prescription is then that individuals should become aware of their defective mental model of the learning process and change it. The new model requires them to enter into open dialogue and disclose the assertions they are making about each other. He recognises that this will be very difficult and reports that, despite training, people hardly ever do it.

From the perspective I am pointing to this finding is hardly surprising. People hardly ever move to the learning process Argyris recommends because it is a completely unrealistic requirement. It amounts to requiring people to disclose the shadow themes organising their experience, so making the shadow public and legitimate. However, they cannot do this without taking the chance of openly undermining current power relations and incurring the retaliation of those they threaten. Some ideologies are unconsciously justifying current power relations and others are unconsciously justifying covert attempts to undermine them. People are passionate about these ideological underpinnings. Requiring people to move to the kind of position Argyris has in mind is the same as requiring them to abandon passion and expose not only their ideological position but the largely unconscious purposes they serve. This is only remotely plausible if you put the individual at the centre of your theory of psychology.

Once you place relationship at the centre, it is evident that the basic nature of human relating, the power relations it immediately implies and the ideologies that underpin these relationships would all have to change completely before the Argyris prescription could work. I cannot imagine that human beings will stop engaging in the kind of covert politics that Argyris has so perceptively identified. These complex responsive processes are always likely to characterise life in organisations. However, while they cannot be removed they can be understood, as can their impact on how an organisation evolves. Skilful participation in covert politics plays an important part in the emergence of strategy as identity narrative.

Covert politics are clearly informal, shadow themes organising experience and the themes are often conscious, although the underlying reasons for them may not be. However, covert politics are not organising experience in isolation from, or as an alternative to, other combinations of themes. For example, over many months colleagues and I engaged in just the kind of covert politics Argyris talks about. One faction in the company I worked for formed around the chief executive and favoured a strategy of investing in the existing business while another faction formed around another powerful figure and favoured diversification by acquisition. I found myself in the latter faction. The chief executive did not publicly dismiss the diversification strategy, although we all knew that he did not favour it. Instead, he called for it to be carefully examined and commissioned a paper on acquisition criteria. After discussion of this, a lengthy report was prepared on possible acquisition targets. At the end of the discussion on this report the chief executive called for a rewording of the acquisition criteria. By the time this had been discussed most of the acquisition targets had been bought by other companies. A further report was prepared. This went on for many months, during which time one small investment after another was made in the existing business. Here we can see the importance of covert politics in the constructing of the strategy narrative.

Everyone engaged in this process knew what was going on and knew that others, including the chief executive, knew what was going on too. No one, however, spoke about this at executive meetings, only privately. Conversations about what was going on were organised by shadow themes while legitimate themes organised silence. Note how the themes were informal, quite conscious and of the shadow. However, the reasons for keeping the conversation in this form were probably less conscious and much of the interaction between the two factions took place at formal meetings organised by legitimate themes. It was all going on at the same time.

From the perspective I am suggesting, covert politics is a social process. In ordinary conversations, legitimate and shadow themes interact in complex ways as people bolster, undermine and shift power positions. Action to remove people from their positions, from the chief executive to the office clerk, all begin as ordinary conversations organised by shadow themes. The important point here is that this form of conversation can shift power relations and patterns of talking but it can just as easily block any such shifts. Obviously this affects the strategy narrative and so how an organisation evolves.

Unconscious themes

Consider now how relationships might be organised by themes that are informal and unconscious and have shadow characteristics.

An example of what I mean occurred during a meeting of a group in which I was a consultant. The chief executive for this company expressed considerable frustration with a group of his most senior executives, claiming that he had empowered them to get on with meeting their targets. Instead of doing this, he said that they still kept referring everything to him and he felt that this was a cause of their company's falling profits. He was unwilling to reflect on why this was happening. Instead, he instructed the managers to attend a meeting at which they were to define their roles in such a way that they took more responsibility. I was to be a consultant at this meeting. He started the meeting by berating them for their lack of initiative and then left to go through the exercise of defining their roles. They refused to do this and spent the entire day in an emotional attack on the chief executive's leadership style. They complained about the unreasonableness of being required to meet conflicting targets. One reported overhearing the chief executive promising to fire the next executive who failed to meet any target whatsoever. This provoked outrage on the part of the managers. How could they be held responsible for changes over which they had no control? During this time, any comment I made was simply ignored and they decided that when the chief executive returned on the next day they would confront him.

However, the next morning one of the executives advised caution and gradually their resolve to confront him ebbed away. Instead they prepared a number of colourful PowerPoints and made a presentation to the chief executive about some rather safe business issues. He responded with a lecture. During the course of this lecture it became clear that there was little truth in the rumour that he would remove anyone who failed to achieve all targets no matter what happened. It was only on the following day, in a somewhat depressed state, that they were able to reflect on what they were doing. We talked about some of the themes organising their experience of being together at that time. For example, one clear theme that they seemed to be unconscious of was one that might be summarised as follows: 'Every casual remark the chief executive makes is an instruction or at least about to become one.' An example was the statement all took to be true that they had to achieve all targets or they would be fired. Other themes were those around flight from their task, the fight dynamic around the chief executive and the dependence on presentations of safe issues. These could be understood as the basic assumption behaviours of the psychoanalytic perspective (*see* Chapter 5), that is, unconscious themes organising the experience of being together. On the chief executive's next visit they were able to discuss their relationship with him.

The themes organising the experience for much of this meeting were informal, unconscious and of the shadow. However, the meeting took place legitimately and when the chief executive appeared it took formal, conscious and legitimate form. However, even when this happened the feelings and silent communications between the senior executives clearly reflected the informal, unconscious and shadow themes organising their experience. Again, interaction between all the kinds of themes identified is taking place simultaneously in the construction of strategy narratives. What emerges does so through the complex interplay of legitimate and shadow, conscious and unconscious and formal and informal themes. How all this is at the same time forming and being formed by power relations is also evident in the example. Again, these processes affect how an organisation evolves.

One of the most important aspects of shadow organising themes is the socially unconscious form they take. What is unconscious here is how members of a group collectively employ, in their talk and their actions, differences between themselves (senior executives in the above example) and other groups (the chief executive and those who report immediately to him) to stir up anger (even hatred) against the others in order to preserve unconsciously sensed power differences. They do this by collectively categorising their experience into binary opposites (meet all the targets or get fired) that become entrenched as ideologies, which make their behaviour seem right and natural. Furthermore, they collectively obliterate some differences and highlight others, so polarising experience.

The dynamics of conversational themes

The institutional themes organising the experience of being together tend to take the formal, conscious, legitimate form and they have the effect of limiting the connections between people, so preserving stability. Hierarchical reporting structures in an organisation are an example of this. In hierarchical structures, people mainly interact with their immediate superior, who in turn interacts with a person higher up in the hierarchy. This clearly cuts down on the number of connections. The accomplishment of hierarchy, habits, routines, customs and traditions is to replace many potentially conflicting constraints with a few in the interests of ongoing joint action.

When current power relations are sustained by this means, stability emerges. Social structures, cultures, bureaucratic procedures and hierarchical arrangements emerge, often as intentions and designs, in local communicative interaction. This is a way of thinking about, say, hierarchy that is more encompassing than the usual way of simply identifying it as a designed structure. What is more encompassing is the inclusion of hierarchy and decisions about hierarchy in the wider process of communicative interaction.

The social process may be one that patterns communicative interaction as clusters of strong connections linked to other clusters by much weaker connections. Such clusters of strong connections would constitute institutions and organisations, in turn patterned as clusters of strong connections with weaker links to others, for example, as departments and project teams within an organisation. This could be understood as an intrinsically stabilising process in that it reduces numbers of connections and hence the numbers of conflicting constraints. In this process, closely linked clusters establish power differences both within and between clusters, so constraining both those within the cluster and those in other clusters. The strong connections take the form of habits. In this way powerful institutions and organisations emerge that constrain the choices open to people.

However, institutionalisation as formal, conscious, legitimate themes organising the experience of being together is only one aspect of the process. At the same time experience is also being patterned by, for example, informal, unconscious, shadow themes. These too form clusters as people organise themselves into shadow pressure groups in organisations, sometimes displaying the kind of fluid communication between people that tends to be stifled by institutionalised themes. These pressure groups and their shadow themes will frequently be antagonistic to institutionalised themes and it is in the tension and the conflict between them that change in institutionalised themes emerges. Another way of putting this is to say that novel strategy narratives emerge in the interplay of shadow and institutionalised strategy narratives.

14.4 Summary

To summarise, organisations exist to enable joint action and people can only act jointly through their relationships with each other. People relate to each other through complex responsive processes that can be understood in terms of interacting propositional and narrative themes. The themes take many forms. They may be ideological themes. They may take the form of intentions, expressions of emotion, descriptions and so on. Simultaneous interaction between many themes taking different forms constitutes the conversational life of an organisation and the strategic narratives that emerge from them. The process of relating through conversation constrains that relating and so establishes power relations. Conversation and power relations are simply different words for the same phenomenon, namely that of relating between people. An organisation is processes of relating where relating is the conversational life of organisational members in which they form patterns of power relations and make ideologically based choices. Conversational life cannot develop according to an overall blueprint since no one has the power to determine what others will talk about all the time. Conversation is thus local interaction continuously producing emergent population-wide patterns as strategy narratives.

Further reading

Ideas in this chapter are further developed by Fonseca (2001), Streatfield (2001) and Shaw and Stacey (2005). Also see Wenger (1998).

Questions to aid further reflection

1. What do you think of those who advocate storytelling as a useful form of intervention in organisations?
2. In what way, if at all, does it make sense to think of strategy as fundamentally a narrative of identity?
3. What stories do you have to tell of shadow conversations in your organisation?
4. What role, if any, do you think humour plays in organisational life?
5. What activities in your organisation lead you to believe that unconscious processes might be at play and how might they affect strategy?

Reflective management narrative 4

Rui Grilo works as a project manager at a telecommunications company in Portugal. He recently graduated from the Doctor of Management programme at the University of Hertfordshire where his research was on his experience of project management. In this narrative he tells the story of a project to redesign an Internet portal. Towards the end of the narrative he tells us that his senior colleague regards the activity of project management as a simple one requiring no further reflection or comment other than to say that it is a step-by-step process of setting goals, defining scope, allocating tasks, monitoring performance, rewarding success and punishing failure. Grilo's experience of an ordinary project in this narrative could be explained in this way – they followed all of these steps and were successful in meeting deadlines and achieving objectives. End of story. However, his reflection on what he and others were doing brings out a much more complicated process. The points in his narrative that stand out for me are as follows:

- The experience of managing this project clearly has the narrative structure discussed in Chapter 14.
- While formal tools of analysis and control (*see* Chapter 15) were used, they were tools only in wider processes of interaction between people, essentially taking the form of political activity. The narrative brings out the roles that power and ideology play in project management, matters that were discussed in Chapter 13.
- The scope of the project was not determined in a simple analytical manner but emerged in the interplay of intentions (*see* Chapter 10) in conversational (*see* Chapter 11) and political processes.
- The project management process was not simply a formal one. The narrative brings out the important part played by informal conversations in the evolution of the project (*see* Chapter 14).
- The narrative also brings out the unconscious processes involved to do with fear of failure and shame, the anxiety this brings with it, and how those involved in the project deal with the anxiety (*see* Chapters 13 and 15).
- Then there are shadow themes, which are not publicly discussed, to do with personal ambitions of those involved in the project (*see* Chapter 14).
- The story also points to the importance of influencing, even manipulating, skills in achieving the aims of the project – the ability to engage in the dominant discourse and deploy the required rhetorical skills (*see* Chapter 11).

Accountability and project control at a telecommunications company

by Rui Grilo

This narrative is an exploration of what it means for a manager to be accountable for the results of a project over which he is not fully in control. I live this theme every day in my professional life. As a manager, I find that I never have enough information to be sure about my decisions. When I do choose, and almost every action in management involves some kind of choice, I face the fact that I cannot control most of what makes the outcome of that decision a success, a failure or something between those extremes. I am, nevertheless, accountable for what I do. By being accountable I mean that I answer for the results of my work and that I am responsible for those results. My performance is evaluated and I can keep my job, be promoted or be fired because of that constant evaluation. Even if I do not experience more severe consequences, every time I fail I feel shame and sometimes guilt. This awareness of my own vulnerability to failure provokes in me varying degrees of anxiety, understood as the reaction to a threat of loss (Bateman et al., 2000), the fear of the shame of failing. This anxiety is difficult to deal with and makes me feel uneasy and insecure when having to choose. I do not accept this discomfort passively. I want to understand what makes me feel the way I do and how my thinking and acting can evolve in a way that may enable me to become a better professional, whatever that means. The motivation of this reflective narrative is to develop my ability to go on with my work in spite of the anxiety I may feel.

I live every day with the expectation that I can be in control of what I do as a manager. But I also live with the paradoxical awareness that I am in control and not in control at the same time. I am in control because I can choose my actions and constrain others. I am not in control because I cannot determine everyone's actions and my success or failure can depend more on things beyond my capacity to influence than on my own actions. Streatfield (2001) examines this paradox in a way that resonates with my experience. He points to how the literature on management builds the expectation that managers are 'in control' of an organisation's movement into the future, that their choices are the cause of the organisation's movement, and that competent managers design their organisation's future in advance of realising it. He then examines his own practice, which leads him to a 'reappraisal of what it means to manage effectively' (p. 80), coming to 'understand effective management as the quality of courage to carry on participating in the creation of personal and collective meaning, if only in small ways, in spite of the anxiety and helplessness engendered by the loss of direction' (p. 80).

While Streatfield's (2001) view on the paradox of control resonates with my experience of controlling and not controlling at the same time as a manager, it does not answer fully my concern about accountability. Regardless of how I understand my role as a practitioner, I cannot change the expectations or the standards by which my performance is evaluated. I still answer for the results of my work and I can still be blamed for failures. Therefore, I want to examine my own practice of participating in management change projects. I will ground my reflection in the framework of project management as a specific discipline of management that was developed to be 'the most efficient way of introducing unique change' (Dixon, 2000, p. 14). Most literature on project management (Andersen et al., 1995; Burke, 1999; Lock, 2003; Pinto, 1998; Turner, 1999) focuses on planning and control techniques, such as CPM (Critical Path Method), PERT (Programme Evaluation and Review Technique) or GDPM (Goal Directed Project Management). Those techniques are refined sets of prescriptions that focus on what a manager should do in order to successfully manage a project, establishing procedures to attribute responsibilities and control the completion of tasks.

I will argue that although those tools and techniques are useful to manage a project, focusing exclusively on them is a way for project managers to avoid dealing with the anxiety of being accountable for the project's success while being vulnerable to events beyond their control. In dealing with the paradox of control in this setting, I found that the quality of my interaction with the people with whom I work enabled me to have the courage, in Streatfield's (2001) sense, to keep on engaging with the change process, being aware of its vicissitudes, while being able to communicate to the top management using the language of project management tools and techniques. In my discussion of this theme, I will acknowledge how some project management literature (Turner et al., 1996) is taking into account the importance of relationships in project work, but I will argue that, without considering the paradox of control, that perspective is still not congruent with my experience as a practitioner.

In order to take into account the paradox of control in human interaction, I will draw on the theory of complex responsive processes (Fonseca, 2002; Shaw, 2002; Stacey, 2001, 2003; Stacey et al., 2000; Streatfield, 2001) as a framework to discuss my experience as a project manager. Understanding the interaction of people in an organisation as an ongoing conversational process, where meaning is constantly formed and reformed, points to the importance of self-organisation and to the role of power, enabling and constraining interactions. I find these aspects of human relating crucial to my practice as a participant in management change projects.

In this narrative, I have changed the names of people and organisations in order to protect their identities. This enabled me to reflect with greater freedom on how my work relationships are constituted, without having to worry too much about how those involved might react to the sense I am making.

The discipline of project management

Project management appeared as a discipline of management in the early twentieth century, associated with the development of major engineering projects, such as building ships, constructing bridges or assembling aircraft. Nowadays, however, the tools and concepts of project management are used in a much wider range of situations, as project management has come to be understood as an effective way to introduce all kinds of change in organisations. The project management approach was even incorporated into general management thinking in the form of project-based management (Turner, 1999). The assumption underlying this enthusiasm is that change is thought to be more controllable if it is managed in the form of a project. Most literature on project management is therefore focused on effective tools and techniques to control project work (Andersen et al., 1995; Burke, 1999; Lock, 2003; Pinto, 1998; Turner, 1999).

This broadening field of project management is clearly illustrated by Dennis Lock (2003) when he identifies four different kinds of projects: construction projects, manufacturing projects, research projects and management projects. The first two kinds of project are clearly industrial, focusing on the production or design of some kind of hardware, reflecting the origins of project management. Research projects aim to produce some kind of new knowledge through the allocation of human, financial and technological resources. Management projects encompass the deliberate introduction of change in organisations, such as headquarters relocation, the development and introduction of a new computer system, the launch of a marketing campaign or an organisational restructuring.

The work I do in the strategy and business development department of a telecommunications group, which I will call the Telco Group, clearly falls in this last category. We organise ourselves into temporary teams of one to three members of the department and we are placed in one of the Group's companies to achieve a certain goal. I spent five months in 2002 developing the telemarketing sales of a broadband Internet access product of the Group. While I was doing that, other colleagues were engaging in projects such as the launch of a new company for the corporate market segment or setting financial targets for the information technology companies of the Group. In developing this kind of work, we use the basic tools of project management: Gantt charts, project task lists, regular progress control and, sometimes, CPM in order to determine how long it will take to complete.

To understand why project management came to be regarded as a controllable way to introduce change in an increasingly dynamic and complex business environment (Turner et al., 1996), one has to trace its roots. The pioneer of project management is commonly accepted to have been Henry Gantt (1861–1919). In order to plan and control shipbuilding projects, he started using bar charts as visual aids in the early 1900s, representing each activity, when it would start and when it would be completed. Those charts are still called Gantt charts today. Using those tools, he managed to visualise the whole process, identifying sequences and interconnections of activities. This enabled him to literally see where time could be saved by doing activities in parallel that were previously done sequentially, thus reducing significantly the time required for building ships (Burke, 1999, p. 11).

Gantt's invention was such a breakthrough that it still influences today's project management. The project management planning and control tools and techniques were developed further in the 1950s, with the advent of development of the Critical Path Method (CPM) developed by Remington Rand Univac as a tool to minimise the turnaround time from production to sales, and the Programme Evaluation and Review Technique (PERT) designed by the US Navy with the management consultants Booz Allen & Hamilton in the late 1950s as a technique for planning and controlling the design and development of the Polaris submarine. As software planning tools developed, both CPM and PERT began to be used almost interchangeably (Lock, 2003).

The usage of this set of tools and techniques of project management started to identify a community of practice and a discipline of management. In 1965, that community took a more formal form with the establishment of the International Project Management Association (IPMA), followed by the creation, in 1969, of the Project Management Institute (PMI) in the United States and, later, the Association for Project Management (APM) in the United Kingdom. These associations have been gathering and updating the body of knowledge of the profession. The PMI was the first one to publish it, in 1986, being followed by the APM in 1992, whose body of knowledge is now in its fourth edition (Dixon, 2000).

The appeal project management has for managers comes, in my opinion, from the seductiveness of breaking down work into small pieces with pre-defined deadlines and clear attribution of responsibilities. A clearly laid out project seems much more 'controllable' than a mere sketch of what one thinks must be done in order to attain a certain goal. But those tools of project management do not provide managers with a straightforward solution to managing change, because there is no shortcut for the two harder aspects to manage: how to get people to work to complete the tasks required to attain a certain goal and, before that, how that goal came to be set in the first place. That last question is what I want to discuss through the following account of my experience of participating in the negotiation of the scope of a project.

Negotiating the scope of a project

From February to April, I worked full time in the restructuring of the Telco Group's Internet portal. Pires, the CEO of Dot Com Company, which owns the portal, phoned Sequeira, the head of my department, to ask for my department's help to restructure the Internet portal. It was part of his responsibilities and he had not yet had the opportunity to improve it. They agreed that it would involve two of us for a two-month period. Sequeira assigned me as the senior business analyst for the project and Alberto as the junior one. Both of us would work under Resende's supervision as project leader. Resende is the senior project manager in my department, sharing with Sequeira the top responsibility for the projects in which we engage. He had joined the department a few months before, coming from the Lisbon branch of a major consultancy company, where he was also senior project leader.

I was enthusiastic about working in that project because I have always been interested in Internet-based businesses, but I was uncomfortable with not having a clear goal or a project scope. Sequeira articulated it to me simply as 'Pires wants us to make a turnaround in the portal' and he told me to contact Pires in order to find out exactly what he wanted. I phoned Pires but, as Pires was away on holiday, Sequeira told me to contact the portal's chief executive, Baltasar. I arranged a meeting with him for the following day. When I arrived, he briefed me on how the Internet portal had been born as a university project in the early 1990s. As the Internet became more and more popular, that Internet portal became a leading Portuguese search engine and directory service. Baltasar was one of the executives of a company who bought the portal and the right to use its brand from the university, selling it afterwards to the Telco Group when the Internet boom started.

When the Telco Group bought the portal, Baltasar kept his position as the portal's chief executive. He told me how the costs did not matter when the Internet businesses had all the hype in the world and the only figures everybody wanted to see were how many page views and visitors they had attained. But after the bust of the Internet boom, the portal's staff was reduced from more than 100 people to little more than 30. He understood this project as Pires's reaction to the poorer performance that fewer people were able to deliver. He argued that although the top management had been focusing on cutting costs by firing people, they were now surprised that the portal did not perform as usual. His views made sense to me as well as the metaphor he used: 'they turned a Ferrari into a Mini and now they want to drive the Mini as if it was a Ferrari'. He was succeeding in his attempt to win my sympathy.

I told him that Pires had told me that they had already prepared some work for the portal's restructuring. He confirmed this, telling me that he had the whole strategy articulated in a 100-page presentation that his team had prepared. But he was having trouble communicating it to Pires. Part of that strategy was to redesign the portal, updating its look and feel, and Pires was focusing just on

▶

that aspect, ignoring everything else. It looked as if Pires was stepping out of his role as CEO of the company to become a senior web designer, giving precise guidelines for the new homepage design. For Baltasar the problem was how to give financial credibility to the new strategy in order to communicate it. That was what he wanted our help for, to translate his team's work into a financial language that Pires might listen to and approve.

At this stage of the conversation I started to feel uneasy. Baltasar engaged in the conversation playing a teacher-like role, telling me about the portal's story, a narrative that I already knew. He was stating that he was the one who knew the business from the start, so I should rely on his opinion. It was a power play, but I had no interest in contesting his superior knowledge on the portal. Then the conversation evolved into another pattern of interaction, as Baltasar tried to persuade me to serve as a translator between himself and Pires. That did not make sense to me. Either there was something for us to do at the portal from which some novelty would arise or being there would be a waste of time. That was the rationalisation I came up with to justify my negative emotional response. How could he presume that I would simply support his conclusions and act only as a go-between?

The meaning that was arising from our interaction was that he was in a position to determine my actions. I did not like that, so I held back during the rest of the meeting and reserved my position about how we would engage with the project for the moment after I had talked to Resende and Sequeira about it. When I reported my impressions to both Sequeira and Resende, it sounded unacceptable to them too. Sequeira thought that it was far from what Pires had in mind so he called him, interrupting his holiday. We improvised a loudspeaker conference call with him, gathering around the phone.

Sequeira started the conversation by telling Pires that Baltasar wanted us to examine the strategy proposal he had come up with and work out the financials. He reacted promptly: 'It is not that at all.' He did not want any financial analysis and he had not listened to the portal's proposed strategy because he did not really trust its conclusions. He wanted us to do four main tasks: analyse the portal's channel structure in order to redesign it (as the portal is composed of several thematic websites),

co-ordinate the design of an innovative new homepage, articulate a plan for a further improvement of the whole portal and prepare the launch of a new broadband channel. After some discussion on how much time this would take, Sequeira and Pires finally agreed that it could be done in about two to three months. But Resende wanted to draw clear boundaries around our work, so he proposed that we should have a start-up meeting to define clearly what would be done, by whom and when. Pires accepted.

After that phone call I talked to Baltasar. Pires had already told him what he had asked us to do and he seemed to accept it, although he displayed some discomfort with the situation. After all, his superior had overridden his point of view. After that conversation, in which Baltasar told me whom he would assign from the portal's staff to assist us, I prepared a small presentation with the project's main objectives (its scope) and the main tasks and deadlines (the milestones). That document constituted the basis for the formal start of the project, serving the purpose of reassuring everyone about what had to be done, by whom and when. Pires chaired the meeting himself and it served the purpose of conveying that he was personally committed to get the results he wanted from it. The first would be to give the portal a new, improved homepage.

Power, control and accountability

The theme running through the narrative of this project's start-up is far from being a distinctive feature of project management. Indeed, the dynamics of power and influence that were at play here can be found daily not only in the business world but in all human activities. The sociologist Norbert Elias (1998) argues that trials of strength are part of all human relationships, as people feel the drive to test who is stronger. In this narrative, that kind of test can be seen, for instance, between Baltasar and me, between Sequeira and Pires or between Pires and Baltasar. According to Elias, power is not something that any of us can possess as if it were a thing. Instead of that reified notion of power he proposes the idea that power is a structural characteristic of all human relationships (Elias, 1998, p. 116) that only exists when at least two people interact. This does not deny the unequal distribution of chances of power. Pires obviously had a position that increases his chances of power when interacting with Baltasar or Sequeira. But the initial distribution of the chances of power does not fully determine the balance of power. The way each person plays out their chances of power in their interaction with others can shift that balance. That was what happened when Sequeira and Resende persuaded Pires to accept a well-defined project scope or when I persuaded Sequeira and Resende not to take the role that Baltasar had asked of me.

What is the function of the plan that we came up with for the start-up meeting? In the light of this discussion of power, I think it became for us a symbol that represented the power figuration underlying our relationships at that moment in time. The plan would influence the chances of power in our future interactions. Someone who wanted to follow the plan would have greater chances of power than someone else who might want to change it. This makes me see the plan as a disciplining tool of control. Having been agreed upon by all of us, we became accountable for its success. If we did not manage to transform the intended achievements into real ones, we would have to account for this failure and be blamed for it. The fear of shame and guilt associated with failure would then have the disciplining effect of keeping our efforts focused on reaching the milestones on time.

This understanding of the role of that initial project plan is illustrative of the interplay I see between control and accountability. On the one hand, Pires took the initiative of starting up this project because he is accountable for the portal's performance and he believed it should be improved. On the other hand, the plan served as a tool of control for Pires to measure our work, making us accountable for meeting the deadlines and delivering tangible results. Having participated in the discussion of the plan and having accepted (or even proposed) the deadlines, I became personally accountable for it and, in my turn, I would try to control the people I would be working with in order to have the work done on time, thus avoiding the shame of failing. This circular relationship between accountability and control, control and accountability seems to me to be an organising theme running through my experience. I believe this theme is especially felt in project management or project-based management because of the highly articulated form of breaking down work into tasks whose completion can be evaluated. But that control is all about managing people, getting them to do what someone intended.

According to J. Rodney Turner, one of the most influential experts in this field of management, project management literature often ignores the role of the project manager as a manager of people (Turner *et al.*, 1996). Turner *et al.* tried to account for that missing aspect, arguing that the project manager is often a change agent, having to influence the organisation without a position of authority but with all the responsibility of completing the project on time. Although the actual word used in the text I am referring to is 'responsibility', it is used in the same sense as I am discussing accountability, understanding it as having to answer to someone or for some activity, being liable or responsible. In this sense, both accountability and responsibility may express the meaning of a kind of force that binds us to do what we come to think we must do.

The way those authors (Turner *et al.*, 1996) propose to succeed in influencing the organisation is to 'treat people as if they were volunteers' (p. 126) and to develop an 'influence strategy'. That strategy would include sequential steps of identifying who needs to be influenced, thinking how those people can be persuaded to support the project and then succeeding in actually influencing them. This step-by-step approach is based on the assumption that 'the key factor in influencing anyone to do anything is to ensure that the rewards for doing it are greater than the risks' (p. 128). This assumption is highly questionable because it only acknowledges the purely rational aspects of human action, ignoring more emotional responses such as the ones evoked by personal loyalty or by a seductive kind of leadership.

Nevertheless, this rational balance of what one may win or lose is present in the form of what one thinks one can win or lose. Being accountable for a project, I have felt the sense of having rewards or punishments waiting for me if I succeed or fail. Sometimes, the fantasy about those rewards and punishment is greatly exaggerated in relation to what actually happens. Succeeding in a very demanding task might only evoke an approving nod as a reward and failing to meet a deadline may mean only that the deadline has to be postponed to some later date. Reminding myself that the world will not end if I fail has been an effective way for me to lower my anxiety, enabling me to have the clarity of spirit that may enable me to succeed.

Jeffrey Pinto, another influential project management theorist, equates power with politics (Pinto, 1998), claiming that those aspects play a substantial role in project management. He argues that political behaviour is 'any process by which individuals and groups seek, acquire, and maintain power' (p. 256). Pinto (1998) identifies three reasons why political processes are so important in project work. First, he argues that project managers seldom have high status or formal authority, which forces them to influence others to get the resources they need. Second, the fact that projects exist outside the functional structure forces project managers to continually negotiate and bargain for what they need. Finally, project managers do not usually conduct the formal performance evaluation of their project team subordinates, which takes away from them an important source of formal power. The reasons he identifies for the importance of political processes in project management resonate with my experience. Stepping into an unknown organisation, with support from the top management but without authority over anyone, I had to work with what is a common theme for almost all projects I engaged with at Telco. That situation leads to a tension between being held accountable by the management for results, while having to bargain for attention and resources to deliver those results.

The approach Pinto (1998) prescribes to deal with the issue of power and politics in project management is based in increasing the awareness project managers have of those issues. He proposes that one should acknowledge and understand the political nature of most organisations, learning appropriate political tactics, accepting conflict, levelling the playing field with line managers and learning how to use the 'fine art of influencing' (p. 263). The techniques described by him are very close to sheer manipulation. For instance, he argues that in order to establish sustained influence, a project manager should 'prioritise social relationships on the basis of work needs' and 'develop a network of . . . persons who can be called upon for assistance' (p. 264). I react strongly against this deliberate manipulation of human relationships in order to gain influence and increase one's chances of power. But even though I feel that reaction, I end up establishing relationships in project work that enable me to do my work.

Getting the project on track

The day after the first meeting of the project, both Alberto and I went down to Dot Com's headquarters, as the Internet portal is part of that company's activities. We had an office assigned for us on the top floor, just besides Pires's own office and quite near to Baltasar's. After settling in, we dropped by Baltasar's office. He was free, so we had the chance to sit together and explore further the next steps we should take.

Our first milestone was to redesign the portal's homepage, updating its look and feel and giving it a fresher, more appealing look. The most important competing portals were increasingly popular and in spite of having strong competitors, the Internet portal's homepage had remained unchanged for more than one year, which is a long time for an Internet business. Baltasar was convinced that the portal had to be appealing both to teenage heavy users and to older occasional users. I agreed with that perception and we discussed the methodology to take it into account. As the portal staff had already done some work benchmarking and sketching some alternative web design options for the homepage, the three of us decided to build upon that work, testing it with one or two focus groups to fine tune it before having a final proposal to submit to Pires at the first control meeting of the project.

After our short meeting, Baltasar introduced us to Tomás, the managing director of the portal. He was in charge of the contents and services department of the portal, composed of about twenty people who worked to keep the portal going. In addition to Tomás's department, there was also a commercial department and a technical department. Baltasar and Tomás assigned one of the staff members to help us almost full time. She would help us gather all the available material and arrange for the focus groups to take place.

Focus groups are often used when trying out new products. We would hire the services of a customer survey company to arrange two meetings of about ten people each, selected in order to be representative of the main customer profiles. The sessions would be conducted by a professional (a trained psychologist or sociologist) and could be observed by the clients through a mirrored glass window. We managed to arrange the focus groups to take place in less than one week before which we had to prepare a clear picture of what the options were, with some drafts to show and test.

Alberto and I started to examine every Internet portal, identifying patterns in their approaches and comparing how different looks were dominant in different national audiences. Having spent some days doing that research, we got deep into the web design options the staff had already come up with. Tomás introduced us to Norberto, the web designer who was assigned to work on the homepage. We discussed with him the reasoning behind some options and asked for his opinion on some of the design issues. Should we use a two-, three- or four-column design? How should we arrange the information in the page? Where should we place the advertisements? How could we lighten up the channel bar (where people can find links to more than twenty thematic channels that are part of the portal)? How should we integrate web mail and the access to other services on the top of the page? Which search options should we provide?

Norberto seemed happy to participate in the discussion. Later he made the remark that we obviously did not work there because we were doing something as strange as asking for his opinion. I smiled at that remark and felt happy for having asked for his active involvement. Baltasar and Tomás joined in afterwards and we narrowed down the options to three alternative sketches. Norberto worked out the changes that we agreed upon and, on the day before the focus groups, we had prepared prints of our new design options as well as hard copies of the most relevant competing portals. Before the first session started, I briefed the person who was going to conduct the sessions and we agreed on a simple sequence. He would first enquire about each one's usage of the Internet, which kind of access they had, which was their favourite portal and why they chose it. Afterwards, he would show the images for the portal that we had selected on a computer screen, discussing what they liked and disliked in each one. Finally, he would show our proposals for a new design, conducting the same kind of discussion. Resende attended because he wanted to personally witness the discussions.

The two focus groups were quite useful for our work and after spending more than six hours listening to customer feedback I felt that we might easily deliver a final product. They considered the current Internet portal homepage to be outdated but very rich in information and resources. We could not make the new design too light. The two groups of users came clearly into focus. The younger ones (whom we started calling the 'broadband generation') always had their computer on and connected to the net, through a broadband connection. They disliked farfetched designs and what they called 'too many letters', while preferring simpler, straightforward approaches with no news or advertisements. The older users (whom we called the 'narrowband generation') connected their computers occasionally to the web, searching for news and entertainment content. The Internet service they use the most is simply e-mail. Surprisingly enough, both the 'narrowband generation' and the 'broadband generation' agreed on the same sketch for the new portal homepage. That sketch happened to be almost everybody's favourite, which we welcomed because it would enable us to get it approved in an easier way.

Resende was quite stressed about the control meeting with Pires that was approaching. He seemed more anxious about the meeting than about getting our work done. He then decided to focus his attention on the Dot Com Company. Although I saw this as a way for him to relieve his anxiety, I nevertheless felt that he was taking the project leadership away from me. I resented that, because I felt it was an attitude that was undermining my ability to do my job. I started reacting in a more aggressive way, in a power struggle, claiming my own space. Some tension built up as a result of it and Alberto was placed in the uncomfortable position of being between the two of us. That emerging rivalry, which seems meaningless to me now, could be traced to the way we were having trouble recognising one another. On one hand, I did not recognise Resende as a legitimate boss because I did not acknowledge the full value of his past career in the consulting business. I tended to view him as a caricature of himself, as someone scared of Pires's power and obsessed with adding charts to build up a PowerPoint presentation. On the other hand, I think Resende could not rely on my ability to effectively lead a project. He did not trust the value of my past experience in the public sector and he knew that I was having my first experience leading a project team of this kind. Tangled in this web of lack of recognition, we made our lives more difficult, taking each web design option as a power struggle.

Eventually, we came up with a solution that had the agreement of Baltasar, Tomás, Resende, Alberto and me. I personally prepared the document that we would present to Pires, grounding our choices both in the results of the benchmark studies we did and in the outcome of the focus groups. The new homepage proposal was presented in the end as the logical outcome of our reasoning, with call-outs explaining the reasons behind each option. I was pretty confident that Pires would agree to it but I was a bit stressed before the meeting started, as I was the one who would be giving the presentation. Our goal was to get the new design approved in order to present it to the public, inviting users to give us their feedback. But, to do that, we needed Pires's approval.

The meeting started. Pires chaired, stating in a good mood that he had big expectations about our work. I smiled and gave him a copy of the document we had prepared. He quickly jumped to the final page to see the proposal. Everybody in the room stood still and silent. Baltasar, Tomás, Resende, Alberto and me waited for his reaction. 'I like it,' he said, and the tension dissipated a little. He then added that he would do some things differently, but I asked him to follow our reasoning in order to understand why we had made those choices. He accepted and I guided everybody's attention through the document, explaining what we had realised while seeing other portals' design, what the two groups of users we had identified were expecting and what the most visited areas of the current homepage were. The presentation was conducted in the logical language that Pires was used to.

Resende added a few ideas but everybody else was silent, including Baltasar, who I had thought would like to take the lead at some point. Pires wanted to change the order of the columns on the homepage design. I did not agree with that option because it would break a balance that I thought we had reached through the progression from thinner to wider columns. I argued my case and both Resende and Baltasar stepped into the discussion, supporting a point of view similar to mine. Pires was hard to convince but he finally agreed to the new homepage. We would post it for two weeks at a test address, inviting users to give us their feedback.

We had reached exactly what we intended and that made us all happy. Baltasar had been struggling to have this decision taken for some time and he was cheerful that we had managed to pull it off. The sense I made from that situation was that it was all a matter of verbal communication. We presented our reasoning to Pires in his consultancy language, where each chart was presented for a reason which was to demonstrate a point leading to the final conclusions. Baltasar communicated to him in a less structured way, taking for granted some of his own assumptions from his intuition or his vast knowledge of the business. We also relied on our intuition and on Baltasar's feelings, but we gave it a 'scientific' flavour. We were making choices with reasons that were presented as objective. I think this way of presenting things greatly lowered Pires's anxiety about taking the risk of changing the face of the leading Internet portal of the country.

The new design was cheerfully welcomed by the users, who gave an extremely positive feedback in a poll we conducted. When the test period was almost over, we had another meeting with Pires to show him the results of the poll and to obtain his approval to make the definitive change. He was delighted with the results and easily agreed to it. The new homepage design was launched on time and I felt that I had accomplished something, at least helping Pires and Baltasar to communicate and reach decisions.

Project control and systems thinking

While writing this account of the development of the project, I started reflecting on the role of the regular meetings as procedures of control. While the plan expresses a power balance in terms of general goals and determining who is accountable for each action, the control meetings enforce that plan, making people answer for its development. Resende's anxiety before the first meeting is illustrative of the dynamics at play. He feared failing in the eyes of Pires and so did I. In that anxious state we politely turned against each other, engaging in a power struggle that could have undermined the actual work that we had to do. And why did that happen? I believe that the anxiety to deliver results and to identify myself with being competent prevented me from understanding Resende's behaviour. I can imagine that a similar process might have happened with him.

In an influential book called *Goal Directed Project Management* (Andersen *et al.*, 1995), the authors claim that 'control is doing something about what the reports show', where purpose 'is not to establish grounds for punishment or reward' but to 'establish whether there is a need for corrective measures' (p. 151). They insist that control is not persecution but deciding instead what needs to be done and doing it. Is this just a politically correct statement or is it what really happens in real-life project management? My experience of control meetings is that the fear of the humiliation and shame aroused by potential failure provokes a state of anxiety that may drive people into action. Those actions, taken in that anxious state, can be effective in fulfilling a goal but at times can actually get in the way of what needs to be done. I think that before the first control meeting that I wrote about, Resende was more anxious than I was. It was his first project with Pires and he wanted to make a good impression. I think I was not that anxious because I already knew Pires for some time as it had been he who had employed me in the Telco Group and he had been my boss before moving to the position of CEO of Dot Com Company. I also knew how he behaved in control meetings and I knew what to expect, how to defend myself and how to communicate with him effectively.

After the last control meeting, when the new homepage was definitely approved, I stayed for a while chatting with Resende. I was in the process of looking for more literature on project management, so I asked him if he could recommend me any project management book that he might have found influential. As he had been managing projects for most of his professional life, it seemed like a straightforward thing to ask. It was not. He looked surprised and stood silent for a short while, as if I had asked him some funny question. He replied with another question, asking me why I would need such a thing. I answered that project management was the obvious framework for our department's practice and, as I was examining my own practice and the ideas that underlie it, I had to explore and make some sense of it. I had already come up with plenty of references, I told him, but I wished to know what his personal influences on the issue were. As an example, I showed him an article published in the *International Journal of Project Management* and a copy of *Body of Knowledge* (Dixon, 2000) published by the Association for Project Management. He looked at what I was showing him and said that he could not understand how people could waste their time writing about the issue. It was my turn to look surprised, so I asked him what he meant. He argued that project management did not require fancy literature. It was as simple as setting tasks, establishing deadlines, appointing who is accountable for each task, and then making regular control meetings, using punishments and rewards. No theory was needed; one had simply to focus on what had to be done. It was as simple as that. And, as he was suddenly in a hurry to leave, the conversation ended there.

This conversation was quite illuminating for me, as I found it quite representative of the community of practice in which I develop my work. Resende's point of view is quite contrary to what is argued by Andersen *et al.* He takes control meetings solely for their explicit function as an arena in which a project's development is measured and corrective measures are taken in the form of 'punishments and rewards'. Although Resende refuses theory, this way of his to make sense is clearly grounded in systems thinking, more specifically in cybernetics. Systems thinking was imported to organisation theory in the mid-twentieth century as an answer to insufficiencies found in the early theories of management proposed by Taylor ([1911] 1967) and Fayol ([1916] 1981).

In this context, a system is defined as an 'organized, unitary whole composed of two or more interdependent parts, components or subsystems and delineated by identifiable boundaries from its environmental supra-system' (Kast and Rosenzweig, 1985, p. 15). From this perspective, control is understood as being a function of management. The manager is supposed to step outside of the organisation to observe and analyse it rationally, in order to plan and design where he wants to lead the organisation and what are the actions he must take to make that desired future state come true (Streatfield, 2001, p. 126). This point of view is grounded on cybernetics, a part of systems thinking.

Cybernetics is based on the notion that a system can be controlled by an outside regulator through feedback (Wiener, 1948). In a system regulated through negative feedback, the outcome of an action is compared with the desired outcome and fed back into the system to determine the next

▶

action so as to reduce the discrepancy until it is eliminated. Organisation theory imported these notions from cybernetics, introducing the notion of desired states such as plans, budgets, forecasts or visions; regulators in the form of control meetings or regular reporting documents; and feedback actions in the form of corrective measures. In his textbook on project management, Dennis Lock (2003) explicitly refers to an electric cybernetic system as an analogous process to project control. He argues that 'the competent manager will ensure that . . . corrective actions do take place, so that the control loop is effectively closed' (p. 470). Because of the particularly close analogies he finds between the two processes, he calls project control 'cybernetic control'.

Resende's way of talking is clearly embedded in this perspective when he draws attention to the importance of control meetings to compare the actual state of development of the project with what had been planned. The feedback that he proposes to use is the distribution of rewards and punishments to the ones who were accountable for each task. Assuming that they can fulfil the task in the given time if they work hard enough, rewards and punishments can make them work harder in order to accomplish the goal that had been set. This is a rather simplistic way of looking at what happens in complex projects, where the ones who answer for the completion of each task are subject to events and actions that they cannot influence or avoid.

Conclusions

Project management literature focuses on how an individual can achieve a greater degree of control, using accountability as a tool to achieve it, making specific people accountable for performing given tasks in a determined time frame. In this narrative, accountability is central for the practice of project management not simply as a tool but as a theme patterning the interaction between the people involved in the project, motivating their quest for control. The interplay between accountability, guilt and shame seems to turn it into a powerful tool that some managers try to use in order to grasp some control of what happens in their organisation.

I also acknowledge how the notions of control and accountability can feed upon each other in a circular way in which one activates the other: being accountable can motivate the quest for control, as the expectation that one should be in control can make one accountable for what actually happens. What makes this perspective different from the mainstream prescriptions is how it deals with the paradox of control instead of collapsing it and how it acknowledges the role of interaction between people as crucial instead of focusing on the individual.

Questions to aid further reflection

1. What do you think it means, in situations such as those in this narrative, to be accountable?

2. What, if anything, is to be gained as a project manager from reflecting on the political nature of project management?

3. Although this project has apparently achieved what it was intended to achieve, what could have obstructed it?

4. What role was personal ambition playing in the project?

5. Does the narrative resonate with your experience of managing and, if so, in what way?

© Rui Grilo

Chapter 15

Complex responsive processes and the traditional concerns of the strategist
Technology, resources, markets, planning, control and performance

This chapter invites you to draw on your own experience to reflect on and consider the implications of:

- The meaning of technology in human interaction.

- Organisational resources as a basis of power relations.

- Markets as patterns of relationships and as ideology.

- Planning and control from the perspective of complex responsive processes.

- The contribution of reasoning and modelling to local interaction.

- Thinking about performance and improvement from a complex responsive processes perspective.

This chapter addresses aspects of organisation and strategy which feature prominently in most discussions on these matters but have hardly been referred to in the chapters of Part 3 so far. The reference to these aspects has been sparse or absent not because they are unimportant but because the concern has been with thinking about the fundamentals of human interaction in a manner that differs from the dominant discourse. Moving in thought to a different way of understanding human interaction leads to different ways of thinking about markets, resources and technology, performance and improvement which are so prominent in the dominant discourse. The purpose of this chapter is to take a brief look at this different way of thinking.

15.1 Introduction

So far, the chapters in this part have been concerned with developing a way of thinking about organisations as ongoing process of local interaction between people in which they accomplish purposeful joint action. Realised organisational strategies are patterns of joint activity, forming identity narratives which emerge across the populations of people constituting organisations. Strategy as realised patterns of joint activity, as the identity narrative people articulate, emerges through the many, many local interactions between members of organisations where those local interactions are fundamentally conversational in nature, characterised by relations of power sustained by ideologies which also form the basis of the choices people make and the intentions and plans they form, including desires, intentions and plans for the emerging population-wide patterns of strategy. The term 'strategy' may refer to 'desired strategy', that is, to the desires and intentions people develop for emerging population-wide patterns and the articulations they make of these desires. However, this definition on its own is inadequate because it is the interplay of such desired strategies in local interactions, not simply any one of them on its own, that will produce the actual population-wide patterns of 'realised strategy'. While organisations are 'real' processes of interaction, they also feature in people's imaginations and fantasy lives. They do so as imaginative constructs of idealised 'wholes', which gives felt unity to experience. The conversational, ideological and power-relating activities of organisation are essentially ongoing processes in which people make particular to their specific contingent situations the generalisations (social objects) and idealisations (cult values) they perceive and articulate about the population-wide patterns. The chapters of this part have focused mostly on the nature of local interaction because of its central role in the emergence of realised strategy, which is understood as the emergence of identity – the narrative of who people are and what they are doing together.

The chapters in this part have, therefore, focused attention on organisations and strategies in a way that differs substantially from the focus of attention in the dominant discourse described in the chapters of Part 1. The main concern of the dominant discourse on strategy is with the performance of a 'whole' organisation, understood as a system, particularly with the cause of successful performance, namely, the organisation's resource base, including technology, and its market position. The concern of the dominant discourse is with whether it is possible to choose, at least to some extent, the resource bases and market positions that will produce successful performance and, if it is possible, how this is to be done. This leads to the interest in planning and learning activities, control, progress and improvement. The debate conducted in terms of the dominant discourse centres on the possibility of choosing direction, resource base and market positions for the whole, with most writers and practitioners claiming that this is possible, whether by rational choice or by some form of learning, and others claiming, at the opposite extreme, that it is not possible to choose, in which case direction, resources base and market position are taken to emerge by chance in activities of muddling through. In terms of the complex responsive processes theory developed in this chapter, the dominant discourse focuses attention on the desires people form for the generalisations (social objects) and idealisations (cult values) of emerging population-wide patterns. In other words, the dominant discourse is concerned with what I have been calling an imaginative construct of a 'whole'. What the dominant discourse largely ignores is the local interaction of people who constitute organisations understood as the interplay of desires for the imagined 'whole'. It is in the interplay of such desires and intentions that the population-wide patterns of realised strategy actually emerge as identity narrative, not at all by chance but through what people are actually doing in their local interactions.

The purpose of this chapter is to explore how we might think about the central concerns of the dominant discourse to do with technology, resources, market positions, control and planning from a complex responsive processes perspective. This is a perspective that provides *a way of thinking about what people in organisations are already doing* in their ordinary, everyday local interactions and includes the activities of strategising. People in organisations do talk about technology, resources, market positions, performance, success and so on. This chapter is concerned with how one might make sense of what they are talking about from a complex responsive processes perspective. People in organisations do also engage in activities to which previous chapters in this part have so far paid little attention. People do reason, they measure many aspects of what they are doing, they make forecasts and prepare plans, they construct models of whole organisations and industries, and they sometimes use all of this in their decision-making processes in various ways. This chapter will, therefore, also look at the role that reasoning, measuring, forecasting and modelling play in complex responsive processes of local interaction. Consider first how we might think about technology from a complex responsive processes perspective.

15.2 Understanding technology as social object

Human beings have always used tools in their joint activities and nowadays local interactions between people in organisations are frequently conducted in the medium of highly sophisticated communication technologies. An understanding of local interaction and emergent strategy in modern organisations therefore requires paying particular attention to how we might understand the role of technology.

Tools, techniques and technology

Mead's notion of social objects provides a way of understanding technology from the perspective of complex responsive processes (Johannessen and Stacey, 2005). First, the social object of technology must be distinguished from technology as physical object. Some of the tools involved in a technology can be understood as physical objects designed and constructed by people to purposefully accomplish their activities. As such, technology is to be found in nature as other physical objects are. However, techniques for using tools, that is, people's knowledge, skills, practices and methods of tool use, always involve complex social acts. As such, technology is a social object to be found only in experience. Technology in the form of physical objects is also, in use, immediately a social object, that is, generalised tendencies for large numbers of people to act in fairly similar ways in using the physical objects of technology. In their particularisation these generalised tendencies evolve further as small differences are amplified – the causality is transformative. Technology is then understood not simply as physical objects to be found in nature, but, at the same time, as social objects to be found in our experience of complex social acts. This gives us an understanding of technology as being perpetually iterated in the particularising of the generalised tendencies to act in the present. As with other social objects, technologies can also be idealised and so form cult values. For example, technology and progress become conflated as cult values offering to people's imaginations a future free of poverty, disease and inequality. Widespread dissemination of technology then also becomes a cult value which suppresses the harmful consequences of technology.

An example of technology as social object is provided by Internet and e-mail technologies. The tools are computers, servers and software programs and these are physical objects. Their mere existence creates tendencies for large numbers of people to communicate with each other through e-mail and accessing databases. This is the generalised tendency to act in similar ways as social objects. These generalised tendencies are iterated in each present as rather repetitive, habitual techniques. In their continual iteration, technologies are particularised in specific situations. We send e-mails to each other and conduct transactions over the Internet, for example, with banks. Such particularisation is inevitably a conflictual process in that techniques are adapted to the demands of particular situations with their specific understanding of the past and expectations of the future. For example, as the use of e-mail spreads in organisations, conflicts arise as to the purposes it can be used for. People start using e-mails for personal use and this often conflicts with business requirements leading to policies specifying what uses are to be allowed or prohibited. The possibility of technological transformation arises in this particularising as techniques are spontaneously adapted to variations in specific situations and then potentially amplified. For example, the Internet has become a means of transacting payments. Then there is the development of fraud, illegal and immoral uses, viruses and ways of dealing with them. Technology as social object exists only insofar as it is taken up, or particularised, in the ordinary everyday local interactions between people. This technology of electronic communication is also idealised and its widespread availability becomes a cult value offering a future of access to communication for all and so greater democracy. Another cult value around this technology is that of control to be achieved by increasing electronic surveillance.

Thinking about technology in this way focuses attention not only on the physical objects of tools but also on the complex responsive processes of relating in which the generalised/idealised social object called technology is particularised. This brings to the fore questions of power, control and identity. Consider some examples.

Reading and writing is a technology that is essential to scientific progress and the development of tools and techniques. However, reading and writing are also social objects. Abram (1996) points out how reading and writing have led to the replacement of the sensuous, embodied style of consciousness found in oral cultures with a more detached, abstract mode of thinking. When concepts such as 'virtue' and 'justice' are recorded in writing, they acquire an autonomy and permanence independent of ordinary experience. Abstraction becomes a way of thinking and speaking as well as of writing. Donaldson (2005) argues that reading and writing not only eclipse nature but also tend to eclipse local, bodily human interaction in the present. Drawing on Elias (2000), she suggests that a new technology (including writing and printing) can be understood as an unplanned process that transforms the society which has produced it. Drawing on Ong (2002), Donaldson points to how literacy and printing have influenced human patterns of relating. The technology of writing fosters logic and abstraction. Writing also sets up the conditions for objectivity. It fosters precision and distanced forms of communication between people. Writing led to a shift from 'hearing dominance' to 'sight dominance' and print continued the trend. The abstract, objective thinking fostered by writing and reading has also been idealised to become cult values of rationality and objectivity.

Modern technologies of information and communication are other examples of social objects that profoundly affect the pattern of our interactions and even the conceptions we have of ourselves. The development of computers has been accompanied by the development of cognitivist psychology in which mind has come to be thought of as an information processing device rather like a computer. The mind has come to be thought of and modelled as a map, again reflecting technology. The development of the camera obscura some 250 years ago was accompanied by a view of mind as an internal world that made representations of objects in outside reality. As social object, technology shapes our thinking in many areas apparently unconnected with that technology itself. Technology provides metaphors for our thinking about everything around us. So we think of organisations as machines or as ships to be steered by their leaders. The social objects of technology, therefore, affect how we experience ourselves, our identities, and they of course impact on patterns of social relations. Through the cult values they give rise to, they become embedded in our ideologies. One only has to think of the technology of fast foods and that of contraception to see what enormous shifts in social relations accompany the evolution of technology.

The relationship between people and technology: social objects and meaning

Most approaches see the relationship between people and technology in an instrumental way. Technology is that which people design and manipulate in order to control their environment. The notable exception is actor-network theory (Callon and Latour, 1981; Latour and Woolgar, 1979), which treats both people and technology as agents in social evolution. As the interaction between people and that between people and technology are regarded as being almost identical, there is no need for a distinction. Some of those appealing to complexity theory also grant agency to things.

In the complex responsive processes perspective on technology outlined above, both of these positions are avoided. First of all, it is argued that humans do not have a relationship with things in anything like the same way as they have with each other, even though they may feel as if they do and metaphorically talk as if they do. People and things do not engage each other in the social act of gesture and response.

The gesture–response is an understanding of the detailed way in which humans interact with each other. It is not just one person doing something and the other reacting to it. In gesturing, one is taking a similar attitude to one's action as the other is taking to it. Furthermore, in human relating, one person is not simply taking the attitude of the specific other but always at the same time the attitude of the generalised/idealised other (which is the same as the social object). Both the gesturer and the responder are self-conscious and selves are social objects. Clearly, nothing like this goes on when using a tool. The key point is that we are not interacting with or relating to a tool in anything like the sense we are when using these words with respect to human relating or interaction. What we are doing is using, even imaginatively playing with, the tool in our interactions with each other.

However, tools and other physical objects in nature are not just objects we operate with and upon, because they have meaning for us, including highly emotional significance. The key point here has to do with *meaning*. We respond emotionally and intellectually to the *meaning* that physical objects such as cars, clothes, jewellery, our own bodies, mountains, lakes and so on have for us. However, Mead makes the profoundly important point that meaning cannot be located in a physical object. Physical objects have no meaning because meaning cannot be 'had'. For Mead, meaning is the social act and the social act is meaning. In this way of thinking, meaning is interacting and it does not exist anywhere, even as the vocal act of the word, let alone in a physical object. So it follows that a physical object can only be meaningful insofar as it is somehow taken up in our interactions with each other. Meaning arises as the particularising of the social object in specific situations. Take a car as an example. The car in itself, as a physical object, has no meaning and can therefore arouse no emotion in those using it. However, a car is not simply a physical object but also, at the same time, a social object, that is, a generalised tendency to act which is common to a number of people. This generalised tendency could take the form of respecting those who own big cars, for example. What is evoking the response of respect here is not the physical object of the big car but the social object of 'big car'. Such social objects can be idealised so that 'big car' becomes a cult value.

Thinking about technology in this way links to the fantasising, imaginative activities of human minds. For example, it is well known that infants become very attached to particular objects such as a teddy bear or blanket. The psychoanalyst Winnicott (1965, 1971) referred to these as transitional objects because they were neither simply reality nor simply fantasy but both at the same time. However, the physical object of the blanket or teddy bear has no meaning in itself. The meaning is the infant's gesture together with the imagined response from the object – the meaning is constituted by the fantasising or imagining activities of the body. In other words, meaning is not in the object but rather it is the activity of mind and there can be no mind without social interaction. So, what is important is not the physical object of blanket or teddy bear, but the corresponding social object. Meaning lies not in the physical object but in the fantasy purpose for which the object is used. A similar argument could be made for adults with respect to their emotional attachments to artefacts like cars, musical instruments, clothes, jewellery and inanimate objects in nature, like a river or a mountain, or resources like money or oil.

The point, then, is that technology is not simply a resource to be analysed and chosen in order to achieve some organisational objective or to produce success, as it is in strategic choice theory. Nor is technology simply some means of managing knowledge or enhancing learning processes in organisations, as it tends to be thought of in organisational learning and knowledge management theories. And technology is also not an agent in the strategy process as in some other views. These are all views which tend to understand technology as physical object. From a complex responsive processes perspective, technology is far more importantly also a social object. Technology has an impact on the local interactions of strategising persons and hence on the emergent population-wide patterns of strategy as identity narrative. This impact takes place in the particularising of the generalisations/idealisations of technology as social object in specific situations. And it is in these activities of particularising that technology continues to evolve. Thinking about technology in these more complex ways has the potential to widen and deepen conversational interaction in organisations.

The next section looks more widely at resources in general.

15.3 Resources and markets

A key concern in the dominant discourse on strategy has to do with competitive advantage and whether this is secured by market position or is due to an organisation's resource base. This section looks at how one would think about resources, markets and strategy from a complex responsive processes perspective. Consider first the resource base of an organisation.

Resources

Resources are the technologies, materials, competences and knowledge that people in organisations use to produce the products and services that justify the continuing existence of their organisation. Money and other financial assets easily converted into money are the resources that provide an organisation's ability to acquire most other forms of resource. In complex responsive processes terms, money is, first of all, a social object. This is so because there is a general tendency on the part of large numbers of people to act in broadly similar ways in relation to money and other related financial assets. Money features in many ways in most social acts. In modern societies most people understand how to gain access to money, how to deal with banks and other financial institutions. Those who have access to large sums of money are treated in very different ways from those who have little access. The social object of money conveys meaning that is far more than simply access to resources. The second, perhaps most important, aspect of money from a complex responsive processes point of view is its role in the figuration of power relations. Since we all need money to live and carry out any enterprise we are interested in, those who have control over money are needed by those who do not. Such need is the basis of power relations with the power balance tilted substantially towards those who have most access to financial resources.

Who controls money is a reflection of a community's history and its institutional arrangements. Hundreds of years ago the acquisition of wealth frequently occurred through the exercise of violence, including force-backed demands for tributes and tax payments, through the patronage and protection of those who had access to force, and through the laws of inheritance, which enabled the passing of wealth from one generation to the next. As Elias, has shown, the development of Western society involved the gradual monopolisation of force by the state, bring with it the monopolisation of authority to demand tax payments. Control over money came to depend more and more on institutional arrangements according to which some people were given the legitimate role of authorising the use of money by others. More recently, changing tax regimes have weakened, to some extent, the inheritance of wealth from one generation by the next. For people in modern societies, therefore, control over the allocation of money resources has come to be vested in organisations and more specifically in legitimately appointed roles in a hierarchy of managers who have authority to allocate money to others and who are held accountable for its use by those in the other organisations, such as banks and investment funds, who provide it.

The most important point about financial resources, from a complex responsive processes point of view, is the institutional arrangements, the procedures and routines, for legitimising the allocation of these resources and the monitoring of how they are used. These routines and procedures establish figurations of power relations and generate a considerable volume of organisational conversation. The ordinary, everyday activities of strategising involve conversations in which those who want to pursue a project must persuade those with authority to allocate resources to them. The more objective and credible the case that applicants make for resources, and, even more important, the more impressive their track record for the previous use of resources, the more likely they are to be allocated resources. Resource allocation activities may, therefore, have the appearance of technical rationality, indeed it is of great importance that it should have such an appearance, but the resource allocation activities themselves are highly political. They are important in sustaining and changing the pattern of power relations and therefore reflect ideologies that are often undiscussable. What the money can be used for and how it can be used reflect the norms and values that have evolved in the organisation and in the wider society. The allocation procedures themselves reflect ideologies to do with surveillance and control.

Resource allocation, then, is not primarily based on rational analysis reflecting choices made about the resource base required to secure competitive advantage. Of course, concern with an appropriate resource base is a factor in the allocation conversation but the rational language of competitive advantage is more often likely to be the rhetoric used to justify allocation decisions that are actually being made on the basis of experience-based judgements and the sustaining and changing of power relations.

While money is the key to acquiring many resources in an organisation, it is only indirectly useful in relation to other important resources, namely, competences and knowledge. Consider first how one might think about competences from a complex responsive processes perspective.

Management competences

Systemic theories of organising and managing encourage a belief in the possibility of identifying necessary skills in a clear way and defining steps to go through in order to acquire them (*see* Chapter 3). The essential skills I am pointing to are much fuzzier and the steps to achieving them even more nebulous. I have been arguing that the main implication of the complex responsive processes perspective is the way in which it refocuses attention not on what members of an organisation should be doing, but on what they are already, and always have been, doing. If there is a prescription, it is that of paying more attention to the quality of one's own experience of relating and managing in relationship with others. This is a reflexive activity requiring each of us to pay more attention to our own part in what is happening around us. This requires a reflective development of self-knowledge. It means taking one's own experience seriously. The reward, in my experience, is to find oneself interacting more effectively, not only for one's own good, but also potentially for the good of those with whom one is in relationship.

However, the skills and competences required for this reflection and reflexivity are difficult to develop and just as difficult to sustain. They are competences that do not usually feature in the skill sets prescribed for managers. Examples of the necessary skills are the capacity for self-reflection and owning one's part in what is happening, skill in facilitating fluid conversation, ability to articulate what is emerging in conversations and sensitivity to group dynamics. These skills become essential to notions of leadership and the role of top executives because their greater power renders their impact on others all the greater. Furthermore, these skills are not easily taught, perhaps they cannot be taught, in an abstract way. They are acquired in the experience of exercising them.

Knowledge and organisations

The theory of complex responsive processes focuses attention on the importance of local communicative interaction in the living present, particularly its thematic patterning, its gesture–response structure and its reflection in ideologies and power relations. This represents a way of understanding the emergence of knowledge in which people use the tools and technologies with which they transform their material environment. This view of knowing as process counters the widespread tendency to focus attention on knowledge as artefact or systems tool. Instead of focusing attention on the tool, the perspective I am suggesting focuses attention on how the tools are used.

The tools are used in wider processes of communicative interaction in which particular ways of talking are 'in' and others are 'out'. A concern with the knowledge-creation process would, therefore, involve an exploration of this dynamic as it manifests in local situations in the living present. What kind of exclusion is operating? What impact does this have in terms of obstructing or encouraging the emergence of new knowledge? Such questions soon lead to reflection on the manner in which ideologically based power relations are being sustained and challenged. What impact does this have on communicative interaction and the emergence of knowledge? A concern with the knowledge-creating process also involves an exploration of the identity-threatening and anxiety-provoking aspects of the process, so focusing attention on these and other aspects of the conversational life of an organisation and its transformative potential.

This refocusing of attention raises important questions with regard to mainstream thinking about knowledge creation in organisations. What can it mean to talk about managing knowledge creation in organisations when knowing is action in local situations in the living present? What can it mean to create a learning organisation? What can it mean to talk about measuring and managing the intellectual capital of an organisation?

As part of the knowledge management theory reviewed in Chapter 4, a number of writers call for steps to measure intellectual capital on the grounds that what is measured can be managed. The aim of measuring intellectual capital is that of managing its contribution to shareholder value. From the perspective of complex responsive processes, meaning, and therefore knowledge, arises in the local, detailed, ordinary communicative interaction of people in organisations in the living present. Knowledge creation is an evolutionary process of reproduction and potential transformation at the same time. In other words, knowledge is neither stored nor shared because it is not an 'it' at all but a process. Knowledge cannot be grasped, owned by anyone or traded in any market and its creation is a process of communicating and power relating that is both stimulating and anxiety provoking at the same time. If one takes a view of knowledge creation along these lines, then it is not only impossible to manage knowledge, even asking the question makes no sense. The whole notion that an organisation can own 'intellectual capital', that is, can own the attitudes, competence and intellectual agility of individuals is a dubious one.

A central feature of the systemic theory of knowledge creation in organisations (*see* Chapter 4) is the split it makes between tacit and explicit knowledge. Tacit knowledge is assumed to arise in individual minds and this is thought to create a problem for organisations. The assumption is that humans are reluctant to share their individual tacit knowledge with others. To the extent that they do, it is in informal exchanges, and systemic views tend to express a profound mistrust of these informal exchanges. This leads to the major emphasis on the conversion of individual tacit knowledge into explicit form and the storing of that explicit knowledge in systems. The complex responsive processes perspective, however, holds that tacit and explicit knowing are facets of the same communicative process and, therefore, that it makes no sense to talk about them separately or to believe that one is converted into the other. Furthermore, knowledge is not simply located in individual minds, nor is it stored in any straightforward sense. Instead, knowledge is continuously replicated and potentially transformed in the communicative interaction between people. Knowledge is not understood to be 'property' at all but active relational processes between human persons and a reflection of human identity, which cannot be captured, stored or owned.

If one starts from the basic assumption that the origins of knowledge are located in tacit form in the heads of individuals, it is a natural step to advocate that organisations pay particular attention to hiring and retaining a professional elite. From the perspective of complex responsive processes it is not particularly clear that simply hiring and retaining individual professionals has very much to do with knowledge creation. If knowledge arises in communicative interaction, then what matters is the process of relating that individual professionals engage in, not simply how clever or competent they are as individuals.

Systemic views of knowledge creation and management also present prescriptions concerned with spreading knowledge around an organisation. If knowledge is created in individual heads, and if human nature is such that individuals selfishly seek to keep it to themselves, then it becomes a prime management task to design structures, systems and behaviours to overcome these selfish tendencies and spread knowledge around the organisation. However, if knowledge is not a thing but a process of making meaning, where meaning is continuously reproduced and potentially transformed in the action of communicative relating between human bodies, then one cannot speak of sharing it, or of spreading it around an organisation. Any concern with 'improving' knowledge-creating capacity becomes a concern with the qualities and the dynamics of human relating in the living present. Attention is then focused on the power relations being sustained and shifted in communicative interaction and on the ideologies unconsciously making patterns of power relations feel natural.

Closely linked to prescriptions for hiring and retaining of professionals are those for training and developing people. Again, these prescriptions reflect the underlying assumption that knowledge is stored in individual heads. The aim of training and development follows, namely, to increase the competence, skill and knowledge of the individual, including the capacity to work as a member of a team. The emphasis is placed on managing not just the activities of training and development but the quality of the learning process itself. Again, management is understood in systemic terms and the prescriptions relate to the design and operation of a system to ensure the quality of the learning process. However, this usually ignores the impact of learning processes on human identity.

Markets

In the dominant discourse on organisations and strategy, reflecting its origins in economics, markets are usually talked about in terms of the 'forces' of demand and supply, as well as the consumer preferences 'driving' demand and the product features required to meet customer needs. The concern is with industry 'structures' and market 'positions'. The forces, drivers, structures and positions are usually quantified to provide information for the analytical techniques to be used in making strategic decisions. As with the dominant discourse on resources, the concern is with the macro level of the 'whole' and with choosing success factors for the 'whole'. This is certainly the terms in which most managers in organisations talk. While not denying that it is useful to talk in these terms, the theory of complex responsive processes seeks to draw attention to the manner in which these concepts abstract from the ordinary experience of managers as they engage daily with their 'markets'. The theory seeks to do this by pointing to how managers and everyone else in an organisation do not actually engage with the abstraction called the 'market' but with *people* in other organisations or households. Managers, marketers, salespeople and purchasers are always meeting people in other organisations and engaging them in conversation, in local interaction, just as they do in any other organisational activity.

Mead used the market as one of his examples of a social object. Markets can be understood as the generalisation, the social object of market, which is constantly being made particular in many, many local interactions. The dominant discourse is primarily concerned with the generalisation, with measuring *it* and articulating trends in *its* movement, while the complex responsive processes view is concerned with just how organisational members are making such generalisations particular in their ordinary everyday local interactions with people in other organisations. As they engage in the social activity of market large numbers of people are acting in largely similar ways in which the actions of purchasing and selling, of all the players in the market, are implicated in the actions of all of them.

The activity of the market is thus conversational in nature and such activity also immediately constitutes figurations of power. Such power figurations are sustained by ideologies. Indeed, the notion of 'the market system' is itself an ideology, a cult value.

15.4 Planning and control

In Chapter 1, I suggested that the phenomenon that strategic management is concerned with is that of the population of interacting organisations and the population of interacting groups and individuals within any organisation. The key question relates to the nature of the processes through which these populations evolve over long time periods.

I have argued that it is too simple to suggest that they evolve in directions chosen separately by groups of senior executives within each of them. The interaction between them simply makes this impossible. Nor can change in any one organisation be chosen by groups of senior executives. The complex interactions between groupings of people within an organisation make this impossible too. I am not arguing that senior executives cannot, do not or should not make such choices. They can, they do, and they should. What I am arguing is that these choices are gestures in an ongoing conversation of gestures out of which the evolution of organisations emerges.

What I have been pointing to is a theory of emergent strategy. Strategies emerge, intentions emerge, in the ongoing conversational life of an organisation and in the ongoing conversations between people in different organisations. Strategic management is the process of actively participating in the conversations around important emerging issues. Actual strategic direction is not set in advance but understood in hindsight as it is emerging or after it has emerged. This is because if small changes can escalate to have enormous consequences, then the distinction between what is strategic and what is, say, tactical becomes very problematic. The distinction can only be identified after the event. Complex responsive processes theory therefore leads to a different conceptualisation of strategy and strategic management.

The role of strategic planning

In the literature on organisations, and in the way managers in organisations talk, strategic planning means deciding on some kind of population-wide outcome for some long-term period ahead, say five years. Once formulated, the plan is then implemented. Clearly, this is thought first and action later. The assumption is that it is possible to design population-wide patterns well before they are realised and this in turn implies that it is possible to predict the outcomes of action taken now to a degree useful enough to enable a choice now between one future action and another. Local interaction is then understood as the process of implementing the plan or design. The plan or design is the 'thought' and the implementation is the 'action'. This is the essence of the planning and design schools of strategic management in the literature, it is how managers think and talk in most organisations and it is what governments have imported from business as the basis of centralised, managerialist forms of public sector governance.

As we have seen in Part 1, a number of writers and practitioners have been critical of this approach for some time and emphasised processes of learning in the formation of strategy. Senge, a key writer in this tradition, claims that organisations develop according to a limited number of general archetypes and that systems thinking allows managers to identify leverage points (thought) in organisations and then operate (action) on them to shift from a dysfunctional archetype. So here too we get the idea that population-wide patterns can be identified beforehand and changed directly through operating at leverage points. Local interaction then becomes working in teams to learn and so shift individual mental models and global archetypes. In both the planning and the learning approaches the focus of attention is on the population-wide and long term, the macro level, and it is thought possible to operate directly on the population-wide in some way so as to actualise prior intention regarding the population-wide patterns. Local interaction in both cases is simply implementation.

A complex responsive processes perspective emphasises the unpredictability of long-term population-wide patterns, holding that any design or plan for these patterns, that is, for the organisation as a 'whole', can only achieve what they claim to achieve with regard to short-term, repetitive and thus reasonably predictable activity. Even then, any plans, designs, visions, or descriptions of archetypes are simply articulations of population-wide generalisations and these articulations have to be made particular in each specific, contingent situation which leads to explorative conflict that must be negotiated. So even with regard to the short term and rather repetitive, it is problematic to think of planning activities as straightforward determinants of what happens. Central to the complex responsive processes perspective is the notion of emergence according to which population-wide patterns continually emerge in local interaction and this means that they are not the consequence of any overall plan or design but of the interplay between local plans and designs. There may well be articulations of desires for realised population-wide patterns in the form of global plans and designs but they cannot function as the cause of the population-wide pattern because such desires and articulations are simply gestures and what actually happens will also depend upon the processes of particularisation, that is, on the interplay of many, many intentions.

So in these circumstances any claims that strategic planning and organisational leverage activities actually cause what happens are highly problematic. Instead of being causes of what happens, plans and designs may well amount to fantasies whose main function is to serve as social defences against anxiety. The problem with such defences is that they might blinker people and, if taken seriously, could easily get in the way of more improvisational, spontaneous behaviour. Such activities might then largely be a distracting waste of time which could be discontinued with the benefits far outweighing any drawbacks. However, if the articulation of population-wide patterns and desires for them are understood as gestures in ongoing processes of local interaction, they may serve provocative, or even inspirational, purposes in generating further conversation. Instead of being planned, however, the population-wide patterns will emerge in those further conversations in the many, many local interactions that they take place in and this is especially true for population-wide patterns displaying any form of novelty. Those engaged in such local interactions do have intentions, perhaps even plans for their own local interaction and desires for the population-wide pattern, but the actual population-wide patterns emerge in the interplay between all of their intentions/plans and desires. Since the interplay cannot be said to be planned, neither can the population-wide pattern. Instead the local interaction takes on the form of improvisational acting with a high degree of spontaneity or, alternatively, of stuck repetition. Such improvisational/spontaneous acting cannot be said to be planning, although it does not mean that there is no intention on the part of those engaging in such activity.

The perspective I am suggesting, therefore, requires us to think much more carefully about what we think we are doing when we articulate long-term plans for whole populations and believe that we can thereby change those whole population. This is a widespread belief reflected in culture change programmes, quality assurance, total quality management, business process re-engineering and many other such global change programmes. A complex responsive processes view turns the dominant discourse on its head. Instead of change occurring as the result of the plan, change programme, or vision of leaders or dominant coalitions, change emerges in many local interactions in which leaders and the most powerful are very influential participants, but participants nonetheless. Instead of being the straightforward cause of change, the activities of planning, forming visions and so on serve many other purposes. They may perform the function of social defences against anxiety. They may be rhetorical tools or ploys in the political processes in which strategies emerge. They may be public relations tools directed at audiences both internal and external to the organisations. They may even be propaganda and spin. They may serve the purpose of avoiding being blamed if things go wrong – people can always point to the rational approaches they used to choose their actions, claiming that it is not their fault if things went wrong.

Control

In the systemic theories of organisation reviewed in Part 1, the role of the manager is always thought to be that of formulating the purpose (visions, aims, goals, objectives, performance targets) of the organisation and controlling its movement into the future so as to achieve its purpose. It is recognised that this is difficult and cannot be perfectly achieved but it is thought that managers nevertheless need to be in control as much as possible, designing and using systems for this purpose. To be 'in control' means to more or less control the movement into the future of the whole organisational system through some kind of monitoring of its progress. Control means ensuring that movement into the future realises or unfolds a future state already enfolded in the present or past as the intention or desire of top managers, or of the democratic intention or desire of organisational members. Control requires organisational members to conform and sustain consensus. The implicit view is that without such control there would be anarchy. Control is ensured through conscious, formal, legitimate decisions based on the assumed possibility of reasonably useful predictions of the future. Some opposites of being 'in control' are taking piecemeal decisions, reacting, not knowing and conflicting. In systemic theories of organisation, effective managers remove the characteristics of 'not in control' so as to avoid 'drifting' or anarchy.

For a long time now, management research has frequently pointed to the messiness of actual decision-making processes in organisations. Chapter 7 referred to Lindblom (1959) who talked about organisational decision making as 'muddling through', whereas March and Olsen (1972) referred to it as 'garbage can' decision making and Mintzberg and Waters (1985) pointed to *both* deliberate *and* emergent strategies in the sense that strategy is sometimes the former and sometimes the latter. It is rare for management theorists, or practitioners for that matter, to think of organisational control in paradoxical terms.

Streatfield (2001) explores his own experience of control as a manager at various hierarchical levels in organisations and comes to think about control in paradoxical terms:

> My experience is that of communicatively interacting with others at all times in the known and the unknown at the same time. I would certainly not label what my colleagues and I were doing as 'muddling' or as an inferior kind of 'garbage can' decision making. I have been arguing for a way of thinking about the dynamics of human relating and joint action, that is, the dynamics of organizations, which is essentially paradoxical. This is the paradoxical dynamic of being 'in control' and 'not in control' at the same time. The apparently messy processes of communicative interaction I have been describing are not some second best but, rather, the only way we know of living with paradox. The very dynamics of organizational life call for the kind of complex responsive processes of relating that I have been describing. It is in these processes that the dynamic is created. The processes only appear to be messy and less than competent from the perspective of mainstream thinking about management. From the complex responsive process way of thinking, management skills and competencies lie in how effectively managers participate in those processes. They provide a way of thinking about what competent managers actually do to live effectively in the paradox of organizing. And what they actually do is continue to interact communicatively, especially in the medium of conversation, in spite of not knowing and not being simply 'in control'. (p. 128)

Streatfield argues that instead of collapsing to either the 'in control' or the 'not in control' pole, we can make more sense of the activities of the manager if we understand that organisational life requires living with paradox. Managers are 'in control' and 'not in control' at the same time and they display the courage to continue participating in the making of meaning in paradox. The essential function of managers cannot be to control the paradoxical movement of continuity and transformation, of the known-unknown, because it is impossible for any participant to be in control of it. But this does not simply mean that managers are not in control. Instead, managers are simultaneously 'in control' and 'not in control' in the sense that they intend their next gestures, which are simultaneously evoked by previous responses. There is coherence, which emerges as continuity and potential transformation of identity in the perpetual construction of the future. The distinguishing feature of management is not control but courage to carry on creatively despite not knowing and not being in control, with all the anxiety that this brings.

The central notion of systemic thinking, that of the manager being 'in control', is therefore much more problematic than is usually assumed because managers are both 'in control' and 'not in control' at the same time. The key question then becomes how managers operate effectively and maintain reasonably orderly states of affairs if they are not simply 'in control'. From the perspective of complex responsive processes, it is transiently stable patterns of meaning arising in local interaction that maintain a sense of order and therefore a sense of control as managers go about their daily activities. Intentional goal-oriented acts emerge in the local conversations of managers and those conversations function as patterning, meaning-making processes. These communicative interactions constitute the way in which managers, individually and collectively, maintain their sense of self and their defences against anxiety. An organisation is local processes of interaction in which intention and meaning emerge and anxiety is lived with. These interconnected processes across an organisation generate collective emergent outcomes that cannot be traced back to specific actions. Processes of decision making, change and performance achievement emerge in the local negotiation of patterns of meaning in which each individual struggles, in participation with others, to maintain a sense of self in an uncertain world. This is the process of an organisation's evolution, the activities of strategising.

> Are managers in control of organizations in which they work? My experience now suggests to me that this is the wrong question. The key management ability is not that of being 'in control' but the ability to participate creatively in the formation of transient meaning, which enables all of an organization's members to continue living with the anxiety generated by change. It is this meaning that creates a felt sense of order, coherence, pattern or control. The ability to participate creatively in the construction of meaning develops as managers struggle to cope with the paradox of control, using legitimate control mechanisms as tools in a wider dynamic of self-organizing communicative interaction. I believe that management practitioners continually hone and develop the capacity to live with paradox as they go about their practice, even if they are not all that aware of doing it.   (Streatfield, 2001, p. 136)

Streatfield is making it clear that when one understands that organisations are emergent processes of communicative interaction and power relating, one does not conclude that things just happen. Instead, he points to how what happens is due to the detail of what managers as interacting individuals are doing, particularly in their ordinary, everyday conversations with each other. Emphasising the emergent nature of social interaction in no way lessens the accountability and responsibility of the interacting individuals. On the contrary, one can no longer blame a system for what is happening, because what happens is due to the detail of how each of us is interacting with others. Each of us has to take ethical responsibility for what we do despite not knowing or being in control of the outcomes of our actions.

15.5 Reasoning, measuring, forecasting and modelling

In reviewing how the processes of organising and strategising are thought about in the dominant discourse, Chapter 7 pointed to the way in which the process of technical rationality was increasingly problematised. In the early days of theorising about organisations and strategy, the emphasis was very much on analytical reasoning applied to quantitative data in order to deduce optimal actions. Strategising was thought about primarily in terms of identifying simple cause and effect links so as to choose actions with a high probability of producing optimal performance. The earliest critiques of technical rationality pointed to how the ideal of analytical, reductionist, linear, instrumental reasoning was impossible to apply in practice because of the costs involved and because of the limited capacity of the human brain. It was argued that the strategy process in practice was a form of bounded rationality. Even this notion of bounded rationality was found to be an idealisation of reason because in practice any reasoning process is highly conditioned by the interpretive frameworks in terms of which people have no option but to think about the situations in which they have to choose actions. As a result of their interpretive frameworks, people would inevitably ignore some features of the situation and reach biased views about the situation, often leading them to inertia and drift. Then, psychodynamic perspectives point to the role of unconscious, irrational processes in determining what people do and how this can obstruct rationality. The limitations of objective reasoning processes were even further stressed by those who argued that people together enact, that is, actively select and create their world of experience. Social constructionists argued that people create the world of their experience in language. Postmodernism, which has not been reviewed in this book, takes this problematising of objective reasoning a step further in arguing that there are as many views of the world as there are people and therefore there is no grand narrative, no theory that can claim to be fundamental in any sense. Taken to its extreme this leads to a view in which there is no reality out there, only our stories, and one story is as good as another.

The theory of complex responsive processes continues with this critique of the strategy process as one of rationality but stops short of postmodernism in arguing for a way of understanding that does, in a sense, offer a grand narrative and makes fundamental claims about human relating. It argues that all human relating is fundamentally conversational and that conversation is, and always was, the conversation of gestures. It argues that all human relating is, and always was, power relating and it argues that the basis of patterns of power relations is ideological. It argues that all human experience has a narrative structure and that the criteria for the choices people make within the ongoing narrative of experience are fundamentally based on the evaluative criteria of ideology. In making these claims, the theory of complex responsive process remains firmly within modernism, just as what I have been calling the dominant discourse does. The theory of complex responsive processes problematises human reason much as the debate in the dominant discourse does, even taking this problematisation a step further in emphasising the fundamentally uncertain and perpetually constructed nature of human futures and in emphasising the fundamental interdependence of human agents.

However, no matter how problematic, the human capacity for reasoning remains of great importance and has enormous consequences. The previous chapters in this part have not mentioned reasoning processes much simply because these chapters have been concerned with understanding the basic nature of human agency and human action of which reasoning is only one aspect. In their communicative inter-action, their power relating and their ideologically based choosing, people employ their capacity to reason and in fact reflect in a reasoned manner on their very processes of reasoning. After all, despite not mentioning reason, all of the chapters in this part have been exercises in reasoning about human interaction in a structured and rational manner. Complex responsive processes of reasoning, therefore, remain of fundamental importance no matter how problematic they might be. What the theory of complex responsive processes seeks to provide is a rigorously reasoned, unashamedly theoretical but hopefully useful way of thinking about human processes of thinking which must include human processes of reasoning. Instead of simply taking rationality for granted the invitation is to reflect on the manner in which we are reasoning in any specific situation.

Just as the theory of complex responsive processes is not some kind of justification or prescription for abandoning reason (the head) in favour of muddling through or in favour of emotion (the body), so it is also not a justification or prescription for abandoning any attempt to measure important aspects or organisational life or to abandon any attempt to forecast anything. Instead it offers a way of thinking about the activities of measuring and forecasting by providing a perspective from which one can ask whether particular measurements and particular attempts to forecast make any sense in a particular situation. For example, take the widely accepted approach to making investment decisions having long-term consequences. When I talk to managers about unpredictable long-term futures, someone will often say that since managers must make investment decisions with very long-term consequences they must be able to predict. And clearly managers do this. But are the predictions actually the basis of their investment decisions?

Prediction and investment decisions

The normal technique for making long-term investment decisions is to undertake a discounted cash flow analysis. This involves modelling the future by measuring the costs and the outcomes of the investment in financial terms and forecasting these variables over a long time period, typically 25 years. It is also usual to specify a number of different scenarios and to calculate the return on the investment for each scenario. This is supposed to enable managers to compare the outcomes of different investment options in different possible situations so enabling them to choose the one most likely to produce a desired outcome. Consider what happened at a meeting of top executives I was consulting to. They arrived at a meeting at which they were going to put forward a recommendation on a particular large investment proposal which would have consequences for many years to come. As they entered the room, the financial analysts handed them a piece of paper which listed twelve scenarios, each based on different assumptions about costs, prices and volumes of product. The rates of return varied across the scenarios from a large negative to a large positive return. The executives started to question the financial analysts, asking why one rate of return was higher or lower than another. The analysts rapidly encountered difficulties in giving satisfactory replies because there were so many different assumptions in the various scenarios that they could not remember them all. Tempers were becoming frayed and then the chief executive laughingly intervened and said, 'Don't get upset – the one thing we all know for sure is that none of these scenarios will ever happen!'

What is happening here? A group of very competent and intelligent executives are going through a procedure in what looks like a highly rational manner, based on what looks like objective data, but in fact they all know that the future is unknowable. They are apparently going to make a decision on the basis of information that they all agree is completely unreliable. They all agree that they cannot forecast in this detail over this time period. Further discussion revealed that there had been a number of informal conversations between the directors in small groups of two or three. They had all already agreed that they would support the investment proposal even though they had not seen any of the forecasts. On what did they base their agreement? They had agreed that if they did not make the investment they would not be 'in the game' in that particular market. They had argued that if they did not make the investment then a rival would and this could make the rival more powerful in the market to the point where that rival might even acquire them. They formed the judgement that although they could not know what would happen, it would nevertheless be better to make the investment than not to. This seems to me to be an entirely reasonable argument and they thought so too. However, they were not proposing to discuss the real reasons for the investment in public because they did not sound rational and objective enough. They needed the cash flow forecasts in order to present a case to the non-executive directors on their board. In other words, the apparently rational analysis was to be used as a rhetorical ploy to persuade others to accept the judgement of the executive directors and, of course, the non-executives knew this but also needed to have a rational case so that they could not be blamed if things went wrong.

The theory of complex responsive processes, therefore, offers managers a way of thinking about what they are doing. It is not possible to make long-term investment decisions on the basis of forecasts because the long-term future is unknowable. It is because of the inherent uncertainty of organisational life that commercial enterprises have the opportunity to earn a profit. In capitalist, market economies, profit is the reward for bearing uncertainty. Uncertainty is unique and unknowable compared with risk, which can be assessed in terms of probability and so insured against. An organisation bearing risk is rewarded with an insurance premium. An organisation bearing uncertainty is rewarded with profit. To earn a profit, managers must make judgements and undertake investments whose outcome they cannot know in advance. In such situations the use of discounted cash flow analyses can only ever be a rhetorical ploy. Knowing this, managers can at least thoroughly explore the real reasons they have for making an investment even if they find they have to present the public case in some other way.

The complex responsive processes perspective, therefore, is a useful one in understanding just when one can forecast, over what time period, and just what measurements make sense for just what purpose in particular situations.

I would like to make one other point about prediction. While a forecast is a quantitative statement, a prediction could take a qualitative form. Chapter 11 presented Mead's explanation of human consciousness in which a person is conscious because he or she has the capacity to take the attitude of the other, including the attitude of the generalised other. In other words, through a life history in a community with a history, each person can predict to some extent how others might respond to his or her next action. As we interact in ordinary ways with each other every day, we are always expecting some response, which is a form of predicting. Our action is always future oriented. At the same time, however, we do not know what the responses will be – we know that our predictions in ordinary social life are going to be far from perfect. For this reason, effective people remain alert to the differences between their predictions and the responses they evoke so that they are able to continually adjust their actions. In other words, alert people are those who are aware of the predictably unpredictable nature of the responses they are likely to evoke. So just knowing that the future is not knowable is not a recipe for despair but a realisation that is essential to effective conduct.

In the investment decision example given above I referred to the decision technique as a model and the next section looks in more detail at the use of models from the complex responsive processes perspective.

Modelling

Second-order and critical systems thinkers (*see* Chapter 6) adopt what is essentially a qualitative modelling approach to their work. First, their immediate concern is with some *problem issue or situation* about which some *group of people* feel that they need to *make decisions* and take actions in order to bring about some improvement. The practitioner aims to *intervene* in this situation in order to identify how this issue or situation *should* be formulated, how the decision *should* be taken and how it *should* be implemented. The purpose is to specify some kind of procedure that the group *should* follow in order to improve the situation, recognising that it will probably be impossible to optimise the decision outcome. Improvement is understood as securing some desired or intended outcomes. The unquestioned assumption is that problem formulation/analysis, decision making and implementation are separate activities. They may overlap, they may circle around many iterations, but conceptually they are separate. The assumption is that thought is apart from action.

The practitioner operating from the complex responsive processes perspective does so on the basis that thinking and talking are action. What is of interest is the conversational process in which a group of people are coming to feel that there is some kind of issue or situation of concern even though as yet they do not know what it is. The perspective is, then, not what people should be doing but what they actually are doing as the practitioner joins them. Here the practitioner joins a group of people as a participant in their conversations, seeking to understand something of the organising themes that are emerging in these conversations.

Second, the systems practitioner prepares for an intervention by gathering data and interviewing those involved or affected by the situation in order to formulate some kind of view of what is going on. The systems practitioner has various techniques for doing this, such as preparing a 'rich picture' of the situation or summaries of evaluations of the situation made by various participants (*see* Chapter 6). This information is prepared as some kind of presentation or feedback to those who will participate in the intervention and it is the basis on which the practitioner advises on who the appropriate group of participants should be.

From a complex responsive processes perspective, the practitioner does not join a group with the intention of structuring or shaping the situation or the conversations in which an issue is emerging. The practitioner has no intention of creating the right conditions for better conversations or identifying the right people to be involved in them. There is no intention to design anything, improve it, or make it right or more creative. Instead, the intention is the same as that of other participants, namely, to understand what they are all doing together, what they are talking about and why. So, for example, Shaw (*see* Chapter 11) explains how she asks people how they came to be involved in the current conversation because their stories begin to indicate what they are actually doing in the living present. In participating in this storytelling she draws attention in certain directions rather than others by emphasising certain moments rather than others and using certain forms of expression rather than others. In so doing she is drawing attention to how these stories create meaning, changing in emphasis as people go on thinking and speaking about them. People identify with each other's stories and so sustain their relationships. This process does not simply reaffirm existing ideas but enlivens the senses of participants, stirring them from the habit of attending to experiences in familiar ways to awaken a fresh appreciation of their experience.

For Shaw (2002), there is no intention to prepare for the work to be done at some later point because in their already conversing, the work is under way in what she calls gatherings. Instead of selecting a key group of influencers, formal or informal, to initiate change, she pays attention to the way in which influence is spontaneously arising in webs of relationships in particular contexts, reflected in people gathering together in some way. Gatherings are provoked by the urgent need to make sense of some dimly perceived issues, making it inevitable that their conversation will be characterised by a vague sense of why they are there. Instead of a clear formulation of an enquiry and special invitations to a representative sample of stakeholders, Shaw seeks ways to connect people so that gatherings will arise spontaneously because of some interest in common. Such gatherings are not representative, fair or consultative but, rather, they are active. The point is to work with the potential for change, finding ways of convening forums that tap people's interests, enthusiasms or frustrations and which demand an intensive interaction to create meaningful forms of activity that 'move things on'. These discussions have an 'everyday quality' – they are branching, meandering, associative and engaging. They are similar to the modes people value and recognise in many informal kinds of conversation. They include formulating and making reference to proposals, analysis and frameworks. They involve speculation, anecdotes and personal revelation. They are characterised by feeling and bodily sensations that all are resonating and responded to in different ways. It is a very active, searching, exploratory form of communication in which the way the future is under perpetual construction is more than usually evident.

Third, the systems practitioner designs some kind of intervention event such as a meeting, workshop or learning event in which participants explore the nature of the issue/situation and possible responses to it. The systems practitioner has a collection of methodologies, methods, tools and techniques to draw upon in designing the intervention events. For example, there are various heuristics, procedures and *models* developed by systems thinkers for application to ambiguous problem situations characterised by power differences and ideological features. The methods and techniques aim to surface multiple evaluations of the situation in what is a pluralistic approach. All of these methodologies, techniques and so on are systemic. This means that they focus attention on some *whole* or system and the interconnections that produce the system. The implicit assumption is that it is only by affecting the whole that improvement can be assured. This is because complex interconnections could overcome attempts at partial improvement. The systems practitioner is seeking to assist people to draw boundaries around the problem situation, identifying the whole system of which it is an aspect. They recognise the difficulties of doing this in complex situations and so advocate the drawing of multiple boundaries and the exploration of ethical and power implications of doing so. Each model or system identified is recognised as only a partial view of the whole, one that depends upon the particular paradigm of those drawing the boundary.

Systems practitioners think of themselves as facilitators who structure, shape and guide workshops and other intervention events using the methodologies of systems thinkers. They keep it rational, to the point and following the agenda. For example, they present lists of questions to workshop participants asking them to evaluate their current situation and how they plan to do things differently. They support workshop participants in looking at where they want to go. Such information may then be used to design subsequent learning events. They give exercises to participants in learning events, such as imagining that they have just climbed out of a time capsule five years into the future.

In relation to the group faced with the problem situation, the stance of the systems practitioner is one of involvement in that the work is done with the people involved. The systems practitioner joins the group but always does so in a particular manner, namely, as the bringer of systematic sets of conceptual paradigms, a system of methodologies, a plurality of methods, techniques, heuristics, lists of questions and models. The systems thinker analyses the situation in order to select appropriate paradigms and methodologies for the situation in accordance with some kind of meta-paradigm or meta-methodology. In other words, the systems thinker sets some kind of agenda.

In the stages leading up to these events, and in the events themselves, then, systems practitioners see themselves as participating with those whom they are advising in the formulation and exploration of the problem situation. However, in an important sense they are all taking the stance of the objective observer of the situation simply because they analyse the situation, design the intervention events and select the appropriate models. The participants also then take this objective position in applying the *models* to their situation.

From the complex responsive processes perspective, Shaw argues that meetings which are carefully orchestrated and over-specified in advance increase the likelihood of people reconstructing the familiar. Outcomes, procedures for working together, agendas, roles to be taken up by those present, forms of contribution and prepared presentations, all conspire to reduce the experience of uncertainty as the experience of acting into the known is engineered. She argues that under-specification increases the experience of diversity and multiplicity, disturbing routine responses and increasing the potential for novelty. For Shaw, facilitating means participating as fully and responsively as possible, voicing one's opinions, associations and ideas along with everyone else. In doing this she is sensing the move towards and away from agreement, of shifts in power difference, the development and collapse of tensions, the variations in engagement, the different qualities of silence, the rhetorical ploys, the repetition of familiar turns of phrase or image, the glimpsing and losing of possibility, the ebb and flow of feeling tone, the dance of mutual constraint. She tries to participate in the conversation in a way that helps to hold open the interplay of sense making rather longer than would occur in her absence, to hold open the experience of not knowing. In doing this she is resisting the enormous pressure for closure.

Notice the difference between the systems and complex responsive processes accounts of practice. The systems practitioner arrives at the situation with a set of methodologies, models, techniques and so on, to shape the discussion. There is a design and something of an agenda. From the complex responsive processes perspective the practitioner's methodology is the ordinary everyday conversational process that is already under way – there are no formal models. The practitioner does not set any agenda at all but seeks to understand the shifting thematic patterning of the self-organising process as the basis on which to contribute to it, just as all the other participants are doing. There is little emphasis on facilitating in the sense of structuring, summarising, writing bullet points on flipcharts, calling for feedback or model building. Instead, by responding to what others are saying, by linking themes, the practitioner is helping to articulate emerging themes and in so doing is influencing the further patterning of the conversation. It is these shifts in communicative patterning, the widening and deepening of communication, which constitute organisational change.

This means that, unlike the systems practitioner, the practitioner from a complex responsive processes perspective is not concerned with any whole or system at all but with the detail of the local interactions between people, the interplay of their intentions, in the living present.

The fourth step in systemic practice is that of working in the intervention to make decisions and take actions to improve the situation. For the complex responsive processes practitioner, the action and the work have been going on all the time and in this work decisions and actions are continually emerging or being blocked.

Systems practitioners are well aware of the highly complex, ill-structured nature of the situations that groups in organisations face. Their response is pluralism, which means employing combinations of given paradigms, methodologies, methods and models. Instead of proposing a single, or even a few consistent hypotheses, they encourage those they work with to explore many hypotheses, selecting particular models according to what the culture allows. From the complex responsive processes perspective, one is sceptical of this notion of pluralism, that is, identifying and selecting different paradigms for evaluation. Instead the practice is concerned with what is emerging, and since what is emerging is individual and collective identities, one is sceptical about the possibility of simply switching paradigms as systemic practice suggests. In the kind of practice I am describing the focus of attention is on emerging themes and there is no notion of anyone drawing boundaries around a system.

The use of qualitative models related to whole organisations focuses attention at the macro level, the population-wide patterns, in the belief that this can be directly affected. The complex responsive processes approach focuses attention on the micro on the basis that population-wide patterns cannot be directly operated on because they emerge in local interaction. The models can help to articulate the population-wide patterns and so provoke conversation but cannot provide a direct intervention tool.

Quantitative modelling

In a very general sense, the previous chapters of this part have outlined a model. This is a model of local interaction between members of a group of people in which they form desires and intentions concerning their own local interactions and concerning the generalisations and idealisations of the population-wide patterns that emerge in their local interactions. This is their experience and they often talk and feel about this experience in terms of a unity expressed as an imaginatively constructed 'whole' directed to the future, although they may usually not be all that aware of the imaginatively constructed nature of this unity of experience. Any theory can be thought of as a model in this kind of way. However, the term 'model' is also used in a much more restricted sense as an analytical, often mathematical construct of a system, sometimes incorporating empirical measurements of some kind. Such models are sometimes used by managers and policy makers as aids to decision making. How would one understand such models and their use from a complex responsive processes perspective?

The formal mathematical modeller usually makes a distinction between a group of decision makers, the problem situation that they are facing, and the alternative strategies they might deploy to deal with the problem situation, just as the qualitative modellers described in the last section do. The decision makers tend to be thought of as acting within or upon the situation and in order to assist them to make an appropriate decision, the modeller constructs a model of the situation to enable them to explore the possible consequences of alterative decisions they could take in order to better achieve their objectives.

The model, therefore, focuses on the situation and the alternative ways of dealing with it, while the group of decision makers slips unnoticed into the background. It is implicitly assumed that the individual decision makers act according to rationalist causality (*see* Chapter 2), rather than the assumption made in the theory of complex responsive process of transformative causality in human action. Leaving the decision makers themselves out of the model is perfectly understandable because a formal mathematical model could not capture the micro-detail of the conversational, ideological and power-relating interactions between them that the theory of complex responsive processes focuses on. The first point to notice, then, is how formal mathematical modelling necessarily abstracts from direct human experience and constructs a set of formal, abstract relationships relating to the whole situation. The situation is normally understood as a system at the macro level and traditional systems models average away any microdiversity and so implicitly assume formative causality (*see* Chapter 2) in which the system model unfolds the hypothesis of the modeller. Second-order systems thinkers referred to in the last section do recognise that the decision makers are not separate from the situation and so the model of the situation is widened to incorporate the decision makers themselves. However, they are then observing themselves observing the situation and we get into infinite regress. There are two problems with a great many formal mathematical models. First, by modelling at a very macro level, they average away diversity and, second, they separate decision makers and situation.

From a complex responsive processes perspective, the situation is not a given that can be modelled apart from the decision makers, although temporarily thinking this might be instructive. Instead, the situation is the history of the decision makers and their processes. This history has produced particular configurations of resources (e.g. a particular configuration of transport facilities) and particular patterns of habits that we call culture or social structure. In the living present, as a group of decision makers are acting, their actions are simultaneously enabled and constrained by these resource configurations and cultural patterns. And in their acting they are continually re-enacting, but in subtly different ways, the configurations and patterns and so potentially transforming them. In this way there is no split causality because both the situation and the decision makers are thought of according to transformative causality. The situation is part of the decision makers and vice versa. The decision makers are co-creating or enacting the situation. They may or they may not construct and use models but if they do, the models are tools and the important point is just how those tools are employed in the complex responsive processes of making decisions.

A few system models (*see* the section on Allen's work in Chapter 9) do partially take account of human diversity and so produce models based on a form of transformative causality (*see* Chapter 10). However, there is still the split causality of rationalist decision makers in the background and the transformative causality of the model itself. Furthermore, since it reflects transformative causality, this kind of model now evolves unpredictably – it takes on a life of its own. Since the model cannot capture all of the details of the situation, it and the situation it is modelling could evolve in completely different ways. The model's microdiversity could amplify in one way, while the situation's microdiversity could amplify in different ways. It follows that the decision makers could not use their models in the rational-calculating manner that might have been hoped for in the traditional models.

However, they could learn a lot about the dynamics of the situation, about the uncertainty and unpredictability of it, even though they could not directly calculate decisions from it. This immediately undermines the rational causality being assumed about the decision makers. I would then argue that the decision makers making the decisions also need to be understood in terms of transformative causality because they are an integral part of the situation. This is what the theory of complex responsive processes seeks to do. From this perspective, models are understood as tools, amongst other tools, used in the communicative processes of decision making.

How might people be using these tools? Decision makers are confronted by many possible futures and so seek to develop some idea of the possible consequences of the actions they choose. A macro-model of the situation, particularly one incorporating diversity, provides a tool for exploring possible consequences in terms of generalisations. In complex responsive processes terms one can think of these as models of social objects, including idealisations thereof. Any problem situation needs to be understood in terms of its wider social contexts – in terms of the generalisations of social objects and cult values, including technology and resources. A model of relationships between such generalisations could give useful insights even though it can never capture how the actual particularisations of these generalisations will be made. For example, Chapter 9 described Allen's model of police targeting suspects and the unintended consequences this can have. This insight could lead to very different conversations about targets.

15.6 Performance and improvement

A central concern of the dominant discourse on strategy, for practitioners and researchers alike, is with securing at least acceptable organisational performance and with continually improving that performance. The dominant discourse overwhelmingly focuses attention at the macro level on the 'whole' organisation. The concern is with identifying the causes of successful performance and the causes of improvement in order to identify strategies and interventions that will operate on the 'whole' so as to secure success and bring about improvement. The problem is that despite many decades of practice and research, which have produced huge libraries of prescriptions and descriptive writings, the identification of how to consistently secure successful performance eludes us. And yet organisations continue to function – some disappear, others appear – and taken together it all more or less works. Over the past two decades, public sector organisations have been subjected to enormous pressure to improve performance. In terms of performance targets there has been some patchy improvement in some sectors but how to secure widespread public sector improvement continues to elude us. And yet it all more or less works.

The theory of complex responsive processes seeks to provide a way of understanding why this is happening and in the course of doing so problematises the way of thinking underlying the dominant discourse. It does so by arguing that generalised/idealised population-wide patterns, imaginatively constructed as 'wholes', emerge in myriad local interactions in which they are made particular and functional. This suggests that the reason why the means of operating directly on the 'whole' to secure performance and make improvements has eluded us is that it is impossible in the first place. Performance, and improvement in it, in general as a 'whole' can only emerge in myriad local interactions.

This in no way amounts to a dismissal of the concern with performance and improvement or to a dismissal of any generalised/idealised statements or policies regarding performance and improvement. Instead it directs attention to the particularising, locally interactive processes in which such generalisations and idealisations are taken up. Performance and improvement are not simply given but, like strategy, are under perpetual construction in the meaning-making activities of local interaction.

15.7 Summary

This chapter has explored how one might think, from a complex responsive processes perspective, about central concerns of organisational strategists to do with technologies, resources, markets and performance. It has looked at the contributions that processes of reasoning and modelling can make to thinking about these matters and how these contributions might be reinterpreted from a complex responsive processes point of view. Finally, it has briefly mentioned certain concerns to do with performance and improvement. The central argument regarding all of these matters is as follows. The dominant discourse approaches all of these matters from a macro perspective and seeks to identify means of operating directly at the macro level on the 'whole' organisation. The complex responsive processes perspective is one in which such a 'whole' is an imaginative construct, a felt sense of unity of experience. And what the imaginative construct amounts to is generalisations and idealisations of population-wide patterns of joint activity. These patterns emerge in local interactions in which the generalisations and idealisations are taken up and made particular and functional. It follows that operating directly on the 'whole' amounts simply to articulating generalisations and idealisations, which may or may not be useful, but what happens will happen through the many local responses to them.

Further reading

Further reading is provided by Streatfield (2001), Stacey (2001, 2005) and Stacey and Griffin (2005).

Questions to aid further reflection

1. If strategy emerges in the interplay of local intentions, how would you think about organisational performance and improvement?
2. What are the strategic implications of thinking about technology as social object?
3. What are the implications of thinking about markets not in terms of abstract forces but as patterns of relationships between people?
4. Is it possible to manage knowledge and measure intellectual capital?
5. What role does modelling play in strategising?
6. If the future is unpredictable how would you thinking about activities of planning in organisations?

Chapter 16

Complex responsive processes
Implications for thinking about organisational dynamics and strategy

This chapter invites you to draw on your own experience to reflect on and consider the implications of:

- The move from a systemic to a responsive processes way of thinking about human interaction.

- The move from understanding individual persons as autonomous to thinking about them as interdependent.

- The move to understanding people as participants in processes of interaction in which it is not possible to take an external position.

- The move from a dual theory of causality to a paradoxical theory of causality.

The purpose of this final chapter is to briefly compare the theory described in Part 3 of this book with the theories reviewed in Part 1 and in so doing point to some implications for thinking about organisational dynamics and strategy.

16.1 Introduction

In Chapter 1, I suggested that this book would be dealing with the following questions. How do populations of interdependent people who constitute organisations, and populations of such organisations, change and evolve over time? How have these populations come to be what they are and how will they become whatever they become? How does one explain the dynamics of evolving organisations? What do strategy, strategic direction and strategic thinking mean? How does a strategy come into being and how is it manifested? I also suggested that the way one answers these questions depends upon the frame of reference from which one approaches them. In Part 1 I reviewed a number of different systemic frames of reference and how they deal with these questions. In this chapter, I want to explore how the theory of organisation as complex responsive processes explored in this part of the book deals with the above questions and in so doing compare this theory with systemic perspectives. The chapter then goes on to consider how the theory of complex responsive processes refocuses attention in thinking about organisations and their strategies. First, however, I give a brief summary of the theory described in Chapters 10 to 15.

16.2 Key features of the complex responsive processes perspective

Chapters 10 to 15 have outlined the basis of a complex responsive process theory of organisations. From this perspective, organisations are iterated patterns of interaction between people. They take the form of social objects, that is, generalised tendencies, on the part of large numbers of people, to act in similar ways in similar situations. When people describe an organisation, they describe who its members are collectively, what they stand for, and what they do. In other words, they articulate generalisations about collective activity, or population-wide patterns. Furthermore, there is a powerful tendency to idealise these generalisations about collective identity, so providing a felt sense of the unity of experience taking the form of an imaginative 'whole' which members co-construct. Such an imaginative 'whole' is fundamentally ideological in nature and people tend to describe it in terms of cult values. Organisations, then, are generalised patterns of interaction, idealised as imaginative 'wholes' which provide powerful experiences of 'we' identity to members. Strategising is the activity of members making sense of and exploring their desires and intentions for the evolution of their 'we' identities which actually emerge in the interplay of their intentions in local interactions. Realised strategy is the population-wide patterns of relationships and activities that emerge in this local interplay of intentions. In both desired and realised forms, strategy is basically expressed as narratives of identity.

Local interaction is then central to understanding organisations and strategising activities because it is in this local activity that there emerges the population-wide patterns of organisation and strategy both desired and realised. The theory stresses the following inextricably intertwined aspects of human local interaction:

- Interaction is always communicative and communication always takes place in the medium of symbols in the conversation of gestures. Symbols are always social acts, that is, the gesture of one body responding to its own gesture by taking the attitude of others and of the generalised/idealised other, while being responded to by others. Meaning emerges in such communicative interaction. Particularly important are the vocal symbols of language, and ordinary, everyday conversation is a particularly important form of communicative interaction in the medium of language. Feelings and other forms of bodily communication are, however, always involved.

- Interaction between human persons is always power relating because in relating to each other people are always simultaneously constraining and enabling each other's actions. Power relations are felt as the dynamics of inclusion and exclusion.

- In the activity of their conversational and power relating, people are always making choices on the basis of evaluative criteria which constitute ideology.
- As experience, the patterning of conversation, power relating and ideologically based choosing simultaneously forms and is formed by themes taking a predominantly narrative form.
- The identities of person in both their collective and individual aspects arise in interaction.

The term 'complex responsive processes of relating', therefore, always encompasses communicative interaction, power relating and ideologically based choices and it is in such responsive processes of relating that human beings create meaning and accomplish sophisticated joint action of any kind. The key feature of all human groups, organisations, institutions and societies is this joint action. Joint action is possible only because complex responsive processes of relating produce emergent, coherent, meaningful patterns of interaction both locally and population-wide at the same time.

The theory postulates that these coherent, meaningful patterns of interaction take the form of narrative and propositional themes that organise and are simultaneously organised by people interacting with each other. In other words, interaction is self-organising in that meaningful patterns emerge in local interactions between people in the living present, in the absence of any prior design, blueprint or plan for population-wide patterns. Self-organisation, understood as local interaction, means that human agents are choosing, intending, their next actions in response to others, where those choices reflect their own local organising principles, based on a life history in a community with a history. This is self-organising in the sense that human agents always have the potential for spontaneity and do not simply follow centrally determined rules of conduct. People do design and they do use blueprints and plans but these are all tools they use in their communicative interaction with each other and what happens depends upon the interplay of intentions, plans and choices. People have desires for these imaginatively constructed 'wholes' but what happens does so because of the interplay of their desires. There are no designs, blueprints or plans for interaction itself, for the interplay of intentions, and the tools emerge in the interaction between people. Although interaction is always local, the emergent patterns of meaning may be very widespread due to the fact that people do not interact in one local situation only. Local interaction produces the emergent population-wide patterns of social objects as such objects are made particular. A particular understanding of experience follows. Experience is the direct interaction between human bodies and the joint action accomplished in that interaction. Experience is participation in direct interaction, not participation in some abstract system.

The thematic patterning of communicative interaction has many continuously intertwining, inseparable aspects. These aspects are formal and informal, conscious and unconscious, legitimate and shadow themes organising and being organised by the experience of interaction. Furthermore, interaction is always evolving as the past is iterated in the living present in which the future is perpetually constructed. Other important aspects of interaction, therefore, are continuity and the spontaneity of the transformation of organising themes at the same time. In other words, in the continual iteration of the living present, thematic patterns are reproduced as habits, norms, routines, customs and so on. Social structures, cultures, organisations, institutions and societies, therefore, are not things but perpetually reproduced thematic patterns of relating between people taking habitual forms. Change, or evolution, in these rather repetitive patterns is possible only because in their iteration they are never reproduced exactly. This is because of the diversity of the people interacting, the imperfection of reproduction (memory) of past habitual interaction, and the inherent spontaneity or human capacity to choose responses, at least to some extent. Since human interaction is nonlinear, its iteration has the capacity to amplify small differences caused by spontaneity and imperfect reproduction into major qualitative changes in population-wide patterns of relating. It is in this manner that human interaction evolves in novel ways.

The theory of complex responsive processes, therefore, reflects a theory of transformative causality. This means that the causality of human interaction is not a dual one as in systems thinking. In systems thinking there is, on the one hand, formative unfolding of that which is already enfolded (the known) in the system of which people are parts through, say, design or some pre-given motivation such as a vision. On the other hand, there is rationalist individual choice. Instead, in responsive processes thinking, human interaction is perpetually constructing the future as the known-unknown, that is, as continuity and potential transformation at the same time. This is a fundamentally paradoxical theory of causality.

Furthermore, what is being perpetually constructed as continuity and potential transformation is human identity, that is, human meaning. Human identity has two inseparably interwoven aspects, namely, individual and collective, that which Elias called 'I' and 'we' identities. From a complex responsive process perspective, *an organisation is evolving identity*. In talking about organisations, the normal practice is to focus almost exclusively on collective or 'we' identities. The complex responsive process perspective, however, encourages us not to lose sight of the fact that 'I' identities are inseparable from 'we' identities. For example, General Electric (GE) is recognised as perhaps the world's largest corporation, which provides a wide range of products and services. It presents itself to, and is recognised by, many of us as a competitive company that operates with integrity and values its people. In other words, GE is a recognisable collective identity and, as such, is a key aspect of the identities of the people who work there. They take pride in telling people that they work for GE and experience a real sense of loss if their part of GE is sold to another corporation. This view of identity makes sense of the trauma individuals experience when they are ejected from an organisation or when their organisation is dissolved or merged with another. What is threatened is far greater than economic well-being; it is the very identities of people that are threatened.

This immediately leads us to the definition of strategy implicit in the theory of complex responsive processes. Strategy is the evolving narrative pattern of organisational identity. It is the evolving pattern of what an organisation is. An organisation is what it is because of a history of relating and it will become what it becomes in the local communicative interaction and power relating between people in the living present. If we want to understand strategy, then we need to understand the evolving complex responsive processes of relating between people who constitute an organisation in their local interaction.

Box 16.1 summarises key points about the dynamics of complex responsive processes.

Box 16.1	**Complex responsive processes: main points on organisational dynamics**

- Organisations are complex responsive processes of relating between people. Since relating immediately constrains, it immediately establishes power relations between people.
- Complex responsive processes are patterned as propositional and narrative themes that organise the experience of relating and thus power relations.
- These themes take many forms. Of great importance are the official ideological themes that determine what it is legitimate to talk about in an organisation and the unofficial ideologies which may be supporting or subverting official ideologies.
- Conversational patterns may take stable forms of repetition in which people are stuck. They may also take more fluid forms, analogous to the dynamics of the edge of chaos.
- Change occurs in novel ways through the presence of sufficient diversity in organising themes. This is expressed in fluid conversation in which shadow themes test the legitimate.
- The evolution of fluid conversation and the emergence of creative new directions are radically unpredictable.
- Fluid conversation is made more possible when people are able to live with anxiety.
- The choices people make are fundamentally based on ideology.
- Population-wide patterns emerge in local interaction.
- There is no guarantee of success.

16.3 How the theory of complex responsive processes answers the four key questions

Four questions were posed in Chapter 1 and used to explore important features of a number of theories of organisation. These questions relate to:

1. How the theory in question understands the nature of interaction.
2. What views the theory takes on human action.
3. The methodological position that the theory adopts.
4. The manner in which it deals with paradox.

This section will examine how the complex responsive processes theory of organisation deals with these questions and how this differs from other theories.

The nature of human interaction

Strategic choice theory is built on a systemic notion of interaction in which organisations adapt to their environments in a self-regulating, negative-feedback (cybernetic) manner so as to achieve their goals. The dynamics, or pattern of movement over time, are those of movement to states of stable equilibrium. Prediction is not seen as problematic. The analysis is primarily at the macro level of the organisation in which cause and effect are related to each other in a linear manner. Microdiversity receives little attention and interaction is assumed to be uniform and harmonious.

Learning organisation theory also adopts a systemic perspective on human inter-action, but one that takes account of positive as well as negative feedback. From the systems dynamics perspective the dynamic is that of non-equilibrium in which unexpected outcomes appear. However, this theory holds that when managers understand the positive and negative feedback structure of the whole system they will be able to identify leverage points through which they can control it. This theory does not explore the implications of radical unpredictability. Here, too, the analysis is at the macro level of the organisation but this time connections between cause and effect take nonlinear forms in which the connections might be distant over time and space. Again, little attention is paid to microdiversity and successful interaction is still assumed to be harmonious, although this theory does recognise obstacles to the achievement of such harmony.

The third theory reviewed, psychodynamics, also takes a systemic perspective on interaction, this time open systems theory. Here the focus is on regulation at permeable boundaries between system and environment and between subsystems of the system. The dynamics of human open systems are somewhat turbulent and the importation of primitive human behaviour disrupts organisational learning. This possibility requires careful management of boundaries and radical unpredictability does not feature as an important characteristic. This theory sees the purpose of man-agement as intervention aimed at enabling equilibrium adaptation to the organisa-tion's environment. The analysis here is at a far more micro level than is the case with strategic choice and the learning organisation, taking account of the behaviour of members of an organisation, particularly the unconscious causes of that behav-iour. Microdiversity is recognised and success is a state of adaptation to reality.

These three approaches to organisations are, therefore, based on a systemic theory of interaction. This means that interaction between people is assumed to create a whole, a system, of which they are parts and so subjected in some way to the purpose of the whole. Later developments in systems thinking in the form of autopoiesis, second-order, soft and critical systems thinking all continue on the basis of a theory of sys-temic interaction. Various strands of systems thinking may differ according to whether they view systems as reality itself or mental constructs of reality but they continue to take a systemic perspective on interaction. This also applies to more recent developments in organisational theory to do with knowledge management.

A number of writers have been moving to a systemic perspective on human action drawn from chaos and complexity theory. Attention is drawn to the dynamics of the edge of chaos and the self-organising, emergent properties of the system. Attention is also drawn to the possibility of unpredictability, but this is often not seen as essen-tial or requiring further exploration. The analysis tends to be at the macro level of the organisation as a whole, although some do focus upon micro diversity to some extent. Most writers apply complexity theory to organisations within the systemic theory of interaction.

The complex responsive processes perspective described in Chapters 10 to 15 is built upon a completely different theory of interaction or process (*see* Chapter 10). It regards interaction between people as iterated processes of communication and power relating. There is no notion here of a system, and what people are produ-cing in their interaction is further patterns of interaction in which they imaginatively construct 'wholes' which they tend to idealise. Such imaginative 'wholes' are under-stood as ideologies rather than systems. The theory of complex responsive processes, therefore, represents a move from a spatial metaphor of inside and outside to temporal processes of continual reproduction and potential transformation. Complex responsive processes are fundamentally conversational in nature, forming and being formed by power relations and ideologically based choices. The analysis focuses at a micro level and concentrates on the paradoxical dynamics of stable instability in which local interaction produces emergent population-wide patterns in relating and these could take novel forms through the amplification of diversity and human spontaneity. This perspective emphasises the importance of diversity and deviance as essential to the internal capacity to change spontaneously. In this evolving, potentially creative process, unpredictability is central, inviting further exploration of how people act into the unknown.

The comparison that I have made above between organisational theories suggests a move from one theory of interaction to another so that uncertainty and unpredictability, and their relationship with diversity and creativity, are increasingly taken into account.

Human psychology

Strategic choice theory takes a cognitivist view of human nature. Here, mind is understood to be a property of the individual brain. The brain/mind processes symbolic information, forming representations and models of a pre-given reality. Humans then act on the basis of their mental models. The individual is primary in that knowing and acting do not depend fundamentally on relationships between individuals. Individuals form groups and being part of a group may then affect individual behaviour. This theory places great emphasis on the importance of the intentions formed and expressed by autonomous individuals. Emotion is often seen as a dangerous disruption of rational choice capacity and power is understood as an attribute of an individual, often in terms of official authority. Creativity is an attribute of an individual.

Learning organisation theories employs the same theory of human nature. However, they also combine this with notions from humanistic psychology in which the central motivation for action is the urge individuals have to actualise themselves, finding their true selves as it were. Again, individuals form groups and these groups may affect their behaviour. Leadership is a competence possessed by individuals and intention is a characteristic of individuals. Emotions of a positive kind are emphasised. Power as an attribute of charismatic individuals comes to the fore. Creativity is in the end seen as an attribute of an individual, although a role is also ascribed to cohesive teamwork. Humanistic psychology also immediately focuses attention on the individual, but in a way rather different from cognitivism. The central tenet here is the belief that the human individual is fundamentally motivated by self-realisation, or self-actualisation. Human knowing and acting, and therefore human learning, are driven by the need to find the self. Others, in the form of community, are very important to emotional well-being but it is not postulated that the group or the community actually forms the individual. In fact, the self-actualising individual has to find his or her true self despite group pressures to conform.

Psychoanalytic perspectives on organisations combine open systems theory with a view of human nature derived from psychoanalysis. The fundamental motivation for human behaviour here is the mental ideas of inherited animal instincts called the drives. Aggressive and libidinal drives blindly seek satisfaction but encounter social prohibition. Individual mental processes are structured by this encounter with the social. Individuals form groups but considerable account is taken of the impact group processes have on individual behaviour, particularly those that are unconscious. The theory focuses on how regression to primitive behaviour can destroy rational thinking and learning. An important insight into the nature of the relationship between individual and group is that about leadership. Individuals may be sucked into leadership positions by unconscious dynamics of the group. Leadership is no longer simply a competence of the individual. Emotion and power play a much more important role in understanding the development of an organisation than they do in the theories of strategic choice and the learning organisation. The impact of emotions of a negative kind and of individual and group fantasy life is taken into account, as are the negative aspects of power. Creativity is an individual attribute arising in the ability to hold anxiety and engage in play.

Many of those developing the knowledge management perspective on organisations, as well as those understanding organisations as communities of practice, adopt a constructivist view of psychology, sometimes combined with the theory of autopoietic systems. Here, individuals are thought of as selecting or enacting the world into which they act. In this way, interacting individuals co-create their worlds. However, the individual still remains primary, although much more importance is attached to social interaction.

The writers reviewed in Chapter 9 import a theory of interaction drawn from chaos and complexity theory into their theory of organisations. They combine this with the same cognitivist, constructivist and humanistic views of human nature as those found in strategic choice, learning organisation theory, as well as knowledge management and communities of practice perspectives. The individual, therefore, remains central, and as a result these writers do not go further, in my view, than the other systemic theories reviewed in Part 1. More attention may be paid to the creative aspects of instability but, for most, the same views on control are retained and creativity continues to be regarded as an attribute of an individual. Individuals, according to this theory, are essentially cybernetic entities who can take the position of objective observer of an external reality.

The complex responsive processes theory of organisations makes a radical departure from systemic thinking when it comes to human psychology. While the systemic theories reviewed in Part 1 combine a theory of interaction with a theory of human psychology, the complex responsive processes perspective is a theory of human psychology that is also a theory of interaction. There is no split between psychology and sociology. While systemic theories distinguish between individual and group as different levels of analysis, the complex responsive processes perspective is one in which the individual is the singular of interdependent people while the group is the plural of interdependent people.

The fundamental proposition is that individuals and groups form and are formed by each other simultaneously. Individual minds are not seen purely as a process of brain computation, nor are they seen as motivated by primitive drives formed in the mind by the clash with the social. From a complex responsive processes perspective, the fundamental motivator of human behaviour is the urge to relate. From this perspective, there can be no human individual outside of relationship. Mind is silent, private conversation structured by, and always resonating and changing with, vocal, public conversation in groups. This theory moves away from the notion of the autonomous individual containing a mind as an internal world to the notion of interdependent people, to social selves. Power relations and the ideologies supporting them, as well as emotions and fantasies, are all central to this theoretical perspective. Intention is no longer an attribute of an individual. Instead, it emerges in conversational relationship to be articulated by an individual. Leadership is no longer simply an individual competence but a form of relationship. Creativity arises in patterns of relationship in which there is sufficient deviance and subversion.

Methodological position

The methodological position adopted by strategic choice and learning organisation theorists is that of the objective observer who stands outside the organisational system and observes it as a pre-given reality. The purpose is to manipulate and control the system. This is part of cognitivist thinking. When the writers reviewed in Chapter 9 take chaos and complexity theory into theorising about organisations, they adopt the same methodological position. The manager is implicitly ascribed the same role and prescriptions are made as to how the manager may control, direct or at least disturb or perturb the system.

Those adopting psychoanalytic perspectives move some way from this position in that they adopt methodologies analogous to the clinical. They advocate action research in which the researcher participates with members of an organisation and uses his or her feelings as information. However, some notion of objective observation is retained. The researcher, and the manager, takes a position at the boundary of the system in order to avoid being sucked into unconscious group processes (Stapley, 1996).

Those who take second-order, soft and critical systems perspectives, as well as some of those who talk of communities of practice and knowledge management, adopt a reflexive and participative methodological position. They display great awareness of the co-constructed nature of knowledge and many actively look for multiple perspectives on any situation.

Many move from the position of the objective observer to methodologies of participative enquiry (Reason, 1988) where researchers understand themselves to be participants in processes of enquiry. This is a reflexive methodology (Steier, 1991) in which organisations are understood to be social constructions (Gergen, 1982). However, while seeking to deal with the fact that humans are both observers and participants in their own action, the writers in the traditions just referred to continue to do so from a systemic perspective. They still understand human interaction as producing a system. This inevitably leads to a methodological dualism in which people move from the participant position to the observer position and back again. Critical systems thinking develops this kind of dualism into a whole system of methodologies.

The complex responsive processes perspective seeks to sustain a methodological position in which people are both participants and observers at the same time.

This has implications for how the role of the manager is understood. Neither researcher nor manager can step outside the conversational processes that are the organisation simply because their work requires them to talk to others. What they say affects what they hear and what they hear affects what they say. From this perspective, then, a manager cannot stand outside organisational processes and control, direct, shape, influence, condition or perturb them in an intentional way. All such intentions are gestures made to others in an organisation and what happens depends on the ongoing responses. The methodology for understanding complex responsive processes is essentially reflexive.

This perspective on the nature of management leads to a completely different understanding of the dynamics of stable instability. The writers reviewed in Chapter 9 tend to equate the dynamics of the edge of chaos with crises. They tend to see the manager as one who stands outside the system and pushes, or nudges, it into instability, disturbance and crisis. One prescription is to place people under more stress so that they will be motivated to change and so 'unleash the power of self-organisation'. The notion of the edge of chaos used in a complex responsive processes perspective is completely different. The analogue of this dynamic is fluid conversation. People can only engage in this when the pattern of their relationships provides good enough capacity for living with the anxiety of facing the unknown. Crisis and stress are not relational qualities that contain anxiety, rather they increase it. The edge of chaos, from the perspective I am suggesting, is safe enough, exciting enough patterns of relationships, not terrifyingly stressful ones.

Paradox

Paradox is not central to the theories of strategic choice, learning organisations, knowledge management and communities of practice or the importation of chaos and complexity theory into organisational thinking through cognitivist and constructivist perspectives on psychology. Contradiction, tension and dilemmas are recognised but they are seen as resolvable. It is indeed the purpose of management, according to these theories, to resolve them. The reason is that all of these theories are fundamentally systemic and it is of the essence of systems thinking to eliminate paradox in dualistic thinking.

Paradox plays a much more important role in psychoanalytic theories and is seen as fundamental to human life. The theory of complex responsive processes places even more emphasis on paradox in that the individual and the group are paradoxically formed by and forming each other at the same time. Particularly important is the emphasis placed on the paradox of predictability and unpredictability at the same time. Paradox, of course, cannot be resolved or harmonised, only endlessly transformed.

In this section I have compared the answers to the four key questions given by various *systemic* theories of organisation with those provided by complex responsive *processes* theory. I suggest that the move from systems to responsive processes leads to a radically different understanding of organisational evolution. It is radical in that it abandons the assumptions of the autonomous individual and the position of the objective observer. It replaces these assumptions with those of the simultaneous social construction of group and individual identities and the methodological position of reflexivity in both individual and social terms. Another move is away from thinking of oneself as manager in terms of the objective designer, towards thinking of oneself as an active participant in complex processes of relating to other people in all its aspects, both good and bad. In the next section of this chapter, I want to explore how this theoretical shift focuses the attention of practitioners and researchers on factors that are, in some respects, very different from other theories.

16.4 Refocusing attention: strategy and change

Strategic choice, learning organisation and knowledge management theories take the methodological position of the objective observer where the manager stands outside the organisation understood as a system and thinks in terms of controlling it. These theories, therefore, immediately have an application to do with the intentional control of the system by the observing manager. It is then a natural step to formulate general prescriptions for the application of control. The prescriptions take the form of tools and techniques of analysis and monitoring. Furthermore, some test of the validity of the tools and techniques is required. This is provided by pointing to how organisations that use particular tools and techniques, or have particular attributes, are successful while those that do not use, or possess, them fail.

It seems to me that psychoanalytic perspectives on organisations hold the position of the objective observer much less firmly. The concern with application then becomes less central and the focus shifts more to understanding what is happening in an organisation. Rather than straightforward prescriptions, those working from a psychoanalytic perspective provide hypotheses for joint discussion with members of an organisation in specific, rather than general, cases.

A theory of organisations as complex responsive processes of relating makes a methodological move away from the notion of the manager as objective observer. Managers are understood to be participants in complex responsive processes, engaged in emergent enquiry into what they are doing and what steps they should take next. They may also be enquiring into the nature of their own complex responsive processes of relating. This is what it means to be reflexive. This theory provides an explanation of what managers are doing, rather than prescribing what they should be doing. Application has little meaning in this endeavour. If you are trying to explain what managers are doing now, you can hardly use this as a prescription. They are already doing it. The whole purpose of the theoretical shift I have been suggesting is to focus attention on processes that managers are held to be engaging in but which the other theories either do not focus upon or tend to do so in a prescriptive way. The purpose is not to apply or prescribe but to refocus attention. When people focus their attention differently, they are highly likely to take different kinds of actions. However, a theory that focuses attention on contingent local interaction and emergent population-wide patterns can hardly yield general prescriptions on how that local interaction should proceed and what should emerge from it. The theory would be proposing to do the opposite of what it is explaining. Instead, the theory of complex responsive processes invites recognition of the uniqueness and non-repeatability of experience.

If you focus your attention according to strategic choice, learning organisation and knowledge management theories, the lack of application and prescription implied by complex responsive processes theory is highly unsatisfactory. The tendency is to dismiss it as useless, as not practical, for this reason. However, if you take the perspective of complex responsive processes theory, rather than trying to make it fit into some other theory, you might come to value what it does, namely refocuses attention. I have found that even if managers accept this, they immediately ask for examples of where people have refocused attention in the way suggested and whether they were then successful. Again, this is approaching the theory of complex responsive processes from the frame of reference of the other theories. One of the main properties of the dynamics of stable instability is the escalation of small changes into qualitatively different patterns. Patterns of stable instability may be similar to each other but they are never repeated in the same way. They are unique and not repeatable at important levels of detail. Organisations characterised by the dynamics of bounded instability will therefore all be unique in some important way. The experience of one cannot be repeated, at important levels of detail, by another. Giving examples of success in one organisation to managers in another is likely to be spurious. Perhaps this is why the track record of identifying attributes of successful organisation is so poor. Instead of looking for understanding in other people's experience one might look for it in one's own experience.

Consistent with the nature of the theory I am talking about, therefore, I will not be providing applications or prescriptions. What I will be trying to point to is how the theory shifts the focus of attention. First, consider how attention is focused on the quality of participation.

Focusing attention on the quality of participation

Whenever I talk to managers about the complex responsive processes perspective, they immediately ask what it says that 'you' need to do to bring about the success of an organisation. When I ask who this 'you' is, they usually say that they mean the top executives of an organisation. The main issue here is how one is thinking about what top executives of an organisation are doing. From the dominant systemic perspective they are implicitly thought of first as standing outside the organisation understood as a system and operating on it in some way, and then as participating in the system as parts of it. From the complex responsive processes perspective, top executives are thought of as participating with other members in evolving processes of communicating and power relating. The meaning of participation is completely different in the two perspectives. In the systemic perspective, participation means participating in an abstract 'whole' or system and in the complex responsive processes perspective it means participating in direct interaction with other people. In the former case, participation creates a 'whole' outside of the direct experience of interaction; in the latter case, participation means creating further interaction.

Strategic choice theory holds that the top executives can form organisation-wide intentions for an organisation's future evolution. It also holds that if they then appropriately motivate other members of their organisation, those members will move according to the intention that top executives have ascribed to the system. In the language of complex responsive processes theory, this amounts to saying that top executives can make an intentional gesture to all members of the organisation and they can also more or less determine the responses to that gesture throughout the organisation. Responses of a deviant kind are to be forestalled by appropriate motivation and unexpected responses from other organisations are to be handled by making further, organisation-wide, intentional gestures. Innovation and creativity are also understood to be intentions formed by top executives. There is no fundamental place for the unexpected.

Learning organisation theory does take account of unexpected response to the organisation-wide, intentional gestures of top executives. However, it holds that they can intentionally operate at leverage points so as to get the responses they want, more or less. Creativity here is the intentional change of mental models by individuals. From psychoanalytic perspectives, top executives can choose task and role definitions and design structures that will hold disruptive unconscious processes at bay. Those employing complexity theory in what I have called an orthodox way point to unpredictability of responses and to their self-organising and emergent nature. However, they hold that top executives can choose simple rules or intentionally create crises that will move their organisation to a dynamic in which it can be successful.

In critical systems thinking, researchers, consultants and managers evaluate a problem situation, invite the 'right' participants to engage with it, encourage them to interact, trigger their enthusiasm and present them with the selected systems models that they think are appropriate to the problem situation. In the communities of practice perspective, someone formulates a design for learning.

In all these cases, the top executives are making choices about how they are to operate on the system as a whole and it is being assumed that they can determine the responses that their gestures call forth. In effect this assumes that there is a special category of person in an organisation who alone has free will and choice, or agency, with all the others reduced to automata. Even members of that special category then have to become a part in the system they have designed, implying that they are only free while they are designing the system.

From the complex responsive processes perspective, no manager can stand outside an organisation and choose how it is to operate. Instead, all managers are active participants with each other in the interactive processes that are the organisation. Top executives can and do form organisation-wide intentions about their organisation. They can and do identify leverage points. They can and do design structures to contain unconscious processes and sometimes they do set simple rules and intentionally cause crises. They can and do prepare designs for learning and they do try to identify the 'right' people. They can and do select and recommend systems models that they think are relevant to particular problem situations. However, all of these intentions and designs emerge in the conversations top executives have with each other and with other people. Furthermore, top executives can never design the responses to these gestures. Small changes may escalate and people will engage in local conversations and power relations, often organised by shadow themes, from which unexpected responses may well emerge. Attention is then focused on the thematic patterning of interaction, such as the pattern of power relations, the patterns of inclusion and exclusion, the ideological themes sustaining them and the feelings of anxiety and shame aroused by shifts in patterns of identity.

I am suggesting, then, that in moving from the position of manager as objective observer of a system to that of manager as participant in emergent enquiry, attention is focused on the unexpected and complex patterning of the responses of organisational members to managers' intentions. Intention and design are understood as emergent and problematic processes and attention is focused on the interplay of intentions. The emphasis shifts from the manager focusing on how to make a choice to focusing on the quality of participation in self-organising conversations from which such choices and the responses to them emerge. It becomes a personal matter of reflecting together on the quality of participation.

Focusing attention on the quality of conversational life

In organisations, relationships between people are organised in conversations that form and are formed by the power relations between them. Conversational relating is organised by themes of an ideological nature that justify the patterns of power relations. Intentions emerge as do other themes organising the experience of relating, as do the responses these intentions call forth. New themes emerge as people struggle to understand each other and as their conversations are cross-fertilised through conversations with people in other communities and disciplines. Organisations change when the themes that organise conversation and power relations change. Learning is change in these themes. Knowledge is language and meaning emerges as themes interact to form conversations.

Attention is thus focused on the conversational life of an organisation as the changing, evolving, local communicative interaction and power relating patterned as intention and design and using communicative tools such as systems models. The quality of that conversational life is thus paramount. Increasingly, systemic theories are focusing on conversations, story and narrative. However, the tendency is to seek to design special forms of conversation known as dialogue and special forums such as communities of practice. From the complex responsive processes perspective the emphasis is on ordinary, everyday conversation. The key role of managers is their participation in those conversations and their facilitation of different ways of conversing. A key implication of this way of understanding life in organisations has to do with being sensitive to the themes that are organising conversational relating. Another is awareness of the rhetorical ploys that are being used to block the emergence of new conversational themes. From this perspective, effective managers are those who notice the repetitive themes that block fluid conversation and participate in such a way as to assist in shifting those themes. They may do this, for example, by repeatedly asking why people are saying what they are saying. Effective managers will seek opportunities to talk to people in other communities and bring themes from those conversations into the conversational life of their own organisation. They will be particularly concerned with trying to understand the covert politics and unconscious group processes they are caught up in and how those might be trapping conversation in repetitive themes. They will also pay attention to the power relations and the ideological basis of those power relations and of the choices people make as expressed in conversations.

Focusing attention on the quality of anxiety and how it is lived with

A theory of organisation as complex responsive processes focuses attention on the importance of fluid conversation in which people are able to search for new meaning. Anxiety is an inevitable companion of shifts in themes that organise the experience of relating because such shifts create uncertainty, particularly uncertainty around individual and collective identities. Themes organising the experience of relating are not only expressed in the vocal, public conversations between people, they also resonate with and change the silent, private conversations that are individual minds. Change in organisations is also, at the same time, deeply personal change for individual members. New ways of talking publicly are reflected in new ways of individuals making sense of themselves. Such shifts unsettle the very way in which people experience themselves. It is because of these deeply personal reasons that shifting patterns of conversation give rise to anxiety, but without this there can be no emergence of creative new themes.

When one thinks in this way, the manner in which people live with anxiety is crucial to organisational change and innovation. When managers focus attention on this matter they begin to pay attention to what it is about particular work, at a particular time, in a particular place, that gives rise to anxiety. They pay attention to the nature of this anxiety. They ask what makes it possible to live with the anxiety so that it is also experienced as the excitement required to enable people to continue struggling with the search for new meaning. This a matter for managers to reflect upon. What are we doing that enables us, or disables us, from living with the anxiety that change generates? Central to this possibility is sufficient trust between those engaging in difficult conversations. Attention is then focused on what in a particular organisation, at a particular time, is promoting or destroying trust.

What will be seriously questioned from the perspective of complex responsive processes is prescriptions that have to do with setting stretching targets and placing people under stress in the belief that this will move them to try harder. What this may do is simply make them feel more anxious and so less likely to develop the kind of conversational life that makes creativity possible.

Focusing attention on the quality of diversity

One of the most distinctive aspects of a theory of complex responsive processes is the way in which it focuses attention on diversity. The other theories reviewed in this book tend to focus attention on consensus. Strategic choice theory focuses attention on the importance of members of an organisation sharing the same commitment to its policies and its chosen strategic direction. Learning organisation theory focuses attention on the importance of people in an organisation being committed to the same vision and working together harmoniously in cohesive teams. Psychoanalytic perspectives focus attention on the importance of people understanding the nature of boundaries and having shared understandings of their roles and tasks. Many of those who import complexity theory into their theorising about organisations in systemic ways stress the importance of people sharing a few simple rules, although some have laid great emphasis on diversity (see Chapter 9). The theory I am suggesting takes a paradoxical perspective.

The paradox is this. If members of an organisation have nothing in common at all, then obviously any kind of joint action will be impossible. However, if they conform too much then the emergence of new forms of behaviour is blocked. Organisations display the internal capacity to change spontaneously only when they are characterised by diversity. This focuses attention on the importance of deviance and eccentricity. It focuses attention on the importance of unofficial ideologies that undermine current power relations. Such unofficial ideologies are expressed in conversations organised by shadow themes. A condition for creativity is therefore some degree of subversive activity with the inevitable tension this brings between shadow and legitimate themes organising the experience of relating.

It is difficult to get one's mind around what this means. It does not make much sense to me to move from noting the importance of deviance to thinking that managers, in their legitimate roles, should promote deviance. It would then not be deviance. It makes little sense to advocate harnessing shadow conversational themes in order intentionally to generate creativity. The shadow so harnessed is no longer the shadow. It makes little sense to say that managers should take steps to unleash self-organisation. This implies that it is not going on already, when the whole point of the theory of complexity is that it is explaining how things already are. It also makes little sense to me to respond to the recognition of diversity by prescribing 'respect' for diversity. I think that this is a form of disengagement in which everyone politely ignores the differences while claiming to respect them. I think this is a defensive manoeuvre which blocks the explorative conflict provoked by diversity, which is how some new understanding might emerge.

For me, the implication of recognising the importance of deviance has to do with people making sense of their own engagement with others in the shadow conversations that express deviance. It means paying attention to how what they are doing may be collusively sustaining the legitimate themes organising experience, so making change impossible. It means developing a greater sensitivity to the unconscious way in which together people create categories of what is 'in' and what is 'out' and the effect that this has on people and organisations. These dynamics of power relating, inclusion–exclusion and shame are central to the complex responsive processes perspective.

Focusing attention on unpredictability and paradox

Perhaps the most radical implication of complex responsive processes theory is the severe limits to certainty and predictability that it points to. This is a major departure from other theories of organisation, which either virtually ignore or at least downplay the radical unpredictability of the long-term evolution of organisations. What does paying attention to such unpredictability imply?

First, for me, it means thinking about how to cope with not knowing and the potential for feelings of incompetence and shame that this arouses. Managers in organisations often find themselves in situations in which they must act without knowing what the outcome of their actions will be over long time periods. They must act because failure to act will also have unpredictable long-term outcomes. Furthermore, managers can and do act, often very creatively, when they do not know what the long-term outcomes of their actions will be – when they do not really know what they are doing.

These situations are made much more difficult, I think, when management is understood from perspectives that lead people to believe that long-term predictability is possible if one is well informed and competent enough. When the inevitable surprise comes then this view leads to a search for whom to blame. The perspective that predictability is possible leads to the view that the surprise must be due to ignorance, incompetence or some form of bad behaviour in that people did not do what they were supposed to do. In my experience, this judgement is frequently completely unjustified in that very intelligent managers do the best they can and still the surprises come. When you take the complex responsive processes perspective then surprise is part of the internal dynamic of the processes themselves. Surprise is inevitable no matter how well informed, competent and well behaved everyone is. Surprise is inseparable from creativity. I believe that thinking in this way is itself a way of living with the anxiety of not knowing. It is quite natural not to know and this does not have to incapacitate one. It is possible to carry on working together even in the condition of not knowing. Emergent meaning, often of a new and creative kind, is produced in conversational processes characterised by 'not knowing'.

This way of thinking encourages one to pay more attention to what one actually does as one holds the position of not knowing long enough for the new to emerge. One implication of this position has to do with the criteria used to judge a quality action. The systemic theories reviewed in Part 1 implicitly assume that the criterion for selecting a quality action is its outcome. Quality actions are those that produce desired outcomes. However, in an unpredictable world, the outcomes of an action cannot be known in advance. It is necessary to act and then deal with the consequences. This does not make action impossible or futile. It simply means that people select actions on the basis of other criteria for quality. For example, in a highly uncertain world a quality action is one that keeps options open for as long as possible. A quality action is one which creates a position from which further actions are possible. That is why the option of doing nothing is such a poor response to uncertainty. If the response to uncertainty is to stay at home then the options opened up by journeying forth will never be available. Another criterion for a quality action is that it should enable errors to be detected faster than do other options. Finally, the most important criteria for quality actions are moral and ethical in nature. An action may be taken without the actor's knowing its outcome simply because the action is judged to be good in itself. One is not absolved of responsibility simply because one does not know the outcome. Even if I do not know how my action will turn out, I am still responsible and will have to deal with the outcome as best I can. In the end, quality action is ideologically based.

Just as the unpredictability arising in complex interactions imposes limits on what it is possible to know about outcomes of actions, so the complexity of the interactions itself imposes limits on how much of it can be understood. Managers often cannot know the long-term outcomes of their actions and they usually cannot understand the full nature of the complex responsive processes of organising. However, this does not disable action either because the process is one in which local interaction produces an emergent population-wide pattern. It is not necessary to understand the 'whole' in order to act; it is simply necessary to act on the basis of one's own local understanding, which will always include one's perceptions and feelings about social objects and cult values. This is a very different notion from that in, say, learning organisation theory where understanding the whole system is essential to learning. Unlike systemic theories of any kind, one is not seeking the whole or trying to be comprehensive.

The focus on long-term unpredictability has implications for the meaning of control. As it is normally understood in other theories of organisation, control is a cybernetic process. It is an activity that ensures the achievement of chosen outcomes. In highly complex processes with emergent and unpredictable long-term outcomes, this form of control is impossible. This does not mean that there is no control, however. It simply means that control has to be understood in a different way. Control then takes the form of constraint. As I have often pointed out in previous chapters, all acts of relating impose constraint on all of those relating. Control takes the form of relating itself, that is, mutual constraint. Control is understood as social processes of power relations, ideology and socialised self-control.

Notions of complexity, long-term unpredictability and control as constraint have implications for many activities that are currently taken for granted by managers. If these notions are taken seriously, they lead to a number of questions. For example: why do people prepare long-term forecasts if it is impossible to make useful long-term forecasts? Why do they adopt investment appraisal methods that require detailed quantitative forecasts over long time periods? Complexity theory suggests that it is impossible to make such forecasts so why do people carry on doing so? If organisations are not simply cybernetic systems why is so much effort expended on cybernetic systems of quality control? One important implication of a complex responsive processes theory of organising may have to do with putting a stop to many initiatives and abandoning control systems and procedures that are not fulfilling the purposes they are supposed to fulfil. The savings in time, resources and human stress might be considerable.

The theory of complex responsive processes particularly focuses attention on the paradoxical nature of organisational life:

- Organising is at the same time intentional and emergent in the interplay of intentions. Intention emerges in local, self-organising processes of conversation while at the same time organising that conversation.
- Conversational patterns in an organisation enable what is being done and at the same time constrain what is done as power relating.
- The performance of complicated tasks requires that they be divided up but at the same time they have to be integrated.
- The same processes of local interaction and emergent population-wide pattern creatively produce new forms while at the same time destroying others. New conversational themes and power relations emerge while older ones are destroyed.
- Themes organising the experience of relating in conversation are both stable and unstable at the same time. They are in control and not in control at the same time.
- The emergence of new themes organising the experience of relating is both predictable and unpredictable at the same time.
- Managers operate in a state of knowing and not knowing at the same time.
- Complex responsive processes organise both conformity and deviance at the same time.

Managing is then a process of continually rearranging the paradoxes of organisational life.

16.5 Summary

Systemic theories of organisation see strategy as the usually rational choice or intention of some or all of the members of an organisation and the intentional overcoming of obstacles to the implementation of such choices. The psychoanalytic approach pays particular attention to how irrational processes might interfere with this choice or intention. Intention is understood as the choice, or design, made by autonomous individuals, usually taking the position of the independent observer. The criteria for the choice focus on desired, predetermined outcomes.

The complex responsive processes perspective makes a substantial move in a number of ways. First, it directs attention to how intention emerges in local inter-action taking the form of ordinary conversation between people. This replaces the notion that intention is the expression of an autonomous individual who reflects and makes choices in the light of expected outcomes, as it were, after consulting with others. So, the first move is to focus on how intention emerges rather than on what it is. The second move is to focus attention on how the irremovable interdependence of people involves the interplay of intentions and it is from this interplay that organisations evolve. The third move is to focus attention on diversity and how the amplification of differences is the process of change. Novel intention initially emerges in the tension between legitimate and shadow themes organising the experience of being together, that is, in ordinary conversations at the margins of the organisation.

Questions to aid further reflection

1. Does taking a complex responsive processes perspective amount to a call for a new kind of organisation?

2. Does the emphasis on widening and deepening conversation, on relationships, mean that people should bring to awareness what they think is going on between them? In other words does it lead to a prescription for managers to spend time discussing their own group dynamics and bringing everything out into the open?

3. Does the emphasis on ordinary conversation lead to the need to develop good conversations?

4. Does the emphasis on relationships amount to a prescription for managers to develop good relationships and pay more attention to the greater good?

5. Are organisations real and can they have an identity?

6. What happens to the emphasis placed on the 'task' by many other perspectives, if one takes the perspective of complex responsive processes?

7. What is wrong with thinking in systems terms?

8. Is emergence a matter of fate?

9. What are the applications of complex responsive processes theory and what is practical about it? Is it blindingly obvious?

10. How does intention feature in the theory of complex responsive processes?

11. Does the theory of complex responsive processes amount to an ideology inviting the formation of a cult?

References

A

Abraham, F. D. (1995), *Chaos Theory in Psychology*, Westport, CT: Praeger.

Abram, D. (1996), *The Spell of the Sensuous*, New York: Vintage Books.

Ackoff, R. L. (1981), *Creating the Corporate Future*, New York: Wiley.

Ackoff, R. L. (1994), *The Democratic Organization*, New York: Oxford University Press.

Aldrich, H. (1979), *Organizations and Environments*, Englewood Cliffs, NJ: Prentice-Hall.

Allen, P. M. (1998a), 'Evolving complexity in social science', in Altman, G. and Koch, W. A. (eds), *Systems: New Paradigms for the Human Sciences*, New York: Walter de Gruyter.

Allen, P. M. (1998b), 'Modelling complex economic evolution', in Schweitzer, F. and Silverberg, G. (eds) (1998), *Selbstorganisation*, Berlin: Duncker & Humblot.

Allen, P. M., Strathern, M. and Baldwin, J. S. (2005), 'Complexity of social economic systems: the inevitability of uncertainty and surprise', in McDaniel Jr., R. R. and Driebe, D. J. (eds), *Uncertainty and Surprise in Complex Systems: Questions on Working with the Unexpected*, Heidelberg: Springer.

Allen, P. M., Strathern, M. and Baldwin, J. S. (2006), 'Evolutionary drive: new understandings of change in socio-economic systems', *Emergence: Complexity and Organization*, vol. 8, no. 2.

Ameriks, K. (ed.) (2002), *The Cambridge Companion to German Idealism*, Cambridge: Cambridge University Press.

Andersen, E. S., Grude, K. V. and Haug, T. (1995), *Goal Directed Project Management: Effective Techniques and Strategies*, 2nd edition, London: Kogan Page.

Anderson, P. W., Arrow, K. J. and Pines, D. (1988), *The Economy as an Evolving Complex System*, Menlo Park, CA: Addison-Wesley.

Andrews, K. R. ([1971] 1987), *The Concept of Corporate Strategy*, Homewood, IL: Irwin.

Ansoff, I. (1965), *Corporate Strategy*, New York: McGraw-Hill.

Ansoff, I. (1990), *Implanting Corporate Strategy*, Hemel Hempstead: Prentice Hall.

Aram, E. (2001), 'The experience of complexity: learning as the potential transformation of identity', unpublished PhD thesis, University of Hertfordshire, UK.

Argyris, C. (1990), *Overcoming Organizational Defenses: Facilitating Organizational Learning*, Boston: Allyn & Bacon.

Argyris, C. and Schön, D. (1978), *Organizational Learning: A Theory of Action Perspective*, Reading, MA: Addison-Wesley.

Ashby, W. R. (1945), 'The effect of controls on stability', *Natura*, vol. 155, pp. 242–3.

Ashby, W. R. (1952), *Design for a Brain*, New York: Wiley.

Ashby, W. R. (1956), *Introduction to Cybernetics*, New York: Wiley.

Axelrod, R. and Cohen, M. D. (1999), *Harnessing Complexity: Organizational Implications of a Scientific Frontier*, New York: The Free Press.

B

Bacharach, S. B. and Lawler, E. J. (1980), *Power and Politics in Organizations*, San Francisco: Jossey-Bass.

Baddeley, A. (1990), *Human Memory: Theory and Practice*, Hove, Sussex: Lawrence Erlbaum Associates.

Baets, W. (1999), *A Collection of Essays on Complexity and Management*, London: World Scientific Publishing Co.

Bales, R. F. (1970), *Personality and Interpersonal Behavior*, New York: Holt.

Balogon, J., Huff, A. S. and Johnson P. (2003), 'Three responses to the methodological challenges of studying strategizing', *Journal of Management Studies*, vol. 40, no. 1, pp. 198–224.

Barney, J. B. (1991), 'Firm resources and sustained competitive advantage', *Journal of Management*, vol. 17, no. 1, pp. 99–120.

Barr, P. S., Stimpert, J. L. and Huff, A. S. (1992), 'Cognitive change, strategic action and organizational renewal', *Strategic Management Journal*, vol. 13, Special Issue, Summer, pp. 15–36.

Bateman, A., Brown, D. and Pedder, J. (2000), *Introduction to Psychotherapy: An Outline of Psychodynamic Principles and Practice*, 3rd edition, London: Routledge.

Bateson, G. (1972), *Steps to an Ecology of Mind*, New York: Ballantine Books.

Baumol, W. J. and Benhabib, J. (1989), 'Chaos: significance, mechanism and economic applications', *Journal of Economic Perspectives*, Winter, vol. 3, no. 1, pp. 77–105.

Beer, S. ([1959] 1967), *Cybernetics and Management*, London: English Universities Press.

Beer, S. (1966), *Decision and Control: The Meaning of Operational Research and Management Cybernetics*, London: Wiley.

Beer, S. (1979), *The Heart of the Enterprise*, Chichester: Wiley.

Beer, S. (1981), *The Brain of the Firm*, Chichester: Wiley.

Belbin, R. M. (1981), *Management Teams: Why They Succeed or Fail*, Oxford: Heinemann.

Bertalanffy, L. von (1968), *General Systems Theory: Foundations, Development, Applications*, New York: George Braziller.

Bion, W. (1961), *Experiences in Groups and Other Papers*, London: Tavistock.

BMA (2004), 'Briefing: measuring performance in the national health service'. Available online at http://www.bma.org.uk.ap.nsf/content/measureper.

Boden, D. (1994), *The Business of Talk: Organizations in Action*, Cambridge: Polity Press.

Boden, M. A. (ed.) (1996), *The Philosophy of Artificial Life*, Oxford: Oxford University Press.

Bogner, W. C. and Thomas, H. (1993), 'The role of competitive groups in strategic formulation: a dynamic integration of two competing models', *Journal of Management Studies*, vol. 30, no. 1, pp. 51–67.

Bohm, D. (1965), *The Special Theory of Relativity*, New York: W. A. Benjamin.

Bohm, D. (1983), *Wholeness and the Implicate Order*, New York: Harper & Row.

Bohm, D. and Peat, F. D. (1989), *Science, Order and Creativity*, London: Routledge.

Bolman, L. and Deal, T. (1997), *Reframing Organizations*, 2nd edition. San Francisco: Jossey-Bass.

Borgatta, E. F., Couch, A. S. and Bales, R. F. (1954), 'Some findings relevant to the great man theory of leadership', *American Sociology Review*, vol. 19, pp. 755–9.

Boulding, K. E. (1956), 'General systems theory: the skeleton of science', *Management Science*, vol. 2, pp. 97–108.

Briggs, J. and Peat, F. (1989), *The Turbulent Mirror*, New York: Harper & Row.

Brown, J. S. (1991), 'Research that reinvents the corporation', *Harvard Business Review*, vol. 69, January–February, pp. 102–11.

Brown, J. S. and Duguid, P. (1991), 'Organizational learning and communities-of-practice: toward a unified view of working, learning and innovation', *Organization Science*, vol. 2, no. 1, pp. 40–56.

Brown, J. S. and Duguid, P. (2001), 'Knowledge and organization: a social practice perspective', *Organization Science*, vol. 12, no. 2, pp. 198–215.

Brown, S. L. and Eisenhardt, K. (1998), *Competing on the Edge: Strategy as Structured Chaos*, Boston, MA: Harvard Business School Press.

Brundin, E. (2002), *Emotions in Motion: The Strategic Leader in a Radical Change Process*, JIBS Dissertation Series No. 12, Jonkoping International Business School.

Brundin, E. and Melin, L. (2003), 'Unfolding the dynamics of emotions in strategizing: how emotion drives or counteracts change activities', *EGOS Colloquium 2003*.

Bruner, J. S. (1986), *Actual Minds, Possible Worlds*, Cambridge, MA: Harvard University Press.

Bruner, J. S. (1990), *Acts of Meaning*, Cambridge, MA: Harvard University Press.

Burgelman, R. A. (1991), 'Intraorganizational ecology of strategy making and organizational adaptation: theory and field research', *Organization Science*, vol. 2, no. 3, pp. 239–62.

Burke, R. (1999), *Project Management: Planning and Control Techniques*, 3rd edition, New York: Wiley.

Burkitt, I. (1991), *Social Selves: Theories of the Social Formation of Personality*, London: Sage.

Burton-Jones, A. (1999), *Knowledge Capitalism: Business, Work and Learning in the New Economy*, Oxford: Oxford University Press.

C

Callon, M. and B. Latour (1981), 'Unscrewing the big Leviathan: how actors macrostructure reality and how sociologists help them to do so', in Knorr-Cetina, K. and Cicourel, V. (eds), *Advances in Social Theory and Methodology: Toward an Integration of Micro- and Macro-Sociologies*, Boston, MA: Routledge & Kegan Paul.

Campbell, A. and Tawady, K. (1990), *Mission and Business Philosophy: Winning Employee Commitment*, Oxford: Heinemann.

Casti, J. (1994), *Complexification: Explaining a Paradoxical World through the Science of Surprise*, London: HarperCollins.

Chakravarthy, B. S. and Doz, Y. (1992), 'Strategy process research: focusing on corporate self-renewal', *Strategic Management Journal*, vol. 13, Special Issue, pp. 5–15.

Chandler, A. D. (1962), *Strategy and Structure*, Boston: MIT Press.

Checkland, P. B. (1981), *Systems Thinking, Systems Practice*, Chichester: Wiley.

Checkland, P. B. (1983), 'OR and the systems movement: mapping and conflicts', *Journal of the Operational Research Society*, vol. 34, p. 661.

Checkland, P. B. and Holwell, S. (1998), *Information, Systems and Information Systems*, Chichester: Wiley.

Checkland, P. B. and Scholes, P. (1990), *Soft Systems Methodology in Action*, Chichester: Wiley.

Child, J. (1972), Organisational structure, environment and performance: the role of strategic choice, *Sociology*, vol. 6, no. 1, pp 1–21.

Child, J. (1984), *Organisation*, London: Harper & Row.

Churchman, C. West (1968), *The Systems Approach*, New York: Delacorte Press.

Churchman, C. West (1970), *The Systems Approach and its Enemies*, New York: Basic Books.

Cohen, J. and Stewart, I. (1994), *The Collapse of Chaos: Discovering Simplicity in a Complex World*, New York: Viking.

Cohen, M. D., March, J. G. and Ohlsen, J. P. (1972), 'A garbage can model of organizational choice', *Administrative Science Quarterly*, vol. 17, pp. 1–25.

Collingridge, D. (1980), *The Social Control of Technology*, Buckingham: Open University Press.

Coopey, J. (1995), 'The learning organization: power, politics and ideology', *Management Learning*, vol. 29, no. 3, pp. 193–214.

Coser, L. A. (1967), *Continuities in the study of social conflict*, New York: Free Press.

Crawley, J. (1992), *Constructive Conflict Management*, London: Nicholas Brealey Publishing.

Cyert, R. M. and March, J. G. (1963), *A Behavioral Theory of the Firm*, Englewood Cliffs, NJ: Prentice-Hall.

D

D'Aveni, R. (1995), *Hypercompetitive Rivalries*, New York: Free Press.

Dalal, F. (1998), *Taking the Group Seriously: Towards a Post-Foulkesian Group Analytic Theory*, London: Jessica Kingsley.

Damasio, A. R. (1994), *Descartes' Error: Emotion, Reason and the Human Brain*, London: Picador.

Davenport, T. H. and Prusak, L. (1998), *Working Knowledge: How Organizations Manage What they Know*, Cambridge, MA: Harvard University Press.

Davies, P. (1987), *The Cosmic Blueprint*, London: William Heinemann.

Davies, P. (2004), 'Star cross'd', *Guardian Unlimited*, 20 November. Available online at: http://society.guardian.co.uk/nhsperformance/comment/0,8146,1362727,00.html.

De Wit, B. and Meyer, R. (2005), *Strategy Synthesis: Resolving Strategy Paradoxes to Create Competitive Advantage*, London: Thomson Learning.

Department of Health, (2000), *The NHS Plan*. London: The Stationery Office.

Dewey, J. (1934), *A Common Faith*, New Haven, CT: Yale University Press.

DiMaggio, P. J. and Powell, W. W. (1991), 'Introduction', in Powell, W. W. and DiMaggio P. J. (eds), *New Institutionalism in Organizational Analysis*, Chicago: Chicago University Press, pp. 1–38.

Dixon, M. (ed.) (2000), *Project Management Body of Knowledge*, 4th edition, Peterborough, UK: Association for Project Management.

Donaldson, A. (2005), 'Writing in organizational life: how a technology simultaneously forms and is formed by human interaction', in Stacey, R. (ed.), *Experiencing Emergence in Organizations: Local Interaction and the Emergence of Global Pattern*, London: Routledge.

Dougherty, D. (1992), 'A practice-centered model organizational renewal through product innovation', *Strategic Management Journal*, vol. 13, Special Issue, Summer, pp. 77–92.

Dugdale, R. (2002), *Pursuing Perfection in the Bradford Health Community*, Bradford Community National Health Service Trust.

Duncan, R. (1972), Characteristics of organizational environments and perceived uncertainty, *Administrative Science Quarterly*, vol. 17, pp. 313–27.

Dunphy, D. C. (1968), 'Phases, roles and myths in self analytic groups', *Journal of Applied Behavioural Science*, vol. 4, pp. 195–226.

E

Easterby-Smith, M. and Araujo, L. (1999), 'Organizational learning: current debates and opportunities', in Easterby-Smith, M., Burgoyne, J. and Araujo, L. (eds), *Organizational Learning and the Learning Organization*, London: Sage.

Edelmann, R. J. (1993), *Interpersonal Conflicts at Work*, Leicester: The British Psychological Society.

Elias, N. ([1939] 2000), *The Civilizing Process*, Oxford: Blackwell.

Elias, N. (1978), *What is Sociology?* London: Hutchinson.

Elias, N. (1987), *Involvement and Detachment*, Oxford: Blackwell.

Elias, N. (1991), *The Society of Individuals*, Oxford: Blackwell.

Elias, N. (1998), *On Civilization, Power, and Knowledge*, Chicago, IL: University of Chicago Press.

Elias, N. and Scotson, J. ([1965] 1994), *The Established and the Outsiders*, London: Sage.

Etzioni, A. (1961), *Complex Organizations*, New York: Holt, Rinehart & Winston.

F

Fayol, H. ([1916] 1948), *Industrial and General Administration*, London: Pitman.

Festinger, L., Schachter, S. and Back, K. (1950), *Social Pressures in Informal Groups: A Study of a Housing Project*, New York: Harper & Row.

Fiedler, F. E. (1967), *A Theory of Leadership Effectiveness*, New York: McGraw-Hill.

Flood, R. L. (1990), 'Liberating systems theory: towards critical systems thinking', *Human Relations*, vol. 43, pp. 49–75.

Flood, R. L. (1999), *Rethinking the Fifth Discipline: Learning within the Unknowable*, London: Routledge.

Floyd, S. W. and Wooldridge, B. (1992), 'Middle management involvement in strategy and its association with strategic type: a research note', *Strategic Management Journal*, vol. 13, Special Issue, Summer, pp. 153–168.

Foerster, H. von (1984), 'On constructing reality', in Foerster, H. von (ed.), *Observing Systems*, Seaside, CA: Intersystems.

Fonseca, J. (2001), *Complexity and Innovation in Organizations*, London: Routledge.

Forrester, J. (1958), 'Industrial dynamics: a major breakthrough for decisionmaking', *Harvard Business Review*, vol. 36, no. 4, pp. 37–66.

Forrester, J. (1961), *Industrial Dynamics*, Cambridge, MA: MIT Press.

Forrester, J. (1969), *The Principles of Systems*, Cambridge, MA: Wright-Allen Press.

Foulkes, S. H. (1948), *Introduction to Group Analytic Psychotherapy*, London: William Heinemann Medical Books.

Foulkes, S. H. (1964), *Therapeutic Group Analysis*, London: George Allen & Unwin.

Frankfurt, H. (1971), Freedom of the will and the concept of a person, *Journal of Philosophy*, vol. 67, no. 1, pp. 5–20.

Friis, P. (2004), 'The relevance of theatre and improvisation to consulting for organisational change', unpublished thesis, University of Hertfordshire.

G

Galbraith, J. R. and Kazanian, R. K. (1986), *Strategy Implementation: Structure, Systems and Process*, St Paul, MN: West.

Gardner, H. (1985), *The Mind's New Science: A History of the Cognitive Revolution*, New York: Basic Books.

Garfinkel, H. (1967), *Studies in Ethnomethodology*, Englewood Cliffs, NJ: Prentice-Hall.

Garud, R. and Van de Ven, A. H. (1992), 'An empirical evaluation of the internal corporate venturing process', *Strategic Management Journal*, vol. 13, Special Issue, Summer, pp. 93–110.

Garven, D. A. (1993), 'Building a learning organization', *Harvard Business Review*, July–August.

Gell-Mann, M. (1994), *The Quark and the Jaguar*, New York: Freeman.

Gergen, K. J. (1982), *Toward Transformation in Social Knowledge*, New York: Springer.

Gergen, K. J. (1985), 'The social constructionist movement in modern psychology', *American Psychologist*, vol. 40, pp. 266–75.

Gergen, K. J. (1991), *The Saturated Self: Dilemmas of Identity in Contemporary Life*, New York: Basic Books.

Giddens, A. (1976), *New Rules of Sociological Method*, London: Hutchinson.

Giddens, A. (1979), *Central Problems in Social Theory*, London: Macmillan.

Giddens, A. (1984), *The Constitution of Society: Outline of the Theory of structuration*, Cambridge: Polity Press.

Ginsberg, A. and Venkatraman, N. (1992), 'Investing in new information technology: the role of competitive posture and issue diagnosis', *Strategic Management Journal*, vol. 13, Special Issue, Summer, pp. 37–54.

Glasl, F. (1999), *Confronting Conflict*, Gloucestershire: Hawthorn Press.

Gleick, J. (1988), *Chaos: The Making of a New Science*, London: William Heinemann.

Goffman, E. (1981), *Forms of Talk*, Philadelphia, PA: University of Pennsylvania Press.

Goldstein, J. (1994), *The Unshackled Organization: Facing the Challenge of Unpredictability through Spontaneous Reorganization*, Portland, OR: Productivity Press.

Goodwin, B. (1994), *How the Leopard Changed its Spots*, London: Weidenfeld & Nicolson.

Goodwin, R. M. (1951), 'Econometrics in business-style analysis', in Hansen, A. H. (ed.), *Business Cycles and National Income*, New York: W. W. Norton.

Goold, M. and Campbell, A. (1987), *Strategies and Styles*, Oxford: Blackwell.

Gould, L., Stapley, L. and Stein, M. (eds) (2001), *The Systems Psychodynamics of Organizations: Integrating the Group Relations Approach, Psychoanalytic and Open Systems Perspectives*, New York: Karnac.

Greiner, L. E. (1972), 'Evolution and revolution as organizations grow', *Harvard Business Review*, vol. 50, July–August, pp. 37–46.

Greiner, L. E. and Schein, V. E. (1988), *Power and Organization Development: Mobilizing Power to Implement Change*, Reading, MA: Addison-Wesley.

Griffin, D. (2002), *The Emergence of Leadership: Linking Self-Organization and Ethics*, London: Routledge.

Griffin, D. and Stacey, R. (eds) (2005), *Complexity and the Experience of Leading Organizations*, London: Routledge.

Griffin, D., Shaw, P. and Stacey, R. (1998), 'Speaking of complexity in management theory and practice,' *Organization*, vol. 5, no. 3, pp. 295–310.

H

Hamel, G. and Prahalad, C. K. (1989), 'Strategic intent', *Harvard Business Review*, vol. 67, May–June, pp. 63–76.

Hamel, G. and Prahalad, C. K. (1990), 'The core competence of the corporation', *Harvard Business Review*, vol. 68, no. 3, pp. 79–81.

Hamel, G. and Prahalad, C. K. (1994), *Competing for the Future*, Boston, MA: Harvard Business School Press.

Hannan, M. T. and Freeman, J. (1989), *Organizational Ecology*, Cambridge, MA: Harvard University Press.

Healthcare Commission (2005), *Acute and Specialist Trust Overview, Healthcare Performance Ratings*. Available online at: http://ratings2005.healthcarecimmission.org.uk/trust/overview/acute_overview.asp.

Henderson, B. D. (1970), *The Product Portfolio*, Boston, MA: Boston Consulting Group.

Hersey, P. and Blanchard, K. (1988), *Organizational Behavior*, Englewood Cliffs, NJ: Prentice-Hall.

Hertzberg, F. (1966), *Work and the Nature of Man*, Cleveland, OH: World.

Hirschhorn, L. (1990), *The Workplace Within: Psychodynamics of Organizational Life*, Cambridge, MA: MIT Press.

Hofer, C. W. and Schendel, D. (1978), *Strategy Evaluation: Analytical Concepts*, St Paul, MN: West.

Holland, J. (1998), *Emergence from Chaos to Order*, New York: Oxford University Press.

Huff, J. O., Huff, A. S. and Thomas, H. (1992), 'Strategic renewal and the interaction of stress and inertia', *Strategic Management Journal*, vol. 13, Special Issue, Summer, pp. 55–76.

Hurst, D. (1995), *Crisis and Renewal: Meeting the Challenge of Organizational Change*, Boston, MA: Harvard Business School Press.

Hurst, D. K. (1986), 'Why strategic management is bankrupt', *Organizational Dynamics*, vol. 12, Autumn, pp. 4–77.

Hurst, E. G. (1982), 'Controlling strategic plans', in Lorange, D. (ed.), *Implementation of Strategic Planning*, Englewood Cliffs, NJ: Prentice-Hall.

Hussey, D. E. (1991), 'Implementing strategy through management education and training', in Hussey, D. E. (ed.), *International Review of Strategic Management*, vol. 2, no. 1.

I

Isaacs, W. (1999), *Dialogue and the Art of Thinking Together*, New York: Doubleday.

Isenhart, M. W. and Spangle, M. (2000), *Collaborative Approaches to Resolving Conflict*, London: Sage.

Iterson, A. van, Mastenbroek, W., Newton, T. and Smith, D. (eds) (2002), *The Civilized Organization: Norbert Elias and the Future of Organization Studies*, Amsterdam: John Benjamins Publishing Company.

J

Jackall, R. (1988), 'Moral mazes: the world of corporate managers,' in Handel, M. J. (ed.), *The Sociology of Organizations: Classic, Contemporary and Critical Readings*, Oxford: Oxford University Press.

Jackson, M. C. (2000), *Systems Approaches to Management*, New York: Kluwer.

Jacques, E. (1955), 'Social systems as a defence against persecutory and defensive anxiety', in Klein, M., Heinmann, P. and Money-Kyrle, P. (eds), *New Directions in Psychoanalysis*, London: Tavistock. (Also published in Gibbard, G. S., Hartman, J. J. and Mann, R. D. (1974), *Analysis of Groups*, San Francisco: Jossey-Bass.)

James, W. (1902), *The Varieties of Religious Experience*, Cambridge, MA: Harvard University Press.

Jarzabkowski, P. (2003), 'Strategic practices: an activity theory perspective on continuity and change', *Journal of Management Studies*, vol. 40, no. 1, pp. 23–55.

Jefferson, G. (1978), 'Sequential aspects of storytelling in conversation', in Shenkein, J. (ed.), *Studies in the Organization of Conversational Interaction*, New York: Academic Press.

Joas, H. (2000), *The Genesis of Values*, Cambridge: Polity Press.

Johannessen, S. and Stacey, R. (2005), 'Technology as social object', in Stacey, R. (ed.), *Experiencing Emergence in Organizations: Local Interaction and the Emergence of Global Pattern*, London: Routledge.

Johnson, G. (1987), *Strategic Change and Management Process*, Oxford: Blackwell.

Johnson, G., Melin, L. and Whittington, R. (2003), 'Guest editors' introduction: micro strategy and strategizing: towards an activity-based view', *Journal of Management Studies*, vol. 40, no. 1, pp. 3–22.

Johnson, G., Scholes, K. and Whittington, R. (2005), *Exploring Corporate Strategy*, 7th edition, Harlow: Pearson Education.

K

Kast, F. E. and Rosenzweig, J. E. (1985), *Organization and Management – A Systems and Contingent Approach*, New York: McGraw-Hill.

Kauffman, S. A. (1995), *At Home in the Universe*, New York: Oxford University Press.

Kellert, S. H. (1993), *In the Wake of Chaos*, Chicago, IL: University of Chicago Press.

Kelly, S. and Allison, A. (1999), *The Complexity Advantage: How the Science of Complexity can Help your Business Achieve Peak Performance*, New York: McGraw-Hill.

Kelsey, D. (1988), 'The economics of chaos or the chaos of economies', *Oxford Economic Papers*, vol. 40, pp. 1–31.

Ketovi, M. and Castener, X. (2004), 'Strategic planning as an integrative device', *Administrative Science Quarterly*, vol. 49, pp. 337–65.

Kets de Vries, M. F. (1989), *Prisoners of Leadership*, New York: Wiley.

Kiel, L. D. (1994), *Managing Chaos and Complexity in Government*, San Francisco, CA: Jossey-Bass.

Kiersey, D. and Bates, M. (1978), *Please Understand Me: Character and Temperament Types*, Del Mar, CA: Prometheus Nemesis Books.

Klein, M. (1975), *The Writings of Melanie Klein*, London: Hogarth Press.

Kleiner, A. and Roth, G. (1997), 'How to make experience your best teacher', *Harvard Business Review*, vol. 68, September–October, pp. 112–22.

Kolb, D. M. and Bartunek, J. M. (1992), *Hidden Conflicts in Organisations*, Newbury Park, CA: Sage.

L

Langley, A. (1999), 'Strategies for theorizing from process data', *Academy of Management Review*, vol. 24, no. 4, pp. 691–710.

Langton, C. G. (1996), 'Artificial life', in Boden, M. A. (ed.), *The Philosophy of Artificial Life*, Oxford: Oxford University Press.

Larsen, H. (2005), 'The experience of change in the profession of clinical psychology in the UK', unpublished thesis, University of Hertfordshire.

Latour, B. and S. Woolgar (1979), *Laboratory Life: The Social Construction of Scientific Facts*, Beverly Hills, CA: Sage.

Lave, J. and Wenger, E. (1991), *Situated Learning: Legitimate Peripheral Participation*, New York: Cambridge University Press.

Lawrence, P. R. and Lorsch, J. W. (1967), *Organization and Environment*, Cambridge, MA: Harvard University Press.

Leonard, D. and Strauss, S. (1997), 'Putting your company's whole brain to work', *Harvard Business Review*, vol. 67, July–August, pp. 111–21.

Levy, D. (1994), 'Chaos theory and strategy: theory, application, and managerial implications', *Strategic Management Journal*, vol. 15, pp. 167–78.

Levy, S. (1992), *Artificial Life*, New York: First Vintage Books.

Lewin, R. and Regine, B. (2000), *The Soul at Work*, London: Orion Business Books.

Lewis, D. S., French, E. and Steane, P. A. (1997), 'Culture of conflict', *Leadership and Organisational Development Journal*, vol. 18, no. 6, pp. 275–82.

Likert, R. (1961), *New Patterns of Management*, New York: McGraw-Hill.

Lindblom, L. (1959), 'The science of muddling through', *Public Administration Review*, vol. 19, pp. 79–88.

Lissack, M. and Roos, J. (1999), *The Next Common Sense: Mastering Corporate Complexity through Coherence*, London: Nicholas Brealey.

Lock, D. (2003), *Project Management*, 8th edition, Aldershot: Gower.

Lohr, K. N. (ed.) (2001), *Crossing the Quality Chasm*, Washington, DC: Institute of Medicine.

Luhmann, N. (1984), *Social Systems*, Stanford, CA: Stanford University Press.

M

Maitlis, S. and Lawrence, B. (2003), 'Orchestral manoeuvres in the dark: understanding failure in organizational strategizing', *Journal of Management Studies*, vol. 40, no. 1, pp. 109–39.

March, J. G. and Olsen, J. P. (1972), 'A garbage can model of organizational choice', *Administrative Science Quarterly*, vol. 17, no. 1.

March, J. G. and Simon, H. A. (1958), *Organizations*, New York: Wiley.

Marion, R. (1999), *The Edge of Organization: Chaos and Complexity Theories of Formal Social Systems*, Thousand Oaks, CA: Sage.

Maslow, A. (1954), *Motivation and Personality*, New York: Harper & Row.

Mastenbroek, W. F. G. (1987), *Conflict Management and Organisational Development*, Chichester: Wiley.

Maturana, H. R. and Varela, F. J. (1987), *The Tree of Knowledge: The Biological Roots of Human Understanding*, Boston, MA: Shambala.

Mayo, E. (1945), *The Social Problems of an Industrial Civilization*, Cambridge, MA: Harvard University Press.

McCleod, J. (1996), 'Qualitative research methods in counselling psychology', in Woolfe, R. and Dyden, W. (eds), *Handbook of Counselling Psychology*, London: Sage.

McCulloch, W. S. and Pitts, W. (1943), 'A logical calculus of ideas imminent in nervous activity', *Bulletin of Mathematical Biophysics*, vol. 5, pp. 115–33.

McGill, I. and Beaty, L. (2001), *Action Learning*, revised 2nd edition, London: Kogan.

Mead, G. H. (1908), 'The philosophical basis for ethics', *International Journal of Ethics* vol. 18, pp. 311–23.

Mead, G. H. (1923), 'Scientific method and the moral sciences', *International Journal of Ethics*, vol. 33, pp. 229–47.

Mead, G. H. (1932), *The Philosophy of the Present*, Chicago: University of Chicago Press.

Mead, G. H. (1934), *Mind, Self, and Society: From the Standpoint of a Social Behaviourist*, Chicago: University of Chicago Press.

Mead, G. H. (1938), *The Philosophy of the Act*, Chicago: University of Chicago Press.

Menzies Lyth, I. (1975), 'A case study in the functioning of social systems as a defence against anxiety', in Coleman, A. and Bexton, W. H. (eds), *Group Relations Reader*, Sausalito, CA: GREX.

Midgley, G. (2000), *Systemic Intervention: Philosophy, Methodology, and Practice*, New York: Kluwer.

Miller, D. and Friesen, P. H. (1980), Momentum and revolution in organizational adaptation, *Academy of Management Journal*, vol. 23, pp. 591–614.

Miller, E. J. (1977), 'Organisational development and industrial democracy: a current case-study', in Cooper, C. (ed.), *Organisational Development in the UK and USA: A Joint Evaluation*, London: Macmillan.

Miller, E. J. (1983), *Work and Creativity*, Occasional Papers, London: Tavistock.

Miller, E. J. (1993), *From Dependency to Autonomy: Studies in Organization and Change*, London: Free Association Books.

Miller, E. J. and Rice, A. K. (1967), *Systems of Organization: The Control of Task and Sentient Boundaries*, London: Tavistock.

Mingers, J. (1995), *Self-Producing Systems: Implications and Applications of Autopoiesis*, New York: Plenum Press.

Mintzberg, H. (1973), *The Nature of Managerial Work*, New York: Harper & Row.

Mintzberg, H. (1983), *Power in and around Organizations*, Englewood Cliffs, NJ: Prentice-Hall.

Mintzberg, H. (1987), 'Crafting strategy', *Harvard Business Review*, vol. 65, no. 4, July–August, pp. 66–75.

Mintzberg, H. (1989), *Mintzberg on Management: Inside Our Strange World or Organizations*, New York: The Free Press.

Mintzberg, H. (1994), *The Rise and Fall of Strategic Planning*, Hemel Hempstead: Prentice Hall.

Mintzberg, H. (1998), 'The manager's job', in Mintzberg, H. and Quinn, J. B. (eds), *Readings in the Strategy Process*, Upper Saddle River, NJ: Simon & Schuster.

Mintzberg, H., Ahlstrand, B. and Lampel, J. (1998), *Strategy Safari*, Harlow: Pearson Education.

Mintzberg, H. and Waters, J. A. (1985), 'Of strategies deliberate and emergent', *Strategic Management Journal*, vol. 6, pp. 257–72.

Mintzberg, H., Théorêt, A. and Raisinghani, D. (1976), 'The structure of the unstructured decision making process', *Administrative Science Quarterly*, vol. 21, no. 2, pp. 246–75.

Morgan, G. (1997), *Images of Organization*, 2nd edition, Thousand Oaks, CA: Sage.

Morrill, C. (1991), 'Conflict management, honour, and organizational change', *American Journal of Sociology*, vol. 97, pp. 585–622.

N

Nelson, R. R. and Winter, S. G. (1982), *An Evolutionary Theory of Economic Change*, Cambridge, MA: Harvard University Press.

Nicolis, G. and Prigogine, I. (1989), *Exploring Complexity: An Introduction*, New York: W. H. Freeman.

Nonaka, I. (1988a), 'Creating organizational order out of chaos: self renewal in Japanese firms', *California Management Review*, Spring, pp. 57–73.

Nonaka, I. (1988b), 'Toward middle-up-down management: accelerating information creation', *Sloan Management Review*, vol. 29, no. 3, pp. 9–18.

Nonaka, I. (1991), 'The knowledge-creating company', *Harvard Business Review*, vol. 69, November–December, pp. 96–104.

Nonaka, I. and Takeuchi, H. (1995), *The Knowledge-Creating Company: How Japanese Companies Create the Dynamics of Innovation*, Oxford: Oxford University Press.

O

Oberholzer, A. and Roberts, V. Z. (1995), *The Unconscious at Work: Individual and Organizational Stress in the Human Services*, London: Routledge.

Ong, Walter J Ong (2002), *Orality and Literacy*, London and New York: Routledge.

Owen, H. (1992), *Open Space Technology: A User's Guide*, Potomac, MD: Abbott Publishing.

P

Pascale, R. T. and Athos, A. (1981), *The Art of Japanese Management*, New York: Simon & Schuster.

Pascale, R. T., Millemann, M. and Gioja, L. (2000), *Surfing the Edge of Chaos: The Laws of Nature and the New Laws of Business*, New York: Crown Business.

Perrow, C. (1972), *Complex Organizations*, London: Scott Foresman.

Peters, E. E. (1991), *Chaos and Order in the Capital Markets: A New View of Cycles, Prices and Market Volatility*, New York: Wiley.

Peters, T. J. and Waterman, R. H. (1982), *In Search of Excellence*, New York: Harper & Row.

Pettigrew, A. M. (1977), 'Strategy formulation as a political process', *International Studies of Management and Organization*, vol. 7, no. 2, pp. 78–87.

Pettigrew, A. M. (1992), 'The character and significance of strategy process research', *Strategic Management Journal*, vol. 13, pp. 5–16.

Petzinger, T. (1999), *The New Pioneers: The Men and Women Who Are Transforming the Workplace and Marketplace*, New York: Simon & Schuster.

Pfeffer, J. (1981), *Power in Organizations*, Cambridge, MA: Ballinger.

Phelan, S. (1999), 'A note on the correspondence between complexity and systems theory', *Systemic Practice and Action Research*, vol. 12, no. 3, pp. 237–46.

Philips, A. W. (1950), 'Mechanical models in economic dynamics', *Econometrica*, vol. 17, pp. 283–305.

Pinto, J. K. (ed.) (1998), *Project Management Handbook*, San Francisco: Jossey-Bass.

Polanyi, M. (1958), *Personal Knowledge*, Chicago: University of Chicago Press.

Polanyi, M. (1960), *The Tacit Dimension*, London: Routledge & Kegan Paul.

Polanyi, M. and Prosch, H. (1975), *Meaning*, Chicago: University of Chicago Press.

Porter, M. (1980), *Competitive Strategy: Techniques for Analyzing Industries and Competitors*, New York: The Free Press.

Porter, M. (1985), *Competitive Advantage: Creating and Sustaining Superior Performance*, New York: The Free Press.

Porter, M. (1987), 'From competitive advantage to corporate strategy', *Harvard Business Review*, vol. 63, May–June, pp. 43–59.

Prigogine, I. (1997), *The End of Certainty: Time, Chaos and the New Laws of Nature*, New York: The Free Press.

Prigogine, I. and Stengers, I. (1984), *Order Out of Chaos: Man's New Dialogue with Nature*, New York: Bantam Books.

Q

Quinn, J. B. (1978), 'Strategic change: logical incrementalism', *Sloan Management Review*, vol. 1, no. 20, Fall, pp. 7–21.

Quinn, J. B. (1980), *Strategic Change: Logical Incrementalism*, Homewood, IL: Richard D. Irwin.

Quinn, J. B., Anderson, P. and Finkelstein, S. (1996), 'Managing professional intellect: making the most of the best', *Harvard Business Review*, March–April, pp. 71–80.

R

Rajagopalan, N. and Finkelstein, S. (1992), 'Effects of strategic orientation and environmental change on senior management reward systems', *Strategic Management Journal*, vol. 13, Special Issue, Summer, pp. 127–42.

Ralls, J. G. and Webb, K. A. (1999), *The Nature of Chaos in Business: Using Complexity to Foster Successful Alliances and Acquisitions*, Houston, TX: Gulf Publishing.

Ray, T. S. (1992), 'An approach to the synthesis of life', in Langton, G. C., Taylor, C., Doyne Farmer, J. and Rasmussen, S. (eds), *Artificial Life II*, Santa Fé Institute, Studies in the Sciences of Complexity, vol. 10, Reading, MA: Addison-Wesley.

Reason, P. (1988), *Human Inquiry in Action: Developments in New Paradigm Research*, London: Sage.

Reason, P. and Heron, J. (1995), 'Co-operative inquiry', in Smith, J. A., Harre, R. and Van Langenhove, L. (eds), *Rethinking Methods in Psychology*, London: Sage.

Regner, P. (2003), 'Strategy creation in the periphery: inductive versus deductive strategy making', *Journal of Management Studies*, vol. 40, no. 1, pp. 57–82.

Regner, R. K. and Huff, A. S. (1993), 'Strategic groups: a cognitive perspective', *Strategic Management Journal*, vol. 14, pp. 103–24.

Reynolds, C. W. (1987), 'Flocks, herds and schools: a distributed behaviour model', Proceedings of Siggraph '87, *Computer Graphics*, vol. 21, no. 4, pp. 25–34.

Richardson, G. P. (1991), *Feedback Thought in Social Science and Systems Theory*, Philadelphia, PA: University of Pennsylvania Press.

Rowe, A. J., Mason, R. O., Dickel, K. E. and Snyder, N. H. (1989), *Strategic Management and Business Policy: A Methodological Approach*, Reading, MA: Addison-Wesley.

Rumelt, R. D. (1974), *Strategy, Structure and Economic Performance*, Boston, MA: Harvard Business School Press.

Rumelt, R., Schendel, D. and Teece, D. J. (1994), 'Fundamental issues in strategy', in Rumelt, R., Schendel, D. and Teece, D. J. (eds), *Fundamental Issues in Strategy*, Cambridge, MA: Harvard Business School Press.

Rush, J. C., White, R. E. and Hurst, D. C. (1989), 'Top management teams and organizational renewal', *Strategic Management Journal*, vol. 10, pp. 87–105.

Rycroft, R. W. and Kash, D. E. (1999), *The Complexity Challenge: Technological Innovation for the 21st Century*, New York: Pinter.

S

Sacks, H. (1992), *Lectures on Conversation*, ed. G. Jefferson, Oxford: Blackwell.

Salvato, C. (2003), 'The role of micro-strategies in the engineering of form evolution', *Journal of Management Studies*, vol. 40, no. 1, pp. 83–108.

Samra-Fredericks, D. (2003), 'Strategizing as lived experience and strategists' everyday efforts to shape strategic direction', *Journal of Management Studies*, vol. 40, no. 1, pp. 141–74.

Sanders, T. I. (1998), *Strategic Thinking and the New Science: Planning in the Midst of Chaos, Complexity, and Change*, New York: The Free Press.

Sarbin, T. R. (1986), 'The narrative as a root metaphor for psychology', in Sarbin, T. R. (ed.), *Narrative Psychology: The Storied Nature of Human Conduct*, New York: Praeger.

Schein, E. H. (1988), *Process Consultation. Vol. II: Lessons for Managers and Consultants*, Reading, MA: Addison-Wesley.

Schendel, D. (1992), 'Introduction to the summer 1992 special issue on "strategy process" research', *Strategic Management Journal*, vol. 13, Special Issue, Summer, pp. 1–4.

Schenkman, L. and Le Baron, B. (1989), 'Nonlinear dynamics and stock returns', *Journal of Business*, vol. 62, no. 3.

Schermerhorn, R., Hunt, J. G. and Osborn, R. N. (1991), *Managing Organizational Behaviour,* New York: Wiley.

Schwenk, C. and Thomas, H. (1983), 'Formulating the mess: the role of decision and problem formulation', *Omega: The International Journal of Management Science*, vol. 11, no. 3, pp. 239–52.

Selznick, P. (1957), *Leadership in Administration: A Sociological Interpretation*, Evanston, IL: Row Peterson.

Senge, P. M. (1990), *The Fifth Discipline: The Art and Practice of the Learning Organization*, New York: Doubleday.

Senge, P. M., Scharmer, C. O., Jaworski, J. and Flowers, B. S (2005), *Presence: Exploring Profound Change in People, Organizations and Society*, London: Nicholas Brealey Publishing.

Shannon, C. and Weaver, W. (1949), *The Mathematical Theory of Communication*, Urbana, IL: University of Illinois Press.

Shapiro, E. R. and Carr, Wesley A. (1991), *Lost in Familiar Places*, New Haven, CT: Yale University Press.

Shaw, P. (2002), *Changing the Conversation: Organizational Change From a Complexity Perspective*, London: Routledge.

Shaw, P. and Stacey, R. (2005), *The Experience of Risk, Spontaneity and Improvization in Organizational Change: Working Live*, London: Routledge.

Shegloff, E. A. (1991), 'Reflections on talk and social structure', in Boden, D. and Zimmerman, D. H. (eds), *Talk and Social Structure*, Cambridge: Polity Press.

Shelton, C. D. and Darling, J. D. (2004), 'From chaos to order: exploring new frontiers in conflict management', *Organisational Development Journal*, vol. 22, no. 3, pp. 22–41.

Shotter, J. (1983), '"Duality of structures" and "intentionality" in an ecological psychology', *Journal for the Theory of Social Behavior*, vol. 13, pp. 19–43.

Shotter, J. (1993), *Conversational Realities: Constructing Life Through Language*, Thousand Oaks, CA: Sage.

Shotter, J. and Katz, A. M. (1997), 'Articulating a practice from within the practice itself: establishing formative dialogues to the use of a "social poetics"', *Concepts and Transformations*, vol. 2, pp. 71–95.

Simon, H. A. (1960), *The New Science of Management Decision*, Englewood Cliffs, NJ: Prentice Hall.

Simon H. A. (1969), *The Sciences of the Artificial*, Cambridge MA: MIT Press. (See in particular Chapter 5, 'The sciences of design: creating the artificial'.)

Skjorshammer, M. (2001), 'Conflict management in a hospital', *Journal of Management in Medicine*, vol. 15, no. 2, pp. 156–66.

Smith, D. (2001), *Norbert Elias and Modern Social Theory*, London: Sage.

Soeters, J. and Iterson, A. van (2002), 'Blame and praise gossip in organizations', in Iterson, A. van, Mastenbroek, W., Newton, T. and Smith, D. (eds) *The Civilized Organization:*

Norbert Elias and the Future of Organizational Studies, Amsterdam: John Benjamins, pp. 25–40.

Springett, N. (1998), 'Producing strategy in the 1990s: the rhetorical dynamics of strategic conversation', Complexity and Management Centre Working Paper no. 21, University of Hertfordshire.

Stacey, R. (2001), *Complex Responsive Processes in Organizations: Learning and Knowledge Creation*, London: Routledge.

Stacey, R. (2003), *Complexity and Group Processes: A Radically Social Understanding of Individuals*, London: Brunner-Routledge.

Stacey, R. (ed.) (2005), *Experiencing Emergence in Organizations: Local Interaction and the Emergence of Global Pattern*, London: Routledge.

Stacey, R. and Griffin, D. (eds) (2006), *Complexity and the Experience of Managing in the Public Sector*, London: Routledge.

Stacey, R., Griffin, J. D. and Shaw, P. (2000), *Complexity and Management: Fad or Radical Challenge to Systems Thinking?* London: Routledge.

Stapley, L. F. (1996), *The Personality of the Organisation: A Psychodynamic Explanation of Culture and Change*, London: Free Association Books.

Steier, F. (1991), *Research and Reflexivity*, Thousand Oaks, CA: Sage.

Stewart, I. (1989), *Does God Play Dice? The Mathematics of Chaos*, Oxford: Blackwell.

Stickland, F. (1998), *The Dynamics of Change: Insights into Organizational Transition from the Natural World*, London: Routledge.

Streatfield, P. (2001), *The Paradox of Control in Organizations*, London: Routledge.

Sveiby, K. E. (1997), *The New Organizational Wealth: Managing and Measuring Knowledge-Based Assets*, San Francisco, CA: Berrett & Koehler.

T

Taylor, F. ([1911] 1967), *Scientific Management*, New York: Harper Brothers.

Taylor, J. (2005), 'Leadership and cult values: moving from the idealized to the experienced', in Griffin, D. and Stacey, R. (eds), *Complexity and the Experience of Leading Organizations*, London: Routledge.

Thietart, R. A. and Forgues, B. (1995), 'Chaos theory and organisation', *Organisation Science*, vol. 6, no. 1, pp. 19–31.

Thompson, J. D. and Tuden, A. (1959), 'Strategies, structures and processes of organisational decisions', in Thompson, J. D. *et al.* (eds), *Comparative Studies in Administration*, Pittsburgh, PA: University of Pittsburgh Press.

Tolbert, P. S. and Zuckner, L. G. (1996), 'The institutionalization of institutional theory', in Clegg, S. R., Hardy, C. and Nord, W. R. (eds), *A Handbook of Organization Studies*, London: Sage.

Traylen, H. (1994), 'Confronting hidden agendas: co-operative inquiry with health visitors', in Reason. P. (ed.), *Participation in Human Inquiry*, Sage: London.

Trist, E. L. and Bamforth, K. W. (1951), 'Some social and psychological consequences of the long wall method of coal getting', *Human Relations*, vol. 5, pp. 6–24.

Tsoukas, H. (1997), 'The firm as a distributed knowledge system: a constructionist approach', Complexity and Management Papers, no. 10, Complexity and Management Centre, University of Hertfordshire Business School.

Turner, J. R. (1999), *The Handbook of Project-Based Management*, 2nd edition, New York: McGraw-Hill.

Turner, J. R., Grude, K. V. and Thurloway, L. (1996), *The Project Manager as Change Agent: Leadership, Influence and Negotiation*, New York: McGraw-Hill.

Turquet, P. (1974), 'Leadership: the individual and the group', in Gibbard, G. S., Hartman, J. J. and Mann, R. D. (eds), *Analysis of Groups*, San Francisco, CA: Jossey-Bass.

Tushman, M. L. and Romanelli, E. (1985), 'A metamorphosis model of convergence and reorientation', in Straw, B. and Cummings, E. (eds), *Research in Organizational Behavior*, vol. 7, Greenwich, CT: Jai Press.

Tustin, A. (1953), *The Mechanism of Economic Systems*, Cambridge, MA: Harvard University Press.

V

Van de Ven, A. (1992), 'Suggestions for studying strategy process: a research note', *Strategic Management Journal*, vol. 13, Special Issue, Summer, pp. 169–91.

Varela, F. J., Thompson, E. and Rosch, E. (1995), *The Embodied Mind: Cognitive Science and Human Experience*, Cambridge, MA: MIT Press.

Volberda, H. W. and Elfring, T. (eds) (2001), *Rethinking Strategy*, London: Sage.

Vroom, V. H. and Yetton, P. W. (1973), *Leadership and Decision Making*, Pittsburgh, PA: University of Pittsburgh Press.

Vygotsky, L. S. (1978), *Mind in Society: The Development of Higher Psychological Processes*, Cambridge MA: Harvard University Press.

W

Waldrop, M. M. (1992), *Complexity: The Emerging Science at the Edge of Chaos*, Englewood Cliffs, NJ: Simon & Schuster.

Webster, G. and Goodwin, B. (1996), *Form and Transformation: Generative and Relational Principles in Biology*, Cambridge: Cambridge University Press.

Weick, K. ([1969] 1979), *The Social Psychology of Organizing*, New York: McGraw-Hill.

Weick, K. (1995), *Sensemaking in Organizations*, Thousand Oaks, CA: Sage.

Wenger, E. (1998), *Communities of Practice: Learning, Meaning and Identity*, New York: Cambridge University Press.

Wernerfelt, B. (1984), 'A resource-based view of the firm', *Strategic Management Journal*, vol. 5, no. 2, pp. 171–80.

Wheatley, M. J. (1999), *Leadership and the New Science*, revised edition, San Francisco: Berrett & Koehler.

Whitehead, A. N. (1978), *Process and Reality*, New York: The Free Press.

Whittington, R. (2001), *What is Strategy – and Does it Matter?* London: Thomson Learning.

Whittington, R. (2002a), 'The work of strategizing and organizing: for practice perspective', *Strategic Organization*, vol. 1, no. 1, pp. 119–27.

Whittington, R. (2002b), 'Practice perspectives on strategy: unifying and developing a field', *Academy of Management Conference Proceedings, Denver*.

Wiener, N. (1948), *Cybernetics: or Control and Communication in the Animal and the Machine*, Cambridge, MA: MIT Press.

Winnicott, D. W. (1965), *The Maturational Processes and the Facilitating Environment*, London: Hogarth Press.

Winnicott, D. W. (1971), *Playing and Reality*, London: Tavistock. (Reprinted in 1993 by Routledge.)

Wood, R. (2000), *Managing Complexity: How Businesses Can Prosper in the Connected Economy*, London: Profile Books.

Wright, P., Pringle, C. and Kroll, M. (1992), *Strategic Management: Text and Cases*, Needham Heights MA: Allyn & Bacon.

Z

Zimmerman, B. J. (1992), 'The inherent drive towards chaos', in Lorange, P., Chakravarty, B., Van de Ven, A. and Roos, J. (eds), *Implementing Strategic Processes: Change, Learning and Cooperation*, London: Blackwell.

Index